Modern Law of Meetings

Third Edition

Modern Law of Meetings

Third Edition

Nicholas Briggs LL.M.
Barrister, Guildhall Chambers and Deputy Registrar of the High Court, Companies Court

Christopher Brockman
Barrister, Guildhall Chambers

David Impey
Solicitor

Olwen Dutton
Partner, Bevan Brittan LLP

Published by
Jordan Publishing Limited
21 St Thomas Street, Bristol BS1 6JS

Copyright Jordan Publishing Limited 2013

All rights reserved. No part of this publication may be reproduced, stored in a retrieval system, or transmitted in any way or by any means, including photocopying or recording, without the written permission of the copyright and database right holder, application for which should be addressed to the publisher.

British Library Cataloguing-in-Publication Data

A catalogue record for this book is available from the British Library.

ISBN 978 1 84661 554 2

Typeset by Letterpart Ltd, Reigate, Surrey

Printed in Great Britain by CPI Antony Rowe, Chippenham and Eastbourne

FOREWORD TO THE FIRST EDITION BY THE HONOURABLE MR JUSTICE LIGHTMAN

Vast numbers of people are involved in meetings every day. They are involved in board or members' meetings of limited companies, meetings of creditors or members of companies in liquidation, meetings of public bodies and meetings of private organisations, such as sports clubs.

What they need is a simple, coherent and universal set of legal rules governing meetings that are: accessible, easy to master, that deal fairly and effectively with the realities of convening, conducting and recording the business at meetings, that take into account the need to give proper notice of the business of the meeting, and fix a location for the meeting that is reasonably accessible, that allow invitees who cannot attend to be represented at the meeting, that enable the meeting to deal swiftly and effectively with the business at hand, taking into account that there may be matters on the agenda that are of great importance to attendees and can become heated, and that make adequate provision for recording decisions, and sometimes discussions leading to them, made at the meeting.

With one or two notable exceptions, that is not what we have. The law that applies to meetings is usually to be found scattered piecemeal (often only with difficulty) in statutes, statutory instruments, custom and case-law and the organisation's constitution, its policies, procedures and standing orders. There are often gaps in the established law and apparent contradictions in the rules.

The rules applying to one organisation will often differ, and sometimes markedly, from those applying to another, apparently similar organisation – a company secretary within a group of companies, for example, will often find that each subsidiary has a slightly (or even markedly) different constitution, so that there are variations between the rules that apply to meetings of each company within the group.

That's why this book is timely and valuable. It draws together in one place all the usual or common rules that might apply to the various types of meetings. Where there are options, it discusses the merits of one against another. And it provides authoritative guidance as to the law and practical help to the lawyer, officer, official or member seeking to establish rules from the outset, or rationalise the rules that already apply, so that they cover all the bases, avoid ambiguities and uncertainty, and promote fair, effective despatch of business at meetings.

Coverage includes a section on local authority meetings, taking full account of the fundamental changes introduced by the Local Government Act 2000 to the way local councils conduct business at meetings and make decisions. The implications of the Human Rights Act 1998, the Anti Social Behaviour Act 2003 and the Criminal Justice Act 2003 on public meetings are also considered. One area of the law of meetings also covered in depth in this book relates to electronic communications between companies and their shareholders regarding notices of members' meetings, proxies and related documents. This work, which incorporates the guidance from the Institute of Chartered Secretaries and Administrators, is manifestly the fruit of much thought and research by those involved day-to-day in the subject matter.

Whatever the involvement with meetings, whatever the nature and activities of the organisation, this book (like no other) provides an authoritative understanding of the law of meetings and the practical means to ensure that meetings are convened and conducted in a manner which is compliant with the law, fair and likely to lead to a productive outcome. I commend this book to all who are concerned to achieve this goal.

Sir Gavin Lightman
Royal Court of Justice
London
March 2005

PREFACE

This new edition of the Modern Law of Meetings has been comprehensively updated. It covers the law relating to private limited companies meetings, insolvency meetings and also local authority meetings, public meetings, and meetings of private organisations. In each area, it highlights and discusses current best practice as well as the latest important case-law.

Our aim has been to provide practical, authoritative and relevant guidance not only to lawyers and other professional advisers, but also to company secretaries and directors, local government and other public sector lawyers, committee administrators, insolvency practitioners and insolvency lawyers, and those involved in running private organisations such as clubs.

We provide a thorough analysis of the meeting process, from deciding when a meeting is needed, convening the meeting, its conduct and management, to keeping lawful and adequate records.

The book deals in detail with the saving provisions that apply to companies whose constitutions pre-date the relevant parts of the Companies Act 2006, which often have an option of either preserving their old way of doing things, or converting to the 2006 Act regime. It covers the legal and practical consequences for companies dealing with issues such as:

- The abolition by the Act of objects clauses and 'authorised share capital'

- The introduction of new rules on directors' powers to allot shares

- The practical impact of a new power for boards to authorise directors' 'situational conflicts' under s 175 of the 2006 Act – subject to conditions.

The new edition also covers the often significant changes made to the original provisions of the 2006 Act by, for example, regulations such as the Companies (Shareholders Rights) Regulations 2009, SI 2009/1632 which, among other reforms, alter the rules governing proxies and corporate representatives, and members' powers to require a general meeting to be called.

Chapter 26 on local authority meetings has been significantly revised to take account of the impact of the Localism Act 2007, which amongst other things removed the previous standards regime brought in by the Local Government Act 2000 (and then amended by the provisions of the Local Government and Public Involvement in Health Act 2007). The Localism Act, and the various regulations made under it are dealt with in some details; although the main planks of local government law as set out, in the main, in the Local Government Act 1972, remain unchanged. A new part to this chapter has been included, dealing with meetings of health bodies, especially important in the light of the Health and Social Care Act 2012 and the closer working between health and government.

The chapters on insolvency and meetings have also been updated to take into account new case-law and the amendments to the insolvency regime to permit remote attendance at meetings and the passing of some resolutions by post. Since the last edition, the rate of change in the law and practice of insolvency has continued to be great and the chapters relating to insolvency meetings have been updated considerably to reflect this.

Nicholas Briggs
Christopher Brockman
David Impey
Olwen Dutton
The law is stated as at 1 January 2013

CONTENTS

Foreword to the First Edition by the Honourable Mr Justice Lightman   v
Preface   vii
Table of Cases   xxi
Table of Statutes   xxxiii
Table of Statutory Instruments   xli
Table of European Materials   xlv
Table of Insolvency Rules   xlvii

Part 1
Company Meetings

Chapter 1
Introduction   3
How meetings started   3
Limited companies   4
Meetings in insolvency   4
Meetings of local authorities   4
Private members' organisations   4

Chapter 2
The Control and Management of Companies   7
Division of powers   7
Articles of association   10
Informal rules   14
Custom   14
General principles   15
How the members make decisions   15
Ultra vires acts and acts beyond the directors' powers   16

Chapter 3
Types of Members' Resolution   19
Introduction   19
Ordinary resolutions   20
   Special notice   21
      Removal of a director   21
      Special notice in other circumstances   25
Special resolutions   28
Extraordinary resolutions   30

Elective resolutions	31
Decisions made without a meeting	33
Statutory written resolutions	34
Regulation 53 of the 1985 Table A	40
Provision for written resolutions in a company's articles	40
Informal corporate acts	40
Registration of resolutions	44
Notifications by listed companies	45

Chapter 4
Meetings of Members (Including Classes of Members and of Debenture Holders)   **47**

Types of members' meeting	47
Meetings convened by the directors	48
Meetings convened by members	49
Meetings 'requested' by members	50
Meeting ordered to be held by the court	52
Resigning auditors' rights to require a meeting	54
Class meetings	55
On the directions of the court pursuant to s 425	60
In relation to compensation to directors for loss of office	63
Meetings of debenture stockholders	63

Chapter 5
Annual General Meetings for Public Companies   **65**

Why annual general meetings are held	65
When annual general meetings are held	66
Special rules for notices of annual general meetings	66
The business of an annual general meeting	67
Dividends	69
Accounts, balance sheets and the reports of the directors and auditors	70
At the meeting	72
Appointing, and fixing the remuneration of, the auditors	73
The election of directors in the place of those retiring	74
Other business at the annual general meeting	77
Directors' authority to allot shares	77
Disapplying statutory pre-emption rights	80
Authority to make a market purchase of own shares	83
Political contributions	85
Circulation of members' resolutions	85
Circulation of members' statements	87
Nominated persons and information rights – ss 145 and 146	88
CREST	92
Explanatory circulars	92

Chapter 6
Notice of General (Members') Meetings   93
Introduction   93
Period of notice   93
The form of the notice   97
  Date, time and place of meeting   97
  Framing resolutions   97
    Ordinary resolutions   98
    Special resolutions   101
  Statement required on notices   102
  Signing the notice   105
To whom notices should be sent   106
  Members   106
  Special classes of members   106
  Joint holders of shares   107
  Persons entitled to a share as a result of the death or bankruptcy of a member   107
  Directors   107
  Auditors   108
  Debenture holders   108
Method of service   108
Notice of proposal to pay compensation to directors   111
Circulation of statement given pursuant to s 314   113
Authentication of notices   115

Chapter 7
The Quorum and the Chairman at General Meetings   117
Introduction   117
Quorum   118
  General rules   118
  One person meetings   120
  Special class quorums   121
  Abuse of quorum provisions   121
Chairman   121
  Appointment   121
  Authority, duties and powers   122
    To regulate the course of the proceedings at the meeting   124
      Right to speak   124
      Relevance of debate   125
      Order of speaking   125
      Amendments to the resolutions proposed   126
      Keeping order   126
      Points of order   126
      Separate resolutions   126
    To close the meeting with its consent   127
    To adjourn the meeting   127
    To make arrangements for taking a poll and to receive or reject proxies   127

To exercise a casting vote	127
To declare the result of voting	128
Disputing the chairman's conduct	129

Chapter 8
Voting and Proxies at Members' Meetings — 131
General principles	131
Entitlement to vote	132
Third-party interests in shares	134
Objecting to a member's right to vote	135
Votes on a show of hands	135
Votes on a poll	137
Voting by corporate representatives	139
Demanding a poll	140
Announcing the results of the poll	146
Appointing proxies, and proxy notices	148

Chapter 9
Adjournments of Members' Meetings — 157
Exercise of the chairman's power to adjourn	157
The court's power to adjourn	159
Procedure on adjournment	159
Business at adjourned meetings	161

Chapter 10
Rights of the Auditor in Relation to Members' Meetings — 163
Appointing and reappointing auditors	163
Private companies	163
Public companies	165
Remuneration of auditors	166
Removal of auditors	166
Changing auditors	166
Special notice	167
Resigning as auditors	168
Requirements on any cessation of office as auditor	170
Specific rights in relation to resolutions and meetings	171
Auditor's rights to raise audit concerns at accounts meetings	171

Chapter 11
Electronic Communications and General Meetings — 173
Introduction	173
The statutory framework	173
The documents and information that can be sent or supplied electronically	174
How documents and information may be sent or supplied	175
Can a company follow the new rules irrespective of what is in its articles?	177

Can a company follow its articles irrespective of what is in the new rules?	182
Mutual, express agreement required	182
Nominated persons	184
Death or bankruptcy of a member	185
The invitation to members to participate	186
Making documents and information available by means of a website	190
A member's deemed agreement to making documents available by means of a website	190
The relationship between an invitation and a request	193
The notification that a document is available on a website	194
Making the document or information available on a website	197
When is an electronic communication 'sent' and 'delivered'?	200
Non-delivery	201
Right to require hard copy version	202
Electronic communications from individual members to their companies	203
Authentication	206
General meetings involving electronic communications	206
Background	206
Entirely virtual general meetings	207
Should companies provide for remote participation in physical meetings?	210
Best interests of the company?	210
Equality Act 2010	211
Amendment of articles	211
Notice of such a general meeting	212
Entitlement to participate	212
Quorum	212
See, be seen, hear and be heard	212
Voting and conduct of the meeting	213
Record keeping generally	213
Breakdowns in electronic communications	213
Remote participation not mandatory	213
Written resolutions in lieu of a meeting, as a solution	214

Chapter 12
Meetings of Directors — 215

Introduction	215
Function of the board	215
Statutory duties	216
Delegation of powers by the board	218
Decisions reserved to the board	218
Exercising the power to delegate	221
Monitoring and reviewing the exercise of delegated powers	222
Convening and conducting board meetings	223
Directors' obligation to meet	223

Who may summon a meeting?	224
Notice of meetings	224
The nature of the business to be conducted	226
Chairman	228
Quorum	231
General rules	231
Abuse of quorum provisions	234
Failure to keep quorum	234
Minimum number of directors	234
Directors' votes	235
General	235
Votes of directors who have a personal interest and/or conflict	235
Alternate directors	242
Committees	243
Resolutions in lieu of a board meeting	244
Companies with a sole director	245
The effect of invalid appointments on board decisions	248

Chapter 13
Electronic Communications and Board Meetings — 249
Introduction	249
Electronic notice of board meetings	250
Electronic board meetings	252
Written resolutions in lieu of a meeting, as a solution	257

Chapter 14
Minutes of Members' and of Board Meetings — 259
Background	259
The minute books	261
Rights to inspect minutes	262
Validating minutes	263
Resolutions agreed to by all members in lieu of a meeting	266

Chapter 15
Admission To and Expulsion From Members' and Directors' Meetings — 267
Admission to meetings (including the press)	267

Part 2
Meetings in Insolvency

Chapter 16
Introduction — 271

Chapter 17
Company Voluntary Arrangements — 279
Introduction	279
Meetings to be held prior to a CVA	280

Notice of meetings	284
Where the nominee is not administrator or liquidator	284
Where the nominee is the administrator or liquidator	287
The chairman	288
Proxies	292
Adjournments	293
Voting at a creditors' meeting	294
Who can vote	294
The calculation of a creditor's voting rights	296
The outcome of the meeting	298
Members' meetings	300
Challenging decisions	302

Chapter 18
Company Administrations — 305

Introduction	305
'Streamlined' and out of court administrations	306
Creditors' meetings	307
Relationship between creditors' voting rights and the administrator's duties	308
The proposals	311
Pre-administration costs	312
Notice	314
Chairman	316
Adjournment	317
Voting	317
Administrator's report	319
Post-meeting revision of proposals	320
Creditors' committee	320

Chapter 19
Administrative Receivership — 321

Creditors' meeting	321
Notice	323
The right to participate in the voting at a creditors' meeting	323
The chairman	325
Adjournment	325
Voting	326
Creditors' committee	326

Chapter 20
Creditors' Voluntary Winding Up — 327

Meetings to be held	327
The section 98 meeting	328
Subsequent meetings: notice	329
Creditors' meetings: chairman	330
Creditors' meeting: adjournment and suspension	331
Creditors' meeting: voting	332

Resolutions by correspondence 332
Final meeting 333
Return to Registrar on final meetings prior to dissolution 335

Chapter 21
Winding Up by the Court 337
Meetings to be held 337
Contributories 338
Notice 338
Final meeting 338
Chairman 339
Adjournment 340
Voting 340
Resolutions by correspondence 340
Report to the court 340

Chapter 22
Members' Voluntary Liquidation 343
The requirements to be satisfied for a members' voluntary liquidation 343
Meetings and resolutions 343
Notice 344
Voting 345
Procedure and meetings subsequent to the passing of the resolution to wind up 345

Chapter 23
Creditors' Schemes under Part 26 (ss 895–901) of the Companies Act 2006 347
Introduction 347
Three stages 349
   Overview 349
Summoning of meeting(s) 350
Information for the meeting 351
Single meeting or separate class meetings? 352
Identification and resolution of creditor issues 353
Proxies 354
   Human rights 355
Schemes versus CVAs 356

Chapter 24
Bankruptcy 359
Introduction 359
Whether to hold a first creditors' meeting 359
Notice of first meeting of creditors 360
Creditors' requisition of a meeting 362
Proxies 363
Admission or rejection of proofs for voting purposes 365
Voting 366

Chairman	368
Chairman and proxies	368
Quorum	369
Opening the meeting	369
No resolution for the appointment of a trustee	371
Creditors' committee	372
Further (general) meetings	372
Release	373
Keeping administrative records	373

Chapter 25
Individual Voluntary Arrangements — **375**

Introduction	375
The proposal	375
Giving and receiving notice of the meeting	377
The meeting generally	378
The meeting: voting rights	380
The meeting: majorities	382
After the meeting	382
Effect of approval	383
Challenging the decision of the meeting	384
Creditor rights in practice: an example	387
The IVA Protocol	388
Fast-track IVAS	389

Part 3
Local Authorities

Chapter 26
Local Authority Meetings — **393**

Introduction	393
Local government structure	394
Local government equals meetings!	394
Types of meeting	395
Impact of the Local Government Act 2000	396
Internal rules – constitution and standing orders	398
Convening meetings	400
What meetings must local authorities hold?	400
Where should meetings be held?	401
Notice of meetings	401
Agenda for meetings	404
Running meetings	406
Chairing meetings	406
Voting at meetings	407
Quorum at meetings	411
Public involvement	411
Right to attend	411
Right to participate	418

Press rights	419
Issues arising during the meeting	420
Conflicts/declarations of interest	420
The position in Wales	424
Disorder at the meeting	424
Defamation	425
After the meeting	426
Minutes	426
Access to papers	427
Challenging decisions	428
Overview and scrutiny	428
Referral within the council	428
Statutory routes of appeal/review	429
Judicial review	429
Local Government Ombudsman	433
Health bodies	435
Bodies subject to the Public Bodies (Admission to Meetings) Act 1960	436
NHS Foundation Trusts	437
Clinical Commissioning Groups	438

Part 4
Meetings of Private Organisations

Chapter 27
Meetings of Private Organisations

Meetings of Private Organisations	443
Background	443
Members' meetings	446
The annual general meeting	446
Special meetings	446
Who can call members' meetings?	446
Notice period	447
How notice is to be given	447
The form of the notice	448
Service of the notice	449
Who is entitled to notice?	450
The chairman	450
Quorum	451
Voting	451
Amendments	453
Adjournments	454
Executive committee meetings	455
When held, and notice period	455
To whom should notice be given?	456
The form of the notice	456
Service of the notice	457
Conduct of the meeting	457
The chairman	457

Quorum	458
Voting	458
Delegation to subcommittees	458
Minutes and records	459

Appendix 1
Summary of Main Matters to be Dealt with by Members under the Companies Act — **463**

Appendix 2
Bushell v Faith clause — **471**

Appendix 3
The UK Corporate Governance Code — **473**

Index — **499**

TABLE OF CASES

References are to paragraph numbers.

A Company (No 004539 of 1993), Re [1995] 1 BCLC 459, [1995] BCC 116	16.16, 17.31, 20.11, 21.10
A Company (No 00789 of 1987) ex parte Shooter, Re [1990] BCLC 384, 5 BCC 792	6.57
A Company, Re BLD 1605021825	4.25
A Debtor (No 101 of 1999), Re [2001] 1 BCLC 54, [2000] BPIR 998, [2000] All ER (D) 949	16.20
A Debtor (No 103 of 1994), Re, Cooper v Fearnley [1997] BPIR 20	25.6
A Debtor (No 222 of 1990), ex p Bank of Ireland, Re [1992] BCLC 137	17.31, 24.26, 25.6, 25.33
A Debtor (No 259 of 1990), Re [1992] 1 All ER 641, [1992] 1 WLR 226	25.32
Abbatt v Treasury Solicitor [1969] 1 WLR 561, [1969] 1 All ER 52, Ch D; [1969] 1 WLR 1575, [1969] 3 All ER 1175, CA	27.36
Abbott v Sullivan [1952] 1 KB 189, [1952] 1 All ER 226, [1951] 2 Lloyd's Rep 573, 96 Sol Jo 119, [1952] 1 TLR 133	12.119, 27.84
Alabama, New Orleans, Texas & Pacific Junction Railway, Re [1891] 1 Ch 213, 60 LJ Ch 221, 2 Meg 377, 64 LT 127, 7 TLR 171, [1886–90] All ER Rep Ext 1143	4.58, 23.5
Allen v Gold Reefs of West Africa Ltd [1900] 1 Ch 656, 69 LJ Ch 266, 82 LT 210, CA	8.1
Alman v Approach Housing Ltd [2001] BPIR 203, [2001] 1 BCLC 530, [2000] All ER (D) 2093	25.25
Alpa Lighting Ltd, Re [1997] BPIR 341, CA	17.68
Altitude Scaffolding Ltd, Re; Re T&N Ltd [2006] EWHC 1401 (Ch), [2007] 1 BCLC 199, [2006] All ER (D) 181 (Jun)	23.24
Andrew v FarmStart (1988) 71 CBR (NS) 124; 54 DLR (4th) 406	17.44
Anglo-International Bank, Re [1943] Ch 233, [1943] 2 All ER 88	6.78
Anglo-Spanish Tartar Refineries, Re [1924] WN 222, 68 Sol Jo 738	4.60
Annamunthodo v Oilfield Workers Trade Union [1961] AC 945, [1961] 3 All ER 621, [1961] 3 WLR 650, 105 Sol Jo 706, 4 WIR 117	27.84
Arnot v United African Lands [1901] 1 Ch 518, 70 LJ Ch 306, 84 LT 309 CA	7.55
Assisco Engineering Ltd, Re [2002] BCC 481, [2002] BPIR 15	16.14, 21.10
Associated Provincial Picture Houses Ltd v Wednesbury Corporation [1948] 1 KB 223, [1947] 2 All ER 680, CA	9.9, 9.10
Automatic Self-Cleansing Filter Syndicate Co v Cunninghame [1906] 2 Ch 34, 75 LJ Ch 437, 13 Mans 156	5.34
Ayles v Romsey and Stockbridge Rural District Council (1944) 42 LGR 210, 108 JP 175, 88 Sol Jo 135	26.78
Bairstow and Others v Queens Moat Houses plc [2001] EWCA Civ 712, [2001] 2 BCLC 531, [2001] All ER (D) 211 (May)	3.114
Ballan Pty Ltd, Re (1993–1994) 12 ACSR 605	18.34
Bank of Credit & Commerce International SA (No 5), Re [1994] 1 BCLC 429	16.13
Barings plc (No 6); Hamilton v Law Debenture Trustees Ltd, Re [2001] 2 BCLC 159, [2002] BPIR 85, [2001] All ER (D) 171 (Jun)	16.10
Baroness Wenlock v River Dee Co (1883) 36 Ch D 675n, 57 LT 402n	6.3

Barron v Potter, Re British Seagumnite Co [1914] 1 Ch 895, 83 LJ Ch 646,
  100 LT 929   12.39
Barton v Taylor (1886) 11 App Cas 197, 55 LJPC 1, 55 LT 158   15.3
Beanby Estates Ltd v Egg Stores (Stamford Hill) Ltd [2003] 1 WLR 2064   27.35
Bentley-Stevens v Jones [1974] 2 All ER 653, [1974] 1 WLR 638, 118 Sol Jo
  345   12.44
Betts & Co v Macnaghten [1910] 1 Ch 430, 79 LJ Ch 207, 53 SJ 521   6.27, 7.57, 27.53
Beverley Group plc v McClue [1995] 2 BCLC 407, [1996] BPIR 25, [1995]
  BCC 751, ChD   17.17
Blair Open Hearth Furnace Co v Reigart (1913) 57 Sol Jo 500, 108 LT 665,
  29 TLR 449   7.50
Blair v Consolidated Enfield Corporation [1995] 4 SCR, (1993) 106 DLR
  (4th) 193   7.30, 7.35, 27.45
Bland v Buchanan [1901] 2 KB 75, 65 JP 404, 70 LJKB 466   7.53
Blue Arrow plc [1987] BCLC 585, 3 BCC 618   6.57
Bluebrook Ltd, Re [2009] EWHC 2114 (Ch), [2010] BCC 209, [2010] 1
  BCLC 338   23.32
Blundell v Christie Hospital NHS Trust [1996] ICR 347   12.14
Blunden v Frogmore Investments Ltd [2002] 2 EGLR 29   27.35
BML Group Ltd v Harman (1994) *The Times*, April 8, CA   4.28
Bond Corporation Holdings Ltd, Re (1991) 5 ACSR 304   23.5
Bonelli's Telegraph Co, Re, Collie's Claim (1871) LR 12 Eq 246, 40 LJ Ch
  567, 19 WR 1022   12.37
Bonham-Carter v Situ Ventures Ltd [2012] EWHC 230 (Ch), [2012] BCC
  717   3.65, 3.101, 3.103, 3.117
Borgelt v Millman NO [1983] 1 SALR 757   23.5
Bournemouth & Boscombe Athletic Football Club Co Ltd, Re [1998] BPIR
  183, ChD   17.65
Bowling & Welby's Contract, Re [1895] 1 Ch 663, 64 LJ Ch 427, 2 Mans 257   7.15
Bradburn v Kaye [2006] BPIR 605   25.33
Bradford Investments Ltd, Re [1990] BCC 740, [1991] BCLC 224, ChD   7.23
Bradley-Hole (A Bankrupt), Re, ex parte Knight [1994] 4 All ER 865, [1995]
  1 WLR 1097, [1995] 2 FLR 838, ChD   17.56
Bradman v Trinity Estates plc (1989) 5 BCC 33, [1989] BCLC 757, ChD   6.18, 27.35
Brady v Brady [1989] AC 755, [1988] 2 WLR 1308, [1988] 2 All ER 617, HL   17.61
British America Nickel Corporation v O'Brien [1927] AC 369, 96 LJPC 57,
  136 LT 615, 43 TLR 195   8.3
British Aviation Insurance Co Ltd, Re [2005] EWHC 1621 (Ch), [2006] 1
  BCLC 665, [2005] All ER (D) 290 (Jul)   23.12
British Flax Producers Co, Re [1889] WN 7, 1 Meg 133, 60 LT 215   8.64
British Sugar Refining Co, Re, ex p Faris (1857) 3 K & J 408, 26 LJ Ch 369,
  5 WR 379   5.15
British Union for the Abolition of Vivisection, Re (1995) 2 BCLC 1, (1995)
  The Times, March 3   4.30, 7.18, 15.6
Brown v Andrew (1849) 18 LJQB 153, 13 Jur 938, 12 LTOS 398   27.83
Browne v La Trinidad (1887) 37 ChD 1, 57 LJ Ch 292, CA   4.9, 12.43, 12.44, 12.51, 27.66, 27.69
BTR plc, *sub nom* BTR plc v Northcote, Re [1999] 2 BCLC 675, [1999] All
  ER (D) 96   4.58, 23.5, 23.7
Burnett v Gill (1906) *The Times* 13 June   8.104
Burton v Bevan [1908] 2 Ch 240, 77 LJ Ch 591, [1908] WN 140   14.27
Bushell v Faith [1970] AC 1099, [1970] 1 All ER 53, [1970] 2 WLR 272, HL;
  affirming [1969] 2 Ch 438, [1969] 1 All ER 1002, [1969] 2 WLR 1067,
  CA   3.22, 3.23, 4.40, 8.73
Business City Express Ltd, Re [1997] 2 BCLC 510, [1997] BCC 826   17.66
Byng v London Life Association Ltd [1990] Ch 170, [1989] 1 All ER 560,
  [1989] 2 WLR 738, CA   9.7–9.9, 11.202, 11.204–11.206, 27.62
Byrne v Kinematograph Renters Society Ltd [1958] 2 All ER 579, [1958] 1
  WLR 762, 102 Sol Jo 509   27.84

Cadburys Schweppes plc v Somji [2001] 1 WLR 615, [2001] 1 BCLC 498,
  [2001] BPIR 172   16.20
Calor Gas Ltd v Piercy [1994] BCC 69, [1994] 2 BCLC 321, ChD   17.44

Table of Cases xxiii

Campbell v Maund (1836) 5 Ad & El 865, 6 LJMC 145, 2 Har & W 457	8.72
Cane v Jones and Others [1980] 1 WLR 1451, [1981] 1 All ER 533, ChD	3.47, 3.65, 3.116, 11.228, 12.62, 14.32
Cannon v Trask (1875) LR 20 Eq 669, 44 LJ Ch 772	6.22, 27.29
Caratal (New) Mines Ltd, Re [1902] 2 Ch 498, 71 LJ Ch 883, [1902] WN 120	7.55
Cardona, Re [1997] BPIR 604, [1997] BCC 697	17.35, 17.64, 24.23
Cassel v Inglis [1916] 2 Ch 211, 85 LJ Ch 569, 114 LT 935	27.75
Catesby v Burnett [1916] 2 Ch 325, 85 LJ Ch 745	9.26
Cawley & Co, Re (1889) 42 ChD 209, 58 LJ Ch 633, CA	14.29
Cazaly Irving Holdings Ltd v Cancol Ltd [1996] 1 All ER 37, [1996] 1 BCLC 100, [1995] BCC 1133	17.66
Ceylon University v Fernando [1960] 1 All ER 631, [1960] 1 WLR 223, 104 Sol Jo 230	27.84
Channel Collieries Trust Ltd v Dover, St Margaret's and Martin Mill Light Rly Co [1914] 1 Ch 568, 83 LJ Ch 417, 110 LT 365	12.80
25 Chesham Place Ltd, Re [1999] Ch D, 26 November 1999	5.54
Chevron (Sydney) Ltd, Re [1963] VR 249, SC, Vic	23.5
Chevron Furnishers Pty Ltd, Re (1992) 8 ACSR 726	18.33, 20.10, 21.9
Chillington Iron Co, Re (1885) 29 Ch D 159, 54 LJ Ch 624	8.62
Chittenden v Pepper; Re Newlands (Seaford) Educational Trust [2006] EWHC 1511 (Ch), [2006] 33 EG 100, [2006] 27 EG 234 (CS)	17.51, 25.18
Choppington Collieries v Johnson [1944] 1 All ER 762, CA	6.29
Citizens Theatre Ltd, Re 1946 SC 14	7.55, 27.47
City Equitable Fire Insurance Co Ltd, Re [1925] Ch 407, [1924] All ER Rep 485, CA	12.6
City Property Investment Trust Corporation Ltd, Petitioners 1951 SC 570, [1951] SLT 371	23.14
Clark & Co, Re 1911 SC 243	7.55
Clark v Workman [1920] 1 IR 107	12.63
Clemens v Clemens Bros Ltd [1976] 2 All ER 268	8.2
Cleve v Financial Corporation (1873) LR 16 Eq 363, 43 LJ Ch 54, 21 WR 839	6.42, 12.54, 27.72
Clydesdale Financial Services Ltd v Smailes (No 1) [2009] EWHC 1745 (Ch), [2009] BCC 810, [2010] BPIR 62	18.16
Colin Gwyer & Associates Ltd v London Wharf (Limehouse) Ltd; Eaton Bray Ltd v Palmer [2002] EWHC 2748 (Ch), [2003] 2 BCLC 153, [2003] BPIR 1099	12.6
Commissioners of Inland Revenue v Conbeer and White [1996] BPIR 398, [1996] BCC 189	17.35, 25.16
Commissioners of the Inland Revenue v The Wimbledon Football Club Ltd [2004] EWHC 1020 (Ch), [2004] All ER (D) 128 (May), ChD	17.66
Conegrade, Re BLD 0511023945 [2002] EWHC 2411 (Ch), [2003] BPIR 358, [2002] All ER (D) 19 (Nov)	3.100
Consolidated Nickel Mines [1914] 1 Ch 883, 83 LJ Ch 760, 21 Mans 273	5.54
Constable v Harris (1824) T&R 496	7.44
Cook v Deeks [1916] 1 AC 554, 85 LJPC 161, [1916–17] All ER Rep 285	8.2
Copal Varnish Co Ltd, Re [1917] 2 Ch 349, 87 LJ Ch 132, [1916–17] All ER Rep 914	12.78
Cortefiel SA, Re [2012] EWHC 2998 (Ch)	23.18
County Bookshops v Grove [2002] EWHC 1160 (Ch), [2003] 1 BCLC 479, [2002] BPIR 772	17.45
Cousins v International Brick Co Ltd [1931] 2 Ch 90, 100 LJ Ch 404, [1931] All ER Rep 229, CA	8.107, 8.111
Criterion Properties plc v Stratford UK Properties LLC [2002] EWCA Civ 1783, [2003] 1 WLR 2108, [2003] 2 BCLC 129	12.6
Cumbrian Newspapers Group Ltd v Cumberland & Westmorland Herald Newspaper & Printing Co Ltd [1987] Ch 1, [1986] 2 All ER 816, [1986] 3 WLR 26	3.23
Cumbrian Newspapers Group Ltd v Cumberland & Westmorland Herald Newspaper & Printing Company [1986] 3 WLR 26	4.40
Currie v Cowdenbeath Football Club [1992] BCLC 1029, 1992 SLT 407	3.8

Davidson v Stanley [2004] EWHC 2595 (Ch), [2005] BPIR 279, [2004] All
 ER (D) 441 (Oct)   25.6
Debtors (Nos 400 IO and 401 IO of 1996), Re [1997] 1 WLR 1319, [1997] 2
 BCLC 144, [1997] BCC 863   17.17, 17.19, 17.23, 17.44, 25.8
Demarco v Perkins [2006] EWCA Civ 188, [2006] BPIR 645, [2006] All ER
 (D) 150 (Jan)   25.3
Dey v Rubber & Mercantile Corporation [1923] 2 Ch 528, 93 LJ Ch 27,
 [1923] All ER Rep 526   4.66
Donaldson v O'Sullivan [2008] EWCA Civ 879, [2009] 1 WLR 924, [2008]
 BPIR 1288   16.2, 16.10
Dorman, Long & Co Ltd, Re, Re South Durham Steel and Iron Co Ltd
 [1934] Ch 635, 103 LJ Ch 316, [1933] All ER Rep 460   4.60
Doyle v Falconer (1866) LR 1 PC 328, 4 Moo PCCNS 203, 36 LJPC 33   15.4
Drax Holdings Limited, Re [2003] EWHC 2743 (Ch), [2004] 1 All ER 903,
 [2004] 1 BCLC 10   23.7
Duce v Commissioner of Inland Revenue (1998) (unreported) 4 December,
 ChD   17.64
Duomatic Ltd, Re [1969] 2 Ch 365, [1969] 2 WLR 114, [1969] 1 All ER 161,
 ChD   3.65, 3.102, 3.111–3.114, 11.228

East Norfolk Tramways Co, Barber's Case, Re (1877) 5 Ch D 963, 26 WR 3   12.38
East Pant-Du United Mining Co v Merryweather (1864) 2 Hem & M 254,
 10 Jur NS 1231, 5 New Rep 166   8.7
East v Bennett Bros [1911] 1 Ch 163, 80 LJ Ch 123, 18 Mans 145   7.16
EIC Services Ltd v Phipps [2003] EWHC 1507 (Ch), [2003] 3 All ER 804,
 [2003] 1 WLR 2360   3.65, 3.101, 3.103
El Sombrero Ltd, Re [1958] Ch 900, [1958] 3 All ER 1, [1958] 3 WLR 349   4.29, 7.21
Eley v Government Security Life Assurance (1875) 1 ExD 20   4.40
Ellis v Hooper (1859) 28 LJ Ex 1   27.41
Enderby Town Football Club v the Football Association [1971] Ch 591,
 [1971] 1 All ER 215, [1970] 3 WLR 1021   27.84
Equitable Life Assurance Society, Re [2002] EWHC 140 (Ch), [2002] BCC
 319, [2002] 2 BCLC 510   4.58, 4.59, 23.4, 23.25
Euro Brokers Holdings Ltd v Monecor (London) Ltd [2002] EWHC 1573
 (Ch), [2003] 1 BCLC 338, [2002] All ER (D) 131 (May)   3.100, 3.103
Express Engineering Works Ltd, Re [1920] 1 Ch 466, 89 LJ Ch 379, 122 LT
 790   3.100

Fender v Commissioners of Inland Revenue [2003] BPIR 1304, [2003] All
 ER (D) 148 (Jul)   17.9, 25.33, 25.35
Fenning v Fenning Environmental Products Ltd [1982] LSG 803   3.14
Finelist, Re [2003] EWHC 1780   16.17
Fireproof Doors, Re, Umney v The Company [1916] 2 Ch 142, 85 LJ Ch
 444, 60 SJ 513   12.69, 12.116, 14.21
Fisher v Keane (1878) 11 Ch D 353, 49 LJ Ch 11, 41 LT 335   27.19
FMS Financial Management Services Ltd, Re (1989) 5 BCC 191   17.68
Forest of Dean Coal Mining Co, Re (1878) 10 Ch D 450, 27 WR 594, 40 LT
 287   12.6
Foss v Harbottle (1843) 2 Hare 461, 67 ER 189   2.52
Foulkes Group plc v Alexander BLD 010202355 [2002] Ch D, 31 January
 2002   3.22
Frontsouth (Witham) Ltd, Re [2011] EWHC 1668 (Ch), [2011] BCC 635,
 [2012] 1 BCLC 818   3.114
Fruit and Vegetable Growers' Association v Kekewich [1912] 2 Ch 52, 81 LJ
 Ch 499, 19 Mans 206   4.18

Gallagher (N T) & Son Ltd (in liq), Re, Shierson v Tomlinson [2002] EWCA
 Civ 404, [2002] 3 All ER 474, [2002] 1 WLR 2380   17.1
Garden Gully United Quartz Mining Co v McLister (1875) 1 App Cas 39,
 24 WR 744, 33 LT 408   12.142

Table of Cases

GJ v Luxembourg (Application No 21156/93) (2003) 36 EHRR 40, [2000] BPIR 1021	16.21, 23.30
Goodfellow v Nelson Line [1912] 2 Ch 324, 81 LJ Ch 564, 19 Mans 265	8.3
Gordon & Breach Science Publishers Ltd, Re [1995] 2 BCLC 189, [1995] BCC 261	16.20
Graham v Van Diemen's Land Co (1856) 1 H & N 541, 26 LJ Ex 73, 2 Jur NS 1191	5.12
Great Northern Salt and Chemical Works, Re, ex p Kennedy (1890) 44 Ch D 472, 59 LJ Ch 288, 2 Meg 46	12.37
Greenhalgh v Arderne Cinemas Ltd [1951] Ch 286, [1950] 2 All ER 1120, 94 SJ 855, CA	4.41, 4.45
Greenwell v Porter [1902] 1 Ch 530, 71 LJ Ch 243, [1902] WN 19	8.1, 8.16
Greymouth-Point Elizabeth Rly and Coal Co Ltd, Re, Yuill v Greymouth-Point Elizabeth Rly and Coal Co Ltd [1904] 1 Ch 32, 73 LJ Ch 92, 11 Mans 85	7.9, 12.76
Greystoke v Hamilton-Smith and Others, Re a Debtor (No 140 IO of 1995) [1997] BPIR 24, [1996] 2 BCLC 429, ChD	17.9
Grimwade v BPS Syndicate (1915) 31 TLR 531	12.87
Grundt v Great Boulder Proprietary Gold Mines Ltd [1948] Ch 145, [1948] 1 All ER 21, [1948] LJR 1100	5.49
Guinness plc v Saunders [1990] 2 AC 663, [1990] 2 WLR 324, [1990] 1 All ER 652, HL, on appeal from Guinness plc v Saunders and Another [1988] 1 WLR 863, [1988] 2 All ER 940, CA	12.14, 12.100, 12.116
H & R Paul & Son Ltd, Re (1974) 118 SJ 166	7.21
Haarhaus & Co GmbH v Law Debenture Trust Corporation plc [1988] BCLC 640	8.70
Hackney Pavilion Ltd, Re [1924] 1 Ch 276, 93 LJ Ch 193, [1923] All ER Rep 524	12.78
Halcrow Holdings Ltd, Re [2011] EWHC 3662 (Ch), [2012] Pens LR 113	23.11
Halifax Sugar Refining Co Ltd v Francklyn (1890) 59 LJ Ch 591, 2 Meg 129, 62 LT 563	12.45
Harben v Phillips (1883) 23 Ch D 14, 31 WR 173, 48 LT 741	8.105, 12.44, 27.49
Harington v Sendall [1903] 1 Ch 921, 72 LJ Ch 396, 51 WR 463	27.18, 27.31
Hartley Baird Ltd, Re [1955] Ch 143, [1954] 3 All ER 695, [1954] 3 WLR 964	12.79
Hawk Insurance Co Ltd, Re [2001] EWCA Civ 241, [2001] 2 BCLC 480, [2001] All ER (D) 289 (Feb)	23.5, 23.7, 23.9, 23.18, 23.21
Haycraft Gold Reduction and Mining Co, Re [1900] 2 Ch 230, 69 LJ Ch 497, 7 Mans 243	4.10
Health & Life Care v SA Asset Mgt (1995) 18 ACSR 153	17.44
Hellenic & General Trust Ltd, Re [1975] 3 All ER 382, [1976] 1 WLR 123, 119 SJ 845	4.55, 4.58, 23.5
Henderson v Bank of Australasia (1890) 45 ChD 330, 59 LJ Ch 794, 63 LT 597, CA	6.30, 6.32, 6.34, 7.36, 27.56, 27.58, 27.59
Hickman v Kent or Romney Marsh Sheep Breeders Association [1915] 1 Ch 881	4.40
Hoare (KG), Re [1997] BPIR 683	17.31, 17.38, 17.49, 17.56
Hockley (William) Ltd, Re [1962] 2 All ER 111, [1962] 1 WLR 555, 106 Sol Jo 308	17.45
Holders Investment Trust Ltd, Re [1971] 2 All ER 289, [1971] 1 WLR 583, (1970) 115 SJ 202	4.40, 4.41, 4.45, 8.3
Holmes v Keyes [1959] Ch 199, [1958] 2 All ER 129, [1958] 2 WLR 772, CA; reversing [1958] Ch 670, [1958] 1 All ER 721, [1958] 2 WLR 540	8.65
Homer District Consolidated Gold Mines, Re, ex p Smith (1888) 39 Ch D 546, 58 LJ Ch 134, 60 LT 97	12.43, 12.44, 27.66
Hood Sailmakers Ltd v Axford; *sub nom* Hood Sailmakers Ltd v Adford and Bainbridge [1996] 4 All ER 830, [1997] 1 WLR 625, [1997] 1 BCLC 721, QBD	12.124
Hook v Jewson Ltd [1997] BPIR 100, [1997] 1 BCLC 664, [1997] BCC 752, ChD	25.6

Hooper v Kerr, Stuart & Co Ltd (1900) 45 Sol Jo 139, 83 LT 729, 17 TLR
162   4.10
Horbury Bridge Coal, Iron and Waggon Co, Re (1879) 11 Ch D 109, 48 LJ
Ch 341, 27 WR 433   6.30, 27.56
Horrocks v Lowe [1975] AC 135, [1974] 1 All ER 662, [1974] 2 WLR 282   26.179
Huth v Clarke (1890) 25 QBD 391, 55 JP 86, 59 LJQB 559   12.118
Hydrodan (Corby) Ltd (in Liquidation), Re [1994] BCC 161, [1994] 2 BCLC
180, (1994) *The Times*, February 19, ChD   12.99

Indian Zoedone Co, Re (1884) 26 ChD 70, 53 LJ Ch 468, 50 LT 547, CA   7.36, 14.21
Industrial Equity (Pacific) Ltd, Re [1991] 2 HKLR 614, HC, Hong Kong   23.5
Industrial Services Group Ltd (No 2), Re [2003] BPIR 597   16.17
IRC v Adam & Partners Ltd [2002] BCC 247, [2001] 1 BCLC 222, [2000]
BPIR 986, CA   23.4
IRC v Bland and Sargant [2003] EWHC 1068 (Ch), [2003] BPIR 1274   23.4
IRC v Conbeer [1996] BCC 189, [1996] BPIR 398   24.22
IRC v Wimbledon Football Club Ltd [2004] EWCA Civ 655, [2004] BCC
638, [2005] 1 BCLC 66   17.68, 25.32
Isaacs v Chapman [1915] WN 413, 32 TLR 183   8.96
Isle of Wight Railway Co v Tahourdin (1883) 25 Ch D 320, 53 LJ Ch 353,
32 WR 297   4.24

Jackson v Greenfield [1998] BPIR 699   25.32
Jackson v Hamlyn [1953] Ch 577, [1953] 1 All ER 887, [1953] 2 WLR 709   9.23
Jacobsson v Sweden (Application 10842/84) (1989) 12 EHRR 56   23.30
Jax Marine Pty Ltd, Re [1967] 1 NSWR 145   23.5
Jeffrey David Rose v Brian Kenneth McGivern and Others, No 2 (1998)
(unreported) 8 June, Ch D   4.19
John v Rees and Others, Martin and Another v Davis and Others, Rees and
Another v John [1970] Ch 345, [1969] 2 WLR 1294, [1969] 2 All ER
274, ChD   9.7, 27.36, 27.42, 27.61, 27.62
Johnson v Davies [1999] Ch 117, [1999] 3 WLR 1299, [1998] BPIR 607, CA   17.56
Jones v Victoria Graving Dock Co (1877) 2 QBD 314, 25 WR 501, 36 LT
347, CA   14.28

Kaye v Croydon Tramways Co [1898] 1 Ch 358, 67 LJ Ch 222, 78 LT 237,
CA   5.15, 6.24
Kayley Vending Ltd, Re [2009] EWHC 904 (Ch), [2009] BCC 578, [2011] 1
BCLC 114   18.1
Kelantan Coconut Estates Ltd and Reduced, Re [1920] WN 274, 64 Sol Jo
700   7.15
Kerr v John Mottram Ltd [1940] Ch 657, [1940] 2 All ER 629   14.21, 27.93
Kerr v Wilkie (1860) 24 JP 211, 6 Jur NS 383, 8 WR 286, 1 LT 501   9.14, 27.63
Keveling v Netherlands (Application No 3171/96) (10 September 1997)   16.21
Khan v Permayer [2001] BPIR 95, CA   17.44
King v Anthony [1998] 2 BCLC 517, [1999] BPIR 73, [1997] All ER (D) 58   16.16
Knowles v Coutts & Co [1998] BPIR 96   25.6
Knowles v Zoological Society of London [1959] 1 WLR 823, [1959] 2 All
ER 595, [1959] 103 SJ, CA   27.44

La Compagnie de Mayville v Whitley [1896] 1 Ch 788, 65 LJ Ch 729, 74 LT
441, CA   12.52, 27.70
La Mutuelle Du Mans Assurance Iard, Re; Re Scottish Eagle Insurance Co
Ltd [2005] EWHC 1599 (Ch), [2006] BCC 11   23.7
Labouchere v Earl of Wharncliffe (1879) 13 ChD 346, 28 WR 367, 41 LT
638   27.24, 27.25
Lam Soon Australia Pty Ltd v Molit (No 55) Pty Ltd [1997] BPIR 481   17.64
Land Credit Co of Ireland, Re (1869) LR 4 Ch App 460   14.5, 27.87
Landmark Corporation Ltd, Re [1968] 1 NSWR 759   23.5
Lands Allotment Co, Re [1894] 1 Ch 616, [1891–4] All ER Rep 1032, 63 LJ
Ch 291, CA   14.27

Lehman Brothers International (Europe) (In Administration), Re [2009] EWCA Civ 1161, [2010] Bus LR 489, [2010] BCC 272	23.4
Lehman Brothers International (Europe) (in administration), Re; Four Private Investment Funds v Lomas [2008] EWHC 2869 (Ch), [2008] All ER (D) 237 (Nov)	18.12
Link Agricultural Pty Ltd v Shanahan (1988) 28 ACSR 498	18.33, 20.10, 21.9
Linter Textiles Corporation Ltd, Re [1991] 2 VR 561	23.5
Liverpool Household Stores Association Ltd, Re (1890) 59 LJ Ch 616, 2 Meg 217, 62 LT 873	12.120
Longfield Parish Council v Wright (1919) 88 LJ Ch 119, (1918) 16 LGR 865	12.55, 27.73
MacConnell v E Prill & Co [1916] 2 Ch 57, 85 LJ Ch 674, 60 Sol Jo 556	3.54, 6.25, 6.39
Mackenzie & Co, Re [1916] 2 Ch 450, 85 LJ Ch 804, 115 LT 440	6.59
MacLelland v National Union of Journalists [1975] ICR 116	12.48
MacPherson v European Strategic Bureau Ltd [2002] BCC 39, [2000] 2 BCLC 683, (2000) 97(35) LSG 36, CA; [1999] 2 BCLC 203, [1999] TLR 144, (1999) *The Times*, March 1, ChD	12.134, 12.135
Magadi Soda Co, Re (1925) 94 LJ Ch 217, [1925] WN 50	4.60
Mahon v Air New Zealand [1984] AC 808, [1984] 3 WLR 884, (1983) *The Times*, 21 October, CA	27.84
March Estates plc v Gunmark Ltd [1996] 2 BCLC 1, [1996] BPIR 439, [1996] 2 EGLR 38, ChD	17.64
Marconi Corporation plc, Re [2003] EWHC 1083 Ch, [2003] All ER (D) 126 (May)	23.4
Marshall's Valve Gear Co Ltd v Manning, Wardle & Co Ltd [1909] 1 Ch 267, 78 LJ Ch 46, 15 Mans 379	2.51
Martin v Walker (1918) 145 LT Jo 377	6.21
Marx v Estates & General Investments Ltd [1975] 3 All ER 1064, [1976] 1 WLR 380, [1975] STC 671	8.18
MB Group plc, Re [1989] BCLC 672, 5 BCC 684	4.56
McLaren v Thomson [1917] 2 Ch 261, 86 LJ Ch 713, 117 LT 417; affirming [1917] 2 Ch 41	8.114
McMillan v Le Roi Mining Co [1906] 1 Ch 331	8.75
Melville v Graham-Yooll (unreported) referred to in [1936] SLT 54	7.37
Menier v Hooper's Telegraph Co (1874) 9 Ch App 350, 43 LJ Ch 330, 22 WR 396	8.2
Mercantile Investment and General Trust Co v International Co of Mexico [1893] 1 Ch 484n, 68 LT 603n, 7 TLR 616	4.67
Minmar (929) Ltd, Re [2011] EWHC 1159 (Ch), [2011] BCC 485, [2012] 1 BCLC 798	22.3
Minster Assets plc, Re [1985] BCLC 200, (1985) 82 LS Gaz 277, (1985) PCC 105, ChD	4.56
Mond v MBNA Europe Bank Ltd [2010] EWHC 1710 (Ch), [2011] Bus LR 513, [2010] BPIR 1167	25.38
Monecor (London) Ltd v Ahmed [2008] BPIR 458, [2008] All ER (D) 22 (Mar)	25.29
Montrotier Asphalte Co, Re, Perry's Case (1876) 34 LT 716	12.58
Moon Development Corporation v Power Boat International [1995] NZLR 56	8.42
Moor v Anglo-Italian Bank (1879) 10 ChD 681, 40 LT 620, 27 WR 652	17.44
Moorgate Mercantile Holdings Ltd, Re [1980] 1 WLR 227, [1980] 1 WLR 227, 123 Sol Jo 557	6.26, 6.37, 6.40
Morgan v Driscoll (1922) 38 TLR 251	27.44
Morgan v Gray [1953] Ch 83, [1953] 1 All ER 213, [1953] 2 WLR 140	6.62
Morris v Kanssen [1946] AC 459, 174 LT 353, 115 LJ Ch 177, HL	4.11
Mourant & Co Trustees Ltd v Sixty UK Ltd (in liq) [2010] EWHC 1890 (Ch), [2010] BCC 882, [2011] 1 BCLC 383	17.6, 17.64
Murray v Newham Citizens Advice Bureau Ltd [2003] All ER (D) 12 (Jan)	5.54
Musselwhite v C H Musselwhite [1962] Ch 964, [1962] 1 All ER 201, [1962] 2 WLR 374	6.58, 8.16

MyTravel Group plc, Re [2004] EWCA Civ 1734, [2005] 2 BCLC 123, [2004]
  All ER (D) 221 (Dec) — 23.4, 23.5, 23.7, 23.32
Mytre Investments Ltd v Reynolds and Others (No 2) [1996] BPIR 464 — 25.8

N (a Debtor), Re [2002] BPIR 1024 — 25.33
National Assembly for Wales v (1) Elizabeth Condron (2) Miller Argent
  (South Wales) Ltd [2006] EWCA Civ 1573, [2007] LGR 87, [2007] 2
  P & CR 38 — 26.213, 26.214
National Bank Ltd, Re [1966] 1 WLR 819, [1966] 1 All ER 1006, ChD — 4.55
National Dwelling Society v Sykes [1894] 3 Ch 159, 63 LJ Ch 906, 1 Mans
  457 — 7.32, 9.1, 9.4, 27.60
National Westminster Bank plc v Scher [1998] BCLC 124, [1998] BPIR 224 — 17.64
NatWest Bank plc v Yadgaroff [2011] EWHC 3711 (Ch), [2012] BPIR 371 — 17.31, 17.51, 25.18
Neal v Quinn [1916] WN 223 — 12.84
Neath Port Talbot CBC v Ware — 26.216, 26.217
Nell v Longbottom [1894] 1 QB 767 — 27.45
Neptune (Vehicle Washing Equipment) Ltd v Fitzgerald (No 2) [1995] BCC
  1000 — 12.129, 12.135, 12.136
New Millennium Experience Co Ltd, Re [2003] EWHC 1823 (Ch), [2004] 1
  All ER 687, [2004] 1 BCLC 19 — 22.1
New York Taxicab Co Ltd, Re, Sequin v New York Taxicab Co Ltd [1913] 1
  Ch 1, 82 LJ Ch 41, 19 Mans 389 — 4.65
Newhaven Local Board v Newhaven School Board (1885) 30 ChD 350, 34
  WR 172, 53 LT 571 — 26.112
NFU (or National Farmers' Union) Development Trust Ltd, Re [1973] 1 All
  ER 135, [1972] 1 WLR 1548, 116 Sol Jo 679 — 4.67
Nordic Bank plc v International Harvester Australia Ltd [1983] 2 VR 298,
  FC, Vic — 23.5
Normandy v Ind Coope & Co Ltd [1908] 1 Ch 84, 77 LJ Ch 82, 97 LT 872 — 6.26
North Eastern Insurance Co, Re [1919] 1 Ch 198, 88 LJ Ch 121, 63 Sol Jo
  117 — 12.76
North-West Transportation Co Ltd and Beatty v Beatty (1887) 12 App Cas
  589, 56 LJPC 102, 36 WR 647 — 12.87
Northern Counties Securities v Jackson and Steeple Ltd [1974] 2 All ER
  625, [1974] 1 WLR 1133, 118 Sol Jo 498 — 8.1, 9.12
NRMA Ltd, Re (1999–2000) 33 ACSR 595 — 23.5

O'Doherty v West Limerick Resources [1999] IESC 39 (14 May 1999) — 6.58
Oliver v Dalgleish [1963] 3 All ER 330, [1963] 1 WLR 1274, 107 SJ 1039 — 8.112
Opera Photographic Ltd, Re [1989] 1 WLR 634, [1989] BCLC 763, 5 BCC
  601 — 4.27, 7.21

Palmer Marine Services Ltd, Re [1986] 1 WLR 573, [1986] BCLC 106, 1
  BCC 99, 557 — 16.20
Parker & Cooper v Reading [1926] 1 Ch 975, 96 LJ Ch 23, [1926] All ER
  Rep 323 — 3.65, 3.100
Parkstone Ltd v Gulf Guarantee Bank plc [1990] TLR 477, [1990] BCLC
  850, [1990] BCC 534 — 6.75, 6.76
Parrott, Re, ex p Cullen [1891] 2 QB 151, 60 LJQB 567, 8 Morr 185 — 8.106
Patent Wood Keg Syndicate v Pearse [1906] WN 164, 50 Sol Jo 650 — 4.18, 8.68
Peña v Dale [2003] EWHC 1065 (Ch), [2004] 2 BCLC 508, [2003] All ER
  (D) 416 (Mar) — 3.100, 3.103
Pearce Duff & Co Ltd, Re [1960] 3 All ER 222, [1960] 1 WLR 1014, 104 Sol
  Jo 764 — 6.13
Pedley v Inland Waterways Association Ltd [1977] 1 All ER 209, 120 Sol Jo
  569 — 27.21
Peel v London and North Western Railway Co [1907] 1 Ch 5, 76 LJ Ch 152,
  14 Mans 30 — 8.84
Pender v Lushington (1877) 6 Ch D 70, 46 LJ Ch 317 — 8.1, 8.71
Peninsular and Oriental Steam Navigation Co, Re [2006] EWHC 3279 (Ch),
  [2007] Bus LR 554 — 4.56

Table of Cases xxix

Philip Alexander Securities & Futures Ltd, Re [1998] BPIR 383, [1999] 1 BCLC 124, [1988] BCC 819, ChD	17.35
Phoenix Electric Light and Power Co Ltd, Re (1883) 31 WR 398, 48 LT 260	8.53
Phoenix Shannon plc v Purkey (No 5) [1997] IEHC 214, [1997] 2 ILRM 381	5.54
Piercy v S Mills & Co [1920] 1 Ch 77, 88 LJ Ch 509, [1918–19] All ER Rep 313	12.6
Polly Peck International Plc, Re [1991] BCC 503	18.41
Poplar Housing and Regeneration Community Association v Donoghue [2001] EWCA Civ 595, [2001] Fam Law 588, [2002] QB 48	16.21
Portuguese Consolidated Copper Mines Ltd, Re, ex p Badman, ex p Bosanquet (1890) 45 Ch D 16, 2 Meg 249, 39 WR 25	12.46
Power Builders (Surrey) Ltd; Power v Latos, Re [2008] EWHC 2607 (Ch), [2010] BCC 11, [2009] 1 BCLC 250	16.16
Practice Note [1934] WN 142	23.21
Precision Dippings Ltd v Precision Dippings Marketing Ltd [1986] Ch 447, [1985] 3 WLR 812, [1985] BCLC 385	3.114
Prudential Assurance Co Ltd v PRG Powerhouse Ltd (in administration) [2007] EWHC 1002 (Ch), [2010] BCC 882, [2011] 1 BCLC 383	17.6, 17.64, 17.67, 25.32
Puddephatt v Leith (No 1) [1916] 1 Ch 200, 85 LJ Ch 185, [1914–15] All ER Rep 260	8.16
Pyle Works (No 2), Re [1891] 1 Ch 173, 60 LJ Ch 114, 2 Meg 327	14.21
Quin & Axtens v Salmon [1909] AC 442, 78 LJ Ch 506, 53 SJ 575, HL; affirming *sub nom* Salmon v Quin & Axtens Ltd [1909] 1 Ch 311, CA	4.40
R (Friends of Hethel) v South Norfolk District Council [2010] EWCA Civ 894, [2011] 1 WLR 1216, [2011] PTSR 630	26.89
R (on the application of Island Farm Development Ltd) v Bridgend County Borough Council [2006] EWHC 2189 (Admin), [2007] LGR 19, [2006] All ER (D) 118 (Aug)	26.215
R (on the application of Lewis) v Persimmon Homes Teesside Ltd, *sub nom* R (on the application of Lewis) v Redcar & Cleveland Borough Council [2008] EWCA Civ 746, [2009] 1 WLR 83, [2008] 2 P & CR 436	26.218, 26.219
R (on the application of Nash) v Chelsea College of Art and Design [2001] EWHC Admin 538, (2001) *The Times*, 25 July, [2001] All ER (D) 133 (Jul)	7.34
R (on the application of Tromans) v Cannock Chase District Council [2004] EWCA Civ 1036, [2004] LGR 735, (2004) *The Times*, 25 August, [2004] All ER (D) 504 (Jul)	26.99
R (on the Application of WB) v Leeds School Organisation Committee [2002] EWHC 1927 (Admin), [2003] ELR 67, [2003] ACD 5	26.145
R v Alnwick District Council ex parte Robson [1997] EGCS 144	26.144
R v Bradford City Metropolitan Council, ex p Wilson [1990] 2 QB 375n, [1989] 3 All ER 140, [1990] 2 WLR 255	26.92, 26.95, 26.96
R v Brent Health Authority ex parte Francis [1985] QB 869, [1985] 1 All ER 74, [1984] 3 WLR 1317	26.167
R v Brent London Borough Council ex parte Assegai (1987) *The Times*, 18 June	26.168
R v Cooper (1870) LR 5 QB 457, 39 LJQB 273	8.53, 27.48
R v County of London Quarter Sessions Appeals Committee ex parte Rossi [1956] 1 QB 682, [1956] 1 All ER 670, [1956] 2 WLR 800	27.35
R v D'Oyly *sub nom* R v Rector and Churchwardens of St Mary, Lambeth (1840) 4 JP 532, 12 Ad & El 139, 9 LJMC 113	7.32
R v Flintshire County Council ex parte Armstrong-Braun [2001] EWCA Civ 345, (2001) 3 LGLR 34, [2001] BLGR 344	26.38
R v Grimshaw (1847) 5 Dow & L 249, 17 LJQB 19, 12 Jur 134	9.1, 27.60
R v Highbury Corner Magistrates' Court ex parte Ewing, *sub nom* Ex p Ewing [1991] 3 All ER 192, [1991] 1 WLR 388	26.98
R v Hill (1825) 4 B & C 426, 3 Dow & Ry MC 219, 6 Dow & Ry KB 593	5.16

R v Kensington and Chelsea Royal London Borough Council ex parte
  Stoop [1992] 1 PLR 58   26.137
R v Liverpool City Council ex p Professional Association of Teachers
  (1984) *The Times*, 22 March   27.83
R v Liverpool City Council ex parte Liverpool Taxi Fleet Operators
  Association [1975] 1 WLR 701, [1975] 1 All ER 379, 73 LGR 143   26.138, 26.238
R v Local Commissioner for Local Government for North and North East
  England, ex parte Liverpool City Council [2000] LGR 571   26.220
R v Mariquita and New Granada Mining Co, *sub nom* R v Maraquita and
  New Granada Mining Co (1858) 1 E & E 289, 28 LJQB 67, 5 Jur NS
  725   14.18
R v Rector etc of St Mary, Lambeth (1838) 2 JP 423, 8 Ad & El 356, 2 Jur
  566   8.74, 27.48
R v Rector of Birmingham (1837) 7 A & E 254   27.48
R v Secretary of State ex parte London Borough of Hillingdon [1986] 1 All
  ER 273   26.20
R v Swansea City Council ex parte Elitestone Ltd (1993) 66 P&CR 422,
  [1993] PLR 65, [1993] 2 EGLR 212   26.59
R v Tavistock Commissioners ex parte Adams (1969) 46 TC 154, 48 ATC
  406, [1969] TR 387   27.35
R v Turner [1910] 1 KB 346, CA   27.23
R v Wandsworth London Borough Council ex parte Darker Enterprises Ltd
  (1999) 1 LGLR 601, [1999] All ER (D) 14 (Jan)   26.136
R v Wimbledon Local Board (1882) 8 QBD 459, 46 JP 292, 51 LJQB 219   8.65
R W Peak (Kings Lynn) Ltd, Re [1998] Ch D, Companies Court, 24
  October 1997   3.113
RAC Motoring Services Ltd (1), Royal Automobile Club Ltd (2) [1998] Ch
  D Companies Court, 8 July 1989   6.26
Rae, Re [1995] BCC 102   16.1
Rankin & Blackmore, Petitioners [1950] SC 218, 1950 S.L.T. 160   23.14
Ravichandran, Re [2004] BPIR 814, ChD   25.3
Regent's Canal Ironworks Co, Re [1867] WN 79   12.69, 27.78
Reid v Hamblin [2001] BPIR 929   25.11, 25.13
Robert v Pinnacle Entertainment Ltd [2003] EWHC 2394 (Ch), [2004] BPIR
  208, [2003] All ER (D) 347 (Oct)   17.38, 25.33
Robson v Premier Oil and Pipe Line Co Ltd [1915] 2 Ch 124, 84 LJ Ch 629,
  [1914–15] All ER Rep 419   8.13
Rolfe v Rolfe [2010] EWHC 244 (Ch), [2010] 2 BCLC 525, [2010] Bus LR
  D99   3.65
Rosen v Bruyns, NO [1973] 1 SALR 815   23.5
Ross v Telford [1997] BCC 945, [1998] 1 BCLC 82, (1997) 94(28) LSG 26,
  CA   4.28, 7.21
Royal British Bank v Turquand (1856) 6 E & B 327, 25 LJQB 317, 2 Jur NS
  663   12.143
Russell v Northern Bank Development Corporation Ltd [1992] 1 WLR 589   8.17

Salcombe Hotel Development Corporation Ltd, Re [1991] BCLC 44, (1989)
  5 BCC 807, (1988) *The Times*, 25 November, ChD   7.23, 20.10
Salisbury Gold Mining Co v Hathorn [1897] AC 268, 66 LJPC 62, PC   9.3
Salomon v Salomon & Co [1897] AC 22, 66 LJ Ch 35, [1895–9] All ER Rep
  33, HL   2.1
Scadding v Lorant (1851) 3 HLC 418, 15 Jur 955, HL   8.114, 9.14, 27.63
Schofield v Schofield [2011] EWCA Civ 154, [2011] 2 BCLC 319   3.65
Sea Voyager Maritime Inc v Bielecki (t/a Hughes Hooker & Co); *sub nom*
  Bielecki, Re [1999] 1 All ER 628, [1999] BCC 924, [1999] 1 BCLC
  133, ChD   17.23, 17.64, 17.66, 25.32
Second Consolidated Trust Ltd v Ceylon Amalgamated Tea & Rubber
  Estates Ltd [1943] 2 All ER 567, 87 Sol Jo 299, 169 LT 324   8.54
Secretary of State for Business, Innovation and Skills v Doffman, Re
  Stakefield (Midlands) Ltd [2010] EWHC 3175 (Ch), [2011] 2 BCLC
  541   3.65

Secretary of State v Deverell [2001] Ch 340, [2000] 2 WLR 907, [2000] 2 All
 ER 365 — 12.99
Seventeenth Canute Pty Ltd v Bradley Air Conditioning Pty Ltd (1986) 11
 ACLC 193 — 17.44
Shaw (John) & Sons (Salford) Ltd v Shaw [1935] 2 KB 113, 104 LJKB 549,
 [1935] All ER Rep 456 — 2.51
Shaw v Tati Concessions [1913] 1 Ch 292, 82 LJ Ch 159, 108 LT 487 — 8.65
Sick and Funeral Society of St John's Sunday School, Golcar, Re [1973] Ch
 51, [1972] 2 All ER 439, [1972] 2 WLR 962 — 27.36
Siemens Bros v Burns [1918] 2 Ch 324, 87 LJ Ch 572, 119 LT 352 — 8.14
Sisu Capital Fund Ltd and others v Tucker and others [2005] EWHC 2170
 (Ch), [2006] BCC 463, [2006] BPIR 154 — 17.69, 25.32
Skipton Building Society v Collins [1998] BPIR 267 — 17.17
Sly, Spink & Co, Re, Hertslet's Case [1911] 2 Ch 430, 81 LJ Ch 55 — 12.80
Smith v Henniker-Major & Co (a firm) [2002] EWCA Civ 762, [2003] Ch
 182, [2002] 3 WLR 1848 — 12.41
Smith v Paringa Mines [1906] 2 Ch 193, 75 LJ Ch 702 — 9.21
Smurthwaite v Simpson-Smith [2006] EWCA Civ 1183; [2006] BPIR 1504,
 [2006] All ER (D) 368 (Jul) — 16.17, 25.37
Smyth v Darley (1849) 2 HLC 789 — 6.1, 6.57, 27.36
Sofaer v Anglo Irish Asset Finance Plc [2011] EWHC 1480 (Ch), [2011]
 BPIR 1736 — 17.31, 17.51, 25.18
Somji v Cadbury Schweppes plc [2001] BPIR 172, [2001] 1 WLR 615, [2001]
 1 BCLC 498, CA — 25.33
Sovereign Life Assurance Co v Dodd [1892] 2 QB 573, CA — 4.58, 23.5
Spiller v Mayo (Rhodesia) Development Co (1908) Ltd [1926] WN 78 — 8.111
Sporrong and Lönnroth v Sweden (Applications 7151/75 and 7152/75)
 (1982) 5 EHRR 35 — 23.30
State of Wyoming Syndicate, Re [1901] 2 Ch 431, 70 LJ Ch 727 — 4.15
Stevens ex parte (1852) 16 JP 632 — 6.31, 27.57
Sticky Fingers Restaurant Ltd, Re [1991] BCC 754, [1992] BCLC 84, ChD — 4.27
Stonegate Securities Ltd v Gregory [1980] Ch 576, [1980] 3 WLR 168, [1980]
 1 All ER 241, CA — 17.45
Stoughton v Reynolds (1736) Fortes Rep 168, 2 Stra 1045, Lee temp Hard
 274 — 9.1, 27.60
Sweatfield Ltd, Re [1998] BPIR 276, [1997] BCC 744, ChD — 17.31

T&N Ltd (No 2) [2006] EWHC 842 (Ch), [2006] 1 WLR 2831, [2006] BPIR
 1268 — 17.19, 17.46, 17.47, 23.7
T&N Ltd (No 4), Re [2006] EWHC 1447 (Ch), [2007] Bus LR 1411, [2007] 1
 All ER 851 — 23.12
T&N Ltd, Re [2005] EWHC 2870 (Ch), [2006] 3 All ER 697, [2006] 1 WLR
 1728 — 23.30
Tack, Re [2000] BPIR 164, ChD — 16.20
Tager v Westpac Banking Corporation and Others [1997] BPIR 543, [1997] 1
 BCLC 313, [1998] BCC 73, ChD — 25.26
Tanner v Everitt [2004] EWHC 1130 (Ch), [2004] BPIR 1026, [2004] All ER
 (D) 192 (May) — 17.68
Taurine Co, Re (1883) 25 Ch D 118, 53 LJ Ch 271, 32 WR 129 — 12.13, 27.82
Tayplan Ltd v Smith [2011] CSIH 8, [2012] BCC 523, 2011 GWD 9-211 — 3.65, 3.101
TDG Plc, Re [2008] EWHC 2334 (Ch), [2009] 1 BCLC 445 — 4.55
Tea Corp Ltd, Re [1904] 1 Ch 12 — 23.32
Telewest Communications plc, Re; Re Telewest Finance (Jersey) Ltd [2004]
 EWHC 924 (Ch), [2005] 1 BCLC 752, ChD — 23.7, 23.9
Tenby Corporation v Mason [1908] 1 Ch 457, 6 LGR 233, 72 JP 89 — 26.115
Thomas v Ken Thomas Ltd [2006] EWCA Civ 1504, [2007] Bus LR 429,
 [2007] BPIR 959 — 25.32
Thomas v York Trustees Ltd BLD 1607012402 [2001] Ch D, 13 July 2001 — 3.24
Tiessen v Henderson [1899] 1 Ch 861, 68 LJ Ch 353, 80 LT 483, 6 Mans
 340, 47 WR 459 — 5.138, 6.23, 6.26, 27.52
Torbuck v Westbury (Lord) [1902] 2 Ch 871, 71 LJ Ch 845, 51 WR 133 — 6.28, 27.55
Torvale Group Ltd, Re [1999] 2 BCLC 605, [1999] All ER (D) 944 — 3.65

Tradition (UK) Limited v Ahmed [2008] EWHC 2946 (Ch), [2009] BPIR
626   25.6, 25.29, 25.33
Transbus International Ltd, Re [2004] EWHC 932 (Ch), [2004] 2 All ER
911, [2004] 1 WLR 2654   18.10
Transport Ltd v Schonburg (1905) 21 TLR 305   4.11
Transvaal Lands Co v New Belgium (Transvaal) Land and Development Co
[1914] 2 Ch 488, 84 LJ Ch 94, 21 Mans 364   12.84
Trident Fashions plc, Re; Anderson v Kroll Ltd [2004] EWHC 293 (Ch),
[2004] 2 BCLC 35, (2004) *The Times*, 23 April   25.33

UDL Argos Engineering v Li Lo Lin [2001] HKCFA 53   23.20
UK Safety Group Ltd v Heane [1998] 2 BCLC 208   12.125
Union Music Ltd v Watson [2003] EWCA Civ 180, [2003] 1 BCLC 453,
[2003] All ER (D) 328 (Jan)   4.28
United Provident Assurance Co Ltd, Re [1910] 2 Ch 477, 79 LJ Ch 639   23.5

Vale of Neath and South Wales Brewery Joint Stock Co, Re, Lawes's Case
(1852) 1 De GM & G 421, 21 LJ Ch 688, 16 Jur 343   5.15
Villatte v 38 Cleveland Square Management Ltd [2002] EWCA Civ 1705,
[2002] All ER (D) 218 (Oct)   5.54

Walker v W A Personnel Ltd [2002] BPIR 621   3.115
Walker v Wimbourne (1976) 137 CLR 1   17.61
Wall v Exchange Investment Corporation [1926] Ch 143, 95 LJ Ch 132,
[1925] All ER Rep 318   7.56
Wall v London & Northern Assets Corporation (No 2) [1899] 1 Ch 550, 68
LJ Ch 248, 6 Mans 312   7.56
Wall v London and Northern Assets Corporation [1898] 2 Ch 480   7.44, 7.53
Wandsworth Gaslight Co v Wright (1870) 22 LT 404   7.32
Warden & Hotchkiss, Re [1945] Ch 270, [1945] 1 All ER 507, 114 LJ Ch 342   6.59, 6.76
Waste Recycling Group Plc, Re [2003] EWHC 2065 (Ch), [2004] BCC 328,
[2004] 1 BCLC 352   23.30
Waxed Papers Ltd, Re [1937] 2 All ER 481, 81 Sol Jo 397, 156 LT 452   8.87, 9.20
West Canadian Collieries Ltd, Re [1962] Ch 370, [1962] 1 All ER 26, [1961]
3 WLR 1416   6.57
Whitchurch Insurance Consultants Ltd, Re [1993] BCLC 1359, [1994] BCC
51   4.27
White v Bristol Aeroplane Co Ltd [1953] 1 All ER 40   4.41, 4.45
Wills v Murray (1850) 4 Ex 843, 19 LJ Ex 209   9.14, 27.63
Wimbledon Local Board, Re (1882) 8 QBD 459, 46 JP 292, 51 LJQB 219   27.48
Wise v Lansdell [1921] 1 Ch 420, 90 LJ Ch 178, 124 LT 502   8.16
Woodford v Smith (1970) 120 LJ News 333, [1970] 1 All ER 1091n, [1970] 1
WLR 806   27.49
Woven Rugs Ltd, Re [2002] 1 BCLC 324   4.27
Wright & Another v Atlas Wright (Europe) Ltd [1999] 2 BCLC 301, [1999]
BCC 163, (1999) *The Times*, 3 February   3.106, 3.115, 3.117
Wright v Official Receiver [2001] BPIR 196, Cty Ct   25.3

York Tramways Co v Willows (1882) 8 QBD 685, 51 LJQB 257, 30 WR 624,
CA   12.65
Young v Ladies' Imperial Club [1920] 2 KB 523, 89 LJKB 563, 36 TLR 392,
CA   12.48, 12.54, 27.31, 27.36, 27.72

TABLE OF STATUTES

References are to paragraph numbers.

Banking and Financial Dealings Act 1971	6.73
Bankruptcy Act 1914	
s 16	17.3
Bankruptcy (Scotland) Act 1985	5.133, 6.61, 11.69
Companies (Tables A to F) Regulations 1985, SI 1985/805	
reg 62	8.72
Companies Act 1862	6.28, 6.76, 27.55
Companies Act 1948	3.58, 6.75, 7.13
s 206	17.2
s 306	17.2
Sch 1	
reg 52	5.12–5.14
Companies Act 1976	7.13
Companies Act 1980	
s 43(3)(c)	3.114
s 88	4.38
Companies Act 1985	2.2–2.4, 2.7, 2.9, 2.28, 2.33, 2.49, 3.1, 3.2, 3.4, 3.28, 3.57, 3.58, 3.60, 3.113, 4.2, 4.13, 4.31, 4.32, 4.42, 5.35, 5.56, 5.67, 5.106, 6.5, 6.6, 6.11, 6.25, 6.76, 8.22, 8.34, 11.7, 11.12, 11.25, 11.55, 12.97, 13.7, 16.3, 23.1, 26.120, 27.63
s 5(8)	6.65
s 8(2)	2.19
s 8(4)	2.28
s 14	4.40
s 35(1)	2.45
s 39	2.47
s 41	6.95
s 80	5.56, 5.59
s 80A	3.55, 5.67, 5.68
s 143	3.113, 4.2
s 159	3.113
s 166(4)	5.95
s 247(3)	17.8
s 270	3.114
s 307	3.54
s 317	12.129–12.131, 12.134–12.136
s 319	3.107–3.109
s 320	3.100
s 327	8.103
s 346	12.97
s 359	3.113
s 368	4.15
s 369(3)	6.39
Companies Act 1985—continued	
s 371	15.6
s 376	4.33
s 378	2.8, 3.48, 3.50, 6.28
s 378(1)	3.50, 3.51
s 378(3)	6.39
s 378(5)	3.52
s 379A(2)(a)	3.56
s 379A(2)(b)	3.56
s 379A(3)	3.56
s 379A(4)	3.56
s 386	3.55
s 394	10.39
s 425	17.46, 18.2, 23.30, 23.32
ss 425–427	23.1
s 431	5.35
s 431(2)	5.35
s 431(3)	5.35
s 431(4)	5.35
s 459	4.28, 6.57
s 744	6.95
Companies Act 1989	3.55, 10.1
Pt II	10.1
Companies Act 2006	1.6, 1.7, 2.1–2.4, 2.9, 2.11–2.14, 2.28, 2.33, 2.37, 2.38, 2.40, 2.42, 2.43, 2.49, 2.52, 3.1, 3.4–3.6, 3.17, 3.42, 3.43, 3.48, 3.57, 3.58, 3.60, 3.62, 3.67, 3.68, 3.71, 3.72, 3.75, 3.77, 3.96–3.98, 3.111, 4.2, 4.21, 4.33, 4.38, 4.41, 4.42, 4.45, 4.51, 5.16, 5.24–5.26, 5.40, 5.43, 5.46, 5.56, 5.59, 5.68, 5.92, 5.100, 5.106, 5.129, 5.132, 6.1, 6.9, 6.11, 6.13, 6.19, 6.25, 6.36, 6.47, 6.57, 6.58, 6.72, 6.73, 6.79, 7.2, 7.6, 7.8, 7.27, 7.32, 7.53, 8.19, 8.22, 8.23, 8.25, 8.49, 8.82, 8.85, 8.93, 8.98, 8.106, 10.1, 11.2, 11.4, 11.11, 11.14–11.16, 11.18, 11.21, 11.24–11.27, 11.33–11.37, 11.39, 11.40, 11.42–11.44, 11.46, 11.47, 11.51, 11.53, 11.54, 11.60, 11.67, 11.72, 11.92, 11.101, 11.123, 11.124, 11.127, 11.130, 11.132, 11.169, 11.186, 11.188, 11.195, 12.1, 12.6, 12.8, 12.10, 12.31, 12.88, 12.136, 12.137, 13.2, 13.6, 13.23, 16.3, 23.1, 26.243, 27.14, 27.22
Pt 9	11.60, 11.61

Companies Act 2006—*continued*		Companies Act 2006—*continued*	
Pt 13	3.1, 4.50, 10.46, 11.5	s 168(5)	3.20
Ch 2	3.64	s 169	3.15
Ch 3	22.3	s 169(2)	3.15
Ch 4	22.3	s 169(3)	3.15
Pt 26	4.47, 23.1, 23.7, 23.9, 23.14, 23.24, 23.30, 23.31	s 169(5)	3.17
		s 171	12.8
Pt 30	4.47	s 172	12.8
Pt 42	10.1	s 173	12.8
s 16(3)	2.48	s 174	12.8
s 19	2.15	s 175	2.18, 12.8, 12.106
s 21	4.40	s 175(2)	12.106
s 21(1)	2.14, 3.43	s 175(4)	12.107
s 28	2.49, 4.42	s 175(6)	12.108
s 29	3.119, 3.120	s 176	12.8
s 30	3.119, 3.120	s 177	12.8, 12.14, 12.31, 12.88, 12.89, 12.93, 12.94, 12.100, 12.115, 12.116, 12.129, 12.136, 14.9
s 30(2)	3.120		
s 30(3)	3.120		
s 31	2.48	s 177(4)	12.93
s 39	2.48, 2.49	s 177(6)	12.136
s 40	2.51, 12.142, 12.143	s 177(6)(b)	12.88
s 40(1)	2.50, 2.51	s 177ff	12.99
s 40(2)(a)	2.50	s 180(4)(b)	12.110
s 40(2)(b)	12.143	s 182	12.10, 12.14, 12.31, 12.88, 12.89, 12.93, 12.94, 12.100, 12.115, 12.116, 12.129, 12.136, 12.137, 12.139, 12.141, 14.9
s 40(5)	2.51		
s 41(4)	2.50		
s 77(1)	3.43		
s 77(2)	3.43	s 182(4)	12.93
s 88(2)	3.43	s 182(6)	12.136
s 88(3)	3.43	s 182(6)(b)	12.88
s 90(1)(a)	3.43	s 182ff	12.99
s 97(1)(a)	3.43	s 184	12.89, 12.95, 12.99
s 98	4.47	s 185	12.89, 12.97, 12.99
s 105(1)(a)	3.43	s 185(3)	12.98
s 125	3.23, 3.113	s 186	12.137–12.139, 12.141
s 125(6)	7.20	s 188	3.71, 3.107, 12.101
s 126	7.9	s 190	3.100, 12.88
s 145	3.76, 3.87, 5.119–5.121, 5.128, 5.129, 6.56, 6.88, 8.82, 11.66, 11.68, 11.93	s 192	12.88
		s 197	3.71
		s 198	3.71
s 145(2)	11.67	s 200	3.71
s 145(4)	11.68	s 201	3.71
s 146	5.29, 5.111, 5.118, 5.124, 5.125, 5.127–5.130, 6.45, 6.56, 6.94, 8.80, 11.93	s 203	3.71
		s 204	3.71
		s 217	3.71, 6.79, 6.83, 6.85–6.87
s 147	5.127, 11.61	s 218	3.71, 6.80, 6.84, 6.85, 6.87
s 147(4)	11.63	s 218(2)	6.80
s 148	5.133	s 219	3.71, 6.81, 6.84, 6.85, 6.87
s 149	6.45	s 219(1)	6.81
s 150	11.65	s 219(2)	6.81
s 150(3)	5.131	s 219(4)	6.81
s 151	5.124	s 220	6.82
s 152	5.130, 5.132	s 221(2)	6.87
s 153	5.110, 5.117, 6.93, 8.79	s 221(3)	6.87
s 154(2)	12.1	s 221(4)	6.87
s 160	4.11, 7.49, 12.142	s 224	3.72
s 160(1)	5.53	s 228	14.14
s 160(2)	5.53	s 231	12.140
s 161	4.11, 12.142	s 237	14.14
s 168	3.7–3.9, 3.15, 3.18, 3.20–3.22, 3.24, 3.25, 3.27, 3.28, 3.42, 3.70, 3.105, 5.37	s 238(2)	5.28
		s 239	8.7, 8.9
		s 248	11.222, 12.96, 12.139, 14.1
s 168(3)	3.27	s 249	14.1, 14.20
s 168(4)	3.26	s 251	12.99

Companies Act 2006—continued
s 252	8.7, 12.97, 12.108
s 252ff	6.79
ss 260–269	2.52
s 281	7.53
s 281(3)	3.4
s 281(4)	3.4
s 282	3.4, 7.53, 8.22
s 282(1)	3.4
s 283	3.45, 4.19, 6.39, 21.1, 27.55
s 283(3)	6.36
s 283(3)(a)	3.86
s 283(6)	6.36
s 283(6)(a)	3.46
s 283(6)(b)	3.46
s 284(2)	8.20
s 284(3)	8.20, 8.31
s 285	3.78, 8.25, 12.143
s 285(1)	8.25
s 285(3)	8.33
s 285(4)	8.33
s 285(5)	8.28
s 286	7.14, 8.5
s 287	8.19
s 288	3.67, 3.96, 3.97, 3.104
s 288(1)	3.97
s 288(2)	3.9, 3.29, 3.42, 3.70, 3.118
s 288(4)	3.97
s 288(5)	3.67
s 288ff	11.231, 14.33
s 291	3.76, 3.93, 5.121, 10.28
s 291(3)	3.73
s 291(4)	3.73
s 292	3.68, 3.87, 5.121, 11.66
s 292(3)	3.87
s 293	3.93, 5.121, 10.28
s 293(3)	10.28
s 296	3.90
s 297	3.90
s 298	11.186
s 300	3.79
s 301	22.3
s 302	4.9
s 303	3.11, 3.12, 3.14, 4.13–4.15, 4.22, 4.50, 5.121, 27.22
s 304	3.12, 4.20, 4.22, 4.50, 6.57
s 305	3.12, 4.22, 4.23, 4.50, 6.57
s 306	4.25, 4.27–4.29, 4.31, 4.32, 4.50, 7.18, 7.19, 7.21, 15.6
s 306(4)	7.19
s 306(5)	7.19
s 307	6.4–6.7
s 307(1)	6.14
s 307(1)–(6)	4.38, 4.50
s 307(2)	6.5, 6.12, 6.14
s 307(A1)	6.4, 6.5, 6.10
s 307A	4.38, 4.50, 6.10
s 308	6.67, 11.22
s 309	11.126, 11.132
s 309(2)	11.116
s 310	5.121, 6.63, 11.66
s 310(1)	6.49, 6.56, 6.59
s 310(2)	6.61
s 311	6.14, 6.20, 6.53

Companies Act 2006—continued
s 311(2)	6.25
s 311(3)	4.50, 6.53
s 311A	4.50, 6.53, 6.54
s 311A(1)	8.102
s 312	3.9, 3.11, 3.117
s 312(1)	3.9, 3.14
s 312(2)	3.10, 6.14
s 312(3)	6.14
s 312(4)	3.14
s 313	6.57, 23.11
s 314	5.112, 5.116–5.118, 5.121, 6.88, 6.92–6.94
s 314(2)	5.112, 6.88
s 314(4)(d)	5.113, 6.14, 6.89
s 315	5.114, 5.115, 6.90, 6.91
s 315(1)	5.114, 6.90
s 316	5.115, 6.91
s 316(1)(b)	5.115, 6.91
s 316(2)(b)	6.14
s 317	5.116, 6.92
s 317(1)	5.116, 6.92
s 317(2)	5.116, 6.92
s 318	4.51, 7.8, 7.16, 7.17
s 319(2)	7.26
s 319A	4.50, 5.121, 6.53, 7.40
s 320	7.55, 8.37
s 321	4.51, 8.43, 8.45, 8.46, 9.18
s 322	8.32
s 322A	3.4, 3.45, 6.53, 8.34, 8.75
s 323	7.8, 7.15, 8.39, 8.41
s 324	5.121, 8.82
s 324A	8.23
s 325	6.44, 6.46
s 326	6.47, 6.51, 8.83
s 326(2)	6.51
s 327	6.50, 8.98
s 327(A1)	4.50, 8.100
s 328	7.27
s 329	8.48
s 329(2)	8.45
s 330(A1)	4.50
s 331	8.21
s 332	9.24
s 333(1)	11.186
s 333(2)	11.186
s 333(4)	8.101
s 333A	4.50, 8.101
s 334	4.50, 4.51, 23.11
s 334(2A)	4.50
s 336	4.3, 5.3
s 336(2)	4.4, 5.4
s 337(1)	5.6
s 337(2)	6.12
s 337(3)	5.6, 6.14
s 338	5.6, 5.106, 5.109–5.111, 5.117, 5.118, 5.121
s 338(2)	5.107
s 338(3)	5.106
s 338(4)	5.106
s 338(4)(d)(i)	6.14
s 338A	5.6, 5.7, 5.121
s 339	5.108, 5.109, 6.57
s 339(1)	5.108

Companies Act 2006—*continued*

s 339(3)	5.106
s 340	5.109
s 340(2)(b)(i)	6.14
s 341	8.77
s 342	8.78–8.80
s 353	8.77
s 355	11.222, 14.33
s 356	14.20
s 357	14.34
s 357(5)	14.34
s 358	14.15, 14.16
s 359	14.17
s 360	5.30, 6.14, 6.18
s 360A	6.53, 11.5
s 360A(2)	11.6
s 360B(2)	6.53
s 360C	4.38, 4.50, 5.1, 5.7, 6.4, 6.12, 6.25, 6.45, 6.53, 7.40
s 367	5.103
s 368	5.104
s 378	5.102
s 382	17.8
s 382(3)	17.8
s 385	10.47
s 390	5.22
s 391	5.22
s 392	4.4, 5.4
s 399	5.21
s 415	5.23
s 417	5.23
ss 420–422	5.23
s 423	5.28, 5.121
s 423(3)	5.28
s 423(4)	5.31
s 424	5.28, 5.31
s 424(4)	5.31
s 425	4.53, 5.31
s 426	5.125
ss 426–429	5.30
s 426(5)	5.125
s 431	5.125
s 432	5.125, 10.41
s 434	11.141
s 437	5.21, 10.13
s 437(1)	5.23
s 437(3)	3.33
s 439	5.23
s 442(2)	5.22
s 442(7)	5.22
s 477	5.24, 5.38, 10.3
s 480	10.3, 10.12
s 485	10.3
s 486	10.11
s 488	10.8
s 489	10.12
s 489(2)	5.39
s 490	10.17
s 491	10.16
s 492	5.40
s 492(1)	10.18
s 492(2)	10.18
s 492(3)	10.18
ss 495–497	5.24

Companies Act 2006—*continued*

s 496	5.24
s 499	14.18
s 502	3.31, 3.69, 10.25, 10.36
s 502(1)	10.46
s 502(2)	6.64, 10.25, 10.36, 10.45
ss 503–505	5.24
s 510	3.28–3.30, 3.32, 3.42, 3.70, 3.105, 10.19
s 510(3)	10.19
s 510(4)	3.30
s 511	3.28, 3.29, 3.117, 10.24
s 511(3)	10.24
s 511(4)	10.24
s 511(5)	3.31, 10.24
s 511(6)	10.24
s 512	10.19
s 513	10.25
s 514	3.91, 10.26
s 515	3.28, 3.33, 10.20
s 515(2)	10.21
s 515(3)	10.24
s 515(4)	10.24
s 515(5)	10.24
s 515(6)	10.24
s 515(7)	10.24
s 516(1)	10.30
s 516(2)	10.30
s 516(3)	10.30
s 517	10.30
s 518	4.34, 10.31
s 518(2)	4.35
s 518(3)	4.35
s 518(4)	4.36
s 518(5)	4.36
s 518(8)	4.36
s 518(9)	4.37
s 519	3.39, 3.40, 10.30, 10.31, 10.37, 10.43
s 519(2)	10.38
s 519(3)	10.39
s 520(2)	10.41
s 521	10.42
s 522	3.37, 3.41, 10.42
s 522(3)	3.37
s 523	3.37, 3.39, 3.41, 10.43
s 524	3.41
s 525	10.42
s 525(1)	3.37
s 527	10.47, 10.51
s 528	10.52
s 529	10.51
s 549	5.56
s 549(1)	5.56
s 549(2)	5.56
s 549(3)	5.56
s 549(4)	5.72
s 549(8)	5.72
s 550	5.56, 5.58, 5.60, 5.61
s 551	5.56–5.58, 5.61–5.67, 5.69, 5.71, 5.72, 5.84–5.86, 5.89
s 551(1)	5.57, 5.65, 5.71
s 551(2)	5.57, 5.62
s 551(3)	5.65
s 551(4)	5.70

Table of Statutes

Companies Act 2006—*continued*
s 551(8)	5.71
s 560(1)	5.74
s 560(2)	5.73
s 560(3)	5.73
s 561	5.78, 5.80–5.84, 5.86, 5.90
s 561(1)	5.86
s 561(1)(a)	5.73, 5.75
s 561(1)(b)	5.75
s 561(4)	5.73
s 564	5.77
s 565	5.76
s 566	5.78
s 567	5.80
s 567(2)	5.80
s 567(3)	5.80
s 568	5.81
s 569	3.43, 5.82, 5.83, 5.90
s 570	3.43, 5.82, 5.84, 5.89, 5.90
s 570(1)	5.85
s 571	3.43, 3.71, 5.82, 5.84, 5.87, 5.89, 5.90
s 571(2)	5.86
s 626	3.43
s 629(1)	4.39
s 629(2)	4.39
s 630	4.41, 4.42, 4.45, 4.47
ss 630–640	3.23
s 630(3)	4.44
s 630(5)	4.43
s 630(6)	4.43
s 631	4.49
s 633	4.46
ss 636–640	4.52
s 641(a)	3.43
s 641(b)	3.43
s 642	3.71
s 656	3.66, 4.2
s 694	3.43, 3.71
s 695(4)	8.49
s 698(4)	8.49
s 701	5.94
s 701(2)	5.94
s 701(3)	5.94
s 701(5)	5.94
s 702(2)	5.98
s 702(3)	5.98
s 716	3.43
s 717(4)	8.49
s 793	8.11
s 836	3.114
s 895	4.53, 4.56, 4.58, 4.60, 4.64, 4.67, 17.2
ss 895–899	23.1
s 895(2)	4.55
s 896(1)	4.56
s 896(2)	4.60
s 897	4.56
s 899(2)	4.60
s 901	4.57
s 969	6.4
s 971(1)	6.4
s 994	2.52, 4.27, 8.4
s 1134	14.13

Companies Act 2006—*continued*
s 1135	14.13
s 1136	14.15, 14.16
s 1138	14.14
s 1143	11.8, 11.9
s 1143(2)	11.8
ss 1144–1148	11.8
s 1145	5.125, 5.127, 11.22, 11.64, 11.163
s 1146	3.83, 3.84, 5.9, 11.188
s 1146(4)	11.191
s 1147	6.14, 6.17, 6.73
s 1147(3)	11.27, 11.150
s 1147(4)	11.27, 11.151
s 1147(6)	6.17, 11.28, 11.33
s 1148(1)	11.54
s 1148(3)	11.9
s 1157(5)	11.152
s 1168	11.14, 11.15, 11.20, 11.21
s 1169	10.3
s 1212	10.1
ss 1214–1216	10.1
Sch 4	3.75, 11.8, 11.167
para 6	11.52
Sch 5	3.75, 6.68, 6.71, 11.8, 11.29, 11.49, 11.92, 11.94, 11.95, 11.167
para 4	6.68
para 6	11.52, 11.168
para 6(a)	11.55
para 7	11.54
para 7(1)	11.55
para 9(a)	11.57, 11.101
para 10	11.42, 11.93, 11.98, 11.101, 11.120
para 10(3)(a)	11.99
para 10(4)(b)	11.100
para 13	11.115
para 13(2)	11.132
para 14(1)	11.132
para 14(2)	11.132
para 16	6.60
para 17	11.69
para 17(5)	6.61
Pt 3	11.63
Pt 4	11.63
Criminal Justice and Court Services Act 2000	26.131
Data Protection Act 1998	11.88
Education Act 1996	
s 325	26.198
Electronic Communications Act 2000	11.7, 11.25
Enterprise Act 2002	18.4, 18.6, 18.11, 18.23, 18.39, 19.1, 23.6, 25.39
Pt X	24.1
Equality Act 2010	11.78, 11.143, 11.212
Financial Services and Markets Act 2000	11.141, 18.29, 19.4
s 19	17.8
s 261	18.45
s 362(3)	18.29

Financial Services and Markets Act 2000—*continued*		Insolvency Act 1986—*continued*	
s 363(4)	19.4	ss 72B–72H	19.1
s 371(4)(a)	20.4	s 79	21.4
		s 84	20.16, 22.7
		s 84(1)(a)	22.2
Health and Social Care Act 2012	26.19, 26.228, 26.240	s 84(1)(b)	3.43, 22.2
		s 84(2A)	22.4
Housing Act 1996		s 84(2B)	22.4
s 202	26.198	s 85	22.8
s 204	26.198	s 85(2)	22.8
Human Rights Act 1998	16.21, 26.146	s 89	20.1, 22.1
s 1	16.21, 23.26	s 89(2)	22.1
s 6	23.29	s 89(3)	22.1
s 6(3)(a)	23.29	s 89(4)	22.1
Sch 1	16.21, 23.26	s 89(6)	22.1
		s 90	20.1
Insolvency Act 1986	3.43, 16.1–16.4, 16.9, 16.10, 16.19, 16.20, 17.1, 17.5, 17.19, 17.35, 17.46, 18.1, 18.47, 19.1, 20.1, 20.2, 22.6, 25.2, 25.11, 25.18, 25.26, 25.33, 27.14	s 91(1)	22.2, 22.8
		s 91(2)	22.8
		s 92(2)	22.8
		s 92(3)	22.8
		s 94(1)	22.2
		s 94(2)	22.9
Pt I	17.46	s 94(3)	22.9
Pt II	23.6	s 94(5)	22.9
Pt VIII	17.3	s 95	20.2
s 1(1)	17.10	s 96	20.1, 20.2
s 1(3)	17.10	s 98	20.1, 20.2, 20.4
s 1A(1)	17.8	ss 98–106	16.10
s 2	17.11, 17.22	s 98(1A)(a)	20.4
s 2(2)	17.11, 17.16	s 98(1A)(b)	20.4
s 2(2)(a)	17.11	s 98(1A)(c)	20.4
ss 3–6	16.10	s 98(1A)(d)	20.4
s 3(1)	17.16	s 98(2)(a)	20.5
s 3(2)	17.14	s 98(2)(b)	20.5
s 3(3)	17.19, 17.23	s 98(3)	20.4
s 4(3)	17.5, 17.15, 17.44	s 98(4)	20.4
s 4(4)	17.5, 17.15	s 99	20.2
s 4(4)(a)	16.19	s 99(1)	20.4, 20.9
s 4(5)	17.29	s 99(3)	20.10
s 4(6)	17.15, 17.31	s 100	20.1, 20.2
s 4A	17.34	s 100(3)	20.2
s 4A(2)(b)	17.61	s 101	20.2
s 4A(3)	17.61	s 104	20.2
s 4A(4)	17.61	s 104A	20.2, 22.2
s 4A(6)	17.61	s 106	20.28, 20.30, 20.32
s 5(2)(b)	17.56, 17.57	s 106(2)	20.8, 20.29
s 5(2)(b)(i)	17.18	s 108(2)	16.2
s 5(2)(b)(ii)	17.18	s 109	22.8
s 6	17.19, 17.64, 17.66, 17.68	s 110	17.2
s 6(3)	17.65	s 122	21.1
s 6(3)(b)	17.19	s 122(1)	3.43, 21.1
s 8	18.2, 18.5	s 122(1)(a)	21.1
ss 8–27	18.5	s 122(1)(g)	2.52
s 8(3)(c)	23.6	s 136(4)	21.2
s 40	16.19	s 136(5)(a)	21.2
s 48	19.4	s 136(5)(c)	21.5
s 48(1)	19.6	s 139	21.2
s 48(2)	19.4–19.6	s 141	21.2
s 48(3)	19.5	s 146	21.9, 21.13
s 48(4)	19.4, 19.5	s 146(1)	21.3
s 48(5)	19.6	s 172(2)	16.2
s 48(7)	19.3	s 175	16.19
s 49	19.15	s 176A	18.6, 21.8
s 72A	22.4	s 176A(2)(a)	18.9, 18.21

Insolvency Act 1986—continued

s 201(2)	20.32, 22.9
s 201(3)	20.32
s 201(4)	20.32
s 214	12.7
s 239	24.5
s 241	3.115
s 246A	16.5
s 246A(9)	16.5
s 246A(10)	16.5
s 249	17.55
s 252(2)	25.4
s 255(1)	25.6
s 255(2)	25.6
s 256	25.6
s 256A(1)	25.4
ss 257–260	16.10
s 258(2)	25.13
s 258(4)	17.5
s 258(5)	17.5
s 258(5)(a)	16.19
s 259	25.28
s 260(2)	25.2
s 260(2)(a)	25.24
s 260(2)(b)	25.24
s 262	25.30, 25.31
s 262(1)	25.27–25.29
s 262(1)(a)	25.26, 25.35
s 262(1)(b)	25.26, 25.29, 25.35, 25.37
s 262(2)	25.27
s 262(2)(b)(ii)	25.28
s 262(3)	25.28
s 262(4)	25.29
s 262(4)(a)	25.30
s 262(4)(b)	25.30
s 262(5)	25.30
s 262(6)	25.30
s 262(7)	25.30
s 295	24.14
s 299(2)	24.60
s 339	25.35
s 386	16.19
s 387	16.19
s 425	17.46
Sch A1	
para 2(1)	17.8
para 2(2)	17.8
para 3	17.8
para 4	17.8
para 7(1)	17.21
para 8(1)	17.21
para 8(2)	17.61
para 8(3)	17.21
para 8(5)	17.61
para 8(7)	17.61
para 12(1)	17.8
para 24	17.33
para 29	17.21
para 29(2)	17.21
para 30	17.21, 17.29
para 31	17.21
para 31(1)	17.21
para 32(1)	17.39
para 32(2)	17.21, 17.39

Insolvency Act 1986—continued

Sch A1—continued	
para 32(2)(a)	17.39
para 32(2)(b)	17.39
para 32(3)	17.33
para 32(4)	17.33
para 32(5)	17.33
para 36(2)	17.61
para 36(3)	17.61
para 36(4)	17.61
para 36(5)	17.61
para 44	17.61
Sch B1	18.5, 18.20, 18.45
para 3(1)	18.5, 18.17, 23.6
para 3(1)(a)	18.9, 18.11, 18.21
para 3(1)(b)	18.9, 18.11, 18.21
para 3(2)	18.11
para 3(3)	18.11
para 3(4)	18.11
para 4	18.11
para 5	18.5
para 14	17.8
para 22	17.8, 18.16
para 49(1)	18.17
para 49(2)	18.17
para 49(2)(b)	18.11
para 49(4)	18.18
para 49(4)(c)	18.27
para 49(5)	18.15, 18.20
para 49(7)	18.20
paras 50–58	16.10
para 50(1)	18.27
para 50(3)	18.24
para 51	18.8
para 52(1)	18.9, 18.21
para 52(2)	18.22
para 52(4)	18.25
para 53(2)	18.8, 18.34, 18.45
para 53(3)	18.45
para 54(2)	18.8
para 57	16.11, 18.47
para 58(3)	18.23
para 62	18.8
para 73(1)(b)	16.19
para 74(1)	18.12
para 74(2)	18.12
para 75	18.12
para 97(2)	16.2, 18.16
para 107	18.25
para 108	18.25
para 111(1)	18.23
Insolvency Act 2000	17.8, 17.9, 17.21, 17.56, 17.57, 17.60, 17.61, 25.4, 25.24
s 256(3)	25.27
s 256A(4)	25.27
s 258(3)	25.27
s 260(2)	25.8

Licensing Act 2003

s 181	26.198
Sch 5	26.198

Local Authorities (Admission of the Press to Meetings) Act 1908	26.115, 26.117, 26.148
s 1(4)(c)	26.150
Local Government Act 1972	26.4, 26.6, 26.38, 26.56, 26.106, 26.114, 26.120, 26.153, 26.178
Pt VA	26.120
s 100	26.119
s 100A	26.59, 26.121
ss 100A–100K	26.64, 26.120
s 100A(3)	26.126
s 100A(6)(a)	26.58
s 100A(6)(c)	26.154
s 100A(7)	26.141
s 100A(8)	26.164
s 100B	26.75
s 100B(4)	26.76
s 100B(4)(b)	26.76
s 100B(6)	26.140
s 100B(7)	26.155
s 100C	26.190
s 100C(1)	26.188
s 100D	26.192
s 100E(1)	26.59
s 100EA	26.120
s 100I	26.127
s 101	26.20, 26.30
s 106	26.34
s 132	26.54
s 134	26.54
s 228(1)	26.188
s 239	26.90
Sch 12	26.4, 26.45, 26.76, 26.87, 26.89
para 1	26.43
para 3	26.45
para 4	26.54
para 4(2)	26.58, 26.73
para 4(5)	26.74
para 6	26.111
para 13	26.97
para 29	26.97
para 39(1)	26.21
para 42	26.34
para 45	26.111
Pt I	
para 5	26.82
Pt II	26.50, 26.80
Pts II–IV	26.60
Pt III	26.52
Pt IV	26.50
Pt V	26.53
Pt VI	
para 39	26.88
para 39(2)	26.91
para 40	26.182
para 41	26.183, 26.189
Sch 12A	26.127
para 10	26.129
Local Government Act 1974	26.222
s 26	26.225
s 27	26.225
Local Government Act 1974—*continued*	
Sch 5	26.225
Local Government Act 1989	
s 15	26.30
Local Government Act 2000	26.5, 26.13, 26.22, 26.23, 26.25, 26.28, 26.62, 26.82, 26.106, 26.159, 26.196
s 9D(2)	26.31
s 37	26.33
Local Government (Access to Information) Act 1985	26.114, 26.120, 26.153
Local Government (Miscellaneous Provisions) Act 1976	
s 41	26.189
Local Government and Housing Act 1989	
s 20	26.35
s 20(2)	26.35
Local Government and Public Involvement in Health Act 2007	26.22, 26.26, 26.225
Pt 9	26.223
s 237	26.120
Localism Act 2011	26.5, 26.25, 26.158–26.160, 26.196, 26.221, 26.225
Ch 7	26.161
s 25(2)	26.221
Sch 2	26.25
London Government Act 1963	26.6
National Health Service Act 2006	26.237, 26.240
s 14A	26.228
s 25	26.228
s 33	26.228
Sch 7	26.234
para 18	26.237
para 27A	26.235
Parliamentary Commissioner Act 1967	26.224
Political Parties, Elections and Referendums Act 2000	5.102
Probation Service Act 1993	26.131
Public Bodies (Admission to Meetings) Act 1960	26.118–26.120, 26.142, 26.149–26.152, 26.154, 26.167, 26.178, 26.229, 26.230, 26.236
s 1(8)	26.165
Statute of Frauds	14.28
Third Party (Rights Against Insurers) Act 1930	25.32
Town and Country Planning Act 1990	
s 78	26.198
Trade Union and Labour Relations (Consolidation) Act 1992	26.161

TABLE OF STATUTORY INSTRUMENTS

References are to paragraph numbers.

Civil Procedure (Amendment) Rules 2009, SI 2009/2092	23.4
Civil Procedure Rules 1998, SI 1998/3132	17.20
Pt 6	17.20
r 6.8	17.20
Pt 8	23.4
r 49.1	23.4
PD 49B	
para 7	23.4
Companies Act 1985 (Electronic Communications) Order 2000, SI 2000/3373	2.22, 3.6, 4.21, 11.7, 11.25
Companies Act 2006 (Allotment of Shares and Right of Pre-emption) (Amendment) Regulations 2009, SI 2009/2561	
reg 2	5.73
reg 2(1)	5.56
reg 2(4)	5.78
Companies Act 2006 (Commencement No 1, Transitional Provisions and Savings) Order 2006, SI 2006/3428	6.95, 11.4
Sch 5	
Pt 2	
para 4	11.55
Companies Act 2006 (Commencement No 3, Consequential Amendments, Transitional Provisions and Savings) Order 2007, SI 2007/2194	2.2, 2.9
Sch 1	
para 15	5.3
Sch 3	
para 23	2.8, 3.3, 3.48
para 32	2.4, 4.5
Sch 4	
para 2	4.41
Companies Act 2006 (Commencement No 4 and Commencement No 3 (Amendment)) Order 2007, SI 2007/2607	2.9
art 4	3.1, 3.3, 3.48
Companies Act 2006 (Commencement No 5, Transitional Provisions and Savings) Order 2007, SI 2007/3495	7.49
Sch 5	
para 2	2.6
para 2(6)	3.59
Companies Act 2006 (Commencement No 6, Saving and Commencement Nos 3 and 5 (Amendment)) Order 2008, SI 2008/674	3.61, 6.11
Companies Act 2006 (Commencement No 8, Transitional Provisions and Savings) Order 2008, SI 2008/2860	
Sch 2	
para 42	6.25
para 44	5.68
Companies (Company Records) Regulations 2008, SI 2008/3006	14.16
Companies (Fees for Inspection and Copying of Company Records) Regulations 2007, SI 2007/2612	14.16
Companies (Fees for Inspection of Company Records) (No 2) Regulations 2007, SI 2007/3535	14.16
Companies (Fees for Inspection of Company Records) Regulations 2008, SI 2008/3007	14.16
Companies (Model Articles) Regulations 2008, SI 2008/3229	2.15, 3.5, 3.96, 4.38, 5.43, 7.22, 12.52, 12.86, 12.112, 12.126, 13.7, 27.63
reg 21	5.41
reg 30	5.18
reg 70	5.18
Sch 1	
reg 3	2.44, 2.46, 3.5, 7.1
reg 4	2.44, 2.46, 7.1
reg 5	12.116
reg 6	12.117
reg 7	12.67
reg 7(2)	12.70, 12.74
reg 7(2)(b)	12.72, 12.74
reg 8	12.70, 12.121, 12.122, 12.124, 13.23, 13.40
reg 9	12.42, 12.47

Companies (Model Articles) Regulations
2008, SI 2008/3229—continued
Sch 1—continued

reg 10	13.25, 13.30
reg 11	12.66, 12.79
reg 11(1)	12.70
reg 11(2)	12.71–12.75
reg 12	12.61
reg 13	12.81, 27.77
reg 14	12.86
reg 38	7.10
reg 39	7.23
reg 41	9.2, 9.14, 9.16
reg 43	7.56, 8.18
reg 44	8.46, 8.50, 8.59, 8.65
reg 45	8.81, 8.85, 8.86
reg 47	6.35, 6.38
reg 48(1)	11.98
reg14	12.85

Sch 2

reg 3	2.44, 2.46
reg 4	2.44, 2.46
reg 7	12.67
reg 8	13.40
reg 9	12.42
reg 11	12.66, 12.79
reg 12	12.61
reg 13	12.81
reg 25	7.23
reg 27	9.2, 9.14, 9.16
reg 29	7.56, 8.18
reg 33	6.35, 6.38

Sch 3

reg 3	7.1
reg 4	7.1
reg 8	12.42, 12.47
reg 10	12.79
reg 11	12.68
reg 12	12.61
reg 13	12.81
reg 17	13.40
reg 18	13.40
reg 28	4.12
reg 31	7.23, 8.86
reg 33	9.2, 9.14, 9.16
reg 35	7.56, 8.18
reg 36	8.50
reg 37	8.60, 8.64, 8.65, 8.69
reg 37(4)	9.18
reg 38	8.81, 8.85
reg 39	8.99
reg 40	6.35, 6.38
reg 41	8.6
reg 79(1)	11.98

Companies (Share Capital and Acquisition by Company of its Own Shares) Regulations 2009, SI 2009/2022   5.94

Companies (Shareholders' Rights) Regulations 2009, SI 2009/1632   4.50, 5.7, 8.20, 8.24, 8.33, 27.22

reg 2	3.45
reg 3	3.45
reg 4	3.11, 4.14

Companies (Shareholders' Rights) Regulations 2009, SI 2009/1632—continued

reg 5	3.4, 3.45, 8.34
reg 6	8.39
reg 7	8.23
reg 8	11.5
reg 9	6.4, 6.53
reg 10	6.25
reg 11	6.54
reg 12	7.40
reg 13	8.100, 8.101
reg 15	5.3
reg 16	5.6

Companies (Tables A to F) (Amendment) (No 2) Regulations 2007, SI 2007/2826   2.22, 3.6, 4.21, 5.43

Companies (Tables A to F) (Amendment) Regulations 1985, SI 1985/1052   2.22, 3.6, 4.21

Companies (Tables A to F) (Amendment) Regulations 2007, SI 2007/2541   2.22, 3.6, 3.98, 4.21, 5.43, 6.8

Companies (Tables A to F) (Amendment) Regulations 2008, SI 2008/739   2.22, 5.43

Companies (Tables A to F) Regulations 1985, SI 1985/805   2.4, 2.22, 2.28, 3.6, 4.21, 5.43, 5.49, 6.77, 9.13, 11.37, 12.51, 12.52, 12.126, 13.7, 13.24, 27.63

reg 31	6.61
reg 37	4.9, 4.12, 4.21
reg 38	6.7, 6.14, 6.20, 6.49, 6.56
reg 39	6.57
reg 40	7.8, 7.22
reg 41	7.11, 9.16
reg 42	7.23
reg 44	7.41
reg 45	9.2, 9.8, 9.14, 9.25
reg 46	8.47, 8.53
reg 47	7.55
reg 49	8.65, 8.69
reg 51	8.60, 9.18
reg 52	8.64
reg 53	3.96, 3.98, 3.99, 7.13
reg 54	7.13, 8.39
reg 55	8.5
reg 56	8.5
reg 57	8.6
reg 58	7.56, 8.18
reg 60	8.85
reg 61	8.85
reg 65	12.112
reg 70	2.44, 2.46, 3.5, 7.1
reg 72	12.116
reg 75	5.53
reg 76	5.50, 5.51
reg 76(a)	5.50
reg 77	5.51
reg 78	5.52

Companies (Tables A to F) Regulations 1985, SI 1985/805—*continued*
reg 79	5.52
reg 85	8.7, 12.91
reg 85(a)–(c)	12.91
reg 88	12.42, 12.45, 12.49, 12.62, 12.81
reg 89	12.66, 12.79
reg 91	12.61, 12.62
reg 92	4.11
reg 93	12.121, 12.123, 12.124, 13.41
reg 95	12.77
reg 100	14.2
reg 102	5.18
reg 103	5.18
reg 111	6.73
regs 111–116	6.72
reg 112	6.73, 6.75
reg 115	6.14, 6.18, 6.73
reg 131	6.75

Large and Medium-sized Companies and Groups (Accounts and Reports) Regulations 2008, SI 2008/410   5.23

Local Authorities (Access to Information) (Variation) Order 2006, SI 2006/88   26.127

Local Authorities (Executive Arrangements) (Access to Information) (England) Regulations 2000, SI 2000/3272   26.63

Local Authorities (Executive Arrangements) (Decisions, Documents and Meetings) (Wales) Regulations 2001, SI 2001/2290   26.72

Local Authorities (Executive Arrangements) (Meetings and Access to Information) (England) Regulations 2012, SI 2012/2089   26.57, 26.63, 26.121, 26.132, 26.141
reg 4	26.130
reg 10	26.68, 26.124
reg 11	26.69

Local Authorities (Functions and Responsibilities) (England) Regulations 2000, SI 2000/2853   26.31

Local Authorities (Model Code of Conduct) Order 2007, SI 2007/1159   26.161

Local Authorities (Model Code of Conduct) (Wales) Order 2008, SI 2008/788   26.162

Local Authorities (Standing Orders) (England) Regulations 2001, SI 2001/3384   26.36

Local Authorities (Standing Orders) (Wales) Regulations 2006, SI 2006/1275   26.36

Relevant Authorities (Disclosable Pecuniary Interests) Regulations 2012, SI 2012/1464
reg 1	26.161
Sch 1	26.161

Uncertificated Securities (Amendment) Regulations 2007, SI 2007/124   5.136

Uncertificated Securities Regulations 2001, SI 2001/3755   5.136

TABLE OF EUROPEAN MATERIALS

References are to paragraph numbers.

Council Regulation 1346/2000/EC (on insolvency proceedings)   17.62, 18.17, 18.39
    Art 32(2)   18.39
    Art 32(3)   18.39
Council Regulation 2157/2001/EC (on the Statute for a European company with regard to
    the involvement of employees)   1.7

Directive 2001/86/EC (on the Statute for a European company with regard to the
    involvement of employees)   1.7

Eighth EC Company Law Directive (84/253/EEC)   10.1
European Convention for the Protection of Human Rights and Fundamental Freedoms
    1950   23.26, 23.28, 26.146
    Art 6   26.146, 26.147
    Art 6(1)   16.21, 23.27
    Art 14   23.28
European Convention for the Protection of Human Rights and Fundamental Freedoms
    1950, Protocol 1
    Art 1   16.21, 23.26, 23.30

TABLE OF INSOLVENCY RULES

References are to paragraph numbers.

Enterprise Act 2002 (Insolvency) Order 2003, SI 2003/2096	22.3, 22.4
Insolvency (Amendment) Rules 1987, SI 1987/1919	
r 3(1)	17.59
Sch, Pt 1, para 5	17.59
Insolvency (Amendment) Rules 2002, SI 2002/1307	18.39
Insolvency (Amendment) Rules 2006, SI 2006/1272	17.47
r 13.12(2)	17.47
Insolvency (Amendment) Rules 2010, SI 2010/686	16.6, 18.19, 18.27, 20.20, 20.26, 20.29, 24.6, 24.19
Insolvency Regulations 1994, SI 1994/2507	24.61
Insolvency Rules 1986, SI 1986/1925	16.1, 16.3, 16.4, 16.9, 16.10, 17.1, 17.5, 17.17, 17.26, 17.27, 17.48, 17.55–17.57, 18.30, 18.34–18.37, 18.43, 19.13, 20.2, 20.11, 21.2, 22.9, 24.63, 25.9, 25.11, 25.24, 25.33
r 1.1(3)	17.26
r 1.7(2)	17.11
r 1.9	16.10
r 1.9(1)	17.16
r 1.9(2)	17.16
r 1.9(2)(a)	17.23
r 1.9(2)(b)	17.24
r 1.9(3)	17.22
r 1.11	16.10, 17.19
r 1.11(1)	17.26
r 1.11(2)	17.27
r 1.12(4)(a)	17.41
r 1.12(6)	17.27
rr 1.13–1.21	16.10
r 1.13(1)	17.60
r 1.13(3)	17.25, 17.60
r 1.13(4)	17.25, 17.27, 17.60
r 1.13(5)	17.22
r 1.14(1)	17.28
r 1.15	17.32
r 1.16(1)(a)	17.24
r 1.16(1)(b)	17.24
r 1.16(2)	17.31
r 1.17(1)	17.44
r 1.17(2)	17.50

Insolvency Rules 1986, SI 1986/1925—*continued*	
r 1.17(3)	17.31, 17.51
r 1.17A(2)	17.31, 17.48
r 1.17A(3)	17.31, 17.48
r 1.17A(4)	17.31
r 1.17A(6)	17.31
r 1.18(1)	17.59
r 1.19(1)	17.27, 17.55
r 1.19(2)	17.55
r 1.19(3)	17.27, 17.54
r 1.19(3)(c)(i)	17.54
r 1.19(3)(c)(ii)	17.54
r 1.19(4)	16.20, 17.27, 17.55
r 1.19(5)	17.31
r 1.20	17.59
r 1.21	17.40
r 1.21(1)	17.40
r 1.21(2)	17.40, 17.58
r 1.21(3)	17.41
r 1.21(5)	17.42, 17.58
r 1.22(1)	17.58
r 1.22(3)(a)	17.58
r 1.22(3)(b)	17.58
r 1.24(2)	17.62
r 1.24(2)(b)	17.58
r 1.24(2)(c)	17.58
r 1.24(3)	17.58, 17.62
r 1.24(4)	17.62
r 1.24(5)	17.63
r 1.32(2)	17.25
r 1.48(1)	17.16
r 1.48(2)	17.16
r 1.48(3)	17.24
r 1.48(4)	17.22, 17.24
r 1.49(1)	17.44
r 1.49(2)	17.53
r 1.49(3)	17.51
r 1.50(2)	17.31, 17.48
r 1.50(3)	17.31, 17.48
r 1.50(4)	17.31
r 1.50(6)	17.31
r 1.52(1)	16.15, 17.22
r 1.52(2)	16.15
r 1.52(3)	17.22
r 1.52(4)	17.22, 17.54
r 1.52(6)	17.31
rr 2.30–2.42	18.40
r 2.33	18.17
r 2.33(2A)	18.19
r 2.33(2B)	18.17, 18.19

Insolvency Rules 1986, SI
1986/1925—*continued*

rr 2.34–2.49	16.10
r 2.34(1)	18.27
r 2.34(1A)	18.27
r 2.34(2)	18.28
r 2.34(4)	18.36
r 2.34(5)	18.36
r 2.35	18.44
r 2.35(2)	18.30
r 2.35(3)	18.31
r 2.35(4)	18.31, 18.32
r 2.35(4A)	18.27
r 2.35(5)	18.31
r 2.35(6C)–(6D	18.36
r 2.36(1)	18.33
r 2.36(2)(a)	18.33
r 2.36(2)(b)	18.33
r 2.37A	18.27
r 2.38	18.31, 18.43
r 2.38(1)(a)	18.34
r 2.38(1)(a)–(c)	18.37
r 2.38(2)	18.34
r 2.38(4)	18.40
r 2.38(5)	18.34
r 2.39(1)	18.34
r 2.39(3)	18.34
rr 2.40–2.42	18.38
r 2.43(1)	18.41
r 2.43(2)	16.20, 18.41
r 2.44(1)	18.35
r 2.44(2)	18.35
r 2.44(4)	18.35
r 2.45(2)	18.46
r 2.45(3)	18.46
r 2.45(4)	18.46
r 2.48	18.32
r 2.48(2)–(4)	18.43
r 2.48(3)	18.43
r 2.48(6)	18.44
r 2.48(7)	18.44
r 2.48(8)	18.44, 18.46
r 2.52(3)	18.47
r 3.9	19.7
r 3.9(5)	19.8
r 3.9(6)	19.8
r 3.9(6A)	19.8
r 3.9(7)	19.8
r 3.10(1)	19.11
r 3.10(2)	19.11
r 3.11	19.9, 19.10
r 3.11(1)	19.8
r 3.11(1)(a)	19.10
r 3.11(1)(b)	19.10
r 3.11(2)	19.12
r 3.11(3)	19.12
r 3.11(4)	19.14
r 3.11(5)	19.9, 19.14
r 3.11(6)	19.9
r 3.11(7)	19.9
r 3.11A	19.9, 19.10
r 3.12(1)	19.12
r 3.12(2)	19.12, 19.14
r 3.12(3)	19.12

Insolvency Rules 1986, SI
1986/1925—*continued*

r 3.12(4)	19.12
r 3.12(5)	19.12
r 3.14(1)	19.13
r 3.15(1)	19.14
r 3.15(2)	19.12
r 3.15(3)	19.12
rr 3.18–3.30A	19.15
r 3.18(1)	19.15
r 4.49(2)	21.6
r 4.49(3)	21.6
r 4.49(4)	21.6
r 4.49D	20.28, 21.7
r 4.49D(1)	20.27, 21.6
r 4.49D(5)	20.27, 21.6
r 4.49E(1)	20.27, 21.6
r 4.49E(1)(b)	20.27
r 4.49E(2)	20.27
r 4.49E(3)	20.27
r 4.49E(4)	20.27
rr 4.50–4.147	16.10
r 4.50(1)	21.5
r 4.50(2)	21.5
r 4.50(4)	21.5
r 4.50(5)	21.5
r 4.50(6)(b)	21.5
r 4.51(2)	20.5
r 4.52	21.2
r 4.53	20.2
r 4.53A	20.16
r 4.54	20.3, 21.3
r 4.54(1)	20.7
r 4.54(2)(a)	20.7
r 4.54(3)	20.7
r 4.54(5)	20.7
r 4.55(2)	21.9
r 4.55(3)	21.9
r 4.56	20.10
r 4.56(2)	20.10
r 4.57	20.3, 21.3
r 4.59	20.4, 20.7
r 4.60(1)	20.5, 20.7, 20.15, 21.5, 22.5
r 4.60(2)	20.5, 20.7, 20.15, 21.5, 22.5
r 4.60(3)	20.5, 20.7, 21.5
r 4.63(1)	20.18, 20.19
r 4.63(4)	20.19
r 4.64(a)	20.12
r 4.64(b)	20.12
r 4.65(2)	20.15
r 4.65(3)	20.15
r 4.65(4)	20.15
r 4.65(5)	20.15
r 4.65(6A)	20.15
r 4.65(7)	20.15
r 4.67(1)(a)	20.17, 20.21, 21.10
r 4.67(1)(b)	20.17
r 4.67(2)	20.17, 21.10
r 4.67(3)	20.18
r 4.67(4)	20.18
r 4.67(5)(a)	20.18
r 4.67(5)(b)	20.18
r 4.68	20.11, 20.17
r 4.70	16.16

Table of Insolvency Rules

Insolvency Rules 1986, SI 1986/1925—continued	
r 4.70(1)	20.11, 20.17, 21.10
r 4.70(2)	20.11
r 4.70(3)	20.11
r 4.71(1)	20.13
r 4.71(2)	20.13
r 4.71(3)	21.10
r 4.71(4)	21.10
r 4.72	20.4
r 4.106	22.8
r 4.122	20.31
r 4.125(1)	21.7
r 4.125(2)	21.8, 21.13
r 4.125(4)	21.13
r 4.125(5)	21.13
r 4.125A	21.7, 21.8
r 4.126(1)	20.8
r 4.126(1A)	20.29
r 4.126(1D)	20.28
r 4.126(1E)	20.30
r 4.126(2)	20.31
r 4.126(3)	20.31
r 4.126(5)	20.30
r 4.139(2)	22.6
r 4.139(3)	22.6
rr 4.151–4.178	16.11
r 5.3(1)	25.5
r 5.3(2)	25.5
rr 5.11–5.13	25.6
r 5.14	25.7
rr 5.17–4.24	16.10
r 5.17(1)	17.44
r 5.17(2)	25.8
r 5.17(3)	25.37
r 5.17(3A)	25.9
r 5.17(5)	25.37
r 5.17(7)	25.35
r 5.18	25.10
r 5.19	25.14
r 5.20	25.15
r 5.21(1)	25.18
r 5.21(2)	25.18
r 5.21(3)	25.18
r 5.22	25.18, 25.26, 25.34
r 5.22(1)	17.38
r 5.22(4)	25.18
r 5.22(7)	25.18
r 5.23(1)	25.19
r 5.23(2)	25.19
r 5.23(4)	16.20, 25.19
r 5.24(3)	25.17
r 5.24(4A)	25.17
r 5.27(2)	25.20
r 5.27(3)	25.21
r 5.27(4A)	25.23
r 5.29	25.23
r 6.73	24.4
r 6.75	24.4
rr 6.79–6.95	16.10
r 6.79(1)	24.2
r 6.79(4)	24.9
r 6.79(7)	24.5

Insolvency Rules 1986, SI 1986/1925—continued	
r 6.80	24.47
r 6.81	24.59
r 6.82(1)	24.38
r 6.83	24.13
r 6.83(2)	24.13
r 6.84(1)	24.5
r 6.84(3)	24.9
r 6.86	24.10
r 6.86(3)	24.16
r 6.87(1)	24.14
r 6.88(2)(a)	24.34
r 6.88(2)(b)	24.34
r 6.88(2)(c)	24.34
r 6.89	24.41
r 6.90	24.48
r 6.91(1)	24.46
r 6.91(2)	24.44
r 6.91(3)	24.49
r 6.91(4A)	24.40
r 6.91(4C)	24.50
r 6.91(5)	24.49
r 6.93(3)	24.27
r 6.95	24.62
rr 6.129–6.130	16.2
r 6.136	24.60
rr 6.150–6.166	16.11
r 6.162	24.61
rr 8.1–8.7	17.36, 20.7
r 8.1(3)	24.15
r 8.1(4)	24.15
r 8.2	17.27, 20.7
r 8.4	17.37, 24.63
r 8.5	17.37
r 8.6	25.15
r 12	17.19
r 12.4(1)	17.19
r 12.4(2)	17.19
r 12.4A	17.58
r 12.4A(2)	19.13
r 12.4A(2)(b)	17.58
r 12.4A(4)	17.58
r 12.5	24.63
r 12.10	17.17
r 12.12	24.6
r 12.16	17.19
r 12A.21(2)(a)	17.58
r 12A.21(2)(b)	17.58
r 12A.21(4)	17.58
r 12A.22(3)	16.5
r 12A.31	24.19
r 12A.55	17.41
r 13.3	17.19
r 21.10A	25.16
reg 8	24.61

Legislative Reform (Insolvency) (Miscellaneous Provisions) Order 2010, SI 2010/18   16.5, 20.2, 22.2, 24.6

Part 1
COMPANY MEETINGS

Part 1
COMPANY MEETINGS

Chapter 1

INTRODUCTION

HOW MEETINGS STARTED

1.1 If humans were less successful at communicating with each other, the odds are that you would not be here to read this book. It has ensured our survival as a species and we do it compulsively, every time two or more of us come into contact. We cannot help it. We put our points of view. We listen to others. We exchange information, analyse and debate. We influence each other and reshape and rearticulate our ideas. We generate new ideas, and test them out on each other. We propose plans, discuss their merits and conjecture on their outcomes. We review the consequences of previous plans and activities. We review external events affecting the topic under discussion. We discuss what we have learnt and how we can do better.

1.2 Often, we communicate collectively in order to make decisions together. We can achieve consensus, even among opposing factions, as minds are changed by new information or a debate, compromise is reached or power exercised to coerce those with opposing views. We can agree the outcomes or objectives we want, and which course of action is most likely to achieve them. We can allocate tasks and resources, decide timescales, and agree how we are going to monitor and assess progress. Group decision-making can be wiser, if many heads are better than one. Often, we are bolder when we know decisions are being taken collectively, as responsibility (and blame) will be spread if they turn out to be wrong.

1.3 Communicating together can have other benefits. It can advance individuals in a hierarchy. It can give stakeholders an opportunity to have their say, and feel listened to – particularly if there are 'rules of engagement' that have patently been observed, so everyone feels fairly treated. It can provide a forum in which praise or punishment can be given. It can provide a public demonstration of accountability, or compliance. It can simply be a way for a powerful participant to demonstrate who is in charge.

1.4 In the past, we had to be face to face to communicate, to carry on a dialogue with others. These days, electronic communications mean we can do so at a distance. We can have a dialogue, in real time, with other people who are many thousands of miles away from us and from each other. Sometimes we can only hear each other. Sometimes we can both hear and see each other. But we can do all the things mentioned above, that we could do if we were physically present together in the same room.

1.5 A dialogue between two or more people, who can all hear each other and be heard, for a purpose, is as good a definition as any of a meeting. How the law regulates meetings in certain circumstances is the subject matter of this book.

LIMITED COMPANIES

1.6 One class of meeting covered here is meetings of directors and members of companies incorporated under the Companies Act 2006. Many provisions regulating meetings – particularly members' meetings – are to be found in that Act.[1] References to sections are to sections in the Companies Act 2006 unless stated otherwise.

1.7 The rules in the Act, and other rules discussed in this book in relation to limited companies, apply to both companies limited by shares and companies limited by guarantee, unless stated otherwise. European companies (*Societas Europaea* or SEs)[2] are, however, not covered. When speaking of limited companies the term 'member' is used wherever possible in this book, rather than 'shareholder', since it encompasses both members of a guarantee company and shareholders in a share company.

MEETINGS IN INSOLVENCY

1.8 Another is meetings in insolvency. There is some overlap with the company law rules when considering meetings in insolvency as, of course, the insolvent may be a limited company. The rules governing meetings in insolvency are covered in Part 2.

MEETINGS OF LOCAL AUTHORITIES

1.9 Meetings of local authorities (council meetings, formal consultation meetings, and one-off meetings with the public or parts of it, including public meetings) are dealt with in Part 3. Local authorities need to take account of specific legislation when conducting council meetings, and their own standing orders when conducting other meetings.

PRIVATE MEMBERS' ORGANISATIONS

1.10 This book also deals, in Part 4, with meetings of private members' organisations, such as clubs and other unincorporated associations (but not charities). There are cases that guide and inform how these bodies should

---

[1] And the many statutory instruments made pursuant to it.
[2] Council Regulation 2157/2001/EC on the Statute for a European company. There is an associated Directive 2001/86/EC that supplements the Statute for a European company in relation to the involvement of employees in the management of such companies.

convene, conduct and record meetings. Such organisations are overwhelmingly choosing to reduce the uncertainties that can arise when trying to apply the facts of a case to particular circumstances by adopting specific constitutions, agreed upon by their members, that deal with matters relating to meetings. Common and sensible provisions to include are discussed, and the case-law that may apply in the absence of a specific constitution is also highlighted and reviewed.

Chapter 2

THE CONTROL AND MANAGEMENT OF COMPANIES

DIVISION OF POWERS

2.1 A company is recognised in law as being a distinct legal person.[1] However, being an artificial entity, it is only capable of acting through its duly constituted organs. The two primary organs are the members (which in a company limited by shares means the shareholders) entitled to vote, and the board of directors.[2] The Companies Acts provide that certain decisions may only be made by one or other organ of the company. For example, they say that articles of association of a limited company may only be altered by a decision (or 'resolution') of the members – they cannot be altered by a resolution of the directors.

2.2 So far as the members are concerned, the Companies Act 1985 (CA 1985) laid down four particular ways in which the members could make a decision. These were by special resolution, extraordinary resolution, ordinary resolution and elective resolution. Special resolutions and extraordinary resolutions required a three-fourths majority of the votes cast at the meeting in order to be passed. An ordinary resolution required a simple majority. Elective resolutions required unanimous agreement by all members entitled to attend and vote.[3] However, between November 2006 and October 2009, CA 1985 was gradually replaced by the Companies Act 2006 (CA 2006). Under CA 2006 extraordinary and elective resolutions ceased to exist – subject to one or two exceptions, discussed below – leaving only special and ordinary resolutions.[4]

2.3 What are the exceptions? In relation to elective resolutions the CA 2006 rules include saving provisions that, in two circumstances, preserve the effect of an elective resolution passed pursuant to CA 1985 – that is, before 1 October 2007.[5]

2.4 The first circumstance in which an elective resolution passed under CA 1985 may still be relevant relates to annual general meetings. To understand

---

[1] *Salomon v Salomon & Co* [1897] AC 22, HL.
[2] Others include committees of the board and the company secretary.
[3] See Chapter 3.
[4] By virtue of the third commencement order – Companies Act 2006 (Commencement No 3, Consequential Amendments, Transitional Provisions and Savings) Order 2007, SI 2007/2194.
[5] 1 October 2007 was the date when the part of CA 2006 which abolished elective resolutions came into force. No new elective resolutions can be passed on or after that date.

why, we need to understand the background circumstances. Under CA 1985 a private company had to hold an annual general meeting every year, but its members could pass an elective resolution dispensing with the requirement. From 1 October 2007, CA 2006 ended the requirement for private companies to have annual general meetings, but there was a saving provision[6] for private companies whose articles expressly required them to hold annual general meetings. The new rules said that such companies must continue to hold annual general meetings. Although the third commencement order clarified that articles based on the 1985 Act Table A default articles[7] (which referred to the retirement of directors by rotation at the annual general meeting) did not count as articles expressly requiring annual general meetings for this purpose, there are still a significant number of private companies whose articles *do* expressly say they must hold an annual general meeting. For example, reg 50 in the 1948 Act Table A states that: 'The company shall in each year hold a general meeting as its annual general meeting', and therefore expressly requires companies to hold an annual general meeting in each calendar year, so any company whose articles apply that Table A still has to hold annual general meetings. Similarly, the 1929 Table A states, in reg 39, that: 'A general meeting shall be held once in every calendar year'. Other, more modern companies – particularly companies limited by guarantee – may also have articles which contain an express requirement to hold an annual general meeting.[8]

2.5 But what if the members of a private company whose articles expressly require it to hold annual general meetings passed an elective resolution under the old 1985 Act rules dispensing with the requirement to hold them? Is the elective resolution still effective so that, even though their articles expressly require an annual general meeting, they do not need to hold one under the new rules?

2.6 The answer is 'yes'. The fifth commencement order contains an amendment to the third commencement order[9] saying that such elective resolutions remain effective. So companies that had chosen, before 1 October 2007, to pass an elective resolution to dispense with the need to hold annual general meetings under the old rules continue to enjoy exemption from the need to do so, irrespective of what is in their articles of association.

2.7 The second circumstance in which an elective resolution passed under CA 1985 may still be relevant is in relation to convening of a general meeting on short notice. This is discussed in detail at **6.11**.

---

[6] In para 32 of Sch 3 to the third commencement order.
[7] See **2.19**.
[8] Of course, members of a company whose articles expressly require an annual general meeting, whether old or modern, can pass a special resolution to alter their articles to remove the requirement, if they wish.
[9] See Sch 5, para 2 of the Companies Act 2006 (Commencement No 5, Transitional Provisions and Savings) Order 2007, SI 2007/3495.

2.8 There is also a saving provision in relation to extraordinary resolutions. The third commencement order[10] carries forward the old 1985 Act rules in relation to extraordinary resolutions in certain circumstances. It says that, if the memorandum or articles of, or any contract (for example, a shareholders' agreement or a subscription agreement) entered into by, a company refer to an extraordinary resolution, the reference continues to have effect. The memorandum, articles or contract will therefore continue to be construed in accordance with CA 1985, s 378. So if, for example, a company's articles require a decision to be made by extraordinary resolution, then an extraordinary resolution is still required in order to make that decision, and the CA 1985 rules governing the notice period and majority required to pass an extraordinary resolution remain effective for this purpose.

2.9 Because extraordinary resolutions ceased to exist under CA 2006, the CA 1985 provisions that required them to be filed at Companies House were, initially, also repealed. However, the Department for Business, Innovation and Skills[11] had to backtrack almost immediately to reinstate the requirement to file extraordinary resolutions at Companies House because it was inconsistent with the saving provisions in the third commencement order discussed in **2.8**. Article 4 in the fourth commencement order[12] therefore provides that the obligation to file extraordinary resolutions at Companies House remains in force, in case one is passed pursuant to a company's memorandum or articles, or a contract.

2.10 Before 1 October 2007, the members of private or public companies could also make decisions without holding a general meeting. Instead, provided all the members who would have been entitled to attend and vote on a matter if it *had* been put to a general meeting signed a resolution in writing, the resolution was treated as passed as if a meeting had been held. Most companies' articles made specific provision for such 'resolutions in writing' in lieu of holding a meeting.

2.11 The rules were changed by CA 2006 for resolutions passed on or after 1 October 2007. After that date, only private companies may pass written resolutions, and must pass them pursuant to the written resolution procedures in the 2006 Act – articles of association, including regulations in the 1985 Table A, that purport to authorise the passing of resolutions in writing in any other way no longer have effect.

2.12 Under the 2006 Act rules, eligible members holding a majority of the total voting rights in a private company can sign a written resolution in lieu of holding a general meeting to pass an ordinary resolution, and eligible members holding a majority of not less than 75% of the total voting rights can sign a

---

[10] At para 23 of Sch 3.
[11] Often referred to as BIS. Formerly the Department for Business, Enterprise and Regulatory Reform, or BERR. Before that the Department of Trade and Industry or DTI.
[12] The Companies Act 2006 (Commencement No 4 and Commencement No 3 (Amendment)) Order 2007, SI 2007/2607.

written resolution in lieu of holding a general meeting to pass a special resolution. They do not all have to sign the same piece of paper – a written resolution can comprise several documents in like form, each signed by one or more members.[13] There are additional rules and requirements, including a period during which the proposed resolution in writing must be passed or it will lapse, and an obligation to send an accompanying statement with each resolution sent for signature. See **3.67ff**.

2.13 Those powers which are not required by CA 2006 to be exercised by a particular organ are normally divided between the corporate organs by the company's articles of association. The provisions of the articles of association cannot, however, have the effect of relaxing the provisions of the Act by making it easier to pass that particular resolution. This means that where the Act requires a certain decision to be made in general meeting by special resolution, the articles may not provide for it to be made by an ordinary resolution, as that requires a lesser majority than a special resolution. On the other hand, anything which may be done by a simple majority can, under the articles of association, be required to be done by a greater majority.

ARTICLES OF ASSOCIATION

2.14 The articles of association lay down the rules by which the company will conduct its affairs including, usually, many matters relating to meetings. The contents of these internal regulations are decided upon by its members. They may only be altered by special resolution,[14] and then only within the parameters laid down by the mandatory provisions of CA 2006.

2.15 For a company incorporated on or after 1 October 2009, CA 2006 provides that one of three sets of articles (collectively called the 'model form' articles) will apply as a company's articles of association by default unless the members decide otherwise. Which model form applies depends on the type of company being formed. The three sets of model form articles of association (which are set out in regulations[15] made under CA 2006, s 19) are for private companies limited by shares, public companies limited by shares and private companies limited by guarantee respectively.

2.16 If the members of a particular company do not wish the relevant model form to apply as its articles at all, or wish to vary some of its provisions to fit the company's circumstances more closely, the company may file articles of its

---

[13] Such written resolutions may also be valid as 'informal corporate acts' if signed by every member who would have been entitled to vote on it if put to a general meeting of the members, and the law relating to the validity or otherwise of such informal corporate acts is, for most purposes, expressly preserved by CA 2006. See Chapter 3.
[14] CA 2006, s 21(1).
[15] Companies (Model Articles) Regulations 2008, SI 2008/3229. Note that there is no model form for an unlimited company. Such companies must draft and file their own articles from scratch.

own at Companies House that either exclude or modify it. If the articles completely exclude the model form they will invariably contain an entire, alternative set of provisions instead.

2.17 If the articles merely modify the relevant model form they usually begin by stating that the relevant model form shall apply 'save as follows'. They then set out the modifications to the model form that the members want to apply, one by one. So the model form continues to be relevant, except for those clauses modified by the filed articles. Officers of such companies, and their advisers, will therefore need to have copies of both the company's filed articles and the relevant model form to hand before they can find out what the rules governing meetings are for that particular company.

2.18 A company's members almost always *will* want the company to file its own articles at Companies House which exclude and/or modify the application of the relevant model form. This is because there are invariably provisions in the model form, whichever version of it applies, that are not completely appropriate to that company's circumstances. A listed public company, for example, will exclude the model form entirely and register its own articles of association at Companies House, since it cannot otherwise comply with Stock Exchange rules. And even a small private company limited by shares or guarantee is highly likely to want to modify the relevant model form in some way – for example, in relation to the powers of the board to authorise situational conflicts under CA 2006, s 175 (see **12.106ff**).

2.19 For companies limited by shares and incorporated before 1 October 2009 the rules governing articles of association were different. Under those rules there was only one default set of articles, which applied to both public and private companies limited by shares. Like the model form articles for such companies, these regulations – called 'Table A' and made by virtue of CA 1985, s 8(2) – constituted the articles of association of a company limited by shares by default, unless its members (or, in the case of a company about to be incorporated, its promoters) decided they wanted to exclude or vary Table A by filing specific articles of their own at Companies House. A company limited by shares, whether public or private, which did not register any articles of its own at Companies House therefore found that the regulations in Table A applied in their entirety as its articles of association.

2.20 However, just as companies formed on or after 1 October 2009 usually file articles that exclude or modify the relevant model form, companies limited by shares formed before then usually filed articles that excluded or modified Table A, and for the same reasons.

2.21 Table A is still relevant to company officers of share companies and their advisers today because, if Table A applied to a share company before 1 October 2009 it continues to apply on or after that date too – unless and until the members adopt a new set of articles. There are therefore very many share companies for which Table A remains the default articles.

2.22 The situation is made more complicated in that there have been many different versions of Table A over the years.[16] So which applies? The starting point is that (unless a company has filed articles that entirely exclude Table A from applying) the Table A that applied to a particular company when it was incorporated continues to apply notwithstanding the subsequent introduction of new versions of Table A, and notwithstanding the introduction of the model form articles, into the general law. It is only if the members of a company subsequently passed a special resolution to adopt an entirely new set of articles that the original version of Table A ceases to apply. Instead, if the resolution was passed before 1 October 2009, the Table A in force at the date of adoption of the new articles applies. If the resolution is passed on or after 1 October 2009, the relevant model form applies instead (except to the extent it is modified or excluded by articles filed at Companies House, as discussed in **2.16ff** above). Mere amendments or alterations (short of the adoption of a whole new set of articles) to the original articles by the members of the company do not have the same effect. The original version of Table A continues to apply – it is just the modifications made to it by the company's articles that have changed.

2.23 A person concerned with meetings of a share company incorporated before 1 October 2009 is therefore likely to need a copy of the company's articles and the right version of the relevant Table A to find out what the rules regarding meetings are for that company.

2.24 As a general principle a company limited by shares should consider adopting a new set of articles at least every time a new set of default articles is introduced, and whenever the Companies Act is amended.

2.25 Even in the case of two companies both of whose articles cross-refer to the same set of model form articles (or same Table A, for older companies) there may be significant differences between the rules which apply in relation to meetings in each case. If the two companies' circumstances are very different, then the members of each may have made very different variations to the relevant model form (or Table A). The need to consult and consider the articles of each individual company to discover exactly what they say about meetings cannot therefore be overstated.

2.26 What of companies limited by guarantee? Before 1 October 2009 (when a set of model form articles was first introduced as the automatic default for

---

[16] The two latest versions for companies limited by shares, prior to the introduction of the model form articles in October 2009, were:
For companies incorporated before 1 October 2007, the Table A to the Companies (Tables A to F) Regulations 1985, SI 1985/805 as amended by the Companies (Tables A to F) (Amendment) Regulations 1985, SI 1985/1052 and the Companies Act 1985 (Electronic Communications) Order 2000, SI 2000/3373.
For companies incorporated on or after 1 October 2007, the Table A to the Companies (Tables A to F) (Amendment) Regulations 2007, SI 2007/2541, as amended by the Companies (Tables A to F) (Amendment) (No 2) Regulations 2007, SI 2007/2826 and the Companies (Tables A to F) (Amendment) Regulations 2008, SI 2008/739.

companies limited by guarantee), the rules for guarantee companies were different from those that applied in relation to companies limited by shares.

2.27 Under those pre-2006 Act rules a company limited by guarantee always had to file its own articles of association at Companies House. If it failed to do so, Table A did not apply in default as it did in the case of a company limited by shares (or as the relevant model forms for both share and guarantee companies do today). Instead the failure to file articles meant the guarantee company had no articles. This was not just a practical problem – it was also a breach of CA 1985.

2.28 So what form did the articles of guarantee companies take before they had their own set of default articles? Under CA 1985,[17] the form of the articles of a company limited by guarantee had to be in the same form as 'Table C' (the latest version of which, prior to CA 2006, was set out in the Companies (Tables A to F) Regulations 1985),[18] 'or as near to that form as circumstances admit'.

2.29 So a guarantee company either had to file a set of articles in the form of Table C or, if the circumstances of the company admitted it, could file articles that either excluded or modified the provisions of Table C.

2.30 In fact, most guarantee companies took advantage of the 'as near to that form as circumstances admit' concession and filed articles that excluded or modified Table C.

2.31 Confusingly, Table C was not a self-contained set of articles in its own right. Instead, it cross-referred to Table A, but excluded and modified those provisions of Table A which referred to share capital (because those provisions were, of course, inappropriate to a company limited by guarantee, which does not have a share capital).

2.32 There are still very many guarantee companies incorporated before 1 October 2009 whose articles remain in the form of the 1985 Table C (or as near to it as their circumstances admit). Officers and advisers concerned with meetings of guarantee companies formed prior to 1 October 2009 which have not updated their articles of association since (so the relevant model form now applies) will therefore need to equip themselves with a copy of their own articles of association, Table C and also Table A (because Table C cross-refers to it) before they can be confident that they know what the company's articles say about meetings.

2.33 The rules in CA 2006, that now provide for a self-contained set of model form articles for a guarantee company, and state that they will apply as a guarantee company's articles of association by default unless the members

---

[17] Section 8(4).
[18] As amended.

decide otherwise (by excluding or varying the application of all or any of the relevant model form) are much clearer and more sensible than the CA 1985 rules.

2.34 And there is no specific requirement for a company limited by guarantee, if it does decide to file its own articles, to follow the form of the new model form articles, ie there is no equivalent of the old 'as near to that form as circumstances admit' requirement.

2.35 Finally, as with share companies, the articles of guarantee companies can be very different from each other. Indeed, the variations likely to be found between, for example, the rules relating to meetings which appear in the constitution of a charitable company limited by guarantee and those which appear in a residents' property management company or incorporated sports club, all of which were (and remain) likely to be companies limited by guarantee, can be significant. This book does not address the particular requirements of such companies. Suffice to say that the warning that each company's articles must be consulted and carefully considered to determine the specific rules applicable to the particular company applies even more forcefully when dealing with guarantee companies than when dealing with share companies.

2.36 The differences in companies' articles are hardly surprising given the many different types of company. The operation of a small private company, a large public company with thousands of shareholders and a not for profit company limited by guarantee will inevitably be quite different and this will be reflected in their constitutions.

2.37 What if neither CA 2006 nor the company's articles regulate a particular matter relating to meetings? How do the company's officers decide upon the right course of action?

INFORMAL RULES

2.38 The company may operate according to informal rules which supplement the requirements of CA 2006 and articles of association. These may be set out in, for example, operating manuals or like documents, decided upon from time to time by the directors.

CUSTOM

2.39 There may also be customs followed by the company generally, or at a number of previous meetings, which have acquired some status by virtue of the fact that members or directors have an expectation that they will be followed.

GENERAL PRINCIPLES

2.40 Finally, in the absence of regulation by CA 2006, the articles, any informal rules or custom, there is a body of general principles which may apply to company meetings by virtue of the common law, as established by the courts over the centuries.

2.41 These various rules operate as a hierarchy. Customs may not be inconsistent with operating procedures; operating procedures may not be inconsistent with articles of association and so on. The common law provides the final layer of guidance in the event that the solution to a problem cannot be found at a higher level in the hierarchy.

HOW THE MEMBERS MAKE DECISIONS

2.42 Unless CA 2006 or the articles otherwise provide, members of a company can authorise any decision by an ordinary resolution (see **3.4**).

2.43 This is, however, limited to matters which the company is legally entitled to transact. If all the members agree to a corporate act which is illegal or unlawful, this is ineffective and the company does not thereby acquire the power necessary for that purpose. It is also the case that if the articles or CA 2006 have removed control of certain matters from the general meeting, then the majority of members will not have any power in relation to those matters. Where the articles (rather than the Act) have deprived the general meeting of power, however, it is always open to the company to alter the articles by special resolution.

2.44 Most company articles provide that the business of the company shall be managed by the directors. For examples, the provisions of the model form articles (regs 3 and 4 in the model form articles for both a private and a public company limited by shares) and Table A (reg 70) confer on the directors the power to manage the company's business.

2.45 Where the articles provide to this effect, then the power of the members in general meeting to interfere with the running of the company is very limited. Nevertheless, there are circumstances where, notwithstanding the fact that the power to manage the business of the company resides with the directors, the general meeting may exercise the management power. This power will transfer to the general meeting if the directors waive their power, are unable to exercise it because of conflicting personal interests, are deadlocked or are inquorate. In these circumstances, the general meeting may act by ordinary resolution.[19]

2.46 If the members of a company disapprove of the action of its directors on a matter which is within the powers of the directors, they cannot, by passing a resolution, annul the directors' decision. The members can remove the directors

---

[19] CA 1985, s 35(1).

by ordinary resolution (see Chapter 3) or, by special resolution, control the directors for the future by altering the articles. Where the company has an article in the form of regs 3 and 4 (model form articles for a share company) or reg 70 (Table A), then the general meeting may also control the directors for the future by giving directions by special resolution; however, such directions cannot invalidate an act which has already been carried out by the directors.

ULTRA VIRES ACTS AND ACTS BEYOND THE DIRECTORS' POWERS

2.47 Section 39 of CA 2006 says that the validity of an act done by a company shall not be called into question on the ground of lack of capacity by reason of anything in its constitution.[20] This means that neither the company nor a third party can try to escape any of their obligations arising from an act of the company – for example, a commercial transaction such as entering into a contract with the third party, or a non-commercial matter such as a donation to a charity – by arguing that the act was beyond the company's capacity because of some restriction in the company's constitution. This means that the contents of the company's constitution will generally be a matter of indifference to third parties.

2.48 Under CA 2006 a new company is capable of exercising all the functions of an incorporated body (s 16(3)) and, unless the company's articles of association specifically restrict the company's objects, it can carry on any lawful activity (s 31). For CA 2006 companies that do not include restrictions in their articles of association s 39 is therefore redundant, as the company has no restrictions in its constitution anyway. However, if the shareholders *have* included restrictions in a company's articles of association, s 39 makes those restrictions irrelevant when considering the validity of any act of the company in relation to outsiders, such as customers, creditors or lenders. (The same is not true as between the company and its directors – see **2.51**.)

2.49 How does this rule apply to companies incorporated under CA 1985, before the CA 2006 rule was introduced? CA 1985 provided that a company's memorandum of association had to include an 'objects' clause setting out what the company was empowered to do. If such a company has not updated its constitution since 1 October 2009 then s 28 of the 2006 Act applies. This states that the provisions of the memorandum (including its objects clause) are treated, with effect from 1 October 2009, as if they were restrictions on what the company can do, and were set out in its articles of association. So, if such a company is treated as having restrictions in its articles, s 39 makes them irrelevant when considering the validity of any act of the company in relation to outsiders, just as if it was a CA 2006 company and the members had expressly decided to include restrictions on what it could do in the company's articles.

---

[20] CA 2006, s 39.

2.50 The situation is more complicated where the issue is whether the directors have exceeded their powers. In relation to the directors s 40(1) says that where a person is dealing with a company in good faith, the power of the directors to bind the company (or authorise others to do so) is deemed to be free of any limitation under its constitution.[21] However, the requirement of good faith is not an onerous one. A person dealing with the company:

- is presumed to have acted in good faith unless it can be proved that he was not; and

- is not bound to ask whether there is any limitation on the powers of the directors to bind the company or authorise others to do so. Indeed, merely knowing that an act is beyond the powers of the directors under the company's constitution is not, in itself, evidence of bad faith.

Members have the right to bring proceedings to restrain an act that is beyond the powers of the directors, although these proceedings cannot be brought where the act to be done is 'in fulfilment of a legal obligation arising from a previous act of the company'.[22]

2.51 It should be noted that s 40(1) does not affect any liability incurred by the directors (or, for that matter, any other person), such as liability for a breach of their duties, if they exceed their powers (s 40(5)). They may only escape liability for a breach of duty if the general meeting passes a special resolution specifically relieving them from their breach. A special resolution which merely ratifies their act or decision (which will also be needed) is, by itself, insufficient to save the directors from the consequences of their breach of duty.[23] However, s 40 does not protect a person who is party to a transaction with a company if that person is an 'insider' (for example, a director of the company or its holding company, or a person connected to such a director). In that case, the transaction will instead be voidable at the option of the company (except in certain circumstances – for example, if restitution is no longer possible). An 'insider' and any director who authorised the transaction is also (irrespective of whether the transaction is avoided) liable to account to the company for any gain he has made as a result of the transaction and to indemnify the company for any loss or damage that it has incurred, unless:

- he is an 'insider' who is not a director of the company; and

- he can show that at the time he entered into the transaction with the company he was unaware that the directors were exceeding their powers.

---

[21] CA 2006, s 40(1). 'Dealing with' a company means being a party to any transaction (or other act) where the company is also a party (s 40(2)(a)).
[22] CA 2006, s 41(4).
[23] Compare the approaches in *Marshall's Valve Gear Co Ltd v Manning, Wardle & Co Ltd* [1909] 1 Ch 267 and *John Shaw & Sons (Salford) Ltd v Shaw* [1935] 2 KB 113, HL.

2.52 The circumstances in which a member or members can bring an action in the name of the company are very limited. They may do so, using a statutory form of action under CA 2006, known as a derivative action.[24] Also, a member, all the members or some part of the membership, including the petitioning member, may petition the court under CA 2006, s 994 on the basis that the affairs of the company are being conducted in a manner which is unfairly prejudicial to company members. They may also petition for the winding up of the company on 'just and equitable' grounds.[25] Otherwise, a member is not permitted to bring an action in his, her or its own name for a wrong done to the company. This would breach the rule in *Foss v Harbottle*,[26] which stipulates that the proper plaintiff for a wrong done to the company is the company itself.

---

[24] CA 2006, ss 260–269.
[25] Insolvency Act 1986, s 122(1)(g).
[26] (1843) 2 Hare 461.

Chapter 3

TYPES OF MEMBERS' RESOLUTION

INTRODUCTION

3.1 There are two types of resolution under the Companies Act 2006 (CA 2006) which may be put to a members' (or general) meeting, or (in most cases) proposed as a statutory resolution in writing in lieu of a meeting. These are ordinary resolutions and special resolutions.

Previously, under the Companies Act 1985 (CA 1985), there were four types of resolution: ordinary, special, elective and extraordinary. However, CA 2006 makes no provision for elective or extraordinary resolutions so that they were effectively abolished from 1 October 2007 when the parts of CA 2006 dealing with members' resolutions and meetings[1] came into force, and replaced the rules previously in CA 1985.[2] However, there is an exception in relation to extraordinary resolutions, which means they can continue to be passed in certain circumstances.

3.2 This is because, for companies formed before 1 October 2007 there are saving and transitional provisions that preserve CA 1985 rules in certain circumstances. These are aimed at saving existing 'bargains' between companies and their shareholders.

3.3 One saving provision[3] says that any reference to an extraordinary resolution in a provision of a company's memorandum or articles, or in a contract, continues to have effect as if the old law remained in force. It is therefore still possible to come across a company that is required to pass an extraordinary resolution in certain circumstances – see **3.48**. The rules requiring extraordinary resolutions to be filed at Companies House also therefore remain in force for such companies.[4]

---

[1] CA 2006, Part 13.
[2] However, while it is no longer possible to pass new elective resolutions under CA 2006, certain elective resolutions that were passed before 1 October 2007 remain effective in certain circumstances (see **3.53**). Since the shareholders of a company can still, technically, pass an ordinary resolution to revoke such elective resolutions, the Companies Act 2006 (Commencement No. 4 and Commencement No. 3 (Amendment)) Order 2007, SI 2007/2607, art 4 also keeps in force those provisions of CA 1985 requiring resolutions to revoke an elective resolution to be filed at Companies House.
[3] In para 23 of Sch 3 to the Companies Act 2006 (Commencement No. 3, Consequential Amendments, Transitional Provisions and Savings) Order 2007, SI 2007/2194.
[4] See the Companies Act 2006 (Commencement No. 4 and Commencement No. 3 (Amendment)) Order 2007, SI 2007/2607, art 4.

ORDINARY RESOLUTIONS

3.4 The term 'ordinary resolution' was not defined in CA 1985, but it is in CA 2006.[5] Where the 2006 Act does not specify a particular type of resolution, but says a matter is to be decided by 'the company in general meeting', then an ordinary resolution is, in fact, what is required (s 281(3)). An ordinary resolution is treated as passed if there is a simple majority vote in favour of it (s 282(1)). What this means depends on whether the members are voting on the resolution by way of a show of hands, or on a poll. If the resolution is put to a show of hands, 'a simple majority' vote means a simple majority of the votes cast by those entitled to vote. If it is put to a poll, a simple majority means a simple majority of the total voting rights of the members who (being entitled to do so) vote (either in person, by proxy or in advance – see the reference to s 322A at **8.34**)[6] on the resolution. Those who are not there to vote, or who abstain, are ignored for these purposes (ss 282(3) and (4)).

3.5 As has been pointed out,[7] the articles of a company may delegate wide powers to the board of directors, so that those powers can no longer be exercised by the members of the company in general meeting – for example, reg 3 of the model form articles for a private company limited by shares, made under CA 2006,[8] provides that the directors are responsible for the management of the company's business, and they can exercise all the powers of the company for that purpose. This wide-ranging delegation of authority to the directors is subject only to (1) those provisions in the Act, or any provisions in the articles of the particular company, that reserve particular decisions to the members, or (2) any direction given by special resolution that directs the directors to take, or refrain from taking, a specified action (although no such special resolution can invalidate anything which the directors have already done before it was passed).

3.6 All matters reserved to the members under CA 2006 (see Appendix 1) and the articles can be decided by ordinary resolution, except those that are required to be made by special resolution by either the Act itself or the company's articles. The following steps should therefore be followed to find out what type of resolution is required for a proposed decision by the members of the particular company:

- Check CA 2006 to see if there is a 'base' requirement – for example, that an ordinary resolution is required.

---

[5] CA 2006, s 282.
[6] Inserted into CA 2006 by the Companies (Shareholders' Rights) Regulations 2009, SI 2009/1632, reg 5.
[7] Chapter 2.
[8] See the Companies (Model Articles) Regulations 2008, SI 2008/3229.

- Check whether a version of the model form articles or (for companies incorporated before 1 October 2009 that have not updated their articles since) a version of Table A[9] applies to the company.

- If a version of the model form or Table A does apply (and it usually will):
    - check it to see if it specifies a particular type of resolution for the decision to be made and, if it does, whether it is a more onerous form of resolution than any specified in the Act;[10] then
    - check the company's own articles to see if they vary the application of the model form or Table A to the company in this respect and, if they do, whether they specify a more onerous form of resolution than that required by the Act, the model form or Table A.

- If the model form or Table A does *not* apply, because the company's own articles exclude it expressly, and the company's articles comprise a stand-alone set of regulations instead, go straight to those articles to see if they specify a particular type of resolution for the decision being proposed and, if they do, whether it is a more onerous form of resolution than any specified in the Act.

Special notice

Removal of a director

3.7 One important circumstance, when special rules apply, is in relation to an ordinary resolution to remove a director under s 168 of CA 2006. Section 168 provides that a company may, 'by ordinary resolution', remove a director before the expiration of his period of office, notwithstanding anything in its articles, or in any agreement between the company and the director.

3.8 Special notice is, however, required of any ordinary resolution to remove a director under s 168, and to appoint a director to replace him at the same meeting.[11]

---

[9] The latest version of Table A before CA 2006 is that set out in the Companies (Tables A to F) Regulations 1985, SI 1985/805, as amended by the Companies (Tables A to F) (Amendment) Regulations 1985, SI 1985/1052, the Companies Act 1985 (Electronic Communications) Order 2000, SI 2000/3373, the Companies (Tables A to F) (Amendment) Regulations 2007, SI 2007/2541 and the Companies (Tables A to F) (Amendment) (No 2) Regulations 2007, SI 2007/2826. However, there were many earlier versions that may still apply. See **2.22**.

[10] The company's articles may not substitute a *less* onerous form of resolution for that specified in the Act. For example, the Act requires a special resolution to change a company's articles. The articles cannot provide for this to be done by (the less onerous) ordinary resolution.

[11] The courts (in Scotland, at least) will restrain the holding of a general meeting under s 168 to remove persons named in a resolution 'if they were presently directors'. Contingent resolutions of that kind are not lawful for the purposes of s 168: *Currie v Cowdenbeath Football Club* [1991] Outer House Court of Session, 2 September.

3.9 The special notice rules are set out in s 312 of CA 2006. These provide that, where special notice is required of a resolution, the resolution shall not be effective unless notice of the intention to move it has been given to the company, not less than 28 days before the meeting at which it is moved (s 312(1)).[12] A member who wishes to propose the removal of a director or directors should therefore give special notice of his intention to do so under s 312. The Act makes no provision, but such notice should be in writing and delivered to the registered office of the company. The notice should be delivered in a way that enables the member to prove receipt, such as registered post.

3.10 Upon receipt of such a notice, s 312(2) provides that the company must give its members notice of any such resolution at the same time and in the same manner as it gives notice of the meeting at which the resolution is to be considered. If that is not practicable, it must give them notice, either by advertisement in a newspaper having an appropriate circulation or in any other way allowed by the articles. Notice must be given not less than 14 days before the meeting.

3.11 Section 312 does not confer on the member giving special notice any automatic right to compel the board to convene the necessary members' meeting to consider the proposed resolution. The member who gives special notice to the company can only insist on a meeting if there is a provision to this effect in the articles, or, more likely, if the member (together with such other members as are needed to make up the necessary proportion of members under the section)[13] also serves a request, pursuant to s 303 (which is discussed in Chapters 4 and 6), requiring the convening of a general meeting.

3.12 If a request is validly given pursuant to s 303, s 304 requires the directors to convene the necessary meeting. If, however, the directors default, the Act allows those making the request (or any of them representing more than one-half of the total voting rights of all of them) to convene it themselves, and to recover the costs from the company (which can in turn recover them from the directors personally) (s 305).

3.13 The member giving the notice of intention to move the resolution will have to consider the interaction between the different but overlapping rules governing (1) the period allowed between the date the special notice is given and the date of the subsequent meeting and (2) the date the relevant request is given and the date of the subsequent meeting, to make sure both are complied with – for he can be sure that the target director will be taking advice, eager to find defects in the procedure being followed.

---

[12] This implies that a meeting is required. Certainly, s 288(2) states that a resolution to remove a director before the expiration of his period of office under s 168 cannot be passed using the statutory written resolution procedure in the Act. It is not so clear whether a director can be removed by unanimous, informal corporate act – see **3.117**.

[13] The required percentage is 5%. See reg 4 in the Companies (Shareholders' Rights) Regulations 2009, SI 2009/1632, which amended s 303 with effect from 3 August 2009.

3.14 If the directors receive a s 303 request requiring them to convene a general meeting to consider a resolution to remove one (or more) of their number, it is the directors who fix the date of the general meeting. A simple way for the directors to make the request ineffective would be to call the meeting for a date that is fewer than 28 days from the date that notice of the intention to move the resolution was given. This would make it ineffective under s 312(1) – were it not for a proviso in s 312(4). The proviso lays down that if, after notice has been given to the company, a meeting is called for a date 28 days or less after the notice has been given, the notice, even though not given within the time required by the section, is deemed properly given. This avenue is therefore closed off.[14]

3.15 On receipt of notice of an intended resolution to remove a director under s 168, the company is bound to send a copy of the notice to the target director 'forthwith', and the director (whether or not a member of the company) is entitled to be heard on the resolution at the meeting (s 169). The director also has a right to make representations in writing to the company, provided they are of a reasonable length, to be circulated to members of the company. Unless the representations are received too late for it to do so, the company must (s 169(2) and (3)):

- state the fact of the representations having been made in the notice of the resolution given to the members; and

- send a copy of the representations to every member of the company to whom notice of the meeting is sent (whether before or after receipt of the representations by the company).

3.16 If a copy of the representations is not sent to the members, either because the representations were received too late or because the company has defaulted in its obligations, the company must allow the representations to be read out at the meeting. This is in addition to the director's general right to be heard on the resolution at the meeting.

3.17 The entitlement to have representations circulated and read out at the meeting is subject, however, to the right of the company or any other aggrieved person to apply to the court to prevent this, on grounds they amount to an abuse of the rights given by CA 2006 – for example, because they are being used to secure needless publicity for defamatory material by the director (s 169(5)). If this happens, the court has discretion to make the director liable for the legal costs and expenses, even though the director is not a party to the application.

3.18 Although s 168 requires that special notice be given of a resolution to remove a director under the section, it does not require that the resolution be

---

[14] *Fenning v Fenning Environmental Products Ltd* [1982] LSG 803.

proposed at the meeting by the person who gave the special notice. Once special notice has been given, any member entitled to vote may propose the resolution at the meeting.

3.19 So far as the director who has been removed at the meeting is concerned, the section does not deprive him of compensation or damages payable in respect of the termination of his appointment as director, or of any other appointment terminating with the appointment as director (for example, as managing director).

3.20 If a company's articles provide an alternative way of removing a director, the company can still choose to follow the s 168 procedure, but also has the option of relying on that alternative procedure if it prefers (s 168(5)). For example, the board of a parent company will often wish to be able to (appoint and) remove directors of a subsidiary without going through the special notice procedure, and without the target director having the right to make representations. It will therefore provide in its subsidiary's articles that it may (appoint and) remove directors of the subsidiary, by serving notice in writing to that effect on the subsidiary's registered office. Assuming that all the directors of the subsidiary have not resigned in disgust immediately such a provision is introduced, a director subjected to that procedure will be removed from office immediately, with no right to special notice or to make representations.

3.21 Another company may decide to try to make it more onerous to remove a director. For example, its articles may include a requirement for a special resolution in order to remove a director, rather than the ordinary resolution required by s 168. That procedure can be followed but, again, the company can still choose to rely on s 168 to remove a director, if it wishes.

3.22 Those considering removal of a director under s 168 (and directors considering how to protect themselves from removal) should be aware of *Bushell v Faith*.[15] In that case, the House of Lords upheld the validity of an article giving extra votes per share to any member who was also a director, in the event of an ordinary resolution being proposed to remove him as a director.[16] The case concerned an attempt to remove a director from office who also held shares in the company. The company's articles purported to give a director under threat of removal extra votes per share on the resolution to remove him. Since the director was entitled to vote as a member on the resolution for his own removal as director, he naturally voted against it. His extra votes meant that the resolution was not passed. It would have been passed had he not had the extra votes. Despite what Lord Morris said in that case by way of dissent, the effect of *Bushell v Faith* is that such articles are effective to safeguard the interests of, for example, shareholder directors in a

---

[15] [1970] AC 1099. See also *Foulkes Group plc v Alexander* BLD 010202355 [2002] Ch D, 31 January 2002.
[16] See Appendix 2 for such an article.

'quasi-partnership' company. On the other hand, larger companies would have little legitimate use for such a provision, and no listed company could have such an article.

3.23 Commentators have suggested that the way to remove the director in *Bushell v Faith* would have been for the members to pass a resolution to alter the company's articles first, to take away his extra votes on a resolution to remove him as a director. He would then have failed to prevent the passing of the subsequent resolution to remove him from office. There is, however, a persuasive argument, following the reasoning in *Cumbrian Newspapers Group Ltd v Cumberland & Westmorland Herald Newspaper & Printing Co Ltd*,[17] that he would have been able to block a resolution to take away his rights in this way, on grounds that this would vary his class rights, and therefore require his sanction or approval pursuant to ss 630 to 640 (see Chapter 4) in order to be effective. In any event, practitioners now invariably draft '*Bushell v Faith* clauses' so that they give the director/shareholder weighted voting rights not only on a resolution to remove him, but also on a resolution to make any change to the articles that would neutralise those weighted voting rights, by whatever means.

3.24 The effect of s 168 may also be avoided if members enter into a shareholders' agreement whereby they agree to vote against a resolution to remove any director (or particular directors). Courts are likely to grant an injunction restraining breach of such an agreement.[18]

3.25 Special notice is also required of a resolution to appoint a new director, if they are being appointed to replace a director being removed under s 168, at the same meeting, and the above will apply equally to that resolution.

3.26 Where the vacancy is filled at the same meeting at which the director is removed, and the company's articles provide for retirement by rotation (see Chapter 5), then the person so appointed is, for the purpose of ascertaining which directors are to retire by rotation, deemed to have been appointed on the day the removed director was last appointed a director (s 168(4)).

3.27 If the vacancy is not filled at the meeting at which a director is removed pursuant to s 168, the vacancy is thereafter treated as a casual vacancy, to be filled in accordance with the usual provisions governing casual vacancies in the particular company's articles (s 168(3)).

Special notice in other circumstances

3.28 Special notice is discussed above in the context of removal of a director under s 168 of CA 2006. Special notice is also required by the Act in relation to certain changes in a company's auditors (as it was under CA 1985) – namely, on

---

[17] [1987] Ch 1.
[18] *Thomas and Others v York Trustees Ltd* BLD 1607012402 [2001] Ch D, 13 July 2001.

removal of an auditor at any time at a general meeting, and on appointment of a new auditor at a general meeting following a failure to reappoint an outgoing auditor (ie changing auditor from one financial year to the next). The procedures are set out in ss 510, 511 and 515, and are aimed at ensuring that the outgoing auditor has the chance to make representations which are seen by the members.

3.29 Section 510 says that the members of a company may remove an auditor from office at any time, provide they exercise their power to do so by ordinary resolution at a meeting[19] and in accordance with s 511 – which is the section requiring special notice of a resolution to remove an auditor.

3.30 If the removal is before the expiration of the auditor's terms of office, s 510(4) says that this *must* be carried out by a resolution passed under s 510.

3.31 The special notice rules regarding removal of an auditor are virtually identical to those for removing a director on special notice, dealt with above. In basic terms, they require notice of the intended resolution to be given to the company at least 28 days before the meeting at which it is to be proposed. In this case, on receipt of the notice of the intended resolution the company must forthwith send a copy of it to the person proposed to be appointed and the outgoing auditor. Again, the auditor may require the company to circulate representations in writing to the members. In each case, the company may apply to the court not to circulate the representations on the basis that the auditor is using the statutory provisions to secure needless publicity for defamatory matter. The auditor is entitled to attend the meeting and be heard orally, because he has these rights in relation to meetings generally under s 502 but, without prejudice to those rights, s 511(5) also provides that, if a copy of any representations is not sent out as required (either because they are received too late or because of the company's default), the auditor can require that they are read out at the meeting. The auditor may be entitled to compensation or damages because of the termination of his appointment as auditor, or of any appointment terminating with that as auditor.

3.32 Where a resolution is passed under s 510, the company must give notice of that fact to the Registrar within 14 days.

3.33 Section 515 regulates resolutions at a general meeting of a company[20] to appoint a new auditor in place of an outgoing auditor:

---

[19] So a meeting is required. This is consistent with s 288(2), which states that a resolution to remove an auditor before the expiration of his period of office under s 510 cannot be passed using the statutory written resolution procedure in the Act. It is probable, but not certain, that a director cannot be removed by unanimous, informal corporate act of the members either – see **3.117**.

[20] If the company is private such a resolution can also be passed by statutory written resolution under s 514. Special rules apply which ensure the auditor still has the right to make representations to the members before they resolve to remove him, even though no meeting is being held.

- whose term of office has ended; or

- if it has not yet ended, whose term of office is to end:
  - in a private company, at the end of the period for appointing auditors; or
  - in a public company, at the end of the next 'accounts meeting' (ie the next general meeting of the company at which the company's annual accounts and reports are laid) (s 437(3)).

3.34 For private companies it provides for special notice of such a resolution if:

- no period for appointing auditors has ended since the outgoing auditor ceased to hold office; or

- the period for appointing auditors has ended and a new auditor should have been appointed, but has not been.

3.35 For public companies it provides for special notice of such a resolution if:

- there has been no accounts meeting of the company since the outgoing auditor ceased to hold office; or

- there has been an accounts meeting (see **3.33**) at which an auditor should have been appointed, but has not been.

3.36 The 'period for appointing auditors' is the period of 28 days beginning with the end of the time allowed for sending out the company's annual accounts and report to members or, if earlier, the day they are actually sent out.

3.37 There is a duty on the outgoing auditor and the company to notify the appropriate audit authority (as defined in s 525(1)) in some circumstance when an auditor ceases to hold office (ss 522 and 523). In the case of a 'major audit', where an auditor ceases for any reason to hold office, the auditor ceasing to hold office must notify the appropriate audit authority. Section 522 defines 'major audit' as a statutory audit conducted in respect of:

- a company whose securities have been admitted to the official list; or

- any other person in whose financial condition there is a major public interest. In determining whether an audit of such a person is a major audit, s 522(3) requires that regard shall be had to any guidance issued by an appropriate audit authority.

3.38 If the audit is not a major audit (as will almost always be the case for a private company), the auditor ceasing to hold office must still notify the appropriate audit authority if he ceases to hold office before the end of his term of office, meaning that he must so notify only if he has resigned or has been dismissed.

3.39 The notification by the auditor to the audit authority must be accompanied by a copy of the s 519 statement. If that s 519 statement to the company said that there were no circumstances that needed to be brought to the attention of members or creditors, the notice to the audit authority must also be accompanied by a statement of the reasons for the auditor ceasing to hold office. It is an offence for a person ceasing to hold office as auditor to fail to comply with these requirements. Section 523 imposes a similar duty on the company to notify the appropriate audit authority where an auditor ceases to hold office before the end of his term of office (ie he resigns or is dismissed). The notice must be accompanied by either:

- a statement by the company of the reasons for the auditor ceasing to hold office; or

- a copy of the s 519 statement deposited by the auditor (provided that the s 519 statement was a statement of circumstances that need to be brought to the attention of members or creditors).

3.40 This notification must be made not later than 14 days after the s 519 statement is deposited at the company's registered office by the auditor.

3.41 Section 524 provides that the audit authority, on receiving notice under s 522 or 523, must inform the accounting authorities.

3.42 Section 288(2) says that the provisions in CA 2006 on written resolutions of private companies do not apply to resolutions removing a director under s 168, or removing an auditor under s 510. However, this does still leave some scope for confusion about the application of the special notice provisions to the law on informal corporate acts. Further attention is given to this question below.

SPECIAL RESOLUTIONS

3.43 Special resolutions are required by CA 2006 or the Insolvency Act 1986 (IA 1986) for various purposes, of which some of the more significant are:

(1) altering the articles (s 21(1));

(2) changing the company's name (s 77(1)) (although changes of name can also be effected by any other means provided for by the company's articles, under s 77(2));

(3) changing the register at Companies House so that, instead of stating the company's registered office is to be situated in England and Wales, it says instead that its registered office is in Wales. This is only possible for a company whose registered office is in Wales (s 88(2));

(4) changing the register at Companies House so that, instead of stating the company's registered office is to be situated in Wales, it says instead that its registered office is in England and Wales. Again, this is only possible for a company whose registered office is in Wales (s 88(3));

(5) re-registering a company from private to public (s 90(1)(a)), public to private (s 97(1)(a)) or unlimited to limited (s 105(1)(a));

(6) disapplying members' statutory pre-emption rights in the case of a private company with only one class of shares (s 569);

(7) disapplying members' statutory pre-emption rights where the directors are acting under a general authorisation to allot shares (s 570);

(8) disapplying pre-emption rights where the directors are authorised to allot shares, whether generally or otherwise (s 571);

(9) reducing share capital in connection with a redenomination (s 626);

(10) reducing share capital, supported by a solvency statement (s 641(a));

(11) reducing share capital, confirmed by court order (s 641(b));

(12) approving, where permissible, the purchase of its own shares by a private company (s 694);

(13) approving a payment out of capital for a purchase of own shares by a private company (s 716);

(14) procuring the winding up of the company by the court (IA 1986, s 122(1)); and

(15) voluntarily winding up the company (IA 1986, s 84(1)(b)).

3.44 In addition, the articles may provide that the company is only able to do certain things by special resolution.

3.45 Section 283[21] lays down the requirements for the passing of a special resolution at a general meeting, namely that it is passed by a majority of not less than 75%. What this means depends on whether the members are voting on

---

[21] As amended by the Companies (Shareholders' Rights) Regulations 2009, SI 2009/1632, arts 2 and 3 with effect from 3 August 2009.

the resolution by way of a show of hands, or on a poll. For a resolution voted on by a show of hands this means it is passed by a majority of not less than 75% of the votes cast by those entitled to vote. If it is put to a poll, it means it is passed by members representing not less than 75% of the total voting rights of the members who (being entitled to do so) vote in person, by proxy or in advance (see the reference to s 322A at **8.34**)[22] on the resolution. Those who are not there to vote, or who abstain, are therefore ignored for these purposes.

3.46 Where a resolution is passed at a meeting, a resolution is not a special resolution unless the notice of the meeting includes the text of the resolution and specifies the intention to propose the resolution as a special resolution (s 283(6)(a). If the notice of the meeting so specifies, the resolution may only be passed as a special resolution (s 283(6)(b)).

3.47 Pursuant to the doctrine of informal corporate acts, a special resolution may be passed with no notice if all members entitled to attend and vote agree to it.[23] Indeed, as discussed at **3.100ff**, a meeting is not even necessary, under the application of the doctrine of informal corporate acts.

EXTRAORDINARY RESOLUTIONS

3.48 As discussed in outline at **3.3**, extraordinary resolutions, and consequently the need to file them at Companies House, were generally abolished by CA 2006, from 1 October 2007. However, the third commencement order provided a saving provision.[24] It says that if a provision of a company's memorandum or articles or any contract require a particular decision of its members to be passed by an extraordinary resolution, then those provisions shall continue to be construed in accordance with s 378 of CA 1985, ie an extraordinary resolution is still required, and is to be passed as if extraordinary resolutions had not been abolished generally. The fourth commencement order[25] provides that the obligation to file extraordinary resolutions also remains in force in such circumstances.

3.49 The sort of decision that articles sometimes provide should be passed by extraordinary resolution include, for example, the removal of a director without going through the formalities of giving special notice (see **3.20**).

3.50 Since CA 1985, s 378 continues to apply to such resolutions, how are they to be passed? Section 378(1) provided that an extraordinary resolution

---

[22] Inserted into CA 2006 by the Companies (Shareholders' Rights) Regulations 2009, SI 2009/1632, reg 5.
[23] *Cane v Jones* [1981] 1 All ER 533.
[24] In para 23 of Sch 3 to the Companies Act 2006 (Commencement No 3, Consequential Amendments, Transitional Provisions and Savings) Order 2007, SI 2007/2194.
[25] See the Companies Act 2006 (Commencement No 4 and Commencement No 3 (Amendment)) Order 2007, SI 2007/2607, art 4.

could only be passed at a general meeting if the notice of the meeting, duly given, specified that it was proposed as an extraordinary resolution.

3.51 Section 378(1) also provided that, on a show of hands, an extraordinary resolution was one which had been passed by not less than three-fourths of such members as, being entitled to do so, voted in person or, where proxies were allowed, by proxy.

3.52 The position on a poll is dealt with by s 378(5), which provides that, in computing the majority on a poll demanded on the question that an extraordinary resolution or a special resolution be passed, reference shall be had to the number of votes cast for and against the resolution.

3.53 In summary, for an extraordinary resolution to be passed on a show of hands, at least 75% in number of the members who vote must vote in its favour; and on a poll 75% of the total votes validly cast, must be in favour of the resolution.

3.54 The notice of the meeting at which it is intended to propose a resolution as an extraordinary resolution must set out the exact words of the resolution or its entire substance, and also that it is intended to propose the resolution as an extraordinary resolution.[26] The length of notice of a meeting (other than the annual general meeting) for the passing of an extraordinary resolution by a company (other than an unlimited company) is 14 clear days, unless a shorter notice is agreed to as specified in s 307.

ELECTIVE RESOLUTIONS

3.55 The Companies Act 1989 introduced an elective regime for private companies into the Act. Elective resolutions could be passed by members of a private company whereby they resolve (or 'elect') to do all or any one of the following things:

(1) to remove or extend the duration of the directors' authority to allot shares (CA 1985, s 80A);

(2) to dispense with the laying of accounts and reports before the general meeting;

(3) to dispense with the holding of annual general meetings;

(4) to reduce the majority required to authorise short notice of a meeting; and

(5) to dispense with the appointment of auditors annually (CA 1985, s 386).

---

[26] *MacConnell v Prill & Co* [1916] 2 Ch 57.

3.56 An elective resolution could only be passed at a meeting of which 21 days' notice in writing is given, and for which the notice states that an elective resolution was to be proposed and also stated the terms of the proposed elective resolution (s 379A(2)(a) of CA 1985). All members entitled to vote in person or by proxy had to agree to the passing of the elective resolution (s 379A(2)(b) of CA 1985). Notwithstanding this stringent requirement, the elective resolution could be revoked by an ordinary resolution (s 379A(3) of CA 1985). It also ceased to have effect if the company became a public company (s 379A(4) of CA 1985).

3.57 CA 2006 makes no provision for elective resolutions but they are still relevant because, for companies formed before 1 October 2007, there are various saving and transitional provisions that preserve the CA 1985 elective regime rules in certain circumstances. These are aimed at saving existing 'bargains' between companies and their shareholders. The net effect of the new rules is as follows.

3.58 CA 2006 ended the requirement for private companies to have annual general meetings, with effect from 1 October 2007. The relevant provisions were brought into effect by the third commencement order. However, the order contained a transitional provision ensuring that any private company whose articles expressly required it to hold an annual general meeting should continue to hold them (although the third commencement order clarified that articles based on the CA 1985 Table A, which referred to the retirement of directors by rotation at the annual general meeting, did not count as expressly requiring one). Such articles are rare in modern companies but, for older companies, the CA 1948 Table A explicitly requires a company to hold an annual general meeting in each calendar year.

3.59 The question therefore arises of the effect of pre-existing elective resolutions dispensing with the requirement to hold an annual general meeting. The fifth commencement order[27] (Sch 5, para 2(6)) also contains an amendment to the third commencement order so that companies which had previously chosen, by means of an elective resolution, to dispense with annual general meetings are relieved of the need to hold them. Such an existing elective resolution therefore continues to have effect for those (few) companies required by their articles to have an annual general meeting.

3.60 CA 1985 provided that a general meeting (other than an annual general meeting) of the members of a company could be held on less than the usual number of days' notice, provided that a majority in number of the members, holding a certain proportion of the total voting rights at the meeting, agreed. This proportion was 95% unless, in the case of a private company, it had passed an elective resolution that enabled meetings to be convened on short notice with the consent of a lower percentage (but not lower than 90%). CA 2006 now

---

[27] The Companies Act 2006 (Commencement No 5, Transitional Provisions and Savings) Order 2007, SI 2007/3495.

provides that the proportion required in order to hold a meeting on short notice is 90% (save in relation to the annual general meetings of private companies, which are no longer required under CA 2006). However, to preserve existing bargains, any existing provisions in a company's articles that require more than 90% to agree before a meeting can be held on short notice continue to have effect.

3.61 Where a company's articles do require a higher proportion, because they were drafted at a time when, in the absence of an elective resolution, the minimum possible percentage required to consent to calling a meeting on short notice was 95%, but they have passed such an elective resolution, the question therefore arises as to the effect of that elective resolution. The sixth commencement order[28] provides that such elective resolutions in force immediately before 1 October 2007 which result in a reduction of the percentage required from 95% to some other percentage continue to have effect, so that any provision in a company's articles specifying a different percentage shall be disregarded.

DECISIONS MADE WITHOUT A MEETING

3.62 Members of companies may pass resolutions without holding a meeting in some circumstances. This may occur where a company passes a resolution by an 'informal corporate act' or by statutory written resolution under CA 2006.

3.63 Where a matter is one that could have been decided by the members in general meeting, and all the members of a private company, who would have been entitled to attend and vote on it if it had been considered at a general meeting, agree it, this can sometimes constitute a valid decision, even though no meeting is actually held.

3.64 One circumstance in which members of a private company may pass valid resolutions without the need to hold a members' meeting is (subject to exceptions) by statutory written resolution pursuant to the statutory provisions in Chapter 2 of Part 13 to CA 2006. These allow written resolutions of members of private companies in lieu of a meeting, provided the rules in that Chapter are followed. Public companies may not pass statutory written resolutions – they must hold a members' meeting or rely on the doctrine of informal corporate acts.

3.65 The doctrine of 'informal corporate acts' (often called the '*Duomatic* principle'),[29] applies if all members (being aware of relevant facts) either give approval or so conduct themselves that it would be inequitable for them to deny they had given approval to a decision, or to a particular course of action. The doctrine applies to both public and private companies. In such circumstances,

---

[28] The Companies Act 2006 (Commencement No 6, Saving and Commencement Nos 3 and 5 (Amendment)) Order 2008, SI 2008/674.
[29] After the case of *Re Duomatic Ltd* [1969] 2 WLR 114.

the courts are often prepared to hold the decision or act valid, even if procedural requirements have not been observed.[30] Approval can be given in advance or afterwards; can be characterised as an agreement, ratification, waiver or estoppel; and can be given in different ways at different times.[31] It applies equally to any particular group of members required to make decisions, such as members holding a particular class of shares, as it does to the main body of the membership.[32]

3.66 Two statutory exceptions to these rules, are the annual general meeting, and the meeting required to be convened by the directors of a public company if its net assets fall to half (or less) than its issued share capital (s 656). In both circumstances an actual meeting must be held.

Statutory written resolutions

3.67 The statutory written resolution procedures under CA 2006 came into effect on 1 October 2007. Key requirements are circulation of copies of the proposed resolution to every 'eligible member' and indication of agreement to the resolution from the required majority of all the eligible members, within the relevant time-limit. It can be used by members of a private company to pass any type of resolution (including a special resolution[33]) which might be put before a general meeting or a meeting of any class of members of the company (s 288(5)). There are two exceptions, discussed below.

3.68 In the vast majority of cases, the board will be the originator of a proposed written resolution of the members. CA 2006 sets out in detail the procedures that must be followed for circulating and obtaining agreement to such a proposal. These are examined in the following sections. However, the Act also recognises that a written resolution might originate from the members, exercising their statutory right to require circulation of a proposed written resolution (s 292).

3.69 Section 502 provides that the company's auditor is entitled to receive all communications relating to a written resolution as if he were a member.

3.70 Under s 288(2) the two exceptions are (1) a resolution to remove a director before the expiration of his period of office (a removal under s 168); or (2) a resolution to remove an auditor (a removal under s 510). Both of these decisions (which, of course, trigger the special notice procedure discussed at **3.7ff** and **3.28ff**) require meetings to be held.

---

[30] *Parker & Cooper v Reading* [1926] 1 Ch 975; *Re Duomatic Ltd* [1969] 2 WLR 114; *Cane v Jones* [1980] 1 WLR 1451; *Secretary of State for Business, Innovation and Skills v Doffman, Re Stakefield (Midlands) Ltd* [2010] EWHC 3175 (Ch); *Rolfe v Rolfe* [2010] EWHC 244 (Ch); *Tayplan Ltd v Smith* [2011] CSIH 8; *Schofield v Schofield* [2011] EWCA Civ 154; *Bonham-Carter v Situ Ventures Ltd* [2012] EWHC 230 (Ch).
[31] *EIC Services Ltd v Phipps* [2003] 3 All ER 804.
[32] *Re Torvale Group Ltd* [1999] 2 BCLC 605.
[33] CA 2006, s 288.

Types of Members' Resolution

3.71 It might be thought that a statutory written resolution could not be used in transactions where CA 2006 requires that a document be put before a general meeting before the transaction is lawful, because that requirement implies that a general meeting must be held. Relevant transactions include:

- disapplication of pre-emption rights on allotment of shares, pursuant to s 571;

- conferring, varying, revoking or renewing authority for a company to make an off-market purchase of its own shares under s 694;

- approval of a director's service contract (s 188);

- loans or quasi-loans to directors or persons connected with them, credit transactions or related arrangements (ss 197, 198, 200, 201 and 203);

- approval of a resolution to fund a director's expenditure in performing his duties (s 204);

- approval of payments to a director as compensation for loss of office in various circumstances (ss 217, 218 and 219); and

- a reduction of capital supported by a solvency statement (s 642).

3.72 However, CA 2006 specifically provides for alternative procedures in each of the relevant circumstances, which allows it to be effected by statutory written resolution. In each case, CA 2006 provides that the relevant document must be sent to the members before, or at the same time as, the written resolution is supplied to them for signature. However, where approvals are sought by written resolution, and a memorandum is required to be sent or submitted to every eligible member before the resolution is passed, then any accidental failure to send or submit the memorandum to one or more members is, subject to the articles, disregarded for the purpose of determining whether the requirement has been met (s 224). In certain circumstances, the rules also prohibit a member holding shares to which the resolution relates from participating in the written resolution.

3.73 Where a written resolution is proposed by the directors of the company, they must send or submit a copy of the proposed resolution to every eligible member by:

- sending copies at the same time (so far as reasonably practicable) to all eligible members in hard copy form, in electronic form or by means of a website; or

- if it is possible to do so without undue delay, submit the same copy to each eligible member in turn (or different copies to each of a number of eligible members in turn); or

- a combination of those two methods (s 291(3)).

The copy of the resolution must be accompanied by a statement informing the member how to signify agreement to the resolution and indicating the date by which the resolution must be passed if it is not to lapse (s 291(4)).

3.74 The validity of the resolution, if passed, is not affected by failure to comply with the above requirements. However, failure to comply is a criminal offence.

3.75 Where the copies are being sent in electronic form or via a website, the provisions of CA 2006 regarding electronic communications by and to the company in Schs 5 and 4 respectively need to be taken into account. See Chapter 11 for relevant details.

3.76 The eligible members who can vote on a written resolution are the members who would have been entitled to vote on it on the circulation date. This includes any person who has been nominated by a member under s 145 and is entitled to receive written resolutions under s 291 (see **5.124**). The circulation date is the date on which copies of it are sent or submitted to members in accordance with the statutory requirements (or if copies are sent or submitted to members on different days, the first of those days). If the persons so entitled to vote change during that day, the eligible members are the persons entitled to vote on the resolution at the time that the first copy of the resolution is sent or submitted to any member for his agreement.

3.77 Subject to any different provision in the company's articles, the voting rights on a vote on a written resolution are:

- in a company limited by shares, every member has one vote for each share that he holds; and

- in a company without share capital, every member has one vote.

The percentage vote required to pass a written resolution depends on whether the resolution is proposed as an ordinary resolution or a special resolution. For an ordinary resolution a simple majority of the total voting rights of the eligible members is required. For a special resolution a majority of not less than 75% of the total voting rights of the eligible members is required. This is a significant difference from the pre-CA 2006 rules, which required the unanimous vote of all the voting members before a written resolution was treated as passed.

3.78 If a resolution is required or authorised by an enactment, it is not possible to provide in the company's articles that a member has a different number of votes in relation to a resolution when it is passed as a written resolution compared with when it is passed on a poll taken at a meeting. If this is attempted, s 285 makes that provision void, and says that a member has the same number of votes in relation to the resolution when it is passed on a poll as he has when it is passed as a written resolution.

3.79 It is not possible for a private company's articles to exclude directors and members from proposing, and members from passing, written resolutions (s 300).

3.80 The period allowed for indications of agreement from eligible members can be set out in the individual company's articles of association. If so, the resolution is passed if adequate indications of agreement are received within that period. If no period is specified for this purpose in the company's articles, then adequate indications must be received within a period of 28 days beginning with the circulation date. If they are not, the resolution lapses and, if the company wants it passed as a written resolution in writing, it must start the procedure again.

3.81 The circulation date is the date on which copies of the proposed resolution are sent or submitted to members (or if copies are sent or submitted to members on different days, the first of those days). If the persons so entitled to vote change during that day, the eligible members are the persons entitled to vote on the resolution at the time that the first copy of the resolution is sent or submitted to any member for his agreement.

3.82 A member's agreement to a written resolution is signified when the company receives from him (or from someone acting on his behalf) an authenticated document identifying the resolution and indicating his agreement to the resolution. The document must be sent to the company either in hard copy or electronic form.

3.83 Section 1146 of CA 2006 provides clarification of what is meant by 'authenticated'. A document supplied in hard copy is sufficiently authenticated if it is signed. A document supplied in electronic form is sufficiently authenticated if:

- the identity of the sender is confirmed in a manner specified by the company; or

- where no such manner has been specified by the company, if the communication contains or is accompanied by a statement giving details of the identity of the sender and the company has no reason to doubt that statement.

3.84 Section 1146 does not affect any provision in the company's articles under which, if the document is sent by one person on behalf of another, the company may require reasonable evidence of the authority of the former to act on behalf of the latter.

3.85 The accuracy of the register of members is vital to carrying out correctly the procedure for written resolutions of the members. So is the availability of an up-to-date copy of that company's articles of association. The person responsible for the company's administration must be sure they can identify who the 'eligible members' are and be able to demonstrate that they were all properly circulated. He must also be able to calculate correctly whether or not the required majority consent has been received in the required time-limit.

3.86 If a company circulates a special resolution as a proposed written resolution, the circulated resolution must state that it is being proposed as a special resolution. If it does not, the resolution is not a special resolution (s 283(3)(a)).

3.87 The members of a private company (including a person nominated by a member under s 145, who is entitled to join in the request that the company circulate a written resolution – see **5.124**), can require the company to circulate a proposed written resolution, that may be properly moved, and is proposed to be moved as a written resolution (s 292). The members must hold at least 5% (or such lower percentage as is specified in the company's articles) of the total voting rights of all members entitled to vote on the resolution and may require the directors to circulate a proposed written resolution. Where they do this, they may also require the company to circulate a statement of up to 1,000 words to accompany the proposed resolution (s 292(3)). The resolution (and any accompanying statement) must be circulated once the company has received requests from members holding a sufficient percentage of the total voting rights. The request can be made in hard copy or electronic form. It must identify the resolution and any accompanying statement, and it must be authenticated by the person(s) making it.

3.88 The expenses of the company in complying with this requirement must be paid by the members who requisitioned the resolution unless the company resolves otherwise. Unless the company has previously so resolved, it is not bound to comply with the requisition unless there is deposited with or tendered to it a sum reasonably sufficient to meet its expenses in complying.

3.89 If the circulation of the written resolution (and any accompanying statement) is validly requested by the members, and subject to payment of costs, and provided that the resolution is not defamatory of any person, is not frivolous or vexatious and would, if passed, be legally effective, then the company must comply with the request. The company must send or submit a copy of the resolution and any accompanying statement to every eligible member by:

- sending copies at the same time (so far as reasonably practicable) to all eligible members in hard copy form, in electronic form or by means of a website; or

- if it is possible to do so without undue delay, submitting the same copy to each eligible member in turn (or different copies to each of a number of eligible members in turn); or

- a mixture of both.

This must be done not more than 21 days after the company becomes subject to the requirement to circulate the resolution (that is, once it has received sufficient requests).

3.90 The copy of the resolution must be accompanied by guidance on how to signify agreement to the resolution (s 296), and the date by which the resolution must be passed if it is not to lapse (see s 297).

3.91 Section 514 applies if a resolution is proposed as a written resolution by a private company, where its effect would be to appoint a person as auditor in place of an 'outgoing auditor' (an auditor whose term of office has expired, or is to expire, at the end of the period for appointing auditors).

3.92 It says that, if no period for appointing auditors has ended since the outgoing auditor ceased to hold office, or such a period has ended and an auditor or auditors should have been appointed but were not:

- the company must send a copy of the proposed written resolution to the person proposed to be appointed and to the outgoing auditor; and

- the outgoing auditor may, within 14 days after receiving the notice, make representations in writing to the company in respect of it (not exceeding a reasonable length) and request their circulation to members of the company.

3.93 The company must circulate the representations together with the copy or copies of the resolution circulated in accordance with s 291 or 293, except that, for this purpose, the period allowed for service of copies of the proposed resolution is extended to 28 days instead of the usual 21 days required under s 291 or 293.

3.94 Copies of the representations need not be circulated if either the company or any other person claiming to be aggrieved can satisfy the court that the auditor is using his rights to secure needless publicity for defamatory matter. The court can order the company's costs (or expenses, in Scotland) to be paid in whole or in part by the auditor, even if he is not a party to the application.

3.95 If any of these requirements are not complied with, the resolution is ineffective.

Regulation 53 of the 1985 Table A

3.96 Regulation 53 of the 1985 Table A, which continues to apply to many companies notwithstanding the introduction on 1 October 2009 of the model form articles made under CA 2006,[34] purports to allow resolutions in writing, without the rules, procedures and exceptions that apply to statutory written resolutions under s 288. However, it is now clear that reg 53, and any article in the form of reg 53 in a company's own articles, is no longer effective as an authority for the passing of resolutions in writing. The only methods are the statutory procedure and the doctrine of informal corporate acts.

3.97 This is because of the combined effect of clauses in s 288 in CA 2006. First, s 288(1) states that a 'written resolution' means a resolution of a private company proposed and passed in accordance with CA 2006. For 'enactments' (which include pre-CA 2006 versions of Table A) made before s 288 came into force (on 1 October 2007), references to a resolution of a company in general meeting, or a resolution of a meeting of a class of members of the company, have effect as if they included references to a written resolution (ie a written resolution proposed and passed in accordance with the Act) of the members, or of a class of members, of a private company (as appropriate) (s 288(4)).

3.98 Further evidence in support of this is that, for companies incorporated on or after 1 October 2007, a transitional version of Table A set out in the Companies (Tables A to F) (Amendment) Regulations 2007[35] (called in this chapter 'transitional Table A') and introduced from that date, applied as the default Table A. Transitional Table A made alterations to the 1985 Table A required to make it consistent with the provisions of CA 2006 then in force, together with some other alterations. Some of the transitional Table A alterations applied to all companies, some to private companies only and some to public companies only. One of the alterations in transitional Table A was the removal of reg 53 – presumably on grounds it was no longer effective.

Provision for written resolutions in a company's articles

3.99 As with reg 53, it is now also clear that express provisions in a company's articles that allow members to pass resolutions in writing in lieu of a meeting are no longer effective.

Informal corporate acts

3.100 The common law doctrine of informal corporate acts applies, in theory, to any type of company, but in practice will probably only arise in those companies with a small membership. As indicated earlier, the effect of the doctrine is that, provided a decision or act is within the company's powers, the agreement to it of all members entitled to attend and vote at a company

---

[34] See the Companies (Model Articles) Regulations 2008, SI 2008/3229.
[35] SI 2007/2541.

meeting is binding on the company.[36] No meeting is necessary,[37] and any procedural formalities are overridden.[38]

3.101 Consent must, however, actually be given, either before or after the decision or act. It is not enough that it would have been given if asked for if it was not, in fact, asked for – the members must have actually addressed their mind to the decision they are alleged to have consented to, so that '... there must have been a proposal of which all parties were aware and it must have been agreed to'.[39]

3.102 There is some confusion as to whether those entitled to attend and be heard at a company meeting, but not to vote, must also consent for there to be an informal corporate act. This issue was raised in *Re Duomatic Ltd*[40] but, on the facts of the case, it was not necessary to decide it because the non-voting shareholders in question had no actual right under the articles to attend or to be heard at the meeting. Subject to the comments in *Duomatic*, the better view is probably that it is not necessary for those with the right to attend and be heard to consent to an informal corporate act.

3.103 The common law doctrine of informal corporate acts and the statutory provisions for written resolutions in lieu of a members' meeting by private companies co-exist slightly uneasily with each other. There is an argument that the statutory provisions supersede the common law doctrine so it no longer applies, but this is very unlikely. The courts have certainly considered and/or applied it several times in recent years.[41]

3.104 The provisions for written resolutions in s 288 are, in some respects, narrower than the doctrine of informal corporate acts, as they apply only to private companies. On the other hand, it is arguable that the statutory provisions for written resolutions cover wider ground than the common law doctrine of informal corporate acts.

---

[36] *Parker & Cooper v Reading Ltd* [1926] Ch 975; *Peña v Dale* [2003] All ER (D) 416; *Re Express Engineering Works Ltd* [1920] 1 Ch 466.
[37] If a meeting is held at which all members are in attendance, but which is categorised as a board meeting, approval of a transaction can constitute members' approval for the purposes of s 190 (requiring members' approval of 'substantial property transactions'): *Re Conegrade* BLD 0511023945 [2002] All ER (D) 19 (a case dealing with s 320 in CA 1985, the forerunner to s 190).
[38] Including any formalities required by a shareholders' agreement: *Euro Brokers Holdings Ltd v Monecor (London) Ltd* [2002] EWHC 1573 (Ch).
[39] *EIC Services Ltd v Phipps* [2003] All ER 257; *Tayplan Ltd v Smith* [2011] CSIH 8. See also *Bonham-Carter v Situ Ventures Ltd* [2012] EWHC 230 (Ch) where the court decided that filing forms at Companies House (mistakenly) stating directors had resigned did not amount to an informal unanimous decision to remove them.
[40] [1969] 2 WLR 114.
[41] *Peña v Dale* [2003] All ER (D) 416; *EIC Services Ltd v Phipps* [2003] All ER 257; *Euro Brokers Holdings Ltd v Monecor (London) Ltd* BLD 1005021715 [2002] Ch D, 9 May; *Bonham-Carter v Situ Ventures Ltd* [2012] EWHC 230 (Ch).

3.105 First, a recurring question is whether a director or auditor can be removed under ss 168 or 510 by an informal corporate act. This is discussed at **3.117**.

3.106 Interesting comments in the case of *Wright & Another v Atlas Wright (Europe) Ltd*[42] also need to be considered. These seem to impose an important limitation on the application of the common law doctrine of informal corporate acts.

3.107 The court had to decide whether a term in a service contract applied, given that s 319 of CA 1985 (which applied to this contract, and required that it be made available for inspection by members, and subsequently approved by them) had not been complied with. The same considerations and reasoning would apply in relation to s 188 of CA 2006, which has now superseded s 319.

3.108 The Court of Appeal held that failure to observe formalities required by statute (such as those in s 319) did not mean the contract was void, provided that, given the statutory purpose and underlying rationale of a particular formality, the failure could legitimately be capable of being overlooked by oversight and curable by assent.

3.109 In this case, the court held that real consent had been given by the sole member of the company, and that there was no statutory purpose underlying s 319 beyond the benefit and protection of members of the company. The contract was not therefore void.

3.110 The result appears to be that the principle that unanimous approval by members is sufficient to validate a company's acts, even if there has been a failure to observe procedural requirements, is not automatic. Unanimous consent by members only overrides procedural failure if, taking into account the underlying purpose of the statutory procedure, it is only the members who are intended to be protected by it.

3.111 Consequently, the question of whether failure to make a document available at a general meeting, when required to do so under apparently similar provisions of the Act,[43] can be overridden with consent of all the members under the *Duomatic* principle will depend upon whether, taking into account the underlying purpose of the statutory procedure in each case, it is intended to protect some wider constituency than merely the members. Certainly, a transaction to which creditors can make objection, such as a purchase of own shares out of capital, will not be considered a transaction concerning only the members.

3.112 The courts have also held that the *Duomatic* principle does not apply in other circumstances.

---

[42] (1999) *The Times*, February 3.
[43] See **3.71**.

3.113 *In the matter of R W Peak (Kings Lynn) Ltd*[44] concerned an application for rectification of the company's register of members pursuant to s 359 of CA 1985 (now CA 2006, s 125). The company had purported to buy back its shares from a member, but had not complied with the provisions of s 159ff of CA 1985. The court commented that (while the matter did not require resolution in that particular case) the *Duomatic* principle presumed assent of the members to something which the company was capable of doing in general meeting. Section 143 of CA 1985 provided a general statutory prohibition against a company buying back its own shares except in certain circumstances (one of them being compliance with s 159ff). If the failure to comply with the Act meant that the transaction no longer fell within an exception to s 143, the prohibition in that section applied and the purchase therefore appeared to be void. Informal assent of all the members could not override the s 143 prohibition.

3.114 In a case[45] in which a dividend was declared in excess of the company's distributable reserves in the accounts, the Court of Appeal held that the 'strict and mandatory' nature of s 270 of CA 1985 (now CA 2006, s 836) was fatal to the argument that even a technical breach might be avoided by the *Duomatic* principle. The fact that there was profit in the subsidiaries that could lawfully have been paid to the company prior to the declaration, and made it valid, went to the issue of relief, not that of liability. That case applied *Precision Dippings Ltd v Precision Dippings Marketing Ltd*,[46] in which a subsidiary in liquidation paid a dividend to its parent on the strength of accounts in which a qualified auditor's report contained no statement of the materiality of the qualification (required at the time by s 43(3)(c) of the Companies Act 1980). A statement that the qualification was not material was later issued by the auditors. Notwithstanding the subsequent statement, the court held that such a statement had to be available *before* payment of the dividend or the payment was ultra vires. That meant that the members could not waive the need for a statement.

3.115 The case of *Walker v W A Personnel Ltd*[47] decided that there was no presumption (under s 241 of IA 1986) that the court would grant relief in respect of a transaction at an undervalue by requiring the recipient of the assets in question to pay monetary compensation rather than requiring the assets to be restored. On the issue of informal consent, the court said it was seriously arguable that informal approval under the *Duomatic* principle was not possible where the company in question was hopelessly insolvent. This seems consistent with the principle in *Wright* (discussed at **3.106**) that unanimous consent by members only overrides procedural failure if, taking into account the underlying purpose of the statutory procedure, it is only the members who

---

[44] [1998] Ch D, Companies Court, 24 October 1997.
[45] *Bairstow and Others v Queens Moat Houses plc* [2001] EWCA Civ 712. See also *Re Frontsouth (Witham) Ltd* [2011] EWHC 1668 (Ch).
[46] [1986] Ch 447.
[47] [2002] BPIR 621.

are intended to be protected by it. Many of the rules which apply in an insolvency (or when insolvency is looming) are intended to protect creditors rather than members.

3.116 Subject to the cases discussed above, an informal corporate act can achieve what may only otherwise be achieved by special resolution,[48] without the need for any of the formalities normally associated with such resolutions.

3.117 Whether an informal corporate act can cure the absence of special notice as required by s 511 (on removal of a director or an auditor) is a more vexed question. On general principles, one might have assumed the answer to be 'yes'. But some doubt arises because the provisions for special notice are intended to protect the director or auditor to be removed rather than the members so, applying the reasoning in the *Wright* case (see **3.106ff**), the better view may therefore be that their unanimous consent is not to the point. This is supported by obiter comments in *Bonham-Carter v Situ Ventures Ltd*[49] which indicate that the statutory purposes of ss 169ff and 510ff are to protect directors and auditors respectively, so members are not therefore competent to waive their application.

3.118 This argument is given added weight by the fact that removal of a director or auditor is expressly stated (s 288(2)) to be a situation in which the *statutory* written resolution procedure cannot be used – precisely in order to protect the director or auditor's right to special notice. The rationale for this exception seems to be that use of a statutory written resolution would take away the director's or auditor's right to make representations and have them presented to or read out at a members' meeting, because there would be no meeting. Since removing a director or auditor by informal corporate act would also take away that right, it follows that there is a strong possibility the courts would refuse to uphold an attempted removal by informal corporate act.

REGISTRATION OF RESOLUTIONS

3.119 Sections 29 and 30 require that certain resolutions and agreements must be lodged with the Registrar of Companies within 15 days of their passing or making. The Registrar is obliged to record the relevant resolution.

3.120 Failure to comply with the provisions of ss 29 and 30 as to lodgement with the Registrar makes the company and every officer in default liable to a fine (s 30(2) and (3)).

---

[48] *Cane v Jones* [1981] 1 All ER 533.
[49] [2012] EWHC 230 (Ch).

NOTIFICATIONS BY LISTED COMPANIES

3.121 Some of the main requirements for a listed company to notify[50] the UK Listing Authority of matters arising around meetings are set out here.

3.122 A listed company must forward to the UK Listing Authority[51] two copies of:

- all circulars, notices, reports or other documents to which the Listing Rules apply, at the same time as they are issued;

- all resolutions passed by the company other than resolutions concerning ordinary business at an annual general meeting, as soon as possible after the relevant general meeting.

3.123 On a change of name, a listed company must inform the UK Listing Authority in writing, as soon as possible, enclosing a copy of the revised certificate of incorporation issued by the Registrar of Companies.[52]

---

[50] A listed company may also have to notify a 'Regulatory Information Service' under the Listing Rules in these and other circumstances.
[51] Listing Rules, paras 9.6.1 and 9.6.2.
[52] Listing Rules, para 9.6.19.

Chapter 4

MEETINGS OF MEMBERS (INCLUDING CLASSES OF MEMBERS AND OF DEBENTURE HOLDERS)

TYPES OF MEMBERS' MEETING

4.1 All meetings of the members of a company other than annual general meetings are called 'general meetings'. Only public companies are required to hold annual general meetings, and private companies whose articles specifically require them to.

4.2 General meetings are usually convened by the directors because a matter is required, by the Companies Acts or the company's articles, to be put to the members for a decision at a meeting and, in the case of a public company, the directors do not wish to wait for the next annual general meeting.[1] Matters required by the Companies Act 2006 (CA 2006) to be referred to the members for decision are listed in Appendix 1. A general meeting may also be requisitioned by certain of the members, by the court or by an outgoing auditor.

4.3 Annual general meetings are different. Section 336 requires every public company to hold an annual general meeting in each period of 7 months beginning with the day following its accounting reference date. This is in addition to any other general meetings held during that period.

4.4 If the company has given notice to Companies House of a change of accounting reference date under s 392, to shorten its current or a previous accounting reference period, and this has caused it to be out of time for holding its annual general meeting under the usual rule, s 336(2) provides that it must hold its next annual general meeting within 3 months of giving that notice.

4.5 Since 1 October 2007, it has not been necessary for private companies to hold an annual general meeting. The one exception is if a private company's articles as at 1 October 2007 expressly required it to hold an annual general meeting, in which case it must continue to comply unless and until it changes its

---

[1] There is also one circumstance in which CA 2006 requires a company to convene a general meeting. Under s 656 the directors of a public company must call a general meeting if the net assets of which fall to one-half or less of its called-up share capital.

articles to remove the requirement.[2] The rules make it clear that a provision of a company's articles specifying that one or more directors are to retire at each annual general meeting of the company is not a provision expressly requiring the company to hold an annual general meeting for these purposes. However, private companies whose articles contain such a 'retirement by rotation' provision should consider altering their articles to remove it, so there is no inconsistency between the rules and the articles.

4.6 Principle E.2 of the UK Corporate Governance Code (formerly the Combined Code) provides that listed companies should use their annual general meetings to communicate with private shareholders (that is, shareholders other than institutions like pension funds) and encourage them to take part. Code Provisions set out particular action for companies to take to comply with the Principle.[3]

4.7 These companies also take into account the guidance and recommendations of bodies like the Financial Reporting Council,[4] in order to maintain good relations with their members.

4.8 The Institute of Chartered Secretaries and Administrators also produces valuable guidance and recommendations for company secretaries, chairmen, directors and practitioners.[5] These are referred to below where applicable.

MEETINGS CONVENED BY THE DIRECTORS

4.9 It is usually the directors who are responsible for convening the annual general meeting and empowered to convene general meetings (see, for example, s 302ff). This power to convene meetings is a power of the board, not of some of the directors only[6] (unless acting as a duly appointed committee with power to convene meetings).

4.10 A notice issued by the secretary without the authority of a resolution of the directors duly assembled at a board meeting is invalid.[7] A notice issued without such authority, either because no instructions have been given by the board for its issue or because the instructions were given by an improperly

---

[2] See para 32 of Sch 3 to the Companies Act 2006 (Commencement No 3, Consequential Amendments, Transitional Provisions and Savings) Order 2007, SI 2007/2194. Or unless it had passed an elective resolution to dispense with the requirement to hold an annual general meeting. See **2.4**.

[3] The UK Corporate Governance Code (September 2012).

[4] Which first published the UK Stewardship Code in July 2010 (although there have been subsequent revisions). Based on the former Institutional Shareholders' Committee guidance 'The Responsibilities of Institutional Shareholders and Agents – Statement of Principles', the Code is available at http://www.frc.org.uk/Our-Work/Codes-Standards/Corporate-governance/UK-Stewardship-Code.aspx

[5] Available to order at www.icsa.org.uk, or from ICSA, 16 Park Crescent, London W1B 1AH or e-mail informationcentre@icsa.org.uk.

[6] *Browne v La Trinidad* (1887) 37 ChD 1, at 17.

[7] *Re Haycraft Gold Reduction Co* [1900] 2 Ch 230.

constituted board, may become a good notice if adopted and ratified by a proper board meeting held prior to the general meeting. As was said in *Hooper v Kerr*:[8]

> 'The question is whether, although the notice was not authorised beforehand, it has been so ratified now as to make it a good and valid notice ... The principle of the cases ... is that the ratification of an act purporting to be done by an agent on your behalf dates back to the performance of the act.'

4.11 In this context, note should also be taken of s 161 which provides that the acts of a person acting as a director are valid notwithstanding that it is afterwards discovered that:

- there was a defect in his appointment;

- he was disqualified from holding office;

- he had ceased to hold office;

- he was not entitled to vote on the matter in question.

This applies even if the resolution for his appointment is void under s 160, which requires the appointment of directors of a public company to be voted on individually. This may, for example, validate a meeting held on notice sent out by an irregularly constituted board.[9]

MEETINGS CONVENED BY MEMBERS

4.12 If there are too few directors in the UK to call a meeting, the articles may provide that general meetings may also be called by any member. For example, reg 37 of the 1985 Table A (which continues to apply to many companies, both private and public, incorporated before 1 October 2009 – see Chapter 2) so provides. For companies with more modern articles, reg 28 in the model form articles[10] for a public company provides that where a public company has fewer than two directors, and its director (if any) is unable or unwilling to appoint sufficient directors to make up a quorum at a board meeting, or to call a general meeting to do so, then two or more members may call a general meeting. However, there is no such provision in the model form articles for private companies.

---

[8] (1900) 83 LT 730.
[9] *Transport Ltd v Schonburg* (1905) 21 TLR 305.
[10] Companies (Model Articles) Regulations 2008, SI 2008/3229.

MEETINGS 'REQUESTED' BY MEMBERS

4.13 Section 303, which expressly overrides any contrary provision in the articles, requires the directors to call a general meeting on the request of members representing at least the 'required percentage' of the voting and paid-up capital of the company (excluding treasury shares) or, for a company not having a share capital, members representing at least the 'required percentage' of the total voting rights of all the members having a right to vote at general meetings. They do so by serving a 'request' on the company. In CA 1985 the title used for the same document was a 'requisition', which was a more accurate name for it because, once received, the company is required to act on it.

4.14 The required percentage is 5%.[11]

4.15 The secretary must wait for the directors to instruct him to call such a meeting – the secretary cannot validly summon a meeting requested under s 303 without the authority of the board of directors.[12]

4.16 The request:

- must state the general nature of the business to be dealt with at the meeting; and

- may include the text of a resolution that may properly be moved and is intended to be moved at the meeting.

4.17 A resolution may 'properly be moved' at a meeting unless it would, if passed, be ineffective because it is inconsistent with any enactment or the company's constitution or otherwise, it is defamatory of any person, or it is frivolous or vexatious.

4.18 The request may be in hard copy form or in electronic form, and must be authenticated by the person or persons making it. Where several documents are used for the requisition, they must be 'in like form'. This requirement does not mean they must be in exactly the same form,[13] but best practice is that they should be. Where those making the request include owners of shares held jointly, the request must be authenticated by all the joint holders.[14]

4.19 If the requests received by the company identify a resolution intended to be moved at the meeting, the notice of the meeting must include notice of that resolution. If the resolution is to be proposed as a special resolution, the directors are treated as not having duly called the meeting if they do not give

---

[11] See reg 4 in the Companies (Shareholders' Rights) Regulations 2009, SI 2009/1632, which amended s 303 to reduce the required percentage to 5% with effect from 3 August 2009.
[12] *Re State of Wyoming Syndicate* [1901] 2 Ch 431; and see also CA 1985, s 368.
[13] *Fruit and Vegetable Growers' Association v Kekewich* [1912] 2 Ch 52.
[14] *Patent Wood Keg Syndicate v Pearse* [1906] WN 164.

the required notice of the resolution in accordance with s 283. If the request is valid, the meeting should be held even if the resolutions proposed have been overtaken by events. However, the directors need not call a meeting if it will in fact only be for the purposes of considering ineffective resolutions. If the stated nature of the business is not set out as resolutions already, but requires conversion into resolutions, it must be capable of being formally regularised and particularised by detailed resolution. If it cannot be, and has not been, so regularised and particularised, the board need not convene the requested meeting.[15]

4.20 Section 304 provides that the directors must convene a meeting (by sending out notice of the meeting) within 21 days of the request, and call such meeting for a date within 28 days from the date of the notice of the meeting.

4.21 There is a curious mismatch between the requirement in CA 2006 that the directors must convene the meeting for a date within 28 days from the date of the notice (which notice must, remember, be given within 21 days from the date of the deposit of the request) and reg 37 of almost all versions of the 1985 Table A which, if it applies to a company, requires the directors to convene a meeting pursuant to a request within 8 weeks of the date of the receipt of the request. For those companies to whom reg 37 of the 1985 Table A still applies, the provisions of the Act should be taken to prevail.[16]

4.22 If the directors do not call a meeting as required by s 303, and in accordance with the procedures and rules in s 304, then the members representing at least half the total voting rights of those who requested the meeting can convene a meeting themselves (s 305). Where the requests received by the company included the text of a resolution intended to be moved at the meeting, the notice of the meeting must include notice of the resolution.

4.23 A meeting convened by members under s 305 must be called for a date not more than 3 months after the date on which the directors become subject to the requirement to call a meeting. When convening such a meeting the members must do so in the same manner, as nearly as possible, as that in which meetings are convened by the directors. The business which may be dealt with at the meeting includes a resolution of which notice is given in accordance with s 305. The company must pay the reasonable expenses of the members making

---

[15] *Jeffrey David Rose v Brian Kenneth McGivern and Others (No 2)* (8 June 1998, unreported), Ch D.
[16] For companies whose articles apply the last version of the 1985 Table A before the model form articles were introduced on 1 October 2009 – ie the version of the 1985 Table A in force from 1 October 2007 to 30 September 2009 – this is not a problem, as reg 37 in that latest version was amended to remove this anomaly. However, for companies to whom the regulations in the Companies (Tables A to F) Regulations 1985, SI 1985/805, as amended by the Companies (Tables A to F) (Amendment) Regulations 1985, SI 1985/1052, the Companies Act 1985 (Electronic Communications) Order 2000, SI 2000/3373, the Companies (Tables A to F) (Amendment) Regulations 2007, SI 2007/2541 and the Companies (Tables A to F) (Amendment) (No 2) Regulations 2007, SI 2007/2826 apply, the anomaly is still there.

the request incurred as a result of the directors' failure to convene a meeting, but may deduct the same amount from fees or other remuneration falling due to the defaulting directors.

4.24 Those making the request are also entitled to convene a meeting if the directors convene a meeting to deal with part only of the business specified in the request. In this case they may convene a meeting only for the purpose of considering the business omitted from the notice sent out by the directors.[17] Presumably, in order to convene such a meeting to deal with the business omitted from the notice sent out by the directors, those representing at least half of the total voting rights of those making the request must be involved in the convening of the meeting.

MEETING ORDERED TO BE HELD BY THE COURT

4.25 If, for any reason, it is impracticable to call or to conduct a meeting of a company, the court may order one to be convened and held, and may give such directions as to the calling and conduct of the meeting as it thinks expedient (s 306). 'Impracticable' includes situations where a meeting could be convened but, if convened by normal means, could not take place sufficiently quickly to transact urgent business vital to the company's survival.[18]

4.26 Application may be made by any director, or a member entitled to vote, or by the court, of its own motion.

4.27 The power under s 306 is useful if there is a dispute as to the identity of the duly constituted directors able to call a meeting, and where one of the members is deliberately avoiding general meetings, so as to render them inquorate. This may be because the member does not wish a particular resolution to be passed (such as one to remove him as a director), or simply because there is a dispute between members and one is staying away from meetings to pressure the other, who wishes a meeting to be held.[19] It has also been used to call meetings in circumstances involving a petition under s 994 that the affairs of the company have been conducted in an unfairly prejudicial manner.[20]

4.28 However, the court will not call a meeting where to do so would override class rights.[21] Nor will it allow use of s 306 to upset a deadlock situation deliberately created by the members, where each agrees to hold equal shareholdings specifically so they can veto each other's actions.[22] The court

---

[17] *Isle of Wight Railway Co v Tahourdin* (1883) 25 Ch D 320.
[18] *Re a Company* BLD 1605021825.
[19] *Re Opera Photographic Ltd* [1989] 1 WLR 634. *Re Woven Rugs Ltd* [2002] 1 BCLC 324.
[20] *Re Sticky Fingers Restaurant Ltd* [1991] BCC 754; *Re Whitchurch Insurance Consultants Ltd* [1993] BCLC 1359.
[21] *BML Group Ltd v Harman* (1994) *The Times*, April 8, CA.
[22] *Ross v Telford* [1997] BCC 945.

may, however, decide differently if the relevant shareholdings are not equal. In *Union Music Ltd v Watson*,[23] members had entered into a shareholders' agreement which required the consent of both members before certain matters could be decided or acted upon. Their shareholdings were unequal. The members fell out and the minority shareholder stopped coming to meetings. There was a need to appoint a new director at a members' meeting. The Court of Appeal allowed the majority shareholder's s 306 application (in fact, its CA 1985 predecessor, s 459). It said that, where there were unequal shareholdings, so that the court could take into account the ordinary right of the majority shareholder to remove or appoint a director in the exercise of his majority voting power, and no rights attached to shares (or exercisable by a member) that could be construed as class rights, the court was under no obligation to assume that the parties had intended that either could veto meetings, let alone that the minority member could.

4.29 If the court decides to exercise its powers under s 306, these are substantial. Its directions may include a provision that one member present in person or by proxy shall constitute a meeting, and it may call a meeting notwithstanding the opposition of some members.[24]

4.30 In *Re British Union for the Abolition of Vivisection*,[25] a previous general meeting of the company had been disrupted by a minority of the members who were also on the company's 'committee' or board of directors. It was possible that the 'near riot' conditions which had prevailed at that general meeting would deter members from attending future meetings. Members could not vote unless present in person – proxies were not permitted. (Such a provision would have been invalid in a company limited by shares at the time, but was valid in this instance because the British Union was a company limited by guarantee.)

4.31 An application was made to the court under the CA 1985 predecessor to s 306 for a general meeting to be held to consider a resolution to alter the articles to allow proxy voting. The court granted the application and, addressing the concern that the disruptive element might use the same tactics as in the past to prevent the resolution being passed, the court also ordered that the general meeting should be attended only by the leaders of the disruptive minority, but that the rest of the membership should be entitled to vote by postal vote.

4.32 The court's powers under the predecessor to s 306 were therefore exercised to override both the articles and the provisions of CA 1985 which would otherwise have applied in relation to voting procedure at general meetings.

---

[23] [2003] All ER (D) 328.
[24] *Re El Sombrero Ltd* [1958] Ch 900.
[25] (1995) 2 BCLC 1.

4.33 The former powers of the Secretary of State, under s 376 of CA 1985, to order that an annual general meeting be held on the requisition of any member of the company, were not re-enacted in CA 2006. It was a rarely used power in any event.

RESIGNING AUDITORS' RIGHTS TO REQUIRE A MEETING

4.34 The only person other than the directors or members entitled to require the holding of a general meeting is a resigning auditor. Pursuant to s 518, where an auditor's notice of resignation is accompanied by a statement of circumstances which, in the auditor's opinion, should be brought to the attention of members or company creditors, then the auditor may requisition the directors to convene a general meeting.

4.35 The purpose of holding such a meeting will be to allow the meeting to receive information about, and consider the circumstances which have given rise to, the auditor's concern (s 518(2)). The auditor may request the company to circulate to its members a statement in writing concerning the circumstances connected with his resignation. Such a statement should be circulated before the relevant meeting (s 518(3)).

4.36 The directors must convene the meeting within 21 days, to be held before the end of 28 days from the date of the notice convening the meeting. Any director who fails to take reasonable steps to secure the convening of such a meeting is guilty of an offence (s 518(5)). Unless the auditor's statement to the members is received too late, the notice convening the meeting should indicate that such a statement has been made and a copy should be sent to every member of the company who is entitled to receive notices convening meetings (s 518(4)). If, for any reason, every member of the company does not receive a copy of the resigning auditor's notice, then the auditor is entitled to require the statement to be read out at the meeting (s 518(8)).

4.37 The right of a resigning auditor to have the contents of his statement made known to the members is subject to the ability of the company or any aggrieved person to apply to the court on the basis that the rights are 'being abused to secure needless publicity for defamatory matter'. Where such an application is made the court may order the auditor to pay the company's costs in part or in full (s 518(9)). The provisions concerning resigning auditors are part of a more general series of provisions which are designed to strengthen the position of the company auditor. These provisions are further considered in Chapter 10.

CLASS MEETINGS

4.38 Where a company's capital is divided into different classes of shares, it was often provided by the articles that the rights attaching to each class (for example, the rate of preferential dividend) could be varied, for example, by a resolution at a meeting of members of that class. However, there has been no such provision in Table A since it was removed, for companies registered after 21 December 1980, by the Companies Act 1980, s 88, and there is no such provision in any of the model form articles prescribed under the 2006 Act for public or private share companies, or companies limited by guarantee.[26] Instead, variation of class rights is governed by CA 2006 itself, to which attention must therefore be paid even in the case of companies whose articles do contain provisions governing variation of class rights. There are no special provisions for traded companies (see s 360C and **6.4**), so that s 307(1)–(6), discussed below, apply to variation of class rights, and s 307A does not.

4.39 What actually *constitutes* a 'class right' is another question. Section 629(1) provides that (for the purposes of CA 2006) shares are of one class if the rights attached to them are in all respects uniform. (A potential problem arises in relation to dividends payable on newly issued shares. This is because a company's articles will sometimes provide that dividends are payable according to the amount paid up on each share during the period of time in respect of which the dividend is paid. If one share has been allotted later than another, then it will have been paid up for a shorter period than that other, and the dividend paid on it in the year of its allotment will therefore be less than the dividend paid on the other share. Section 629(2) therefore clarifies that the fact one share does not carry the same rights to dividends in the 12 months immediately following its allotment as other shares already in issue does not make it a share of a different class.) Applying s 629(1), the 'norm' is the case where particular shares have special rights or benefits attached to them (usually in the articles,[27] by a resolution of the members or in the terms of issue of the shares) which are not attached to other shares (for example, voting rights, a right to dividend or a right to share in any surplus on winding up).

4.40 However, rights or benefits that are specific to a particular member while he holds shares in the company (in the sense that they come to an end when he transfers the shares and do not 'go' with the shares to the new registered shareholder), can also be class rights in some circumstances. They cannot be class rights if they are purely personal rights, not attaching to any particular shares, and not affecting the member *qua* member – ie in his capacity as a member. Thus, a provision in a company's articles that one of the members should be the company's solicitor was held by the courts not to amount to a

---

[26] The Companies (Model Articles) Regulations 2008, SI 2008/3229.
[27] Best practice is to include share rights in the articles. If shares are to be issued as redeemable shares (ie on terms that they can be cashed in, at the option of the shareholder, the company or both), the rights of redemption *must* be included in the articles. Rights of redemption cannot be attached to shares after they have been issued – the shares must be issued as redeemable shares from the outset.

class right, as it affected no particular shares and did not affect the member in his capacity as a member.[28] However, if, while a particular person or category of person is owner of certain shares, they clearly constitute a block – or class – to which special rights are attached for the time being, those rights may constitute class rights. Thus, in *Bushell v Faith*,[29] the articles of a small private company conferred three votes per share on any director who held shares, in the event of a resolution to remove him. The right attached to no specific shares, merely to the shares which a director held from time to time. This court said that this created two classes of shares, and the relevant provisions in the articles could not be altered without class shareholder consent. Similarly, in *Cumbrian Newspapers Group Ltd v Cumberland & Westmorland Herald Newspaper and Printing Company*,[30] a company's articles were amended to give a new member rights of pre-emption, rights to appoint a director, and certain rights over unissued shares, provided that the member held a certain proportion of shares in the company. This was to put the new member in a position to block a takeover. These rights only applied while the shares were held by the particular shareholder – the rights would not have 'gone with' the shares if they had been transferred to a new owner. However, the court ruled that they were class rights, because they were rights the member enjoyed qua member, and were attached to the shares held for the time being by the new member. This meant they could not be altered except in accordance with the procedures required on a variation of share rights at that time; they could not therefore be altered merely by passing a special resolution to alter the articles at a general meeting of the company (CA 2006, s 21) any more than would be the case if they were attached to particular shares in the usual way.

---

[28] As in *Eley v Government Security Life Assurance* (1875) 1 ExD 20 (the case turning, however, on the contract contained in the articles, which does not extend to purely 'personal' benefits). This, at least, is the general interpretation of the *Eley* decision. In fact, the most likely ratio of the *Eley* case is that Eley failed because he sued as the solicitor named in the articles of the company. Accordingly, the statutory contract was, in the words of Lord Cairns, 'res inter alios acta [he was] no party to it': at 90. In other words, he failed because he had sued in the wrong capacity. In a later case, *Hickman v Kent or Romney Marsh Sheep Breeders Association* [1915] 1 Ch 881, Astbury J analysed the *Eley* decision by saying that 'no right merely purporting to be given by an Article to a person, whether a member or not, in a capacity other than that of a member, as, for instance, as solicitor, promoter, director, can be enforced against the company'. This analysis seems to have been adopted by the vast majority of the textbooks. Astbury J however, seems to have ignored earlier cases where the courts have allowed enforcement of articles giving rights to a member other than in his capacity as a member. For example, in *Quin and Axtens Ltd v Salmon* [1909] AC 442, a power was given to a member in his capacity as managing director of the company to veto the disposal of certain assets of the company. The House of Lords held that he could enforce this Article notwithstanding that he was doing so as a director rather than as a shareholder. In acting as a director, the conduct of the director is overlaid with a fiduciary duty. This would not have been the case had the power been vested in him in his capacity as a shareholder. This distinction between the orthodox approach to the CA 1985, s 14 contract and what really was the decision in *Eley* was first pointed out by Lord Wedderburn in [1957] Camb LJ 183. See also Gregory (1981) 44 MLR 526.
[29] [1970] AC 1099.
[30] [1986] 3 WLR 26.

4.41 If there *are* class rights, the consent of class members must always be obtained before those rights can be varied. How this is done depends on a combination of CA 2006 and the company's articles.

Section 630 provides that class rights can only be varied in accordance with any provisions for variation in the company's articles or, if there are none, if either:

(a) three-quarters or more of the members of the class consent in writing to the variation; or

(b) a special resolution[31] sanctioning the variation is passed at a separate general meeting of the members of that class.

If the class rights are conferred by the articles, and the articles make specific provision for variation of those rights, then those provisions must be followed instead of the statutory rights. The articles can prescribe a less stringent procedure than the statutory requirement – for example, they could specify that a mere majority vote of the class members is required, or an ordinary resolution passed at a separate general meeting of the members of that class. Alternatively, they may prescribe a more onerous procedure – for example, they may require a higher percentage than the statutory minimum.

4.42 Class rights that were originally set out in a company's memorandum of association (which means that the company must have been formed pursuant to the 1985 or some earlier Companies Act, because it is not possible to include class rights in the memorandum under the 2006 Act), including any provisions for variation of the class rights, are now treated, by virtue of s 28, as if they were provisions in the company's articles of association. Section 630 will therefore apply to such a company too.

4.43 An alteration or insertion of a provision in a company's articles for the variation of class rights is itself treated as a variation of those rights, and references to a variation include the abrogation of any right: s 630(5) and (6).

4.44 If there is some other restriction on variation of class rights, such as a restriction outside the articles (for example, in the resolution to issue the shares), this must also be complied with: s 630(3).

4.45 Section 630 does not affect the question of what amounts to a 'variation' and two decisions in particular may weaken the statutory protection:

(a) that the alteration of voting rights of *other* shares under a power in the articles is not a variation of the *class* rights;[32] and

---

[31] Changed from an extraordinary resolution by the Companies Act 2006 (Commencement No 3, Consequential Amendments, Transitional Provisions and Savings) Order 2007, SI 2007/2194, Sch 4, para 2.
[32] *Greenhalgh v Arderne Cinemas Ltd* [1950] 2 All ER 1120.

(b) that the issue of new shares of the same class is not a variation.[33]

Such action obviously weakens the position of the existing class members. It is possible, but no more, that objection could be taken on the general principle of lack of good faith, without resort to a complaint under CA 2006.[34]

4.46 A variation of share class rights may be reviewed by the courts under s 633, which seeks to ensure that variations within the meaning of the Act will not operate unfairly. The holders of 15% or more of the class shares who did not agree to or vote for the variation may, within 21 days of consent being given or the resolution passed, apply to the courts for cancellation of the variation, which is then suspended until and unless confirmed by the courts. The application may be made on their behalf by any one or more of their number that they appoint to do so in writing. The courts may disallow the variation if satisfied, in all the circumstances, that it would unfairly prejudice class members; otherwise, it must confirm the variation.

4.47 In any event, nothing in s 630 above affects the court's powers:

(a) under s 98 (objection to a public company re-registering as private);

(b) under Part 26 (arrangements and reconstructions); or

(c) under Part 30 (protection of members against unfair prejudice).

4.48 The company must forward a copy of the order to the Registrar of Companies within 15 days after it is made.

4.49 Section 631 introduces, for the first time, specific provisions governing variation of members' rights in a company limited by guarantee. Such companies may have, for example, different classes of members with different voting rights. The provisions are identical to those for share companies save that, if they apply, the statutory majorities required to give the relevant class consents or to sanction the variation at a class members' meeting are:

(a) consent in writing to the variation from three-quarters or more of the members of the class; or

(b) a special resolution passed at a separate general meeting of the members of that class sanctioning the variation

and, where an application is made to the court, objecting to the variation, it must be made by (or on behalf of) members amounting to not less than 15% of the members of the class affected (being persons who did not consent to or vote in favour of the resolution approving the variation).

---

[33] *White v Bristol Aeroplane Co Ltd* [1953] 1 All ER 40.
[34] *Re Holders Investment Trust Ltd* [1971] 1 WLR 583.

Meetings of Members (Including Classes of Members and of Debenture Holders) 59

4.50 Section 334[35] states that the provisions of Part 13 of that Act (governing general meetings of the members generally, eg length of notice, voting and members' resolutions), and the ordinary provisions of the articles, govern the procedure for class meetings except for:

(a) ss 303–305 (members' power to require directors to call general meeting);

(b) s 306 (power of court to order meeting);

(c) sections 311(3), 311A, 319A, 327(A1), 330(A1) and 333A (additional requirements relating to traded companies).

4.51 Section 334 also says that, in addition to the above, ss 318 (quorum) and 321 (right to demand a poll) do not apply to meetings in connection with the variation of rights attached to a class of shares (a 'variation of class rights meeting') either. In those respects, CA 2006 specifically provides that:

(a) the quorum for a variation of class rights meeting is:

   (i) for a meeting other than an adjourned meeting, two persons present, holding at least one-third in nominal value of the issued shares of the class in question (excluding any shares of that class held as treasury shares);
   (ii) for an adjourned meeting, one person present holding shares of the class in question.

(b) at a variation of class rights meeting, any shareholder may demand a poll.

4.52 Sections 636 to 640 require companies to file various notices at Companies House within one month of doing so if:

(a) being a company with a share capital, it assigns a name or other designation to a class of shares or it varies class share rights (including assigning a new name or other designation to them); or

(b) being a company without a share capital, it assigns a name or other designation to a class of members; or it varies the rights of any class of members.

---

[35] Section 334(2A), as inserted by the Companies (Shareholders' Rights) Regulations 2009, SI 2009/1632, provides that ss 307(1)–(6) also apply in relation to a meeting of holders of a class of shares in a traded company as they apply in relation to a meeting of holders of a class of shares in a company other than a traded company. This means that s 307A, which would otherwise apply to a traded company, does not. See s 360C and **6.4** for the definition of a 'traded company'.

This applies even if the name, designation or variation will also appear on the public record because they are in the articles of association, or a special resolution or an agreement that must be filed with the Registrar of Companies. The relevant forms are:

- SH08 – Notice of name or other designation of class of shares;
- SH09 – Return of allotment by an unlimited company allotting new class of shares;
- SH10 – Notice of particulars of variation of rights attached to shares;
- SH11 – Notice of new class of members;
- SH12 – Notice of particulars of variation of class rights;
- SH13 – Notice of name or other designation of class of members.

For a company with a share capital, a statement of capital is not required unless there has been a change in the aggregate amount of the company's subscribed capital.

On the directions of the court pursuant to s 425

4.53 Class meetings are largely convened in the same way as meetings of the company are convened, but there is another kind of class meeting which may be held, under s 895. Under this section, where a 'compromise or arrangement' is proposed between a company and its creditors, or any class of them, or between the company and its members, or any class of them, the court may, on the application of the company, or of any creditor or member of the company, or, in the case of a company being wound up or subject to an administration order, of the liquidator or the administrator, order a meeting of the creditors or class of creditors, or of the members of the company or class of members, as the case may be, to be summoned in such manner as the court directs.

4.54 If a majority in number representing three-fourths in value of the creditors, or class of creditors, or members, or class of members, as the case may be, present and voting either in person or by proxy at the meeting, agree to any compromise or arrangement, the compromise or arrangement, if sanctioned by the court, becomes binding on all the creditors, or the class of creditors, or on the members, or class of members, as the case may be, and also on the company or, in the case of a company in the course of being wound up, on the liquidator and contributories of the company.

4.55 A 'compromise or arrangement' may include a complete change in the company's capital structure, and may even amount to its acquisition by another company.[36] In the latter case, however, the court will impose a heavy burden on those who support the scheme to show that it is a fair one.[37] The expression 'arrangement' includes a reorganisation of the share capital of the company by the consolidation of shares of different classes or by the division of shares into shares of different classes or by both those methods (s 895(2)).

4.56 A company proposing a scheme of arrangement under s 895 is required to give certain specified information regarding the effect of the scheme and the interests of directors and debenture stock trustees (s 897). This information must be contained in a statement which must accompany every notice summoning the required meeting under s 895. Failure to provide such a statement makes the company and every defaulting officer liable to a fine. Liquidators, administrators and trustees under a debenture trust deed are deemed to be officers for this purpose (s 896(1)). Mere compliance with the statutory requirement about what must be disclosed in this statement may not be sufficient to ensure the court's sanction of the scheme. In particular, if there has been a subsequent change in the directors' material interests which is not disclosed to or before the relevant meeting, the court will need to be satisfied that no reasonable person would have changed their mind, and their vote, in the light of that information, before it will sanction the scheme of arrangement.[38]

4.57 Section 901 requires a company to deliver to the Registrar a court order that alters the company's constitution. It also requires that every copy of the company's articles subsequently issued must be accompanied by a copy of the order, unless the effect of the order has been incorporated into the articles by amendment. These changes are included for consistency with other provisions in the Act concerning such orders.

4.58 Section 895 is a useful provision enabling all the members and creditors to be bound by a scheme of which the majorities of the various classes approve. Sometimes difficult questions are raised about what constitutes a separate class for the purposes of the section. The courts have always balanced the fact that unnecessary sub-division of a class might thwart a proper scheme by affording a veto to a small minority, against the potential for oppression or unfairness on the part of the majority in a larger, undivided class.[39] Certainly, a single meeting is appropriate where members possess not different rights but merely different 'interests'.[40] Generally speaking, if either:

(1) certain shares have different rights from other shares, and those rights are relevant for consideration of the scheme; or

---

[36] *Re National Bank Ltd* [1966] 1 WLR 819.
[37] *Re Hellenic & General Trust Ltd* [1976] 1 WLR 123. It is not an objection to a proposed scheme that there is an alternative legal means of achieving the same end which would give smaller members greater potential to block the transaction – see *Re TDG Plc* [2008] EWHC 2334 (Ch).
[38] *Re Minster Assets plc* [1985] BCLC 200; *Re MB Group plc* [1989] BCLC 672; *Re Peninsular and Oriental Steam Navigation Co* [2006] EWHC 3279 (Ch).
[39] *In the matter of the Equitable Life Assurance Society* [2002] Ch D Companies Court, 8 February 2002.
[40] *Re BTR plc, sub nom BTR plc v Northcote* [1999] 2 BCLC 675.

(2) certain shares are treated differently under the scheme from others,

then separate classes exist for the purpose of the section. It was certainly once thought that a single type of share with similar rights and which was to be treated uniformly by the scheme constituted a single and indivisible class.[41] In *Re Hellenic & General Trust Ltd*,[42] however, a single shareholder with 53% of the shares was the subsidiary of the bank which would, under the scheme, obtain all the new ordinary shares to be issued by the company (the old shares being cancelled in return for cash compensation). It was held that the subsidiary had an interest in the 'purchaser's camp' distinct from the interest of the other shareholders. Consequently, the subsidiary formed a separate class, so that separate class meetings should have been held to approve the scheme. It is generally thought that the decision somewhat strains the meaning of 'class rights' and it seems that this notion of class rights should be confined strictly to the rules on schemes of arrangement under s 895.

4.59 In the event of a dispute about the way creditors (and, presumably, members too) have been divided into classes, the court will take into account the voting figures in favour of a scheme as a 'powerful starting point' when deciding whether to sanction it.[43]

4.60 The meetings for the purpose of consenting to a scheme of arrangement are summoned by the order of the court, and in accordance with its directions. Section 899(2) makes clear that the persons who may apply for a court order sanctioning a compromise or arrangement are the same as those who may apply to the court for an order for a meeting (under s 896(2)). Failure to comply with the court's directions may result in the court refusing to sanction the scheme.[44] Proxies may be used in meetings under s 895, provided the company is not in liquidation.[45] The form of a proxy for these purposes will be settled in chambers. Directors who hold proxies for or against a scheme must use them.[46]

4.61 The class meetings themselves do not constitute general meetings of the company. If the scheme requires either the consent of the company in general meeting or some corporate act which has to be performed in general meeting, such as an increase or reduction of capital, then a general meeting must be convened for this purpose. Such a meeting is convened by the directors in the ordinary way, and is not called on the direction of the court. Proxies for such general meeting must follow the form required by the articles. On proxies, see Chapter 8.

---

[41] *Re Alabama, New Orleans, Texas & Pacific Junction Railway* [1891] 1 Ch 213. 'Classes' of creditors may be a more flexible concept. For example, holders of matured insurance policies constitute a class separate from other policy-holders: *Sovereign Life Assurance Co v Dodd* [1892] 2 QB 573.
[42] [1976] 1 WLR 123.
[43] *In the matter of the Equitable Life Assurance Society* [2002] Ch D Companies Court, 8 February 2002.
[44] Cf *Re Anglo-Spanish Tartar Refineries* [1924] WN 222.
[45] *Re Magadi Soda Co* [1925] WN 50.
[46] *Re Dorman, Long & Co* [1934] Ch 635.

In relation to compensation to directors for loss of office

4.62 As to class meetings that may be required to be held in connection with compensation to directors for loss of office, see Chapter 6.

MEETINGS OF DEBENTURE STOCKHOLDERS

4.63 Meetings of debenture stockholders are akin to meetings of class shareholders. These will be convened and conducted in accordance with the provisions contained in the debenture stock trust deed. The provisions in old stock deeds are often inadequate for modern requirements. The quorum requirements are often so high that in practice they are difficult to attain, and these requirements often extend through to a meeting adjourned from the original date, through lack of quorum, to a later date. A second defect is often the very restricted powers for amendment of the deed; frequently, they cannot be used to enable the substitution of a similar debenture stock of another company in place of that under the trust deed. Such substitution is often very desirable in the case of a takeover bid for the company concerned, or if the parent company in a group wishes to rationalise the financial structure and borrowing of the group.

4.64 If the provisions under the trust deed are inadequate, the company has to have recourse to a scheme under s 895.

4.65 Where a meeting of debenture holders is held, each holder may vote in his own interests, but if the holder has conflicting interests in a capacity as a member of the company, or as a creditor of a different class, he must not vote in favour of the other interest, or, if he does, his vote may be open to challenge.[47]

4.66 A person may be entitled to vote at a meeting of debenture holders if debentures have been allotted to him, his name is in the register of debenture holders and he has the right to call for duly sealed debentures and is bound to accept them.[48]

4.67 Debentures are often issued on the terms that the rights of the holders may be varied with the consent of a certain proportion of the holders, or with the consent of a resolution passed by a particular majority at a meeting of the holders. Any such variation must, to be valid, be strictly in accordance with the terms of the debentures. A power of this kind to vary rights will not justify abandoning rights and a power to compromise can only be exercised if there is some dispute to compromise,[49] or if there is some compromise (but not

---

[47] *Re New York Taxi Cab Co* [1913] 1 Ch 1.
[48] *Dey v Rubber & Mercantile Corporation* [1923] 2 Ch 528.
[49] *Mercantile Investment Co v International Co of Mexico* [1893] 1 Ch 484n.

abandonment) of rights.[50] Where there is no power to compromise then, in order to achieve a compromise, it will be necessary to resort to s 895.

---

[50] *Re NFU Development Trust Ltd* [1972] 1 WLR 1548.

Chapter 5

ANNUAL GENERAL MEETINGS FOR PUBLIC COMPANIES

WHY ANNUAL GENERAL MEETINGS ARE HELD

5.1 Since 1 October 2007, it has not been necessary for private companies to hold an annual general meeting unless (very unusually) they are traded companies (see s 360C and **6.4**) or if a particular private company's articles as at 1 October 2007 specifically required it to hold an annual general meeting, in which case it must continue to comply unless and until it changes its articles to remove the requirement. This chapter is therefore mainly only relevant to public companies.

5.2 The overriding rationale for the annual general meeting is that it is the opportunity for members of public companies to question the directors about their stewardship of the company, and its commercial and financial performance and status. For example, the UK Corporate Governance Code (formerly the Combined Code on Corporate Governance),[1] which sets out standards of good practice for UK companies with a Premium listing on the Main Market of the London Stock Exchange, provides that the boards of such companies should use the annual general meeting to communicate with investors and to encourage their participation,[2] and that the chairman of such companies should arrange for all directors to attend and for the chairmen of the audit, remuneration and nomination committees to be available to answer questions at the annual general meeting.[3] The attendance of directors at the annual general meeting is highly recommended for all public companies. And, among the members, the UK Stewardship Code (which sets out the principles of effective stewardship by investors in UK listed companies and helps them exercise their stewardship responsibilities better) provides that institutional investors[4] should attend the general meetings of companies in which they have a major shareholding, where appropriate and practicable.[5]

---

[1] *The UK Corporate Governance Code* (September 2012). This version applies to accounting periods beginning on or after 1 October 2012 and applies to all companies with a Premium listing of equity shares regardless of whether they are incorporated in the UK or elsewhere.
[2] Main Principle of E.2.
[3] Provision E.2.3.
[4] Which effectively means asset owners, such as pension funds, insurance companies, investment trusts and other collective investment vehicles, and the asset managers and companies which have day-to-day responsibility for managing investments.
[5] Principle 3.

WHEN ANNUAL GENERAL MEETINGS ARE HELD

5.3 Section 336 of the Companies Act 2006 (CA 2006) requires every public company to hold an annual general meeting in each period of 7 months[6] and every private company that is a traded company to hold an annual general meeting in each period of 9 months[7] beginning, in each case, with the day following its accounting reference date, in addition to any other meetings held during those periods.

5.4 However, if either a public, or a private traded, company has given notice to Companies House of a change of accounting reference date under s 392, to shorten its current or a previous accounting reference period, and this has caused it to be out of time for holding its annual general meeting under the usual rule, s 336(2) provides that it must hold its next annual general meeting within 3 months of giving that notice.

SPECIAL RULES FOR NOTICES OF ANNUAL GENERAL MEETINGS

5.5 The rules governing the form of notices of annual general meetings are virtually identical to those for a notice of a general meeting (see Chapter 6), and those rules can therefore be followed. However, there are differences.

5.6 The main difference is a simple one – that the notice of an annual general meeting must specify that the meeting being called is the annual general meeting (s 337(1)). However, there are also special rules relating to traded companies in s 337(3),[8] which are more complex. These say that, where a notice calling an annual general meeting of a traded company is given more than 6 weeks before the meeting, the notice must include:

- if the company is public, a statement of the right under s 338 to require the company to give notice of a resolution to be moved at the meeting; and

- whether it is public or not, a statement of the right under s 338A to require the company to include a matter in the business to be dealt with at the meeting.

5.7 Under s 338A[9] the 'requisite members' of a traded company can make a request that it include in the notice of its annual general meeting any matter (other than a proposed resolution) which can properly be included in the

---

[6] Changed from 6 to 7 months by the Companies Act 2006 (Commencement No. 3, Consequential Amendments, Transitional Provisions and Savings) Order 2007, SI 2007/2194, Sch 1, para 15.
[7] By virtue of s 336(1A), inserted by the Companies (Shareholders' Rights) Regulations 2009, SI 2009/1632, reg 15.
[8] Inserted by the Companies (Shareholders' Rights) Regulations 2009, SI 2009/1632, reg 16.
[9] See the Companies (Shareholders' Rights) Regulations 2009, SI 2009/1632.

business to be dealt with at an annual general meeting. For these purposes a traded company is a company which has voting shares that are admitted to trading on a regulated market in an EEA State (s 360C). Regulated markets in the UK include the London Stock Exchange main market and the listed elements of ISDX, the ICAP Securities & Derivatives Exchange (previously the PLUS stock exchange), but not AIM.[10] A matter can 'properly be included' unless it is defamatory, frivolous or vexatious.

5.8 For these purposes, the requisite members are those representing at least 5% of the total voting rights of all the members who have a right to vote at the meeting, or at least 100 members who have a right to vote at the meeting and hold shares in the company, and each member has paid up, on average, at least £100.

5.9 The request can be given in hard copy or electronic form. It must identify the matter to be included in the business of the meeting, and it must be accompanied by a statement setting out the grounds for the request. The members making the request must authenticate it (s 1146) and it must be received by the company not later than 6 weeks before the meeting, or the time at which notice of the meeting is given, whichever is later.

THE BUSINESS OF AN ANNUAL GENERAL MEETING

5.10 General meetings other than the annual general meeting are convened to consider particular resolutions required to be put to the members for decision. It is self-evident that the business of the meeting is to consider those resolutions, and they should be set out in the notice of the meeting. What is the business of an annual general meeting, and what should appear in the notice to convene it?

5.11 This will depend upon the answers to a range of questions, including the following.

- Do the company's articles distinguish between 'special' and ordinary' business at the annual general meeting?

- Does the company wish to put resolutions to declare dividends to the members at the annual general meeting?

- Will the company present the accounts to the members at the annual general meeting and, if so, does it have auditors?

These and other questions are considered below.

---

[10] AIM is instead a Multilateral Trading Facility as defined under the Markets in Financial Instruments Directive 2004.

5.12 The 1948 Table A (reg 52) drew a distinction between 'special' business, the general nature of which had to be specified in the notice of a general meeting before it could validly be considered at the meeting,[11] and 'ordinary' business, that could be considered whether or not it had been specified in the notice.[12] Regulation 52 of the 1948 Table A will apply to companies incorporated, or which last adopted a new set of articles, before 1 July 1985, while that 1948 version of Table A was in force.[13]

5.13 Specifically, reg 52 provides that all business transacted at a general meeting is deemed special, and also all business transacted at the annual general meeting, with the exception of:

- declaring a dividend;

- the consideration of the accounts, balance sheets and the consideration of the reports of the directors and auditors;

- the appointment of, and fixing of the remuneration of, the auditors; and

- the election of directors in the place of those retiring.

So if reg 52 of the 1948 Table A (or a like article) does apply to a company, any of these items of 'ordinary' business may be transacted at the annual general meeting, without the need to include them in the notice.

5.14 For completeness, however, even the notices issued by companies to whom reg 52 applies often include an item along the lines of 'To transact any ordinary business of the company'. Even better practice is for items of ordinary business to be included in the notice, irrespective of the distinction in the articles, in the same detail as if they were items of special business. (An alternative, sometimes adopted by such companies, is to convene an annual general meeting to transact the ordinary business, followed immediately by a general meeting, to conduct special business.)

5.15 Whether it is to be considered at an annual or some other general meeting, the purport of the special business must be stated in the notice convening the meeting. The transaction of that special business will otherwise be invalid.[14] (However, the transaction at a meeting of some business outside

---

[11] *Graham v Van Diemen's Land Co* (1856) 26 LJ Ex 73.
[12] The use of the words 'ordinary' and 'special' to classify the business of a general meeting in this way has nothing to do with the classification of members' resolutions as 'ordinary' or 'special' for the purposes of determining appropriate notice periods or majorities required to pass them, discussed in Chapter 3.
[13] However, no corresponding provision appears in the 1985 Table A, which applied (in various versions) to companies incorporated on or after 1 July 1985, or any of the model form articles prescribed under CA 2006, which applied to companies incorporated on or after 1 October 2009.
[14] *Lawes' Case* (1852) 1 De GM & G 421; *Kaye v Croydon Tramways Co* [1898] 1 Ch 358.

the object specified in the notice will not make the whole meeting irregular.[15]) Best practice is probably that, if any special business appears on the notice, it should also be accompanied by a full explanation, setting out the consequences of passing it.

5.16 The distinction between special and ordinary business does not apply to companies whose articles adopt the CA 1985 Table A or the CA 2006 model form articles. Such companies must, therefore, specify all items of business to be considered at the annual general meeting in the notice, or those items may not be transacted at it.[16]

5.17 Whether or not the distinction between special and ordinary business applies, it is clear that company law envisages the items specified as ordinary business in the 1948 Table A as being items that may usually be dealt with at the annual general meeting. The company's officers should therefore consider each in turn, to see if they need to be included in the notice for a particular annual general meeting.

Dividends

5.18 Both the model form articles for private companies and those for public companies (at regs 30 and 70 respectively)[17] say that directors can pay interim dividends; and that the company in general meeting may resolve, by ordinary resolution, to declare dividends, provided that the directors must make a recommendation as to the amount to be paid, and no dividend may exceed that amount. For public companies this means that it is in order to propose an ordinary resolution to declare a dividend, provided it is recommended by the director, at an upcoming annual general meeting.

5.19 However, there is no requirement to do so. The reference to dividends payable by directors as being 'interim' dividends does not imply any requirement for a company to have to pay a 'final' dividend at a general meeting as well in relation to a particular financial year. The directors may quite lawfully pay only one or more interim dividends for a particular year, with none being declared in general meeting.[18]

5.20 The company's officers should therefore consider, at the board meeting at which they resolve to convene an annual general meeting, whether they wish to put a resolution to declare a dividend to the meeting. Since the members may not declare a dividend that exceeds the amount recommended by the directors, the directors should (if they do wish to include such a resolution in the notice of meeting) also decide, at that board meeting, the amount of the dividend that they recommend. Decisions by the board of directors of a listed company on

---

[15] *Re British Sugar Refining Co* (1857) 26 LJ Ch 369.
[16] *R v Hill* (1825) 4 B & C 426.
[17] For companies to which the 1985 Table A applies, regs 102 and 103 say the same.
[18] And vice versa. Or it may have done both. Or neither.

dividends, distribution of profits and other matters requiring announcement must be notified to a Regulatory Information Service as soon as possible.[19]

Accounts, balance sheets and the reports of the directors and auditors

5.21 Section 437 of CA 2006 requires the directors of a public company to lay a copy of the profit and loss accounts and a balance sheet for each financial year before a general meeting. They may also be required to lay a copy of the group accounts (see s 399) before the meeting.

5.22 This must be done within 6 months, for public companies, after the end of the 'relevant accounting reference period' (s 442(2)). The end of the relevant accounting reference period is, effectively, the same as the end of the company's financial year (s 442(7)).[20]

5.23 The directors' report must also be laid before the general meeting, with the accounts (s 437(1)). The requirements for the directors' report are found in s 415ff. These sections require, among other things, that (unless the company is subject to the small business regime) the directors' report should contain a business review – a fair review of the company's business and a description of the principal risk and uncertainties facing the company (s 417). There are detailed requirements about the content of the business review, including special provisions for quoted companies. There are also a number of other requirements for the directors' report contained in these sections and in statutory instruments made pursuant to them. A quoted company must also prepare a directors' remuneration report for the members[21] and, in practice, will also include brief details, including relevant experience, of directors retiring by rotation at the annual general meeting (see **5.41**).

5.24 The auditors' report (and, if the company is quoted, an auditor's report on the auditable parts of the directors' remuneration report[22]) should also be laid with the accounts (unless the company is exempt from the provisions of the Companies Acts relating to the audit of accounts in a particular year under s 477 – ie it is an 'audit exempt' company). The requirements for the auditor's report are laid down in ss 495–497 and 503–505. In particular, it should be noted that under s 496 the auditors are required, if they consider that the information given in the directors' report for the relevant financial year is not consistent with the annual accounts for that year, to state that fact in their report.

---

[19] Listing Rules, para 9.7A.2.
[20] As to the calculation of the company's financial year end and the 'accounting reference period', see ss 390 and 391 of CA 2006.
[21] CA 2006, ss 420–422 and 439. See also the Large and Medium-sized Companies and Groups (Accounts and Reports) Regulations 2008, SI 2008/410.
[22] Ibid.

5.25 CA 2006 does not require that the general meeting at which the accounts and reports are laid should be the annual general meeting. However, if the company is able to plan its annual general meeting, and the preparation of its accounts, so that the annual general meeting is due to take place just when the accounts are ready to be laid, this is very convenient for the company. The alternative is to lay the accounts at a general meeting – often one that has to be convened specifically for this purpose.

5.26 CA 2006 does not require that the accounts and reports be approved by the members in general meeting, simply that they are laid before the members in general meeting. The accounts are the accounts, after all, and cannot be rejected. Companies will, however, invariably hold a vote on the accounts – and, for listed companies, the UK Corporate Governance Code says that companies should propose a resolution at the annual general meeting relating to the report and accounts, if they are considered.[23]

5.27 The notice of a general meeting at which accounts are to be laid should therefore include a resolution relating to the accounts, but this should be along the lines of 'That the report and accounts be received by the meeting' or 'The report and accounts be adopted by the meeting'. The members may vote against the resolution, but this does not stop the accounts being filed at Companies House subsequent to the meeting, as the valid statutory accounts of the company.

5.28 Under ss 423 and 424, copies of the annual accounts together with copies of the directors' report and (unless the company is audit exempt) the auditor's report must be sent to every member of the company, every debenture holder of the company and to all other persons entitled to receive notices of general meetings of the company (for example, the auditors), for whom, in each case, the company has a current address, at least 21 days before the date of the meeting at which the documents are to be laid. (Under s 423(3), a company has a 'current address' if the person has notified an address to the company as an address to which documents may be sent to them, and the company has no reason to believe that documents sent to him at that address will not reach him.) The annual accounts and report must therefore be sent to members or debenture holders, even if they are not entitled to receive notices of meetings, the exception being if the company does not know the address of any such person. If, however, joint holders of shares and debentures are not all entitled to notices of meetings, copies need only be sent to those joint holders who are entitled to notices or, if none is entitled, to one such joint holder (s 238(2)).

5.29 The company may also have to take into account the rights of 'nominated persons' under s 145, and a person's 'information rights' under s 146. See **5.122**.

---

[23] Code Provision E.2.1.

5.30 In the case of listed companies, the UK Corporate Governance Code also requires, in addition to the '21 clear days' rule' (see s 360), that the accounts and reports (and related papers) are sent 20 working days before the meeting at which they will be laid.[24] A listed company, however, may choose to send an annotated version of the accounts, known as a Summary Financial Statement, to members instead of the full accounts (ss 426–429).

5.31 In the case of companies not having a share capital, the accounts and reports need not be sent to anyone who is not entitled to receive notices of meetings of the company (s 423(4)). If in the case of a public company copies are sent out later than is required by s 424, they shall, despite that, be deemed to have been duly sent if it is so agreed by all the members entitled to attend and vote at the meeting (s 424(4)), but in the absence of such agreement the company and every officer in default commits an offence if there is failure to comply with the time-limit (s 425).

AT THE MEETING

5.32 At the meeting, the chairman usually comments on the accounts and then explains the position of the company, giving such further information concerning its affairs as he thinks proper. He concludes by moving that the reports and accounts be adopted. This is usually seconded by another director. The members present at the meeting are then free to comment on or criticise the reports, the accounts and the chairman's speech. As long as it is consistent with their fiduciary duties, the directors should answer all questions about the accounts and the company's affairs. However, they are not bound to answer any questions which they consider undesirable, in the best interests of the company, to answer.

5.33 There is usually very little that the members can do at an annual general meeting if they are dissatisfied with the accounts and the report or the conduct of the directors. They can vote against the resolution for the adoption of the report, but even if the resolution is lost, this has no effect other than to indicate the disapproval of a majority at the meeting.

5.34 Attempts are sometimes made by dissatisfied members to appoint a committee of inspection from among their number to look into the affairs of the company, but this cannot be done without proper notice of a resolution to this effect having been given. This procedure is, in any case, valueless, since the members cannot confer any powers of investigation on their committee. So long as the directors remain as the directors of the company, they retain their powers as such and the company cannot remove the control of its affairs from them.[25] Where a meeting proves hostile, the directors may voluntarily agree to

---

[24] Code Provision E.2.4.
[25] *Automatic Self-Cleansing Filter Co v Cunninghame* [1906] 2 Ch 34.

give certain information to a committee appointed by the dissatisfied members, and will adjourn the meeting until that has been done. They are not, however, bound to do so.

5.35 Dissatisfied members are entitled to make an application to the Secretary of State to investigate a company under s 431 of the Companies Act 1985 (CA 1985) (which remains in force), but only if, together, they number 200 shareholders or 10% of the holders of the issued shares (or, where the company has no share capital, one-fifth of the persons on the register of members) (s 431(2)). The applicants for such an investigation must give supporting evidence showing they have good reason for requiring an investigation (s 431(3)) and they may also be required to give security (s 431(4)).

5.36 Even after all this has been done, there is no guarantee that an investigation will be ordered.

5.37 A final option is for the members to instigate the procedures in CA 2006, s 168, to remove the directors by ordinary resolution and appoint others in their place by like resolutions (see Chapter 3). This, however, can only be done if the requisite notices have been given. If the necessary notices have not been given in time before the annual general meeting, a subsequent meeting will have to be requisitioned for this purpose so that the procedures can be complied with.

Appointing, and fixing the remuneration of, the auditors

5.38 A private company may be exempt from the requirement that its accounts be audited, or a company, whether private or public, may be exempt because it is dormant.[26] In all other cases, the appointment of auditors must be dealt with at each general meeting at which accounts are laid, unless the directors reasonably resolve otherwise on the ground that audited accounts are unlikely to be required.

5.39 In a public company, the auditor (or auditors) so appointed then holds office until the conclusion of the next such meeting.[27] If the accounts are laid at the annual general meeting, it follows that the appointment of auditors must be dealt with too.

5.40 CA 2006 requires that the same general meeting should fix the remuneration of the auditors, or determine how it will be fixed (s 492). Since the remuneration at issue is for the audit for the year in which the general meeting is taking place, which is, at best, incomplete, the usual outcome is that the general meeting authorises the directors to fix the auditor's remuneration.

---

[26] CA 2006, s 477.
[27] CA 2006, s 489(2).

The election of directors in the place of those retiring

5.41 The articles may contain provisions relating to the standing down, and re-election, of directors at the annual general meeting. This process is often called 'retirement by rotation'. If the company is limited by shares and its articles adopt the model form articles for a public company under CA 2006, then reg 21 provides for retirement by rotation. Retirement by rotation also applies to companies with older articles (whether public or private) which pre-date 1 October 2007. If any version of Table A in force before that date applies, and a company's own articles amend Table A in this respect, retirement by rotation provisions will apply. Typically, they will say that, at the first annual general meeting, all the directors shall retire from office; and at subsequent annual general meetings one-third of the directors (being those who have been longest in office) shall retire. And, invariably, where retirement by rotation applies, the directors affected must, if they wish to stay in office, submit themselves to a vote for their re-election as directors at the annual general meeting.

5.42 The articles of private companies, however, will often disapply any requirement that directors retire by rotation, without including any alternative regime.

5.43 However, if the company was incorporated on or after 1 October 2007 (but before 1 October 2009, when the model form articles under CA 2006 came into force), a transitional version of Table set out in the Companies (Tables A to F) (Amendment) Regulations 2007[28] (called in this chapter 'transitional Table A') applied as the default Table A. Transitional Table A made alterations to the 1985 Table A required to make it consistent with the provisions of CA 2006 currently in force, together with some other alterations. Some of the transitional Table A alterations applied to all companies, some to private companies only and some to public companies only. One of the alterations in transitional Table A was that, if the company was a private company limited by shares, the retirement by rotation provisions were no longer applicable. However, if the company was a public company, transitional Table A continued to require directors to retire by rotation.

5.44 If it applies, the intention behind retirement by rotation is that directors who know that they must periodically stand down and submit themselves for re-election will be particularly mindful of their duties and responsibilities as a director and their need to perform to members' satisfaction.

5.45 A listed company (that will disapply Table A in its entirety and adopt a self-contained set of articles tailored to its circumstances), will invariably include its own retirement by rotation regime in its articles. For listed companies, the UK Corporate Governance Code says that all directors of

---

[28] SI 2007/2541, as amended by the Companies (Tables A to F) (Amendment) (No 2) Regulations 2007, SI 2007/2826 and the Companies (Tables A to F) (Amendment) Regulations 2008, SI 2008/739.

FTSE 350 companies should be subject to annual retirement by rotation and, directors of other listed companies should be subject to retirement by rotation at the first annual general meeting and then at regular intervals, and at least every 3 years.[29]

5.46 The UK Corporate Governance Code makes rigorous provision for non-executive directors of listed companies. It provides that they should be appointed for specified terms subject to re-election and to the CA 2006 provisions relating to the removal of a director. The board should set out to shareholders, in the papers accompanying a resolution to elect a non-executive director, why they believe he should be elected. The chairman should confirm to shareholders when proposing re-election that, following formal evaluation, the individual's performance continues to be effective and to demonstrate commitment to the role. Any term beyond 6 years (for example, two 3-year terms) for a non-executive director should be subject to particularly rigorous review and should take into account the need for progressive refreshing of the board. Non-executive directors may serve longer than 9 years (for example, three 3-year terms), subject to annual re-election after those 9 years. Serving more than 9 years could be relevant to the determination of a non-executive director's independence.[30]

5.47 For companies to which the retirement by rotation provisions in Table A apply, or that have their own retirement by rotation provisions, the notice of the annual general meeting must include items relating to the standing down and re-election of the relevant directors. For companies that have no retirement by rotation regime at all, the notice need make no reference to it.

5.48 Best practice is for details of directors being proposed for re-election following retirement by rotation to be included in the notice, and in proxy forms, and that a brief description, including relevant experience, should go out with the notice of the annual general meeting. The UK Corporate Governance Code[31] says that listed companies should provide sufficient biographical details of each director to enable members to make an informed decision on whether to elect directors standing down and seeking election for the first time, or to re-elect directors standing down and seeking re-election on second or subsequent occasions.

5.49 For companies to which the pre 1 October 2007 version of the 1985 Table A applies, and there continue to be many of them, the retirement by rotation rules are that, if the company does not fill the vacated office at the meeting at which a director retires, the retiring director is (if willing to act) deemed reappointed. The exceptions are:

- if it is resolved not to fill the office; or

---

[29] Code Provision B.7.1.
[30] Code Provisions B.7.1 and B.7.2.
[31] Ibid.

- if a resolution for the retiring director's re-election is put to the meeting and lost.[32]

5.50 If a member (being a member entitled to vote at the relevant general meeting) wants to propose a person (other than a retiring director or a person recommended by the directors) for appointment to the board at any general meeting, he must, if reg 76 of the 1985 Table A applies to the company, give notice to the company, executed by him, together with a notice from the proposed director, indicating his willingness to act, not less than 14 or more than 35 clear days before the meeting (reg 76(a)). The member's notice must include the details that will need to be entered in the Register of Directors, if the proposed director is appointed.

5.51 Where the directors propose to recommend someone other than a retiring director for appointment to the position of director, or if a notice has been received from a member proposing a new appointee under reg 76, then the directors must give notice of that fact to the members entitled to attend and vote at the meeting at which the appointment is to be considered, not less than 7 or more than 28 clear days before the meeting (reg 77).

5.52 Subject to all these provisions, appointments under Table A to the office of director may be made by ordinary resolution (reg 78); and, in the period between annual general meetings, the board may (subject to certain provisos) appoint someone to be a director (reg 79).

5.53 In the case of a public company, the appointment of each director must, to be valid, be effected by a separate resolution unless the meeting agrees, without a dissentient, to a motion for the appointment of two or more directors being made by a single resolution (s 160(1)). A resolution moved in contravention of that section is void and the persons thereby intended to be appointed directors will not be so appointed (s 160(2)). The section also provides that if an election is thereby avoided, and the office of a retiring director is in consequence not filled, no provision for the retiring director's automatic reappointment (such as in reg 75 of Table A, discussed in Chapter 2) is to apply (s 160(2)).

5.54 Finally, there have been a number of cases dealing with the consequences of a failure to hold an annual general meeting by companies whose articles require retirement by rotation at each annual general meeting. The outcomes vary according to the specific wording of the articles in each case. Suffice to say that several of the cases decide that, on the construction of the particular articles, the directors of the company due to retire by rotation at the annual general meeting that does not, in fact, take place are deemed to have submitted themselves for re-election on the last day on which that annual general meeting

---

[32] See *Grundt v Great Boulder Proprietary Gold Mines Ltd* [1948] Ch 145.

could have been held. Since the meeting was not in fact held, they could not have been re-elected and therefore cease to be directors from that date.[33]

OTHER BUSINESS AT THE ANNUAL GENERAL MEETING

5.55 An annual general meeting may also consider any ordinary or special resolutions that it is convenient to put before the members at that time which would otherwise be put before a general meeting convened specifically for the purpose.

Directors' authority to allot shares

5.56 Section 549(1) of CA 2006 provides that directors of a company shall not exercise any power of the company to:

- allot its shares;[34] or

- grant rights to subscribe for or to convert any security into shares in the company[35]

unless the company is exempt from that requirement under s 550, or they have a specific authority to do so from the members under s 551 (which we will call 'a s 551 authority' in this chapter). The requirement for a s 551 authority repeats the previous requirement under CA 1985, s 80, now repealed, which required a 's 80 authority' in these circumstances.

5.57 If a s 551 authority is required it can be included in the company's articles, or given by the company in general meeting (s 551(1)). It can be unconditional or subject to conditions, and it may be given for a particular exercise of the power to allot shares, or generally (s 551(2)).

---

[33] *Murray v Newham Citizens Advice Bureau Ltd* [2003] All ER (D) 12; *Consolidated Nickel Mines Ltd* [1914] 1 Ch 883; *In the matter of 25 Chesham Place Ltd* [1999] Ch D, 26 November 1999. For cases which, on the facts, went the other way, see *Villatte v 38 Cleveland Square Management Ltd* [2002] All ER (D) 218; and, in Ireland, *Phoenix Shannon plc v Purkey (No 5)* [1997] IEHC 214.

[34] Section 549(1) does not apply to an allotment of shares under an employees' share scheme, or to the grant of a right to subscribe for, or to convert any security into, shares allotted under such a scheme (s 549(2)).

[35] In relation to the grant of a right to subscribe for, or to convert any security into, shares, s 549 does not apply to a subsequent allotment of shares pursuant to any such grant (ss 549(3)). The drafting of s 549 of CA 2006 did not originally include this exemption. Regulation 2(1) of the Companies Act 2006 (Allotment of Shares and Right of Pre-emption) (Amendment) Regulations 2009, SI 2009/2561 therefore replaced the original s 549(3) in order to reinstate it – so the law is now the same under the 2006 Act as it was under the 1985 Act.

5.58 The exemption in s 550 says that, from 1 October 2009, directors of private companies with only one class of share capital do not require a s 551 authority to allot shares. They may simply go ahead with the allotment.

5.59 However, for companies who already had an existing authority under the old CA 1985, s 80 (and which therefore must have been incorporated before 1 October 2009 when this part of CA 2006 came into force), there are saving provisions which say that any such existing authority will continue to have effect in accordance with the terms on which it is given.

5.60 However, such a company's members can choose to relax this by passing an ordinary resolution to remove the 'carry forward' effect of the old authority, so that s 550 applies immediately.[36]

5.61 Otherwise, the old authority will run its term to expiry but, at the end of that term, the directors will be able to rely on the provisions in s 550. This means that, on a proposed allotment by a private company with only one class of shares, incorporated before 1 October 2009, once the old authority expires (and if, after the proposed allotment the private company would continue to have one class of shares), then no further authority for the directors to allot shares is required. Conversely, once the previous authority expires, if the private company has (or will have after the proposed allotment) more than one class of shares, then the directors must then be authorised under s 551 to allot shares.

5.62 Section 551(2) says a s 551 authority may be given for a particular exercise of the power or for its exercise generally, and may be unconditional or subject to conditions. If the directors are required to have a s 551 authority they will usually want to be sure they have one, and that it be general and unconditional, so they can allot shares for as long as it is current without having to convene a general meeting to get authority from the members each time.

5.63 One circumstance in which a s 551 authority may be sought for a particular exercise of the power to allot shares, rather than generally, is in a takeover, where the directors of an acquiring company need to allot its shares to shareholders of a target company as payment for the transfer by those shareholders to the acquiring company of their shares in the target company.

5.64 If one is required, a company's articles invariably include a s 551 authority on incorporation, or an authority may have been given subsequently.

5.65 One limitation that applies when members give a s 551 authority is that every authority must state the 'maximum amount of shares that may be allotted under it' (s 551(3)(1)).

---

[36] See clause 43 in Sch 2 to the Companies Act 2006 (Commencement No 8, Transitional Provisions and Savings) Order 2008, SI 2008/2860.

5.66 A s 551 authority must also state the date upon which it will expire, and this cannot be more than 5 years from the date of the resolution conferring it (or, in the case of an authority contained in a company's articles at the time it is incorporated, the date of incorporation).

5.67 There is one exception, when an authority may be effective for more than 5 years. Under CA 1985[37] members of a private company were able to pass an 'elective resolution' (see Chapter 3), allowing an authority to be given for a period of more than 5 years, or given indefinitely. In those circumstances, the resolution to give the s 551 authority could include the expiry date, exceeding 5 years, provided for in the elective resolution or, if the elective resolution provided that the authority could continue indefinitely, the authority could also be given indefinitely.

5.68 The power to pass elective resolution was abolished by CA 2006 but there is a saving provision[38] which says that, if a company had taken advantage of the elective regime provisions of CA 1985, s 80A, before 1 October 2009, to extend the period during which shares could be allotted so it either exceeded 5 years or was indefinite, it may continue to rely on that elective resolution.

5.69 If the period specified in a s 551 authority has expired, the directors can still allot shares (or grant rights to subscribe for or to convert any security into shares) provided the shares are allotted (or rights granted) pursuant to an offer or agreement made by the company before the authorisation expired, and provided the relevant s 551 authority allowed the company to make an offer or agreement which would or might require shares to be allotted, or rights to be granted, after the authorisation had expired.

5.70 Otherwise, the members can either be asked to give a fresh authority, or to renew or vary the existing one (s 551(4)). Generally, it is more convenient to give a completely fresh authority.

5.71 Section 551(1) provides that the s 551 authority can be given by 'resolution of the company', which means an ordinary resolution, notwithstanding that a resolution to include the authority in the company's articles amounts to an alteration of the articles, which normally requires a special resolution (s 551(8)). This is, however, one of those unusual circumstances in which a copy of the ordinary resolution has to be filed at Companies House within 15 days after it is passed, as if it were a special resolution.

5.72 A s 551 authority can be revoked by ordinary resolution, which must also be filed at Companies House within 15 days after it is passed (ss 549(4) and (8)).

---

[37] CA 1985, s 80A.
[38] See clause 44 in Sch 2 to the Companies Act 2006 (Commencement No 8, Transitional Provisions and Savings) Order 2008, SI 2008/2860.

Disapplying statutory pre-emption rights

5.73 Section 561(1)(a) of CA 2006 says that a company proposing to make an 'allotment of equity securities' for cash must first offer them to the existing members, on the same or more favourable terms, in proportion (as nearly as practicable) to the proportion in nominal value of the ordinary shares already held by them.[39] For these purposes an 'allotment of equity securities' includes the grant of a right to subscribe for (or to convert any securities into) ordinary shares in the company – but not a subsequent allotment of shares pursuant to such a right.[40] It also includes the sale of ordinary shares in the company that, immediately before the sale, were held by the company as treasury shares.[41]

5.74 An 'equity security' means an ordinary share in the company, or a right to subscribe for, or to convert securities into, an ordinary share in the company, and an 'ordinary share' is a share that does not, as respects dividends and capital, carry a right to participate only up to a specified amount in a distribution (s 560(1)).

5.75 Under s 561(1)(b) shares may only be allotted following an offer under s 561(1)(a) if either the period during which the offer can be accepted has expired or the company has received notice of the acceptance or refusal of every offer so made. Securities that a company has offered to allot to a holder of ordinary shares may be allotted to him, or anyone in whose favour he has renounced his right to their allotment, without contravening s 561(1)(b).

5.76 However, there are exceptions to the requirement to offer equity securities to existing members. An important one is that the statutory pre-emption rights do not apply if the allotment is for a non-cash consideration, whether in whole or in part (s 565).

5.77 Another is that the statutory pre-emption rights do not apply to an allotment by way of a bonus issue (s 564).

5.78 Nor does s 561 apply to an allotment of equity securities that would (apart from any renunciation or assignment of the right to their allotment), be held under, allotted or transferred pursuant to an employees' share scheme.[42]

5.79 The requirement can also be excluded or disapplied, and often is, both in private and public companies. It is either excluded or disapplied because the

---

[39] When making the offer, ordinary shares held by the company itself as treasury shares at the date of the offer are disregarded (s 561(4)). This means that the company is not treated as a holder of ordinary shares to whom a proportion of the proposed new shares must be offered, and nor are the treasury shares treated as part of the company's ordinary share capital.

[40] Section 560(2), as amended by reg 2 of the Companies Act 2006 (Allotment of Shares and Right of Pre-emption) (Amendment) Regulations 2009, SI 2009/2561.

[41] Section 560(3), as amended by reg 2 of the Companies Act 2006 (Allotment of Shares and Right of Pre-emption) (Amendment) Regulations 2009, SI 2009/2561.

[42] Section 566, as amended by reg 2(4) in the Companies Act 2006 (Allotment of Shares and Right of Pre-emption) (Amendment) Regulations 2009, SI 2009/2561.

directors wish to have a complete discretion to allot equity securities to whoever they want (subject always to their fiduciary duties) or because the company wants to substitute its own, specially drafted pre-emption rights for the statutory pre-emption rights, because of perceived deficiencies in the statutory pre-emptive regime. For example, the statutory pre-emption rights make no provision for the procedure if an offer of shares to members in proportion to their shareholdings will result in an offer of fractions of shares (for example, if 11 shares are being offered to ten members). A company that substitutes its own pre-emption regime for the statutory regime can correct this deficiency.

5.80 If the company is private, s 567 allows the members to exclude all or any of the requirements of s 561 generally, or its application to a particular allotment, by provision in the company's articles of association. The provision can specifically exclude all or any such requirement in general or in relation to a particular allotment (s 567(2)). However, a provision is also effective to exclude s 561 if it is merely inconsistent with it (s 567(3)).

5.81 Any company, private or public, can also exclude s 561 by conferring corresponding rights in the articles (s 568).

5.82 Sections 569, 570 and 571 provide alternative ways of disapplying s 561. Section 569 can only be used by private companies with only one class of share. Sections 570 and 571 can be used by both private and public companies, but are more complicated than using s 569, so private companies with only one class of share rarely rely on them.

5.83 Under s 569, members of a private company with only one class of shares can give the directors power by the articles, or by a special resolution, to allot equity securities of that class as if s 561 did not apply to the allotment, or applied to it, but with such modifications as the directors decide.

5.84 Sections 570 and 571 apply to both public and private companies, provided the members of a particular company have authorised the directors to allot shares pursuant to s 551. They differ in that the method of disapplying the statutory pre-emption rights in s 561 in each depends upon the type of s 551 authority to allot shares that has been given to the directors.

5.85 Section 570(1) says that, where the directors of the company are generally authorised to make allotments for the purposes of s 551, the members may give them power, by the articles or by a special resolution, to allot equity securities pursuant to that authority as if the pre-emption rights in s 51 did not apply to the allotment, or as if the pre-emption rights did apply, but with such modifications as the directors may determine.

5.86 Section 571(2) says that, where the directors of the company are authorised, *whether generally or otherwise* (emphasis added) to make allotments for the purposes of s 551, the members of the company may, by special resolution, resolve either that s 561(1) shall not apply to a *specified* (emphasis added) allotment of equity securities to be made pursuant to that authority, or that s 561 shall apply, but with such modifications as may be specified in the resolution.

5.87 However, if a company relies on s 571, the special resolution (and any special resolution to renew such a resolution) must be recommended by the directors, and the directors must have made a written statement setting out their reasons for making the recommendation, the amount to be paid to the company in respect of the equity securities to be allotted, and the directors' justification of that amount.

5.88 If the special resolution is put as a written resolution, the statement must be sent or submitted to every eligible member at the same time as (or before) the time the written resolution is sent or submitted to him. If the special resolution is put to a general meeting, it must be circulated with the notice of the meeting.

5.89 As both ss 570 and 571 resolutions to disapply the statutory pre-emption rights are dependent upon the existence of a s 551 authority for their validity, it stands to reason that when the s 551 authority to which they relate is revoked or expires, so does the disapplication of the pre-emption rights. The company must consider their disapplication of s 561 anew, in the light of any new s 551 authority that is being proposed.

5.90 The main differences between s 569, 570 and 571 are therefore that:

- under ss 569 and 570 the statutory pre-emption rights in s 561 may be disapplied by the articles or by special resolution, whereas under s 571 the disapplication must be by special resolution;

- s 571 permits disapplication in relation to a specified allotment only, whereas a disapplication under s 570 may be in relation to allotments in general, particular types of allotment (such as a rights issue) or one specified allotment only;

- the modifications to s 561 permitted under s 570 are such as 'the directors may determine' whereas those permitted under s 571 are such as 'may be specified in the resolution', ie are determined by the members; and

- a special resolution under s 571 may not be proposed unless it is recommended by the directors, and a written statement from the directors has been circulated, with the notice of meeting at which the special resolution is to be proposed, setting out:

    – their reasons for making the recommendation;
    – the amount to be paid to the company in respect of the equity securities to be allotted; and

– the directors' justification of that amount.

5.91 If a listed company wants to disapply the pre-emption rights completely in relation to any allotment of equity securities for cash, ie they want the directors to be able to offer equity securities other than to holders of shares on a pro-rata basis, then it must comply with the Pre-Emption Group Statement of Principles. These are designed to prevent wholesale changes arising in the composition of the membership, or even control, of a company arising from exercise of discretion by the directors. The Principles say a company can disapply the pre-emption rights in respect of not more than 5% of the company's issued ordinary share capital, as shown in the latest published annual accounts, provided that, in any 'rolling' 3-year period prior to that allotment, not more than 7.5% of the company's issued ordinary share capital has been issued for cash on a non-pre-emptive basis.

Authority to make a market purchase of own shares

5.92 A company may buy its own issued shares back from a member or members pursuant to CA 2006. The procedure varies according to the type of purchase. (It also varies according to the source of funds from which the purchase is made, but this aspect does not affect proceedings at the annual general meeting.)

5.93 The two type of purchase are a 'market' purchase and an 'off-market' purchase. A purchase is a market purchase if it is of shares purchased on a 'recognised investment exchange', such as the London Stock Market, that are subject to a marketing arrangement on that exchange. A purchase of shares otherwise than on a recognised investment exchange (or shares purchased on a recognised investment exchange but not subject to a marketing arrangement) is an off-market purchase.

5.94 A company cannot make a market purchase of its own shares unless the purchase has first been authorised by a resolution of the members of the company (s 701). This authority can either be general or can be limited to the purchase of shares of a particular class or description; and may be unconditional or subject to conditions (s 701(2)). It must state the maximum number of shares it authorises the company to acquire; must determine both the maximum and minimum prices which may be paid for the shares; and must specify a date upon which it will expire, which may not be more than 5 years from the date the authority is given (s 701(3) and (5)).[43]

5.95 For listed companies with a Premium listing, there are Listing Rules[44] restricting the manner, timing and pricing of any purchase. Notwithstanding

---

[43] The period in s 701(5) was extended from 18 months to 5 years by clause 4 in the Companies (Share Capital and Acquisition by Company of its Own Shares) Regulations 2009, SI 2009/2022.
[44] Paragraph 12.

s 166(4), companies with institutional shareholders should be aware that the Association of British Insurers requires that the authority be renewed annually.

5.96 Such companies also need to take into account the Association of British Insurers' recommendation that, where authority is given to purchase more than 5% of a company's ordinary share capital, the directors should consider the effect on the ratio of the company's share capital to borrowing (the 'gearing'). Above 5%, it considers that its members are unlikely to object to authority being given for a purchase of between 5 and 10% of the company's issued ordinary capital, provided all other requirements are complied with. Anything over 10% will be treated by institutions on a case-by-case basis.

5.97 The maximum and minimum price, or either of them, may be determined either by specifying a particular sum or by providing a basis, or formula, for calculating the price (provided that this is not by reference to any person's discretion or opinion).

5.98 The annual general meeting of a public company whose shares are on a recognised investment exchange will therefore usually include a general and unconditional authority to the directors authorising the company to buy its own shares back from members by way of a market purchase that complies with s 702(2) and (3).

5.99 For listed companies, the Listing Rules[45] require that details of a proposed resolution to authorise a market purchase of own shares should notify a Regulatory Information Service (unless a renewal of an existing authority), stating whether the authority is general or relates to proposed purchases from specific members. If the latter, it should give the names of the sellers.

5.100 Under CA 2006, the authority is to be given by ordinary resolution, which does not have to be filed at Companies House. For listed companies with institutional shareholders, the Association of British Insurers' recommendation is that it be proposed as a special resolution. A special resolution must be filed at Companies House within 15 days of being passed. The Listing Rules[46] also require that the giving of the authority be notified to the Stock Exchange.

5.101 A company does not need approval of a general meeting to make off-market purchases – although the draft contract for each particular off-market purchase has to be approved by special resolution in advance of the purchase.

---

[45] Paragraph 12.4.5.
[46] Paragraph 12.4.5.

Political contributions

5.102 A resolution of the members is required before a company may make a contribution to a political party of more than £5,000[47] or incur any EU political expenditure.[48] A political party means any registered political party or any other EU political organisation, and a donation or expenditure includes gifts, sponsorship, subscriptions, membership fees, payment of party expenses, loans on other than commercial terms and providing property, services or facilities other than on commercial terms.

5.103 The form of such a resolution is regulated by the Act.[49]

5.104 The resolution can give authority for up to 4 years (s 368), after which it must be renewed, so that it is likely to become a regular, although perhaps not annual, item at the annual general meeting. Companies wishing to make political donations regularly may wish to update the resolution annually, so it becomes a regular item at every annual general meeting.

5.105 The resolution is ordinary unless the articles, or the directors, specify otherwise and therefore does not need to be filed at Companies House.

CIRCULATION OF MEMBERS' RESOLUTIONS

5.106 In addition to those matters required by the articles of association and CA 2006 to be dealt with at annual general meetings, s 339(3) provides that the business of an annual general meeting of a public company must also include any resolutions validly proposed by members (or nominated persons – see **5.122ff**) under s 338. This section permits members holding 5% or more of the total voting rights, or at least 100 members of the company holding shares paid up to an average sum of at least £100 (s 338(3)), to require the company to give all members notice of any resolution which may properly be moved and which it is intended to be moved at the meeting. In each case, the shares must carry the right to vote on the relevant resolution – a new requirement under CA 2006 that did not appear in the previous CA 1985 provisions. The request can be given in hard copy or in electronic form. It must be received by the company not later than 6 weeks before the annual general meeting to which it relates or, if later, the time at which notice of the meeting is given (s 338(4)).

5.107 Section 338(2) clarifies when a resolution is 'properly moved'. It says that a resolution may properly be moved unless (1) it would be ineffective if passed (for example, because it is inconsistent with any enactment or with the company's constitution), (2) it is defamatory or (3) it is frivolous or vexatious.

---

[47] CA 2006, s 378.
[48] Political Parties, Elections and Referendums Act 2000.
[49] CA 2006, ss 367.

5.108 Section 339 provides for the method of serving the resolution. Section 339(1) provides that a copy of the resolution should be sent to all members of the company entitled to notice of the annual general meeting, in the same manner as the notice of the meeting itself and either at the same time or as soon as reasonably practicable after it gives notice of the meeting.

5.109 Under s 340 of CA 2006, the expenses of complying with s 339 need not be paid by the members who request the circulation of the resolution, provided that sufficient requests under s 338 to trigger the requirement to circulate details of the resolution are received before the end of the company's financial year preceding the meeting. If they are not, the members making the request must deposit with, or tender to, the company a sum reasonably sufficient to meet its expenses. They must do this either not later than 6 weeks before the annual general meeting or, if later, when the notice of it is given. However, the company can resolve that any such notice should not be at the expense of the requisitionists, so requisitionists are likely to continue to include in their resolutions one which provides that the expenses of the requisition shall not be paid by them, but with the new proviso that such resolution is only put to the vote of the meeting if the members fail to satisfy s 340.

5.110 Under s 153 a company is required to act on a request received under s 338, if the following conditions are met:

(a) it is made by at least 100 persons;

(b) it is authenticated by all the persons making it;

(c) in the case of any person who is not a member of the company, it is accompanied by a statement:

> (i) of the full name and address of a person ('the member') who is a member of the company and holds shares on behalf of that person;
> (ii) that the member is holding those shares on behalf of that person in the course of a business;
> (iii) of the number of shares in the company that the member holds on behalf of that person;
> (iv) of the total amount paid up on those shares;
> (v) that those shares are not held on behalf of anyone else or, if they are, that the other person or persons are not among the other persons making the request;
> (vi) that some or all of those shares confer voting rights that are relevant for the purposes of making a request under the section in question; and
> (vii) that the person has the right to instruct the member how to exercise those rights;

(d) in the case of any of those persons who is a member of the company, it is accompanied by a statement:

(i) that he holds shares otherwise than on behalf of another person; or
(ii) that he holds shares on behalf of one or more other persons but those persons are not among the other persons making the request;

(e) it is accompanied by such evidence as the company may reasonably require of the matters mentioned in paragraphs (c) and (d);

(f) the total amount of the sums paid up on:

(i) shares held as mentioned in paragraph (c); and
(ii) shares held as mentioned in paragraph (d),
divided by the number of persons making the request, is not less than £100; and

(g) the request complies with any other requirements of the section in question as to contents, timing and otherwise.

5.111 This is to ensure that, where indirect investors have been nominated to enjoy certain rights of membership by members pursuant to s 146, they are able to count towards the total required under s 338, subject to certain conditions. The conditions are intended to ensure that only genuine indirect investors are allowed to count towards the total, that the same shares cannot be used twice and that the indirect investor's contractual arrangements with the member allow the former to give voting instructions.

CIRCULATION OF MEMBERS' STATEMENTS

5.112 Section 314 also provides that members holding 5% or more of the total voting rights, or at least 100 members of the company holding shares paid up to an average sum of at least £100 (s 314(2)), may require the company to circulate a statement of not more than 1,000 words to all members of the company entitled to receive notice of a general meeting. The meeting can be an annual general meeting, but may also be any other general meeting.

5.113 The statement must relate to (1) a matter referred to in a proposed resolution that is to be put to the meeting or (2) any other business to be dealt with at the meeting. In the case of (1), the shares must carry the right to vote on the relevant resolution. In the case of (2), they must carry the right to vote at the meeting. The request can be given in hard copy or in electronic form, must identify the statement to be circulated and must be received by the company at least one week before the meeting (s 314(4)(d)).

5.114 Section 315 provides for the method of serving the statement. Section 315(1) provides that a copy of the statement should be sent to all members of the company entitled to notice of the general meeting, in the same manner as the notice of the meeting itself, and either at the same time or as soon as reasonably practicable after it gives notice of the meeting.

5.115 Under s 316 of CA 2006, the expenses of complying with s 315 need not be paid by the members who request the circulation of the statement, provided that the meeting to which the request relates is an annual general meeting of a public company, and requests sufficient to trigger the requirement to circulate it are received before the end of the company's financial year preceding the meeting. If these conditions are not met, the expenses must be paid by the members making the request, who must deposit or tender to the company a sum reasonably sufficient to meet those expenses. However, even then, the company can resolve that the expenses be paid by the company (s 316(1)(b)).

5.116 Section 317 sets out the circumstances in which the company will not be obliged to circulate a copy of the statement received under s 314. These are where the company or any other person who claims to be aggrieved by the terms of any such statement applies to the court and the court is satisfied that the rights conferred by the section are being abused (s 317(1)). Section 317(2) provides that the court can order the members who requested circulation of the statement to pay the costs of the application, even if they are not parties to it.

5.117 Under s 153 a company is required to act on a request received under s 314, if the same conditions are met as those which apply in relation to s 338 – see **5.109ff**.

5.118 As in relation to s 338, this is to ensure that, where indirect investors have been nominated to enjoy certain rights of membership by members pursuant to s 146, they are able to count towards the total required under s 314, subject to certain conditions. The conditions are intended to ensure that only genuine indirect investors are allowed to count towards the total, that the same shares cannot be used twice and that the indirect investor's contractual arrangements with the member allow the former to give voting instructions.

Nominated persons and information rights – ss 145 and 146

5.119 Section 145, which applies to all companies, whether public or private, provides that a company's articles may enable a member to nominate another person or persons as being entitled to enjoy or exercise all or any specified rights of the member in relation to the company. The aim is to allow company articles to enfranchise indirect investors (that is, those holding an interest in shares registered in the name of another person).

5.120 Section 145 provides that, to the extent necessary to give effect to the provision in a company's articles, anything to be done by or in relation to the member shall or may instead be done by, or in relation to, the nominated person (or each of them) as if he were a member of the company. Therefore, where a company makes relevant provision in its articles, all the relevant references in the Companies Acts to 'member' should be read as if the reference to member was a reference to the nominated person or persons, and not to the actual member – the nominated person enjoys rights to the exclusion of the member.

5.121 The particular rights specified in s 145 are the rights conferred by:

- ss 291 and 293 (right to be sent proposed written resolution);

- s 292 (right to require circulation of written resolution);

- s 303 (right to require directors to call general meeting);

- s 310 (right to notice of general meetings);

- s 314 (right to require circulation of a statement);

- s 319A (right to ask question at meeting of traded company);

- s 324 (right to appoint proxy to act at meeting);

- s 338 (right to require circulation of resolution for the annual general meeting of a public company); and

- s 338A (traded companies: members' power to include matters in business dealt with at AGM);

- s 423 (right to be sent a copy of annual accounts and reports).

5.122 However, the list is non-exhaustive, so nominated persons could, it seems, enjoy rights in addition to those specified – for example, to attend and vote at general meetings or to receive dividends directly, provided the articles were correctly drafted. The only rights that cannot be given to a nominated person are rights to transfer or otherwise dispose of the whole or any part of the member's interest in the company. The articles may specify that the entitlement is only to certain rights, or to all rights.

5.123 The rights remain enforceable by the member whose name is in the register, and not the nominated person so that, if the company refuses to observe them, it is the member who must take action. So it may be that the company must also send a copy of the accounts and reports to the nominated person instead of the member who appointed him.

5.124 There are quite separate rights under s 146 for members of 'traded companies', that is, companies whose shares are admitted to trading on a regulated market (although s 151 does give the Secretary of State power to extend or limit the classes of companies to which these provisions apply). The aim is to enable registered members to nominate indirect investors as entitled to receive information that is sent to members by the company.

5.125 Section 146ff provides that a member of such a company who holds shares on behalf of another person may nominate that person to enjoy information rights. There is no need to alter the company's articles to authorise such a nomination. 'Information rights' means:

- the right to receive a copy of all communications (including the company's annual report and accounts) that the company sends to its members generally or to any class of its members that includes the person making the nomination; and

- the rights conferred by s 431 or 432 (right to require copies of accounts and reports) and s 1145 (right to require hard copy version of document or information provided in another form).

For the application of s 426 (option to provide summary financial statement) in relation to a person nominated to enjoy information rights, see s 426(5).

5.126 If the person to be nominated wishes to receive hard copy communications, he must, before the nomination is made, request the person making the nomination to notify the company of that fact, and provide an address to which such copies may be sent. Once the member making the nomination has notified the company, and provided the address given, the right of the nominated person to receive hard copy communications takes effect.

5.127 If he does nothing, s 147 provides that, where a company must provide copies to a person nominated under s 146, the nominated person is taken to have agreed that documents or information may be sent or supplied to him by the company by means of a website (see Chapter 11) unless he revokes his deemed agreement. If he is taken to have agreed to this, it does not affect his right under s 1145 to require a hard copy version of a document or information provided in any other form.

5.128 Unlike rights conferred on a nominated person pursuant to s 145, the rights conferred by a nomination pursuant to s 146 are in addition to the rights of the member himself. They do not affect any rights exercisable by virtue of any such provision included in a company's articles by virtue of s 145. The two regimes – under each of s 145 and s 146ff – operate independently of each other.

5.129 However, like rights conferred under s 145, rights under s 146 must be enforced by the member. They cannot be enforced directly by the nominated person. If the member does need to enforce them, CA 2006 provides that they are enforceable against the company by the member as if they were rights conferred by the company's articles.

5.130 A member who exercises rights under s 146 but does not exercise *all* his rights, must inform the company to what extent he is exercising the rights. A member who exercises such rights in different ways must inform the company of the ways in which he is exercising them and to what extent they are exercised in each way. If a member exercises such rights without informing the company of these, then the company is entitled to assume that he is exercising all his rights and is exercising them in the same way (s 152).

5.131 Under s 150(3), any enactment, and any provision of the company's articles, which has effect in relation to communications with members has a corresponding effect (subject to any necessary adaptations) in relation to communications with the nominated person. In particular:

- where under any enactment, or any provision of the company's articles, the members of a company entitled to receive a document or information are determined as at a date or time before it is sent or supplied, the company need not send or supply it to a nominated person:

    - whose nomination was received by the company after that date or time; or
    - if that date or time falls in a period of suspension of his nomination; and

- where under any enactment, or any provision of the company's articles, the right of a member to receive a document or information depends on the company having a current address for him, the same applies to any person nominated by him.

5.132 CA 2006 specifically provides that, where a member holds shares in a company on behalf of more than one person, the rights attached to the shares, and rights under any enactment exercisable by virtue of holding the shares, need not all be exercised and, if they are all exercised, need not all be exercised in the same way (s 152).

5.133 Under s 148, a nomination may be terminated at the request of the member or of the nominated person, and also ceases to have effect if either the member or the nominated person:

- in the case of an individual, dies or is made bankrupt; and

- in the case of a body corporate, is dissolved or an order is made for the winding up of the body otherwise than for the purposes of reconstruction.

For these purposes, 'bankruptcy' includes (1) the sequestration of a person's estate and (2) a person's estate being the subject of a protected trust deed (within the meaning of the Bankruptcy (Scotland) Act 1985).

5.134 The effect of any nominations made by a member is suspended at any time when there are more nominated persons than the member has shares in the company. Where the member holds different classes of shares with different information rights and there are more nominated persons than he has shares conferring a particular right, the effect of any nominations made by him is suspended to the extent that they confer that right.

5.135 A company can inquire of a nominated person whether he wishes to retain information rights. If the company does not receive a response within the period of 28 days beginning with the date on which its inquiry was sent, the nomination ceases to have effect at the end of that period. However, the company cannot make such an inquiry more than once in any 12-month period.

CREST

5.136 If a company holds shares through CREST, the notice of the annual general meeting can include a note stating the time (which must not be more than 48 hours for the time fixed for the meeting) by which a person must be entered into the register of members if he is to be entitled to attend and vote at the meeting.[50]

EXPLANATORY CIRCULARS

5.137 A listed company must, if the meeting is to consider anything other than routine business, prepare an explanatory circular[51] to go out with the notice of the annual general meeting that explains the background to the non-routine items. This can be included in the directors' report or can be a separate document. Including the circular, notice, reports and accounts in the same document, as often happens, can save costs.

5.138 If the annual general meeting is to consider only ordinary business, and the circular and other documents convening the annual general meeting comply with Chapter 13 of the Listing Rules, they do not need to be submitted to the UK Listing Authority for prior approval. Otherwise they do. If they do have to be submitted, they must, together, provide sufficient information to allow a shareholder to decide whether or not to attend the annual general meeting.[52]

---

[50] Uncertificated Securities Regulations 2001, SI 2001/3755, as amended by the Uncertificated Securities (Amendment) Regulations 2007, SI 2007/124.
[51] See LR 13.
[52] *Tiessen v Henderson* [1899] 1 Ch 861.

Chapter 6

NOTICE OF GENERAL (MEMBERS') MEETINGS

INTRODUCTION

6.1 Members are only able to make decisions at a general meeting if proper notice has been given of the meeting, in accordance with the Companies Act 2006 (CA 2006), the company's articles and, if applicable in the circumstances, the common law. Failure to give proper notice will invalidate the meeting.[1] This chapter deals with the rules relating to notices of general meetings other than annual general meetings, unless specifically stated otherwise. Such meetings used to be called 'extraordinary' general meetings, but the word 'extraordinary' has been dropped in CA 2006, so that they are now referred to simply as general meetings.

6.2 Additional rules governing the notice for annual general meetings for public companies are dealt with in Chapter 5. The rules that apply when notices of general meetings are given electronically are dealt with in Chapter 11.

6.3 The doctrine of informal corporate acts, which cures any defect in the giving of notice if all the members entitled to be present at the meeting attend and agree on the course proposed,[2] is discussed in Chapter 3.

PERIOD OF NOTICE

6.4 Section 307(A1) of CA 2006[3] says that the rules in s 307 governing notice periods apply to:

- General meetings of companies that are not traded companies.

- General meetings of traded companies if they are opted-in companies (as defined by s 971(1)) and the meeting is held to decide whether to take any action that might result in the frustration of a takeover bid for the company; or the meeting is held by virtue of s 969 (power of offeror to require a general meeting to be held).

---

[1] *Smyth v Darley* (1849) 2 HLC 789.
[2] *Baroness Wenlock v River Dee Co* (1883) 36 ChD 675n.
[3] As inserted by the Companies (Shareholders' Rights) Regulations 2009, SI 2009/1632, reg 9.

For these purposes a traded company is a company which has voting shares that are admitted to trading on a regulated market in an EEA State (s 360C). Regulated markets in the UK include the London Stock Exchange main market and the listed elements of PLUS, but not AIM.

6.5 For companies within the definition in s 307(A1), s 307 provides that a general meeting (except an adjourned meeting) must be called on a minimum of at least 14 days' notice. Section 307(2) provides that a general meeting of a public company (other than an adjourned meeting) must be called on at least 21 days' notice if the meeting is an annual general meeting, and 14 days' notice in any other case. This represents a change from the Companies Act 1985 (CA 1985) rules, which required 21 days' notice for a meeting to consider a special resolution.

6.6 Section 307(3) makes it clear that a company which is subject to s 307 can specify a longer notice period in its articles in each case but, where its articles are silent as to the period of notice (or void because they contravene s 307), then s 307 applies.

6.7 However, most companies in existence prior to 1 October 2007 (when s 307 came into force) *are* likely to have provisions in their articles that require 21 days' notice for annual general meetings *and* for meetings called to pass a special resolution. This is because reg 38 in the 1985 Table A as prescribed prior to 1 October 2007 did require 21 days' notice of a meeting called to consider a special resolution. If this provision applies it will override s 307 and so, for such companies, the longer period of notice specified in the articles will still be required. It is also appropriate to check shareholder agreements.

6.8 Companies incorporated between 1 October 2007 and 30 September 2009 which adopted Table A will not have this issue, as the Companies (Tables A to F) (Amendment) Regulations 2007[4] amended Table A from 1 October 2007 to remove the provision for 21 days' notice.

6.9 Companies incorporated on or after 1 October 2009 which have adopted the relevant set of model form articles will not have this issue either. None of the three model form articles prescribed under CA 2006 require more than 14 days' notice of general meetings, whether to consider ordinary and/or special resolutions.

6.10 The rules are different for companies that are not within the definition in s 307(A1). For these companies s 307A says that the notice required for a general meeting is (subject to any contrary provision in the company's articles) 21 days or, if all of the following three conditions are satisfied, 14 days:

- The general meeting is not an annual general meeting.

---

[4] SI 2007/2541.

- The company offers electronic voting, accessible to all members holding shares that carry rights to vote at general meetings. (This is met if there is a facility to appoint a proxy by means of a website that meets these criteria.)

- A special resolution has been passed reducing the period of notice to not less than 14 days – either at the immediately preceding annual general meeting, or at a general meeting held since that annual general meeting. If the company has not yet held an annual general meeting, the condition is that a special resolution reducing the period of notice to not less than 14 days has been passed at a general meeting. If it has held one, the special resolution must have been passed either at the immediately preceding annual general meeting, or at a general meeting held since that annual general meeting.

A company to which s 307A applies can require longer periods of notice in its articles, so provisions in the articles governing notice periods should be carefully checked.

6.11 Periods of notice shorter than those stipulated in CA 2006 or in the articles may be given, provided that the 'requisite percentage' of members agree:

- For a private company limited by shares, this means a majority in number of the members having a right to attend and vote at the meeting, being a majority who together hold not less than 90% (or such higher percentage, not exceeding 95%, as may be specified in the company's articles) in nominal value of the shares giving a right to attend and vote at the meeting (excluding any shares in the company held as treasury shares).

- For a company limited by guarantee, this means a majority in number of the members who together represent not less than 90% (or such higher percentage, not exceeding 95%, as may be specified in the company's articles) of the total voting rights at that meeting of all the members.

- For a general meeting of a public company, this means a majority in number of the members having a right to attend and vote at a general meeting, being a majority who together hold not less than 95% in nominal value of the shares giving a right to attend and vote at the meeting (excluding any shares in the company held as treasury shares).

- Under CA 1985, the requisite percentage was 95% unless a company, being a private company, had passed an elective resolution (see Chapter 3) that enabled meetings to be convened on short notice with the consent of at least 90% in nominal value of the total voting rights at the meeting. As CA 2006 makes no provision for elective resolutions, and the ability to pass elective resolutions relating to short notice ceased to exist from 1 October 2007, a doubt therefore arose as to the effect of existing elective resolutions that varied the 95% requirement. The sixth commencement order[5] provides that such elective resolutions in force immediately before 1 October 2007 which resulted in a reduction of the percentage required from 95% to some other percentage (of 90% or more) continue to have effect, so that any provision that was in a company's articles before 1 October 2007 specifying a different percentage shall be disregarded if the company has passed such an elective resolution.

6.12 For public companies that are not traded companies (see s 360C and **6.4**), s 337(2) provides that an annual general meeting may be called by shorter notice than that required by s 307(2) or by the company's articles, provided that all the members entitled to attend and vote at the meeting agree to the shorter notice.

6.13 It has been held that if a meeting is convened on short notice, the members present must be aware of this to comply with CA 2006.[6] If they are not, they cannot have consented to its being held on short notice. It seems that attendance at the meeting does not imply consent to short notice if consent was not in fact given.

6.14 The number of days' notice must be clear.[7] This means that in calculating whether the period of notice has been given, the day upon which the notice is given (or deemed to be given) and the day upon which the meeting is to be held must be excluded. Saturdays, Sundays and bank and other holidays are counted when calculating these notice periods unless the company's articles say otherwise. Under s 1147, which applies to documents and information sent or supplied by a company by post (whether in hard copy or electronic form) to an address in the United Kingdom, provided the company can show its post was properly addressed, prepaid and posted, it is deemed to have been received by the intended recipient 48 hours after it was posted.

6.15 In some circumstances (see Chapter 11) documents or information can be sent or supplied 'by means of a website'. If so, they are deemed to have been received by the intended recipient either when the material was first made available on the website, or when the recipient received (or is deemed to have received) notice of the fact that it was available, whichever is later.

6.16 Any hours falling on a non-working day are ignored for these purposes.

---

[5] Companies Act 2006 (Commencement No 6, Saving and Commencement Nos 3 and 5 (Amendment)) Order 2008, SI 2008/674.
[6] *Re Pearce Duff & Co Ltd* [1960] 3 All ER 222.
[7] See CA 2006, s 360. Section 360 provides that the 'clear days' rule' applies to s 307(1) and (2) (notice required of general meeting), s 312(1) and (3) (resolution requiring special notice), s 314(4)(d) (request to circulate members' statement), s 316(2)(b) (expenses of circulating statement to be deposited or tendered before meeting), s 337(3) (contents of notice of AGM of traded company), s 338(4)(d)(i) (request to circulate member's resolution at AGM of public company) and s 340(2)(b)(i) (expenses of circulating statement to be deposited or tendered before meeting).

6.17 These provisions of s 1147 are subject to the company's articles, so these should be checked carefully.[8]

6.18 There are no provisions varying s 360 in any of the model form articles, and Table A, reg 115 provides that notices are deemed to have been given 48 hours after they have been posted anyway. Reliance on this provision by a company during a postal strike may, however, be a ground for the grant of an injunction to a member who did not receive the notice in good time to restrain the holding of the meeting.[9]

6.19 The Institute of Chartered Secretaries and Administrators recommends that larger, non-listed companies consider giving longer notice than required under CA 2006, and suggests 20 working days as a useful starting point.

THE FORM OF THE NOTICE

Date, time and place of meeting

6.20 Notice of a general meeting must be written. It must state the time, date and place of the meeting (s 311).

6.21 The fixing of these is at the discretion of the directors[10] (taking into account their general duties, including the duty to treat members fairly), and older articles may specifically say this (see, for example, reg 38 of Table A).

6.22 Although the court will not usually interfere with the powers and duties of directors in their management of the internal affairs of a company, directors will be restrained from fixing a particular date for holding the annual general meeting of the company for the purpose of preventing members from exercising their voting powers.[11]

Framing resolutions

6.23 The vote of the majority at a general meeting must be a vote given on proper information, as it binds both dissentient and absent members. This rule is consistent with the general principle that matters must be fairly put before the meeting and the meeting itself must be conducted in the fairest possible manner.[12]

---

[8] And, where the recipients are debenture holders, they are subject to the provisions of the debenture. Where the recipients are receiving documents or information in a capacity other than member or debenture-holder, they are subject to the provisions of any agreement between the company and that person. See s 1147(6).
[9] *Bradman v Trinity Estates plc* [1989] BCLC 757.
[10] *Martin v Walker* (1918) 145 LT Jo 377.
[11] *Cannon v Trask* (1875) LR 20 Eq 669.
[12] *Tiessen v Henderson* [1899] 1 Ch 861.

6.24 Subject to the rules governing 'ordinary' business at the annual general meeting, discussed in Chapter 5, the common law rule is therefore that a notice of any company meeting must give a sufficient, fair, candid and reasonable explanation of the business intended to be transacted.[13]

Ordinary resolutions

6.25 The common law applies to ordinary resolutions save where overridden by the Act or the articles[14] (but see **6.36ff** for special resolutions). Section 311(2) provides that notice of a general meeting must state the general nature of the business to be dealt with at the meeting, although this can, for companies that are not traded companies (see s 360C and **6.4**), be varied by the company's articles.[15] If the general nature of business to be dealt with does have to be stated, a notice of ordinary resolutions should therefore contain sufficient detail, and be sufficiently clear, for a member to be able to decide whether he should attend the meeting, and, if necessary, ask questions; or whether he may, without concern, allow the meeting to pass the resolution without his attendance or inquiry. In *MacConnell v E Prill & Co Ltd*,[16] however, notice of a resolution to increase a company's authorised share capital (under the 1985 Act – CA 2006 has abolished the concept of an authorised share capital, subject to transitional and saving provisions preserving it in certain circumstances),[17] without specifying the amount of the increase, was held invalid, and an individual member could apply for an injunction to restrain the company from acting on it. The company should therefore err on the side of caution when drafting notice of ordinary resolutions.

6.26 The rule will not be satisfied if the notice merely says that resolutions may be inspected at the company's offices or that copies will be forwarded on request.[18] Giving facilities for obtaining information is not equivalent to giving the information. If, however, a circular is sent with the resolution, members are expected to read it. If, together, they meet the criteria above, the rule is satisfied.[19]

6.27 In *Betts & Co v MacNaghten*,[20] the notice stated that the meeting was for the purpose of considering the resolution 'That A, B, and C be appointed directors', but allowed for such amendments and alterations as should be determined upon at the meeting. The notice was taken as read at the meeting, and two other persons were appointed as directors in addition to A, B and C. It

---

[13] *Kaye v Croydon Tramways* [1898] 1 Ch 358.
[14] See Chapter 2.
[15] See the Companies (Shareholders' Rights) Regulations 2009, SI 2009/1632, reg 10.
[16] [1916] 2 Ch 57.
[17] See the Companies Act 2006 (Commencement No 8, Transitional Provisions and Savings) Order 2008, SI 2008/2860, Sch 2, para 42.
[18] *Normandy v Ind Coope & Co* [1908] 1 Ch 84.
[19] *Tiessen v Henderson* [1899] 1 Ch 861; *Re Moorgate Mercantile Holdings Ltd* [1980] 1 WLR 227; *(1) In the matter of RAC Motoring Services Ltd (2) In the matter of the Royal Automobile Club Ltd* [1998] Ch D Companies Court, 8 July 1989.
[20] [1910] 1 Ch 430.

was held that the notice sufficiently indicated the business to be transacted and that the particularity of the names did not put greater restriction upon the meeting than there would have been had the notice been in general terms. Accordingly, all five were properly appointed. In that case, however, notice was given of the resolution with the addition of the words 'with such amendments as shall be determined on at the meeting', so the court may have been more than usually ready to find that an amendment to the ordinary resolution which had been set out in the notice would not invalidate the resolution.

6.28 But this rule will only apply if the amendment at the meeting renders the resolution less, and not more, onerous to the company or its members; for example, where the remuneration to be paid to directors is, under the amended resolution, less than that proposed in the notice.[21] The reason for this is that shareholders may have decided not to attend, or merely appointed proxies, because they were content with the stated proposal, but might have taken a different course of action had the more onerous proposal been proposed originally.

6.29 In *Choppington Collieries v Johnson*,[22] the articles provided that the election of directors in place of those retiring by rotation was not special business. Notice was sent out of an annual general meeting stating that the business was (among other business) to elect directors (in the plural) and also stating that one retiring director offered himself for re-election. It was held that the meeting could appoint persons other than the retiring director to be directors up to the maximum number allowed by the articles. The rationale appears to be that it was clear to members that there was a possibility that new directors might be appointed, other than the retiring director standing for re-election.

6.30 A proposed amendment to an ordinary resolution need not be put to the meeting in writing unless the articles expressly provide (as to which, see **6.35**), but it should be sufficiently definite.[23] It need not be seconded unless the articles specifically require this. 'If the chairman put the question without its being proposed or seconded by anybody, that would be perfectly good.'[24] A chairman is, therefore, not justified in refusing a motion or amendment because there is no seconder unless the articles expressly provide that all motions and amendments shall be seconded.

6.31 Where there is more than one amendment, these should be put to the meeting in the order in which they affect the main resolution. The main resolution, as finally amended, should then be put to the meeting. Strict adherence to the formality of putting motions and amendments is not essential,

---

[21] *Torbuck v Westbury (Lord)* [1902] 2 Ch 871. The resolution in this case was a special resolution under the Companies Act 1862.
[22] [1944] 1 All ER 762.
[23] *Henderson v Bank of Australasia* (1890) 45 ChD 330.
[24] *Re Horbury Bridge Coal Co* (1879) 11 ChD 109, at 118.

provided they are put to the meeting in such a way that those present understand what they are called upon to decide.[25]

6.32 If there is the slightest doubt as to whether an amendment is in order or not, it should be allowed to be put. The chairman is bound to allow the proposal of all legitimate and germane resolutions and amendments, and a refusal to do so will invalidate that part of the proceedings, because such refusal may amount to the withdrawal of a material and relevant question from the meeting. In *Henderson v Bank of Australasia*, Cotton LJ observed:[26]

> '... the chairman was entirely wrong in refusing to put the amendment, and ... the resolutions which were passed cannot be allowed to stand, because the chairman, under a mistaken idea as to what the law was which ought to have regulated his conduct, prevented a material question from being brought before the meeting.'

6.33 So accepting an amendment to an ordinary resolution will safeguard the ultimate resolution if it turns out in the end that the amendment is in fact relevant and germane. The chairman often has to make up his mind at once upon the validity of amendments, and when the chairman is fairly certain that the amendment will be lost there is no real harm done in allowing an amendment which may not be covered by the notice of the meeting. Thus, a chairman should not reject an amendment, if proposed, on the grounds that it has no chance of success. To do so would put the passing of the original resolution in danger of a technical objection.

6.34 Where the chairman does rule an amendment out of order, there is no obligation on the part of the mover of the amendment to contest that ruling or to leave the meeting in order to challenge it subsequently. It is not necessary for the mover to keep up an altercation with the chairman, nor does the mover lose any right later to object by acting under the ruling of the chairman.[27]

6.35 For modern companies to which the model form articles apply, some guidance is given by regs 47 (for a private company limited by shares), 33 (for a guarantee company) and 40 (for a public company). These all say that an ordinary resolution proposed at a general meeting may be amended by another ordinary resolution if:

(a) notice of the proposed amendment is given to the company secretary in writing by a person entitled to vote at the general meeting at which it is to be proposed;

(b) the notice is given not less than 48 hours before the meeting is to take place (or such later time as the chairman of the meeting determines); and

---

[25] *Stevens ex parte* (1852) 16 JP 632.
[26] (1890) 45 ChD 330, at 346.
[27] *Henderson v Bank of Australasia* (1890) 45 ChD 330.

(c) in the reasonable opinion of the chairman of the meeting, the proposed amendment does not materially alter the scope of the resolution.

They also say that, if the chairman of the meeting, acting in good faith, wrongly decides that an amendment to a resolution is out of order, the chairman's error does not invalidate the vote on that resolution.

Special resolutions

6.36 For special resolutions,[28] CA 2006 overrides the common law rule. It requires that the notice of the meeting at which a special resolution is to be proposed must specify that the resolution is to be passed as a special resolution (s 283(3)). Since this intention must be specified in relation to 'the resolution', the text of the resolution – its entire substance – must be set out in the notice, exactly as it will be put to the meeting (s 283(6)). The rule includes circulars accompanying such notices.

6.37 Unless all the members entitled to attend and vote agree, the basic rule is therefore that no amendment may be made to a proposed special resolution, unless the articles say otherwise.[29]

6.38 For companies with modern articles they may well say otherwise. Regulations 47 (for a private company limited by shares), 33 (for a guarantee company) and 40 (for a public company) all say that a special resolution proposed at a general meeting may be amended by ordinary resolution, if:

(a) the chairman of the meeting proposes the amendment at the general meeting at which the resolution is to be proposed; and

(b) the amendment does not go beyond what is necessary to correct a grammatical or other non-substantive error in the resolution.

They also say that, if the chairman of the meeting, acting in good faith, wrongly decides that an amendment to a resolution is out of order, the chairman's error does not invalidate the vote on that resolution.

6.39 There is no point in adding words such as 'with such amendments and alterations as may be determined at the meeting' to the notice with a view to taking amendments at the meeting, because no amendment may be made to a special resolution once the notice has been given. If the resolution actually proposed and/or passed at the meeting is different from that specified in the notice, it will not be valid, even if passed by the required majority,[30] because notice of intention to propose it will not have been given as required by s 283.

---

[28] See Chapter 2.
[29] *Re Moorgate Mercantile Holdings Ltd* [1980] 1 WLR 227.
[30] *MacConnell v Prill & Co* [1916] 2 Ch 57.

6.40 The exception is if the resolution passed at the meeting is different from that in the notice only because it corrects a mere typographical error or other slip, obvious in the light of the proposal and the information given. In that case, the resolution passed will be effective; it is not necessary to reconvene the meeting. The courts have, on various occasions, acted on this principle when confirming reductions of capital. In *Moorgate Mercantile Holdings Ltd*,[31] a derogation from this general rule was allowed. It was held that a special resolution:

> '... as passed can properly be regarded as "the resolution" identified in the proceeding notice even though (a) it departs in some respects from the text of a resolution set out in such notice (for example by correcting those grammatical or clerical errors which can be corrected as a matter of construction, or by reducing the words to more formal language) or (b) it is reduced into the form of a new text which was not included in the notice, provided only that in either case there is no departure whatever from the substance.'

6.41 Where particularly complex proposals or changes are put forward, best practice is that, as well as setting these out, the notice should also summarise the proposals and, if these involve changes from existing provisions, summarise the differences. Such a procedure is often disliked by directors, who prefer not to attempt to explain resolutions in case some aspect is unwittingly summarised incorrectly, or overlooked, but the information is more likely to be presented clearly using this procedure.

6.42 Where the notice deals with two separate resolutions the failure of the one will not invalidate the other, even in cases where they are closely associated.[32] If it is intended that one proposal should take effect only if another does, they should either be put in a single resolution or made interdependent in their terms.

6.43 For listed companies, the UK Corporate Governance Code provisions say that companies should propose a separate resolution at general meetings on each substantially separate issue.[33]

Statement required on notices

6.44 Any member of the company entitled to attend and vote at a general meeting is entitled to appoint one or more other persons as his proxy or proxies, to attend, speak and vote instead of him. A company's articles may also provide proxies with additional rights, over and above their statutory rights. A proxy need not be a member of the company. A statement to that effect, together with information about any more extensive rights conferred by the company's articles, must appear 'with reasonable prominence' on every notice calling a general meeting (s 325).

---

[31] [1980] 1 WLR 227.
[32] *Cleve v Financial Corporation* (1873) LR 16 Eq 363.
[33] Provision E.2.1.

6.45 Where members of 'traded companies' (that is, companies whose shares are admitted to trading on a regulated market) – see s 360C and **6.4** have nominated others to enjoy some of the benefits of membership under s 146 (see **5.122**), s 149 provides that the copy of the notice of a meeting sent to such a nominated person must be accompanied by a statement that:

- he may have a right under an agreement between him and the member by whom he was nominated to be appointed, or to have someone else appointed, as a proxy for the meeting; and

- if he has no such right or does not wish to exercise it, he may have a right under such an agreement to give instructions to the member as to the exercise of voting rights.

6.46 Section 325 states that the requirement that a notice of a general meeting must contain a statement of a member's rights in relation to the appointment of a proxy or proxies does not apply to the copy, and the company must either omit the notice required by that section, or include it but state that it does not apply to the nominated person.

6.47 It is common practice to send out a form for appointment of a proxy (or proxies) with the notice of meeting, with instructions on how to complete and return it for an effective proxy appointment. CA 2006 (s 326) regulates how this is done. If the company issues (at its own expense) invitations to appoint as proxy a specified person or a number of specified persons, the invitations must be issued to all the members entitled to vote at the meeting, unless:

- the form of appointment naming the proxy or a list of persons willing to act as proxy is issued to a member at his request; and

- the form or list is available on request to all members entitled to vote at the meeting.

6.48 For listed companies, the proxy form must also:

- provide for at least three-way voting by proxies on all resolutions (except procedural resolutions); and

- state that (if lodged without an indication as to how the proxy should vote on any matter) the proxy will exercise his discretion as to whether, and if so how, he votes.

6.49 If the meeting includes resolutions to re-elect retiring directors and the number of them standing for re-election is more than five, the proxy form may give shareholders the opportunity to vote for or against the re-election of the retiring directors as a whole, but must also allow votes to be cast for or against the re-election of the retiring directors individually.[34]

6.50 Section 327 of CA 2006[35] also regulates requirements in company articles relating to how early any appointment of a proxy (including any document necessary to show the validity of, or otherwise relating to, the appointment of a proxy) must be received. See Chapter 8 for a discussion of these rules.

6.51 Where a company invites members to appoint a particular person or persons as proxy, the invitation must be issued to all members entitled to vote at the meeting (s 326), unless:

- the member has requested a form of appointment naming the proxy (or a list of persons willing to act as a proxy); or

- the form or list is available on request to all members entitled to vote at the meeting (s 326(2)).

6.52 Before 1 October 2007, there was no right for a member of a company limited by guarantee to appoint a proxy unless the articles so provided. From then, there has been a statutory right to appoint a proxy, and include the necessary statement on the notice. However, multiple proxies are not provided for in a guarantee company.

6.53 There are special rules requiring additional statements to be included on notices of general meetings called by traded companies (see s 360C and **6.4**) in certain circumstances. Section 311(3)[36] says that the notice of a general meeting of a traded company must also include:

- A statement of the website address where the information required by s 311A (traded companies: publication of information in advance of general meeting) is published.

- A statement that the right to vote at the meeting is determined by reference to the register of members, and of the time when that right will be determined (in accordance with s 360B(2)).

- A statement of the procedures members must comply with in order to be able to attend and vote at the meeting (including the date by which they must comply).

- A statement giving details of any forms to be used for the appointment of a proxy.

---

[34] Listing Rules, paras 9.3.6 and 9.3.7.
[35] As amended by the Companies (Shareholders' Rights) Regulations 2009, SI 2009/1632, reg 13.
[36] Inserted by the Companies (Shareholders' Rights) Regulations 2009, SI 2009/1632, reg 9.

- If the company offers the facility for members to vote in advance (see s 322A) or by electronic means (see s 360A), a statement of the procedure for doing so (including the date by which it must be done, and details of any forms to be used),

- A statement of the right of members to ask questions in accordance with s 319A (traded companies: questions at meetings).

6.54 The rules in s 311A[37] also require a traded company to ensure that the following information is made available on a website:

- the matters set out in the notice of the meeting;

- the total numbers of shares in the company, and the number of shares of each class, in respect of which members are entitled to exercise voting rights at the meeting;

- the totals of the voting rights that members are entitled to exercise at the meeting in respect of the shares of each class;

- members' statements, members' resolutions and members' matters of business received by the company after the first date on which notice of the meeting is given.

The website must be one maintained by or on behalf of, and must identify, the company. Fees for (or any other restrictions on) access to the information, or the ability to obtain a hard copy of it, are prohibited. The information about the matters set out in the notice of the meeting, the total numbers of voting shares (and class shares) in the company, and totals of the voting rights that members are entitled to exercise at the meeting must be made available on or before the first date on which notice of the meeting is given. The information about members' statements, resolutions and matters of business received after the first date on which notice of the meeting is given must be made available as soon as reasonably practicable. All the information must then be kept available for 2 years, starting from the date it is first made available on the website (unless it is available for part of that period only, and the failure is wholly attributable to circumstances that it would not be reasonable to have expected the company to prevent or avoid).

Signing the notice

6.55 Notices should be signed by the secretary (or, if the company is private and has chosen not to have a secretary, some other person authorised by the directors), qualified by the words 'By Order of the Board', and the secretary or other authorised person should see that the board meeting which has

---

[37] Inserted by the Companies (Shareholders' Rights) Regulations 2009, SI 2009/1632, reg 11.

authorised the convening of a general meeting was itself properly convened, and that a quorum of directors was present.

TO WHOM NOTICES SHOULD BE SENT

Members

6.56 Subject to any limitations in the articles, all members on the register of members, every director, and any person entitled to a share in consequence of the death or bankruptcy of a member that has been notified to the company, are entitled to receive notice of meetings.[38] There may also be a right for nominated members under either or both of ss 145 and/or 146 to receive notice (see **5.122**).

6.57 In most instances, where a company gives notice of a general meeting (or a resolution intended to be moved at a general meeting), an accidental failure to give notice to one or more persons is disregarded for the purpose of determining whether notice of the meeting or resolution is duly given.[39] However, a company can choose to make alternative provision in its articles, saying that accidental failure to give notice should *not* be disregarded – unless the notice is given pursuant to s 304 (notice of meetings required by members), s 305 (notice of meetings called by members) or s 339 (notice of resolutions at annual general meetings proposed by members). However, articles normally restate the provisions of CA 2006, and provide that accidental failure to give notice will not invalidate a meeting or the proceedings.[40]

6.58 The situation is different, however, if the failure to send a notice is deliberate. For example, where the company believes that notice to the address in a register will not reach the member and accordingly does not send one to that member, neither CA 2006 nor such an article will help the company, as the failure is not accidental.[41] Similarly, it has been held in the Republic of Ireland that a bona fide but mistaken view that notice need not be sent is nevertheless a 'deliberate' failure for corresponding purposes under Irish law.[42]

Special classes of members

6.59 Articles often prescribe that certain classes of members shall not be entitled to receive notice in respect of their class shares. However, if the articles

---

[38] CA 2006, s 310(1).
[39] CA 2006, s 313. *Smyth v Darley* (1849) 2 HLC 789. Note also that in *Re A Company (No 00789 of 1987) ex parte Shooter* [1990] BCLC 384, it was held that the holding of a general meeting without adequate notice, at which new shares were created, was grounds for a petition alleging unfairly prejudicial conduct under s 459 of CA 1985. However, in *Blue Arrow plc* [1987] BCLC 585, it was held that the proper course of action is to bring an action claiming the resolution to be passed is invalid, rather than petitioning under s 459.
[40] *Re West Canadian Collieries* [1962] Ch 370; Table A, reg 39.
[41] *Musselwhite v C H Musselwhite* [1962] Ch 964.
[42] *O'Doherty v West Limerick Resources* [1999] IESC 39 (14 May 1999).

specify that, for example, preference shares do not carry voting rights, but make no special provision regarding notice, it is unclear whether the preference shareholders will be entitled to notice.[43] To exclude all doubt, articles which provide that certain classes of members are not to have a vote should also provide expressly that they shall not be entitled to receive notices of or to attend meetings.

Joint holders of shares

6.60 Subject to a company's articles, documents or information to be sent or supplied to joint holders of shares (or debentures) of a company can either be sent or supplied to each of the joint holders, or to the holder whose name appears first in the register of members (or the relevant register of debenture holders) (CA 2006, Sch 5, para 16).

Persons entitled to a share as a result of the death or bankruptcy of a member

6.61 As indicated above, persons who become entitled to a share as a result of the death or bankruptcy[44] of a member are automatically entitled to notice of meetings (s 310(2)). It is unclear what such people should do with this notice, since articles invariably provide that before being registered as the holder of a share, a person entitled to a share as a result of death or bankruptcy is not entitled to attend or vote at any meeting of the company.

6.62 It should be noted in this context that a member who becomes bankrupt remains a member and is able to exercise the votes attached to his shares, notwithstanding that by taking appropriate steps under the appropriate provisions the trustee in bankruptcy might be able to secure registration as the holder of the shares.[45] A company cannot, therefore, treat a member who is known to be bankrupt differently from other members, whether in connection with sending notices to that member or accepting the votes of that member.

Directors

6.63 As indicated above, and subject to any limitations in the articles, every director is entitled to receive notice of meetings (s 310). Articles commonly require that notice of meetings be given to the directors in any event.

---

[43] *Re Mackenzie* [1916] 2 Ch 450; *Re Warden & Hotchkiss* [1945] Ch 270, at 278, but see s 310(1) of CA 2006.
[44] Bankruptcy, for these purposes, includes the sequestration of the estate of a person, a person's estate being the subject of a protected trust deed (within the meaning of the Bankruptcy (Scotland) Act 1985 as amended). If so, the permanent or interim trustee (within the meaning of that Act) on the sequestrated estate or, as the case may be, the trustee under the protected deed is treated as the trustee in bankruptcy): CA 2006, Sch 5, para 17(5).
[45] *Morgan v Gray* [1953] Ch 83.

Auditors

6.64 The auditor is entitled to attend any general meeting and to receive all notices and other communications relating to such a meeting. The auditor is also entitled to be heard on any part of the business affecting him as auditor (s 502(2)).

Debenture holders

6.65 As a result of a special provision in s 5(8) of CA 1985 (which is still in force), notice of a special resolution to alter the objects clause of a company's memorandum must be given not only to members, but also to holders of any debentures secured by a floating charge issued or first issued before 1 December 1947, or debentures which form part of the same series as any debentures so issued. The subsection requires the same notice to be given to debenture holders as is given to members of the company. The provision does not confer on relevant debenture holders the right to attend the meeting; rather its purpose is to give them the right to object to the alteration.

6.66 Provision can be made in, or authorised by, a company's articles for notice to be given by advertisement in some instances. Such advertisement may be required to be inserted in a particular newspaper or posted in some specified place. If the requirements are complied with, the notice is duly given. This is, however, unusual except in cases where the persons entitled to notice are unknown, such as holders of bearer warrants or untraced members. In the first instance, the relevant provisions are invariably included in the terms of issue of the bearer warrants and printed on the reverse of each. In the latter instance, they are invariably included in the articles.

METHOD OF SERVICE

6.67 Section 308 of CA 2006 requires a notice of general meeting to be given in hard copy or electronic form, or 'by means of a website' (or partly by one such means, and partly by another). Giving of notices electronically, including by means of a website, is dealt with in Chapter 11. This chapter deals with giving of notice in hard copy form.

6.68 Schedule 5 to CA 2006 regulates service of documents or information by a company on its members, including notices of general meetings. It provides that a document or information is validly sent or supplied by a company if it is sent or supplied in hard copy form in accordance with Sch 5. This applies irrespective of what is in its articles. Schedule 5 says that notices in hard copy form must either be handed to the intended recipient or sent or supplied by hand or by post (that is, posted in a prepaid envelope) to his address as shown in the company's register of members. If the company does not have such an address, para 4 of Sch 5 provides alternative addresses that the company can use.

6.69 Subject to the company's articles, documents or information required or authorised to be sent or supplied to the member may be sent or supplied to the persons claiming to be entitled to the shares in consequence of the death or bankruptcy by name, or by the title of representatives of the deceased, or trustee of the bankrupt, or by any like description.

6.70 The documents or information should be sent to the address in the UK supplied for the purpose by those so claiming. Until such an address has been so supplied, a document or information may be sent or supplied in any manner in which it might have been sent or supplied if the death or bankruptcy had not occurred.

6.71 However, Sch 5 also says that a document or information that is sent or supplied otherwise than in hard copy or electronic form or by means of a website is validly sent or supplied if it is sent or supplied in a form or manner that has been agreed by the intended recipient. So the company and a member or members can agree alternatives.

6.72 The provisions of CA 2006 may be supplemented by the articles. For example, regs 111–116 in the 1985 Table A may apply to some companies, and the rules are set out below. The rules in articles governing electronic notice of members' meetings are dealt with in Chapter 11.

6.73 Regulation 111 in the 1985 Table A provides that notice for a company meeting shall be in writing. Regulation 112 provides that a hard copy notice may be given to a member personally, by post or by leaving it at the registered address of the member. Section 1147 provides that a document or information that the company can show was properly addressed and sent by prepaid post to an address in the UK is deemed to have been received 48 hours after it was posted. Only hours in 'working days' count. A 'working day' means any day other than a Saturday or Sunday, Christmas Day, Good Friday or a bank holiday under the Banking and Financial Dealings Act 1971 in the part of the UK where the company is registered. However, a company may make alternative provision in its articles. Where the notices are to be given by post, then reg 115 in the 1985 Table A restates CA 2006 and provides that the notice is deemed to have been given at the expiration of 48 hours after the envelope was posted. The same regulation further provides that it shall be conclusive evidence that notice was given if it was proved that an envelope containing the notice was properly addressed, stamped and posted.

6.74 Articles that predate the 1985 version of Table A usually stipulate that notice served by post shall be deemed given 24 hours after it was posted – again, proof that an envelope containing the notice was properly addressed, stamped and posted is conclusive evidence that notice was given. It has been suggested that a notice sent by second class post may not be 'properly stamped' for the purposes of this provision, so caution dictates that notices should always be sent by first class post.

6.75 An important feature of the regulations on notice in the 1985 Table A is the provision which entitles a member whose registered address is outside the UK to have notices given at a stipulated address within the UK. The regulation goes on to provide, however, that if such a member does not provide a UK address, he will have no entitlement to receive any notices from the company (reg 112). The equivalent regulation in Table A to the 1948 Act was the subject of *Parkstone Ltd v Gulf Guarantee Bank plc*.[46] In this case, a member with an address in Gibraltar had also given the company an address in the UK for the service of notices. The company, however, sent a notice to the address in Gibraltar. The court held that this was a valid notice under reg 131 of the 1948 Table A. It seems unlikely that a similar result would have been produced on these facts if the regulation in question had been in the form of reg 112 of the 1985 Table A. This is because reg 112, unlike the older reg 131, 'entitles' members to have notices given to them at their stipulated UK address.

6.76 In *Re Warden & Hotchkiss Ltd*,[47] the articles did not provide (as the 1985 Table A does for companies to which it applies) that notice need not be given to members whose only address is outside the UK. But they did provide that a notice would be deemed to be delivered when the letter containing it would have been delivered in the ordinary course of post. The court decided that notice need not be given to members with registered addresses abroad – it treated in the 'ordinary course of post' as meaning in the 'ordinary course of post within the UK'. It seems, however, that this decision should now be regarded as applying only to companies whose articles are in exactly the same form as those in Table A to the 1862 Act. In other cases, a reference to the ordinary course of post should not be construed as including post within the UK only.[48]

6.77 Of course, it is open to members of a company to alter the articles by special resolution, to provide that all members, including those registered with an overseas address only, are entitled to notice at that address. It may also be sensible in such a case to alter articles to extend the period at the end of which notices are deemed to have arrived, if sent by post.

6.78 Persons situated abroad who do not have the right to receive notices of company meetings are those persons who are enemies, or who are situated in enemy territory. The right of such people to receive notices is suspended so long as they remain an enemy or in enemy territory, and meetings are properly convened though no notice has been served upon a person who, if not an enemy, would be entitled to notice.[49]

---

[46] [1990] TLR 477.
[47] [1945] Ch 270.
[48] *Parkstone Ltd v Gulf Guarantee Bank plc* [1990] TLR 477.
[49] *Re Anglo-International Bank* [1943] Ch 233.

NOTICE OF PROPOSAL TO PAY COMPENSATION TO DIRECTORS

6.79 CA 2006 contains important provisions about disclosing proposals to pay compensation (including any non-cash benefits) for loss of office to directors and past directors (but not shadow directors). Under s 217, a company may not make any payment to a director or past director, or to a 'connected person' as defined in s 252ff, of the company or its holding company:

- in compensation for loss of office as a director of the company;

- in compensation for loss of any other office or employment in connection with the management of the affairs of the company or any subsidiary of it;

- in consideration of, or in connection with, his retirement from office as a director of the company; or

- in consideration for, or in connection with, his retirement from office or employment in connection with the management of the affairs of the company or any subsidiary of it,

unless the particulars of the proposed payment, and the amount, are disclosed to the members of the company and, if applicable, the holding company, and the proposal for payment is approved by them (unless the company is a wholly-owned subsidiary) and, if applicable, by the members of the holding company. Therefore, when any such payment is proposed, a meeting of the company and, if applicable, the holding company, must be held, and the notice must contain the particulars required by this section.

6.80 Section 218 requires similar disclosure and approval by the company and, if appropriate, its subsidiary company, of any payment made to any director or connected person of compensation for loss of office (or as consideration for, or in connection with, retirement from office) when any such payment is proposed to be made in connection with the transfer of the whole or any part of the undertaking and property of the company or of any subsidiary (s 218(2)). The section applies whether the proposed payment is by the company itself or some other person, for example, a bidder for the shares.

6.81 Section 219 deals with the situation when a similar payment is proposed to be made to a director or connected person in connection with transfers of shares in the company, or any subsidiary of it, resulting from certain classes of offers to purchase the shares mentioned in the section. This includes all transfers of shares in the company or in a subsidiary resulting from a takeover bid (s 219(1)). In such cases it is the duty of the director to see that the particulars and amount of the proposed payment are disclosed in the offer to purchase the shares. Section 219(2) provides that any such proposed payment must be approved by a meeting of the holders of all the shares to which the offer relates and of all the other shares of that class or those classes of shares. The provisions of CA 2006, and the articles as to the holding of general meetings, apply to meetings to be held under s 219, except that the persons making the offer for shares in the company, and any of their associates, may not vote on the resolution to approve the payment for loss of office in connection with a share transfer (s 219(4)).

6.82 Section 220 creates exceptions for certain payments in discharge of legal obligations. Approval is not required for payment made in good faith:

- in discharge of an existing legal obligation;

- by way of damages for breach of such an obligation;

- by way of settlement or compromise of any claim arising in connection with the termination of a person's office or employment; or

- by way of pension in respect of past services.

6.83 For the purposes of s 217, an existing legal obligation means an obligation of the company, or any body corporate associated with it, that was not entered into in connection with, or in consequence of, the event giving rise to the payment for loss of office.

6.84 For payments within s 218 or 219 (payment in connection with transfer of undertaking, property or shares) an existing legal obligation means an obligation of the person making the payment that was not entered into for the purposes of, in connection with or in consequence of, the transfer in question.

6.85 If the payment is within both ss 217 and 218, or within both ss 217 and 219, an existing legal obligation means an obligation of the company, or any body corporate associated with it, that was not entered into in connection with, or in consequence of, the event giving rise to the payment for loss of office.

6.86 If a payment falls partly within s 217 and partly not, it is treated as if the parts were separate payments.

6.87 There is also an exception for small payments made by the company or any of its subsidiaries, that is, where the amount or value of the payment, together with the amount or value of 'any other relevant payments',[50] does not exceed £200.

---

[50] Where the payment in question is one to which s 217 (payment by company) applies, a payment for loss of office is 'any other relevant payment' if it was or is paid by the company making the payment in question or any of its subsidiaries, to the director to whom that payment is made and in connection with the same event. Where it is one to which s 218 or 219 applies (payment in connection with transfer of undertaking, property or shares), the conditions are that the

CIRCULATION OF STATEMENT GIVEN PURSUANT TO S 314

6.88 Section 314 also provides that members (including any person nominated by a member pursuant to s 145 – see **5.122**) holding 5% or more of the total voting rights, or at least 100 members of the company holding shares paid up to an average sum of at least £100 (s 314(2)), may require the company to circulate a statement of not more than 1,000 words to all members of the company entitled to receive notice of a general meeting.

6.89 The statement must relate to (1) a matter referred to in a proposed resolution that is to be put to the meeting or (2) any other business to be dealt with at the meeting. In the case of (1), the shares must carry the right to vote on the relevant resolution. In the case of (2), they must carry the right to vote at the meeting. The request can be given in hard copy or in electronic form, must identify the statement to be circulated and must be received by the company at least one week before the meeting (s 314(4)(d)).

6.90 Section 315 provides for the method of serving the statement. Section 315(1) provides that a copy of the statement should be sent to all members of the company entitled to notice of the general meeting, in the same manner as the notice of the meeting itself, and either at the same time or as soon as reasonably practicable after it gives notice of the meeting.

6.91 Under s 316 of CA 2006, the expenses of complying with s 315 need not be paid by the members who request the circulation of the statement, provided that the meeting to which the request relates is an annual general meeting of a public company, and requests sufficient to trigger the requirement to circulate it are received before the end of the company's financial year preceding the meeting. If these conditions are not met – and they will, of course, never be met in relation to a general meeting other than the annual general meeting – the expenses must be paid by the members making the request, unless the company resolves otherwise (s 316(1)(b)). The rule is that the members must deposit or tender to the company a sum reasonably sufficient to meet those expenses, not later than one week before the meeting, or the company is entitled to ignore the request.

6.92 Section 317 sets out the circumstances in which the company will not be obliged to circulate a copy of the statement received under s 314. These are where the company or any other person who claims to be aggrieved by the terms of any such statement applies to the court and the court is satisfied that the rights conferred by the section are being abused (s 317(1)). Section 317(2) provides that the court can order the members who requested circulation of the statement to pay the costs of the application, even if they are not parties to it.

---

other payment was (or is) paid in connection with the same transfer, to the director to whom the payment in question was made, and by the company making the payment or any of its subsidiaries: s 221(2), (3) and (4).

6.93 Under s 153 a company is required to act on a request received under any of s 314, if the following conditions are met:

(a) it is made by at least 100 persons;

(b) it is authenticated by all the persons making it;

(c) in the case of any person who is not a member of the company, it is accompanied by a statement:

    (i) of the full name and address of a person ('the member') who is a member of the company and holds shares on behalf of that person;
    (ii) that the member is holding those shares on behalf of that person in the course of a business;
    (iii) of the number of shares in the company that the member holds on behalf of that person;
    (iv) of the total amount paid up on those shares;
    (v) that those shares are not held on behalf of anyone else or, if they are, that the other person or persons are not among the other persons making the request;
    (vi) that some or all of those shares confer voting rights that are relevant for the purposes of making a request under the section in question; and
    (vii) that the person has the right to instruct the member how to exercise those rights;

(d) in the case of any of those persons who is a member of the company, it is accompanied by a statement:

    (i) that he holds shares otherwise than on behalf of another person; or
    (ii) that he holds shares on behalf of one or more other persons but those persons are not among the other persons making the request;

(e) it is accompanied by such evidence as the company may reasonably require of the matters mentioned in paragraphs (c) and (d);

(f) the total amount of the sums paid up on:

    (i) shares held as mentioned in paragraph (c); and
    (ii) shares held as mentioned in paragraph (d),
divided by the number of persons making the request is not less than £100;

(g) the request complies with any other requirements of the section in question as to contents, timing and otherwise.

6.94 This is to ensure that, where indirect investors have been nominated to enjoy certain rights of membership by members pursuant to s 146, they are able to count towards the total required under s 314, subject to certain conditions. The conditions are intended to ensure that only genuine indirect investors are allowed to count towards the total, that the same shares cannot be used twice and that the indirect investor's contractual arrangements with the member allow the former to give voting instructions.

AUTHENTICATION OF NOTICES

6.95 A notice must be properly authenticated. The old s 41 in the 1985 Act provided that a document requiring authentication *by* a company may be signed by an officer and s 744 provided that a notice is a document for this purpose. This was repealed with effect from 6 April 2007 by the Companies Act 2006 (Commencement No 1, Transitional Provisions and Savings) Order 2006,[51] and not replaced in the 2006 Act.

6.96 The government repealed this rule because it believed it had been overtaken by common law developments, and by scope to use a company's own articles to provide rules for authentication of a document by a company.

---

[51] SI 2006/3428.

Chapter 7

THE QUORUM AND THE CHAIRMAN AT GENERAL MEETINGS

INTRODUCTION

7.1 The majority of the day-to-day powers to manage their company are delegated to the directors by the members, in the articles of association (see Chapter 2). Members can even delegate powers (not reserved to them by statute) to the directors in such a way that those powers can no longer be exercised by the members themselves. This is the effect of, for example, regs 3 and 4 in the model form articles for both a private company limited by shares and a public company and, for companies with older articles, reg 70 of Table A to the Companies Act 1985, if any of them apply. The exercise by the directors of the powers delegated to them under these regulations can only be controlled, in advance, by a special resolution of the company in general meeting.

7.2 The Companies Act 2006 (CA 2006), however, reserves certain decisions to the members (see Appendix 1). The members may also, in the articles of association, reserve additional matters to themselves. In both circumstances, a general meeting, open to all the members of the company entitled to attend under the articles, must be convened and properly conducted.

7.3 Some aspects of the conduct of members' meetings are governed by statute. Beyond those, the company's members may establish rules for the conduct of general meetings in the articles of their company. The directors may also establish formal procedures for the conduct of members' meetings by means of policies or internal procedures.

7.4 Such policies and procedures are of great help to the chairman, members and officers alike. From them the chairman obtains most of his power, and they form an invaluable authority to which the chairman can appeal. They prevent misapprehension of the powers of the meeting, avoid confusion and disorder and facilitate the dispatch and conduct of business. They are also particularly valuable for the company secretary (if the company has one – they are optional for private companies), who is responsible to the company chairman for the proper administration of meetings of the members (and of the board and any committees).[1]

---

[1] 'Good Boardroom Practice. A Code for Directors and Company Secretaries' from the Information Centre, ICSA, 16 Park Crescent, London W1B 1AH or informationcentre@icsa.org.uk. See also www.icsa.org.uk.

7.5 There may also be informal customs, established over time, which are tacitly agreed and followed. In the absence of any rules at all, a difficulty may be overcome by the chairman exercising his common sense – bearing in mind that it is his duty to ascertain the views of the meeting and act in a way that complies with his statutory and other duties as a director of the company.

7.6 The formal policies and procedures, any informal customs and any 'decisions of the chairman in the absence of a rule' must not be inconsistent with CA 2006 or the articles. They must also comply with the common law – they must be unambiguous, fair and reasonable, and they must be interpreted in an impartial manner. They should safeguard the general rights of those entitled to attend the meeting and should not infringe or breach the rights of minorities.

7.7 Once agreed to, any alteration to policies and procedures or custom should be made only after proper notice has been given to the persons affected.

QUORUM

General rules

7.8 Every meeting must have a quorum. The quorum is the number of members needed before the meeting can validly transact business that binds all members, even if not present. Any business conducted at a gathering of the members purporting to be a general meeting, but which is inquorate, is invalid because there is no 'meeting' for the purposes of CA 2006 – although this is subject to any contrary provision in a company's articles. At common law, and under reg 40 of Table A (if it applies), only persons entitled to vote on the matter to be voted on are counted in a quorum for the purposes of that decision.[2] However, s 318 now provides statutory authority to allow one person to be a quorum. It says that, in the case of a company limited by shares or guarantee and having only one member, one qualifying person present at a meeting is a quorum. A 'qualifying person' means an individual who is a member of the company, a person authorised under s 323 (representation of corporations at meetings) to act as the representative of a corporation in relation to the meeting or a person appointed as proxy of a member in relation to the meeting. Otherwise, s 318 provides that, subject to the articles, two 'qualifying persons' present at a meeting are a quorum, unless:

- each person present is a qualifying person only because they are representatives (appointed under s 323) of the same corporation in relation to the meeting;

---

[2] *Young v South African Syndicate* [1896] 2 Ch 268; cf *Re Greymouth-Point Elizabeth Railway Co* [1904] 1 Ch 32.

- each is a qualifying person only because he is appointed as proxy of a member in relation to the meeting, and they are proxies of the same member; or

- the company is limited, and has only one member, in which case one qualifying person present at a meeting is a quorum.

In companies incorporated before 1 October 2009, so that the 1985 Table A, or some earlier version, applies, the default provisions are usually unnecessary because the company's articles do generally provide how many members are needed to make a quorum at a general meeting – for example, reg 40 in the 1985 Table A. For companies incorporated on or after that date, the model form articles make no provision for the quorum at general meetings, so the default provisions do apply.

7.9 If a company's articles require a quorum of three, however, and there are two people present, it has been held[3] that the articles are satisfied if one is a member in his own right and also holds shares as trustee for a third party. This was, however, a Scottish case and, under Scots law, notice of trusts may be entered in a company's register of members. This is prohibited by s 126 in relation to English companies.

7.10 Articles normally state what is to happen if no quorum is present when the meeting is due to begin. For example, reg 38 in the model form articles for a private company limited by shares simply says that the members at an inquorate meeting may not transact any business other than the appointment of the chairman of the meeting. The same applies if the meeting becomes inquorate later, after it has started – for example, if a member has to leave.

7.11 For companies with older articles, reg 41 of the 1985 Table A provides that if within half an hour no quorum is present, the meeting stands adjourned for one week exactly and is to be held at the same place, or at such other time and place as the directors may determine. Under reg 41, this also applies if at any time during the meeting a quorum ceases to be present. See Chapter 9 in relation to adjournment of meetings.

7.12 Some companies may regard this requirement for a meeting to remain quorate throughout as inconvenient, as it may permit members who are unhappy with the progress of the meeting to bring it to a halt by walking out. Problems such as this may, to some extent, be dealt with under the principles of law preventing abuse of quorum provisions (discussed at **7.21**), but some companies specifically provide in their articles that a quorum needs to be present only at the beginning of the meeting.

7.13 Older articles (such as regs 53 and 54 of Table A to the Companies Acts 1948–1976), provide that a quorum only needs to be present when the meeting

---

[3] *Yuill v Greymouth-Point Elizabeth Railway Co* [1904] 1 Ch 32.

proceeds to business, in any event. They also provide that, if a meeting is adjourned and a quorum is not present within 30 minutes of the time appointed for the adjourned meeting, the members present shall be a quorum. This means that one member may constitute a quorum at the adjourned meeting under those provisions.

7.14 A question arises whether two joint holders, present personally or by proxy, can be counted for the purpose of a quorum, because s 286 says that the first-named in the register in respect of a joint holding may vote so as to exclude the votes of the other. Ordinarily, a member who is not entitled to vote is not entitled to be counted in the quorum. On principle, the answer must be that both joint holders can be counted in the quorum, as both are members and both can be entitled to vote in certain circumstances. The votes of the second-named are excluded only if the first-named votes all the jointly held shares, but the first-named is not bound to do that and will not necessarily do so. It is not clear if that leads to the conclusion that the two joint holders can constitute a quorum if they are the only people present at the meeting. At best, that is a moot point.

7.15 For the purpose of calculating the quorum, a corporate member which has authorised some person or persons to act as its representative(s) at any meeting of the company, under the provisions of s 323 of CA 2006, is regarded as personally present if a representative is present.[4] A person present by his attorney is not present in person. Nor, it seems, is an executor of a deceased member counted for the purpose of a quorum if the article requires the members to be personally present,[5] even if the executor is entitled to be on the register though not yet entered.

One person meetings

7.16 The general principle that one person cannot constitute either a meeting or a quorum at a general meeting has already been noted, together with the exception in s 318. Some other exceptions to this principle are, however, recognised. In relation to class shares, it was held in *East v Bennett Bros*[6] that the assent of the only preference shareholder was equivalent to a resolution passed by a separate meeting of preference shareholders.

7.17 In the case of general meetings, there is also a second statutory exception (in addition to s 318) to the rule that one person cannot constitute a meeting.

7.18 This is s 306, which deals with the power of the court to order a general meeting on application by a director or member, or of its own motion.[7]

---

[4] *Re Kelantan Coconut Estates Ltd* [1920] WN 274.
[5] For example, where it is anticipated that a meeting will be disrupted: *Re Bowling & Welby's Contract* [1895] 1 Ch 663.
[6] [1911] 1 Ch 163.
[7] See Chapter 4 for commentary on *British Union for the Abolition of Vivisection* [1995] 2 BCLC 1.

7.19 Again, s 306(4) and (5) allows the court to direct that the meeting called, held and conducted in accordance with an order under s 306 is deemed for all purposes to be a meeting of the company duly called, held and conducted, and that one member of the company present at the meeting is deemed to constitute a quorum. The fact that s 306 uses the expression 'deemed' implies that one person could not ordinarily constitute a meeting, or a quorum at it and, therefore, reinforces the general rule that one person cannot constitute a meeting of the members.

Special class quorums

7.20 In the case of class meetings held to resolve a proposed variation of class rights, s 125(6) requires a quorum of two persons holding or representing by proxy at least one-third in nominal value of the issued shares of the class in question. So high a quorum is not always easy to assemble, and if no quorum is obtained the meeting will be adjourned. The subsection provides that, at the adjourned meeting, the quorum is one person, either in person or by proxy, holding shares of the class in question.

Abuse of quorum provisions

7.21 Where a member refuses to attend a meeting and thus prevents the formation of a quorum, this will be a ground for the court ordering the holding of a meeting under s 306.[8] One exception is where the calling of a meeting would go against the original intention of the parties – for example, if they deliberately intended to create deadlock in the event of a dispute[9] – or where to do so would override class share rights (see Chapter 4 for discussion of s 306 generally).

7.22 Presumably, the same consequence would follow in a situation where the articles require that the meeting remains quorate throughout, as in the model form articles and reg 40 in the 1985 Table A, and members persistently frustrate the transaction of business by leaving the meeting.

CHAIRMAN

Appointment

7.23 Every meeting, whether of the board or of members, must have a chairman. The articles generally provide who may or may not take the chair at a general meeting. For example, regs 39, 25 and 31 in the model form articles for a private company limited by shares, a guarantee company and a public company respectively (and, for companies with older articles, reg 42 of the 1985 Table A) provide for the chairman of the board of directors to chair the

---

[8] *Re El Sombrero Ltd* [1958] Ch 900; *Re H & R Paul & Son Ltd* (1974) 118 SJ 166; *Re Opera Photographic Ltd* [1989] BCLC 763.
[9] *Ross v Telford* [1997] BCC 945.

general meeting. If no chairman has been appointed, or if he is unwilling to act, or if the chairman is not present within a specified time (usually 10 or 15 minutes from the time fixed for starting the meeting) the directors present (or, if there are none, the meeting itself) must appoint a director or a member[10] to chair the general meeting. The appointment of the chairman of the meeting must be the first business of a general meeting.

7.24 There are additional considerations for companies with a Premium listing on the London Stock Exchange, to whom the UK Corporate Governance Code (formerly the UK Combined Code) applies on a 'comply or explain' basis. Code Provision A.3.1 says a person to be appointed as chairman of such a company should meet the same independence criteria as non-executive directors (set out in Code Provision B.1.1) and the company's nomination committee should prepare a job specification, including an assessment of the time commitment expected, recognising the need for availability in the event of crises. A chairman's other significant commitments should be disclosed to the board before appointment and included in the annual report. Changes to such commitments should be reported to the board as they arise, and their impact explained in the next annual report.[11]

7.25 These rules apply even if the chairman of the board of directors, or some other director appointed to chair the general meeting, is not himself a member of the company.

7.26 In the absence of any provisions in the articles as to who may or may not be chairman of a general meeting, any member elected by the members present may be a chairman (s 319(2)).

7.27 In addition, CA 2006, s 328 says that, in the absence of any provisions in the articles as to who may or may not be chairman of a general meeting, any proxy elected by the members present may be a chairman.

Authority, duties and powers

7.28 The chairman's authority is delegated to him by the company under its articles, or by that meeting by which he is appointed or by a combination of the two. Where a number of persons assemble and put a person in the chair they confer on that person by agreement the conduct of that assembled body.

7.29 The person presiding over a general meeting of members is, in the capacity as chairman of the meeting, acting as the representative of the members present at the meeting, not as the representative of the directors.

---

[10] *Re Salcombe Hotel Development Corporation Ltd* [1991] BCLC 44. See also *Re Bradford Investments* [1991] BCLC 224, in which a proxy assumed the position of temporary chairman in order to elect a proper chairman.
[11] Code Provision B.3.1.

7.30 The fact that the chairman has an interest in the outcome of a decision does not, in itself, impugn the integrity of the process at a meeting. No company contemplates that the chairman will be totally disinterested in every matter, and he is presumed to act in good faith unless it is proven otherwise.[12]

7.31 The chairman's authority, because it comes from the meeting, must be exercised to ascertain the opinion of the majority; to allow a proper discussion of the questions to be decided; and to ensure that the proceedings are conducted in accordance with the articles. He must act honestly and fairly towards all individual interests at the meeting, and his duty is directed generally towards the best interests of the company. This means he must allow all members who wish to speak to a motion to have a reasonable opportunity to do so, even if there is clearly a majority who have already made up their minds.

7.32 It follows that it is the chairman's duty to conduct the meeting in such a way that the business is facilitated and the results of that business clearly defined. He must control and organise meetings; preserve order so they proceed effectively; conduct the proceedings in a proper manner; and take care that the sense of the meeting is properly ascertained on any question properly before it.[13] In the absence of express provisions in the articles, 'the details of the proceedings must be regulated by the persons present and by the chairman, and if his decision is quarrelled with it must be regulated by the majority of those present'.[14] But where CA 2006 or the articles expressly provide for the conduct of meetings, they must be followed.

7.33 The UK Corporate Governance Code (formerly the UK Combined Code) which applies to companies with a Premium listing on the London Stock Exchange on a 'comply or explain basis, says that the chairman is responsible for leadership of the board and ensuring its effectiveness on all aspects of its role.[15] The Code goes on to say that the chairman is responsible for setting the board's agenda and ensuring that adequate time is available for discussion of all agenda items, in particular strategic issues. It also says that the chairman should promote a culture of openness and debate by facilitating the effective contribution of non-executive directors in particular and ensuring constructive relations between executive and non-executive directors. The chairman is also responsible, under the Code, for ensuring that the directors receive accurate, timely and clear information. The chairman should ensure effective communication with shareholders.[16]

---

[12] *Blair v Consolidated Enfield Corporation* [1995] 4 SCR, on appeal from the Court of Appeal for Toronto.
[13] *National Dwelling Society v Sykes* [1894] 3 Ch 159; *R v D'Oyly* (1840) 12 A&E 139.
[14] *Wandsworth Gaslight Co v Wright* (1870) 22 LT 404.
[15] Main Principle A3.
[16] Code Provision A.2.1 also says that, in companies to which the Code applies, the roles of chairman and chief executive should not be exercised by the same individual, and the division of responsibilities between them should be clearly established, set out in writing and agreed by the board. Code Provision A.3.1 says that if, exceptionally, a board decides that a chief

7.34 The chairman has no power to determine the matters or issues which a meeting takes into account when considering resolutions; those are matters for the whole meeting.[17]

7.35 If legal advice is taken, the chairman's reliance on it must be reasonable and in good faith. If it is, the chairman is acting honestly and in good faith in the best interests of the company.[18]

7.36 It is the duty of a chairman to rule on points of procedure. If the chairman's ruling is wrong, he may, of course, be called upon to answer for his conduct and legal proceedings may follow, which may result in the proceedings of the meeting being declared invalid.[19] Generally, however, the chairman of a general meeting has prima facie to decide all incidental questions which arise at such a meeting, and require a decision at that time.[20]

7.37 This general power of the chairman and its concomitant limitations have been summarised as follows:[21]

> 'Where a chairman frustrates the business of a meeting by wilfully and without good reason preventing that business from being considered, the meeting may in view of his gross violation of duty supersede him as chairman and go on to transact the business. But if in good faith the chairman gives a decision upon a matter of difficulty, such as has arisen in connection with the notice in this case, I am not prepared to hold that his decision can be ignored and overturned there and then. In my opinion in such a case his decision must stand until it is set aside by the Court, or by a general meeting properly convened for that purpose.'

7.38 In more detail, the chairman's duties and powers in relation to general meetings are as follows.

To regulate the course of the proceedings at the meeting

Right to speak

7.39 Every member should, where practicable, have an opportunity of speaking upon each resolution – the chairman should impartially allow supporters and opponents of the resolution equal opportunities of speaking, and have regard to the rights of minorities. No second speech should be

---

executive should become chairman, the board should consult major shareholders in advance and should set out its reasons to shareholders at the time of the appointment and in the next annual report.

[17] *Alletta Nash v Chelsea College of Art & Design* [2001] EWHC 538, a case concerning judicial review of a decision of an academic decision.
[18] *Blair v Consolidated Enfield Corporation* [1995] 4 SCR, on appeal from the Court of Appeal for Toronto.
[19] *Henderson v Bank of Australasia* (1890) 45 ChD 330.
[20] *Re Indian Zoedone Co* (1884) 26 ChD 70.
[21] These words are believed to have been used by Lord Wark in *Melville v Graham-Yooll*, an unreported case referred to in [1936] SLT 54.

allowed except that the mover of the resolution should have a right of reply. Every speech should be addressed to the chairman in his capacity as chairman.

7.40 There are special rules for a 'traded company'. Section 319A,[22] provides that, if the company is a traded company (see s 360C and **6.4**), any question put by a member at the meeting and related to the business being dealt with at the meeting must be answered unless:

- It has already been answered on a website, in the form of an answer to a question.

- It is undesirable in the interests of the company or the good order of the meeting that the question be answered.

- To answer it would:
    - Interfere unduly with the preparation for the meeting.
    - Involve the disclosure of confidential information.

7.41 The articles usually provide that any director may speak at a general meeting, irrespective of whether he is a member or not.

Relevance of debate

7.42 Every member who speaks should direct their speech strictly to the resolution under discussion, or to an explanation or to a question of order. The chairman is entitled to prevent discussion taking place which is not relevant to the business of the meeting. Sometimes a time-limit on the length of speeches is fixed, which may be varied with the consent of the meeting.

Order of speaking

7.43 The order in which members should speak is determined by the chairman, who should endeavour to ascertain either the implied or express wishes of the meeting on this matter. In the case of dispute the chairman is entitled to determine who should address the meeting, and to protect the speaker from interruption.

7.44 According to custom, the member who is entitled to address the meeting is the one who first rises to speak or otherwise indicates a desire to speak and who is observed by the chairman. If a meeting declines to accept the choice of the chairman as to who shall speak, for example, when several members simultaneously indicate a desire to address the meeting, it is open to the meeting to resolve this matter by formal motion (for example, that Mrs A be

---

[22] Inserted by the Companies (Shareholders' Rights) Regulations 2009, SI 2009/1632, reg 12.

now heard). However, deference to the chairman is a principle which should be observed. Furthermore, it is not open to the majority to prevent the views of the minority being put forward.[23]

Amendments to the resolutions proposed

7.45 The business transacted must come within the scope of the notice given, and the chairman should refuse to allow any proposed resolution to be put to the meeting which does not come within the scope of the notice.

7.46 Much difficulty may arise from amendments. There is some scope for amendment of ordinary resolutions, but it seems that no amendments (other than to correct typographical errors) should be accepted to a special resolution (see Chapter 6).

Keeping order

7.47 The chairman should insist on members refraining from unseemly interruptions or making a running commentary on the remarks of the speaker. Similarly, the holding of private conversations sotto voce during the debate, or any other conduct tending to disturb the meeting, should be prevented by the chairman. The chairman should call a member to order for repetition, unbecoming language, imputation of improper motives to other attendees or any other breach of order, and may direct such member, if speaking, to discontinue his speech. If cautions from the chairman are persistently disregarded, the offending member should be requested to retire from the meeting, and, if necessary, be removed from the meeting. If there is total disorder, the chairman will adjourn the meeting – see Chapter 9.

Points of order

7.48 Points of order which may be raised by any member, whether the member has previously spoken or not, should be taken as soon as they are brought to the notice of the chairman. Explanations, which should be brief and to the point, must not introduce new topics. The chairman should not allow a speech or debate to follow an explanation. The chairman's decision on points of order is final.

Separate resolutions

7.49 Where notice has been given of several resolutions, each resolution must, if any member so requires, be put separately and not en bloc. Any poll on a resolution must be taken separately.[24] In this context, it should also be noted that at a meeting of a public company a motion for the appointment of two or more directors cannot be made by a single resolution unless that course is

---

[23] *Constable v Harris* (1824) T&R 496; *Wall v London and Northern Assets Corporation* [1898] 2 Ch 480.
[24] Companies Act 2006 (Commencement No 5, Transitional Provisions and Savings) Order 2007, SI 2007/3495.

resolved upon by the meeting without dissent. If it is not so resolved, the appointment of each director must be resolved upon by a separate resolution (s 160).

To close the meeting with its consent

7.50 When the views of the minority have been heard, it is competent for the chairman, with the sanction of a vote of the meeting, to declare the discussion closed and to put the question to vote.[25] This procedure can be important if a minority are wasting time and repeating arguments or digressing into irrelevancies.

To adjourn the meeting

7.51 With the consent of the meeting, and in various other circumstances, the chairman may adjourn it. See Chapter 9.

To make arrangements for taking a poll and to receive or reject proxies

7.52 The chairman's decision as to the rejection of proxies will be decisive until reversed by the court. See Chapter 8.

To exercise a casting vote

7.53 Sections 281 and 282 of CA 2006 have the inadvertent effect of making void a resolution passed on a show of hands at a company meeting by use of a casting vote of the chairman. A company may not therefore be formed with, or (subject to the exception mentioned below) alter its articles to include, a casting vote on a show of hands. However, the fifth commencement order[26] to CA 2006 includes a saving provision for the chairman's casting vote for those companies that had a provision in their articles conferring a casting vote on the chairman immediately before 1 October 2007. Such companies may continue to be able to take advantage of that provision. The saving also allows companies that had such a provision immediately before 1 October 2007, but have since removed it, to reinstate it should they wish to do so. If the articles are effective to confer a casting vote on the chairman, it may only be exercised if there is an equality of valid votes. If the chairman does not exercise his casting vote in such a situation, the motion is not carried. A chairman may also have an ordinary vote if he is a member of the company (as is usually the case). A chairman may cast a contingent or hypothetical vote to come into operation if, in the course of subsequent proceedings, it should appear that there has been an equality of valid votes.[27]

---

[25] *Blair Open Hearth Furnace Co v Reigart* (1913) 108 LT 665.
[26] *Wall v London & Northern Assets Corporation* [1898] 2 Ch 469.
[27] *Bland v Buchanan* [1901] 2 KB 75.

7.54 Since a casting vote, if one applies, is conferred on the office of chairman, and not on the individual, it must be exercised as a fiduciary power in what the chairman considers to be the interests of the company as a whole.

To declare the result of voting

7.55 Section 320 provides that, unless a poll is demanded and not subsequently withdrawn, the chairman's declaration that a resolution has or has not been passed, or is passed by a particular majority, is conclusive without proof of the number or proportion of the votes recorded for or against the resolution. An entry in respect of the declaration in the minutes of the meeting is also conclusive evidence of that fact, without such proof. The articles of some companies (for example, where reg 47 of the 1985 Table A applies) extend this principle to the voting on all resolutions by providing that, unless a poll is demanded, a declaration by the chairman that a resolution has been carried, carried unanimously, carried by a particular majority, lost or lost by a particular majority and an entry made in the minutes to that effect is conclusive, without proof of the number or proportion of the votes recorded for or against the resolution. A properly made and bona fide chairman's declaration under these provisions will prevent the question being reopened in legal proceedings even if evidence is forthcoming that the chairman's declaration was wrong.[28] The only exceptions to this are:

- where there is an apparent error, such as where the chairman states the number of votes given and they are insufficient[29] or where it is plain on the face of the proceedings that the requisite majority was not obtained;[30] or

- where there is no apparent opposition to a proposal, but the chairman omits to put it to a show of hands, as required by the articles.[31]

7.56 If any of them apply, regs 43, 29 and 35 in the model form articles for a private company limited by shares, a guarantee company and a public company respectively (and, for companies with older articles, reg 58 of the 1985 Table A) say that the chairman has the final and conclusive power to decide on the qualification of any person to vote at a company meeting. In the absence of bad faith or fraud, the court will not interfere with the exercise by the chairman of this power.[32]

7.57 Finally, it should be noted by way of a proviso to the foregoing that no decision of the chairman will be conclusive if it relates to a resolution that was not in accordance with the notice for the meeting. In *Betts & Co v*

---

[28] *Arnot v United African Lands* [1901] 1 Ch 518.
[29] *Re Caratal (New) Mines* [1902] 2 Ch 498.
[30] *Re Clark & Co* 1911 SC 243.
[31] *Re Citizens Theatre Ltd* 1946 SC 14.
[32] *Wall v London & Northern Assets Corporation (No 2)* [1899] 1 Ch 550; *Wall v Exchange Investment Corporation* [1926] Ch 143.

MacNaghten,[33] it was held that notwithstanding a declaration by the chairman, the notice of the meeting is part of the proceedings and may be looked at to see if the resolution is in accordance with it. If it is not, the chairman's declaration that the resolution was passed is not conclusive. Neither is a chairman's declaration conclusive where there is no quorum, since there would be no properly constituted meeting.

DISPUTING THE CHAIRMAN'S CONDUCT

7.58 An attendee at the meeting may dispute the chairman's conduct of the meeting. But even if the attendee does not, or does not persist with his complaint, he still has the right to seek to impeach the validity of the chairman's conduct after the meeting. If the chairman has improperly deprived the attendee of a right to which he is legally entitled, the validity of the proceedings may be impeached afterwards in any event.

---

[33] [1910] 1 Ch 430.

Chapter 8

VOTING AND PROXIES AT MEMBERS' MEETINGS

GENERAL PRINCIPLES

8.1 Subject to certain contractual and equitable restrictions in favour of third parties (discussed at **8.14**ff), company law[1] allows members holding voting shares to vote as they please.[2] They are not subject to a fiduciary duty to the company, and motive is immaterial:[3]

> 'There is no obligation on a shareholder of a company to give his vote merely with a view to what other persons may consider the interests of the company at large. He has a right, if he thinks fit, to give his vote from motives or promptings of what he considers his own individual interest.'

8.2 This rule is itself, however, subject to the qualification that a majority of the members will not be allowed, by the exercise of their votes, to commit a fraud on the minority.[4] This means, in effect, that a member must not vote so as to give himself (alone, or with other members) something which belongs to, or ought to belong to, the company.[5] Nor may a member vote in a way which benefits that member, or that member and others in their capacity as members, in a way which is detrimental to the interests of other members[6] or which differentiates them, unless, of course, the other members all agree.

8.3 This qualification on the general rule becomes of greater significance in the case of meetings of a class of members:[7]

> 'While usually a holder of shares or debentures may vote as his interests direct, he is subject to the further principle that where his vote is conferred on him as a member of a class he must conform to the interest of the class itself when seeking to exercise the power conferred on him in his capacity of being a member.'

---

[1] Members may also, as a matter of contract law, be restrained by the courts from acting in breach of a shareholders' agreement – for example, one that provides that they will vote in favour of or against certain resolutions: *Greenwell v Porter* [1902] 1 Ch 530.
[2] *Allen v Gold Reefs of West Africa* [1900] 1 Ch 656.
[3] *Pender v Lushington* (1877) 6 ChD 75. For an extreme application of this principle, see *Northern Counties Securities v Jackson and Steeple Ltd* [1974] 1 WLR 1133.
[4] *Menier v Hooper's Telegraph Co* (1874) LR 9 Ch 350.
[5] For examples see *Menier v Hooper's Telegraph Co*, ibid; *Cook v Deeks* [1916] 1 AC 554.
[6] *Clemens v Clemens Bros Ltd* [1976] 2 All ER 268.
[7] *British America Nickel Corporation v O'Brien* [1927] AC 369, at 373; *Goodfellow v Nelson Line* [1912] 2 Ch 324; *Re Holders Investment Trust Ltd* [1971] 1 WLR 583.

One of the most important applications of this qualification is found when members of one class are also members of another class. Such members may not exercise votes at one class meeting to benefit themselves as members, perhaps to a greater extent, of the other class. The court will, however, only interfere to restrain or set aside votes if it is clear that the member was exercising the votes improperly. If there has been a full explanation of the proposal, and it is supported by members with no interest in shares of the other class, the courts will be slow to conclude that the votes of members with an interest in both classes were invalidly cast.

8.4 Members should also be aware of s 994 of the Companies Act 2006 (CA 2006), which allows any member to petition the court for relief on grounds that the company's affairs are being conducted in a manner which is unfairly prejudicial to all, or some part of, the membership (including the petitioner). The powers of the court to grant relief are extremely wide, and include forcing the petitioner, or any other members, to sell his shares to other members, or to the company itself, at fair value.

ENTITLEMENT TO VOTE

8.5 If shares are held jointly then, subject to a company's articles, only the vote of the senior holder who votes (and any proxies duly authorised by him) may be counted by the company. The 'senior holder' is the first-named of the joint holders to appear in the register of members (s 286). In older articles where the 1985 Table A applies, members found to be of unsound mind are also restricted from voting (regs 55 and 56 of the 1985 Table A).

8.6 Regulation 41 of the model form articles for a public company (and, under older articles, reg 57 of the 1985 Table A) provides that a member may not vote in respect of any share unless all monies presently payable in respect of it have been paid. So a share in respect of which a call has been made but not paid carries no voting rights. The model form articles for a private company limited by shares assume that all shares will be issued as fully paid. There is therefore no reference in them to making a call on shares, or the effect on a member's voting rights if a call is not paid.

8.7 Articles normally contain restrictions on the power of directors to vote at board meetings on transactions or arrangements in which they are interested.[8] In addition, s 239 says that, if a director or former director (including a shadow director) is also a member, and they vote on a member's resolution to ratify their own conduct[9] amounting to negligence, default, breach of duty or breach of trust in relation to the company, their vote does

---

[8] See regs 14 and 16 in the model form articles for a private and public company limited by shares respectively. See also regs 85 and 86 of the 1985 Table A.

[9] 'Conduct' for these purposes includes both acts and omissions. *East Pant-Du United Mining Co v Merryweather* (1864) 2 H & M 254.

not count.[10] This applies whether the resolution is proposed to a meeting, or as a written resolution. The same applies to the vote of any other member who is 'connected' to them, as defined in s 252.

8.8 They can, however, attend, count towards the quorum and take part in the proceedings at any meeting at which the resolution is considered.

8.9 However, nothing in s 239 affects:

(a) the validity of a decision taken by unanimous consent of the members;

(b) any power of the directors to agree not to sue, or to settle or release a claim made by them on behalf of the company;

(c) any other enactment or rule of law imposing additional requirements for valid ratification; or

(d) any rule of law as to acts that are incapable of being ratified by the company.

8.10 Articles frequently provide that certain classes of shares (for example, preference shares):

- confer no vote at general meetings;

- confer a right to vote only on certain specified matters; or

- confer a right to vote only if the preference dividend is in arrears for a certain period.

8.11 Listed UK companies may impose sanctions on members who do not provide information pursuant to a notice served under s 793 of CA 2006 (requesting information about the beneficial ownership of its shares), which may include cessation of voting rights.[11]

8.12 Very infrequently, provisions in older company's articles state that a member may not exercise votes in respect of shares until that member has held them for a specified period. In other cases, voting rights are exercisable by a member only upon a limited number of shares; thus, if the member held more

---

[10] So, in practice, it is better for them not to vote at all.
[11] Listing Rules, para 9.3.9. Such sanctions may not be imposed earlier than 14 days after service of the notice. The only sanction that may be imposed on a member holding less than 0.25% of the relevant class (calculated exclusive of treasury shares) is a prohibition against attending at meetings and voting. For members holding 0.25% or more of the relevant class (calculated exclusive of treasury shares), the articles may also provide for withholding of dividends and restrictions on transfer of shares, for a specified period.

than that number, he had no (or reduced) voting rights in respect of the excess. Neither of these restrictions is common today, but they are still found on occasions.

8.13 Under case-law, it is clear that the right of an alien enemy to vote personally or by proxy in respect of shares in an English company is suspended during war.[12]

THIRD-PARTY INTERESTS IN SHARES

8.14 As between the company and a member, the member is entitled to vote as he pleases even if the company is aware that he is, or may be, under an obligation to a third person (including another member) to vote in a certain way, or as that other person directs, and is, or may be, in breach of that obligation. The company is not entitled to question or reject the member's vote, provided it is cast in accordance with the articles.[13]

8.15 As between the member and the third party, however, the court will (if an application is made to it by the third party), restrain the exercise of a vote in breach by the member. There are two general classes of cases in which the court will require a member to exercise his vote in a way dictated by another person.

8.16 The first is when a member holds shares in which another person has an interest. For example, a member who holds shares as nominee (ie as a bare trustee for another) is bound to vote as the beneficial owner directs.[14] Similarly, in the absence of a contract to the contrary, a mortgagee to whom shares have been transferred as security for a loan, and who is therefore registered as the owner of the shares, may vote as he pleases. But if he agrees, for valuable consideration, to vote at general meetings of the company in accordance with the wishes of the mortgagor (ie the borrower to whom the shares will have to be retransferred once the loan is repaid), the court will enforce the agreement by mandatory injunction.[15] An agreement made between a member and a buyer of his shares, whereby the member agrees to vote as the buyer directs until the share transfer is registered, is valid and can be enforced.[16] If the member has received payment in full for the shares, such an agreement is probably implied. On the other hand, in the absence of an express agreement to the contrary, a member who has not yet been paid in full for his shares retains the right to decide how those shares should be voted, until the share transfer to the buyer is registered.[17]

---

[12] *Robson v Premier Oil & Co* [1915] 2 Ch 124.
[13] *Siemens Bros v Burns* [1918] 2 Ch 324.
[14] *Wise v Lansdell* [1921] 1 Ch 420.
[15] *Puddephatt v Leith (No 1)* [1916] 1 Ch 200.
[16] *Greenwell v Porter* [1902] 1 Ch 530.
[17] *Musselwhite v CH Musselwhite* [1962] Ch 965.

8.17 The second (of considerable commercial importance) is where that member has entered into a voting agreement with other members to vote in a certain way on a certain issue, as a purely personal obligation.[18] (However, the company itself may not be a party to such a contract.[19])

OBJECTING TO A MEMBER'S RIGHT TO VOTE

8.18 Where there is an objection to a member's right to vote, articles frequently provide that the objection must be raised at the meeting (or adjourned meeting) at which the voter tenders a vote, and the articles make the chairman of the meeting the person who decides upon any such objection (see, for example, regs 43, 29 and 35 in the model articles for a private company limited by shares, private company limited by guarantee and public company respectively and, for older articles, eg 58 in the 1985 Table A). This is an awkward and, in one respect, misleading provision. It is awkward because very often other members who might well wish to object may be unaware that a particular person has voted, or may not then know of a conflict of interest which that person has. It is misleading in the sense that, if a member has voted for improper reasons, the court will interfere, if asked, despite the wording of the article. On the other hand, such an article does seem to mean that objections to the *qualification* of a voter must be taken at the meeting – where they may be answered – and not later. Every vote not disallowed is valid and the chairman's decision is conclusive, whether or not his mind was directed to the point by an objection.[20]

8.19 However, such provisions in a company's articles are given authority by s 287, which says that none of the other statutory provisions in CA 2006 affect:

(a) any provision of a company's articles requiring an objection to a person's entitlement to vote on a resolution to be made in accordance with the articles, and for the determination of any such objection to be final and conclusive; or

(b) the grounds on which such a determination may be questioned in legal proceedings.

VOTES ON A SHOW OF HANDS

8.20 Unless a company's articles provide otherwise, members vote initially on a show of hands, and each member who is present in person has one vote.[21]

---

[18] *Russell v Northern Bank Development Corporation Ltd* [1992] 1 WLR 588.
[19] *Russell v Northern Bank Development Corporation Ltd* [1992] 1 WLR 588.
[20] *Marx v Estates & General Investments Ltd* [1975] STC 671.
[21] Section 284(2), as amended by the Companies (Shareholders' Rights) Regulations 2009, SI 2009/1632.

8.21 In relation to proxy votes on a show of hands, members of both public and private companies have the right to appoint a proxy, or more than one proxy (provided that each proxy is appointed to exercise the rights attached to a different share or shares held by that member) – see **8.81**. This right cannot be diluted by the articles, but may be extended by the articles (s 331).

8.22 Proxies' voting rights on a show of hands were extended by CA 2006 to allow proxies to attend, speak and vote at general meetings on a show of hands, as well as on a poll (s 282). Under CA 1985, they could not vote on a show of hands. A company's articles may also provide proxies with additional rights, over and above their statutory rights.

8.23 CA 2006 also makes it clear, in s 324A,[22] that a proxy is statutorily obliged to vote in accordance with any instructions given by the member appointing him.

8.24 Section 285(1)[23] adds detail by providing that, on a resolution on a show of hands, every proxy present who has been duly appointed by one or more members entitled to vote on the resolution has one vote.

8.25 Section 285(1) is subject to any contrary provision in the company's articles but there are specific limitations in CA 2006 on a company's ability to vary proxy rights in its articles. These are:

- To the extent a company's articles provide for a proxy or proxies to have fewer votes on a resolution by show of hands than the member appointing him would if present in person, they are void, and the proxy or proxies have the same number of votes as the member (s 285).

- The number of proxies appointed by a member cannot exceed the number of shares held by him.

The overall effect is that (unless the articles say otherwise) each of multiple proxies appointed by one member has one vote on a show of hands. This means there is a possibility that, say, an activist member with more than one share could appoint multiple proxies to attend a meeting, and each of them would have a vote (and also be able to speak) on a show of hands whereas, if the activist member attended in person himself, he would only have one vote on a show of hands.

8.26 It is lawful for the articles of a company to restrict the number of votes of proxies, provided that they still have at least one vote between them. One option is therefore for a company to change its articles so that e g they provide that all the proxies of one particular member have only one vote between them. However, this is likely to be unpopular with members, who often want to

---

[22] Inserted into CA 2006 by the Companies (Shareholders' Rights) Regulations 2009, SI 2009/1632, clause 7.
[23] As amended by the Companies (Shareholders' Rights) Regulations 2009, SI 2009/1632.

instruct some proxies to vote one way, and others another. Instead, the Institute of Chartered Secretaries and Administrators (ICSA) suggests (in its *ICSA Guidance on the Implementation of the Shareholder Rights Directive*) that, if the multiple votes of a number of proxies appointed by one member could lead to a different result from that of the single vote that could be cast on a show of hands if the member himself was present, the chairman should demand a poll. It says '... The fact that a shareholder can potentially appoint a different proxy in respect of each share in his holding could result in an anomalous result if a vote is taken on a show of hands. Therefore the chairman of the meeting should be alert to this possibility and require a vote to be taken by way of a poll if necessary.' Another alternative would be to require automatic poll voting on all resolutions, but this would be unusual and, often, administratively inconvenient.

8.27 Chairmen who have not dealt with it before should be briefed before general meetings on this multiple proxy regime and its impact on voting on a show of hands. Clearly the opportunity for a single registered shareholder to appoint multiple proxies who can now all speak and vote on a show of hands brings with it a risk of disruption from activists at general meetings and companies that have not already moved to automatic poll voting may feel that this is an appropriate time to consider doing so.

8.28 Another practical problem arises if different members appoint the same person as their proxy. In that case the proxy only has one vote on a show of hands (and not one vote for each member he represents). The only exception to this is if he has been instructed by one or more of those members to vote for the resolution and by one or more of them to vote against it. In that case, he has one vote for and one vote against the resolution – unless the articles say otherwise (and s 285(5) expressly says they can).

8.29 The position is unclear where a proxy appointed by more than one member has a discretionary vote. What if one shareholder has instructed him to vote for a resolution, and another has given him discretion, and the proxy wants to vote against? Does he have a vote each way, as if he had been instructed by the second appointor to vote against, or just one vote?

8.30 ICSA suggests that the chairman should be alert to situations where the application of each rule would lead to a different result, and demand a poll if that happens. They do not recommend altering the articles.

VOTES ON A POLL

8.31 If there has been a vote on a show of hands, but sufficient members then demand a poll in accordance with the company's articles, members vote on a 'poll' basis instead. On a poll vote in a share company, each member votes according to the number of voting shares he holds (s 284(3)), so the result can be quite different.[24]

8.32 Section 322 provides that, on a poll, a member entitled to more than one vote need not use all his votes, or cast all the votes used in the same way. The object of this provision is to enable a person holding shares as trustee or nominee for more than one person, or appointed as a proxy for more than one member, to vote as he is instructed, even if different instructions require him to vote in different ways.

8.33 Proxies' voting rights on a poll vote at a meeting of a company are dealt with by ss 285(3) and (4).[25] These say that all or any of the voting rights of a member may be exercised by one or more duly appointed proxies provided that, if the member appoints more than one proxy, those proxies, taken together, may not exercise more extensive voting rights than the member could exercise if he were voting in person. These provisions cannot be varied by the articles.

8.34 Proxy voting on a poll were made more flexible than under CA 1985 by s 322A,[26] which says that a company can include provisions in its articles allowing advance voting on a resolution on a poll taken at a meeting.[27]

8.35 If the company is a traded company (see **6.4**), the provisions may not include any restrictions or requirements unless they are both:

- necessary to ensure the identification of the person voting, and

- proportionate to the achievement of that objective.

The company always has power to require reasonable evidence of any non-member's entitlement to vote.

8.36 There are time limits on an advance vote. Articles are void if they require any document casting a vote in advance to be received by the company or another person earlier than:

- in the case of a poll taken more than 48 hours after it was demanded, 24 hours before the time appointed for the taking of the poll;

- in the case of any other poll, 48 hours before the time for holding the meeting or adjourned meeting.

---

[24] In a guarantee company every member has one vote on a poll as well as on a show of hands, so voting on a poll will not affect the result.
[25] As amended by the Companies (Shareholders' Rights) Regulations 2009, SI 2009/1632.
[26] Inserted into CA 2006 by the Companies (Shareholders' Rights) Regulations 2009, SI 2009/1632, clause 5.
[27] Although there are no such provisions in any of the model form articles.

As usual, only working days (or parts of working days) count when calculating these time limits.

8.37 Section 320 says that, unless a poll is demanded and not subsequently withdrawn, the chairman's declaration that a resolution has or has not been passed, or is passed by a particular majority, is conclusive without proof of the number or proportion of the votes recorded for or against the resolution (see **7.55**). An entry in respect of the declaration in the minutes of the meeting is also conclusive evidence of that fact, without such proof.

8.38 Generally, the chairman should make sure proxies are distinguishable from members present in person by use of, for example, different coloured attendance cards.

VOTING BY CORPORATE REPRESENTATIVES

8.39 Under CA 2006, s 323,[28] a member which is a 'corporation' (which includes a body incorporated outside the UK) can appoint one or more 'representatives' to attend general meetings on its behalf.

8.40 If a corporation authorises only one person as its representative, that person is treated as the corporate member present in person, and so can exercise the same powers (including the rights to vote on a show of hands and on a poll) as if he were an individual member in his own right. So, on a vote on a resolution on a show of hands at a meeting of the company, each authorised person has the same voting rights as the corporation would be entitled to if it were an individual member.

8.41 However, if a corporation authorises more than one person then, on a show of hands, each authorised person has the same voting rights as the corporation would be entitled to. On a poll, the situation is more complicated. If more than one authorised person purports to exercise a power (such as voting) in respect of the same shares then:

(a) if they purport to exercise the power in the same way as each other, the power is treated as exercised in that way;

(b) if they do not purport to exercise the power in the same way as each other, the power is treated as not exercised.

Section 323 cannot be overridden by the articles and the articles cannot provide more extensive rights.

8.42 There is no requirement to lodge an appointment of a corporate representative with the company in advance of the meeting, as there is with a

---

[28] As amended by the Companies (Shareholders' Rights) Regulations 2009, SI 2009/1632, clause 6.

proxy notice. While it is prudent for the representative to bring a certified copy of the board resolution of the corporate member appointing him to the members' meeting, his authority rests on the validity of the resolution appointing him, not on his ability to produce evidence of it.[29] A representative could probably insist on a right of entry to a meeting, and to exercise his rights at it.

DEMANDING A POLL

8.43 Since voting is by show of hands unless a poll is demanded, and a poll vote can often change the outcome of a resolution, it is important to understand who can demand a poll. Section 321 provides that a provision of a company's articles is void insofar as it would have the effect of excluding the right to demand a poll at a general meeting on any question (other than the election of the chairman of the meeting, or the adjournment of the meeting).[30]

8.44 A provision is also void if it would make ineffective a demand for a poll on any such question which is made:

- by not less than five members having the right to vote on the resolution;

- by a member or members representing not less than 10% of the total voting rights of all the members having the right to vote on the resolution (excluding any voting rights attached to any treasury shares); or

- by a member or members holding shares in the company conferring a right to vote on the resolution, being shares on which an aggregate sum has been paid up equal to not less than 10% of the total sum paid up on all the shares conferring that right (excluding shares in the company conferring a right to vote on the resolution which are held as treasury shares).

8.45 Section 329(2) goes on to provide that, in applying the provisions of s 321, a demand by a proxy counts for the purposes of the first point above, as a demand by the member; for the purposes of the second point, as a demand by a member representing the voting rights that the proxy is authorised to exercise; and for the purposes of the third point, as a demand by a member holding the shares to which those rights are attached.

8.46 Section 321 overrides any article that purports to make it more difficult to demand a poll. Modern articles, however, usually make it easier to demand a

---

[29] *Moon Development Corporation v Power Boat International* [1995] NZLR 56.
[30] So it is possible for articles to provide that no poll at all may be demanded on the election of a chairman or on a question of adjournment. Accordingly, although it is rare, articles can provide that the election of the chairman or a motion for an adjournment must be determined on a show of hands.

poll. For example, reg 44 in the model form articles of a private company limited by shares says that a poll may be demanded by:

(a) the chairman of the meeting;

(b) the directors;

(c) two or more persons having the right to vote on the resolution; or

(d) a person or persons representing not less than one-tenth of the total voting rights of all the members having the right to vote on the resolution.

8.47 For companies with older articles, reg 46 of Table A provides that a poll may be demanded by:

(a) the chairman;

(b) at least two members having the right to vote at the meeting;

(c) a member or members representing not less than one-tenth of the total voting rights of all the members having the right to vote at the meeting; or

(d) a member or members holding shares conferring a right to vote at the meeting being shares on which an aggregate sum has been paid up equal to not less than one-tenth of the total sum paid up on all the shares conferring that right.

8.48 Section 329 also provides that appointment of a proxy to vote on a matter at a general meeting authorises the proxy to demand or join in demanding a poll on that matter.

8.49 Notwithstanding anything in the articles, there are special rights for members, and proxies for members, to demand a poll in relation to certain aspects of the transaction when a company buys back or redeems its shares under CA 2006.[31]

8.50 Articles will usually also regulate *when* a poll can be demanded. For example, reg 44 in the model form articles for a private company limited by shares, and reg 36 in the model form articles for a public company, provide that a poll can either be demanded in advance of the general meeting where it is to be put to the vote, or at the meeting, either before a show of hands on that resolution or immediately after the result of that show of hands is declared.

---

[31] CA 2006, ss 695(4), 698(4) and 717(4).

8.51 Often, the chairman will demand a poll as soon as a resolution is put (or, sometimes, will demand a poll in relation to all resolutions to be put, at the beginning of the meeting), if the result on a poll could be different from a vote on a show of hands.

8.52 The disadvantage of this, however, is that, in larger companies with institutional members whose votes will always carry the day on a poll, individual members may feel disenfranchised, so that they do not feel it is worth attending – or even continuing as members. Chairmen may want to prepare members for the fact that some matters will go straight to a poll by explaining this in the notice of meeting or a covering letter. Best practice may, however, be to go through the show of hands (so that, even though the ultimate result of the vote will be the same, individual members have the satisfaction, however briefly, of casting their vote on an equal basis with the largest shareholders) but, if the chairman feels that the result might be different, for him to demand a poll.

8.53 If a demand for a poll by members and/or proxies is challenged, it need not be justified if the chairman knows privately that the demand is, in fact, supported by the requisite number.[32] In such a case, it is usually simpler and preferable for the chairman to resolve the point (if entitled under the articles) by demanding the poll himself. If a poll is not taken after a proper demand for a poll has been made, the resolution which has been challenged is void.[33]

8.54 If the chairman thinks that the result of a vote may be different if a poll is demanded, it is his duty to demand one[34] – where, for example, he has been appointed as proxy for a member or members and has been instructed how to vote, and it is extremely likely that his votes cast as proxy on a poll will create a different result from that achieved on a show of hands. He should therefore make sure he has calculated, in advance of the meeting, how many votes he is required to cast, one way or the other, as proxy for members on each resolution.

8.55 What of the converse – a poll is duly demanded but the chairman knows that it will not affect the outcome? Best practice is probably that it is acceptable for the chairman to inform 'anyone demanding a poll' (presumably, in practice, the whole meeting would be informed) of the likely outcome, given the proxies he holds, and ask if they wish to persist with their demand.

8.56 If they do, however, the chairman must comply – they may wish to gauge support for the resolution, or simply to exercise their statutory rights (regardless of the futility of doing so), and the chairman should not prevent them from doing either.

---

[32] *Re Phoenix Electric Light Co* (1883) 48 LT 260.
[33] *R v Cooper* (1870) LR 5 QB 457.
[34] *Second Consolidated Trust Ltd v Ceylon Amalgamated Tea & Rubber Estates Ltd* [1943] 2 All ER 567.

8.57 Another reason why the chairman must accept the demand for a poll is that the presence of a member in person, who votes, overrides the right to vote of his proxy. It is conceivable that the chairman's votes as proxy will be overridden and the outcome will be different, if sufficient of the members who appointed him as proxy attend in person and vote (even though, for the result to be different they would, of course, have to vote contrary to the instructions they actually gave to the chairman in their forms of proxy).

8.58 The articles may provide that the demand for a poll may be withdrawn – often provided that the poll has not yet been taken, and with the consent of the chairman, in which case any pre-existing vote on a show of hands will remain valid.

8.59 If a poll is duly demanded, it is the chairman's duty to fix the time and place for the poll, in accordance with the articles. Articles (for example, reg 44 in the model form articles for a private company limited by shares) frequently provide that a poll must be taken immediately and in such manner as the chairman of the meeting directs.

8.60 However, some differentiate. Regulation 37 in the model form articles for a public company say that a poll on the election of the chairman of the meeting, or a question of adjournment, must be taken immediately, but that polls on other resolutions are to be taken when, where and in such manner as the chairman of the meeting directs, but within 30 days of their being demanded. For older articles, reg 51 in the 1985 Table A is in very similar terms. The articles usually also say that business other than that on which the poll is demanded may proceed in the meantime.

8.61 If the articles give the chairman a power to fix the time and date for a particular poll (rather than requiring him to hold it forthwith), this power is a fiduciary power. It must be exercised in a reasonable way, in the best interests of the company, to enable the members and proxies who are entitled to vote on a poll to record their votes.

8.62 If the articles do not require an immediate poll, but the chairman thinks that the matter is urgent, or that members have already had the opportunity to consider and express their views, he should hold the poll as soon as possible[35] – perhaps immediately, or at the end of the meeting at which it has been demanded. The decision is the chairman's, not the meeting's.

8.63 If the articles allow, and the chairman thinks that, in order to obtain the considered views of members, the poll should be fixed for a future date, he should follow this course, but it would not, for example, be reasonable, or in the best interests of the company, to direct that the poll be taken at midnight on a Saturday, or in a place that members could not conveniently attend.

---

[35] See *Re Chillington Iron Co* (1885) 29 ChD 159.

8.64 Where a poll is not held immediately, articles usually provide that notice need not be given of the time and place for the poll, provided these are announced at the meeting. For example, see reg 37 in the model articles for a public company or, for older articles, reg 52 of the 1985 Table A. If not so announced, both reg 37 and reg 52 require that 7 days' notice be given to members. Where the articles provide that a poll shall be taken within 7 days of the meeting, at a time and place to be fixed by the directors, such time and place must be fixed after a poll has been demanded and cannot be fixed in advance.[36]

8.65 The common law says that a poll is regarded as part of the proceedings of the original meeting. 'The taking of a poll is a mere enlargement of the meeting at which it was demanded.'[37] The poll is complete from the day when the result is ascertained and declared, and not from the end of the voting.[38] Articles usually also expressly provide that the result of the poll is to be deemed to be the resolution of the meeting at which the poll was demanded. For example, see regs 44 and 37 in the model form articles for a private company limited by shares and a public company respectively and, for older articles, reg 49 in the 1985 Table A.

8.66 The usual method for taking a poll in larger companies is to require every member who is entitled to vote to sign a paper (in order to prevent impersonation) headed 'for' or 'against' the motion; the number of votes to which each member is entitled under the articles is inserted against the signature of the member, and these having been added, the chairman declares accordingly. The paper may be a poll card, given to attendees as they arrive, or may be a part of the proxy form or admission card that members bring with them.

8.67 The chairman should explain the reasons for the poll and describe the process, so that members know what is happening.

8.68 Resolutions must be put to the poll separately and not en bloc, otherwise the poll is invalid.[39] All the resolutions may, however, be included on one sheet of paper, to be separately marked by the voters. Usually, members will be asked to complete their poll card(s) as each resolution is proposed.

8.69 It is not obligatory to appoint scrutineers to administer the poll, unless the articles specifically say so. Usually, articles merely give the chairman the option of appointing scrutineers – reg 37 in the model form articles for a public company or, for older companies, reg 49 of Table A, for example, provide that

---

[36] *Re British Flax Producers Co* (1889) 60 LT 215.
[37] *R v Wimbledon Local Board* (1882) 8 QBD 459; *Shaw v Tati Concessions* [1913] 1 Ch 292.
[38] *Holmes v Keyes* [1958] Ch 670. Whether a declaration of the result is strictly necessary is not clear, but it would be difficult, for example, for newly elected directors to act unless they know the result of the vote.
[39] *Patent Wood Keg Syndicate Ltd v Pearse* (1906) WN 164.

the chairman may appoint scrutineers, who need not be members. It seems that, even if the articles do not provide for the appointment of scrutineers, they may still be appointed by the chairman.

8.70 Scrutineers are advisable in larger companies for two reasons. First, the presence of independent scrutineers reduces the danger of a poll being challenged subsequently by a dissident member. Secondly, if, as is usual, the auditors or the company's registrars are appointed as scrutineers, they have the staff and experience necessary for conducting the poll. Where there is a dispute, scrutineers representing the warring parties are sometimes appointed jointly, but dissident members have no right to insist on the presence of scrutineers appointed by themselves. There is no duty of confidence on scrutineers or organisers of the poll in relation to the way in which votes are cast, as it is necessary to know how votes are cast in order to determine the validity of the poll.[40] For smaller companies, their value is questionable.

8.71 The right to vote and the number of shares held are determined by reference to the register of members:[41]

> 'The register of shareholders, on which there can be no notice of a trust, furnishes the only means of ascertaining whether you have a lawful meeting or a lawful demand for a poll, or of enabling the scrutineers to strike out votes.'

8.72 A member may vote personally on a poll held subsequent to an original meeting, even if he was not present at the meeting at which the poll was demanded.[42]

8.73 For circumstances in which members may enjoy enhanced voting rights on a poll under the rule in *Bushell v Faith*,[43] see Chapter 3.

8.74 The chairman should fix the hours during which the poll is to take place. If the chairman does not do so, he cannot close the poll so long as votes are coming in. After waiting a reasonable time, if no more voters present themselves, the chairman may declare the poll closed. The improper exclusion of a voter may invalidate a poll.[44]

8.75 Unless the articles specifically provide to the contrary (which the model form articles do not), a poll cannot be taken by sending voting papers to the members, to be lodged with the company. They must attend personally, or their proxies must, in order to vote on the poll.[45] However, s 322A says that a company's articles may provide for advance voting (see **8.34**), subject to restrictions for traded companies, so this may become more common.

---

[40] *Haarhaus & Co GmbH v Law Debenture Trust Corporation plc* [1988] BCLC 640.
[41] *Pender v Lushington* (1877) 6 ChD 70, at 78.
[42] *Campbell v Maund* (1836) 5 A & E 865.
[43] [1970] AC 1099.
[44] *R v Rector etc of St Mary, Lambeth* (1838) 8 A & E 356.
[45] *McMillan v Le Roi Mining Co* [1906] 1 Ch 331.

ANNOUNCING THE RESULTS OF THE POLL

8.76 If a poll is held subsequent to the meeting, members need to be made aware of the results in due course. Listed companies must make a regulatory announcement to the market, and some may publish results in the paper press. The September 2012 version of the *UK Corporate Governance Code* (Provision E.2.2) provides that a listed company to which the Code applies should count all proxy votes and, except where a poll is called, should ensure that the following information is given at the meeting and made available as soon as reasonably practicable on a website maintained by or on behalf of the company:

(a) the number of shares in respect of which proxy appointments have been validly made;

(b) the number of votes for the resolution;

(c) the number of votes against the resolution; and

(d) the number of shares in respect of which the vote was directed to be withheld.

The company should ensure that votes cast are properly received and recorded.

8.77 There are a number of additional requirements for quoted companies. One is that they must disclose the results of all polls taken at a general meeting on a website (s 341). There are also rules as to the minimum information to be disclosed, and as to the website and its availability (s 353).

8.78 Members of a quoted company holding 5% of the voting rights or 100 members holding on average £100 of its paid-up capital can require a report by an independent assessor of any poll taken, or to be taken, at a general meeting, for example, where there is a controversial resolution or where there appears to be a problem relating to voting procedures. They must make their request before, or within one week of, the meeting where the poll is taken (ss 342 to 351).

8.79 Under s 153 of CA 2006 a company is also required to act on a request received under s 342, if the following conditions are met:

(a) it is made by at least 100 persons;

(b) it is authenticated by all the persons making it;

(c) in the case of any person who is not a member of the company, it is accompanied by a statement:

- (i) of the full name and address of a person ('the member') who is a member of the company and holds shares on behalf of that person;
- (ii) that the member is holding those shares on behalf of that person in the course of a business;
- (iii) of the number of shares in the company that the member holds on behalf of that person;
- (iv) of the total amount paid up on those shares;
- (v) that those shares are not held on behalf of anyone else or, if they are, that the other person or persons are not among the other persons making the request;
- (vi) that some or all of those shares confer voting rights that are relevant for the purposes of making a request under the section in question; and
- (vii) that the person has the right to instruct the member how to exercise those rights;

(d) in the case of any of those persons who is a member of the company, it is accompanied by a statement:

- (i) that he holds shares otherwise than on behalf of another person; or
- (ii) that he holds shares on behalf of one or more other persons but those persons are not among the other persons making the request;

(e) it is accompanied by such evidence as the company may reasonably require of the matters mentioned in paragraphs (c) and (d);

(f) the total amount of the sums paid up on:

- (i) shares held as mentioned in paragraph (c); and
- (ii) shares held as mentioned in paragraph (d),

divided by the number of persons making the request, is not less than £100;

(g) the request complies with any other requirements of the section in question as to contents, timing and otherwise.

8.80 This is to ensure that, where indirect investors have been nominated to enjoy certain rights of membership by members pursuant to s 146, they are able to count towards the total required under s 342, subject to certain conditions. The conditions are intended to ensure that only genuine indirect investors are allowed to count towards the total, that the same shares cannot be used twice and that the indirect investor's contractual arrangements with the member allow the former to give voting instructions.

APPOINTING PROXIES, AND PROXY NOTICES

8.81 The word 'proxy' is often used, confusingly, to describe both the person appointed in the place of another to represent him at a general meeting and also the instrument by which such a person is appointed. The articles usually provide that there must be such an instrument – for example, regs 45 and 38 in the model form articles for a private company limited by shares and a public company respectively, say proxies must be appointed by a notice in writing, which the model articles refer to as a 'proxy notice'. Here the person is referred to as a 'proxy', and the instrument appointing him is referred tor (following the model form articles) as a 'proxy notice'.

8.82 The right for a member (including any person nominated by a member pursuant to s 145 – see **5.122**) of a company to appoint another person as his proxy to exercise all or any of his rights to attend and to speak and to vote at general meetings is statutory (s 324).

8.83 It is common practice to send out a proxy notice for appointment of a proxy (or proxies) with the notice of meeting, together with instructions on how to complete and return it for an effective proxy appointment. Larger companies often issue (at their own expense) invitations to appoint as proxy a specified person (such as the chairman) or a number of specified persons. If they do CA 2006 s 326 imposes conditions. Section 326 says that, in those circumstances, the invitations must be issued to all the members entitled to vote at the meeting, unless:

- the form of appointment naming the proxy or a list of persons willing to act as proxy is issued to a member at his request; and

- the form or list is available on request to all members entitled to vote at the meeting.

8.84 The expenses incurred by a board in sending out forms of proxy are properly payable by the company. In *Peel v London and North Western Railway Co*,[46] it was held that it was the duty of the directors to inform the members of the facts of their policy, and the reason why they considered that this policy should be maintained and supported by the members, and that they were justified in trying to influence and secure votes for this purpose, and accordingly that expenses which had thus been bona fide incurred in the interest of the company were properly payable out of the funds of the company. These expenses included the issuing of stamped proxy papers containing the names of three directors as proposed proxies, with a stamped envelope for return. This is an important decision in relation to takeover bids and in cases where a group of members is attacking the directors, for it enables directors to use the company's funds to defend their policy.

---

[46] [1907] 1 Ch 5.

8.85 CA 2006 does not specify any particular form of proxy notice, and neither do the model form articles. However, the model form articles (in regs 45 and 38 for a private company limited by shares and a public company respectively) do give a company power to require that proxy notices be delivered in a particular form, and to specify different forms for different purposes. Particularly, they say a proxy notice can specify how the proxy is to vote (or that he must abstain) on each resolution. However, they go on to say that, unless a proxy notice says otherwise, the default position is that:

(a) a proxy has discretion how to vote on any ancillary or procedural resolutions put to the meeting; and

(b) appointing a person as a proxy for a meeting also means he is appointed proxy in relation to any adjournment of that meeting as well.

However, for companies with older articles, Table A offers two types of proxy notice: one where there is an open discretion to the appointee as to how to vote (reg 60); the other where the proxy is directed how to vote (the 'two-way' form) (reg 61). The Stock Exchange requires, for listed companies, that members are sent a three-way form.[47]

8.86 Regulations 45 and 31 also say that a proxy notice must:

(a) state the name and address of the member appointing the proxy;

(b) identify the person appointed to be that member's proxy and the general meeting he is appointed to attend;

(c) be signed by or on behalf of the member appointing the proxy, or authenticated in a way determined by the directors may determine; and

(d) be delivered to the company in accordance with the articles and any instructions contained in the notice of the relevant general meeting.

Companies should consider carefully whether they will include any electronic address (such as an email address) on the proxy notice (or any other documents relating to the relevant general meeting), as this can amount to an implied acceptance that members may return their proxy notices electronically to that address. See Chapter 11.

8.87 Some of the difficulties which have arisen from use of two-way proxies in the past could have been avoided by a more carefully worded proxy notice. For example, the form should make clear whether the proxy may exercise discretion how he votes on an amendment or on a motion to adjourn the meeting. These points can be important if (as is usually the case) the chairman has been appointed proxy for a large number of members and he is uncertain as to his

---

[47] Listing Rules, para 9.3.6.

powers. In some cases, the proxy's course of conduct will be easy to decide,[48] but on other occasions the proxy may be unclear as to what he can and should do.

8.88 The usual rule in the case of a proposal to adjourn is that, if the intention of the adjournment is to muster support to defeat a resolution, a proxy instructed to vote in favour of the resolution must oppose the adjournment. If instructed to vote against the resolution, he should support the adjournment. There may, however, be less clear-cut circumstances, in which his only course is to cast his appointor's vote in what he honestly believes to be the best interests of his appointor, or (if he considers that to be in his appointor's best interests and he is not under a fiduciary duty to vote – see **8.14**) abstain.

8.89 Amendments are more difficult for proxies. Ordinarily, if the proxy has been instructed to vote in favour of the resolution to be amended, he can infer that his appointor(s) wished the resolution to be passed as it stands. He should therefore oppose any amendment. But what if the proxy has been directed to vote in favour of a scheme which the directors had initially recommended, but now finds that a more favourable scheme is offered. Should he vote against the amendment if he honestly believes that the new scheme is in his appointor's best interests? In such a case, it seems that the proxy may not vote contrary to his authority, but is probably entitled to refrain from using the vote altogether – ie to abstain.

8.90 The situation is different if the proxy is under some contractual or fiduciary obligation to the member, for example, as the member's solicitor. In that case, the proxy must in principle exercise the vote. This may be as directed or in the member's interests, depending on the nature of the obligation.

8.91 It is sometimes suggested that those who solicit proxies (as the chairman will frequently do, by including 'the chairman' as default proxy on the proxy notice) are also under an obligation to exercise the member's vote(s), and may not abstain. The rationale for this argument is that, if he were able to abstain on a two-way proxy notice, the chairman might abstain from casting proxy votes that did not accord with his view of the best interests of the company. But it would be a brave chairman who thought he could breach his duty to his appointor in this way, as analysis of his voting record would soon reveal what he was up to.

8.92 The better view is therefore that the chairman appointed by two-way proxy notice should (like any other proxy) always vote in accordance with his instructions or, if they do not cover the situation, in what he honestly believes would be the wishes of his appointor, but, if he has no idea what his appointor would want, he may abstain.

---

[48] See *Re Waxed Papers Ltd* [1937] 2 All ER 481.

8.93 This is supported in Guidance Notes issued by ICSA,[49] which suggest abstention as a possible course of action for a chairman if (i) instructed to vote against a resolution, (ii) an amendment to that resolution is proposed and (iii) the chairman has no way of knowing what his appointor's view of that amendment would be.

8.94 Where a proxy holder votes contrary to the instructions given in the proxy form, without any apparent justification for doing so, the chairman (or scrutineers) should note the proxies concerned, and if this affects, or could affect, the result of the resolution, application should be made to the court to determine whether the votes be accepted as cast; accepted as the proxy notice directed; or rejected.

8.95 What if the proxy notice does not comply with the articles? Two conflicting principles of law arise, and a chairman may sometimes find it difficult to decide whether to accept or reject a vote which a person claims to exercise as a proxy. The first principle is that it is the duty of the chairman to obtain, if possible, the decision of the members. The second is that, since the right to appoint a proxy is given by contract (that is, the contract constituted by the articles), any member who seeks to exercise the right to appoint a proxy must carry out and comply with whatever the articles specify.

8.96 In accordance with the first principle, it has been decided[50] that where articles prescribed that forms of proxy must be in a specified form 'or as near thereto as circumstances should permit', and the specified form was a proxy applicable to a single meeting, general proxies covering several meetings were permissible.

8.97 On the other hand, where particular formalities are prescribed, they must be followed. If they are not, it is not merely the chairman's right, but his duty, as representing the shareholders, to reject them.

8.98 One formality usually required by the articles is that forms of proxy be deposited with the company in advance of the meeting. CA 2006 prohibits a longer period than 48 hours from being specified (s 327), by making void any provision in a company's articles which would have the effect of requiring the form (and any supporting documents) to be received by the company or another person earlier than the following time:

- in the case of a meeting or adjourned meeting, 48 hours before the time for holding the meeting or adjourned meeting;

---

[49] ICSA Guidance Note 'The Chairman's Obligations Regarding Polls & Proxies', no 020228, available from the Information Centre, ICSA, 16 Park Crescent, London W1B 1AH or e-mail informationcentre@icsa.org.uk. See also www.icsa.org.uk. Note that, whilst this guidance still contains useful pointers that continue to be relevant, it was published in 2002, long before CA 2006 and its associated statutory instruments, came into force.

[50] *Isaacs v Chapman* (1915) 32 TLR 183.

- in the case of a poll taken more than 48 hours after it was demanded, 24 hours before the time appointed for the taking of the poll; and

- in the case of a poll taken not more than 48 hours after it was demanded, the time at which it was demanded.

8.99 The model form articles for a public company (reg 39) provide that any notice of a general meeting must specify the address or addresses (which they call a 'proxy notification address') at which the company or its agents will receive proxy notices relating to that meeting, or any adjournment of it, delivered in hard copy or electronic form. A proxy notice must be delivered to the proxy notification address not less than 48 hours before the general meeting or adjourned meeting to which it relates. It also says:

(a) If a poll is taken more than 48 hours after it is demanded, the notice must be delivered to a proxy notification address not less than 24 hours before the time appointed for the taking of the poll.

(b) If a poll is not taken during the meeting but taken not more than 48 hours after it was demanded, the proxy notice must be delivered to the proxy notification address not less than 48 hours before the general meeting or adjourned meeting to which it relates and, at the meeting at which the poll was demanded, to the chairman, secretary or any director.

If a proxy notice is not signed by the person appointing the proxy, it must be accompanied by written evidence of the authority of the person who executed it to execute it on the appointor's behalf.

8.100 There are additional rules for traded companies (see **6.4**). Section 327(A1)[51] says that the appointment of a person as proxy for a member must be notified to the company in writing, and the company may require reasonable evidence of the identities of both the member and of the proxy, the member's instructions (if any) as to how the proxy is to vote, and where the proxy is appointed by a person acting on behalf of the member, that person's authority. However, it may not impose any further requirements.

8.101 Section 333A[52] provides that a traded company must provide an electronic address (see s 333(4)) for the receipt of any document (which, in this section, includes the appointment of a proxy for a meeting, any document necessary to show the validity of, or otherwise relating to, the appointment of a proxy, and a notice of the termination of the authority of a proxy) or information relating to proxies for a general meeting. For the purposes of this section, the company is deemed to have agreed that any such document or

---

[51] Inserted by the Companies (Shareholders' Rights) Regulations 2009, SI 2009/1632, para 13.
[52] Also inserted by the Companies (Shareholders' Rights) Regulations 2009, SI 2009/1632, para 13.

information relating to proxies for the meeting may be sent by electronic means to that address – although subject to any limitations specified by the company when providing it.

8.102 It must do so either by:

- giving it when sending out an instrument of proxy for the purposes of the meeting or issuing an invitation to appoint a proxy for those purposes; or

- ensuring that it is made available, throughout the period beginning with the first date on which notice of the meeting is given and ending with the conclusion of the meeting, on the website on which the information required by s 311A(1) (see **6.53**) is made available.

8.103 There are two changes in s 327 from the previous CA 1985 provision. The first is that weekends, Christmas Day, Good Friday and any bank holiday are excluded when calculating the minimum 48-hour notice required to appoint proxies. The second is that polls which are not taken immediately are covered by the rules as well as meetings and adjourned meetings.

8.104 The importance of strictly complying with formalities specified in the articles about place or time of deposit, or the form of address on an envelope, is illustrated by *Burnett v Gill*.[53] In this case, the articles provided that no person should be entitled to vote as a proxy unless the instrument appointing that person was deposited at the office of the company 48 hours before the meeting. The company's registered office was the office of the secretary, a chartered accountant. It was held that a proxy addressed to 'The Chairman of the Meeting, c/o The Secretary' whose name only was mentioned, was not duly deposited at the office.

8.105 In *Harben v Phillips*, Cotton LJ explained the principle which justifies requiring compliance with formalities in the articles:[54]

> 'The right of a shareholder to vote by proxy depends on the contract between himself and his co-shareholders, and where parties have a right depending upon the contract between them and the other parties, then, in my opinion, all the requisitions of the contract as to the exercise of the right must be followed.'

8.106 In that case, it was held that the proxy papers which were not attested as required by the articles were improperly admitted by the chairman. Presumably, even though the right of members of a company limited by shares to appoint a proxy is now conferred by CA 2006, the articles may still validly require attestation of the proxy notice. If they do, the person appointed as proxy cannot act as an attesting witness.[55]

---

[53] (1906) *The Times*, June 13.
[54] (1883) 23 ChD 14, at 32.
[55] *Re Parrott* [1891] 2 QB 151.

8.107 Articles may provide that a vote given in accordance with the terms of an instrument of proxy is to be regarded as valid, notwithstanding the death or insanity of the principal, or revocation of the proxy or authority under which it was executed or the transfer of the share under which it was given, unless notice of the event giving rise to the invalidity is received at the registered office before the meeting (or adjourned meeting) at which the proxy is to be used. In *Cousins v International Brick Co*,[56] the articles contained a similar provision, but it was held that a member who had given a proxy notice, and had not revoked it, could attend the meeting personally and vote, in which case his proxy could not vote for him.

8.108 The provision for revocation of a proxy notice by 'a transfer of the share under which it is given' is a dangerous one: in order to give it any meaning, the word 'transfer' must mean something less than registration of the transfer in the register of members. If so, sending of a transfer form to the company probably constitutes notice of the transfer for this purpose. The result will be that, until the transfer is registered, the shares concerned may be effectively disenfranchised. The transferor remains on the register, but is treated as having revoked any proxy notice which he had given previously, and will probably be disinclined to go to the meeting personally (just to vote as the transferee wishes) or appoint a new proxy (and direct him to vote as the transferee wishes) or to go to a general meeting because, by that time, the transferor will probably not be concerned as to whether the votes are exercised or not.

8.109 Difficult problems frequently arise as to which of two or more forms of proxy is valid. It is sometimes thought that a later form automatically revokes an earlier one, but this is not so. There are two aspects to the problem: first, what was the intention of the appointor; secondly, what is the evidence of this intention? It will normally be the intention of a person who makes a new appointment that a former appointment be revoked and replaced by the new one, but this will not necessarily be the case. The appointor may forget about the earlier proxy; the appointor may intend that both appointments should be effective, perhaps in order to increase his voting rights; the appointor may think that he is required to fill up a second proxy form which has been sent to him; or the appointor may wish to confuse the matter for the sake of confusion. As to the evidence of the intention, there is usually none – except perhaps a date on the proxy notice or the date when it is received. But with modern postal delays, date of receipt is little guide, and dates on the forms themselves are by no means conclusive. The matter may be further complicated if an earlier proxy is stated to be irrevocable, or if the company is on notice that it was given, irrevocably, for valuable consideration.

---

[56] [1931] 2 Ch 90.

8.110 The problem should be avoided (as far as possible) by some provision in the articles, along the lines set out below. Even if not included in the articles, the following may be treated as guidelines, to enable a chairman or scrutineer to decide on proxy problems:

(1) if there are two or more forms of proxy for the same member, or the same shares, the later in date (if given) should be accepted, to the exclusion of the earlier;

(2) if there is no date, the one which appears on the evidence to have been signed later should be accepted to the exclusion of the others;

(3) if there is no sufficient evidence, and both proxy holders claim the right to vote, they should both be excluded since neither can establish the right;

(4) if a later proxy notice is received too late to be used at the meeting, it will, nevertheless, constitute notice of revocation of the earlier proxy. If the meeting is adjourned, or a poll is held later, the later proxy notice may be valid for that purpose;

(5) if the earlier proxy notice, in any of the above cases, was made irrevocable for valuable consideration and the proxy holder claims that he is still entitled to the vote, that claim should be recognised as being the valid compliance with the requirements of the articles for voting by proxy. A shareholder must not be assumed to intend to commit a breach of the contract with the earlier proxy holder, and any later proxy should be rejected so long as the first proxy holder claims the right to vote; and

(6) if the member is personally present at the meeting, this presence will not of itself revoke the authority given to the proxy. If the member seeks to vote, this will displace his proxy on that resolution, but the authority revives for subsequent purposes unless, once again, the member acts to displace the proxy's authority.

8.111 It has been decided that, if the articles provide that a proxy notice shall be valid, notwithstanding that it has been revoked, unless notice of revocation is received before the meeting, then that provision means exactly what it says. Accordingly, a revocation notice received after the commencement of the meeting but before a poll is taken is ineffective.[57] If, however, the member votes in person, this will constitute valid revocation.[58]

8.112 A proxy notice for a specified meeting is not valid for a different meeting. This will be so even if the specified meeting never takes place and another meeting is called instead, but to consider identical business. A similar

---

[57] *Spiller v Mayo* [1926] WN 78.
[58] *Cousins v International Brick Co Ltd* [1931] 2 Ch 90.

type of issue arose in *Oliver v Dalgleish*,[59] where various forms of proxy appointed X as proxy for a number of shareholders, for a meeting to be held on a particular day. The forms described the meeting as an annual general meeting whereas it was, in fact, an extraordinary general meeting. Some of the forms instructed X to vote against the resolutions. X simply marked his voting paper 'for' the resolutions, without stating how many votes he cast. The chairman rejected all his votes.

8.113 It was held (a) that the misdescription of the meeting did not invalidate the forms of proxy and (b) that the failure to obey the instructions on some of the proxy forms did not invalidate all the votes cast by X. He should be taken to have cast his votes in favour of the resolutions in all those circumstances where he was entitled to do so. The more difficult question – about the votes he was instructed to cast against the resolution – did not arise since they were insufficient to affect the outcome of the vote.

8.114 An adjourned meeting, as regards notice, is regarded in law as a continuance of the original meeting.[60] Consequently, where the articles require proxies to be lodged before 'the meeting' this means the original meeting.[61]

8.115 Forms of proxy may now be lodged with the company electronically (see Chapter 11).

---

[59] [1963] 1 WLR 1274.
[60] *Scadding v Lorant* (1851) 3 HLC 418.
[61] *McLaren v Thomson* [1917] 2 Ch 261.

Chapter 9

ADJOURNMENTS OF MEMBERS' MEETINGS

EXERCISE OF THE CHAIRMAN'S POWER TO ADJOURN

9.1 Where the articles make no provision for adjournment, the power of adjournment of a quorate meeting is vested in the meeting.[1] The chairman cannot adjourn the meeting without its authority. If he purports to do so, the meeting may proceed in any event. Motions for adjournment can generally be brought forward at any period of the meeting, and take precedence over any matter then under consideration.

9.2 Usually, however, the articles do provide for the question of adjournment of a quorate meeting. Regulations 41, 27 and 33 in the model form articles for a private company limited by shares, a guarantee company or a public company respectively (and, for companies with older articles, reg 45 of the 1985 Table A), for example, provide that the chairman of the meeting may, with the consent of a meeting at which a quorum is present (and shall, if so directed by the meeting), adjourn the meeting. Under an article such as this the power for adjournment is given absolutely to the meeting.

9.3 Sometimes, however, the articles provide only that the chairman may adjourn with the consent of the meeting – they do not *require* the chairman to adjourn if directed by the meeting. In that case the chairman cannot adjourn without the consent of the meeting, but cannot be compelled to adjourn the meeting against his wishes, even if a majority of the members are demanding an adjournment.[2]

9.4 Any power of the chairman to adjourn – or not to adjourn – is fiduciary. The chairman is not entitled to adjourn a meeting capriciously before the business of the meeting has been transacted, and if he purports to do so without good reason, the meeting may appoint another chairman and proceed with the business.[3] Similarly, the chairman may not adjourn to a place or time which would be unreasonable for shareholders.

9.5 Since the chairman's power is fiduciary, he will sometimes be under a duty to adjourn, or ask for an adjournment. If, for example, he believes that

---

[1] Cf *R v Grimshaw* (1847) 11 Jur 965; *Stoughton v Reynolds* (1736) 2 Strange 1045; *National Dwellings Society v Sykes* [1894] 3 Ch 159.
[2] *Salisbury Gold Mining Co v Hathorn* [1897] AC 268.
[3] *National Dwellings Society v Sykes* [1894] 3 Ch 159.

shareholders should be given an opportunity to reconsider a proposal, or to consider an alternative, or to review the matter in the light of changed circumstances, the chairman should exercise any power he has to adjourn, or ask for members' consent to an adjournment, and should explain why he is doing so.

9.6 In the unusual situation where the meeting is in disorder, all of the model form articles give the chairman power to adjourn the meeting if it appears to him that it is necessary to do so to protect the safety of any attendee, or ensure that the business of the meeting is conducted in an orderly manner.

9.7 If the articles make no provision, and the disorder is such that the views of the members cannot be ascertained (even after 'earnest and sustained efforts'[4]), the chairman has an inherent power (whatever the provisions of the articles) to adjourn the meeting. This should be for as short a time as possible, and he should take steps, so far as possible, to ensure that all present know of the adjournment.[5] In some circumstances he will have a duty to adjourn – where, for example, the safety of members is at risk.

9.8 Aspects of the inherent power of the chairman to adjourn were considered by the Court of Appeal in *Byng v London Life Association Ltd*.[6] The article considered in this case gave the chairman, with the consent of a quorate meeting, the power to adjourn. The Court of Appeal held that, even if it was not possible for the chairman validly to ascertain the views of the meeting on an adjournment, the article did not reduce the chairman's fundamental common law duty to ensure that all who were entitled to be heard and to vote were given the opportunity to do so.

9.9 The reason that it had become impossible to proceed with the meeting and impossible to ascertain the views of the members on adjournment in *Byng* was that the meeting was being held in a series of rooms which were supposedly linked by audio-visual means. However, the audio-visual system broke down and it became impossible to communicate adequately between the rooms. While the Court of Appeal upheld the residual common law power of the chairman to adjourn in these circumstances, it held that it was not sufficient that the chairman merely exercised the power of adjournment in good faith. Rather, the power must be exercised upon the basis of the principles laid down in *Associated Provincial Picture Houses Ltd v Wednesbury Corporation*[7] for the proper exercise of a discretion.

9.10 In the context of company meetings, this meant:[8]

---

[4] *John v Rees* [1970] Ch 345.
[5] *John v Rees* [1970] Ch 345; *Byng v London Life Association Ltd* [1989] BCLC 400.
[6] [1989] BCLC 400.
[7] [1948] 1 KB 223.
[8] [1989] BCLC 400, at 419, per Browne-Wilkinson LJ.

'The chairman's decision will not be declared invalid unless on the facts which he knew or ought to have known he failed to take into account all relevant factors or reached a conclusion which no reasonable chairman, properly directing himself as to his duties could have reached.'

9.11 On the facts of the case, the chairman's behaviour in adjourning the meeting showed he had fallen short of this requirement. He had neglected to take into account a number of matters relevant to the exercise of his discretion to adjourn. These matters included the objections of members to the adjournment of the meeting to that afternoon; the fact that any members unable to attend the adjourned afternoon meeting in person would not be able to vote by proxy since it was too late for them to lodge their proxies; and the fact that the chairman was wrong in believing that it was necessary for the company to pass a special resolution on that day.

THE COURT'S POWER TO ADJOURN

9.12 There are circumstances in which the court has a power to adjourn a company meeting. Such a power may be exercised where, for example, circulars sent to shareholders by the directors with the notice of the meeting are misleading.[9]

PROCEDURE ON ADJOURNMENT

9.13 When a meeting is adjourned, the model form articles all provide that the chairman must either specify the time and place of the adjourned meeting there and then, or state that it is to continue at a time and place to be fixed by the directors. They also require him to have regard to any directions given by the meeting at the time, about where and when the adjourned meeting is to be held. For companies with older articles, the 1985 Table A says the same. The model form articles also say that no business is to be transacted at any adjourned meeting other than the business left unfinished at the meeting from which the adjournment took place.

9.14 However, regs 41, 27 and 33 in the model form articles for a private company limited by shares, a guarantee company or a public company respectively (and, for companies with older articles, reg 45 of the 1985 Table A) provide for a fresh notice to be given if the adjournment is for 14 days or more. In that case, 7 clear days' notice must be given, specifying the time and place of the adjourned meeting and the general nature of the business to be transacted.[10] Otherwise, upon adjournment to a fixed date, notice of the adjourned meeting is not necessary.[11] This is because the adjourned meeting is

---

[9] *Northern Counties Securities v Jackson* [1974] 1 WLR 1133.
[10] Notice of an adjourned meeting can be given electronically. See Chapter 11.
[11] *Wills v Murray* (1850) 4 Ex 843.

treated as merely a continuation of the original meeting[12] (although resolutions passed at the adjourned meeting are treated as passed on the date the adjourned meeting is held – see **9.24**). Business is therefore confined to that specified in the original notice.[13]

9.15 In some instances, articles differ from the model form or Table A in that they require notice to be given of adjourned meetings, but do not specify the notice period. In such cases, the same notice must be given as for the original meeting. It is therefore clear that, if the meeting is the annual general meeting of a public company, 21 clear days' notice will be required.

9.16 Regulations 41, 27 and 33 in the model form articles for a private company limited by shares, a guarantee company or a public company respectively provide that, if there is no quorum within half an hour of the start time for the meeting, or if during a meeting it becomes inquorate, the chairman of the meeting must adjourn it. For companies with older articles, reg 41 of Table A provides that, where a quorum is not attained, or ceases to exist, the meeting will be adjourned 'to the same day in the next week at the same time or place or to such time and place as the directors may determine'.

9.17 However, if the articles do not allow adjournment of an inquorate meeting, then not only does that 'meeting' lack the power to transact business but generally it will also lack power to resolve upon an adjournment.

9.18 Generally, s 321 of the Companies Act 2006 (CA 2006) stops a company's articles placing restrictions on members' rights to demand a poll in its articles. However, there is an exception where the poll relates to the adjournment of a general meeting (and also when the poll relates to election of a chairman of the meeting). In those circumstances a company's articles *can* exclude the right to a poll. However, this would be unusual. In fact, articles, such as reg 37(4) in the model for articles for a public company say that a poll on a question of adjournment must be taken immediately while, for companies with older articles, reg 51 of the 1985 Table A permits a poll to be called on a proposal to adjourn to be taken immediately. If they do not so provide in express terms, this is probably implied.

9.19 If a poll is taken on the issue of adjournment, how should proxy holders vote? Sometimes they will have been given specific directions for this purpose, but in other cases they may be in doubt whether they can exercise their proxy votes and, if so, how, on a vote to adjourn.

9.20 In the absence of a specific direction, proxy holders should act on the principle that they are agents for their appointors. They are therefore entitled to vote in whatever way they feel is in the interests of their appointor, or in the way their appointor would have wished them to vote. In some situations, it will

---

[12] *Scadding v Lorant* (1851) 3 HLC 418.
[13] *Kerr v Wilkie* (1860) 1 LT 501.

be plain how they should exercise their votes in the best interests of their appointor.[14] If it is not, a decision made by a proxy holder, in good faith, will not be open to successful challenge by the appointor, the company or anyone else. If the proxy holder feels unable to decide, he may take no action. The agency is in the proxy holder personally; even if the proxy was canvassed by the board, it is the proxy, and not the board, who has the right and duty to decide.[15]

9.21 Directors will occasionally wish to postpone putting a decision before the members because circumstances have changed or changes are expected. The directors of a company, in the absence of express authority in the articles of association, have no power to postpone a properly convened general meeting of the company.[16] If they purport to do so the shareholders can, if they think fit, meet at the place, time and day appointed by the notice and transact all the business which could properly be put before the meeting. If the directors wish to change the date of a meeting, their only option is to hold the meeting and persuade attendees to adjourn it to the date they want.

9.22 In such situations the directors should, therefore, if time permits, inform shareholders of their intention to ask for an adjournment of the meeting and the reason for this, either by circular or, where time is too short, by newspaper advertisement. The purpose of notifying shareholders is to indicate that the meeting will be a mere formality and it will be a waste of the members' time to attend the meeting – unless they want to oppose the adjournment.

9.23 Finally, it should be noted that a meeting may, in certain circumstances, be continued on a later date without any adjournment in the strict sense having taken place.[17]

BUSINESS AT ADJOURNED MEETINGS

9.24 Section 332 of CA 2006 provides that where a resolution is passed at an adjourned meeting of a company, or a similar meeting of the holders of any class of shares of a company or of the directors of a company, the resolution shall for all purposes be treated as having been passed on the date on which it was in fact passed and shall not be deemed to have been passed on any earlier date.

9.25 The articles usually provide what business may be conducted at an adjourned meeting. All of the model form articles and, for companies with older articles, reg 45 of Table A, say that only business which could properly have been transacted at the original meeting, had it not been postponed, can be transacted at the adjourned meeting.

---

[14] See *Re Waxed Papers Ltd* (1937) 2 All ER 481.
[15] See further on proxies, Chapter 8.
[16] *Smith v Paringa Mines* [1906] 2 Ch 193.
[17] *Jackson v Hamlyn* [1953] 1 Ch 577.

9.26 Sometimes, however, it is possible to transact business at an adjourned meeting which could not have been transacted at the original meeting. In *Catesby v Burnett*,[18] the articles provided that no member should be elected a director unless, 14 clear days before *the day of election* (emphasis added), notice of the intention to so elect a member was given to the company. At the date of the annual general meeting (for, at the time, private companies were obliged to hold an annual general meeting) there were two directors due for retirement, but the necessary notice to elect two members as new directors was not received 14 clear days before the meeting. In fact, the meeting was adjourned without any election of new directors. At the adjourned meeting the two new directors were elected, and the election was held valid. This was because the notice was given 14 clear days before the adjourned meeting, ie the 'day of election' for the purposes of the articles. If the articles had provided for 14 days' notice before the meeting at which they were elected (rather than 14 days' notice before the day of election), the election would not have been valid, because the adjourned meeting is treated as a continuation of the original meeting, which had been held too early.

9.27 For similar reasons, proxies will sometimes be available for use at an adjourned meeting where they would not have been available at the earlier meeting, as, for example, where they have to be deposited not less than 48 hours 'before the meeting or adjourned meeting' (see Chapter 8).

---

[18] [1916] 2 Ch 325.

Chapter 10

RIGHTS OF THE AUDITOR IN RELATION TO MEMBERS' MEETINGS

APPOINTING AND REAPPOINTING AUDITORS

10.1 The Eighth EC Company Law Directive[1] made provision with respect to the eligibility of a person to become a company auditor. The requirements of the Directive in this respect were implemented initially by Part II of the Companies Act 1989, but are now enacted in Part 42 of the Companies Act 2006 (CA 2006). CA 2006 regulates a wider range of auditors than the 1989 Act – for example, auditors of companies incorporated outside the EU, but listed in the UK – and the term 'statutory auditor' is therefore used in parts of CA 2006, where this wider definition applies. Under the CA 2006 provisions, either an individual or a firm may be appointed as auditor (s 1212), provided, of course, that they comply with the other requirements as to eligibility, including the requirement of sufficient independence in ss 1214–1216. Bodies corporate may also be appointed as auditors, subject to compliance with similar eligibility requirements.

10.2 The provisions on appointment and reappointment of auditors are dealt with separately in CA 2006 for private and public companies.

PRIVATE COMPANIES

10.3 For private companies, s 485 provides that the company must appoint an auditor for each financial year of the company 'unless the directors reasonably resolve otherwise on the ground that audited accounts are unlikely to be required'. It is unclear whether this resolution can be made once only, on a once-and-for-all basis, or must be made every financial year, so the prudent approach is to treat it as an annual requirement. Audited accounts are unlikely to be required if the company is either likely to be a dormant company[2] or an audit exempt company (s 477), neither of which are required to audit their accounts.

---

[1] Directive 84/253/EEC.
[2] A company is defined by s 1169 as 'dormant' during any period when it has no transaction that is required to be entered in the company's accounting records (disregarding any transaction arising from the taking of the subscriber shares by a subscriber to the memorandum and fees and penalties payable to the Registrar) (s 480).

10.4 The auditor may be appointed either by:

- ordinary resolution of the members in general meeting; or

- the directors if the appointment is:

    - the first appointment after incorporation;
    - following a period during which the company had no auditor because it was audit exempt, and the appointment is made at any time before the company's next period for appointing auditors; or
    - to fill a casual vacancy.

10.5 If an appointment is required in a financial year other than the company's first financial year, it must be made before the end of the period of 28 days after the end of the time allowed for sending out copies of the company's annual accounts and reports for the previous financial year or, if earlier, the day they are actually sent out. This is called the 'period for appointing auditors'.

10.6 After the first financial year, therefore, an appointment of auditors by the members of a private company will generally be made within 28 days after the company circulates the accounts for the previous financial year to the members.

10.7 The auditor's term of office runs from the end of that 28-day period until the end of the corresponding period in the next year, even if the auditor is appointed at a general meeting at which the company's accounts are laid before the members.

10.8 However, once an auditor has been appointed, he is deemed reappointed at the end of his period of office unless the members in general meeting decide otherwise, except in five circumstances:

- he was previously appointed by the directors;

- the company's articles require actual re-appointment;

- enough members have given notice to the company under s 488 (which enables members holding at least 5% of the voting rights – or such lesser percentage as provided for in the articles – to give notice to the company to prevent an auditor being deemed automatically re-appointed);

- there has been a resolution that the auditor should not be reappointed; or

- the directors decide that they do not need auditors for the following year.

10.9 For administrative convenience therefore, many companies may wish to appoint the first auditors after incorporation or after a period of audit

Rights of the Auditor in Relation to Members' Meetings 165

exemption has ended, and to fill casual vacancies, by ordinary resolution in general meeting, rather than allow the directors to make the appointment, so that the deemed reappointment provisions then apply.

10.10 Generally, when a company changes auditor, the incoming auditor's term of office does not begin before the end of the previous auditor's term. This means that a new auditor's term will typically begin immediately after the end of the 28-day period for appointing auditors.

10.11 If a company fails to appoint an auditor within 28 days of circulation of its accounts, it must notify the Secretary of State, who has power to appoint an auditor for it (s 486).

PUBLIC COMPANIES

10.12 For public companies, s 489 provides that an auditor must be appointed for each financial year, 'unless the directors reasonably resolve otherwise on the ground that audited accounts are unlikely to be required'. It is unclear whether this resolution can be made once only, on a once-and-for-all basis, or must be made every financial year, so the prudent approach is to treat it as an annual requirement. Audited accounts are unlikely to be required of a public company if it is likely to be a dormant company (s 480), as dormant companies are not required to audit their accounts.

10.13 If an auditor is to be appointed, the appointment must be made before the end of the general meeting of the company at which its annual accounts and reports for the previous financial year are laid in accordance with s 437 (an 'accounts meeting').

10.14 The directors may appoint the auditor:

- at any time before the company's first accounts meeting;

- following a period during which the company (being exempt from audit) did not have any auditor, at any time before the company's next accounts meeting; or

- to fill a casual vacancy in the office of auditor.

10.15 The members may appoint an auditor or auditors by ordinary resolution:

- at an accounts meeting;

- if the company should have appointed an auditor or auditors at an accounts meeting but failed to do so; or

- where the directors had power to appoint the auditor, but have failed to do so.

10.16 Under s 491, a public company's auditor remains in office until the end of the meeting at which the accounts are laid, unless reappointed. On a change of auditor, the incoming auditor's term of office does not begin before the end of the previous auditor's term. So the new auditor's term will typically begin immediately after the end of the accounts meeting.

10.17 If a company fails to appoint an auditor within 28 days of circulation of its accounts, it must notify the Secretary of State, who has power to appoint an auditor for it (s 490).

REMUNERATION OF AUDITORS

10.18 The remuneration of auditors is fixed by the company in general meeting, or in such manner as the company in general meeting may determine (s 492(1)). Where auditors are appointed by the directors or the Secretary of State, their remuneration may be fixed by the directors or the Secretary of State, respectively (s 492(2) and (3)).

REMOVAL OF AUDITORS

10.19 The company has power by ordinary resolution in general meeting to remove an auditor before the expiry of his term of office (s 510); however, such a resolution requires special notice (s 510). Notice that such a resolution has been passed must be given to the Registrar of Companies within 14 days (s 512). The removal is effective even though it may amount to a breach of contract between the company and the auditor, who in that case retains the right to compensation or damages for the termination of his appointment or of any other appointment which terminates along with his appointment as auditor (s 510(3)).

CHANGING AUDITORS

10.20 If a company changes its auditor at a general meeting, between one financial year and the next, special notice may be required under s 515. The section applies if an incoming auditor is to be appointed, by ordinary resolution of the members, in place of an outgoing auditor whose term of office has ended, or is to end:

- in a private company, at the end of the period for appointing auditors; or

- in a public company, at the end of the next accounts meeting.

10.21 If the change meets the criteria in s 515(2), then special notice of the resolution is required. Section 515(2) provides that special notice is required if:

- In a private company:

  – no period for appointing auditors has ended since the outgoing auditor ceased to hold office; or
  – such a period has ended and an auditor or auditors should have been appointed but were not.

- In a public company:

  – there has been no accounts meeting of the company since the outgoing auditor ceased to hold office; or
  – there has been an accounts meeting at which an auditor or auditors should have been appointed, but no appointment was made.

10.22 So, for example, if a public company does not propose to reappoint its auditor at its accounts meeting, it would need to give special notice of the meeting in order to be able to appoint replacement auditors.

SPECIAL NOTICE

10.23 The requirement of special notice where the auditor is being removed or not reappointed is a requirement designed to bolster the independence of auditors. Special notice is considered in Chapter 3, but the following points relating to the procedure leading up to the meeting to consider the relevant resolution are covered here.

10.24 On receiving a resolution requiring special notice in relation to the position of auditor, the company must immediately send a copy of the resolution to the person it is proposed to appoint or remove (ss 511 and 515(3)). Where it is proposed to appoint someone other than a retiring auditor to the position of auditor or to remove an auditor before the auditor's term of office expires, the retiring auditor or the auditor whose removal is proposed may make written representations concerning the resolution to the company and may request the company to notify its members of those representations (ss 511(3) and 515(4)). The company must then state that representations have been received in any notice of the resolution given to members and must send a copy of the representations to every member to whom notice of the meeting is to be, or has been, sent (ss 511(4) and 515(5)), unless the representations are received too late to allow this to be done. If the representations are received too late for inclusion in the notice sent to members or the company fails to comply, the auditor may (without prejudice to his right to speak at the meeting – see below) demand that the representations are read out at the meeting (ss 511(5) and 515(6)). This is subject to the usual proviso that the court may accede to the request of the company or an aggrieved person that the representations are not sent out or read at the meeting if it is satisfied that the rights are being used to secure needless publicity for defamatory material (ss 511(6) and 515(7)). If such an application is made, the court may order the outgoing auditor to pay company's costs (in Scotland, expenses) in whole or in part, even though he is not a party to the application.

10.25 An auditor removed in mid term by a general meeting may attend and speak at the general meeting at which his term of office would normally have expired (for example, an accounts meeting of a public company) and any general meeting at which it is proposed to fill the vacancy caused by his removal (ss 513 and 502(2)). The auditor must, accordingly, be given all relevant notices of, and other communications relating to, such meetings which any member is entitled to receive. For these purposes, where appropriate, references in s 502 to matters which concern the auditor 'as auditor' are to be construed as references to matters concerning him as a former auditor.

10.26 It is not possible to remove an auditor by resolution in writing in lieu of a meeting, but it is possible to propose a written resolution of a private company whose effect would be to appoint a person as auditor in place of an outgoing auditor whose term of office has expired, or is to expire, at the end of the period for appointing auditors (s 514).

10.27 If no period for appointing auditors has ended since the outgoing auditor ceased to hold office, or such a period has ended and an auditor or auditors should have been appointed but were not, then the company must send a copy of the proposed written resolution to both the incoming and outgoing auditor.

10.28 Within 14 days after receiving the notice, the outgoing auditor may make representations in writing to the company in respect of it (not exceeding a reasonable length) and request their circulation to members of the company. The company must circulate them with the copy or copies of the resolution circulated in accordance with s 291 (resolution proposed by directors) or s 293 (resolution proposed by members). In this case, the period allowed under s 293(3) for service of copies of the proposed resolution is 28 days instead of 21 days.

10.29 As usual, copies of the representations need not be circulated if, on the company's application (or that of any other person who claims to be aggrieved), the court is satisfied that the auditor is using his rights to secure needless publicity for defamatory matter.

RESIGNING AS AUDITORS

10.30 An auditor may resign by depositing written notice of resignation at the company's registered office (s 516(1)). The resignation will be effective only if it is accompanied by a s 519 statement (s 516(2)). It takes effect either on the date it is deposited or on any later date specified in it (s 516(3)). The company must send a copy of an auditor's notice of resignation to the Registrar of Companies within 14 days after it is deposited (s 517).

10.31 Under s 518, where an auditor's notice of resignation is accompanied by a s 519 statement, he may also deposit with the notice a signed requisition calling on the directors 'forthwith' to call a general meeting to receive and consider any explanation of the circumstances connected with his resignation that he wishes to place before the meeting.

10.32 He may also request the company to circulate a statement in writing (not exceeding a reasonable length) of the circumstances connected with his resignation to its members:

- before the meeting convened on his requisition; or

- before any general meeting at which his term of office would otherwise have expired or at which it is proposed to fill the vacancy caused by his resignation.

10.33 Unless it receives the statement too late to comply, the company must:

- state the fact of the statement having been made in any notice of the meeting given to members of the company; and

- send a copy of the statement to every member of the company to whom notice of the meeting is or has been sent.

10.34 Within 21 days from the date of the deposit of such a request, the directors must convene a meeting for a day not more than 28 days after the date on which the notice convening the meeting is given.

10.35 If a copy of the statement mentioned above is not sent out as required because it was received too late or because of the company's default, the auditor may (without prejudice to his right to be heard orally) require that the statement be read out at the meeting. As usual, copies of a statement need not be sent out and the statement need not be read out at the meeting if, on the company's application (or that of any other person who claims to be aggrieved), the court is satisfied that the auditor is using his rights to secure needless publicity for defamatory matter.

10.36 An auditor who has resigned has, notwithstanding his resignation, the rights conferred by s 502(2) in relation to any such general meeting of the company, and references in s 502 to matters concerning the auditor 'as auditor' are to be construed as references to matters concerning him as a former auditor.

REQUIREMENTS ON ANY CESSATION OF OFFICE AS AUDITOR

10.37 Section 519 provides separate regimes for quoted and unquoted companies on cessation of office as an auditor.

10.38 If the auditor of an unquoted company ceases for any reason (including resignation) to hold office, he must deposit a statement of the circumstances connected with the cessation that need to be brought to the attention of members or creditors of the company at the company's registered office. If there are none, he must still deposit a statement, but it must be to the effect that there are no circumstances in connection with his ceasing to hold office that need to be brought to the attention of members or creditors of the company (s 519(2)).

10.39 If the auditor of a quoted company ceases for any reason to hold office, he must deposit at the company's registered office a statement of the circumstances connected with his ceasing to hold office. This means that auditors ceasing to hold office in respect of quoted companies must always make a statement of such circumstances – it is no longer open to them to make a statement saying there are none (as they could do previously under s 394 of the Companies Act 1985) (s 519(3)).

10.40 In either case, the statement must be deposited:

- in the case of resignation, with the notice of resignation;

- in the case of failure to seek re-appointment, not less than 14 days before the end of the time allowed for next appointing an auditor; or

- in any other case, not later than the end of the period of 14 days, starting with the date on which the auditor ceases to hold office.

10.41 If, in the case of an unquoted company, the notice contains a statement of the circumstances connected with the cessation that needs to be brought to the attention of members or creditors of the company or, in the case of a quoted company, the company must either send a copy of it to every person who is entitled to be sent copies of the accounts under s 432 or apply to the court on the ground that the statement is being used to secure needless publicity for defamatory material, within 14 days of the deposit of the statement (s 520(2)) and, in the latter case, notify the auditor that it has done so.

10.42 If the auditor has not received notification of a court application within 21 days after he has deposited a statement, he has 7 further days to send a copy of the statement to the Registrar of Companies (s 521). In certain cases, the auditor is required by s 522 to notify the 'appropriate audit authority', as defined in s 525.

10.43 In addition, under s 523, if an auditor ceases to hold office before the end of his term of office, the company must notify the appropriate audit authority. The notice must inform the appropriate audit authority that the auditor has ceased to hold office, and be accompanied by either:

- a statement by the company of the reasons for his ceasing to hold office; or

- if the copy of the statement deposited by the auditor at the company's registered office under s 519 contains a statement of circumstances in connection with his ceasing to hold office that need to be brought to the attention of members or creditors of the company, a copy of that statement.

10.44 The company must give notice under this section not later than 14 days after the date on which the auditor's statement is deposited at the company's registered office.

SPECIFIC RIGHTS IN RELATION TO RESOLUTIONS AND MEETINGS

10.45 Under s 502(2), a company's auditor is specifically entitled to receive all notices of, and other communications relating to, any general meeting which a member of the company is entitled to receive. He is also entitled to attend general meetings of the company, and be heard at them on any business which concerns him as auditor. Where the auditor is a firm, the right to attend or be heard at a meeting is exercisable by an individual authorised by the firm in writing to act as its representative at the meeting.

10.46 For private company resolutions in writing in lieu of a meeting, s 502(1) provides that the auditor is entitled to receive the same communications as a member of the company (see Chapter 2, Part 13 of CA 2006).

AUDITOR'S RIGHTS TO RAISE AUDIT CONCERNS AT ACCOUNTS MEETINGS

10.47 Under s 527, members of a quoted company (that is, a company that is quoted within the meaning of s 385 in relation to the financial year covered by the accounts in question) holding the necessary voting rights may require the company to publish a statement on a website setting out any matter that the members propose to raise at the next accounts meeting of the company relating to:

- the audit of the company's accounts (including the auditor's report and the conduct of the audit) that are to be laid before the next accounts meeting; or

- any circumstances connected with an auditor of the company ceasing to hold office since the previous accounts meeting.

10.48 The voting rights required are either:

- at least 5% of the total voting rights of all the members who have a relevant right to vote (that is, a right to vote at the accounts meeting, but excluding voting rights attached to treasury shares); or

- at least 100 members who have a relevant right to vote and hold shares in the company on which there has been paid up an average sum, per member, of at least £100.

10.49 The request must:

- identify the statement to which it relates;

- be authenticated by the person or persons making it, and

- be received by the company at least one week before the meeting to which it relates.

There is the usual exception if the court is satisfied that the rights conferred by this section are being abused.

10.50 If a company is required to do so, it must forward the statement to its auditor not later than the time when it makes the statement available on the website, and the business at the accounts meeting must include any statement that the company has been required to publish on a website.

10.51 Under s 529, a quoted company must draw attention to the possibility of a statement being placed on a website in pursuance of members' requests under s 527, and the effect of the provisions of s 529, in the notice it gives of the accounts meeting.

10.52 There are special rules about the website where the information is published, how it is to be published to ensure access and for how long (s 528).

Chapter 11

ELECTRONIC COMMUNICATIONS AND GENERAL MEETINGS

INTRODUCTION

11.1 Traditionally, companies had to give notice of general meetings and any other documents or information required or authorised to be sent or supplied by them under the Companies Acts, to members personally or by post, in hard copy format. Documents required or authorised to be lodged or deposited with the company by members also had to be in hard copy format, delivered – usually – to the company's registered office by post or personally. Technological advances, coupled with greater geographical spread of company membership, have led to recognition of the use of electronic communications between companies and their members, both in the courts and in legislation.

11.2 Unsurprisingly, electronic communications are more attractive to companies with large numbers of members (for whom, for example, the electronic despatch of the annual report and accounts to members creates significant savings in printing and postage costs), such as listed plcs and large guarantee companies, than to smaller companies. However, new rules in the Companies Act 2006 (CA 2006) are also intended to be attractive to smaller companies.

11.3 Many larger companies subcontract the set-up and management of electronic communications between themselves and members to commercial registrars; but, whether managed in-house or by third parties, companies wishing to communicate electronically with members under the new rules need a thorough understanding of those rules.

The statutory framework

11.4 Statutory rules in CA 2006 permit documents and information to be sent or supplied by companies to their members, and vice versa, electronically, including by means of a website (that is, by posting a document or information on a website and notifying members that it is there), provided certain conditions are satisfied. Virtually all of the relevant provisions in CA 2006 were introduced with effect from 20 January 2007.[1]

---

[1] Companies Act 2006 (Commencement No 1, Transitional Provisions and Savings) Order 2006, SI 2006/3428.

11.5 However, one provision – s 360A – was introduced with effect from 3 August 2009.[2] This provides that nothing in Part 13 of the Act, dealing with meetings and resolutions, is to be taken as precluding the holding and conducting of a meeting in such a way that persons who are not present together at the same place may attend, speak and vote at it by electronic means.

11.6 For traded companies, s 360A(2) limits the requirements and restrictions that the company can impose on use of electronic means for the purpose of enabling members to participate in a general meeting to those that are:

(a) necessary to ensure the identification of those taking part and the security of the electronic communication; and

(b) proportionate to the achievement of those objectives.

However, it is permissible to require reasonable evidence of the entitlement of any person who is not a member to participate in the meeting.

11.7 CA 2006 rules superseded earlier rules, set out in the Electronic Communications Act 2000 and the Companies Act 1985 (Electronic Communications) Order 2000[3] made pursuant to it. Whilst there is some overlap, there are certain key differences between the current rules and the pre-2006 Act rules, which are highlighted below as each new rule is discussed.

The documents and information that can be sent or supplied electronically

11.8 A key provision in CA 2006 in relation to electronic communications between companies and their members is s 1143. This deals with the application of what it refers to as the 'company communications provisions' to companies.[4] The company communications provisions are ss 1144–1148, and Sch 4 and 5 of the Act.[5]

---

[2] By reg 8 in the Companies (Shareholders' Rights) Regulations 2009, SI 2009/1632.
[3] SI 2000/3373.
[4] Note that the company communications provisions do not deal only with electronic communications. They also deal with the sending or supplying of documents or information by or to a company in hard copy format. They also apply in relation to electronic communications between companies and Companies House.
[5] Under s 1143(2) the company communications provisions are subject to any 'requirements imposed, or contrary provision made, by or under any enactment'. This means that, if an enactment requires a particular method of communication between companies and their members, or makes a provision which is contrary to the company communication provisions, the provisions of that enactment will override the company communication provisions. If, however, a contrary provision in another enactment does not require, but merely authorises, a particular method, then it will not override the company communication provisions. It does not matter whether the authorisation is express or implied – it still does not override the company communication provisions. An example of provisions in another enactment is that companies whose shares are traded on a regulated market such as the London Stock Exchange are also subject to the Financial Services Authority's Disclosure and Transparency Rules (DTR), which set out specific electronic communications requirements for such companies.

11.9 Section 1143 provides that the company communication provisions 'have effect for the purposes of any provision of the Act that authorises or requires documents or information to be sent or supplied by or to a company'. 'Company' here includes any body corporate, and also any director acting on behalf of a body corporate (s 1148(3)).

11.10 If, therefore, a provision of the Act requires or authorises a document or information to be sent or supplied in electronic form, or by electronic means, or by means of a website, then the parts of the company communications provisions regulating electronic communications and/or making documents available by means of a website will apply.

11.11 Virtually every provision of the Act that requires or authorises the sending or supply of documents or information by a company to its members, or by a member to their company, does specifically say that they may be sent or supplied electronically – in electronic form, by electronic means or by means of a website. The company communications provisions therefore apply to virtually every document or piece of information that must or may be sent or supplied by a company to its members and vice versa.

11.12 This is in contrast to Companies Act 1985 (CA 1985) rules which were in force before 20 January 2007. Under those rules the documents which could be sent or supplied electronically by a company to its members were limited to:

- notice of members' meetings;

- associated documents, such as proxy forms;

- the annual, and interim, report and accounts; and

- summary financial statements.

11.13 The only documents that a member could supply to a company electronically were documents relating to appointment of a proxy.

How documents and information may be sent or supplied

11.14 There are a number of definitions that apply to the whole of CA 2006, in s 1168, in relation to the sending or supply of documents or information electronically. They apply whether the Act uses the actual words 'sent' or 'supplied' or whether it uses other words (such as 'deliver', 'provide', 'produce' or, in the case of a notice, 'give') to refer to the sending or supply of a document or information.

Issue 14 of the UK Listing Authority newsletter, *List!*, provides guidance on the relationship between CA 2006 rules and the DTR. The DTR provisions are not covered in this book.

11.15 First, under s 1168 a document or information is sent or supplied 'in electronic form' if it is sent or supplied either by electronic means (for example, by e-mail or fax), or by any other means while in an electronic form (for example, sending a disk by post). References to electronic copy in CA 2006 have a corresponding meaning.

11.16 Secondly, a document or information is sent or supplied 'by electronic means' if it is sent initially and received at its destination by means of electronic equipment for the processing (which expression includes digital compression) or storage of data, and entirely transmitted, conveyed and received by wire, radio, optical means or other electromagnetic means. References in the Act to electronic means have a corresponding meaning.

11.17 These definitions are intended to be future-proof (ie to be sufficiently wide to cover future forms of electronic communication, not yet devised). Current forms of communication within the definition of 'electronic means' include e-mails, faxes, telephone calls (including mobile phone calls), VOIP systems such as Skype, text messaging, making information available on a website, sending of a CD-ROM, DVD, floppy disk or audio tape, digital TV broadcasts and communications via WAP (wireless application protocol). The communication can include sounds or images, and can be a communication effecting payment.

11.18 The fact that there is a different definition for each of 'electronic form' and 'electronic means' means those construing CA 2006 should take special notice of which form of words is being used in any particular section. The same is true for those construing – or drafting – a company's articles of association or other legal documents.

11.19 Generally, a document or information authorised or required to be sent or supplied in electronic form must be sent or supplied in a form, and by a means, that the sender or supplier reasonably considers will enable the recipient to read it, and to retain a copy of it.

11.20 A document or information can be read for the purposes of s 1168 if it can be read with the naked eye, or (to the extent that it consists of images – for example, photographs, pictures, maps, plans or drawings) it can be seen with the naked eye.

11.21 The requirement that the recipient is able to retain a copy casts doubt on the use of a telephone call to send documents or information electronically, as it is hard to see how a 'copy' of a call can be retained. A record of a text message to a mobile phone can be retained, but it is not clear whether the record is a 'copy'. Even if the message is downloaded to a PC, and perhaps printed out, the question still remains whether this is a sufficient 'copy' within the meaning of CA 2006. The Institute of Chartered Secretaries and Administrators (ICSA) has produced the useful and authoritative 'ICSA

Guidance on Electronic Communications with Shareholders 2007'[6] (the '2006 Act ICSA Guidance'). In paragraph B2 of the 2006 Act ICSA Guidance, ICSA says that 'when reviewing any electronic means (such as telephone or text) you might be considering for communications with your shareholders you need to be mindful of the need for the shareholder to be able to retain a copy of the document/information under s 1168'.

11.22 In relation to notices of general meetings, s 308 provides that the notice must be given in hard copy form, in electronic form, by means of a website or partly in one way and partly in another. Paragraph B4 of the 2006 Act ICSA Guidance states that it may be preferable to offer electronic communications as a complete package (reserving the right to send hard copy at any time). After all, those receiving everything electronically can always print any of the documents made available to them, or exercise their right under s 1145 and request a hard copy of a particular document at any time.

11.23 Despite the wide range of ways in which a company can communicate with its members (because the definition of 'electronic means' – see **11.16** – is so wide), there are two main ways that companies and members are using to communicate with each other electronically:

- both companies and members are sending or supplying documents or information to each other by e-mail, either in the body of the e-mail itself, or as an attachment; and

- for communications from a company to its members, companies are placing documents or information on a website and notifying members (electronically or otherwise) of the address of the relevant web page on the site where the documents or information appear.

Can a company follow the new rules irrespective of what is in its articles?

11.24 Existing companies that have made no provision in their articles of association may simply follow CA 2006 rules regarding electronic communications, as there are no provisions in their articles that may conflict with the new rules.

11.25 However, articles of association of existing companies, that were incorporated prior to 20 January 2007, will often include provisions governing how the company and its members may communicate with each other electronically. For companies incorporated after 2000, or that have adopted new articles since then, these will invariably be drafted pursuant to provisions

---

[6] Guidance Note no 070216 (August 2008), available online at www.icsa.org.uk/assets/files/pdfs/guidance/070216.pdf.

in the Electronic Communications Act 2000 and the Companies Act 1985 (Electronic Communications) Order 2000[7] made pursuant to it. These are often inconsistent with the CA 2006 rules.

11.26 The wording of CA 2006 makes it clear that a company and its members can use the company communications provisions to communicate electronically with each other, irrespective of what is in the company's articles of association, unless the Act specifically says otherwise – for example, it may specifically say that a particular provision is subject to a company's articles, or that authority to undertake a certain act is required in the articles.

11.27 One circumstance where CA 2006 is stated to be subject to the articles is in relation to the rules governing deemed delivery of documents and information. Sections 1147(3) and (4) provide that:

- where a document or information is sent or supplied by electronic means, and the company is able to show that it was properly addressed, then it is deemed to have been received by the intended recipient 48 hours after it was sent; and

- where a document or information is sent or supplied by means of a website, it is deemed to have been received by the intended recipient either when the material was first made available on the website or, if later, when the recipient received (or is deemed to have received) notice of the fact that the material was available on the website.

11.28 However, s 1147(6) specifically provides that, in its application to documents or information sent or supplied by a company to its members, these rules are subject to the company's articles.

11.29 Another circumstance is in relation to joint holders of shares or debentures. Paragraph 16 of Sch 5 to CA 2006 states that, in relation to documents or information to be sent or supplied to joint holders of shares or debentures of a company, anything agreed or specified by the holder must be agreed or specified by all the joint holders.

11.30 However, anything authorised or required to be sent or supplied to the holder may be sent or supplied either to each of the joint holders or to the holder whose name appears first in the register of members or the relevant register of debenture holders.

11.31 This inconvenient rule, that draws a distinction between agreeing (where all joint holders must agree) and sending or supplying (when documents or information need only be sent to the first-named) is specifically stated under para 16(4), to be subject to the company's articles.

---

[7] SI 2000/3373.

11.32 Companies may wish to consider amending their articles so that the rules are consistent for the two – either every joint holder has to agree, and all receive documents and information, or only the first-named has to agree and only the first-named receives documents or information. If the former is chosen, companies may also need to change their articles to ensure that every joint holder has to supply an address (whether postal and/or electronic), as articles often provide that only the first-named has to provide an address. Otherwise, a company will find it has no address for holders other than the first-named.

11.33 Therefore, there is scope for a company to include in its articles provisions varying the usual rule in relation to the time at which documents or information sent or supplied electronically are deemed received, and in relation to joint holders. If a company already has an inconsistent provision in its articles in this respect, that will still override CA 2006, even though it was not drafted in contemplation of s 1147(6). Articles of existing companies should be reviewed to see if they contain such overriding provisions and whether the company still wants them to apply.

11.34 As discussed at **11.12**, before the relevant rules in CA 2006 came into force in January 2007, the documents which could be given electronically under the previous rules were limited to:

- notice of members' meetings;

- associated documents, such as proxy forms;

- the annual, and interim, report and accounts; and

- summary financial statements.

11.35 Consequently, a company whose articles were drafted while those former rules were in force may find that its articles specify one or more of those documents as being the documents that the company may send or supply electronically, implying that the sending of other documents or information electronically (depending on the wording of the articles) is in breach of the articles. At the least, there will be an inconsistency in what it can do under CA 2006 (which applies irrespective of what is in the company's articles) and what its articles say. Many companies will wish to update their articles to remove such inconsistencies.

11.36 There are also various practical issues, arising out of use of electronic communications, solutions to which are not provided by CA 2006. If these are not resolved in a company's articles, it means the company's electronic communication regime will run less smoothly than it could. For example, there is no provision in the Act governing the format in which documents sent as attachments to e-mails should be sent, yet the issue of whether members can easily open and read such attachments is obviously of great practical importance.

11.37 Many of these practical issues are not new. They were also issues under the pre-CA 2006 rules. For the purposes of dealing with them under that pre-2006 Act law, ICSA produced a 'Best Practice Guide On Electronic Communications With Shareholders, 2000', and an update to it called the 'ICSA Electronic Communications Update'. The Guide and Update (which, for convenience, are referred to here as the '2000 ICSA Guide') flagged up very many of these practical issues and recommended solutions to them. Their recommendations were so authoritative and useful that amendments made to the 1985 Table A to cater for electronic communications at the time included a cross-reference to the Guide.

11.38 The recommended solution to a number of the issues raised was that they should be addressed in a company's articles, before it offered the option of electronic communications to its members.[8]

11.39 Many of the practical issues that arose under the pre-2006 Act rules also arise under CA 2006, so the 2000 ICSA Guide is still a relevant document. It enables officers of or advisers to a company to identify a number of practical issues that still need solutions, and what those solutions might be. As before, the solution is often to make specific provision dealing with that issue in a company's articles.

11.40 In addition, ICSA has now also produced a CA 2006 version, the 'ICSA Guidance on Electronic Communications with Shareholders 2007', referred to in **11.21**, that is equally useful and authoritative. The 2006 Act ICSA Guidance is available free of charge on the ICSA website.[9]

11.41 Companies that wish to introduce electronic communications between the company and its members may therefore wish to change their articles of association to implement some of the best practice recommendations in both the 2000 ICSA Guide and the 2006 Act ICSA Guidance – not to authorise electronic communications, but to supplement and support the statutory rules by adding rules for dealing with various practical issues not dealt with in those rules, for a smoother and more user-friendly electronic communications regime.

11.42 Another circumstance where a company may decide to alter its articles is if it wishes to take advantage of the new CA 2006 provisions allowing it to make documents or information available to a member by means of a website (that is, the company posts them on a website and notifies the member that they are there). This was also possible under the pre-2006 Act rules but the key difference is that CA 2006 contains a 'deeming' provision (Sch 5, para 10),

---

[8] 2000 ICSA Guide, para 2.2.
[9] Reference no 160207.

whereby a member who does not respond to the request within 28 days is deemed to have agreed to receive documents or information by means of a website. There was no corresponding provision under the pre-2006 Act law.

11.43 This deeming provision is dealt with in more detail below but, for the purpose of this paragraph, the key point is that, under CA 2006 rules, a member is deemed to have agreed that the company can make the relevant documents or information available on a website only to the extent that either:

- the members of the company have resolved, by ordinary resolution, that the company may do so; or

- the company's articles contain provision to that effect.

11.44 One option for a company that wishes to take advantage of the deeming provisions is therefore to alter its articles, although it does not have to – it may instead opt for the ordinary resolution route.[10] However, the 2006 Act ICSA Guidance recommends that a change to the company's articles is the better option, so most companies are likely to choose this route. ICSA's reasons for preferring a change to the articles are that future shareholders will more easily be able to spot such a provision in the articles, and because a company will usually be making changes to its articles as a result of CA 2006 rules anyway, so this change can be swept up and dealt with at the same time as the other changes being made.

11.45 The 2006 Act ICSA Guidance debates whether an existing company's pre-2006 articles might already contain wording that is sufficient for this purpose; for example, if they refer to communications 'allowable by law'. ICSA's view is that:

> '... whilst this is a matter for each company to decide with its advisers, and is dependent on the exact wording in the articles, the "deemed agreement" provisions to communication by means of a website are new and unlikely to have been contemplated specifically by companies in the earlier drafting of their articles. If companies are contemplating using deemed agreement to website communications it is therefore recommended best practice to seek shareholder approval via an authorising resolution or article change, unless it is absolutely clear that the articles have already been drafted in clear anticipation of the deemed agreement provisions. This will reduce the likelihood of shareholder complaints that the new regime came in with inadequate profile and, particularly where the articles are changed, will be easily apparent to new shareholders.'

11.46 A company may also wish to review its existing articles to ensure that any use in them of terms such as 'by electronic means', which are now statutorily defined, does not inadvertently create an inconsistency between its articles and CA 2006.

---

[10] The rules are different for companies subject to the DTR made by the Financial Services Authority – companies whose shares are traded on a regulated market, such as the London Stock Exchange. These usually require a shareholder resolution in general meeting.

11.47 A company may also wish to send or supply non-statutory documents or information to members electronically, or to allow them to send or supply non-statutory documents or information to it electronically (that is, documents or information that are not required or authorised to be sent or supplied by one to the other under CA 2006). If so, as the 2006 Act ICSA Guidance points out, there is no reason why the company should not apply the company communications provisions to such documents or information too, in its articles of association.

Can a company follow its articles irrespective of what is in the new rules?

11.48 While it is clear that a company can generally follow the company communication provisions, perhaps supplemented by additional provisions in its articles, irrespective of what is in its articles, can it choose to follow its articles of association instead of the company communications provisions if it has made its own provision for electronic communications in its articles?

11.49 The effect of the Act and the transitional arrangements[11] are that, if a company wants to continue to operate according to existing, pre-2006 electronic communication provisions in its articles, it may do so provided – and to the extent that – the company and the member have expressly agreed to electronic communications under those provisions

11.50 For example, if a member has expressly agreed that the company may communicate with it 'via a website' under the pre-2006 Act rules, the company may continue to do so, but subject to the limitations that applied under those old rules. For example, it may not send or supply documents other than notices, accounts, financial summary statements and forms of appointment of proxies. If, however, it wishes to take advantage of the new provisions, for example to extend the power to send or supply any document or information electronically, it should therefore update its Articles.[12]

Mutual, express agreement required

11.51 A cardinal principle of the rules in CA 2006 is that neither the company nor a member can be forced to communicate electronically if they do not wish to – there must be express, mutual agreement – unless one of the two exceptions to the principle applies, in which consent to electronic communications is deemed given. These are discussed below.

---

[11] CA 2006, Sch 5, paras 9(a) and 10(2)(b).
[12] There is a similar saving for companies traded on a regulated market, that follow the UK Listing Authority's electronic communication regime, as set out in Issue 14 of its newsletter, *List!*. In effect, such companies can continue to communicate via a website in circumstances where it would have been lawful to do so before 20 January 2007. See the Disclosure and Transparency Rules Sourcebook, Transitional Provision 12.

11.52 Express agreement may be either general or specific, and must not have been revoked (Sch 4, para 6 and Sch 5, para 6). The requirement that agreement can be 'general or specific' means that it can be a general consent which relates to all documents or information, or a specific consent relating to a specific document or piece of information.

11.53 The requirement for express agreement was also a requirement under the pre-CA 2006 law. The issue therefore arises whether agreement given under that law can be carried over, and treated as agreement under the new CA 2006 provisions.

11.54 CA 2006 also requires a company and a member who consents to electronic communications to supply an address for that purpose (Sch 5, para 7). In this context, 'address' includes a number or address used for the purposes of sending or receiving documents or information by electronic means (s 1148(1)). The requirement to supply an address for these purposes was also a requirement under pre-2006 Act law. The issue therefore arises as to whether an address given previously can be carried over and used as the address to be used for electronic communications under CA 2006.

11.55 The first Commencement Order[13] that brought the company communications provisions into force provides that where an address had been notified by a person to a company for certain purposes of CA 1985, it had effect as a notification indicating agreement to receiving documents and information electronically under para 6(a) of Sch 5 to CA 2006 'in relation to the matters to which it relates', and also as a notification of the address to use for those purposes under para 7(1).

11.56 The purposes specified are the sending or supply by means of electronic communication of:

- accounts and reports;

- summary financial statements; and

- notices of meeting.

11.57 Similarly, where an agreement between a person and a company had previously been entered into relating to the sending or supply of the following by means of a website:

- copies of accounts and reports;

- summary financial statements; or

---

[13] Companies Act 2006 (Commencement No 1, Transitional Provisions and Savings) Order 2006, SI 2006/3428, Sch 5, Part 2, para 4.

- notices of meeting,

then any such agreement also has effect, in relation to the matters to which it relates, as an agreement to accept documents or information by means of a website under para 9(a) of Sch 5 to CA 2006.

11.58 However, where a company wishes to send or supply a wider range of documents or information electronically than is referred to above, it is recommended that it should ask for a fresh express agreement from each member and a confirmation of the address to be used.

11.59 An agreement, including deemed agreement (see below), can be revoked at any time.

Nominated persons

11.60 Wherever CA 2006 requires a document or information to be sent to a member, this includes, for companies admitted to trading on a regulated market, a person on whose behalf a registered member is holding shares and who has been nominated by the member to receive 'information rights' – often referred to as 'indirect investor rights' – under Part 9 of the Act.

11.61 Under s 147 in Part 9, a person nominated to enjoy information rights is treated as having agreed that documents or information may be sent or supplied to him by the company by means of a website, rather than as hard copy communications, unless:

- he requests the member nominating him to notify the company of that fact, and provide an address to which such copies may be sent, before the nomination is made; and

- such a request having been received, the person making the nomination notifies the company that the nominated person wishes to receive hard copy communications, and provides the company with that address.

11.62 If no such notification is given (or no address is provided), therefore, the nominated person is taken to have agreed to making documents or information available by means of a website.

11.63 Section 147(4) provides expressly that this is subject to the provisions of Parts 3 and 4 of Sch 5 (communications by company) under which the company may take steps to enable it to communicate in electronic form or by means of a website.

11.64 The deemed agreement may, however, be expressly revoked by the nominated person. Also, it does not affect his right under s 1145 to require a hard copy version of a particular document or information provided in any other form.

11.65 The 2006 Act ICSA Guidance therefore recommends that companies should consider these indirect investor rights when setting a communications strategy and developing new systems. ICSA also points out that it is not necessary for a company's articles specifically to provide for the information rights of these indirect investors, because s 150 provides that the corresponding provisions in the articles will apply to them in relation to company communications. However, as discussed below, there are special rules regarding the agreement to electronic communications required in relation to such nominated members.

11.66 A similar but quite separate right for a member to nominate a person to enjoy or exercise rights of membership is conferred by s 145 of CA 2006. Under that section, any company may include provisions in its articles enabling a member to nominate a person to enjoy or exercise all or any specified rights of the member (other than rights in relation to the transfer or other disposition of a share) in relation to the company. For example, such a person may be given the right to require circulation of a written resolution under s 292 or the right to general notice meetings under s 310.

11.67 Where such rights are given, s 145(2) states that, so far as is necessary to give effect to that provision, anything required or authorised by any provision of CA 2006 to be done by or in relation to the member shall instead be done, or (as the case may be) may instead be done, by or in relation to the nominated person (or each of them) as if he were a member of the company.

11.68 This appears to mean that it is the nominated person whose agreement to electronic communications must be obtained in relation to such rights as are enjoyed or exercised by him (and who will receive or be able to send, documents or information electronically in relation to the specified rights), rather than that of the member who nominated him. However, it is clear from s 145(4) that any rights enjoyed or exercised by virtue of s 145 can only be enforced against the company by the member, not the nominated person.

Death or bankruptcy of a member

11.69 Under para 17 of Sch 5, documents or information required or authorised to be sent or supplied to a member may, in the event of his death or bankruptcy, be sent or supplied to the persons claiming to be entitled to his shares in consequence either by name or by their title (for example, representatives of the deceased, or trustee of the bankrupt,[14] or by any like description), at the address in the UK supplied by them for the purpose.

---

[14] In para 17, bankruptcy includes the sequestration of the estate of a person, or a person's estate being the subject of a protected trust deed (within the meaning of the Bankruptcy (Scotland) Act 1985). In such a case, the reference to the trustee of the bankrupt is to be read as the permanent or interim trustee (within the meaning of that Act) on the sequestrated estate or, as the case may be, the trustee under the protected deed.

11.70 Until they have supplied such an address, any document or information may be sent or supplied in any manner in which it might have been sent or supplied if the death or bankruptcy had not occurred. If, therefore, the deceased or bankrupt member had agreed, or was treated as deemed to have agreed, to receiving documents or information electronically at a particular address, the company may continue to send them to that address.

11.71 Paragraph 17 has effect subject to anything in the company's articles, so a company may wish to change its articles to vary the rules in this respect.

The invitation to members to participate

11.72 Where the company wishes to seek the express agreement of its members to electronic communications under the CA 2006 rules it will usually offer its members the option of receiving documents and information, or particular documents and information, electronically, by sending each member an invitation to sign up to electronic communications. However, this is not a statutory requirement.

11.73 Invitations to members to sign up to electronic communications can be sent out as often as the company wishes, and whenever it wishes. Some companies will wish to invite new members to sign up immediately, so that they can be sent documents and information electronically as early as possible. Once the electronic regime is in place, the 2000 ICSA Guide (at para 5.3) recommends that a company offering electronic communications should, within 3 months of their registration, provide new members with a copy of the invitation, together with a statement about the company's policy on electronic shareholder communications.

11.74 However, other companies may wish to 'batch' new members, only sending invitations to them at fixed dates in the year, or when there are sufficient new members to warrant it (although, in the meantime, of course, documents and information have to be sent to those members in hard copy form).

11.75 For existing members, the 2000 ICSA Guide also provides (at para 4.8) that a fresh invitation should be sent out at least annually to members still receiving documents by post. The 2000 ICSA Guide recommended that, at the latest, this should be sent out with the notice of the annual general meeting. Since private companies no longer need to hold annual general meetings, this is now only a consideration for public companies.

11.76 When considering the contents of its invitation, the company will need to decide:

- the documents and information it will offer to send or supply electronically;

- the means by which it wishes to send or supply them;

- the format it will use for documents sent in electronic form; and

- the means by which members will be able to respond to the offer.

11.77 ICSA believes, at para B4 in the 2006 Act ICSA Guidance, that companies may choose to offer shareholders a tick list so that the latter can choose which documents they would like to receive electronically and which in hard copy. It does not have to be all or nothing. However, companies may want to be mindful of the impact of any decision on the mailing matrix – which may already be complex. If they do offer a tick list, ICSA suggests they might want to include a fallback presumption as it may not always be possible to list every single type of possible document.

11.78 These decisions should not be made lightly. Particularly, recommended best practice in the 2006 Act ICSA Guidance, at para B1, is that the invitation to participate (and provision of a facility) to communicate with shareholders electronically should not discriminate between shareholders of the same class, and should be made available to all shareholders on equal terms and in such a way as to make it as simple as possible for shareholders to participate. Companies should also beware the Equality Act 2010 when deciding which options to offer.

11.79 Paragraph C1 of the 2006 Act ICSA Guidance recommends as best practice that members:

> '... electing to communicate with the company in electronic form are warned that a communication containing a virus may not be accepted by the company but that every effort would be made to inform the sharcholder of the rejected communication and that companies ensure that outgoing communications are, as far as reasonably practical, virus free.'

Companies concerned about their technological capabilities can outsource the construction and maintenance of a dedicated website, on which their accounts (and other documents) are posted, to a commercial provider. The company should also consider its own interests, such as the extent to which it may make itself vulnerable to hackers, viruses or other security breaches under each of the options, and the administrative burdens each option will create.

11.80 As indicated above, the usual methods of electronic communication that the company asks members expressly to agree to are:

- sending or supplying a document or information to the member by attaching it to an e-mail to the member; and

- making it available to the member by means of a website (that is, posting it on a website and sending the member a notification that it is there, containing a hyperlink to it).

11.81 If a member does not expressly agree to the second option, all is not lost for the company. It may be able to rely on a member's deemed consent to making documents and information available to them by means of a website in certain circumstances (see **11.95ff**).

11.82 When deciding on the means of electronic communication they will offer, companies must, in practice, ensure they are up to date with technological developments. For example, if members' firewalls are weeding out e-mails containing hyperlinks as a measure against unsolicited e-mails (e-mailing hyperlinks to targets is a popular technique of bulk e-mail advertisers and spammers), companies need to be aware of this, and ensure either that its e-mails are not weeded out or that it switches to an alternative method of communicating with members.

11.83 If a document is sent as an e-mail attachment, companies should consider the format it will be sent in, given the technology likely to be available to members. If provided as a Microsoft Word file or an Adobe pdf file, most members should be able to read it, but what about a tif or jpg file? Companies must find out, and prefer, the options most likely to be convenient for their members.

11.84 The size of the document in each format should be considered. Creating an electronic version of a set of accounts can result in a very large file. If e-mailed to members, is it likely to be rejected by many internet service providers' e-mail systems and therefore unlikely to reach many members, on account of its size. Companies should check the rules of the most popular service providers in this respect.

11.85 Companies should also consider how members will respond to the offer. The 2000 ICSA Guide recommends that they should be able to do so by post, fax, e-mail or online (for example, by submitting a form made available on a website), or by phone – in which case a verification procedure is advisable (para 5.1).

11.86 Once it has established an electronic communications policy in relation to these matters, the company can finalise the invitation it will send to members, setting out its offer. The invitation is best sent by post to members, in hard copy format, but it is common for only parts to appear in a hard copy version, with the rest set out on a website to which members are directed in the event they are minded to take up the invitation. In any event, taken as a whole, it should include the following:

- the alternative options being offered. It should detail which documents will be made available, in what format, and by which electronic means, and explain the procedures that will be adopted in each case (2000 ICSA Guide, para 4.4). The options on offer must include the option to continue receiving documents in hard copy format, by post (2000 ICSA Guide, para 4.4);

- information about the hardware/software the member must have, if the company is to communicate effectively with him (2000 ICSA Guide, para 3.10);

- a unique code for use by that member if he agrees that the company may communicate with him electronically (companies can also include this unique code on members' dividend documentation and share certificates);

- a request for the member's relevant e-mail address, fax number etc, to be used when communicating with the member electronically, dependent on the option chosen by the member;

- mechanisms for the member to use to respond, notifying their preference, and clear advice on how to use them (2000 ICSA Guide, para 5.1); and

- a warning to members that a company's legal obligation to give notice is satisfied when it transmits it – it is not liable if failure in transmission is beyond its control.

11.87 Each member can then choose his preferences. When members reply, the secretary or other person responsible for the registers (or, for many larger companies, a registrar looking after the administration of the company's register of members on its behalf) should take care that, if they record a member's phone or fax number, or e-mail address, in the register of members (as it is sensible to do), these are not in any part of the register to which the public have access (2006 Act ICSA Guidance, para C2).

11.88 Any e-mail address, phone or fax number or any other 'address' supplied by a member for the transmission of electronic communications is not statutorily required to be included in the register of members. It is not therefore covered by the standard exemptions under the Data Protection Act 1998. It should not therefore be released to third parties, such as a person inspecting the register of members. The secretary (or registrar) should also ensure compliance with the Data Protection Act 1998 by both the company and, if any, its registrars.

11.89 The same considerations apply to other information, such as any unique identifier used by or in relation to a member for the purposes of electronic communications between companies and their members.

11.90 Internally, companies need to consider who has access to which non-statutory information and their levels of authority.

11.91 The fact that a member has expressly agreed that the company may communicate with him electronically does not mean that the company always has to do so. It may choose to continue to communicate with that member using hard copy, by post, or do so occasionally – for example, if there has been a software or hardware failure at the time it wants to send documents to members. A company will therefore, for convenience, often ask members if it may make all permitted documents and information available electronically, so it has the option whether or not to do so in respect of each.

Making documents and information available by means of a website

11.92 CA 2006 provides that a document or information is validly sent or supplied by a company if it is made available via a website in accordance with the rules set out in Sch 5. A common option being offered by companies is therefore to make documents and information available to members by means of a website (that is, placing documents or information on a website, and notifying members (electronically or otherwise)), with companies making sure that members agree that the notification (called the 'Notice of Availability' in the 2000 ICSA Guide) can be sent electronically, rather than by post. In essence, the company is offering to e-mail to members a hyperlink to web pages containing the document or information – for example, a notice of a general meeting and/or the statutory accounts, for example.

11.93 Under Sch 5, para 10 the rules apply to a document or information to be sent or supplied to a person as a member of the company in their own right, to a person nominated by a member in accordance with the company's articles to enjoy or exercise all or any specified rights of the member in relation to the company (s 145), and to a person nominated by a member under s 146 to enjoy information rights.

11.94 Such persons can either give their express agreement (general or specific) to receiving documents or information via a website or the company can rely on the 'deemed consent' provisions in Sch 5. If express agreement is sought, an invitation can be sent, as discussed above.

A member's deemed agreement to making documents available by means of a website

11.95 The deemed consent provisions in Sch 5 say that a member is deemed to have agreed that the company can send or supply documents or information by making them available via a website in certain circumstances, and provided a certain procedure is followed. In addition to, or instead of, asking a member for express agreement to making documents or information available by means of a website, a company may choose to follow the procedure that can lead to deemed consent from the member.

11.96 The members must first either:

- pass an ordinary resolution that the company may communicate with members through a website (the ordinary resolution must be filed at Companies House within 15 days); or

- the company's articles must contain a provision to this effect.

11.97 As discussed at **11.45**, it is unlikely that older articles will contain appropriate provisions, so companies with pre-2007 articles must either alter their articles or pass the requisite resolution.

11.98 However, for companies that adopt the model form, it is a moot point whether reg 48(1) or 79(1) for private companies limited by shares or public companies respectively, are sufficient to satisfy the requirements of Sch 5, para 10.

11.99 In addition, each member must be individually asked by the company to agree to communication by means of a website (either generally or in relation to specific documents), by sending him a 'request'. If the member fails to respond within 28 days, starting with the date on which the request is sent, he is deemed to have agreed that the company may send or supply documents or information to him by making them available via a website (para 10(3)(a) of Sch 5).

11.100 A request must:

- clearly state the effect of a failure to respond by the member (for example, that he would be deemed to have consented if he does not reply within 28 days starting with the date on which the request is sent); and

- not be sent less than 12 months after a previous request made to that member in respect of a similar class of documents (Sch 5, para 10(4)(b)).

11.101 The 2006 Act ICSA Guidance also recommends that the company consider including the following in the request:

- the software/hardware a member will need to see the documents or information on the website;

- any time-limit, at the end of which the deemed consent will be treated as expiring (although it can be indefinite);

- a statement that the member can limit the documents or information he is prepared to receive via a website;

- a statement making it clear that where a member agrees to the use of a website, that this constitutes actual agreement (general or specific) under Sch 5, para 9(a), not deemed agreement under para 10; and

- a statement making it clear whether a member's consent or deemed consent will be treated as continuing to apply if he ceases to be a member, but then rejoins again in the future. ICSA points out that 'on this basis the consent could continue until cancelled, or any nil holding is removed from the register (currently after 20 years but ... reduced to 10 years under the Companies Act 2006)'.

11.102 Some companies will wish to send members a request as soon as they become members. This means the company can make documents and information available via a website to those who either agree to this expressly, or who do not respond and are therefore deemed to have agreed, as early as possible. However, as ICSA points out, companies that do this will need to manage the fact that the 12-month anniversaries for members who respond within 28 days saying they do *not* want documents or information to be made available by means of a website will vary.

11.103 The alternative is to send a request to all relevant shareholders (those who have not yet agreed to receive documents and information by means of a website, whether expressly, or by virtue of the deemed consent provisions) on the same date. This way there is less complication in keeping track of when the 12-month anniversaries fall, as they all share the same anniversary. On the other hand, there will be a period between new members joining the company and the next date for sending out requests when the company will not be able to communicate with them by means of a website.

11.104 Particularly, ICSA warns public companies to beware dispatching a 'deeming' request invitation with their annual general meeting mailings in circumstances where the annual general meeting date may have been brought forward for any reason, as this may inadvertently reduce the period since the last request to fewer than 12 months. In any event, ICSA states that:

> '... it is anyway our view that, in normal circumstances, recommended best practice is to consult no more frequently than every other mailing cycle. This is because we do not believe that those that want hard copy should be unduly pestered by the company into having to reaffirm this preference too often.'

11.105 The 2006 Act ICSA Guidance also deals with the debate about whether the request can be sent before the articles have been changed or a resolution passed allowing the deeming provisions. The ICSA view is that there is no reason why it cannot, but it points out that 'legal opinion does, however, vary on this point, with some taking the view that the power to issue the invitation cannot be exercised until the authority to use website as the default communication has been obtained. Companies will want to take their own advice'.

11.106 ICSA also suggests that, if companies do decide to send out the request in advance of the article change/authorising resolution and the period between the date the invitation is sent and the date of the meeting is greater than 28 days, the company consider extending the deadline for responses until the day after the meeting. In any event, it points out, the deemed agreement would not take effect until the authorising resolution or article change was passed.

11.107 ICSA also recommends that companies consider whether it is preferable for them to explain the new regime in advance, for example, in an explanation sent out with the notice of general meeting, and then follow this up with the actual request later in the year (possibly as a separate mailing, or with any dividend). ICSA sees this as having benefits in terms of managing communications with shareholders and from a reputational perspective.

11.108 Once a request has been sent, there are three possible outcomes:

(1) If a member replies within 28 days, agreeing to the company making documents or information available via a website, that constitutes an express agreement to it.

(2) If the member replies within 28 days saying he does not agree, the company may not send or supply documents or information to him via a website (although it may be able to send documents or information to him electronically by other means if he has expressly consented to that). The company must wait 12 months before it can ask him again for consent in relation to the class of documents for which consent was originally sought.

(3) As stated above, if a member fails to respond within 28 days starting with the date on which the request is sent, he is deemed to have agreed that the company may send or supply documents or information to him by making them available via a website.

11.109 The 2006 Act ICSA Guidance recommends that responses requesting hard copy arriving after the 28-day cut-off should be treated as a revocation of the shareholder's deemed agreement, and communications should revert to hard copy. If a record date for posting a hard copy document has been recently missed, ICSA's recommended best practice is that the company send that person a hard copy of that document.

11.110 Similar rules apply for debenture holders, except the power to allow the company to communicate via a website will be set out in the debenture.

The relationship between an invitation and a request

11.111 A company will usually wish to seek express agreement to the use of electronic communications by sending out an invitation as discussed above, and will also usually wish to send out a request in relation to making documents available by means of a website in order to take advantage of the deemed consent provisions that flow if the recipient does not respond to the request.

11.112 Some companies have combined the two into one document, taking care to differentiate between the part that is the invitation and the part that is the request. However, given that there are specific statutory requirements in relation to the request, but not for an invitation, many companies send them as separate documents, so there is a clear differentiation between the two.

11.113 The two can usually be sent together, subject to the prohibition against sending a request to the same member in relation to the same or a similar class of documents within 12 months after the last such request.

The notification that a document is available on a website

11.114 If a document or information is to be made available by means of a website, the company must send each relevant member (those who have consented, or are deemed to have consented, to receive documents or information by means of a website) a notification that it is there.

11.115 Under CA 2006, Sch 5, para 13, the notification must notify the intended recipient of:

- the presence of the document or information on the website;

- the address of the website;

- the place on the website where it may be accessed; and

- how to access the document or information.

11.116 Under s 309(2), if the document on the website is a notice of general meeting, the notification must also contain other statutory information, namely:

- that it concerns a notice of a general meeting;

- the place, date and time of the meeting; and

- if the company is a public company, whether the meeting will be an annual general meeting.

11.117 Paragraph A4 of the 2006 Act ICSA Guidance states that notifications, whether by electronic means or in hard copy, should be kept short and to the point to keep the interest of the reader. To ensure consistency, apart from any necessary adaptation for the specific medium, ICSA recommends that the content of the electronic and hard copy notification should be identical. The notifications should provide signposts to the more detailed information on the website.

11.118 When the notification of availability is in respect of a general meeting, it is also recommended best practice that the notification spells out any proxy appointment deadlines. Companies may also want to consider highlighting any non-routine business.

11.119 Paragraph A5 of the 2006 Act ICSA Guidance deals with the danger that notifications of availability of documents or information on a website discourage shareholder voting and participation. ICSA points out that the issue is that, in the process of changing the communications environment with shareholders, voting and participation levels may be negatively affected.

11.120 ICSA states that, where a company chooses to use the website as a default, it is likely that in the first few years of the new regime a number of members will inadvertently be deemed to have accepted the website by failing to respond to the request sent to them under para 10 of Sch 5. During this transitional phase, until shareholders become accustomed to the new communications regime, ICSA's recommended best practice is that any notification of website availability for general meeting material should not only give the website link but, where sent in hard copy, should include a hard copy personalised proxy card (possibly with return envelope) and details of any online voting facility or, where sent by e-mail, a direct link to any online voting facility. Details of any telephone voting options should also be made clear.

11.121 ICSA says that it is not good practice to post blank proxy cards on the company website as unpersonalised proxy cards with unclear signatures often have to be rejected by registrars.

11.122 If the notification is sent by e-mail, the 2000 ICSA Guide specifically stated that it must:

- contain a hyperlink to the relevant webpage (at para 7.3); and

- alert the member that the company's obligation to notify the member is satisfied when it transmits the notification – it is not liable if failure in transmission is beyond its control (at para 8.9).

11.123 Paragraph A4 in the 2006 Act ICSA Guidance deals with the issue of when the notification must be sent. In terms of annual report mailings for public companies, as is the practice now for those signed up to electronic communications, ICSA's recommended best practice is that the notification of availability, if an e-mail:

- is sent on the publication date for the annual general meeting material (ie the date on which the material would be both on the website and expected to land on the doorsteps of shareholders receiving hard copy); and

- that the company's articles state that an e-mail is deemed to be delivered on the same day that it is sent (the default position in CA 2006 is that e-mails are deemed to have been received 48 hours plus non-working days after sending).

11.124 Where the notification is sent in hard copy, ICSA recommends it should be sent at the same time as the full hard copy mailing (the default position in CA 2006 in relation to hard copy is also that it is deemed to have been received 48 hours plus non-working days later, subject to any contrary provisions in the articles).

11.125 ICSA states that it does not support the concept of advance notification, for example, with the publication of an annual calendar, as shareholders should not have to diarise a future event. When the shareholder receives the notification, the material should be available; clearly an advance notification also has the disadvantage of being subject to unforeseen events and change.

11.126 In any event, as regards notices of meeting, s 309 of CA 2006 states that the notice must be available on the website at the time the notification is sent.

11.127 A notification may itself only be sent or supplied to a member electronically if the member concerned has expressly agreed that it may be sent or supplied to him electronically. There are no provisions in CA 2006 providing for deemed consent in relation to the notification.

11.128 A company may therefore find itself in a situation where it has sent a member:

- an invitation to agree to electronic communications, including a notification that a document or information is available by means of a website; and

- a request (failure to respond to which within 28 days results in the member being deemed to have agreed to communication by means of a website).

11.129 The member having failed to respond to either, the company is treated as having his deemed consent to making documents or information available by means of a website but, when it comes to post its first document or information on the website, the company may find that it has to send him the notification that it is there by post, or give it to him personally, because it does not have his express agreement that it can be sent or supplied to him electronically.

11.130 In practice, this could work out just as expensive as simply sending the document that is made available on the website to the recipient in hard copy form in the first place. There is no provision in CA 2006 whereby members are deemed to have agreed to the sending or supply of a notification by electronic means, for example, e-mail. The company must therefore ask members for their express agreement to the sending of a notification by electronic means.

Making the document or information available on a website

11.131 There are specific rules governing how a document or information is made available via a website. These apply whether a member has expressly agreed to receiving documents or information by means of a website or is deemed to have agreed.

11.132 The company must also ensure the following:

- The document or information on a website must be made available in a form, and by a means, that the company reasonably considers will enable the recipient to read it and retain a copy of it.

- The company must make the document or information available on the website throughout the period specified by any applicable provision of CA 2006 (for example, if the document on the website is a notice of general meeting, it must be available on the website throughout the period beginning with the date of the notification and ending with the conclusion of the meeting – s 309). If no such period is specified, the document or information must be available for a period of 28 days beginning with the date on which the notification that the document is available on the website is sent or supplied to the person in question or, if later, the date on which the document or information first appears on the website (Sch 5, paras 14(1) and 13(2)).

- A failure to make a document or information available on a website during the period is disregarded if it is made available on the website for part of that period and the failure to make it available throughout that period is wholly attributable to circumstances that it would not be reasonable to have expected the company to prevent or avoid (Sch 5, para 14(2)).

11.133 Given the first requirement above, companies need to decide the format to be used when posting documents on a website.

11.134 Para A6 of the 2006 Act ICSA Guidance deals with website management issues. When designing the website pages which carry the documents or information the company is communicating to shareholders, ICSA recommends that it consider the varying levels of technology available to those shareholders. It is recommended best practice that any invitation to shareholders about the use of electronic communications gives details, or provides a link to details, of any particular software or equipment specifications which will be required to enable the shareholder to take advantage of the options being made available. Guidance on where the relevant software can be downloaded free of charge should also be provided.

11.135 The 2000 ICSA Guide recommended that a document posted to a website should always be made available in basic HTML format, even if also provided in some other format, so it can be read by browsers likely to be available to members, such as Internet Explorer or FireFox. The 2000 Guide cites the example of a company wishing to make a document available in a higher level code that might not be accessible to all, such as XBRL (Extensible Business Reporting Language), and says that the document should also be made available in HTML. However, the recommendation would also seem to apply to a company wishing to provide a document in a more common, accessible format, such as an Adobe pdf file or Microsoft Word, so that, even then, the company should also provide an HTML version of the document.

11.136 Para A6 of the 2006 Act ICSA Guidance also states that care needs to be taken to distinguish carefully between audited and non-audited information on websites. To avoid the risk of sections of the website being deemed to be part of the company's report and accounts, it is currently recommended best practice not to allow any hyperlinks from the online report and accounts to any other part of the website.

11.137 If a company posts accounts and reports on its website, and sends members a notification that the accounts can be found there, the accounts will invariably be split up and parts posted to different pages, with appropriate hyperlinks so the visitor to the site can navigate around them. The 2000 ICSA Guide specified certain rules designed to ensure members can differentiate between statutory and other information when navigating around the relevant site.

11.138 Each page on the website must identify clearly whether the information on it is statutory or not, and whether it forms part of the audited accounts (2000 ICSA Guide, para 15.4). A simple way of dealing with this is to include a prominent banner on the side of the relevant pages saying whether it is statutory and/or audited or not. ICSA also suggests a warning window that appears whenever visitors enter or leave a statutory part of the site.

11.139 The company must check with its auditors before it displays audited information, and/or the audit report on its website (2000 ICSA Guide, para 15.6), to make sure the auditors are happy with the fact of the report going online, and the way in which the audited accounts and the report will appear in the particular circumstances. This should happen early, to make sure the auditors can produce a report that will translate easily into the company's preferred online layout.

11.140 The company must check parts of the site containing statutory information periodically for tampering and hacking, and the home page of that part of the site where the accounts appear must give the date and time the contents were last checked (2000 ICSA Guide, para 15.8). In most cases, periodic checking should merely mean extending existing security checks to that part of the site.

11.141 The company must be careful that financial information it posts to its site does not constitute a financial promotion that contravenes the Financial Services and Markets Act 2000, or breach the provisions of s 434 of the 2006 Act which prohibits publication of any of its statutory accounts without the relevant auditor's report. It must also ensure that price-sensitive information is not posted to the website before reported to any appropriate authorities.

11.142 There may also be restrictions on publication of certain information in other jurisdictions. ICSA (2000 ICSA Guide, para 16.2) recommends that access to pages that should not be published in particular jurisdictions should be limited to those who acknowledge, online, the restrictions, and, maybe, confirm that they are not resident in that jurisdiction.

11.143 The 2006 Act ICSA Guidance states that companies need to bear in mind that the shareholder needs to be able to retain a copy of the document or information being made available to him, and that the document must be able to be read and pictures seen with the naked eye. A format that can be retained/saved by the shareholder may not be the best format type for online printing, viewing and navigation, so companies may want to offer more than one format. Providing more than one format may also be helpful in compliance with the requirements of the Equality Act 2010.

11.144 In the current environment, ICSA's 2006 Guidance also recommends that it is generally better to provide a link to a holding webpage, from which a pdf (or similar) can be accessed, rather than providing a link directly to a pdf. This holding webpage approach does not assume the recipient has the software to open a pdf and provides opportunity to offer explanations and options. It would be bad practice to give people who may have a slow internet connection a direct link to download a very large document.

11.145 Given the third requirement at **11.132**, the 2000 ICSA Guide discusses the possibility of sites going down, and recommends that companies give 'serious thought' to arranging a form of back-up facility for their websites (2000 ICSA Guide, para 19.6).

11.146 If a site does go down during part of a period when documents or information are supposed to be available, commentators consulted during the period leading up to publication of the Companies Act 1985 (Electronic Communications) Order 2000 suggested that it would be reasonable to expect a company to anticipate the number of possible impressions ('hits') it might receive on its site following posting of particular documents or information (and also during other potential peaks, such as posting of a notice of a meeting and during periods allowed for filing of proxies online), and to expect the company to prevent or avoid the site going down in consequence of them.

When calculating the possible numbers of hits, the company should take into account other potential visitors to the site, such as analysts, the press, competitors etc, as well as members. Consequently, if a site goes down because of the number of hits it receives at such times, such a failure is likely to invalidate proceedings at the meeting.

11.147 The 2000 ICSA Guide (para 6.2) recommends that the company's website should include a phone and fax number, and an online election form, whereby any member can alter his preferences and/or notify the company of any changes in his contact details, ie the e-mail address, phone or fax numbers to be used to communicate electronically with him. These should be continuously available on the company's website. The company should also ask for periodic confirmation of contact details, for example, when sending dividend vouchers.

11.148 It is also ICSA's recommended best practice that the company's and/or registrar's website should either include an online facility to enable shareholders to notify the company of any change in their choice of communication medium or electronic address details or inform them as to how they may do so.

11.149 It is clearly increasingly important to ensure the availability of the website at all times.

When is an electronic communication 'sent' and 'delivered'?

11.150 Section 1147(3) of CA 2006 deals with deemed delivery of documents and information sent or supplied by a company by electronic means, and if the company is able to show that it was properly addressed, it is deemed to have been received by the intended recipient 48 hours after it was sent.

11.151 Under s 1147(4), documents or information sent or supplied by means of a website are deemed to have been received by the intended recipient when the material was first made available on the website or, if later, when the recipient received (or is deemed to have received) notice of the fact that the material was available on the website.

11.152 Section 1157(5) provides that, in calculating the relevant period of hours for the purposes of this section, no account shall be taken of any part of a day that is not a working day.

11.153 These rules are, however, subject to a company's articles.

11.154 Any notice period runs from the expiry of that 48-hour period after the notice has been sent. For example, the notice period for a notice of general meeting communicated electronically runs from the expiry of that 48-hour period. See 'Non-delivery' at **11.156**ff for the rules as to notice period following failed delivery.

11.155 Given that electronic messages are supposed to be instantaneous, 48 hours may seem an unreasonably long time. ICSA recommends that companies should consider whether that is an appropriate period for their needs, and suggests that some may prefer to amend Table A to provide for a shorter deemed delivery time. However, ICSA research shows that some e-mails do not arrive at their destinations until 36–48 hours after being sent, and ICSA therefore 'strongly recommends' companies to retain the 48-hour provision unless there is good reason.

Non-delivery

11.156 It is important that the company monitors e-mails sent (whether notification that documents or information are available on a website or e-mails with documents attached) for non-delivery. It should use a system that confirms the total number of e-mails sent and, ideally, records recipients (2000 ICSA Guide, para 8.8). The company should keep a certified copy of that record, including notices of failed transmissions and resendings. (An 'out of office' message is not to be treated as failed.)

11.157 Similar precautions apply if a notification, or documents or information, is served by fax. If served by fax, a transaction report or log should be printed and certified (2000 ICSA Guide, para 8.7).

11.158 Companies should consider how long they will keep such records – 6 years is recommended, bearing in mind that litigation can be instituted for up to 6 years after a cause of action has arisen.

11.159 If electronic transmission consistently fails, ICSA recommended in the 2000 ICSA Guide that the company send a hard copy of the document to the member within 48 hours of the first attempt to send it, together with a notice telling the member why he is being sent a hard copy by post (2000 ICSA Guide, para 8.10). It would also be prudent to ask the member to confirm his contact details by return, in case the failure is due to a change in those details or the contact details held by the company are wrong. A company may wish, in its electronic communications policy, to specify how many transmissions it will attempt, and at what intervals, before resorting to sending a hard copy.

11.160 In the event that an electronic transmission relating to a notice of a general meeting fails, but is either:

(1) successfully re-sent; or

(2) a transmission having consistently failed, a hard copy is sent within 48 hours after the first attempt to send it,

then ICSA recommends that the notice period runs from the time that the first attempted transmission would have been deemed delivered if it had been successfully 'sent' – ie 48 hours after the first attempted transmission. The fact the first transmission failed, and that the subsequent successful transmission, or the sending of hard copy, may have occurred up to 48 hours later, is ignored.

11.161 In the case of companies sending documents by e-mail, some are carrying out regular 'test' e-mailings to check the e-mail addresses held (particularly before major e-mailings).

11.162 The company should, if it maintains a branch register and wishes to communicate electronically with members whose details are recorded on that register, ensure that the law of the country in which the relevant members are located allows electronic communications.

Right to require hard copy version

11.163 Generally, under s 1145, a member of a company or a holder of a company's debentures who has received a document or information from the company otherwise than in hard copy form, can require the company to send him a hard copy version. The company must comply within 21 days of receiving a member's request that it do so. The company may not charge the member. ICSA recommends, at para B4 in the 2006 Act ICSA Guidance, that the document that is sent in hard copy in response to a request under s 1145 can be a version of what was sent electronically (ie it does not have to be identical) but it must not exclude any information or exclude any text or exclude any visuals (photographs, charts etc) if they add anything of substance to the text: for example, by showing shareholders a new design of a company product. If the document was originally sent to the shareholder electronically there is no time limit to this right under s 1145 for as long as he remains a shareholder.

11.164 Paragraph B5 in the 2006 Act ICSA Guidance recommends that it is important to set up a system to meet requests for hard copies of all information made available electronically as the company has the statutory 21 days within which to supply the hard copy. ICSA also reminds companies that they will need to keep records of those who have revoked consent to electronic or website communication.

11.165 Paragraph A8 points out an issue for a company that is relying on the deemed consent rules (see **11.95**ff) in relation to documents and information made available by means of a website (which relies on a member having failed to respond to a request sent to him in this respect). ICSA warns that such companies may find, on the first posting of a document or information on a website and notification to members that it is there, that an unknown number of members, not having taken on board the result of their inaction, may later come forward and request hard copies. ICSA therefore recommends that a contingency figure should be added to the company's hard copy print run of, say, accounts and reports. In subsequent years, experience will make this number easier to estimate. It is also possible that it may impact on practice regarding summary financial statements, including whether these are sent at all.

ELECTRONIC COMMUNICATIONS FROM INDIVIDUAL MEMBERS TO THEIR COMPANIES

11.166 The statutory rules now permit any document or information required or authorised to be sent or supplied by an individual member to their company to be sent electronically – for example, to an e-mail address or fax number notified to members for that purpose by the company. Members may not post documents or information on a website, and notify the company they are there, as the company may sometimes do for documents and information for members, as discussed above.

11.167 The rules for electronic communications by individual members (but not corporate members, to which Sch 5 applies – see below) to their companies are set out in Sch 4 of CA 2006.

11.168 The individual member may only send or supply information and documents to the company electronically if the company has expressly agreed (generally or specifically) to that means of communication, has provided an electronic address to be used for that purpose and has not revoked that agreement (Sch 5, para 6), or if the 'deemed consent' provisions discussed below apply.

11.169 Any existing agreement to the sending or supply of documents or information electronically under the pre-CA 2006 rules can be carried over and treated as an agreement made under the new rules (see below). Similarly, an electronic address provided for the purposes of the pre-CA 2006 rules can continue to be used under the new rules.

11.170 The 2000 ICSA Guide (para 3.15) recommended that members are warned that electronic communications containing a virus will not be accepted by the company.

11.171 The agreement with the member should include:

- clear instructions regarding the address, to which it should be returned; and

- a warning that the form will only be valid if lodged at the address supplied by the company.

11.172 For forms of appointment of proxies, the 2000 ICSA Guide recommended that an online form of appointment should include a field that enables a member to key freeform instructions – for example, if the member wants to instruct the proxy to abstain on a particular resolution or otherwise add to or qualify his voting instructions to the proxy. The exception is where the proxy to be appointed is the chairman of the meeting, and the form makes it clear that the chair is not prepared to accept an appointment subject to such additional instructions.

11.173 The 2006 ICSA Guide recommended that, in all circumstances, the members appointing the proxy should be required to state their unique identifiers on the form of appointment itself. If forms of appointment may be deposited by fax, companies should ask that the form be signed by the appointor, as well as including the unique identifier, so that the signature is visible on the fax.

11.174 If the appointment is made by completing an online form, and the company's register of members is held in electronic format, the company may wish to compare the information given in the online form (including, in each case, their unique identifiers) against the register electronically, to flag up duplicates. In that case, the 2000 ICSA Guide also suggested that the online facility should allow a member to visit the share register to check his holding, in case the member wishes to split his votes.

11.175 Another ICSA suggestion is that appointors should see a 'thank you' message on screen following submission of an online form, as evidence that the data elements keyed by them have at least been recorded in the correct format, even if not yet checked.

11.176 If a form of appointment is deposited by e-mail, the company should consider automatically acknowledging receipt by return e-mail, even if the form will not be read straight away. At the least, an acknowledgement should be sent to those who specifically ask for one.

11.177 It is recommended (2000 ICSA Guide, para 14.3) that forms of appointment filed electronically should be kept for one month after the meeting if no poll was demanded, and for one year after if a poll was demanded.

11.178 ICSA also recommend (2000 ICSA Guide, para 14.4) that e-mail or other addresses are recorded but are not included in any part of the register of members that is publicly available.

11.179 During consultation on the new rules, it was suggested that companies should establish 'record dates' – a fixed date and time at which the register will be 'frozen' – when convening meetings. Only members on the register on the record date would be entitled to receive notices and other documents sent out in advance of a meeting, and to attend and vote at the meeting.

11.180 One suggestion was to mimic the CREST rules for settlement and registration, used in relation to listed companies' shares. This provides that registers can be frozen at the close of business 2 days before the relevant general meeting.

11.181 Companies should consider providing a secure part of a website where members can log on to check that their proxy form has been received and that their instructions have been correctly construed and recorded.

11.182 Companies should consider the possibility that a proxy may wish to change his mind – perhaps several times. For example, he may decide he wants to change the person he wishes to appoint as his proxy or his voting instructions to his proxy. The 2000 ICSA Guide suggests (but this is not a formal recommendation in the ICSA Guide) that companies may wish to establish a policy in these respects, and alter their articles to include it, so that it is clear and available to all members.

11.183 Many of the commercial registrars' online electronic communications services (to companies wishing to offer members the option of sending and receiving electronic communications to and from them) include management of electronic filing of proxies.

11.184 Companies may have members who are members of Euroclear's CREST electronic proxy voting service. If a company is considering offering this facility to its CREST members, it should seriously consider setting up an online service for its non-CREST members too, if it does not wish to be criticised by non-CREST members.

11.185 The Euroclear website at www.euroclear.com is useful reading for companies that are setting up their own individual electronic proxy voting facility or using the services provided by a registrar.

11.186 There is provision in CA 2006 for a company to have deemed to have agreed to receive documents or information from a member in certain circumstances. A company is deemed to have agreed to receive in electronic form:

- any document or information relating to proceedings at a meeting, if the notice of meeting includes an electronic address, which, for these purposes, means any address or number used for the purposes of sending or receiving documents or information by electronic means, such as an e-mail address or fax number (s 333(1));

- any document or information relating to proxies for that meeting (including the appointment of a proxy in relation to a meeting, any document necessary to show the validity of, or otherwise relating to, the appointment of a proxy, and notice of the termination of the authority of a proxy), if the form of proxy or proxy invitation sent in relation to the meeting includes an electronic address (s 333(2)); and

- any document containing or accompanying a proposed written resolution of the members, if it includes an electronic address (s 298).

11.187 In each case, this is subject to any conditions or limitations specified in the document itself. Companies should therefore beware of e-mail addresses/phone numbers in such documents or, if they include them, make it clear if they are not intended to indicate deemed agreement to receipt of documents electronically.

Authentication

11.188 There are constant references throughout CA 2006 to the need for documents or information sent or supplied by a person to a company to be authenticated. Under s 1146, a hard copy document or information is sufficiently authenticated if it is signed by the person sending or supplying it.

11.189 For a document or information sent or supplied in electronic form, there is sufficient authentication if the identity of the sender is confirmed in a manner specified by the company, or if it has not specified a way to confirm the sender's identity:

- the communication contains or is accompanied by a statement of the identity of the sender; and

- the company has no reason to doubt the truth of that statement.

11.190 In order to create certainty, a company may wish to provide in its articles how a sender is to confirm their identity of the sender. In any event, there is no need for documents sent or received by electronic communication to be signed with a digital signature, or to be encrypted, but the company may wish to consider these.

11.191 Where a document or information is sent or supplied by one person on behalf of another, s 1146(4) makes it clear that nothing in the section affects any provision of the company's articles under which the company may require reasonable evidence of the authority of the former to act on behalf of the latter.

GENERAL MEETINGS INVOLVING ELECTRONIC COMMUNICATIONS

Background

11.192 Traditionally, general meetings of members of a company have been held in one geographic location, with members coming together face to face to conduct business. However, case-law and statutory provisions now permit, in certain circumstances, electronic participation in members' meetings. There are differing degrees to which members can participate electronically in meetings, and each is considered below.

Entirely virtual general meetings

11.193 The most extreme example of electronic participation would be a meeting at which members communicated electronically with each other but none were physically together in the same location, and they could neither see nor hear each other. This 'virtual' meeting would have no physical location, ie there would be no one place where two or more members meet together, face to face.

11.194 Such a virtual general meeting could be held on the internet, using SMS, a bulletin board, blog, social networking site or chatroom facility that allows members to post their comments to a web page in real time. All members could see each other's postings and could therefore exchange views, debate and make decisions – many of the elements of a meeting – but all online. Can a company hold an entirely virtual general meeting in this way under UK law?

11.195 Consultees were asked, during the consultation that led eventually to CA 2006, by the Department for Business, Innovation and Skills (at the time called the Department of Trade and Industry),[15] whether entirely virtual general meetings should be allowed. Responses were informed and useful. The debate assumed that they were not currently possible under UK law – and consultees felt generally that neither members, nor advisors, nor investor and professional bodies were ready for them.

11.196 Many consultees[16] believed, however, that entirely virtual general meetings are inevitable in the UK, at least for private companies. There was therefore much discussion of potential practical problems in calling and holding such meetings. For example, a notice of general meeting would not specify a physical location, but a web address, and a time at which participants would log on to take part in the meeting in real time. Some means of authenticating members would be needed – at least, a password protected sign on. Current technology means members can only post their comments to the site one at a time. Rules would be required to determine the order in which members could post comments. If many members wanted to contribute, the meeting would proceed very slowly. Exchanges might take place over several days, or even longer. The chairman would need the means to intervene both throughout the meeting (for example, to keep postings to a reasonable length, to bring debate on each resolution to a close and to prevent debate from becoming personal or even defamatory) and at the end (to close the meeting). Some form of electronic voting would be required, or provision made for a subsequent vote at a time determined by the chairman of the virtual meeting or, more probably, specified in advance, in the notice of meeting.

---

[15] 'Modern Company Law for a Competitive Economy: Final Report' URN 01/942 and URN 01/943.
[16] Including the Law Society for England and Wales.

11.197 For general meetings other than annual general meetings, many respondents approved of virtual meetings for routine business, but favoured face-to-face meetings for contentious business, such as sacking a director. Can business easily be classified as routine or contentious? A resolution might be routine in one circumstance, but deeply controversial in another. The Law Society expressed concerns about dealing effectively with 'the genuinely difficult meeting', which could take into account the circumstances surrounding the meeting. The Society was also concerned about the potential for hijacking of virtual meetings by dissenting elements or, alternatively, the stifling of minority shareholders' views, if virtual meetings were allowed, but suggested a possible solution – a right for any member of a company to demand a face-to-face general meeting on any matter.

11.198 There was a strong body of opinion that annual general meetings should always be held as physical meetings. For directors to be truly accountable, members should be able to 'see the whites of their eyes'. Their reactions to questions, body language and other cues should be visible to members who wished to assess these face to face.

11.199 Despite the quality of consultees' contributions, we seem to be a long way from identifying all the issues surrounding entirely virtual general meetings, let alone resolving them. Many of the issues need resolution by legislation. Nor is there confidence in the available technology. There are concerns about how to validate entitlement to participate and vote online. Digital certificates are not sufficiently ubiquitous, and conventional passwords, limiting access to the relevant site or audio visual facility, could be stolen, abused by hackers or, in extreme cases, lead to coercion or influencing of members by extremist groups wishing to gain access to the virtual meeting. There are also record-keeping problems – how could the secretary be sure a quorum has been maintained, and what records should be kept of online participation?

11.200 So, even if legislation can be drafted that addresses all the problems and issues raised in the consultation, it is doubtful, given the current state of the relevant technology, that any company or member will wish to hold an entirely virtual general meeting. No UK company has, as far as the authors are aware, purported to hold an entirely virtual meeting using an internet facility, and there is no direct legal authority for such meetings. Companies are strongly advised not to purport to hold entirely virtual meetings.

11.201 Another way of holding a members' meeting using electronic communications might be for each member to have access to audio and video conferencing facilities, so all participants can see each other, and be seen, and hear each other and be heard. They can then debate, exchange views and make decisions – hold a meeting as if they were all physically present in the same room, even if some are not. The technology already exists.

11.202 Can members' meetings be held in this way? In the appeal court case of *Byng v London Life Association*,[17] the London Life company gave notice of an extraordinary general meeting (as they were then called) to be held, as a physical, face-to-face meeting, in a cinema in the Barbican. The venue proved too small for the numbers who turned up. The company tried to accommodate members in outer rooms, connected to the cinema by an audiovisual facility. The intention was that those in the outer rooms would be able to see, hear and be heard by those in the cinema. The facility broke down. The chairman adjourned the meeting to the Café Royal for the same afternoon. The case concerned the powers of the chair to adjourn the meeting and the validity of the resolutions purportedly passed at the adjourned meeting. These concerned a potential takeover of the company and were therefore important.

11.203 One argument was that there was no meeting at the Barbican because, for there to be a meeting, all participants had to be in the same place, face to face. This was rejected outright by the Court of Appeal. Browne-Wilkinson LJ said the rationale behind the requirement for meetings in the Companies Acts was that members should be able to attend in person to debate and vote on matters affecting the company. Technological advances meant that this could now be achieved without all the members coming together face to face. The fact that such advances could not be foreseen when the statutory requirements for meetings were laid down did not require the court to hold that a gathering at which not all members were face to face was not a 'meeting' for the purposes of the Companies Acts.

11.204 Had he stopped there, a case could be made for treating his words as judicial acceptance of entirely virtual meetings whereby members, all of whom were physically remote from each other, debated and voted electronically on matters affecting the company. However, the judge's comments were, of course, addressed to the situation in front of him – one in which there was a traditional face-to-face meeting of at least some of the members, but with others attempting to participate electronically. His subsequent words made it clear that he was not authorising entirely virtual general meetings per se. For example, he said that he had no doubt that, *in cases where the original venue proved inadequate to accommodate all those wishing to attend* (emphasis added), valid general meetings of a company could be held using overflow rooms. He also imposed two conditions. First, that all due steps should be taken to direct those unable to get into the main meeting room to the overflow rooms. Secondly, that there should be adequate audio-visual links to enable those in all the rooms to see and hear what was going on in the other rooms. These words are based on the assumption, which applied in *Byng*, that the original intention of those calling the meeting was that members should meet face to face in one physical location. If there are problems in holding such a meeting then, Browne-Wilkinson LJ says, it is acceptable to use electronic communications as a fall-back solution, subject to certain conditions, designed to protect members' rights to participate.

---

[17] (1989) BCLC 400.

11.205 This can safely be extended to cover situations where the overflow rooms are designated in advance. The best construction of *Byng v London Life Association*, therefore, is probably that it supports the principle that members can participate in a general meeting through remote electronic access, but that such participation must be built around a physical meeting – a 'hub' meeting – and that precautions must be taken to protect members' rights to participate. Many consultees in the (then) Department for Trade and Industry's company law review were firmly of the view that this was the effect of *Byng*. Some referred to companies that were already holding annual general meetings in this way – with a 'hub' meeting and electronic links in from other locations.

11.206 While *Byng* clearly contemplates use of electronic facilities in overflow rooms at the same venue as the hub meeting, a member could theoretically participate with the 'hub' meeting from elsewhere – for example, via a webcam facility on a PC in his living room. If companies are to allow remote participation, and many have authorised this in their articles of association already, they must consider the practical issues it raises – many of which have been discussed above in relation to entirely virtual meetings. For example, many of the respondees to the (then) Department for Trade and Industry's company law review consultation were of the view that the remote locations should be organised as physical meetings, attended by company officials or independent scrutineers, who ensure that the same or similar rules and procedures are observed at both the 'hub' and at each remote location.[18] The following paragraphs assume that this is the way that companies will choose to conduct general meetings involving electronic participation.

Should companies provide for remote participation in physical meetings?

11.207 Should companies make provision for remote participation in meetings, and what rules should they apply?

Best interests of the company?

11.208 Directors should consider whether remote participation is in the best interests of the company and its members. Certainly, remote participation offers greater opportunities for participation by both institutional and individual shareholders.

11.209 A concern expressed in the consultation, however, was that electronic participation in general meetings might be discriminatory against those without technological expertise or access. A member who could neither attend a general meeting nor participate electronically would be at a disadvantage compared with one who could not attend, but could participate electronically. This

---

[18] In which case the remote location (or one of them) could, indeed, be a member's living room, and be attended only by that member, but the officials or scrutineers would ensure the same (or similar) proprieties as at the 'hub' meeting.

argument is hard to sustain. A similar point could be made in relation to physical meetings – if some members can attend and some cannot, is that not discriminatory against those who cannot?[19] In any event, members who are uncomfortable with, or do not have access to, appropriate technology always have the option, just as they do now, to attend the physical, 'hub' meeting.

11.210 More of a possibility is that it is the remote participants who might be discriminated against. The consultation showed general concern that they should not be prejudiced. There were references to remote participants being sidelined; the difficulties of providing audio-visual facilities that enabled all members to see and be seen, hear and be heard, if there were too many remote locations; members in different time zones might be inconvenienced; remote participants might find their opportunities to ask questions were fewer than those attending the 'hub' meeting, especially if there were disruptive or disorderly elements at the 'hub', and they might feel themselves generally excluded from debate; the difficulty of giving remote participants the same opportunity to see directors' reactions to questions and body language as those attending the 'hub' meeting.

11.211 A general requirement is likely to be that members should know the location which the directors will attend, as many may decide they wish to attend that location in preference to others. All directors attending should go to the same location, and that should be the 'hub' meeting.

Equality Act 2010

11.212 Companies should also consider the potential application of disability discrimination legislation, which might prevent remote participation. However, the barriers to participation presented by audio-visual communication for, for example, people who are blind or deaf are no greater than those presented by physical meetings. It could be said that remote participation can reduce these problems as, for example, it means no travel is required and subtitles can be provided.

Amendment of articles

11.213 Any company that wishes to cater for electronic participation in members' meetings should amend its articles to address some or all of these matters. It is recommended that the relevant resolution should be proposed separately from other resolutions (including resolutions to make any other amendments to the articles). A public company might also offer members the opportunity, periodically, to vote whether to continue to allow electronic participation in meetings – perhaps every 3 years, at the annual general meeting. This might be put as an ordinary or special resolution – although

---

[19] One respondent made the point that access to many annual general meetings is confined to retired people living within reasonable travelling distance of the venue.

some companies may wish to provide for a greater majority than required for either. What sort of issues might a company cover?

Notice of such a general meeting

11.214 The notice of general meeting would have to specify all the venues at which members can attend, and say which will be the 'hub' meeting. The articles might specify a maximum number of locations for the hub and satellite meetings, in case of member demands for multiple venues nationally, or even worldwide, to ensure that the logistics of providing audio-visual communication that enables all to see, be seen, hear and be heard, are not too problematic.

Entitlement to participate

11.215 Provided that there are company officials or independent scrutineers at each venue, the means of proving entitlement to attend will remain the same as in a traditional meeting – save that steps will need to be taken to ensure that attendees are cross-checked across venues, to make sure that two different people do not present themselves at two locations, each claiming to be the same member. The same is also true of voting, both on a show of hands and on a poll.

Quorum

11.216 The question of quorum also needs to be considered, and the articles amended. Do all members count towards the quorum, irrespective of the venue they attend (as would seem sensible) so that, even if no one turns up at the hub meeting but there are sufficient in other venues to constitute a quorum, the meeting would proceed in any event? Or does there have to be a quorum at the hub?

11.217 What if, during the meeting, communications fail, so that not all members can see and hear each other, or be seen and heard? How will the chairman and secretary know this? Perhaps there should be periodic checking, or a procedure whereby disconnected members can phone in or otherwise alert the meeting of the failure? If the remaining members (who can still see etc) do not constitute a quorum, does the meeting continue, at least for the purpose of adjourning? Whichever options are appropriate, they should be specified clearly in the articles.

See, be seen, hear and be heard

11.218 A particular requirement might be that directors must attend the 'hub' meeting, so that members who want to be able to 'see the whites of their eyes' know which venue to attend. For remote participants, there might be more than one screen, or split screens, one of which is always focused on the directors, so that members can see their reactions and body language throughout.

11.219 A roving camera at each location might better ensure that all members feel part of the proceedings, instead of a fixed camera.

Voting and conduct of the meeting

11.220 The directors must be sure that voting procedures are sufficient to record every vote, whether on a show of hands, poll or demand for a poll, and taking into account the respective rights of proxies and corporate representatives. Care should be taken to check that a member and a proxy for that member, each in a different location, are not both permitted to vote the member's shares.

11.221 How the chairman exercises his powers regarding taking questions or points from remote locations, and how he judges the wishes of the meeting on, for example, adjournment, need to be considered, to ensure that he is still able to act in the best interests of the company when chairing a meeting involving remote participants.

Record keeping generally

11.222 The statutory minutes[20] of the meeting should record the different venues, who was present at each venue and who therefore took part in the meeting by electronic means.

Breakdowns in electronic communications

11.223 Directors should be sure that there are adequate systems to monitor for general breakdowns in electronic communications, and their immediate reporting to the chairman of the meeting, in addition to the procedures for members whose individual communications are broken.

11.224 Many respondents to the company law review consultation recommended that electronic systems be trialled internally first – perhaps for the company's internal management meetings.

Remote participation not mandatory

11.225 Even if authorised to do so by the articles, the board should not be required to offer remote electronic participation at every general meeting. The directors' duty to act in the company's best interests means they should consider whether there are any special circumstances that require *particular* general meetings to be held face to face.

11.226 Certain Companies Acts procedures, matters such as a buy back of own shares or approval of a director's service contract, require physical documents and/or statements to be presented at general meetings if the relevant

---

[20] Companies Act 2006, ss 248 and 355.

transaction is lawfully to be effected. This appears to preclude the holding of electronic meetings to consider these matters. Companies might decide that these matters should always be dealt with at face-to-face meetings, or under the statutory written resolution procedures.

11.227 If the agenda includes consideration and approval of the accounts, can members discuss the accounts properly without the degree of physical interaction – body language, free and frank discussion etc – that comes only at a face-to-face meeting? There have been comments among those responding to the Government's consultations during its major company law review, to the effect that meetings concerning the accounts (both directors' and members' meetings) should be face-to-face meetings. Directors should factor such considerations into their consideration of whether it is in their company's best interests that meetings to consider accounts can be held electronically.

Written resolutions in lieu of a meeting, as a solution

11.228 Companies wishing to take advantage of electronic communications, but reluctant to use them for actual meetings, can do so. The *Duomatic* case,[21] *Cane v Jones*[22] and related cases say that members' unanimous agreement on a matter generally overrides procedural rules otherwise required for a valid resolution of the members (see Chapter 3), even on a special resolution. So a unanimous decision of all members, reached following virtual exchange of views via, say, an internet bulletin board, would be held valid in circumstances covered by these cases.

11.229 Similarly, articles of association often permit written resolutions in lieu of a meeting, provided all members who would have been entitled to attend and vote if the resolution were to have been put to a meeting, sign a paper version of the resolution (or two or more identical paper versions of it).

11.230 An electronic debate can therefore be held (for example, by telephone) under each set of rules, culminating in the members each agreeing to sign such a resolution, the wording being agreed between them on the phone. The articles could provide that the written resolution itself is signed using electronic signatures.[23]

11.231 The procedure under s 288ff of CA 2006 also provides for written resolutions in lieu of a meeting. A virtual meeting could be the forum at which it is agreed to sign such a statutory written resolution. Again, the articles could provide that the written resolution itself is signed using electronic signatures.

11.232 None of these is authority to say that virtual general meetings may be held. The technology merely provides a way for members to communicate, prior to agreeing a decision under the relevant written resolution regime.

---

[21] [1969] 2 WLR 114.
[22] [1981] 1 All ER 533.
[23] For circumstances in which the resolution in writing can be signed electronically, see Chapter 3.

Chapter 12

MEETINGS OF DIRECTORS

INTRODUCTION

Function of the board

12.1 Section 154(2) of the Companies Act 2006 (CA 2006) provides that a public company must have at least two directors and every private company must have at least one director. Day-to-day management decisions are (unless reserved to the members by the Act or a company's memorandum or articles, or made subject to members' consent by virtue of a members' or other agreement) the collective responsibility of these directors, acting as a board.

12.2 The UK Corporate Governance Code[1] says that:[2]

> 'The board's role is to provide entrepreneurial leadership of the company within a framework of prudent and effective controls which enables risk to be assessed and managed. The board should set the company's strategic aims, ensure that the necessary financial and human resources are in place for the company to meet its objectives and review management performance. The board should set the company's values and standards and ensure that its obligations to its shareholders and others are understood and met.'

12.3 The UK Corporate Governance Code applies only to companies with a Premium listing of equity shares on the London Stock Exchange (and then only on a 'comply or explain', rather than mandatory, basis), but these words serve as a valuable summary of the role of the board of any UK company.

12.4 The UK Corporate Governance Code (Supporting Principles to B1) also provides that the board of a listed company should not be so large as to be unwieldy. It should, however, be of sufficient size that the balance of skills and experience is appropriate for the requirements of the business, and that changes to the board's composition can be managed without undue disruption. To ensure that power and information are not concentrated in one or two individuals, there should be an 'appropriate combination' on the board of both executive and non-executive directors. For most listed companies,[3] at least half

---

[1] At the time of writing, the latest version was published in September 2012. The UK Corporate Governance Code was previously called *The Combined Code on Corporate Governance* (June 2008). The UK Stewardship Code, which provides guidance on good practice for investors, operates in parallel with the UK Corporate Governance Code.
[2] Supporting Principles to A.1.
[3] See Provision B.1.1. But not 'smaller companies', ie companies below the FTSE 350

the board (excluding the chairman) should be independent non-executive directors. One of the non-executive directors should be appointed as 'senior independent director' (SID) by the board. The role of the SID is to be available to shareholders if their concerns have not been addressed by contact through the (normal channels) of chairman, chief executive or finance director, or if contact with those officers is inappropriate.[4]

12.5 The company secretary's role is also critical in a UK listed company. The UK Corporate Governance Code says that:[5]

> '... under the direction of the chairman, the company secretary's responsibilities include ensuring good information flows within the board and its committees and between senior management and non-executive directors, as well as facilitating induction and assisting with professional development as required. The company secretary should be responsible for advising the board through the chairman on all governance matters.'

And further provides that:

> '... all directors should have access to the advice and services of the company secretary, who is responsible to the board for ensuring that board procedures are complied with. Both the appointment and removal of the company secretary should be a matter for the board as a whole.'

Statutory duties

12.6 In carrying out their functions, and exercising their powers, the directors must comply with a wide range of legal duties that restrict how they may act, and require them to make certain disclosures where, for example, their own personal interests may conflict with those of their company. This is because the directors do not own the business that they manage – it belongs to the company. They are therefore managing the business in a fiduciary capacity – ie for the ultimate benefit of a number of stakeholders.[6] Stakeholders include the company's members, its employees and, in the event of financial difficulties, its creditors.[7] Before CA 2006, many of these duties derived from decisions of the courts – they were 'common law' duties. Directors' fiduciary duties were expressed in many different ways by the courts, but their main duties could be summarised as being:

---

throughout the year immediately prior to the reporting year. A smaller company should have at least two independent non-executive directors: Provision B.1.2.

[4] Provisions A.4.1 to A.4.3.
[5] Supporting Principles to B.5, and B.5.2.
[6] The word 'stakeholder' is used as a term of art here. It does not have a strict legal definition in this context.
[7] *Colin Gwyer & Associates Ltd v London Wharf (Limehouse) Ltd; Eaton Bray Ltd v Palmer* [2002] All ER (D) 226.

- To act bona fide in what they honestly believe to be the company's best interests (even if those conflict with their own).[8]

- To act for what the courts call 'proper purposes'.[9] Directors must exercise their powers for the purposes for which they have been given to the board by the members. For example, members invariably give the directors power to issue shares, but the power is, usually, intended to be exercise to raise capital for the company. If the directors decide to issue shares to all or some of their number to dilute the shareholding of a non-director, then they will have difficulty arguing they have exercised their powers for a proper purpose (even if they honestly believe that what they were doing was in the best interests of the company).

- Not to make a personal profit out of their position, unless authorised by the members.

Although not a fiduciary duty, directors were also obliged to exercise due skill, care and diligence in their role.

12.7 The directors of any company therefore had to carry out their functions effectively, and in accordance with their fiduciary duties. If directors failed to do this – and to demonstrate that they were doing it – they could be disqualified from being a director and, in some circumstances, made personally liable for losses arising from their breach of duty.[10]

12.8 However, the many different ways in which the courts had expressed the various duties meant that court cases could be lengthy and expensive, and their outcomes uncertain. To improve the situation, seven new duties have now been 'codified' – made statutory – in CA 2006 (except in relation to charitable companies, for which there are special rules).[11] These are:

(1) duty to act within constitution and powers (s 171);

(2) duty to promote the success of the company (s 172);

(3) duty to exercise independent judgement (s 173);

(4) duty to exercise reasonable care, skill and diligence (s 174);

---

[8] *Re Forest of Dean Coal Mining Co* (1878) 10 ChD 450; *Re City Equitable Fire Insurance Co* [1925] Ch 407.
[9] *Piercy v S Mills & Co* [1920] 1 Ch 77; *Criterion Properties plc v Stratford UK Properties LLC* [2002] All ER (D) 280.
[10] Under the Insolvency Act 1986, s 214.
[11] There is also a statutory 'derivative' action, and a provision that prevents conflicted directors – or persons 'connected' with them (see CA 2006, s 252) who also hold shares – from participating in a resolution to ratify a breach, that makes it easier than before to bring a court action against a director for breach of these duties.

(5) duty to avoid situations creating, or that could create, a direct or indirect conflict of interest (s 175);

(6) duty not to accept benefits from third parties (s 176); and

(7) duty to declare an interest in a proposed transaction or arrangement (s 177).

12.9 All of these are to continue to be regarded as fiduciary duties of directors, save for the duty to exercise reasonable care, skill and diligence, which was not a fiduciary duty previously, either.

12.10 There is also a provision in CA 2006 (s 182) under which a director who is directly or indirectly interested in an existing transaction or arrangement (one that has already been entered into by the company) must declare the nature and extent of the interest to the other directors. (Note that this is a different provision from the duty to declare an interest in a *proposed* transaction or arrangement.) This provision is not a 'general duty' under CA 2006 and non-compliance is merely an offence under the Act, rather than a breach of a director's duties (although non-compliance may also involve breach of a statutory duty, such as the duty to avoid conflicts of interest).[12]

12.11 Whether or not board meetings are held, how they are conducted and the matters discussed and decisions taken at them can be crucial evidence of whether or not directors are discharging their duties and responsibilities properly. In practice, how often directors' meetings are held; which business is put before them; how they conduct their proceedings, etc will depend on the company's circumstances. Matters such as the company's size and geographic spread, the nature and diversity of its products and markets, its objectives, its stage of development, its values and culture, whether the directors and members are substantially the same people or not and whether ownership is spread or concentrated in a few hands will all affect how its board should operate.

DELEGATION OF POWERS BY THE BOARD

Decisions reserved to the board

12.12 Boards of directors therefore operate in many different ways. In a business that has a sole director (who also owns the company) and few employees, the 'board' may make all decisions. In most companies, however, even the most effective board cannot make every decision itself. The directors

---

[12] The requirement to declare the nature and extent of an interest in an existing transaction or arrangement of the company does not apply if or to the extent that the interest has been declared under the separate duty to declare this in respect of a proposed transaction or arrangement. So the original declaration is sufficient, provided that neither the nature nor the extent of the interest changes.

will therefore often delegate certain powers to committees made up of one or more of their number (for listed companies, these will include a remuneration committee to monitor the remuneration of the directors; an audit committee to monitor internal financial matters, financial risk management and relations with the auditor; and a nomination committee to lead the process for board appointments and make recommendations to the board).

12.13 'A committee means a person or persons to whom powers are committed which would otherwise be exercised by another body.'[13] It exercises limited powers, which may be modified or withdrawn by its appointing authority. The powers of committees should be clearly set out in their appointment.

12.14 It is not possible for directors to declare or notify a personal interest in a contract, transaction or arrangement under s 177 or 182 of CA 2006 to a committee. It must be declared or made to a full board meeting.[14]

12.15 The board will also delegate powers to non-directors such as the company secretary, or to other personnel. Delegates directly authorised by the board may also be given power to delegate in their turn. Delegation is, like any power of the directors, a fiduciary power. It must be exercised in accordance with the principles in **12.6ff**.

12.16 If there is to be delegation, the directors should make it clear which matters are reserved for a decision of the full board. If their company is listed, the UK Corporate Governance Code[15] recommends that the board approve a formal schedule of matters reserved to them (and that the annual report should contain a 'high level statement of which types of decisions are to be taken by the board and which are to be delegated to management'). The Institute of Chartered Secretaries and Administrators (ICSA) has issued a Guidance Note[16] suggesting matters to be reserved for this purpose.

12.17 Which matters should be reserved to the board of non-listed companies? Again, ICSA has issued useful guidelines in the form of a *Code of*

---

[13] *Re Taurine Co* (1883) 25 ChD 118.
[14] *Guinness plc v Saunders* [1990] 2 AC 663. It may also be the case that boards cannot delegate (and nor can they ratify) quasi-judicial decisions, such as a decision whether to reject an appeal against dismissal of an employee where, under the relevant procedure, the employee was entitled to consideration of the dismissal by the full board: *Blundell v Christie Hospital NHS Trust* [1996] ICR 347. However, this was a case involving an NHS Trust rather than a limited company and may therefore be distinguishable.
[15] Provision A.1.1.
[16] ICSA Guidance Note 'Matters Reserved for the Board', no 031119, available free at www.icsa.org.uk or from the Information Centre, ICSA, 16 Park Crescent, London W1B 1AH or e-mail informationcentre@icsa.org.uk. See also www.icsa.org.uk. These are organised under 12 headings: strategy and management; structure and capital; financial reporting and controls; internal controls; contracts; communication; board membership and other appointments; remuneration; delegation of authority; corporate governance matters; policies; and other.

Good Boardroom Practice (the 'GBP Code').[17] The GBP Code recommends that a board should specify the matters that require its prior approval. This ought to include all 'material' contracts and any contracts 'not in the ordinary course of business'. The board should specify what these terms mean in the context of its activities, and set financial limits where appropriate.

12.18 A company wishing to comply with the GBP Code might decide to use the guidance in the ICSA Guidance Note as a starting point when deciding which contracts are 'material' and which 'in the ordinary course of business' in the context of its own activities.

12.19 The GBP Code provides that, in the event of uncertainty as to whether or not any contract is material, or in the ordinary course of business, the company should err on the side of caution and bring it before the directors.

12.20 Once the matters to be reserved, and appropriate definitions, are agreed, the GBP Code recommends that they be brought to the attention of 'all relevant persons'. This will include the board, the company secretary, senior managers who might otherwise believe themselves to have authority to enter into such contracts, and the auditors (if any).

12.21 Both the UK Corporate Governance Code and the GBP Code recommend that companies establish procedures for those occasional circumstances when a board decision is required between board meetings. In each case, the procedures must take into account two fundamental principles. One is that each director should receive the same information at the same time as the others, and the other is that he should be given sufficient time to consider it. (New directors should be given sufficient information to enable them to perform their duties and, particularly in the case of non-executive directors, this should include guidance on how they can obtain information concerning the company and how they can requisition a board meeting.[18])

12.22 The GBP Code recommends that phone or video conference meetings can be held to deal with such emergency decisions, in which as many directors as possible should participate.[19] Those who cannot attend should be sent papers and given the opportunity to give their views to the chairman, to another director or to the secretary, before the meeting.

12.23 Alternatively, and exceptionally, a written resolution in lieu of a meeting may be circulated for signature by all the directors, without any debate.

---

[17] *Good Boardroom Practice. A Code for Directors and Company Secretaries*, available from the Information Centre, ICSA, 16 Park Crescent, London W1B 1AH or e-mail informationcentre@icsa.org.uk. See also www.icsa.org.uk.

[18] This will, presumably, form part of the information given to new directors on induction. Main Principle B4 and Provision B.4.1 in the *UK Corporate Governance Code* recommends that listed companies give new directors a full, formal and tailored induction. There are checklists of induction matters in the ICSA Guidance Note 'ICSA Guidance: Induction of Directors', no 120606, of June 2012. See www.icsa.org.uk.

[19] See Chapter 13 for discussion of electronic communications and board meetings.

When choosing the means of dealing with emergency decisions, however, the need for urgency should always be balanced against the two fundamental principles in **12.21**. If, therefore, there is some contentious and significant decision that cannot be made without a full airing of opposing views in face-to-face discussion, then dealing with it by written resolution may result in a director not having the information he needs to make the decision, or not having sufficient time to consider it. In that instance, an emergency board meeting may need to be requisitioned and convened.

Exercising the power to delegate

12.24 Having decided what they will reserve to themselves for decision, and what they will delegate, the directors should ensure they delegate in accordance with their fiduciary duties. For example, delegation to a committee in order to exclude one or more directors from the forum where the board's decisions are taken is likely to be an improper purpose.

12.25 Committees of directors are usually appointed for one of three main purposes:

(1) to deal with a matter which requires speedy decision where the whole board could not be contacted quickly enough;

(2) to deal with a matter where it is desirable to have discussion free from the embarrassing presence of a director who is personally concerned in the matter, for example, for the appointment or removal of a director to or from executive office (although the minutes, as distinct from a report on the discussions, are open to inspection by directors who were not on the committee, including the one being discussed); or

(3) for routine matters such as affixing of the company seal to documents, in which case standing committees are often appointed.

12.26 The directors should ensure delegates are capable of exercising the powers delegated to them, given the circumstances in which the committee is established. They should also set the parameters within which delegated authority may be exercised, and require their delegates to do the same if they sub-delegate. The GBP Code recommends that, where the articles of association allow the board to delegate any of its powers to a committee, the board should give its prior approval to:

(1) the membership and quorum of any such committee;

(2) its terms of reference; and

(3) the extent of any powers delegated to it.

12.27 The same principles must be applied to any other delegation by the board – to managers and other employees, wherever located and whatever their job – because, in the event of any problem arising, it is the directors who are ultimately, and collectively, responsible. Internal policies, job descriptions, staff handbooks and like documents should make the scope of each employee's responsibilities and authority clear.

12.28 Detailed discussion of meetings of nomination, audit and remuneration committees of listed companies (see **12.12**) is beyond the remit of this book, but they operate as any other committees of the board, subject to the additional provisions of the UK Corporate Governance Code.

Monitoring and reviewing the exercise of delegated powers

12.29 Directors must also be able to demonstrate that they are monitoring and reviewing the exercise of delegated powers by the delegates if they are to discharge their responsibilities (see **12.6**). Leaving the delegates to their own devices will be a breach of their fiduciary duties, because directors must keep themselves informed about what is going on in their company. Otherwise, they will find themselves punished for the acts or omissions of employees whom they do not adequately monitor, if the employees exceed their authority.[20]

12.30 Different boards monitor and review what is going on in their company in different ways.

12.31 Some smaller companies may hold board meetings only as and when a particular director considers that a matter requires a collective, formal board decision, or when CA 2006 or the company's articles require it. (For example, when a declaration of a personal interest needs to be made by a director to a meeting pursuant to s 177 or 182 of CA 2006; or when a transfer of shares requires approval by the board and the articles require that this is dealt with at a meeting.) Otherwise, implicit consensus about the company's strategy, direction, values and culture means that directors can be relied upon to carry out their functions effectively and in accordance with their fiduciary duties.

12.32 Larger companies will hold regular board meetings, often monthly, but may simply consider reports submitted and make strategic or policy decisions. Executive powers are exercised outside the meeting by committees of the board or individual directors. This is often the case if the board has many non-executive directors. Alternatively, the boards of larger companies may, like the smallest companies, consider a comprehensive range of matters, including operational issues, at every board meeting.

---

[20] As in the case of Nick Leeson, the Barings bank trader who, for lack of adequate supervision and monitoring while trading in derivatives in Singapore, brought Barings down. A key error was that the bank allowed Leeson to be both chief trader and also responsible for settling his trades. This dual role, which is usually held by different people, enabled him to hide the mounting losses that finally led to the collapse of the bank.

CONVENING AND CONDUCTING BOARD MEETINGS

12.33 The way that meetings are convened, conducted and recorded may also vary. Articles will invariably contain provisions relating to board meetings.

12.34 The GBP Code is also valuable in this respect, particularly to the company secretary (if, being a private company, it has one) who (according to the GBP Code) is responsible to the company chairman for the proper administration of meetings of the members, of the board and of any committee of the board.

12.35 The GBP Code recommends that boards should establish written procedures for conducting their business (including the matters covered by the GBP Code), give a copy to every director and monitor compliance. It recommends that monitoring be by 'an' audit committee. The term 'audit committee' is used in the UK Corporate Governance Code, where the expectation is that the audit committee (made up of two or three independent non-executive directors) will monitor financial matters, and relations with the auditor and internal risk management. It is not clear whether monitoring should, in the case of a listed company, be by its audit committee within the meaning of the UK Corporate Governance Code.

12.36 If non-listed companies wish to comply with the GBP Code, they might consider establishing a specific committee of the board for monitoring purposes and (if they have them) ensure that its members include non-executive directors.

Directors' obligation to meet

12.37 Where a directors' decision is required, directors must either act at a duly constituted meeting or by unanimous decision, arrived at informally, in lieu of a meeting.[21]

12.38 This requirement for the necessary formality for there to be a board meeting was illustrated starkly in *Barber's Case*.[22] The articles of the company provided that no person should be eligible to be a director unless he had been recommended by the board of directors for election or, at the time, had held 20 shares for 2 months. B, who was not a shareholder, was elected unanimously as a director at a general meeting of the members. Six out of seven directors, who were then the only shareholders, were present. It was held that B's election was void. 'Six directors out of seven met in a different capacity and for a different purpose, and such a meeting does not make them a board of directors.'[23]

12.39 A board meeting can usually, however, be held under informal circumstances provided all directors agree. But, for example, a casual meeting

---

[21] *Collie's Claim* (1871) 12 Eq 246, at 258; *Ex parte Kennedy* (1890) 44 ChD 472, at 481.
[22] *Re East Norfolk Tramways Co, Barber's Case* (1877) 5 ChD 963.
[23] *Re East Norfolk Tramways Co, Barber's Case* (1877) 5 ChD 963 at 697.

of the only two directors of a company at a railway station will not be treated as a board meeting at the option of one, against the will of the other.[24] The dividing line can, however, be narrow. In one case, one of the only two directors did not attend a meeting, proper notice of which had been given. He met the other director shortly after in the passage, and that other director proposed a resolution. He objected, whereby the other declared it passed by virtue of his casting vote. This resolution was held to have been duly passed.[25] In any case, a subsequent meeting can ratify the business done at an informal meeting.[26] It can also ratify an unauthorised act of an agent of the company.[27]

12.40 Even where directors are unanimous, there are circumstances in which a board meeting may have to be held. See Resolutions in lieu of a meeting at **12.121ff**.

12.41 If there is more than one director, a single director cannot constitute a board meeting, even if he honestly misunderstood the articles, if he is also the chairman and is personally responsible for the error by which he purported to turn himself into a one-person board.[28]

Who may summon a meeting?

12.42 Regulation 9 in both the model form articles for a private company limited by shares and a guarantee company, and reg 8 in the model form articles for a public company all say that any director may call a directors' meeting by giving notice of the meeting to the directors or by authorising the company secretary (if any) to give such notice. For companies with older articles, reg 88 of the 1985 Table A says the same. It is probable that the same rules apply even if there is no express provision in the articles. The secretary should not convene board meetings unless instructed to do so, or unless he is also a director and therefore entitled to do so in that capacity.

Notice of meetings

12.43 Reasonable notice must be given of the meeting. This will depend on the facts in any particular case, but the recommendation in the GBP Code (that directors must have sufficient time before the meeting to consider the information sent to them) is likely to influence decisions in the future. If, however, a practice develops of giving a particular period of notice, this will be held to be reasonable in the absence of any particular circumstances which would make that period inappropriate. In *Re Homer Gold Mines*,[29] a shorter notice than any previously given was held invalid, since the court came to the conclusion that the notice had been so given with a view to excluding certain

---

[24] *Barron v Porter* [1914] 1 Ch 895.
[25] *Smith v Paringa Mines* [1906] 2 Ch 193.
[26] *Re Portuguese Consolidated Copper Mines* (1889) 42 ChD 160.
[27] *Molineaux v London, Birmingham etc Co* [1902] 2 KB 589.
[28] *Smith v Henniker-Major & Co (a firm)* [2002] EWCA Civ 762, BLD 2307022826.
[29] (1888) 39 ChD 546.

directors. A notice period may, however, be extremely short if all the directors are able to attend, and if any director wishes to object to the shortness of the notice that director should make such an objection at once.[30]

12.44 It might be thought that failure to give proper notice to each director will invalidate all proceedings at the meeting (unless all the directors do attend).[31] But although the matter is not free from doubt, it seems that a director who does not receive proper notice merely has the right to a second meeting if he does not attend the first; that the failure of that director to seek a second meeting within a reasonable time of discovering the first will amount to a waiver of that right; and that in this event the proceedings of the meeting become effectively unchallengeable.[32]

12.45 There is, however, no need to send notice when the directors have decided to hold meetings at regular intervals; that is, when there is a fixed day and time of which all directors have knowledge and, therefore, notice (for example, weekly meetings on Fridays at 3 pm or every first Thursday in the month at 11 am). And even if articles require notice of meetings to be given to directors outside the UK (which would mean that reg 88 of the 1985 Table A, which says notice need not be given to any director who is abroad, does not apply to the company) in certain circumstances notice need not be given to a director who is abroad and out of reach.[33] In these days of mobile phones and e-mail, however, the circumstances in which a director can be said to be 'out of reach' have shrunk dramatically.

12.46 There is case-law to the effect that a director cannot waive in advance his right to notice – notice must be given even if the director indicates that he will not attend. In *Re Portuguese Consolidated Copper Mines*[34] a director of a company, on being told a meeting would be held next week, said 'I cannot be there'. It was held that this could not be relied on as a waiver of his right to notice. In another case a director said 'I shall not be able to come, you need not summon me', but the court still held he should have been given notice.[35]

12.47 However, the model form articles (in reg 9 for private companies limited by shares and guarantee, and reg 8 for public companies) say that notice of a directors' meeting does not need to be given to directors who waive their entitlement to notice by giving notice to that effect to the company not more than 7 days after the date on which the meeting is held. Each regulation goes on to say that, where such notice is given after the meeting has been held, it does not affect the validity of the meeting, or of any business conducted at it.

---

[30] *Browne v La Trinidad* (1887) 37 ChD 1.
[31] *Re Homer Gold Mines Ltd* (1888) 39 ChD 546; *Harben v Phillips* (1883) 23 ChD 14.
[32] *Browne v La Trinidad* (1887) 37 ChD 1 (10 minutes' notice not specifying the business); *Bentley-Stevens v Jones* [1974] 1 WLR 638 (notice sent of meeting the following day and not received because director away from home until the evening of that day).
[33] *Re Halifax Sugar Co* (1890) 62 LT 563.
[34] (1889) 42 ChD 160.
[35] *Re Portuguese Consolidated Copper Mines* (1889) 42 ChD 160.

12.48 Perhaps if a director were at such a distance that it would be absolutely impossible for him to attend, then the secretary might be excused for not giving notice to the director and the meeting would be properly convened? Possibly the same exception might apply when a director was so dangerously ill that he could not be moved.[36] However, such exceptions are unlikely to hold good except on very particular facts in very particular cases.

12.49 For companies with older articles, reg 88 of the 1985 Table A provides that notice need not be given to a director who is absent from the UK. The overriding requirement to treat directors fairly and equally probably means that a director who deliberately waits for a colleague to leave the UK before calling a board meeting is liable to find decisions made at that meeting overturned by the courts.

12.50 It is therefore highly desirable to give notice to all directors for all meetings, whatever the articles say – even to those who may be abroad, and whatever the company's knowledge of their intentions, state of health or other circumstances, and even though it cannot possibly reach the director until after the meeting has taken place.

12.51 The notice need not be in writing unless the articles so provide.[37] The 1985 Table A does not so provide. The model form articles for private share, guarantee and public companies all specifically say notice need not be in writing. It is, however, highly desirable to give written notice if possible.

The nature of the business to be conducted

12.52 One view is that the notice need not specify each item of business to be considered at the meeting unless the articles so require.[38] Neither the model form articles or the 1985 Table A so requires. Directors of a company to which the model form or the 1985 Table A applies can, therefore, deal with all the affairs of the company that require attention or arise, at any board meeting provided:

- they do not exceed their powers; and

- by doing so, they are not acting unfairly towards a director who has decided, on the strength of the notice, not to attend.

12.53 In some companies, therefore, the practice is not to give any indication of the nature of the business, unless there is something unusual to be considered, and no agenda are included in or attached to notices of meetings.

---

[36] *Young v Ladies' Imperial Club* [1920] 2 KB 523. If a meeting may legitimately be summoned in an emergency, it may be enough for those convening it to serve notice on all members who can with proper effort be found: *MacLelland v NUJ* [1975] ICR 116, at 135.
[37] *Browne v La Trinidad* (1887) 37 ChD 1.
[38] *La Compagnie de Mayville v Whitley* [1896] 1 Ch 788.

12.54 However, certain cases, inconsistent with this practice, have been decided on the basis that the object of requiring proper notice of the purposes for which the meeting is to be held is to enable a person entitled to attend to exercise his own judgment as to whether to attend. For example, it has been held that the heading 'Any other business' in a notice will generally authorise the transaction of business of a purely formal nature but not business of any substantial importance. In *Young v Ladies' Imperial Club*,[39] it was held that, as the notice of a meeting did not state the object of the meeting with sufficient particularity, it was invalid and consequently the proceedings of that meeting were invalidated. It has also been held that a notice may be good in part and bad in part, and it is not wholly invalid because it extends to something which cannot be done at the meeting.[40]

12.55 A better view, therefore, is that the notice must provide, or be accompanied by, a description of the nature of (all) the proposed business of the meeting, in sufficient detail for the director to decide whether or not to attend, and that the meeting cannot, in ordinary cases, go outside the business described in that notice.[41] Such a notice or agenda gives directors an opportunity to consider issues in advance and can shorten meetings by reducing ill-informed discussion or misapprehensions based on insufficient information.

12.56 The GBP Code recommends that the chairman and company secretary (or other person involved) should consult each other on the content and presentation of the agenda for each meeting and, whatever the content of a notice or agenda, it recommends that the chairman of a board meeting should permit any director, or the company secretary, to raise any matter concerning compliance with the GBP Code, the articles or any other legal or regulatory requirement, even in the absence of any formal agenda item.

12.57 The UK Corporate Governance Code provides that, in the case of UK listed companies, the board 'should be supplied in a timely manner with information in a form and of a quality appropriate to enable it to discharge its duties'.[42]

12.58 Irrespective of the information as to actual business given in the notice of a board meeting, a director should make every effort to attend every board meeting if he is to avoid the allegation that he is failing to discharge his fiduciary duties. For listed companies, the UK Corporate Governance Code provides[43] that the annual report should set out the number of meetings of the board and those committees and individual attendance by directors, so that members can take issue with directors with poor attendance records.

---

[39] [1920] 2 KB 523.
[40] *Cleve v Financial Corporation* (1873) LR 16 Eq 363.
[41] *Longfield Parish Council v Wright* (1919) 88 LJ Ch 119.
[42] Main Principle B.5.
[43] Provision A.1.2.

Attendance is not, however, a statutory requirement, and a director is not liable for misfeasance committed by co-directors without his knowledge at a board meeting at which he is not present.[44]

Chairman

12.59 To constitute a valid board meeting the proper person must be in the chair. The UK Corporate Governance Code says that:[45]

> '... the chairman is responsible for leadership of the board, ensuring its effectiveness on all aspects of its role.'

And that:

> 'The chairman is responsible for setting the board's agenda and ensuring that adequate time is available for discussion of all agenda items, in particular strategic issues. The chairman should also promote a culture of openness and debate by facilitating the effective contribution of non-executive directors in particular and ensuring constructive relations between executive and non-executive directors.
>
> The chairman is responsible for ensuring that the directors receive accurate, timely and clear information. The chairman should ensure effective communication with shareholders.'

For further guidance, the Association of British Insurers, in its report 'Report on Board Effectiveness; Updating progress, promoting best practice; December 2012' said: 'the chairman is key to an effective board. There is no "one size fits all" approach to the role, with different chairmen having different approaches based on what is best for the individual company and board.' The report can be said to be from the coal face, as it is based on a survey of FTSE 350 chairmen and company secretaries. It also found that:

> 'there was a significant amount of consensus about the role and responsibilities of the chairman. Chairmen emphasised a number of aspects to their role, all a variation on the following five themes:
>
> - Creating the right board dynamic and having the right people around the boardroom table;
> - Helping to set the board agenda, ensuring the board has the right information and is debating the right issues;
> - Managing the board's relationship with the executives and in particular the chief executive;
> - Being an ambassador for the company; and
> - Being fully engaged in the business and understanding what is happening on the ground.'

---

[44] *Perry's Case* (1876) 34 LT 716.
[45] Main Principle A3, and the Supporting Principle to A.3.

12.60 There is further guidance on the role of the chairman in the Higgs Report.[46]

> 'The chairman is pivotal in creating the conditions for overall board and individual director effectiveness, both inside and outside the boardroom. Specifically, it is the responsibility of the chairman to:
>
> - run the board and set its agenda. The agenda should take full account of the issues and the concerns of all board members. Agendas should be forward looking and concentrate on strategic matters rather than formulaic approvals of proposals which can be the subject of appropriate delegated powers to management;
> - ensure that the members of the board receive accurate, timely and clear information, in particular about the company's performance, to enable the board to take sound decisions, monitor effectively and provide advice to promote the success of the company;
> - ensure effective communication with shareholders and ensure that the members of the board develop an understanding of the views of the major investors;
> - manage the board to ensure that sufficient time is allowed for discussion of complex or contentious issues, where appropriate arranging for informal meetings beforehand to enable thorough preparation for the board discussion. It is particularly important that non-executive directors have sufficient time to consider critical issues and are not faced with unrealistic deadlines for decision-making;
> - take the lead in providing a properly constructed induction programme for new directors that is comprehensive, formal and tailored, facilitated by the company secretary;
> - take the lead in identifying and meeting the development needs of individual directors, with the company secretary having a key role in facilitating provision. It is the responsibility of the chairman to address the development needs of the board as a whole with a view to enhancing its overall effectiveness as a team;
> - ensure that the performance of individuals and of the board as a whole and its committees is evaluated at least once a year; and encourage active engagement by all the members of the board.
>
> The effective chairman:
>
> - upholds the highest standards of integrity and probity;
> - sets the agenda, style and tone of board discussions to promote effective decision-making and constructive debate;
> - promotes effective relationships and open communication, both inside and outside the boardroom, between non-executive directors and executive team;
> - builds an effective and complementary board, initiating change and planning succession in board appointments, subject to board and shareholders' approval;
> - promotes the highest standards of corporate governance and seeks compliance with the provisions of the Code wherever possible;
> - ensures clear structure for and the effective running of board committees;

---

[46] *Higgs Suggestions for Good Practice: Guidance on the Role of the Chairman* (January 2003).

- ensures effective implementation of board decisions;
- establishes a close relationship of trust with the chief executive, providing support and advice while respecting executive responsibility; and
- provides coherent leadership of the company, including representing the company and understanding the views of shareholders.'

12.61 The appointment of the chairman is generally governed by the articles. All of the model form articles (at reg 12 in each case) and, for companies with older articles, reg 91 of Table A provide that the directors may elect a chairman of their meetings and terminate the chairman's appointment at any time. If no chairman is elected, if the chairman is unwilling to preside or if at any meeting the chairman is not present within 10 minutes (or 5 minutes, if the 1985 A Table A applies) after the time at which it was to start, the directors participating in the meeting may choose one of their number to be chairman of the meeting.

12.62 The election of a chairman may be a general one or merely for a particular meeting. It is important that a clear record of this is kept in the minutes, since confusion and dispute will often result if it is not clear who the chairman is – especially if the articles give the chairman a casting vote, as they usually do.[47] Moreover, confusion may be compounded by the fact that reg 91 requires no particular formality for the resignation of the chairman.[48]

12.63 An appointment of a chairman of directors made in contravention of the articles is void. It is not regularised by mere acquiescence, and consequently resolutions carried by the casting vote of such a chairman are inoperative.[49]

12.64 For Premium listed companies the UK Corporate Governance Code[50] provides that a job specification should be prepared by the nomination committee for the chairman, including the time commitment expected and the need for availability in the event of crises. A chairman's other significant commitments should be disclosed to the board before appointment and changes reported as they arise (and included in the annual report).[51] If neither an external search consultancy nor open advertising was used to find the chairman, the nomination committee's section in the annual report should explain why.[52] The issue of whether 'undue reliance is not placed on particular individuals' should be taken into consideration when deciding who to appoint as chairman. On the same basis, the Code recommends a clear division of responsibilities at the head of the company between the running of the board and the executive responsibility for the running of the company's business. It therefore recommends that the roles of chairman and chief executive should not be exercised by the same individual – and nor should a chief executive go on to be chairman of the same company subsequently. The division of

---

[47] For example, reg 13 in each of the model form articles for a private company limited by shares, a guarantee company and a public company respectively, and reg 88 of the 1985 Table A.
[48] *Cane v Jones* [1981] 1 All ER 533.
[49] *Clark v Workman* [1920] 1 IR 107.
[50] Provision B.3.1.
[51] Provision B.3.1.
[52] Provision B.2.4.

responsibilities between the chairman and chief executive should be clearly established, set out in writing and agreed by the board. If, exceptionally, a board decides that a chief executive should become chairman, the board should consult major shareholders in advance and should set out its reasons to shareholders at the time of the appointment and in the next annual report. The chairman should, at the time of his appointment, also meet the independence criteria set out in the UK Corporate Governance Code for non-executive directors,[53] and have enough time available to do the job, given any other commitments.[54] It is the chairman's responsibility to act on the results of the 'formal and rigorous annual evaluation of its own performance and that of its committees and individual directors' by the board, which assesses each director's contribution and commitment (including commitment of time for board and committee meetings and any other duties). In practice, this means recognising the strengths and addressing the weaknesses of the board and, where appropriate, proposing new members be appointed to the board or seeking the resignation of directors. The UK Corporate Governance Code also provides that:[55]

> '... the chairman should hold meetings with the non-executive directors, without the executives present. Led by the senior independent director, the non-executive directors should meet without the chairman present at least annually to appraise the chairman's performance and on such other occasions as are deemed appropriate.'

QUORUM

General rules

12.65 Business at a board meeting can only be validly transacted by the directors who attend if it has been properly convened[56] and held, and there is a quorum as prescribed by the articles.

12.66 Regulation 11 in both the model form articles for a private company limited by shares and a guarantee company say that, where the company has more than one director, the quorum for a board meeting can be fixed by board decision but can never be less than two. If no quorum is fixed, the default is two directors. It then clarifies that, if there are enough directors to form a quorum, but they are not present at the meeting, no proposal can to be voted on except a proposal to call another board meeting. However, if there are simply not enough directors to form a quorum at all (for example because directors have died or resigned), the directors must not take any decision except to appoint further directors (or call a general meeting so the members can do so). For companies with older articles, reg 89 of the 1985 Table A provides that the

---

[53] Provisions A.2.1 and B.1.1.
[54] Provision B.3.1.
[55] Provision A.4.2.
[56] *York Tramways Co v Willows* (1882) 8 QBD 685.

quorum necessary for the transaction of the business of the directors may be fixed by the directors and, unless so fixed, shall be two.

12.67 For private companies, reg 7 in both the relevant sets of model form articles (one for private companies limited by shares, and the other for guarantee companies) provide that, if a company's articles do not require it to have more than one director and, in fact, it does only have one director in office, that sole director may take decisions without regard to any of the provisions of the articles relating to directors' decision-making – including the rules requiring a quorum at board meetings.

12.68 The model articles for a public company are slightly more complex. Regulation 11 says that, where the total number of directors is less than the number required for a quorum, and there is only one director, that director may either appoint sufficient directors to make up a quorum or call a general meeting to do so. However, if there is more than one director, a board meeting can be held, provided at least two directors participate, but may only appoint sufficient directors to make up a quorum or call a general meeting to do so. However, if a board meeting is called and only one director attends at the time and date fixed for it, that director may appoint sufficient directors to make up a quorum or call a general meeting to do so too.

12.69 Alternatively (and unusually) the articles could also provide that one director can constitute a quorum in any case.[57] If no provision on quorum is made by the articles, a majority of the directors will constitute a quorum, but under certain circumstances it seems the necessary number may be determined by the practice of the board.[58]

12.70 Where a company has a sole director, some practitioners have seen a problem in the interplay between regs 7(2) and 11(1) in the model form articles for a private company limited by shares. Regulation 7(2) says:

'If –

(a) the company only has one director, and
(b) no provision of the articles requires it to have more than one director,

the general rule does not apply, and the director may take decisions without regard to any of the provisions of the articles relating to directors' decision-making.'

The 'general rule' referred to is the rule in reg 7(1) that decisions by directors must be by majority decision at a meeting or in accordance with reg 8 (directors indicate to each other that they share a common view).

---

[57] *Re Fireproof Doors* [1916] 2 Ch 142.
[58] *Regent's Canal Ironworks* [1867] WN 79.

12.71 However, reg 11(2) provides that the quorum for directors' meetings may be fixed by a decision of the directors, but must never be less than two, and unless otherwise fixed is two.

12.72 The concerned practitioners have argued that reg 11(2) is a provision of the articles requiring a company to have more than one director, within the meaning of reg 7(2)(b). If this is right, then the general rule *does* apply, and the director *cannot* take decisions without regard to any of the provisions of the articles relating to decision-making.

12.73 Therefore, a private company limited by shares which adopts the model for articles and which wishes to operate with only one director should file articles at Companies House modifying reg 11(2).

12.74 However, the alternative, and more commonly held view, is that the provision in reg 7(2) is intended only to deal with the quorum requirement at a board meeting. It does not impose a requirement that there be a minimum number of at least two directors. A company to which reg 11(2) applies does not, on this view, have a provision in its articles requiring it to have more than one director (which, if it did, would mean reg 7(2)(b) applied).

12.75 On that view, there is no need to file articles at Companies House that modify the director quorum provisions in reg 11(2) as they simply do not apply if the company has a sole director – unless the articles contain some other provision that requires more than one director.

12.76 A quorum of directors means a quorum competent to transact and vote on the business before the board. Therefore, in *Yuill v Greymouth-Point Elizabeth R Co*,[59] where the articles prohibited interested directors from voting, a resolution passed at a meeting of three directors, two of whom were interested in the subject matter of the resolution, was held invalid. In *Re North Eastern Insurance Co*,[60] articles provided that directors could contract with the company, but should not vote in connection with such contracts, and that until otherwise determined three should be a quorum. Four directors were present at a meeting. At that meeting a resolution was passed for the issue of a debenture to one of the directors present. He did not vote on that resolution. A similar resolution was passed to issue another debenture to another director who was present, but did not vote on this latter resolution. It was held in the circumstances of the case that the issue of both debentures was part of one entire transaction, in which the directors to whom the debentures were issued were jointly interested. There was therefore no quorum and the debentures were not validly issued. It was subsequently resolved that in future a quorum should be two so as to remove the difficulty. One of the directors interested in the transaction was one of the three directors present when that resolution was

---

[59] [1904] 1 Ch 32.
[60] [1919] 1 Ch 198.

passed and, being interested, was unable to count towards a quorum. The purported reduction of the quorum was consequently ineffective.

12.77 The principle that those who are not entitled to vote on a resolution at a board meeting cannot form part of the quorum is embodied in reg 95 of Table A, although these cases make it clear that the principle stands even in the absence of such an article.

Abuse of quorum provisions

12.78 It seems that in certain circumstances the court will be prepared to step in and make an appropriate order where a director refuses to attend and thus deprives the board meeting of a quorum. An example of this occurred in *Re Copal Varnish Co*.[61] One director out of a board of two refused to attend meetings summoned to consider transfers of shares, in order to prevent a quorum being formed. It was held that the transferees were entitled to an order directing the company to register the transfers, since a shareholder has a property in his shares which he has the right to dispose of, subject only to an express restriction in the articles. Even if the articles give directors a power to decline to register a transfer, such a power is not exercised where the directors have not passed a resolution declining so to register.[62]

Failure to keep quorum

12.79 Where there is a quorum at the beginning of a meeting, but some of the directors leave the meeting, so that the number remaining is less than the quorum, any subsequent acts are invalid. This would not be the case if the articles provided that 'the quorum shall be two directors present when the meeting proceeds to business', as was found in relation to general meetings in *Re Hartley Baird*,[63] but such a provision would be most unusual. The normal provision is similar to that found in reg 11 of the model form articles (for private companies limited by shares, or guarantee companies) or reg 10 (for public companies) or, for companies with older articles, reg 89 of the 1985 Table A, which all require (albeit implicitly) that a quorum be present throughout the meeting.

Minimum number of directors

12.80 Older articles sometimes fix what is to be the maximum and minimum number of the directors. Where a minimum is fixed and the number of the directors has never reached the minimum, they cannot act even though they are sufficient to form a quorum.[64]

---

[61] [1917] 2 Ch 349.
[62] *Re Hackney Pavilion* [1924] 1 Ch 276.
[63] [1955] Ch 143.
[64] *Re Sly, Spink & Co* [1911] 2 Ch 430.

DIRECTORS' VOTES

General

12.81 Unless the articles otherwise provide, each director has only one vote at a board meeting. In the event of a disagreement the majority view will prevail, though the chairman is usually given a casting vote (see, for example, reg 13 in each of the model form articles for private companies limited by shares, guarantee companies and public companies and, for companies with older articles, the 1985 Table A, reg 88).

12.82 In some circumstances, there may be a departure from the usual provision that decisions will be arrived at by a majority vote. For example, where there are special classes of shares each with rights to appoint directors, or where the company is, in effect, an incorporated partnership, articles frequently provide that all or some matters require an affirmative resolution from all directors, or from a specified majority, or from a majority including directors of both (or all) classes or factions.

Votes of directors who have a personal interest and/or conflict

12.83 Directors stand in a fiduciary relation to the company, and under the general rules relating to such a relationship a director cannot (in the absence of express provision in the articles) have a personal interest, whether direct or indirect, in any actual or proposed transaction or arrangement to be entered into by the company without the sanction of the company in general meeting or under some dispensation in the articles. So a director is precluded from dealing on behalf of the company with himself, and from entering into any engagement in which he has a personal interest that conflicts (or may possibly conflict) with the interests of the company unless certain conditions are satisfied.

12.84 This rule extends not only to transactions or arrangements between the company and the director but also to those with any people with whom the director is connected, and any firms or companies in which that director has an interest, either as director or member, and even if the director holds the shares in the other company as a trustee. The smallest conceivable conflict of interest will be sufficient to bring this rule into operation.[65] Even the allotment of shares or the issue of debentures by directors to themselves will fall within this rule unless sanctioned by the company in general meeting, or allowed under the articles.[66]

12.85 Invariably, articles do specify exemptions. Some will provide that such conflicts of interest are allowed, but the interested director is not to vote. In that case, a director prohibited from voting usually does not count towards a quorum either. For example, reg 14 in the model form articles for a private

---

[65] *Transvaal Lands Co v New Belgium Land Co* [1914] 2 Ch 488.
[66] *Neal v Quinn* [1916] WN 223.

company limited by shares says that, if a proposed decision of the directors is concerned with an actual or proposed transaction or arrangement with the company in which a director is interested, that director is not to be counted as participating in the decision-making process for quorum or voting purposes.

12.86 The articles of private companies will, however, almost invariably vary the model form articles (or for companies with older articles, the 1985 and previous Tables A) to allow directors to vote and be counted in the quorum in relation to certain, specified matters in which they have an interest. For example, reg 14 referred to above provides several exceptions, when the director can vote and be counted in the quorum. For example, one says a director can vote and be counted in the quorum if the director's conflict of interest arises because of what the regulation calls a 'permitted cause' – such as a subscription by the director, or an agreement to subscribe, for shares or other securities of the company.

12.87 In the case of companies with a sole director such variations are essential if the director is to enjoy any benefits from the company at all. In any event, prohibitions as to voting and quorum which apply to a person as director will not prevent him from voting as a member at general meetings of the company upon contracts in which that director is interested,[67] and a director is entitled to attend board meetings even when that director is not entitled to vote at the board meeting.[68]

12.88 Whether any such transactions or arrangements are permitted by the articles or by CA 2006 or not[69] the provisions of ss 177 and 182 of CA 2006 must be observed.[70] Those sections declare that it is the duty of a director who is in any way, whether directly or indirectly, interested in a *proposed* transaction or arrangement with the company to declare the nature and extent of his interest to the directors of the company, and also that he must do the same in the case of an *existing* contract or other arrangement or transaction (unless he has already done so when it was a proposed contract, arrangement or transaction (s 192)).

12.89 Whether made under s 177 or 182, the declaration must be made:

- at a meeting of the directors;

- by notice in writing under s 184; or

---

[67] *North-West Transportation Co v Beatty* (1887) 12 App Cas 589.
[68] *Grimwade v BPS Syndicate* (1915) 31 TLR 531.
[69] It should be stressed that certain contracts between directors (or those connected with them) and their companies are, under CA 2006, either generally forbidden or tightly circumscribed (see, for example, the provisions in s 190ff on substantial property transactions involving directors).
[70] Unless the company, being a private company, and being entitled to do so under its articles, has only one director. This is the effect of s 177(6)(b) and 182(6)(b).

- by general notice under s 185.

12.90 It is to be noted that it is not sufficient for a director merely to declare the existence of an interest: he must declare the nature and extent of the interest. For example, if the interest that a director has is 100 shares in the other contracting company, the director must declare that he holds the shares, and the number held. In addition, if, for example, the director's shareholding in the other company were a controlling one, this fact would alter the nature of the interest held and the director would have to disclose not merely that he is a shareholder, and the number of shares, but also that he is the controlling shareholder. The principle to be observed in deciding what has to be disclosed is that any aspect of the interest which could or might affect the attitude of the director or of the other members of the board is part of the 'nature' of the interest and must be disclosed.

12.91 If the interest is 'material', the articles may also require the director to disclose the extent of his interest, not just its nature. If, for example, reg 85 of Table A applies to the company, a director may only enjoy the concessions conferred by reg 85(a)–(c) if he has disclosed to the directors the nature 'and extent' of any 'material' interest.

12.92 The fact that a director discloses the nature or extent of an interest at a meeting and may not vote or be counted in the quorum does not absolve that director from his other statutory and fiduciary duties with regard to the matter. The director is entitled to speak on it and if he feels it is against the interests of the company, he must say so. After having disclosed an interest, the director is not entitled merely to sit back and wash his hands of the matter.

12.93 In the case of a s 177 declaration, it must be made before the transaction or arrangement is entered into (s 177(4)). Any declaration required by s 182 must be made as soon as is reasonably practicable (s 182(4)).

12.94 Both s 177 and s 182 exclude a director from the obligation to declare an interest:

- if the director is not aware of the transaction or arrangement (for which purpose he is treated as being aware of matters of which he ought reasonably to be aware – so directors must take sufficient proactive steps to ensure they are informed of transactions or arrangements entered into by their company);

- if the interest cannot reasonably be regarded as likely to give rise to a conflict of interest;

- if (and to the extent) the other directors are already aware of it (and they are also treated as aware of anything of which they ought reasonably to be aware); or

- if (or to the extent) it concerns terms of his service contract, and the contract has been, or is to be, considered by a meeting of the directors, or by a committee of the directors appointed for the purpose under the company's constitution.

12.95 Under s 184, a declaration made by notice in writing must be given by hand or sent by the director in the post to the other directors, in hard copy form, unless the recipient has agreed to receive it in electronic form. If the latter applies, it must be sent in the electronic form they have agreed (for example, Word document or pdf) and by the electronic means they have agreed (for example, e-mail).

12.96 If a director declares his interest by such a notice in writing, then the making of the declaration is deemed to form part of the proceedings at the next meeting of the directors, and it must be minuted under s 248 as if the declaration had been made at that meeting.

12.97 Under s 185, a general notice given by the director to the board is deemed to be a sufficient declaration of interest if it gives notice that:

(1) he has an interest (as member, officer, employee or otherwise) in a specified company or firm and is to be regarded as interested in any transaction or arrangement which, after the date of the notice, the company may make with that company or firm; or

(2) that the director is to be regarded as interested in any transaction or arrangement which, after the date of the notice, the company may make with a specified person (other than a body corporate or firm).[71]

12.98 The notice must state the nature and extent of the director's interest in the body corporate or firm or, as the case may be, the nature of his connection with the person (s 185(3)). But it has no effect until either it is given at a meeting of the directors or the director in question takes reasonable steps to secure that it is brought up and read at the next meeting of the directors after it is given.

---

[71] Under s 252 of CA 2006, persons connected with the director include the director's spouse, children and stepchildren under 18 years of age; the director's business partner; companies with which the director is associated through control of one-fifth of the nominal equity capital or voting rights; and certain trustees. In addition, unlike the CA 1985 definition, it includes the director's parents; children or stepchildren of the director who are over 18 years old (those under 18 were already included under s 346 of CA 1985); persons with whom the director lives as partner in an enduring family relationship; and children or stepchildren of the director's unmarried partner if they live with the director and are under 18 years of age. This implements the Law Commission and Scottish Law Commission's recommendation that the definition of connected person be extended so as to include cohabitants, infant children of the cohabitant if they live with the director, adult children of the director and the director's parents (in *Company Directors: Regulating Conflicts of Interests and Formulating a Statement of Duties*). However, the recommendation that the definition be extended to siblings has not been implemented.

Meetings of Directors 239

12.99 The provisions of s 182ff (but not s 177ff) also apply to shadow directors,[72] with the following adaptations.

- the declaration cannot be made at a meeting of the directors;

- in s 185, the requirement that a general notice be given at or brought up and read at meeting of directors does not apply; and

- general notice by a shadow director is not effective unless given by notice in writing in accordance with s 184 (that is, a general notice given by a shadow director must comply with both s 184 and the first three subsections of s 185).

12.100 Apart from any specific exemptions found in the articles which permit a director to vote and be counted in the quorum despite his interest, articles often provide in addition that the prohibitions may at any time be suspended or relaxed to any extent, and either generally or in respect of any particular arrangement or transaction, by the company in general meeting. However, even if the articles permit a director to vote on a resolution in which that director is interested, this does not absolve the director from disclosure, under s 177 or 182 of the nature of the interest. That disclosure has to be made so that the other directors can give due weight to the opposing interest while assessing the director's views. It is not sufficient for a director to disclose his interest to a mere subcommittee of the board. It must be to the full board.[73]

12.101 Articles frequently permit a director to hold any other office or place of profit under the company (other than the office of auditor) in conjunction with the office of director for such period and on such terms (as to remuneration and otherwise) as the directors may determine.[74] The articles usually go on to provide that, as long as disclosure of a director's interests has been made to the other directors, a director may be a party to or interested in any transaction or arrangement in which the company is interested, or may be associated with another body which is a party to a transaction or arrangement in which the company is interested. An article in these terms will usually go on to provide that a director so contracting, or being so interested, shall not be liable to account to the company for any profit realised by any such transactions or arrangement by reason of holding that office.[75]

---

[72] The concept of 'shadow director' is defined in s 251 of CA 2006, as 'a person in accordance with whose directions or instructions the directors of a company are accustomed to act', although those giving advice in a professional capacity are specifically excluded. For recent cases on the definition of 'shadow director', see *Re Hydrodan (Corby) Ltd* [1994] BCC 161 and *Secretary of State v Deverell* [2000] 2 WLR 907.
[73] *Guinness plc v Saunders and Another* [1988] 1 WLR 863.
[74] Subject, however, to s 188 of CA 2006 requiring the approval of the members to any proposal to employ a director for more than 2 years when the contract is not freely terminable by the company during that period.
[75] This is subject, however, to the statutory rules on directors' contracts with the company.

12.102 In addition, the articles may permit a director, notwithstanding that director's interest, to be counted in the quorum present at any meeting at which that director or any other director is appointed to hold any such office or place of profit under the company or at which the terms of any such appointment are arranged, and allow a director to vote on any such appointment or arrangement other than his own appointment or the arrangement of the terms of that appointment.

12.103 The articles may also provide that a director may act, or his firm may act, in a professional capacity for the company, and that the director or the director's firm shall be entitled to remuneration for professional services as if that person were not a director. However, these provisions are stated not to authorise a director or a director's firm to act as auditor to the company.

12.104 Many articles (particularly those of private companies) do not contain such an elaborate provision, but it is often useful to permit the restrictions imposed by the articles to be relaxed by the company in general meeting, especially where there are only two or three directors of the company.

12.105 It should be noted that all the provisions regarding disclosure and prohibitions on voting where there is an interest apply to 'transactions and arrangements' – a far wider range of circumstances than merely contracts. These wide provisions reinforce the director's fiduciary duty to disclose his interest in any matter which the board might consider, whether technically a contract with the company or not.

12.106 However, there is one instance when the articles may not permit a director in a conflict situation to vote and be counted in the quorum in relation to a matter at a board meeting. This is when s 175 applies. The section imposes a duty on a director to avoid situations in which he has, or can have, a direct or indirect interest that conflicts, or possibly may conflict, with the interests of the company (often called a 'situational conflict'). Section 175(2) provides that this applies in particular to the exploitation of any property, information or opportunity (and it is immaterial whether the company could take advantage of the property, information or opportunity itself).

12.107 However, there are a number of exceptions, when a situational conflict is permitted. One is under s 175(4), which provides that those members of the board of directors who are not themselves conflicted may authorise a situational conflict of another director, provided the conflict has been proposed to the board and provided the company's constitution:

- in the case of a private company, does not prohibit this and, in the case of a private company incorporated before 1 October 2008, the members also pass an enabling ordinary resolution; or

- in the case of a public company, specifically permits it.

12.108 However, the key point for the purposes of this discussion is that s 175(6) says that the authorisation by the impartial directors is only effective if:

- any requirement as to the quorum at the meeting at which the matter is considered is met without counting the director in question or any other interested director;[76] and

- the matter was agreed to without their voting or would have been agreed to if their votes had not been counted.

12.109 The board will therefore have to make sure it can comply with the usual requirements in its articles as to quorum, but without the conflicted director, or any other director who is interested, counting in the quorum or voting at the meeting in relation to his situational conflict. This is so irrespective of any article purporting to give directors a right to vote and be counted in the quorum even if they are conflicted.

12.110 A company that wants to allow the impartial members of its board to authorise conflicts of their fellow directors should consider including provisions in its articles that set out *how* the board should do so. For example, it may want to make it clear that:

- A conflicted director should give a written notification to the board of any prospective situational conflict, setting out the nature and extent of his interest, as soon as possible and, if it is not immediately clear, explaining why there is a conflict.

- He should not count in the quorum at the relevant board meeting (or, if the conflict is authorised by a directors' written resolution in lieu of a meeting, that the conflicted director(s) consent to the decision is not required).

- The impartial directors must not vote to authorise a conflict if that would breach their other general duties, such as the duty to promote the success of the company.

It may also want to specify in the articles whether an authorisation can be made conditional so that, for example, the board can give authority for a director to be a director of another company, but make it conditional on:

- his not disclosing any confidential information or trade secrets to that other company; and

- his exclusion from board meetings if matters concerning that other company are discussed.

---

[76] The Act does not define what 'interested' means in this context, but it is sensible to treat a person as interested if they are connected to the conflicted director within the definition in s 252.

ALTERNATE DIRECTORS

12.111 Sometimes articles provide that directors may appoint alternate directors to act for them – for example, because they are going abroad or otherwise unable to attend board meetings. There is no common law power to appoint alternates. If the articles do not allow for alternates, they cannot be appointed. Invariably, an alternate may be either an existing director or, if he is not, must be approved by resolution of the directors. Under normal articles, a person may be alternate for more than one director.

12.112 The power to appoint alternates can be very useful, particularly where directors are in some remote place, away from the company's central operations. For modern public companies to whom the model form articles for a public company apply, and older companies for whom regs 65 et seq in the 1985 Table A apply, these provide for appointment of alternates. However, there is no such provision in the model form articles for a private company limited by shares or for a guarantee company and, if such companies want directors to be able to appoint alternates, they will have to file articles at Companies House varying the relevant model form to include such powers.

12.113 Articles usually say that an alternate who is not also a director in his own right is counted as a director for the purposes of both voting and the quorum provided, in each case, his appointor is not present at the meeting. If his appointor is present, the alternate has no vote and cannot count in the quorum.

12.114 If the alternate is also a director in his own right, articles usually say he counts as two persons for voting purposes, provided his appointor is not present. If the appointor is present, the alternate can exercise only his own vote as a director. He counts as only one person when calculating the quorum, whether his appointor attends the meeting or not.

12.115 It is important to recognise that, under most articles, an alternate director is not deemed to be the agent of the director appointing him. Instead, he is deemed for all purposes to be a director and is liable for his own acts and omissions. An alternate director appointed pursuant to an article in such terms is therefore subject to all the duties and responsibilities which apply to a full director. He should, for example, ensure that his acts and decisions as an alternate director are made in the best interests of the company; he should notify or declare his interests in transactions or arrangements to the board under either s 177 or 182; he should not vote or be counted in the quorum if his appointor would not be, and he should be entered in the company's registers as a director and his appointment notified to Companies House. Particularly, he should not act or vote blindly in accordance with instructions given to him by his appointor, but should apply his mind to the company's affairs and come to his own, independent judgment, or he may be liable for breach of his fiduciary duties to the company.

COMMITTEES

12.116 As we have seen above, the directors may, if the articles contain the necessary authority, delegate their powers to a committee. The articles generally do – for example, see reg 5 in the model form articles for a private company limited by shares. Usually, directors may delegate their powers to a committee of one.[77] However, a declaration made or notice given to a subcommittee of the board by a director with a personal interest in an actual or proposed transaction or arrangement of the company is not sufficient to satisfy the requirements of s 177 or 182.[78]

12.117 A committee of the directors can only act within the limits prescribed by its appointing authority, ie the board. For example, reg 6 in the model form articles for a private company limited by shares requires committees to follow procedures based (as far as they are applicable) on the articles governing how the main board makes decisions – unless the board has made specific rules for all or any committees which, if they have, prevail over the articles. Such a provision does not, however, remove the need to ensure that, in all cases of delegation of powers to a committee, the committee's powers and authority are clearly stated in the resolution affecting the delegation.

12.118 However, unlike the delegation of their powers to the directors by the members,[79] delegation of their powers by directors to a committee of the board does not imply a parting with the powers granted by the board. The board remains responsible for the decisions and acts of its committees. Such powers delegated to the committee can be resumed at any time by the board.[80] A committee of the board must report to the board regularly and fully.

12.119 A committee may come into existence and have certain powers even without being expressly appointed. In such a case the powers and jurisdiction of the committee will be implied. An example of such a committee, and the limits on its jurisdiction, is found in the trade union case of *Abbott v Sullivan*.[81]

12.120 When a board of directors delegates their power to a committee without any provision as to the committee acting by a quorum, all acts of the committee must be done in the presence of all members of the committee, and the committee has no power to add to their number or to fill a vacancy.[82]

---

[77] See, also, *Re Fireproof Doors* [1916] 2 Ch 142.
[78] *Guinness plc v Saunders and Another* [1998] 1 WLR 863.
[79] See Chapter 4 (members' meetings).
[80] *Huth v Clarke* (1890) 25 QBD 391.
[81] [1952] 1 KB 189.
[82] *Re Liverpool Household Stores* (1890) 59 LJ Ch 616.

RESOLUTIONS IN LIEU OF A BOARD MEETING

12.121 Articles frequently allow the directors, if acting unanimously, to make decisions without holding a meeting. For example, reg 8 in the model form articles for a private company limited by shares and, for companies with older articles, reg 93 of the 1985 Table A.

12.122 Regulation 8 envisages more ways to pass directors' resolutions than simply by written resolution. It says:

> '(1) A decision of the directors is taken in accordance with this article when all eligible directors indicate to each other by any means that they share a common view on a matter.
>
> (2) Such a decision may take the form of a resolution in writing, copies of which have been signed by each eligible director or to which each eligible director has otherwise indicated agreement in writing.
>
> (3) References in this article to eligible directors are to directors who would have been entitled to vote on the matter had it been proposed as a resolution at a directors' meeting.
>
> (4) A decision may not be taken in accordance with this article if the eligible directors would not have formed a quorum at such a meeting.'

So, under reg 8, a written resolution is just one way directors can show they have indicated to each other that they share a common view on a matter. However, in practice, directors are only using resolutions in writing in lieu of a board meeting, signed or agreed to by all the directors entitled to vote on the particular decision, to satisfy reg 8.

12.123 For companies with older articles, a resolution in writing is usually the only way they can pass a decision outside a board meeting. For example, reg 93 says that a resolution in writing, signed by all the directors entitled to receive notice of a meeting of the directors, shall be as valid and effectual as if it had been passed at a meeting of the directors duly convened and held. However, there are limits to this power.

12.124 In the event that the number of directors entitled to receive notice is less than the number of directors required to constitute a quorum (for example, because a number of directors are overseas and therefore not entitled to notice under the articles) it appears that a resolution passed pursuant to an article in terms of reg 8 or reg 93 (and even their predecessor, reg 106 of the 1948 Table A) will not be valid: *Hood Sailmakers Ltd v Axford*.[83] The members of the board in the UK cannot pass resolutions in writing in the absence of overseas colleagues unless the directors in the UK signing the resolution constitute a quorum in their own right.

---

[83] [1997] 1 WLR 625.

12.125 In the case of *UK Safety Group Ltd v Heane*,[84] it was held in the Chancery Division that a service contract entered into by one of the directors on behalf of the company was not binding on the company unless it had been approved at board level. This was because the articles vested the authority to enter into such contracts with the directors of the company as a 'board'.

12.126 There is no reason why a company cannot amend the model form or Table A in its articles, or disapply it and replace it with an alternative provision, to allow all the directors who would have been entitled to attend and vote on it at a general meeting, to agree to a resolution electronically, in lieu of holding a meeting and without requiring a written document.

12.127 The board should, however, make sure that there is adequate security against abuse. ICSA says that, in some circumstances, it may be sufficient that the director's agreement comes from a known or specified e-mail address.[85] In other circumstances, the board may wish to require that each director provide a unique personal identifier, issued for this purpose, when giving electronic consent to a resolution. The company secretary may wish to circulate a subsequent document in writing, confirming that the relevant consents have been obtained.

COMPANIES WITH A SOLE DIRECTOR

12.128 In the case of a company with a sole director it might be thought that the common law rule that one person cannot, in general, constitute a meeting would preclude the company from holding board meetings. Instead, best practice would be for the sole director to record decisions (which would, in the event that there had been more than one director, have been considered at a board meeting) as resolutions in writing, signed by the sole director.

12.129 However, in *Neptune (Vehicle Washing Equipment) Ltd v Fitzgerald (No 2)*,[86] the court considered the application of s 317 of CA 1985 to companies with a sole director. Section 317 (which has been overtaken by ss 177 and 182 of CA 2006 and is no longer in force) required directors who were directly or indirectly interested in a contract or proposed contract (or any transaction or arrangement) entered into by their company to declare the nature of their interest at a board meeting. In that case a sole director purported to hold a meeting at which he resolved to terminate his own contract of employment and authorise payment to himself of £100,892.62 allegedly due to him under that contract. The payment was then made and he retired as director.

---

[84] [1998] 2 BCLC 208.
[85] 'Electronic Communications Order 2000 – ICSA's Guide to Recommended Best Practice' (December 2000).
[86] [1995] BCC 1000.

12.130 Subsequently, the company (under new management and ownership) sought to recover the sum paid, by way of summary judgment. The former director appealed against the summary judgment, seeking leave to defend. In considering the appeal, the court had to consider whether there was a sufficient case to argue, that s 317 might apply to a company with a sole director, so that he should have held a board meeting at which he declared his interest in the transaction.

12.131 The court granted him leave to defend. In the course of so deciding, it held that the words of s 317 required a sole director to purport to hold a board meeting at which he could make the required declaration. There could therefore be a meeting of one person, and that person could constitute a quorum at it. The court said that the making of the declaration had to be a distinct happening at the meeting, and the occasion for a statutory pause for thought, during which the director should reflect upon the existence of the conflict between his interests and those of the company. The director should consider the possibility that he might, by virtue of the matter under consideration, be in breach of his duties to the company, or at greater risk of committing such a breach in the future. The director should then make the declaration required by s 317. If no other person was in attendance the declaration could be made by the director to himself – 'although not necessarily aloud'. If another person was in attendance, such as the secretary, it should be made aloud in the hearing of those attending.

12.132 The court further held that the declaration, whether made aloud or not, should be recorded in the minutes of the meeting – although omission of such a minute was not conclusive as to whether the declaration had in fact been made or not.

12.133 Implicit in the court's decision is the assumption that a sole director can constitute a meeting – at least in circumstances where there is a statutory provision which appears to require a board meeting to be held.

12.134 In the case of *MacPherson v European Strategic Bureau Ltd*,[87] however, it was held that a failure by directors (who were also members of the company) to declare an interest in an agreement pursuant to s 317 at a formal board meeting did not vitiate the agreement. As all members knew of the agreement and of the precise nature of the other's interest there was, in substance, unanimous approval of the transaction by the members. No amount of formal disclosure would have increased the other's relevant knowledge.

12.135 However, *MacPherson* can be distinguished from *Neptune* because in *Neptune* the members had no knowledge of what the director had done – and in such circumstances, *Neptune* does seem to require a board meeting if s 317 is to be complied with. Faced with the inconsistency between the Act and the usual common law rule that one person may not constitute a meeting, prudence

---

[87] [2000] 2 BCLC 683.

dictated that a sole director, who is not also the sole member, should purport to hold a board meeting at which to make his declaration, should ensure that the declaration is a distinct event at that meeting, should pause for thought sufficient to satisfy the statute and should ensure that all of this is sufficiently minuted.

12.136 What effect does CA 2006 have? The wording of ss 177 and 182 (which are the closest equivalent provisions in CA 2006 to s 317) means that, in relation to declarations of a director's personal interest in both existing and proposed transactions or arrangements to be entered into by their company, *Neptune* is no longer relevant. This is because, under ss 177(6) and 182(6), a director need not declare an interest if, or to the extent that, the other directors are already aware of it (and for this purpose the other directors are treated as aware of anything of which they ought reasonably to be aware). So where a company is permitted to have a sole director, and does so, the sole director already knows about the interest and therefore need not declare it.

12.137 However, where a company has a sole director, but its articles require it to have two or more, s 186 of the Act applies. As stated in the Explanatory Notes to CA 2006, prepared by what was then the Department of Trade and Industry (which became the Department for Business, Enterprise and Regulatory Reform and is now the Department for Business, Innovation and Skills):

> 'This is a new provision. Where a company has only one director, it is not possible for the director to declare his interests to the other directors, because there are no other directors. Therefore, a sole director does not need to comply with section 182 (declaration of interest in existing transaction or arrangement).'

12.138 A reading of s 186 shows that it applies where a company has a sole director but should have two – for example, where it is a public company. (Presumably it will also apply to a private company whose articles require two directors, but only has a sole director for the time being, although this is uncertain.)

12.139 In any event, when it does apply, the effect of s 186 is to require a sole director to make a declaration of interest under s 182 (that is, in relation to an *existing* transaction or arrangement). However, in those circumstances, a meeting need not be held – instead, s 186 states that:

- such a declaration must be recorded in writing;

- the making of the declaration is deemed to form part of the proceedings at the next meeting of the directors after the notice is given; and

- the provisions of s 248 (minutes of meetings of directors) apply as if the declaration had been made at that meeting.

12.140 It goes on to say that these requirements are in addition to the statutory requirement that terms of contracts entered into by a company with a sole member who is also a director must be set out in writing or recorded in minutes (s 231).

12.141 Section 186, therefore, only requires a declaration from a sole director in circumstances where the company should not have a sole director. However, it has no application to a company where sole directors are permitted. In those circumstances, we have to go back to s 182 itself to decide whether the sole director must make a declaration.

THE EFFECT OF INVALID APPOINTMENTS ON BOARD DECISIONS

12.142 Subject to what is said at **12.125** concerning s 40ff, acts done as directors by persons who have not been validly elected do not bind the company,[88] unless, in certain circumstances, this is only discovered afterwards – for s 161 provides that the acts of a person acting as a director shall be valid notwithstanding that it is discovered afterwards that there was a defect in their appointment, or that they were disqualified from holding office, or that they had ceased to hold office or that they were not entitled to vote on the matter in question. Section 161 applies even if the resolution appointing them is void because it contravened the s 160 requirement that appointments of directors of a public company should be voted on individually.

12.143 Outsiders are, in the absence of knowledge to the contrary, entitled to assume that the domestic affairs of a company are properly conducted, the basis for this principle being known as the rule in *Royal British Bank v Turquand*.[89] The importance of the *Turquand* rule has been significantly lessened by s 40 of CA 2006. The reason for this is that s 40 makes the acts of the directors binding on the company in favour of a person dealing with it in good faith, notwithstanding any constitutional limitations on the directors' powers. Knowing that an act is beyond the power of the directors does not show bad faith (s 40(2)(b)). The effect of this provision seems to be to make concerns about the proper constitution of the board relevant in most cases only to internal disputes, and then subject only to s 285.

---

[88] *Garden Gully United Mining Co v McLister* (1875) 1 App Cas 39.
[89] [1843–60] All ER Rep 435.

Chapter 13

ELECTRONIC COMMUNICATIONS AND BOARD MEETINGS

INTRODUCTION

13.1 Traditionally, companies have had to give notice of board meetings to directors personally or by post, in hard copy format, and board meetings have been held face to face, with directors assembling together in one physical location. Technological advances, coupled with greater geographical spread of company personnel, have led to widespread use of electronic communications, both for the purpose of calling and of conducting board meetings.

13.2 There is, however, very little legislation covering electronic communications in relation to board meetings – certainly nothing corresponding to the Companies Act 2006 (CA 2006) provisions[1] that govern electronic communications relating to members' meetings – and very little case-law. This means that almost none of the practices discussed below have a statutory authority or have been tested in the courts.

13.3 But this is an endorsement of them. Legislation is unnecessary, and case-law scarce, precisely because these practices are useful to the boards that adopt them, and accepted by their members and third parties. Legal doubts that once existed about certain uses of electronic communications have largely been steamrollered as they have been adopted wholesale across boardrooms in the UK. Their authority therefore rests rather on custom – the fact that they are in common use, without challenge.

13.4 Where, however, they should be adopted only after specific, specialist advice has been taken, this is flagged in the discussion. And boards will always need to bear in mind that the particular circumstances of their company may make electronic communication, or some aspect of it, inappropriate. Generally, however, officers adopting these practices can take comfort from the fact that they are following in the footsteps of established, well-advised companies.

---

[1] See Chapter 11.

ELECTRONIC NOTICE OF BOARD MEETINGS

13.5 Notice of a board meeting can be given electronically provided the articles of the company do not specifically prohibit it, and (in accordance with existing case-law on the giving of notice) provided electronic notice is reasonable in the circumstances.

13.6 Notice by phone is already common, and notices can also be sent by e-mail, electronic message or via the Internet. The High Court in England & Wales (following various decisions in the courts in Australia and New Zealand) has sanctioned service of certain documents in legal proceedings by posting them on the intended recipient's page on a social networking site in certain circumstances.[2] This may become acceptable in the UK in relation to notice of board meetings and other documents or information for directors. Documents and information required or that may be sent or supplied to members under CA 2006 can now, provided both sides agree, be given to a member by the company by sending e-mails to him, containing a hyperlink to a web address where the notice of the meeting can be found. This may also become an accepted way of giving notice of board meetings. However, a company should take specific, specialist advice before adopting either of these latter practices. Particularly, since notices of board meetings can contain confidential and sensitive information, the security issues would be far more important than is the case with notice of members' meetings.

13.7 Generally, the authors' view is that neither the model form articles prescribed under CA 2006, nor the 1985 Table A to the Companies Act 1985 (CA 1985) prohibit electronic notice of board meetings. If any of them applies the directors can therefore decide that such notices may be given electronically. The board should, though, establish appropriate rules in internal policies and procedures.

13.8 If a board does wish to ask its members to authorise electronic notice of board meetings in the company's articles (perhaps to avoid censure at a general meeting for using a less secure means of communication than previously – see **13.4**), they may still, in the main, leave the detailed rules to be settled by the directors.

13.9 The rules will often require that directors must unanimously agree to the use of electronic communications generally. They may specify that a director, or a specified proportion of the board, can notify the company that they have withdrawn their agreement at any time. The rules will also specify the form or forms of electronic communication that the company can use to give notice of board meetings, such as phone, fax or e-mail. They will also specify the format

---

[2] *AKO Capital LLP & another v TFS Derivatives & others* UK High Court, 17 February 2012. For Australian and New Zealand cases, *see MKM Capital Property Limited and Carmela Rit Corbo and Gordon Kingsley Maxwell Poyser (A Bankrupt)* (No SC 608 of 2008) *and AXE Market Gardens v Craig Axe* CIV 2008-485-2676.

of the notice – for example, if sent as an attachment to an e-mail, should it be in Microsoft Word and, if so, which version?

13.10 While it would be unusual for a director to agree that electronic notices are permitted generally, but to opt out of the regime himself, the board may decide that each director should have the right to decide whether he, personally, wishes to receive notices electronically. If he does not, the rules might provide that notice must be given to him in some other way acceptable to him.

13.11 Assuming all directors are to receive notice electronically, the rules will require each to provide a specific telephone number, e-mail or other electronic address, to be used for this purpose. Notice is properly given only if transmitted to such a number or address.

13.12 As with any notice, the board should consider rules for ensuring the notice has been received, or is deemed received. In the case of a telephone call, the rules might provide that the telephone must be answered by the director, and the notice given to him personally. Companies might allocate unique personal identifiers that directors can quote as proof of their identity for this purpose. Alternatively, it might be deemed sufficient to record the content of the notice on an answering machine or voice-mail, or to provide it to a third party, to be relayed to the director. Only an engaged tone or a complete failure to answer the phone would be treated as non-delivery.

13.13 In the case of e-mails, the guidelines might require the sender to use a system that provides electronic confirmation of receipt of the e-mail. Some e-mail systems record whether the e-mail has been opened or not.

13.14 In each case, notice may be deemed to have been given immediately, or upon expiry of some period, such as 24 hours.

13.15 The board may wish to provide for personal or postal delivery of a notice within a certain time after the first attempt at electronic transmission, if it has not been given, or deemed given, under the rules.

13.16 Giving notice of directors' meetings electronically will probably be considered reasonable if all the directors are likely to become aware of the particular meeting by virtue of the electronic communication. The board should also consider security issues. Business at board meetings can be extremely sensitive and confidential, so the need to consider security is correspondingly greater than for members' meetings.

13.17 Unauthorised access can be gained to electronic communications, particularly e-mail messages sent over the internet. For reasons which often have no basis in fact, the public perception is that this danger is greater on the internet than over, say, a phone system or the post.

13.18 If a notice is to be given as an attachment in an e-mail or other electronic system, then encryption, passwords and other security devices should be considered, or the directors could be in breach of their general statutory and other duties. The directors may therefore wish to consider security issues if notices are to be given by such electronic means. The security of internet communications is beyond the remit of this book, but there are means of restricting access to e-mails and other electronic communications, using passwords allocated only to particular users, by creating an intranet or extranet using 'firewalls' or by using encryption techniques. The board may wish to consult its IT department or buy in specialist IT expertise to deal with this issue. If the meeting itself is to be held electronically, the board should also consider how it will send out sensitive and confidential documents for the directors to consider prior to the meeting. It is strongly recommended that a more secure method be found to deliver them than e-mail, such as a secure courier service.

ELECTRONIC BOARD MEETINGS

13.19 It is increasingly common for directors' meetings to be held electronically, often by phone conference call, without having to meet face to face in one physical location. Unlike members' meetings, the ability to see other members, and be seen by them, is not necessary – although if it can be achieved using webcam or like facilities, this will usually be preferable to 'voice only' communications.

13.20 Directors must decide whether sanctioning and using electronic board meetings breach any of their general or other duties, and act reasonably in all decisions relating to such board meetings. Key issues are:

- Does the means chosen allow proper debate and interaction?

- Do all directors have access to the appropriate equipment?

- Could any director be disadvantaged?

- Are the methods of communication to be used sufficiently secure?

13.21 Generally, the ability to hold board meetings electronically will be beneficial, particularly where directors are geographically dispersed. To avoid disputes, the board may decide that its decision to approve electronic participation must be unanimous, and that individual directors can notify the company, subsequently, that they have withdrawn their consent to electronic participation in meetings.

13.22 Companies should also, however, consider whether their electronic communication will result in an electronic record that could be obtained at the discovery stage in litigation, or seized on injunction, or simply hacked or stolen. Encryption of electronic communications may provide a solution.

13.23 It may be that a court would hold an electronic board meeting valid without there being authority to hold such meetings in the company's articles (unless electronic meetings were specifically prohibited). To avoid disputes, however, electronic participation at board meetings should be authorised by the articles. There is an argument that this is implicit in the model form articles prescribed under CA 2006 for each of private and public share companies, and companies limited by guarantee respectively. For example, reg 9 in the model form articles for a private company limited by shares says that notice of any directors' meeting must indicate, if it is anticipated that directors participating in the meeting will not be in the same place, how it is proposed that they should communicate with each other during the meeting. There are identical provisions in the model form articles for public and guarantee companies respectively.

13.24 For companies with older articles, there is no such provision in the 1985 Table A. This means a resolution to alter the articles must be put to the members. The item should be put to the members as a distinct resolution, to be voted on separately from other, routine amendments to the articles. In the US, some corporations also ratify all decisions made using electronic communications at the next face-to-face meeting of the board.

13.25 The articles should define the conditions necessary to hold a valid electronic meeting. The overriding requirement will usually be that directors can hear and be heard by all the other participants at all times. This means there can be a debate or exchange leading to a resolution in the best interests of the company, as there would be at a conventional meeting. For example, the model form articles for a private company limited by shares say (in reg 10) that (subject to the articles) directors participate in a directors' meeting, or part of a directors' meeting, when (amongst other conditions) they can each communicate to the others any information or opinions they have on any particular item of the business of the meeting and, in determining whether directors are participating in a directors' meeting, it is irrelevant where any director is or how they communicate with each other. There are identical provisions in the model form articles for public and guarantee companies respectively.

13.26 Most commonly, directors hold electronic meetings using telephone or video, conference facilities. Technologically, it would be possible to link directors by e-mail or through an instant messaging service or via an electronic bulletin board on a website. Such internet-based means of communication would allow directors to see and contribute to a written debate in real time. However, the author's view is that use of such facilities would create many practical problems, particularly in relation to verification of the identities of the participants, the slowness of proceedings and the inability to debate issues properly – to refine arguments, to interrupt etc. (Inability to interrupt etc might be considered beneficial by some chairmen and company secretaries, but is not conducive to good, commercial decision-making generally.) In practice, the author is not aware of board meetings being held electronically in the UK other than via phone or video conferencing.[3]

13.27 One way of drafting articles would be on the basis that board meetings will be called for a particular physical location, but directors can participate remotely using electronic communications. Questions that arise include whether there is a valid meeting if all have chosen to participate remotely (so all can hear and be heard by each other), but no one has turned up at the specified physical location. In some jurisdictions, such issues have been addressed in specific legislation, but they are still uncertain in the UK. The articles of a UK company should therefore avoid providing, or even implying, that a board meeting in which directors participate electronically must have a physical location at all. If they simply specify that a board meeting can validly be held by electronic means, provided that all the participants can communicate interactively and simultaneously with each other – that they can hear each other and be heard (so that there can be proper debate) – then such thorny issues are avoided.

13.28 If all directors are present in the UK when participating in an electronic board meeting, the fact that the specific location of the meeting is not ascertainable is not a problem. There are, however, territories (that do not include the UK) that claim jurisdiction to levy tax on companies that are 'managed and controlled', or 'centrally managed and controlled', in that territory.

13.29 If, in fact, all (or a significant number of) meetings of a UK company are held electronically, and a majority of the directors invariably participate from such a territory, it is possible that the company will receive a tax assessment from the fiscal authority there.

13.30 Where central management and control is exercised will be a question of fact under the law of the territory concerned. However, the articles of association may be persuasive under that law. It may, therefore, be important that they prescribe where the company deems electronic meetings to be held, or the basis upon which that question should be resolved. The local tax authority can then be referred to those articles. For example, common options are to say the meeting is deemed held where the majority of the participants are located, where the chairman is physically present or at such location as the directors agree. The model form articles for a private company limited by shares say (in reg 10) that, if all the directors participating in a meeting are not in the same place, they may decide that the meeting is to be treated as taking place wherever

---

[3] Internet-based meetings are authorised under, for example, California Non-Profit Corporation Law, subject to a requirement that the corporation verify that a person participating is entitled to do so and that all actions/votes are, in fact, taken by directors. Verification is always going to be problematic in jurisdictions like the UK, in which citizens do not have access to an accessible, ubiquitous, common system for issuing and recognising digital certificates.

any of them is. There are identical provisions in the model form articles for public and guarantee companies respectively.

13.31 However, articles will be unpersuasive in many territories. If a majority of directors are in such a 'problem' territory, the company's articles may need to prohibit, or treat as invalid, electronic meetings in which a majority of the directors participating would be physically present in that particular territory. Such directors would either have to forego their right to participate, travel to another territory or, if authorised by the articles, appoint an alternate director. But the tax problem would be avoided.

13.32 These problems should not be overstated. They already arise in other, familiar situations. For example, where is the decision made if directors, the majority of whom are physically present in a 'problem' territory, sign a unanimous resolution in writing in lieu of a meeting? The issue of where a company is 'managed and controlled' is not, therefore, an issue that arises solely in relation to electronic meetings. It is just that it needs to be addressed if the benefits of electronic meetings are to be fully enjoyed without legal mishaps. The lesson for the board is to make sure that the question of whether to hold a particular meeting electronically should also include consideration of the tax implications in other territories if there are directors who will be participating outside the UK.

13.33 It will not be necessary to provide for the fine details of electronic board meetings in the articles. These can be dealt with in policies and procedures, approved by the board. Again, unanimity is recommended.

13.34 These might include a means whereby directors indicate that they are joining in the meeting, or leaving it. For example, the company may want to establish standard statements and responses that the relevant director, and either the chairman or the secretary, make to each other when joining or leaving the meeting, so it is clear to all what is happening. The chairman may also want to check periodically that everyone is still connected to the meeting – that there has not been a technological failure. The secretary can then safely record that a quorum is present at the beginning of the meeting, and record 'arrivals' and 'departures'.

13.35 The board may also want a system for ensuring that the directors participating electronically are who they say they are. This can be particularly important if, for example, alternate directors have been appointed, who are not personally known to the other participants. A person organising an electronic board meeting in the form of a conference call, through a commercial provider like BT, can ask for a 'participant number' to be issued. The organiser then provides the conference call number and the participant number, separately and in confidence, to each intended participant. The participant must key both numbers when he first joins the meeting. The organiser could also ask each intended participant to provide the phone number from which they will call to join the meeting. After the meeting, the organiser receives a report (often integrated into the provider's bill), that shows the phone numbers of participants who took part in the meeting, which can be compared with the numbers they said they would call from. A less sophisticated alternative is for the secretary to issue passwords that participants must give as they join the meeting.

13.36 Generally, good practice is for the chairman to establish attendees by a roll call, at the formal start of business. To enable debate, the chairman will sometimes ask participants to make their contributions to the meeting in a rota, or at least to state their names before making any point.

13.37 The board should also consider a voting procedure that makes it crystal clear to each participant that they are being asked to vote, that they have cast their vote and that their vote has been recognised and recorded by the meeting. Taking votes on the basis of a roll call is a useful procedure that ensures the chairman stays in control and the secretary can be sure votes are being recorded accurately.

13.38 The secretary needs to consider asking the board to approve the form of various minutes, to record the fact of electronic participation in a board meeting and observance of any rules established for the conduct of an electronic meeting.

13.39 Finally, even if generally authorised by the articles to hold electronic meetings, the requirement that directors comply with their general statutory and other duties means they should consider whether there are any special circumstances that require *particular* board meetings to be held face to face. For example, if the agenda includes an important and sensitive item, can discussion safely be held over an open phone line? Is the method of electronic communication being used sufficiently secure, so that their debate cannot be intercepted, tampered with or overheard? If the agenda is to consider and approve the accounts for signature, prior to laying them before the members in general meeting, can directors discuss the accounts properly without the degree of physical interaction – body language, free and frank discussion etc – that comes only with a face-to-face meeting? There have been comments among those responding to the government's various consultations during its major company law review, to the effect that meetings concerning the accounts (both directors' and members' meetings) should be face-to-face meetings.[4] Directors should factor such comments into their consideration of whether it is in their company's best interests for particular meetings to be held electronically.

---

[4] *Modern Company Law for a Competitive Economy: Final Report* URN 01/942 and URN 01/943.

WRITTEN RESOLUTIONS IN LIEU OF A MEETING, AS A SOLUTION

13.40 Companies wishing to take advantage of electronic communications, but reluctant to use electronic communications to hold an actual meeting, can still do so. For example, the model form articles for a private company limited by shares and also a guarantee company say (at reg 8 in both instances) that the directors can take a decision if all eligible directors (meaning directors who would have been entitled to vote on the matter had it been proposed as a resolution at a directors' meeting) indicate to each other, by any means, that they share a common view on a matter – which can be done by all signing (or otherwise indicating in writing their agreement to) a copy of a resolution in writing. However, the number of eligible directors who sign or indicate agreement must be enough to have formed a quorum had a meeting actually been held, or the unanimous resolution is not valid. The model articles for a public company also make provision for written resolutions of the directors (although these are different – see regs 17 and 18) which, because of the definition of 'writing' in the definitions section, can be circulated and signed by electronic means.

13.41 If a company has older articles which apply reg 93 of Table A (or a provision like it), the unanimous agreement of the directors who would have been entitled to attend and vote on a resolution if it had been put to a meeting is sufficient to pass that resolution, provided all sign a paper version of it (or two or more identical paper versions of it).

13.42 An electronic debate can therefore be held (for example, by phone), culminating in the directors each agreeing to sign such a resolution, the wording being agreed between them on the phone. Each copy can then be sent to the company secretary at the registered office as soon as possible.

13.43 Instead of a paper record of the directors' unanimous agreement, there seems no reason why directors cannot unanimously consent electronically, provided the articles allow it. For example, if each director indicates consent in a group e-mail to all the other directors, or via a messaging system, or by posting their consent onto a web page, there seems no legal reason why this should not be a valid resolution in writing. However, many of the practical issues discussed above in relation to electronic board meetings apply equally to electronic resolutions in writing. The board will want to be sure that it has thought these issues through – particularly in relation to ensuring the directors are who they say they are and the security issues raised by the fact that electronic communications may be susceptible to eavesdropping, interception or tampering.

Chapter 14

MINUTES OF MEMBERS' AND OF BOARD MEETINGS

BACKGROUND

14.1 Sections 248 and 249 of the Companies Act 2006 (CA 2006) provide that every company shall cause minutes of all proceedings of general meetings and all proceedings at meetings of its directors (and where it has managers, at meetings of its managers) to be entered in books kept for that purpose.

14.2 For companies with older articles, reg 100 of the 1985 Table A supplements and extends the directors' obligation in this respect. It says they must ensure that minutes are kept of the proceedings of the company, any class of shareholders, the directors or any committees of directors. It also specifically requires minutes to be kept of any appointment of officers by the board.

14.3 Minutes do not need to be recorded by the secretary of the company personally. The chairman of a meeting may, with the express or implied consent of the board, delegate this task to anyone. If delegated to the secretary then, in the absence of a specific prohibition, he can delegate the task in turn. If, however, there is a failure to keep minutes of a meeting then the company, and every officer in default, is liable to a fine. The directors (including the chairman) and secretary must therefore ensure that any person to whom the task is delegated is a proper and competent person. In any event, the chairman should ensure the meeting is conducted in a way that enables effective minutes to be taken. Guidelines for the conduct of board meetings issued by the Institute of Chartered Secretaries and Administrators[1] (ICSA) recommend that the secretary should be entitled to be present (or represented) at the meeting, and to prepare (or arrange the preparation of) minutes of the proceedings.

14.4 One purpose of minutes is to provide an accurate record of what was decided at the meeting. This does not mean that it is always necessary to record the speeches or arguments at the meeting. For meetings of the members (general meetings), this would be very unusual. The minutes will usually record only what was done or agreed upon. If the company wants a record of what

---

[1] *Good Boardroom Practice. A Code for Directors and Company Secretaries*, available from the Information Centre, ICSA, 16 Park Crescent, London W1B 1AH or e-mail informationcentre@icsa.org.uk. See also www.icsa.org.uk.

was said, this record should be created as a separate report, outside the minutes. The minutes of a general meeting will be evidence only of those matters properly entered in them.

14.5 The situation is different for minutes of board meetings. There may be occasions when recording reasons for a decision, or key points made during debate at the meeting, is appropriate. It is open to the directors to decide the form and content of the record of the meeting, and they can require inclusion of such background information if they wish.[2] If they do so, the resulting minutes are usually called 'minutes of narration'. Directors will often ask for minutes of narration because they want the record to demonstrate that they are complying with their duties and discharging their statutory and/or common law obligations, and can only do this if the minutes contain more than a list of what was decided. For example, minutes of narration may be appropriate if a matter is important or contentious. If the company is in a parlous financial state the directors may be keen to demonstrate the reasoning behind their decision, with a view to avoiding liability in a potential insolvency.

14.6 This is why ICSA recommends that minutes of meetings should 'record the decisions taken *and give sufficient background to those decisions*' (emphasis added).[3] Whatever the circumstances, the directors' wishes must be complied with by the secretary.

14.7 Traditionally, the secretary's position has been less clear if an individual director requests that the reasons for his dissent on a particular matter be recorded in the minutes. If there has been doubt among board members as to the propriety of doing this, the matter is referred to the chairman for decision in the best interests of the company. The chairman could, if he was uncertain, refer the matter to the board for a decision – and remind them that their decision is, like any other board decision, to be taken in accordance with their general statutory and other duties.

14.8 For listed companies, however, Provision A.4.3 in the UK Corporate Governance Code (formerly the Combined Code)[4] makes it clear that where directors have concerns which cannot be resolved about the running of the company or a proposed action, they should ensure that their concerns are recorded in the board minutes. On resignation, a non-executive director should provide a written statement to the chairman, for circulation to the board, if they have any such concerns. This is now likely to be treated as best practice for all companies.

14.9 Another function of the minutes of a board meeting is to record any necessary declarations to be made by directors. Particularly, this includes

---

[2] *Re Land Credit Co* (1869) LR 4 Ch App 460, at 473.
[3] *Good Boardroom Practice. A Code for Directors and Company Secretaries*, available from the Information Centre, ICSA, 16 Park Crescent, London W1B 1AH or e-mail informationcentre@icsa.org.uk. See also www.icsa.org.uk.
[4] As revised in September 2012.

declarations of any direct or indirect personal interest of his in an existing or proposed contract, transaction or arrangement, required to be made under s 177 or 182 of CA 2006 (see Chapter 12).

14.10 A function of minutes of all meetings is to show that decisions have been taken properly and in accordance with the statutory rules, articles, operating procedures and customs of the company, and the common law. The minutes should be:

(1) an exact account of what was actually agreed upon;

(2) sufficiently detailed and complete, so that a member who was absent can fully understand what was decided at that meeting; and

(3) concise.

14.11 The minutes should contain, among other things:

(1) in cases where the meeting is of a comparatively small body, for example, of the board of directors of a company or of a committee of the directors, the names of those present. It is usual in the meetings of small bodies to record in the minutes the names of those persons who vote against a specific resolution, if they request this to be done;

(2) identification of all papers presented to the meeting. These should be retained for reference;[5]

(3) full and exact details of all contracts and questions involving financial considerations;

(4) the exact words of all resolutions which have been passed;

(5) if relevant, appointments, salaries, powers and duties of officers (these should be very explicit); and

(6) instructions to officers, and all transactions authorised at that meeting.

THE MINUTE BOOKS

14.12 As the minutes of general meetings are required to be open for inspection by the members and those of directors' meetings are not, separate books are generally kept for each class of minutes.

14.13 Section 1135 provides that company records (defined in s 1134 as any register, index, accounting records, agreement, memorandum, minutes or other

---

[5] For board meetings, this is a recommendation of the *Good Boardroom Practice. A Code for Directors and Company Secretaries* guidelines discussed in Chapter 12. See fn 3 above.

document required by the Companies Acts to be kept by a company, and any register kept by a company of its debenture holders) may be kept in hard copy or electronic form, and may be arranged in such manner as the directors of the company think fit, provided that the information in question is adequately recorded for future reference. Where the records are kept in electronic form, they must be capable of being reproduced in hard copy form.

14.14 Under s 1138, adequate precautions must be taken to guard against falsification, and to facilitate the discovery of falsification where company records are kept otherwise than in bound books, although there is an exception for copies of directors' service contract or memoranda of their terms kept under s 228, or qualifying indemnity provisions kept under s 237. The company and every officer of the company who fails to take adequate precautions are liable to a fine and daily default fines in the case of continued contravention. Ideally, hard copy minutes should be kept in a secure place, such as a fireproof safe or other like place.

14.15 Under s 1136, the Secretary of State may make regulations about where certain company records may be kept available for inspection. These include records of resolutions (s 358). The regulations may specify a place by reference to the company's principal place of business, the part of the UK in which the company is registered, the place at which the company keeps any other records available for inspection or in any other way. To date, none have been made.

RIGHTS TO INSPECT MINUTES

14.16 Section 358 requires the minutes of proceedings of general meetings of a company relating to the previous 10 years to be kept at the registered office of the company, or any place (called a Single Alternative Inspection Location or 'SAIL' in the regulations) specified by regulations made under s 1136 and to be open to the inspection of any member without charge. Regulations[6] require the company to make the minutes available for inspection for at least 2 hours between 9am to 3pm for a private company and 9am to 5pm for a public company on each working day. For private companies, the Regulations require a person wishing to inspect the company's records to give the company advance notice. The notice period is generally ten days, but is two days in certain specified circumstances. The regulations permit the person inspecting the minutes to make a copy of the whole or any part of the minutes. If the person requests a hard or electronic copy, the company must provide it. This is because s 358 entitles any member to be furnished with a copy of any such minutes within 14 days of making a request to the company for a copy. The same section allows the company to charge a fee for this purpose. This fee is prescribed in Regulations[7] as 10p per 500 words or part thereof, together with the reasonable costs incurred by the company in delivering the copy of the

---

[6] The Companies (Company Records) Regulations 2008, SI 2008/3006.
[7] The fees for inspection of any of a company's records and registers are set out in the Companies (Fees for Inspection and Copying of Company Records) Regulations 2007,

company record to the person entitled to be provided with that copy. The company and every officer in default under the section is liable to a fine, and the court may make orders for inspection or direct copies to be sent to the persons requiring them. These provisions regarding the right to inspect minutes apply equally to minutes embodying written resolutions.

14.17 Section 359 specifically provides that the same provisions apply (with necessary modifications) to resolutions and meetings of holders of a class of shares and, in the case of a company without a share capital, a class of members, as they apply in relation to resolutions of members generally and to general meetings.

14.18 There is no requirement that minutes of directors' meetings be available for inspection by members of the company. A director is, by virtue of his office, entitled to see minutes of directors' meetings, but, in the absence of an express provision in the articles or an agreement to which the company is a party such as a subscription or shareholders' agreement, shareholders have no such right. The reasoning behind this was stated in 1859, as follows:[8]

> 'It is highly proper that an inspection of the books containing the proceedings of directors should be obtained on special occasions and for special purposes: but the business of such companies could hardly be conducted if anyone, by buying a share, might entitle himself at all times to gain a knowledge of every commercial transaction to which the directors engage, the moment that an entry of it is made in their books ... the proposed daily and hourly inspection and publication of all their proceedings ... would probably ere long be found very prejudicial to shareholders.'

However, the minutes should be accessible to directors and the secretary. Auditors also are entitled under s 499 to see the minutes for the purposes of audit.

14.19 In addition, minutes should be kept of committees of the board. These, like minutes of board meetings, should be available for inspection by all the directors, whether or not they were members of the committee. Even if the matter discussed was concerned with a particular director, or affairs in which that director was concerned, and the director was excluded from the committee for that very reason, he is entitled as a director to know what decision was taken.

VALIDATING MINUTES

14.20 Sections 249 (for directors' meetings) and 356 (in relation to members' meetings) provide that minutes of a meeting shall be evidence of the

---

SI 2007/2612, the Companies (Fees for Inspection of Company Records) (No 2) Regulations 2007, SI 2007/3535 and the Companies (Fees for Inspection of Company Records) Regulations 2008, SI 2008/3007.

[8] *R v Mariquita Mining Co* (1858) 1 E & E 289.

proceedings if purporting to be signed by the chairman of that meeting or by the chairman of the next succeeding meeting. Further, those sections say that where minutes have been made at any general meeting of the company or meeting of directors or managers:

(1) the meeting is to be deemed to have been duly held and convened until the contrary is proved;

(2) all proceedings are deemed to have duly taken place; and

(3) all appointments of directors, managers or liquidators are to be deemed to be valid.

14.21 The effect of this is that the burden of disproving the accuracy of the minutes rests with a person alleging they are inaccurate. They are assumed accurate unless proven otherwise.[9] To discharge this burden, evidence may be given to show what in fact was done even if this contradicts the minutes, and evidence may be given of a resolution passed but not recorded in the minutes.[10] Articles sometimes provide that the minutes of a meeting if purporting to be signed by the chairman shall be 'conclusive evidence without any further proof of the facts therein stated'. According to the only reported decision on such an article, evidence cannot be given in such a case to contradict minutes so signed unless it can first be shown that the minutes have been written up fraudulently.[11] There is much doubt whether this decision is correct, and an article framed in this way is inadvisable.

14.22 Good boardroom practice guidelines issued by ICSA recommend that companies should establish procedures in relation to circulation and approval of minutes of board meetings.[12] Particularly, they recommend that the minutes of all board meetings (or a written summary of them) should be circulated before the board meeting at which they are presented, and the board should have an opportunity to ask questions about them.

14.23 Certainly, common practice is for minutes to be read or, if previously circulated to the members of the meeting (which is more likely), taken as read, at the next following meeting. They are then submitted to the meeting for approval. If regarded as a correct report of the proceedings by those members present at that meeting, they are signed by the chairman. If considered incorrect, they may be modified and then signed. Any discussion on the minutes, except as to their accuracy, is out of order, and the chairman should rule accordingly.

---

[9] *Re Indian Zoedone Co* (1884) 26 ChD 70, at 77.
[10] *Re Fireproof Doors* [1916] 2 Ch 142; *Re Pyle Works (No 2)* [1891] 1 Ch 173, at 184.
[11] *Kerr v John Mottram Ltd* [1940] Ch 657.
[12] *Good Boardroom Practice. A Code for Directors and Company Secretaries*, available from the Information Centre, ICSA, 16 Park Crescent, London W1B 1AH or e-mail informationcentre@icsa.org.uk. See also www.icsa.org.uk.

14.24 If there is a conflict of opinion about their accuracy, an amendment to the motion that they are correct, setting out any suggested alteration, should be put to the meeting. Those who were not present at the preceding meeting should not take part in the discussion or vote.

14.25 The approval of the minutes by a meeting merely verifies their accuracy; it does not necessarily mean that such minutes are adopted or that the resolutions therein have been confirmed or ratified by the subsequent meeting.

14.26 There is no statutory requirement that the minutes be approved by the attendees at the meeting to which they relate, or at the next succeeding meeting, before they are signed by the chairman. They can be signed at any time. This is the case even if, being signed by the chairman of the succeeding meeting, that person was not the chairman of (or even present at) the meeting to which the minutes relate. This means that minutes can still be signed in the event of an emergency or of a comprehensive change in the members or directors of the company. However, best practice is for the minutes to be put before the members or directors at the next succeeding meeting before they are signed, if possible.

14.27 A director who is present at a meeting of the board at which the minutes of a previous board meeting are approved is not thereby made responsible for the decisions of the previous board meeting if the resolution has been acted upon before the minutes are confirmed.[13]

14.28 The signature of the chairman to minutes which embody the terms of a contract may be sufficient to satisfy the Statute of Frauds,[14] where the Statute requires contracts to be evidenced by a memorandum in writing.

14.29 Once minutes have been signed, they should not be altered or corrected internally. 'I trust I shall never again see or hear of the secretary of a company, whether under superior directions or otherwise, altering minutes of meetings, either by striking out anything or adding anything.'[15] If they are found to be incorrect the proper procedure is to add an additional minute or note correcting the mistake and for the chairman to sign that addition. This makes it clear exactly what the changes are. If the original minutes were approved at a meeting, the addition should also be approved and a record made of it.

14.30 For similar reasons, pages should not be removed from the minute book, the pages of which should be numbered consecutively.

14.31 The benefits of holding a set of minutes signed by the chairman mean it is undesirable to keep computerised records of minutes without also printing out a hard copy of those minutes and obtaining the signature of the chairman to them.

---

[13] *Re Lands Allotment Co* [1894] 1 Ch 616, at 635; *Burton v Bevan* [1908] 2 Ch 240.
[14] *Jones v Victoria Graving Dock* (1877) 2 QBD 314.
[15] *Re Cawley & Co* (1889) 42 ChD 209, at 226.

RESOLUTIONS AGREED TO BY ALL MEMBERS IN LIEU OF A MEETING

14.32 The fact that a resolution agreed to by all members under case-law like *Cane v Jones*[16] is not in writing does not affect its validity. The difficulty is in proving that it is passed if there is a dispute whether a particular member agreed to it or not and there is nothing in writing. It is strongly recommended that a written record be obtained wherever possible.

14.33 Statutory written resolutions, passed pursuant to s 288ff, must be recorded, along with the signatures of the members, in the same way as the minutes of a general meeting of the company.[17]

14.34 Where a company has only one member, then s 357 requires that single member to provide the company with a written record of any decision (other than one taken by written resolution in any event) taken by the member which might have been taken by the company in general meeting or has effect as if agreed by the company in a general meeting (although failure to comply with this requirement in relation to single member companies does not affect the validity of any decision arrived at by the single member[18]).

---

[16] [1981] 1 All ER 533.
[17] CA 2006, s 355.
[18] CA 2006, s 357(5).

Chapter 15

ADMISSION TO AND EXPULSION FROM MEMBERS' AND DIRECTORS' MEETINGS

ADMISSION TO MEETINGS (INCLUDING THE PRESS)

15.1 One of the matters which must sometimes be decided in connection with meetings is who should be invited to attend. Generally speaking, in the case of private meetings such as a meeting of members or directors of a company, there is no right to attend for the public or press, but the meeting itself may decide whether outsiders of any kind shall be permitted to be present. Large public companies, for example, generally desire that their general meetings shall be reported in the papers, and so invite the attendance of reporters, but they are not bound to do so.

15.2 When a meeting of a company takes place in premises which are private property or to which a stranger has no right of access,[1] a stranger may only remain so long as no objection is made to his presence. If the stranger is requested to leave and refuses to do so then he becomes a trespasser and may be ejected with such reasonable force as is required. It is unnecessary for these purposes that any reason be given to support the request that the stranger leave.

15.3 The expulsion, however, of a person who is entitled to attend a meeting (except for disorderly conduct of a serious nature) is unlawful unless the articles or operating procedures (if any) of the company provide otherwise:[2]

> 'The power, therefore, of suspending a member guilty of obstruction or disorderly conduct during the continuance of any current sitting, is ... reasonably necessary for the proper exercise of the functions of any legislative assembly of this kind; and it may very well be, that the same doctrine of reasonable necessity would authorise a suspension until submission or apology by the offending member; which, if he were refractory, might cause it to be prolonged (not by the arbitrary discretion of the assembly, but by his own wilful default) for some further time.'

15.4 Similarly, in *Doyle v Falconer*,[3] it was said that if a member of a colonial House of Assembly was guilty of disorderly conduct in that House while sitting, he might be removed or excluded for a time or even expelled, and that if the conduct of the members was not such as to secure order and decency of

---

[1] It is an offence to use or threaten violence to secure entry into any premises.
[2] *Barton v Taylor* (1886) 11 App Cas 197, at 204, a case concerned with the New South Wales Assembly.
[3] (1866) LR 1 PC 328, at 340.

debate, the law would sanction the use of that degree of force which might be necessary to remove the person offending from the place of meeting and to keep him excluded, and that the same rule would apply even more so to obstructions caused by a non-member. In either case, if the violation of order amounted to a breach of the peace, recourse might be had to the ordinary courts.

15.5 It is the duty of the chairman to preserve order at the meeting and, consequently, in the event of a person otherwise entitled to attend a meeting being so disorderly as to interfere unduly with the reasonable conduct of the meeting or to prevent the proper transaction of business, the chairman may order that person to withdraw. If the person concerned refuses to comply with this order, he may be ejected with reasonable force. If the disorderly person resists ejection, this may constitute a breach of the peace. It is usually desirable, however, that the chairman should be supported by the majority of the meeting before ordering a person to withdraw, and should take care not to give instructions for ejection unless he is quite sure such instructions will be expeditiously and efficiently carried out.

15.6 If it is anticipated in advance of a proposed general meeting of members of the company that the meeting will be 'so disrupted by a minority that no orderly business can be conducted' an application can be made to the court under s 306 of the Companies Act 2006. The court can make an order which will enable the meeting to be called and held in such a way as to avoid the anticipated disruption. The order made can even override the company's articles of association.[4]

---

[4] *Re British Union for the Abolition of Vivisection* (1995) *The Times*, March 3. The statutory provision then in force was s 371 of the Companies Act 1985, which was re-enacted in s 306 of the 2006 Act. See Chapter 4 for a discussion of the case.

Part 2

MEETINGS IN INSOLVENCY

Chapter 16

INTRODUCTION

16.1 When a company is placed into a formal insolvency procedure, the interests of its creditors intervene between the company's shareholders, its directors and its assets. This intervention is regulated and protected by the statutory scheme on insolvency embodied in the Insolvency Act 1986 (IA 1986) and the Insolvency Rules 1986[1] ('the Rules'). The menu of different insolvency procedures which effect the intervention ranges from administrative receivership (principally for debenture holders and now largely replaced in practical terms by the administration regime), company voluntary arrangements, administrations to liquidations (voluntary or compulsory). The same principles are in operation for personal insolvency where, for all intents and purposes, the creditors intervene and they must choose between an individual voluntary arrangement (if one is proposed by the debtor) or bankruptcy.[2] However, the individual debtor retains certain property rights against his creditors because, unlike a company, he is a human being.[3]

16.2 In all cases IA 1986 requires that a licensed insolvency practitioner (or the official receiver in the case of a fast track voluntary arrangement) is appointed to oversee the administration of the particular insolvency process in the interests of creditors. The insolvency practitioner is remunerated out of the insolvent's assets and is paid ahead of the unsecured creditors. In this sense, the insolvency practitioner is paid out of the creditors' moneys and, as such, is subject to their control. Ultimately, he may be removed by a majority of the creditors at a duly convened creditors' meeting.[4] The role of the insolvency practitioner is a complex one. It will vary according to the function he is performing. This explains why he has been described variously as an agent, trustee, fiduciary, officer of the court[5] and a creature of statute.

16.3 As a matter of principle, it is the creditors who have ultimate control over the getting in, realisation and distribution of the insolvent's assets by the insolvency practitioner. The pre-insolvency importance of the company's constitution (ie its memorandum and articles of association) and the

---

[1] SI 1986/1925.
[2] In smaller cases where the debts are below £15,000, it may be possible for a debtor to apply for a Debt Relief Order under the supervision of the Official Receiver – but there is no meeting of creditors so it is beyond the scope of this work.
[3] As to the relevance of the distinction in this context, see, for example, *Re Rae* [1995] BCC 102.
[4] See, for example, ss 108(2) and 172(2) of IA 1986 (liquidations); para 97(2) of Sch B1 to IA 1986 (administration); rr 6.129–6.130 of the Rules (bankruptcy).
[5] See *Donaldson v O'Sullivan* [2008] BPIR 1288.

Companies Act 1985 and/or the Companies Act 2006 as the sources for the regulation and conduct of meetings all but disappear and are replaced by the provisions of IA 1986 and the Rules when corporate insolvency is the issue.

16.4 Generally, IA 1986 and the Rules allow a creditor to express his views and to influence the insolvency procedure in one of the following ways:

- before the onset of formal insolvency by (one or more) creditors exercising statutory rights to have recourse to the court with insolvency jurisdiction (to wind up the company or to make a bankruptcy order in respect of the individual debtor);

- by a resolution passed at a validly convened creditors' meeting;

- by a resolution passed at a validly convened creditors' committee meeting; or

- by an application to the court in the relevant insolvency proceeding.

16.5 IA 1986 and the Rules were amended with effect from 6 April 2010 to enable remote attendance at meeting of creditors summoned under either where the person considers it appropriate,[6] for example by video link, telephone conference or electronic means. The person organising the meeting has to ensure that it is held in a manner which enables the person attending remotely to speak and to vote. The convener of a meeting can be requested to specify a place to hold a meeting.[7] Such a request must be made by either not less than 10% in value of the creditors or contributories or, in the case of a members' meeting, not less than 10% of the total voting rights.[8] Such a request must be made within 7 business days of the date on which the convener sent notice of the meeting in question.[9] Where the request is properly made the convener must call a meeting within 28 days of the original meeting and must give 14 days' notice of the time and venue to all of those originally given notice of the meeting.

16.6 In addition the I(A)R 2010[10] introduced provisions enabling the submission of information to office holders, including the official receiver, by electronic means from 6 April 2010. These provisions[11] enable documents relating to meetings (largely these provisions will relate to proxies) to be submitted electronically provided that the following criteria are met:

---

[6] IA 1986, s 246A, inserted by the Legislative Reform (Insolvency) (Miscellaneous) Order, SI 2010/18.
[7] IA 1986, s 246A(9).
[8] IA 1986, s 246A(10).
[9] Insolvency Rules 1986, SI 1986/1925, r 12A.22(3).
[10] SI 2010/686.
[11] IR 1986, r 12A.31.

- the convener of the meeting must have agreed to receipt of the proxy electronically;

- further they must be satisfied with the format by which the proxy is being sent;

- the electronic submission must contain all of the information that would have been required in the prescribed form; and

- the recipient must be able to provide the information submitted in a legible form.

16.7 To satisfy the requirements for authentication of documents submitted by electronic means, the identity of the sender must be confirmed in a way specified by the recipient. If the recipient has not specified how the sender's identity should be confirmed, the proxy or information is sufficiently authenticated if it is accompanied by a statement of the identity of the sender and the recipient has no reason to doubt the truth of that statement.

16.8 In practice, a scanned proxy containing an original signature and submitted to the official receiver by email can be accepted for the purposes of a meeting provided that the official receiver has no reason to doubt its authenticity. Similarly, a proof received electronically from the creditor or their intermediary, and containing an electronic signature (authentication), may be accepted if the named individual can be traced to the originating organisation and is a known party within that organisation.

16.9 In this section, we are principally concerned with the law relating to full creditors' meetings. IA 1986 and the Rules stipulate when, for what purpose and how full creditors' meetings should be convened and held, as well as regulating how voting is undertaken and the effect of the creditors' votes. The statutory code is supplemented by common law rules on meetings based on justice and common sense – for instance, that any adjournment of a meeting must be on reasonable terms as to notice and venue.

16.10 In broad terms, the sources in IA 1986 and the Rules for the regulation of creditors' meetings within the various statutory regimes are as follows:[12]

- company voluntary arrangements (CVAs) – IA 1986, ss 3–6 and rr 1.9, 1.11, 1.13–1.21 of the Rules;

---

[12] Superimposed over these provisions is the general supervisory power of the court to give appropriate directions in relation to meetings to insolvency office-holders either on their application, on the application of an interested party or, more seldom, of the court's own mention: see *Donaldson v O'Sullivan* [2008] EWCA Civ 879, [2008] BPIR 1288. For a case where the court directed the office-holders not to convene a meeting, see *Re Barings plc (No 6); Hamilton v Law Debenture Trustees Ltd* [2001] 2 BCLC 159.

- administrations – IA 1986, Sch B1, paras 50–58 and rr 2.34–2.49 of the Rules;

- company voluntary liquidations (CVLs) – IA 1986, ss 98–106;

- winding up by the court (or compulsory liquidations) – rr 4.50–4.178 of the Rules;

- individual voluntary arrangements (IVAs) – IA 1986, ss 257–260 and rr 5.17–5.24 of the Rules; and

- bankruptcy – rr 6.79–6.95 of the Rules.

16.11 It would be unduly cumbersome and costly for the insolvency practitioner always to have to report to or consult a full creditors' meeting on each occasion. For this reason, provision is made for the delegation of some of the creditors' powers to the creditors' committees as follows:

- administrations – IA 1986, Sch B1, para 57;

- CVLs and compulsory liquidations – rr 4.151–4.178 of the Rules; and

- bankruptcy – rr 6.150–6.166 of the Rules.

In CVAs and IVAs, the proposals will often provide for the appointment of a creditors' committee for similar purposes.

16.12 Before dealing in the following chapters more specifically with the various provisions relevant to creditors' meetings, it is appropriate to mention some features common to some or all of the insolvency regimes.

16.13 First, it is necessary to distinguish between a *first* meeting of creditors and all subsequent meetings. For several reasons, first meetings tend to be the most eventful and unpredictable. These are the meetings at which the insolvency practitioner is first appointed or confirmed in his appointment. Appointments can be hotly contested and results can rest on a knife-edge. It is also at these meetings that statutory proposals (ie in administrations and voluntary arrangements) are considered and the future direction of the particular insolvency process is shaped. It is no coincidence that much of the law concerning insolvency meetings arises out of disputes over the conduct of first meetings. In one case,[13] voting at a first meeting was anticipated to be so controversial that the court was requested to consider an application by a person claiming to be a creditor before any chairman had been appointed or decision made. The conduct of subsequent meetings rarely excites to the same extent.

---

[13] *Re Bank of Credit & Commerce International SA (No 5)* [1994] 1 BCLC 429.

16.14 Secondly, the terms 'proof' and 'prove' are used in this context to mean at least two different things. A creditor submits a proof for voting purposes and that proof is either admitted or rejected in whole or in part for the purposes of calculating the votes for or against a particular resolution. At a later stage, the creditor will be asked to submit a proof for the purposes of calculating the amount of any dividend payable out of the company's assets. The former proof is a procedural matter (although the decision as to the validity of the proof might nevertheless alter the balance of power and have important consequences), whereas the decision on the proof submitted for dividend purposes is more dispositive in nature and affects substantial rights. It follows that a decision to accept a creditor's proof for voting purposes, as a matter of mere procedure, is not binding or conclusive in respect of a later decision as to the nature and extent of the same creditor's right to participate in a dividend.[14]

16.15 Thirdly, a creditor should be astute to discover not only the requisite majority (ie 50%, 75% or 100%) for the meeting in question, but also whether votes must be counted by number, value or both. So, for example, at a creditors' meeting for any resolution to pass any proposal or modification in respect of a CVA there must be a majority in excess of three-quarters in value of the creditors present in person or by proxy and voting on the resolution,[15] whereas any other resolution at the same meeting will be carried if a majority in excess of one-half in value of the creditors present in person or by proxy vote in favour.[16]

16.16 Fourthly, in many cases, a dissatisfied creditor has recourse to court either expressly or by invoking the court's residual supervisory role[17] over disputes concerning classes of creditors. So, for instance, a creditor whose proof has been rejected in whole or in part on a vote to determine who should be appointed liquidator at a first creditors' meeting in a winding up by the court may 'appeal' to the court and seek an order that the chairman admit the proof in full for voting purposes.[18] However, in this context, the court's supervisory role should not normally be invoked on purely technical grounds. So, for instance, where a proof of debt, which had been marked as objected to at a creditors' meeting, was later found to be invalid, it was held to be not necessary to summon a further creditors' meeting under r 4.70 of the Rules because it was clear that the outcome of the vote would have been the same.[19]

16.17 Fifthly, even at first meetings, it is usually an insolvency practitioner who will either chair or oversee the conduct of a creditors' meeting. The Council of the Association of Business Recovery Professionals (known as R3)

---

[14] See *Re Assisco Engineering Ltd* [2002] BCC 481.
[15] Rule 1.52(1).
[16] Rule 1.52(2).
[17] As to which, see *King v Anthony* [1999] BPIR 73, CA.
[18] Rule 4.70(2) – 'appeal' is a misnomer in that the court hears the matter as if for the first time and is not limited to a review of the chairman's decision or his reasons – see *Re a Company (No 004539 of 1993)* [1995] 1 BCLC 459; see also r 2.39(2) in respect of administrations; and r 5.23(7) (IVAs).
[19] *Re Power Builders (Surrey) Ltd; Power v Latos* [2008] EWHC 2607 (Ch).

has issued a series of Statements of Insolvency Practice (called SIPs) with a view to harmonising the approach of members to questions of insolvency practice. Insolvency practitioners regard the SIPs as statements of best practice and they have been so received by the courts.[20] Of particular relevance is SIP 12, which requires that the responsible insolvency practitioner should always create a record of the meeting, which should be prepared in accordance with SIP 12. Several other SIPs deal with creditors' meetings in some detail – see SIP 3 dealing with corporate and individual voluntary arrangements. Further, on 1 January 2009, a new Code of Ethics came into force for insolvency practitioners. It is the product of 3 years' work by a subcommittee of the Joint Insolvency Committee which, in turn, represents all the insolvency regulatory bodies. One of the themes of the new Code is to stipulate that office-holders must be able to justify their actions and to have recorded the same in writing. These professional duties (owed to the public at large) are consistent with the power of the court, in an appropriate case, to visit an insolvency office-holder with personal liability for the legal costs incurred by others as a result of his unreasonable conduct. So, for instance, an office-holder was directed personally to pay legal costs of an aggrieved creditor who had successfully challenged the office-holder's decision as chairman to allow another creditor to vote at a meeting where that decision constituted conduct which fell below that to be expected of an insolvency practitioner acting reasonably.[21]

16.18 Sixthly, mention should be made of the position of secured creditors. Insofar as they hold security for their debts, they stand outside of the creditors' meetings and do not participate. To the extent that they are under-secured or unsecured, they must assess the value of their security and vote as an unsecured creditor in respect of any shortfall. Without the consent of the secured creditor, the unsecured creditors may not resolve to deal with the assets in a manner which prejudices the security.

16.19 Seventhly, whilst IA 1986 entrenches the priority rights of preferential creditors in respect of dividends,[22] they enjoy no such special status as regards voting rights. In other words, the votes of preferential creditors are counted and treated in the same way as the votes of the unsecured creditors as a whole.

16.20 Lastly, although the voting rights of preferential creditors are not elevated, some unsecured creditors are more equal than others. Both IA 1986[23] and the courts[24] distinguish between creditors who are connected, or 'insiders', and those who are genuinely independent creditors. It is recognised that a

---

[20] See, for example, *Re Industrial Services Group Ltd (No 2)* [2003] BPIR 597; and *Re Finelist* [2003] EWHC 1780 (Ch).
[21] *Smurthwaite v Simpson-Smith* [2006] EWCA Civ 1183; [2006] BPIR 1504.
[22] See, for example, s 4(4)(a) (CVAs); s 40 (administrative receiverships); s 175 (liquidations); s 258(5)(a) (IVAs); para 73(1)(b) of Sch B1 (administrations); and ss 386–387 and Sch 6 (categories of preferential debts).
[23] See, for example, r 1.19(4) (CVAs); r 2.43(2) (administrations); and r 5.23(4) (IVAs).
[24] See, for example, *Re Palmer Marine Services Ltd* [1986] BCLC 106; and *Re Gordon & Breach Science Ltd* [1995] 2 BCLC 189.

debtor, whether corporate or individual, might unscrupulously determine the outcome of a meeting (usually a first meeting to determine the identity of the insolvency practitioner) by the introduction or artificial enhancement of alleged debts (and therefore votes) of family and friends. There are many reported instances of such attempts.[25] In any ensuing dispute in which the court has a discretion, it will place little weight on the wishes of the insiders as expressed in the voting insofar as they clash with the wishes of independent creditors.

16.21 As a postscript, some mention should be made of the Human Rights Act 1998. It is certainly arguable[26] that, as officers of the court, compulsory liquidators, trustees in bankruptcy and administrators are 'public authorities' within the meaning of the human rights legislation. In *GJ v Luxembourg*,[27] the European Court of Human Rights determined that a shareholder's human rights had been violated due to the unreasonable length of a liquidation in that a period of 6 years had not been a 'reasonable time' for the determination of the shareholders' civil rights within the meaning of Art 6(1) – which had been breached accordingly. This decision raises many questions, but for present purposes it is sufficient to note that, to the extent that certain meetings are to be treated as conducted by public authorities within the meaning of the legislation, creditors affected by such meetings might find remedies in the Human Rights Act 1998 where hitherto there were none.[28]

---

[25] For recent examples see, for example, *Re Tack* [2000] BPIR 164; *Cadburys Schweppes plc v Somji* [2001] 1 WLR 615; *Re a Debtor (No 101 of 1999)* [2000] BPIR 998.

[26] Cf the analysis in a different context in *Poplar Housing and Regeneration Community Association v Donoghue* [2001] EWCA Civ 595.

[27] [2000] BPIR 1021.

[28] Creditors whose claims are affected by decisions of office-holders might have rights under the European Convention on Human Rights by virtue of s 1 of and Sch 1 to the Human Rights Act 1998 and Art 1, Protocol 1 – see Chapter 23 at **23.21** and *Keveling v Netherlands* (Application No 3171/96) (10 September 1997).

Chapter 17

COMPANY VOLUNTARY ARRANGEMENTS

INTRODUCTION

17.1 A voluntary arrangement has been called a form of statutory contract made between a debtor and its creditors. Voluntary arrangements were one of the main inspirations of the reforms now embodied in the Insolvency Act 1986 (IA 1986) and the Insolvency Rules 1986[1] (the Rules). In *Re NT Gallagher & Son Ltd*, Peter Gibson LJ described the purpose of company voluntary arrangements (CVAs):[2]

> 'Parliament plainly intended to encourage companies and creditors to enter into CVAs so as to provide creditors with a means of recovering what they are owed without recourse to the more expensive means provided by winding-up or administration, thereby giving many companies the opportunity to continue to trade.'

17.2 Prior to 1986, the only way in which an insolvent corporate debtor could force a dissentient creditor into a binding arrangement was by means of court-approved schemes under the Companies Act 1948, s 206 or 306 (now Companies Act 2006, s 895 and IA 1986, s 110 respectively). The Cork Committee,[3] having recommended the introduction of (what are now) individual voluntary arrangements (IVAs) for individual debtors,[4] went on to consider[5] the difficulties for insolvent companies wishing to rely on s 895 schemes and recommended that a company should have 'the same facility as an individual to effect, out of court, a formal and binding arrangement with its creditors'.[6]

17.3 In this way, the model for CVAs mirrored that for IVAs. The Committee's recommendations for IVAs (which became Part VIII of IA 1986) were drawn from various sources, including the Bankruptcy Act 1914, s 16 (Compositions and schemes of arrangement).

---

[1] SI 1986/1925.
[2] [2002] EWCA Civ 404, [2002] BPIR 565, at [50].
[3] *Report of the Review Committee on Insolvency Law and Practice*, Cmnd 8558 (1982).
[4] Ibid, paras 366–399.
[5] Ibid, paras 414–418.
[6] Ibid, para 428.

17.4 The Cork Committee considered that there were four matters of 'paramount importance' in its proposals for IVAs. The second of these[7] was the ability to achieve a basis of distribution other than *pari passu*. This was justified by reference to the availability of third party funds:

> 'Unless such flexibility exists, the advantages accruing to the creditors from the provisions of third party moneys or from any after-acquired property of the debtor will be lost.'

17.5 Parliament adopted most of the recommendations, in particular, flexibility and the ability to introduce third party monies into an arrangement. Nevertheless, it was considered important to protect the rights of secured and preferential creditors by IA 1986, ss 4(3), (4) and 258(4), (5). A regular and properly convened meeting of the unsecured creditors may approve any proposals as a substitute for formal insolvency. The creditors have limited protection. They may seek relief from the court on the grounds that any approved proposals unfairly prejudice their interests as a creditor. Thus, the meeting of creditors to consider and, if thought fit, approve proposals for a CVA takes centre stage. IA 1986 and the Rules provide a time frame in which a proposal has to be placed before the creditors for their approval. The following makes reference to the statutorily imposed timetable, considers the types of meeting that have to take place and some of the issues that may arise.

17.6 In the recent past CVAs have been used by national retail chains as a method of reorganisation particularly as a way of dealing with landlords and unsustainable rents; however they must not be used as a method of guarantee stripping by forcing the release of a guarantee without the consent of the holder of the guarantee.[8] In reality they only work with prior landlord agreement.

MEETINGS TO BE HELD PRIOR TO A CVA

17.7 Those affected by a proposal for a CVA need to meet in order to consider the detail and vote. The two classes of persons affected will be the creditors and the members of the debtor company. Thus there are two types of meeting: a meeting of creditors and a meeting of the debtor company's members. The creditors should have an opportunity to air their views and make an informed decision as to whether their interests are best served in a formal insolvency process or by way of a binding agreement outside a formal process. The requirement therefore is for an open meeting of creditors, who are asked to vote on a proposal put forward through an insolvency practitioner as a nominee of the debtor company. The proposal should provide the creditors with full and frank information regarding the financial position of the debtor company. It

---

[7] Ibid, para 364(2).
[8] See for example: *Prudential Assurance Co Ltd v PRG Powerhouse Ltd* [2007] EWHC 1002 (Ch), [2007] BPIR 839; and *Mourant & Co Trustees Ltd v Sixty UK Ltd (in liq)* [2010] EWHC 1890 (Ch), [2010] BPIR 1264.

should provide all relevant information necessary for the creditors to be able to make an informed decision as to the future prospects of the company and (usually of more importance for the creditor) the predicted returns to the creditors. The debtor company is reliant on the support and agreement of the creditors, who may otherwise force the company into insolvent liquidation. The members of the debtor company meet to consider the proposals and vote on whether they as members think them appropriate.

17.8 Prior to 2003, a debtor company could not shelter behind a moratorium while the procedure for obtaining the approval of creditors at a creditors' meeting was running its course. The Insolvency Act 2000 (IA 2000) came into full effect on 1 January 2003, introducing an optional moratorium.[9] This assists a debtor company as the interim moratorium will protect the company whilst a proposal for a CVA is formulated, and placed before the creditors for approval at a meeting. This change is in line with the then Labour Government's promotion of the rescue philosophy. However, the ability to apply for a moratorium is not universal. It is restricted to small companies[10] that are eligible[11] within the meaning of IA 2000. In fact the use of a CVA moratorium is rare, with the insolvency process of choice becoming the administration procedure which has a similar moratorium but with far less risk of personal liability for an office holder. The effect of the moratorium is to prevent creditors from taking any prejudicial action, prevent the directors from calling any meeting of the debtor company (save with the consent of the nominee or with leave of the court), preclude an appointment of an administrator under IA 1986, Sch B1, para 14 or 22 and preclude the directors from passing a resolution to wind up the company.[12] Nevertheless the directors remain in day-to-day control of the debtor company. The moratorium procedure for 'small' companies also gives rise to the possibility that the nominee of a small company may call a meeting of creditors simply to seek their consent to extend the moratorium period pending the creditors' meeting called for the purpose of approving or rejecting the proposal.

17.9 In addition, IA 2000 made a change as regards who may act as a nominee. Prior to 1 January 2003, a nominee had to be a qualified insolvency practitioner, who was required to supervise the implementation of any

---

[9] 'Where the directors of an eligible company intend to make a proposal for a voluntary arrangement, they may take steps to obtain a moratorium for the company': IA 1986, s 1A(1).
[10] As defined by the Companies Act 2006, s 382(3) which copies the Companies Act 1985, s 247(3) and provides qualifying conditions. If two or more of the qualifying conditions are met the company will qualify as a small company and take the benefit of less stringent account and reporting requirements.
[11] There are six situations that will render a company unable to apply for a moratorium where the directors propose the arrangement, by reason of their insolvent past, notwithstanding that they are 'small companies' as defined by the Companies Act 2006, s 382: see IA 1986, Sch A1, paras 2(1), 3 and 4. Certain other companies are also excluded by reason not of their insolvent history but due to the nature of the business carried out, for example, companies that carry out contracts of insurance but are not exempt from the general prohibition within the meaning of s 19 of the Financial Services and Markets Act 2000: IA 1986, Sch A1, para 2(2).
[12] IA 1986, Sch A1, para 12(1) provides a full list of the effects of a moratorium.

arrangement and to assist the debtor company to put forward a proposal for a CVA. This requirement has been liberalised by an extension of the category of persons who may act as a nominee to those who have the approval of the Secretary of State although this has not been acted upon and it remains the position that the nominee has to be a qualified insolvency practitioner.[13]

17.10 As regards the requirements of a particular meeting, these depend upon whether the proposal for a CVA is being put forward by an insolvency practitioner who is a liquidator or administrator of the debtor company, or a nominee elected by the debtor company's directors prior to a formal insolvency process commencing. A proposal may be made by the directors to the company and its creditors at a time when the company is not in administration and is not being wound up (IA 1986, s 1(1)), but if the debtor company is in administration or has been wound up, a proposal may only be made by the administrator or the liquidator (IA 1986, s 1(3)) and the administrator or liquidator may appoint himself to be the nominee.

17.11 The relevant procedure where the nominee is not the administrator or liquidator is provided for by IA 1986, s 2, and this also applies where the administrator or liquidator nominates someone other than himself as the nominee. In such cases the nominee must, within 28 days after he is given notice of the proposal for a voluntary arrangement, submit a report to the court. The report has to state whether (in the opinion of the person submitting the report) a meeting of the debtor company and its creditors should be summoned so as to consider the proposal and, if so, the date, time and place where the meeting should be held. The time for reporting may be extended by the court. The report delivered to the court will include a copy of the directors' proposal and a summary of the company's statement of affairs. It is not always the case that a meeting of members and creditors will be required (see IA 1986, s 2(2)). This has the effect of enabling a nominee to save costs and time where he submits a negative report[14] to the effect that the proposal should not be taken forward. The decision as to whether or not to summon a meeting has to be based on a criterion that was first formulated by the courts and is now incorporated in version 4 of SIP 3. The nominee should consider a three-stage test:[15]

- first, that the company's true position as to assets and liabilities is not materially different from that which is represented to the creditors to be;

---

[13] For a consideration of the duties of the nominee to test the proposal see *Re Greystoke v Hamilton-Smith* [1997] BPIR 24; and *Fender v Commissioners of Inland Revenue* [2003] BPIR 1304 (cases concerning IVAs – see **25.3**ff); for best practice see SIP 3.
[14] See r 1.7(2), which provides that the nominee should annexe to the report his comments on the proposals, and if he holds a negative opinion of the proposal, those views should be stated, with reasons provided.
[15] See *Re Greystoke v Hamilton-Smith* [1997] BPIR 24; and *Fender v Commissioners of Inland Revenue* [2003] BPIR 1304 (cases concerning IVAs – see **25.3**ff); for best practice see SIP 3.

- secondly, that the directors' proposal has a real prospect of being implemented in the way it is represented it will be – he should not put forward a proposal unless he knows that there is a reasonable prospect of it being adopted; and[16]

- thirdly, that there is no manifest yet unavoidable prospective unfairness.

17.12 A nominee will in large part rely upon the information provided to him by the directors of a debtor company and thus the first and second tests can only be satisfied if the nominee is satisfied that the information he is being provided with is accurate and that the directors are not making promises based on over-optimistic forecasting.

17.13 Where the nominee reports in the affirmative he is required to set out his comments on the proposal and to annex them to his statement or report. SIP 3 provides guidance upon the matters which the nominee should normally include comment upon:

(a) the extent to which the nominee has investigated the company's/debtor's circumstances;

(b) the basis upon which assets have been valued;

(c) the extent to which the nominee considers that reliance can be placed upon the directors'/debtor's estimate of the liabilities to be included in the voluntary arrangement;

(d) information on the attitude adopted by the directors/debtor with particular reference to instances of failure to co-operate with the nominee;

(e) the result of any discussions between the nominee and secured creditors or other interested parties upon whose co-operation the performance of the voluntary arrangement will depend;

(f) information on the attitude of any major unsecured creditor which may affect the approval of the arrangement by creditors;

(g) details of any previous history of failures in which (any of) the directors/debtor has been involved, insofar as they are known to the nominee;

(h) an estimate of the result for the creditors if the voluntary arrangement is approved, explaining why it is more beneficial for creditors than any alternative insolvency proceeding;

(i) the likely effect of the proposal's rejection by the creditors;

---

[16] This is effectively the statutory test set out in IA 1986, s 2(2)(a).

(j) details of any claims which have come to his attention which might be capable of being pursued by a liquidator/administrator/trustee in bankruptcy if one were appointed; and

(k) if the nominee is not able to state that the proposal has a reasonable prospect of being approved and implemented and still wishes to call a meeting, the basis on which he is recommending that a meeting be held.

17.14 Where the nominee is the administrator or liquidator, IA 1986, s 3(2) provides that the office holder must call a meeting of members and creditors to consider the proposal.

17.15 The purpose of the meeting in both cases is to consider the proposals for the CVA and decide whether to agree to them, or to agree to them in some amended form with modifications. Neither the creditors nor the members have an absolutely unfettered right to agree to any proposal at their respective meeting (see the limitations in IA 1986, s 4(3), (4) and (6)), but once the meeting to consider the proposal is held, the agreement of that meeting is essential for any proposal to go ahead.

NOTICE OF MEETINGS
Where the nominee is not administrator or liquidator

17.16 Where the nominee is not the administrator or liquidator and has reported to the court under IA 1986, s 2(2) that the meetings should be held, then the nominee should, unless the court directs otherwise, summon the meetings for the time and place proposed in the report (IA 1986, s 3(1)) unless the court makes an order to the contrary. The date of each of the necessary meetings should be not more than 28 days after the filing of the report with the court (r 1.9(1) where there is no moratorium). A similar provision applies in respect of cases where a moratorium is in force – see r 1.48(1) (the provisions provide that at least 14 days' notice has to be given – r 1.48(2) where there is a moratorium and r 1.9(2) where there is no moratorium). This minimum notice period of 14 days excludes the day of sending the notice and the day of the meeting.

17.17 Prior to the introduction of IA 2000, the Rules required 'receipt' of the notice by the creditor and r 12.10 treated such notice as being received on the second or fourth day after posting (depending on whether it was sent by first or second class post) unless the contrary was proved by the 'recipient'.[17] This requirement had the potential to lead to protracted and expensive court action. As the onus was on the 'recipient' to prove a negative regarding receipt, such contests could not be determined by affidavit evidence alone but required oral evidence. This was ameliorated by the courts in several different ways. First, it was held that as long as the requisite documents were sent to a creditor and

---

[17] *Skipton Building Society v Collins* [1998] BPIR 267.

that creditor in fact became aware of the meeting before it took place, the strict requirement of the Rules as to notice would be complied with.[18] Secondly, it was held that creditors would be entitled to attend and vote at a meeting of which they had actual notice, regardless of whether they were given notice of it by the nominee or in accordance with the Rules.[19] These judicial findings remain good, but IA 2000 introduced a radical change.

17.18 The aim of the legislation is to provide more certainty to the approval procedure of a proposal. Thus a voluntary arrangement takes effect as if made by the company at the creditors' meeting, and binds:[20]

> '... every person who in accordance with the rules –
>
> (i) was entitled to vote at the meeting (whether or not he was present or represented at it), or
> (ii) would have been so entitled if he had had notice of it as if he were a party to the voluntary arrangement.'

17.19 Accordingly, every creditor of the debtor company who would have been entitled to vote at the creditors' meeting will be bound by the outcome of the meeting regardless of whether or not they received the requisite notice. If a creditor has actual knowledge of the meeting but has not been given notice of the meeting by the nominee or in accordance with the Rules, he may still attend and vote.[21] By remedying the difficulty of 'receipt' of notice in this way the legislators have undoubtedly introduced a degree of unfairness to those creditors who were never sent a notice or never received a notice. To counteract the unfairness, such creditors are able to challenge a decision of a meeting once the outcome of the meeting comes to their attention (see IA 1986, s 6(3)(b)). The time is limited to 28 days after the decision comes to the creditor's attention and that period cannot be extended. The issue of notice arose in *T&N Limited (No 2)*,[22] where it was submitted that for proper service to be effected, r 12 needed to be followed so that the notice must be in writing (r 12.4(1)) and accompanied by the relevant documents and a form of proxy. The notice may be sent by post, and any form of post may be used (r 13.3). Posting of the notices may be proved by a certificate as provided by r 12.4(2). The court accepted that those responsible for convening a meeting to consider a CVA or an IVA must take proper steps to summon the meeting and their duty is to give notice to every creditor of the company of whose claim and address they are aware (as required by s 3(3) and explained by r 1.11). David Richards J said:

> 'I agree also that r 12.16 applies in those cases where notice has been duly sent but has not been received. In such a case the meeting is presumed to have been duly summoned and held, and there will not, as it seems to me, be an irregularity of which complaint can be made under s 6. It does not, however, follow that if notice

---

[18] *Beverley Group plc v McClue* [1996] BPIR 25.
[19] *Re Debtors (Nos 400 IO and 401 IO of 1996)* [1997] BPIR 431.
[20] IA 1986, s 5(2)(b)(i) and (ii), as amended.
[21] *Re Debtors (Nos 400 IO and 401 IO of 1996)* [1997] BPIR 431.
[22] [2006] BPIR 1268.

is not sent to a particular creditor, the meeting is therefore invalid and the CVA is incapable of taking effect. Such a failure will undoubtedly be an irregularity for the purposes of s 6. Its impact is a matter for the court under that section but relevant factors are likely to include whether the result of the meeting would or might have been different, the number of creditors involved and the value of their debts and whether the failure was wilful. Given the right of challenge conferred by s 6, it would not in my view be a correct construction of the 1986 Act that any failure to give notice of the meeting would automatically lead to the invalidity of the meeting.'

17.20 Considering the method of service the court viewed the incorporation of Part 6 of the Civil Procedure Rules (CPR) as introducing a desirable degree of flexibility. The CPR permits service by document exchange, fax or other means of electronic communication, subject to the relevant practice direction. The court's powers to permit service by an alternative method or to dispense with service under r 6.8 of the CPR could prove useful in particular circumstances. The power to order alternative methods of service would be particularly important in the event of any prolonged interruption in postal services.

17.21 For those cases where a moratorium is in force, the nominee[23] has to call a meeting of members and creditors within 28 days of the commencement of the moratorium (see IA 1986, Sch A1, para 8(3)). The consequence of failing to have a meeting before the end of the 28-day period is that the moratorium will end unless it is extended under para 32(1) and (2) of Sch A1. The moratorium commences at the time the documents specified in para 7(1) of Sch A1 are filed or lodged with the court: IA 1986, Sch A1, para 8(1). The nominee has to serve notice of the meeting[24] on every creditor of whose claim the nominee is aware.[25]

17.22 As regards the form of the notice sent by the nominee to the creditors, the Rules provide (r 1.9(3) where there is no moratorium and r 1.48(4) where there is a moratorium) that each notice must contain the following matters:

- where a moratorium is in place, a statement identifying the court in which the documents relating to the obtaining of a moratorium were filed and stating the effect of paras (1), (3) and (4) of r 1.52 (requisite majorities for creditors);

- where there is no moratorium, a statement giving the name of the court to which the nominee's report under IA 1986, s 2 has been delivered and stating the effect of r 1.19(1), (3) and (4) (requisite majorities for creditors);

- a copy of the directors' proposal;

---

[23] IA 1986, Sch A1, paras 29 and 31.
[24] The conduct of the meeting is governed by IA 1986, Sch A1, para 30, as inserted by IA 2000.
[25] IA 1986, Sch A1, para 29(2).

- a copy of the statement of affairs or, if the nominee thinks fit, a summary of the statement (a summary has to include a list of creditors and the amount of their debts);

- the nominee's comments on the proposal; and

- a form of proxy (r 1.13(5)); the proxy must not in any way be pre-completed.

17.23 So far as the creditors' meeting is concerned, notice must be given to all creditors specified in the statement of affairs and to any other creditor of whose name and address the nominee is aware (IA 1986, s 3(3); see also r 1.9(2)(a)).[26]

17.24 So far as the members' meeting is concerned, notice must be sent to all persons who are members, according to the nominee's belief (r 1.9(2)(b) where there is no moratorium and r 1.48(3) where there is a moratorium). Fourteen days' notice of both meetings should also be given to the directors and officers and to any person who the convenor considers should be present if he believes that that person was a director or officer of the company during the 2 years immediately preceding the notice (r 1.16(1)(a) and (b) and r 1.48(5) where a moratorium is in force).

17.25 For both creditors' and members' meetings the notice should, of course, stipulate the time and place of the meeting. The time of the meeting must be fixed for between 10 am and 4 pm on a business day (r 1.13(2)), and although both the members' and creditors' meetings may be held on the same day and at the same place (r 1.13(3)); if they are not they must be held no more than 7 days apart (r 1.13(4)). In either case the creditors' meeting has to be held in advance of the members' meeting (r 1.13(3)).

Where the nominee is the administrator or liquidator

17.26 Where the nominee is the administrator or liquidator (referred to in the Rules as the 'responsible insolvency practitioner' – see r 1.1(3)) there is no question of a moratorium as the company is already protected by an insolvency process. In these circumstances the responsible insolvency practitioner should do the following:

- fix a venue for the creditors' meeting and the company meeting (r 1.11(1));

---

[26] By giving notice of the meeting to a creditor, the nominee is acknowledging his status as a creditor for the purpose of the meeting. For this reason, the inclusion of a creditor in the statement of affairs can have important procedural consequences both for the creditor and the company/debtor: see, for example, *Re Debtors (Nos 400 IO and 401 IO of 1996)* [1997] BPIR 431; and *Re Bielecki* [1998] BPIR 655.

- in the case of a creditors' meeting, give at least 14 days' notice to all the creditors specified in the company's statement of affairs, and to any other creditor of whose address the insolvency practitioner is otherwise aware; and

- in the case of a company meeting, to all persons who are, to the best of the insolvency practitioner's belief, members of the company.

17.27 In addition to stating the time and place of the relevant meeting, the notice must also state the effect of r 1.19(1), (3) and (4) on requisite majorities, include a copy of the responsible insolvency practitioner's proposal and include a copy of the statement of affairs (r 1.11(2)). If the responsible insolvency practitioner thinks it appropriate, he may dispense with a copy of the statement of affairs in favour of a summary. The notice must be accompanied by a proxy form (r 1.13(4)). Importantly, the proxy form must not be pre-completed by the insertion in it of the name or description of any person, ie for appointment as an insolvency office holder or for appointment as a member of a committee or as proxy holder (r 8.2).[27] Where the debtor company is being wound up the responsible insolvency practitioner has an obligation to send a copy of the proposal to the official receiver (r 1.12(6)) ensuring that the official receiver is informed of the name and address of the insolvency practitioner who has agreed to act as nominee.

THE CHAIRMAN

17.28 The convenor of the members' and creditors' meetings (the nominee or responsible insolvency practitioner) is also to be the chairman of the meetings (r 1.14(1)). If for any reason the convener is unable to attend the meeting or meetings, he may nominate another person to act as chairman, but the alternate person has to be qualified to act as an insolvency practitioner in respect of the company, be authorised by the company or be an employee of the convener, or his firm, who is experienced in insolvency matters.

17.29 The role of the chairman is to present his report to the creditors at the meeting. He must decide whether or not it would be useful to have the directors and officers of the company attend the meeting and to adjudicate on any dispute arising in relation to the voting rights claimed by creditors. In all these matters the chairman must have regard to the provisions of the Rules: see IA 1986, s 4(5), or Sch A1, para 30 where there is a moratorium. In order to prepare thoroughly for the creditors' meeting a nominee is recommended[28] to take the following steps beforehand:

- record all proxies received in advance of the meeting, and details of their claims;

---

[27] See SIP 10.
[28] SIP 3, version 4 (April 2007), paras 7.4–7.6.

- complete the meeting record as far as possible, detailing the names and voting value of the creditors;

- discuss with the directors/debtors any modifications suggested by creditors prior to the meeting;

- review the proposal in the light of creditors' responses and possible changes in circumstances;

- prepare a report for presentation at the meeting, summarising the proposal, outlining the likely effects of acceptance or rejection and giving details of any changes in circumstances which have arisen since the proposal was sent to creditors; and

- consider voting rights and requisite majorities.

17.30 Once the chairman has presented his report to the creditors' meeting, he should allow creditors an opportunity to make comments, ask questions or propose modifications to the proposal. Although it is not a statutory requirement for directors to consent to modifications, SIP 3 recommends that the nominee should find out and report to the meeting the views of the directors on any proposed modifications which they may be required to implement if approved. The advantages of such an approach are that the meeting will know whether or not the directors' are likely to buy-in to the arrangement or whether the modifications are, in the view of the company's management, unlikely to be workable. The creditors' meeting has the power to modify any of the terms of the proposal, including those as to remuneration of the insolvency practitioners.[29] SIP 3 recommends that if modifications are proposed by a creditor, the chairman should give careful consideration to the manner in which he will use specific instructions given to him by creditors to vote for either the acceptance or the rejection of the original proposal.

17.31 The Rules lay down a number of powers to be enjoyed by the chairman in addition to the chairman's usual power to regulate the meeting:

- The chairman may exclude any director, officer, former director or former officer from attending all or part of a meeting, even where that person has been sent a notice of the meeting (r 1.16(2)).

- The chairman has to be satisfied as to the amount in respect of which the creditor's vote is to be permitted to be cast.[30]

- Under r 1.17(3) a creditor may vote in respect of a debt for an unliquidated amount or any debt whose value is not ascertained and for

---

[29] See para 2.5.2 of SIP 9 'Remuneration of insolvency office holders'.
[30] *Re KG Hoare* [1997] BPIR 683.

the purposes of voting (but not otherwise) his debt shall be valued at £1 unless the chairman agrees to place a greater value on the debt.[31]

- The chairman also has a discretion to reject the whole or part of a creditor's claim to be entitled to vote (r 1.17A(2) and r 1.50(2) if there was a moratorium), although if the chairman is in doubt as to the validity of the claim he may mark the claim as objected to but allow the creditor to vote (r 1.17A(4) and r 1.50(4) where there was a moratorium). The meeting is not the place to go into lengthy debates as to the exact status of a debt, nor is it the time to consider such matters that the court frequently has to consider such as whether a debt is bona fide disputed upon substantial grounds, an issue which leads to a great deal of litigation and frequently takes a day or so to decide. That is not a suitable process to be embarked upon at a creditors' meeting.[32]

- The decision of a chairman to reject the claim to vote of a creditor is subject to appeal to the court by a member or creditor[33] (r 1.17A(3) and r 1.50(3) if there was a moratorium), but any appeal must be made within 28 days from the day that the report on the meeting under IA 1986, s 4(6) has been made to the court (r 1.17A(6) and r 1.50(6) where there was a moratorium).

- On such an appeal, it is likely that the court will not be limited to consideration of the evidence which was before the chairman, but will come to a conclusion on all the evidence subsequently filed at court, whether on balance a creditor's proof should be admitted in whole or in part for voting purposes.[34]

- Particular powers of the chairman in relation to creditors' meetings are conferred by r 1.19(5) and r 1.52(6) where there was a moratorium. This sub-rule confers on the chairman power to decide whether creditors' votes ought to be left out of account (it may be that they are secured in some way) and also power to decide whose votes should be discounted on the basis that they are a connected person (these matters are discussed further below).

- All these powers (conferred by r 1.19(5) where there is no moratorium and r 1.52(6) where there was a moratorium) should be exercised by the chairman in reliance upon the company's statement of affairs.

---

[31] The Chairman is not obliged to value a claim at £1 if the evidence available suggests that it should be given a higher value: *Sofaer v Anglo Irish Asset Finance Plc* [2011] BPIR 1736 and *NatWest Bank plc v Yadgaroff* [2012] BPIR 371 which although relating to individual voluntary arrangements are equally applicable to company voluntary arrangements.
[32] See *Re A Debtor (No 222 of 1990)* [1992] BCLC 137.
[33] See *Re Sweatfield* [1998] BPIR 276.
[34] *Re A Company (No 004539 of 1993)* [1995] BCC 116, at 120F–120G.

17.32 There is one important limitation on the chairman's power when exercising proxy votes. Unless specifically directed to do so by the appointor, the chairman cannot use proxies to change the amount of remuneration and expenses of the nominee or any supervisor of the proposed arrangement (r 1.15).

17.33 In cases where a moratorium has been in force and the meeting has resolved to extend the moratorium the nominee is under a duty:

- to inform the meeting what he has done to comply with his duty pursuant to IA 1986, Sch A1, para 24 (that is, his duty to monitor the company's affairs for the purpose of forming an opinion as to whether the proposal has a reasonable prospect of being approved and implemented, and whether the company is likely to have sufficient funds available to it during the remainder of the moratorium to enable it to continue to trade);

- to inform the meeting what he is intending to do in order to continue to comply with his para 24 duty if the moratorium is extended or further extended; and

- to inform the meeting of the expected cost of his actions for the debtor company (the meeting can then resolve whether or not to approve the expected costs);[35]

- to ask the meeting to vote on whether or not to approve his expected costs during the extended period.[36] If the decision of the meeting is to not approve the expected costs of the moratorium during the extended or further extended period, the moratorium will come to an end.[37]

17.34 It is possible that the outcome of the meeting of creditors and the outcome of the meeting of members will differ. If that is the case SIP 3[38] recommends that the chairman should draw the creditors' attention to the provisions of IA 1986, s 4A (the right of a member to make an application to the court for an order that the members' decision should prevail over the resolution passed by the creditors). It is thought that the reason for drawing the attention of the creditors to this provision is to explain to them that although the members have only a short period (28 days) in which to make an application, the resolution passed by the creditors should not be considered to be final until after the expiry of the challenge period.

---

[35] IA 1986, Sch A1, para 32(3).
[36] IA 1986, Sch A1, para 32(4).
[37] IA 1986, Sch A1, para 32(5).
[38] Paragraph 7.15.

PROXIES

17.35 Each notice has to contain a form of proxy so as to maximise the number of the debtor company creditors able to vote on the proposal. If a creditor cannot attend and wants to vote he will have to ensure that a proxy has been returned to the chairman prior to the meeting. As was noted in the first edition of this book, the courts are increasingly flexible when interpreting IA 1986 and the accompanying Rules when deciding whether proxies are valid and proxy holders are entitled to vote. It is likely that a proxy holder is entitled to vote provided the proxies are lodged before the vote is taken, even if not presented before the meeting started.[39] In this context the courts have accepted that a proxy may be:

- withdrawn and replaced with another as long as it is done prior to the vote;[40]

- faxed for the purposes of voting at a meeting;[41] and

- lodged by electronic means where permitted.

17.36 If modifications are proposed by a creditor, the chairman should give careful consideration to the manner in which he uses specific instructions given to him by creditors to vote for either the acceptance or the rejection of the original proposal.[42] If the words in the proxy form allowing the exercise of discretion in the absence of specific instructions have not been deleted so as to entitle the proxy holder to vote only as directed, the proxy holder will be entitled to vote or abstain on any proposed modification at his discretion.[43]

17.37 However, the chairman should consider most carefully the impact of the exercise of his discretion upon the expressed intentions of any creditor who has completed a proxy requiring a vote on any particular resolution. He should bear in mind that if a creditor is aggrieved that a vote on proposed modifications has taken place and a decision reached which might have been different if creditors represented by proxy had been present at the meeting or had been given the opportunity of amending their proxy, the aggrieved creditor may subsequently challenge the decision (see below). In these circumstances it is suggested that the chairman should consider an adjournment to give him time to explain the modifications to the creditors from whom he holds proxies and to obtain further instructions.[44] All proxies used must be retained by the chairman and delivered to the responsible insolvency practitioner forthwith

---

[39] *Re Philip Alexander Securities & Futures Ltd* [1998] BPIR 383.
[40] *Re Cardona* [1997] BPIR 604.
[41] *Commissioners of Inland Revenue v Conbeer and White* [1996] BPIR 398.
[42] Rules 8.1–8.7 deal with representation of a creditor by proxy.
[43] See para 7.11 of SIP 3.
[44] See para 7.12 of SIP 3.

after the meeting and he must, so long as they are in his hands, allow them to be inspected by the creditors at all reasonable times, on any business day (rr 8.4 and 8.5).

17.38 In reality, the court will not allow substance to triumph over form when assessing the validity of a proxy. In *Roberts v Pinnacle Entertainment Ltd*,[45] Evans-Lombe J had to decide whether a proxy which did not contain details of the debt was valid. The following passage demonstrates a healthy pragmatism:

> 'By the same token any ordinary person would regard the sending of a written proxy by a creditor to the chairman, to be written notice by that creditor to the chairman that he had a claim on the estate of the debtor or bankrupt in respect of which he wished to vote. In my judgment that is enough to satisfy the requirements of subr (3)(a). However, the chairman, in discharge of his duty under r 5.22(1) of the 1986 Rules must be satisfied as to the amount in respect of which that creditor's vote is permitted to be cast. "[I]t is incumbent on a creditor who wishes to vote in respect of his debt to state to the best of his ability the total amount that is owing to him by the debtor ...": see *Re Kenneth George Hoare and Others* [1997] BPIR 683, at 695 per EG Nugee QC sitting as a deputy judge of the Chancery Division. A proxy in the form used in this case without more would not be sufficient to justify a creditor being admitted to vote. It would be necessary for him to satisfy the chairman, either before the meeting or at it, as to the amount of the debt in respect of which he sought to vote. In the present case that was not necessary because the chairman was in possession of evidence which demonstrated that the debtor admitted his indebtedness to Pinnacle in the sum of £135,290.'

ADJOURNMENTS

17.39 Where a debtor company has the benefit of a moratorium, the meeting may resolve to adjourn any decision and if necessary further adjourn. Whether the word 'further' in this context means that a meeting can only be adjourned once or that there is no limit to the number of adjournments has not been the subject of judicial comment. It is thought that Parliament would not have intended to restrict the number of adjournments that can take place. If there is a perception that an abuse may arise (keeping alive a moratorium without resolving the insolvency issue), then it should be recognised that the creditors of the debtor company will have some control by reason of their position, and it can fairly be anticipated that they will be keen to ensure that the meetings are not unnecessarily adjourned. If it is resolved that the meeting be adjourned, or further adjourned, the meeting may go on to resolve (and should in most circumstances) that the moratorium also be extended or further extended.[46] Conditions may be attached to the extension of the moratorium if required by the meeting. The time period over which a moratorium may be extended or further extended is restricted. The moratorium may not be extended or further extended to a day later than the end of 2 months from the date of the original

---

[45] [2004] BPIR 208.
[46] IA 1986, Sch A1, para 32(1).

meeting.[47] The 2-month period begins either on the day that both the creditors' and members' meetings are held (if on the same day) or, if on different days, the day that the last meeting is held.[48] This limitation produces a natural restraint on the number of meetings that are likely to occur.

17.40 Where the debtor company is not subject to a moratorium the governing provisions on adjournment of meetings convened for the purpose of approving a company voluntary arrangement are those contained in r 1.21, as amended. The chairman of the meeting has power (if he thinks fit) to procure that the creditors' meeting and the company meeting should be held together (r 1.21(1)). For this purpose he may adjourn the meetings for not more than 14 days (r 1.21(2)). The chairman must adjourn the meeting if at the meeting a resolution is passed to the effect that the meetings of creditors and members should be held together.

17.41 However, even where the meetings are adjourned several times, the final meetings must take place within 14 days of the day originally set down for the holding of the meetings (r 1.21(3)). Once in the course of the meeting the chairman may suspend it for any period up to 1 hour (r 1.12(4A)). Although the rule governing the time frame within which the adjournment must take place appears strict the court has a general power to extend time in relation to time prescribed by the rules which can be exercised in appropriate circumstances (r 12A.55).

17.42 If the proposal has not been approved by the creditors' meeting after the final adjournment (with or without the modifications), then the proposal will be deemed to have been rejected (r 1.21(5)).

VOTING AT A CREDITORS' MEETING
Who can vote

17.43 Creditors' voting rights have given rise to great difficulty in the past. The reason for this is that there is much at stake with the potentially serious adjustment of a creditor's right which occurs when an arrangement is approved. This has now, largely, been resolved by way of judicial decisions. What follows is an analysis of who can vote, how those votes are calculated and who is bound by the resolutions passed at the creditors' meeting.

17.44 Every creditor who has been given notice of the meeting is entitled to vote at the meeting or at the adjourned meeting (r 1.17(1) without moratorium). Similarly, where a debtor company has the benefit of a moratorium the creditors entitled to vote are 'every creditor who has notice of the creditors' meeting' (r 1.49(1)). If a creditor has not had formal notice of the meeting but learns of the meeting and attends, he may also vote if he is able to

---

[47] IA 1986, Sch A1, para 32(2).
[48] IA 1986, Sch A1, para 32(2)(a) and (b).

satisfy the chairman that he is a genuine creditor.[49] A secured creditor may vote in respect of the unsecured part of his debt.[50] Voluntary arrangements cannot generally affect the proprietary rights of a creditor without that creditor's consent. This is recognised by statute because a meeting cannot approve any proposal or modification which affects the right of a secured creditor of the debtor company to enforce his security, unless the secured creditor gives consent (s 4(3)). However, it is implicit in most proposals that during the periods of payment established by the arrangement, and thereafter if payment is made in full, the previous right of the secured creditor is novated into the rights conferred on it by the arrangement. A bank would not be able to appoint a receiver during the currency of an arrangement and take for itself the entire income of a business while it was still receiving the instalments it had voted for at the meeting. Accordingly, where a secured creditor votes in favour of an arrangement and accepts a dividend an estoppel or waiver of rights operates, as it would be inconsistent for him to rely on his pre-arrangement position and also rely on his security.[51] Thus a creditor with security over the company's assets must proceed with care in case he should be taken by his conduct in voting to have surrendered his security.[52]

17.45 Some creditors may claim as 'contingent' or 'prospective' creditors and this may cause problems for the chairman when it comes to putting a value on such a claim. The expression 'contingent creditor' is not defined, but has been said to arise where the debtor company may or will become subject to a present liability upon the happening of a future event or will become liable at some future date.[53] The term is not a term of art and each case will depend upon the context in which the term is used.[54] A prospective creditor, on the other hand, is 'a creditor in respect of a debt which will certainly become due in the future either on some date which has already been determined or on some date determinable by reference to future events'.[55]

17.46 Difficulties arise at times as there is no definition of the term 'creditor' in IA 1986. The issue surfaced in a case where the court was asked to consider whether a potential claimant in tort could vote and be bound by an arrangement. It was acknowledged by the court that it was 'a significant step to go from saying that a person with a contingent claim on the basis of an existing contractual obligation is a "creditor" to saying that a person who has suffered no loss and who therefore has no claim in tort is a "creditor" because he may in the future suffer loss, giving him then a cause of action in tort'. The court in

---

[49] *Re a Debtor* [1997] BPIR 431 (Rimer J considering r 5.17(1) in the context of an IVA).
[50] *Calor Gas Ltd v Piercy* [1994] BCC 69.
[51] *Khan v Permayer* [2001] BPIR 95.
[52] *Moor v Anglo-Italian Bank* (1879) 10 ChD 681; *Seventeenth Canute Pty Ltd v Bradley Air Conditioning Pty Ltd* (1986) 11 ACLC 193; *Andrew v FarmStart* (1988) 71 CBR (NS) 124; 54 DLR (4th) 406; and *Health & Life Care v SA Asset Mgt* (1995) 18 ACSR 153.
[53] *Re William Hockley Ltd* [1962] 1 WLR 555, at 558, per Pennycuick J.
[54] *County Bookshops v Grove* [2002] BPIR 772; [2003] 1 BCLC 479.
[55] *Stonegate Securities Ltd v Gregory* [1980] Ch 576.

T&N Ltd[56] thought that the appropriate test was to look closely at the nature of the contingent liability. David Richards J said:[57]

> 'Although contained in the 1986 Act and although envisaged as a mechanism for a company in financial difficulties, there is no clear requirement that creditors for the purposes of CVAs should be restricted to persons with provable debts. As a mechanism which is intended as an alternative to schemes of arrangement, there is every reason for concluding that "creditors" should have as wide a meaning in Part I of the Insolvency Act as in s 425 ... I conclude therefore that T&N is subject to contingent liabilities in respect of future asbestos claims, as defined in the administrators' application and that the future asbestos claimants, being those persons who have been exposed to asbestos and who will have claims in negligence against T&N if they develop asbestos-related diseases, are "creditors" of T&N for the purposes of s 425 of the 1985 Act and Part I of the 1986 Act dealing with CVAs.'

17.47 The Insolvency (Amendment) Rules 2006[58] made a key change in r 13.12(2) of the Rules following *T&N Ltd*[59] so as to include a claim in tort if the elements necessary to establish a cause of action exist at the relevant date even if damage has not been suffered. Although these are stated to apply in the case of winding up only, there is no reason why the same reasoning should not apply to CVAs, particularly given the reasoning of David Richards J in *T&N Ltd*.

17.48 Although the chairman is given a discretion as to whether to admit or reject a claim in whole or in part (r 1.17A(2) and r 1.50(2) where there is a moratorium) for voting purposes, it is implicit in the Rules that the chairman should do all he reasonably can in order to put a value on a claim. If the chairman is unsure or in doubt as to whether a particular creditor's claim should be admitted or rejected for voting purposes (whether the creditor claims to be a liquidated, unliquidated, contingent or prospective creditor), he should mark it as objected to and allow the creditor to vote. In any event the Rules provide a right of appeal against any decision of a chairman to disallow or allow a person to vote (r 1.17(A)(3) and r 1.50(3) where a moratorium is in force).

The calculation of a creditor's voting rights

17.49 It is incumbent on a creditor who wishes to vote in respect of his debt to state to the best of his ability the total amount that is owed to him, and, if the value of his debt or some part of it is not ascertained, to state that fact, and to supply the chairman with as much information as is available to enable the chairman to put an estimated value upon it. It does not lie in the mouth of a

---

[56] [2006] BPIR 1268.
[57] Ibid.
[58] SI 2006/1272.
[59] [2006] BPIR 1268.

creditor who remains silent to say subsequently that he is not bound in respect of a claim which he has not mentioned.[60]

17.50 The calculation of a creditor's voting power is made according to the quantum of the creditor's debt at the date of the meeting/adjourned meeting or, where the company is in administration or compulsory liquidation, at the date of the administration or liquidation order (r 1.17(2)).

17.51 It is axiomatic that the creditor has to have a debt in order for him to vote. Where the debt is liquidated the quantum is known. However, where the creditor's debt is unliquidated or where it is for an unascertained amount, the quantum is less obvious. In these circumstances the Rules provide that unless the chairman agrees to an estimated value, the debt shall be valued at £1 (r 1.17(3) where there is no moratorium and r 1.49(3) where there is a moratorium). The issue of whether the chairman placed the right value on an unliquidated debt (r 1.17(3)) arose in *Re Newlands (Seaford) Educational Trust v Pepper and Others*.[61] The court was asked whether for the purposes of voting at the creditors' meeting the failure of the chairman to value a landlord's claim at more than £1 was open to him. The landlord's claim was for future rent, breach of covenant and dilapidations. The court considered the claims to be both unliquidated and unascertained. On the facts the court found that the chairman was correct to value the claims at £1. In respect of unliquidated claims falling with r 1.17(3):[62]

> 'The chairman should not speculate. Nor is he obliged to investigate the creditor's claim. But he must examine such evidence, and I do not use that word in any technical sense, as the creditor puts forward and any relevant evidence provided by any other creditor or the debtor. If the totality of that evidence leads him to the conclusion that he can safely attribute to the claim a minimum value higher than £1 then he should do so.'

17.52 As regards contingent claims, it has been held that by taking into account subsequent events greater certainty can be introduced into the process of calculation. As the 'process of estimation is designed to put a figure on a contingent claim by reference to what may happen in the future, it would be pure conceptualism not to take account of subsequent events which have occurred before the estimation is made'. Hindsight is used because it is not considered fair to a creditor to value a contingent debt at what it might have been worth at a certain date when prescience would have shown it to be worth more. The same must be true of a contingent debt which prescience would have shown to be worth less.

---

[60] *Re KG Hoare* [1997] BPIR 683.
[61] [2006] BPIR 1230. See also: *Sofaer v Anglo Irish Asset Finance Plc* [2011] BPIR 1736 and *NatWest Bank plc v Yadgaroff* [2012] BPIR 371.
[62] Ibid, at [28].

17.53 Where a debtor company has entered a moratorium, votes are calculated according to the amount of the creditor's debt as at the beginning of the moratorium, after deducting any amounts paid in respect of that debt after that date (r 1.49(2)).

17.54 Certain parts of a debt for an ascertained amount are also to be discounted in the voting process. The discounted interests are laid down in the Rules (r 1.19(3) where there is no moratorium and r 1.52(4) where there is a moratorium), which exclude:

- any part of a debt which is in any way secured;

- debts in respect of which written notice has not been given to the chairman or convener of the meeting either at the meeting or before it; and

- a debt which relates wholly or in part to a current bill of exchange or promissory note.[63]

17.55 The required majority in the creditors' meeting for approval or modification of the proposed arrangement is three-quarters by value (r 1.19(1)). For any other resolution the required majority is one-half by value of the creditors present in person or by voting by proxy and voting on the resolution (r 1.19(2)). Any resolution will be invalid if those voting against it include more than one-half in value of the creditors, counting in these latter only those who are not, to the best of the chairman's belief, persons connected with the company (r 1.19(4)) as defined in IA 1986, s 249.

The outcome of the meeting

17.56 In the event that a creditor is bound by the approved arrangement, his debt will usually be released or suspended and replaced by the bundle of rights set out in the arrangement. Uncertainty as to who is bound by an approved CVA inevitably leads to disruption and sometimes failure of the CVA. Before the coming into force of IA 2000, the approved CVA bound[64] 'every person who in accordance with the rules had notice of, and was entitled to vote at, the meeting (whether or not he was present or represented at the meeting) as if he were a party to the voluntary arrangement'.[65] Thus it may be surmised that two hurdles had to be overcome in order to show that a creditor was bound by the approved arrangement. First, it had to be shown that a formal notice (ie a notice that complied with the Rules) had been received by the creditor (various

---

[63] The exception to this is provided by r 1.19(3)(c)(i) and (ii).
[64] For an analysis of the effect of approval of an arrangement on creditors and third parties such as co-sureties, see *Johnson v Davies* [1998] 2 All ER 649. As to whether a creditor served with notice of the meeting in respect of one debt will be bound if the proposals are approved in respect of other debts, see *Re Bradley-Hole* [1995] BCC 418; and *Re KG Hoare* [1997] BPIR 683.
[65] IA 1986, s 5(2)(b).

rules applied to this as set out in the first edition of this text). In short, if the creditor could show that he did not receive notice he would not be bound by the arrangement. It was, however, always open for a creditor to claim that he was not bound by the arrangement with the potential of causing great harm. The second element required before a creditor would be bound by the arrangement was simply that the creditor had to be entitled to vote.

17.57 In the interests of certainty, the approved CVA had to bind all creditors regardless of whether or not a creditor received notice. The substituted s 5(2)(b) of IA 1986 provides that a CVA binds 'every person who in accordance with the rules was entitled to vote at the meeting (whether or not he was present or represented at it) or would have been so entitled if he had had notice of it, as if he were a party to the voluntary arrangement'.[66] Accordingly, whether or not someone is bound by the approved arrangement will not depend upon receipt of a formal notice but will depend on whether or not the creditor was entitled to vote in accordance with the Rules as set out above.

17.58 As with all meetings in insolvency proceedings, the meeting will be valid if at least one person who is entitled to vote as a creditor is present, or by proxy present, at the place of the meeting (r 12A.21(2)(a)). In the case of a meeting of contributories, there have to be at least two contributories entitled to vote or all the contributories if their number does not exceed two (r 12A.21(2)(b)). However, where there is a quorum that comprises the chairman and one voting creditor or proxy, the meeting has to be delayed by 15 minutes if the chairman is aware that there are other persons entitled to vote but who are not present (r 12A.21(4)). It should be noted that the provisions in relation to remote attendance at creditors' meetings do not apply to CVAs. The chairman has a discretion to adjourn the meeting for a period of not more than 14 days from the appointed date and time (r 1.21(2)), but where the meeting goes ahead he has to be careful to record what resolutions are being voted upon, the decision on each resolution (r 1.24(2)(b)) and how each creditor votes on every resolution (r 1.24(2)(c)), as he has to include these details in his report to the court (which has to be filed within 4 days of the meetings being held), which will then form part of the court record (r 1.24(3)). The proposal shall be deemed to have been rejected if both the creditors' and members' meetings fail to approve it, or a modified version of it (r 1.21(5)). If the proposal is approved (with or without modification) and two or more supervisors are appointed, a further resolution may be taken by the creditors as to whether acts may be done (in connection with the arrangement) by any one or more of them, or whether the acts must be done by all of them (r 1.22(1)). If the creditors pass a resolution that someone other than the nominee is to be appointed as the supervisor, then the chairman must have produced to him at or before the meeting both (a) the written consent of that person to act as the supervisor (unless he is present at the meeting and there and then signifies his consent); and (b) his written confirmation that he is qualified to act as an insolvency practitioner in respect of the debtor company (r 1.22(3)(a) and (b)).

---

[66] Substituted by IA 2000.

MEMBERS' MEETINGS

17.59 As has been noted above, the nominee summons both the meeting of creditors and the meeting of members, and the meetings may be held on the same day. The calculation of members' voting rights is considerably more straightforward than those of creditors. Members of the debtor company generally vote according to the rights attaching to their shares in accordance with the articles (r 1.18(1)). References to a person's shares in r 1.18(1) include any other interest which he may have as a member of the debtor company. The exercise of such a vote seems largely symbolic. This is because such votes are discounted when calculating the requisite majority, which is one-half in value of the members unless the articles otherwise provide (r 1.20). The value of members' votes is determined by reference to the number of votes conferred on each member by the company's articles.[67] However, the ability to vote does have the benefit of binding the members.

17.60 Before the introduction of IA 2000, the creditors' meeting had to be held in advance of the members' meeting. This often was inconvenient, inefficient and led to unnecessary costs being wasted. In recognition of the potential inconvenience, the convenor of the meetings now has a discretion as to whether to hold the meetings on the same day and in the same place. If the convenor favours the meetings being held on the same day and in the same place he has to ensure that the meeting of creditors is fixed for a time in advance of the meeting of members (r 1.13(3)).[68] When fixing the time, date and venue of the meeting the convenor of the meeting has to give priority to the creditors' wishes (r 1.13(1)). If different days are to be allocated to the creditors' and members' meetings then they must be held within 7 days of each other (r 1.13(4)), with the creditors' meeting being held first.

17.61 As to the approval of an arrangement, it is possible that the creditors' meeting and members' meeting may have a different outcome in respect of the resolution to approve. In these circumstances the resolution passed by the creditors' meeting prevails over that passed at the members' meeting (s 4A(2)(b) or Sch A1, para 36(2) where a moratorium was in force).[69] This reflects the position that creditors' rights may displace those of the general body of shareholders where the debtor company is insolvent or near insolvent[70] and adds a degree of certainty to the outcome of the meetings. Nevertheless, the members may feel aggrieved if a creditors' meeting resolves to approve a proposal when the majority of members believe that it is unsuitable or if the creditors do not resolve to approve a proposal where the majority believe that it is in the best interests of the debtor company to approve the proposal. In these circumstances the members may apply to court (s 4A(3) and Sch A1, para 36(3)

---

[67] An amendment to the rules inserted by the Insolvency (Amendment) Rules 1987, SI 1987/1919, r 3(1), Sch, Pt 1, para 5.
[68] As substituted by IA 2000.
[69] This is a radical departure from the pre-IA 2000 position, which required unanimity by both creditors and members.
[70] *Brady v Brady* [1989] AC 755; *Walker v Wimbourne* (1976) 137 CLR 1; *West Mercia Safetywear v Dodd* 1998 BCLC 250.

where a moratorium is in force) within 28 days (s 4A(4) or Sch A1, para 36(4) with a moratorium) from the later of the day on which the decision was taken at the creditors' meeting or the members' meeting, for an order that the resolution of the members' meeting should prevail over the resolution of the creditors' meeting. On such an application the court has a discretion to order that the decision of the members' meeting is to have effect instead of the decision of the creditors' meeting and a wide power is given to the court to make any such order as it sees fit (s 4A(6) or Sch A1, para 36(5) where a moratorium is in force).[71] There is no guidance as to the sort of circumstances where the court may order that the decision of the members should prevail over that of the creditors, but it is thought that some serious misconduct, material irregularity or equivalent behaviour would have to be demonstrated before the court would overturn the decision of the creditors. Once the proposal is approved, any moratorium in force automatically comes to an end (Sch A1, para 8(2), (5) and (7)).

17.62 After the meetings the chairman must report his decision to the court, which will entail the preparation of a written report of those meetings (s 4(6) or Sch A1, para 30(3) where a moratorium is in force). The time for the lodging of the report is short as the chairman is required to report the result to the court within 4 days of the holding of the creditors' and members' meetings (r 1.24(3)). Immediately after reporting to the court the chairman has to give notice of the result of the creditors' and members' meetings to all those persons who were sent notices of the meetings (r 1.24(4)). There is no prescribed form for the report, but the following matters may be included:

- whether the proposal was approved by the creditors alone or by both the creditors and members and in either case whether the approval was made with any modifications;

- the details of all the resolutions taken and the decisions on the resolutions at each of the meetings;

- a list of the creditors and members who attended or were represented and how they voted on each of the resolutions;

- a statement as to whether in the opinion of the supervisor the EC Regulation on insolvency proceedings[72] applies to the arrangement and if it does whether the proceedings are main, secondary or territorial proceedings; and

- as a catch-all, any other information that the supervisor thinks should be included in the report (r 1.24(2)).

---

[71] These provisions also provide that where a member of a regulated company, as defined by Sch A1, para 44, applies to the court, the Financial Services Authority is entitled to be heard on an application.
[72] Council Regulation 1346/2000/EC.

17.63 Where a voluntary arrangement has been approved, a copy of this report must also be sent to the Registrar of Companies (r 1.24(5)).

CHALLENGING DECISIONS

17.64 It is inevitable that different creditors will have different views and concerns as to how their particular interests are protected or advanced. However, it has been held that the statutory scheme envisaged this and, subject to the protection of the minority in cases of unfair prejudice, the minority would be bound by the majority. A person entitled to vote at either of the meetings (including a person entitled to vote if he had had notice of the meeting) may apply to revoke or suspend the approval of a voluntary arrangement on the grounds that it unfairly prejudices the interests of a creditor, member or contributory of the company. Alternatively, such a person may claim that there has been some material irregularity at or in relation to the meetings. The more recent challenges came with the increase of CVAs in the retail sector where they have been utilised in an attempt to avoid guarantee liabilities[73] or without objectively justifying the proposal.[74] The class of person entitled to apply to the court extends to the nominee or, if the company is being wound up or an administration order is in force, the liquidator or administrator of the debtor company (s 6).[75]

17.65 There is a time restriction on when an application to the court may be made. It cannot be made after the end of the period of 28 days beginning with the first day on which each of the reports (mentioned above) has been made to the court or, in the case of a person who was not given notice of the creditors' meeting, after the end of the period of 28 days beginning with the day on which he became aware that the meeting had taken place. The court has no power to extend the 28-day period.[76] However an application can be made by a creditor who did not have notice of the meeting, after the arrangement ceases to have effect (unless it comes to an end prematurely), if he can show that the arrangement prejudices his interests (s 6(3)).

---

[73] *Prudential Assurance Co Ltd v PRG Powerhouse Ltd* [2007] EWHC 1002 (Ch), [2007] BPIR 839.
[74] *Mourant & Co Trustees Ltd v Sixty UK Ltd (in liq)* [2010] EWHC 1890 (Ch) [2010] BPIR 1264.
[75] For cases on what can constitute 'unfair prejudice' see the review of the cases concerning both individual and company voluntary arrangements in Stephen A Lawson *Individual Voluntary Arrangements* (Jordans, Chapter 13), at para 6.3.3; and see *March Estates plc v Gunmark Ltd* [1996] BPIR 439; *Lam Soon Australia Pty Ltd v Molit (No 55) Pty Ltd* [1997] BPIR 481; *Re Cardona* [1997] BPIR 604; and *Re Bielecki* [1998] BPIR 655. For cases on 'material irregularity', see Lawson, ibid, at para 6.3.4; *National Westminster Bank plc v Scher* [1998] BPIR 224; and *Duce v Commissioner of Inland Revenue* (unreported) 4 December 1998, ChD.
[76] *Re Bournemouth & Boscombe Athletic Football Club Co Ltd* [1998] BPIR 183.

17.66 In *Re Wimbledon Football Club Ltd*,[77] Lightman J summarised the case-law relating to the grounds upon which proposals might properly be alleged to be unfairly prejudicial as follows:[78]

> 'Section 6 provides that a creditor may apply to the court for an order to revoke or suspend a decision approving a voluntary arrangement on the ground that the "voluntary arrangement unfairly prejudices the interest of [the] creditor". The authorities establish that: (1) to constitute a good ground of challenge the unfair prejudice complained of must be caused by the terms of the arrangement itself; (2) the existence of unequal or differential treatment of creditors of the same class will not of itself constitute unfairness, but may give cause to inquire and require an explanation; (3) in determining whether or not there is unfairness, it is necessary to consider all the circumstances including, as alternatives to the arrangement proposed, not only liquidation but the possibility of a different fairer scheme; (4) depending on the circumstances, differential treatment may be necessary to ensure fairness (see *Cazaly Irving Holdings Ltd v Cancol Ltd* [1996] BPIR 252 at 269–270D and *Sea Voyager Maritime Inc v Bielecki* [1999] 1 All ER 4 628 at 642c–643b and 647e–g); and (I would add) (5) differential treatment may be necessary to secure the continuation of the company's business which underlies the arrangement: (consider *Business City Express Ltd* [1997] BCC 826).'

17.67 In *Prudential Assurance Co*[79] Etherton J further elaborated upon the exercise the Court has to carry out:

> 'In broad terms, the cases show that unfairness may be assessed by a comparative analysis from a number of different angles. They include what I would describe as vertical and horizontal comparisons. Vertical comparison is with the position on winding up (or, in the case of individuals, bankruptcy). Horizontal comparison is with other creditors or classes of creditors.'

17.68 In *Re Wimbledon Football Club Ltd* in the Court of Appeal,[80] Neuberger LJ emphasised the importance of keeping in mind the 'commercial realities' when assessing a challenge to a CVA. Such considerations are particularly relevant when a CVA is challenged on the grounds of material irregularity at a creditors' meeting.[81] An application of the 'commercial realities' principle arose where a CVA contained a release of officeholders such that the applicant creditors bound by the CVA were unable to bring claims against them for breach of their duties in carrying out their functions. The court found a conflict of interest and a breach of professional rules were not enough, by themselves, to establish unfair prejudice, and accordingly there was no prospect of success. Further, even if there were a prospect of success, the

---

[77] [2004] EWHC 1020 (Ch).
[78] Ibid, at [18].
[79] *Prudential Assurance Co Ltd v PRG Powerhouse Ltd* [2007] EWHC 1002 (Ch), [2007] BPIR 839.
[80] [2004] EWCA Civ 655.
[81] See *Tanner v Everitt* [2004] EWHC 1130 (Ch).

court would not exercise its discretion under IA 1986, s 6 due to the complexities of the interlocking CVAs in question.[82]

17.69 When it comes to a challenge, it should be noted that unless express provision is made in the proposals as approved, the court has no jurisdiction to amend an arrangement without the unanimous consent of the creditors.[83] It is not for the court to speculate whether the terms of a proposed CVA were the best that could have been obtained. The court's power is restricted to revoking or suspending any decision approving the arrangement or any decision taken at the meeting if the challenge has been made on the ground of material irregularity. The court may then give a direction to any person to summon another meeting to reconsider the proposal or modified proposals.

---

[82] See *Re Alpa Lighting Ltd* [1997] BPIR 341. Cf *Re FMS Financial Management Services Ltd* (1989) 5 BCC 191; *Tanner v Everitt* [2004] EWHC 1130 (Ch).
[83] *Sisu Capital Fund Ltd and others v Tucker and others* [2005] EWHC 2170 (Ch), [2006] BCC 463.

Chapter 18

COMPANY ADMINISTRATIONS

INTRODUCTION

18.1 The Insolvency Act 1986 (IA1986) introduced an administration process which affords an ailing company the possibility of recovering from its financial difficulties. At the core was a statutory 'breathing-space', during which creditors were restrained from moving in on a company's assets whilst an insolvency practitioner formulated proposals for a rescue which were then put to a creditors' meeting for consideration. It is now the rescue option of choice and with the development of the 'pre-pack'[1] is frequently used to sell on the business of the company immediately on the appointment of an administrator. Pre-packs are frequently viewed with suspicion by creditors with an apparent seamless transfer of the business to a new company frequently under the control of the same directors. As a result of this concern the Association of Business Recovery Professionals (R3) produced the Statement of Insolvency Practice 16 (SIP 16) which has an impact on when a meeting should be called and what information should be provided to creditors before the meeting. Whilst this does not have statutory force, it is a statement of best practice and is regarded as such by the courts.[2] In addition the Department of Business, Innovation and Skill monitors adherence to SIP 16 and produces an annual report setting out its findings. The failure to abide by SIP 16 can be the subject of disciplinary action by an insolvency practitioner's regulating body. This will be dealt with in more detail below.

18.2 Originally s 8 of IA 1986 gave the court the jurisdiction to make an order appointing an insolvency practitioner as an administrator (investing a power in the administrator to manage the affairs, business and property of the company) for a certain period. The court had to be satisfied that the company was or was likely to become unable to pay its debts and that the making of an administration order would be likely to achieve one or more of the following purposes:

- the survival of the company, and the whole or any part of its undertaking, as a going concern;

- the approval of a company voluntary liquidation (CVA);

---

[1] Defined in SIP 16 'as an arrangement under which the sale of all or part of a company's business or assets is negotiated with a purchaser prior to the appointment of an administrator, and the administrator effects the sale immediately on, or shortly after, his appointment'.
[2] *Re Kayley Vending Ltd* [2011] 1 BCLC 114.

- the sanctioning of a compromise or arrangement under the Companies Act 1985, s 425; and/or

- a more advantageous realisation of the company's assets than would be effected on a winding up.

18.3 The administration process, unlike the CVA process, was originally purely a court-based procedure. Accordingly, there could be no meeting of creditors summoned for the purpose of agreeing to the proposals prior to the court hearing. There was a need for the administrator to call a meeting of creditors within 3 months of the making of the administration order. The purpose of the meeting was to obtain agreement from the creditors as to how the insolvency practitioner would achieve the purposes specified in the court order.

'STREAMLINED' AND OUT OF COURT ADMINISTRATIONS

18.4 The administration process was revolutionised by the Enterprise Act 2002, which came into force (in part) on 15 September 2003. The changes brought by the new provisions are fundamental. Formerly, administration was merely a gateway to another insolvency process – usually liquidation or a CVA. Now, an administration can be, and frequently is, a one-stop insolvency process from which a company can be dissolved and with the approval of the court one in which distributions to creditors may be made. Moreover, administration is the chosen insolvency process for the majority of secured lenders with debentures, although they will frequently put pressure on directors to make the appointment rather than make it themselves.

18.5 Sections 8–27 of IA 1986 are replaced by s 8 and Sch B1 which contains the substantive provisions in relation to the administration procedures. An administrator remains an officer of the court[3] and can be appointed by court order, but may alternatively be appointed 'out of court'. The main priority is the rescue of the company as a going concern and it is only if an insolvency practitioner is of the opinion that this cannot be achieved that the other objectives can be considered. They are set out as follows:[4]

> 'The administrator of a company must perform his functions with the objective of –
>
> (a) rescuing the company as a going concern, or
> (b) achieving a better result for the company's creditors as a whole than would be likely if the company were wound up (without first being in administration), or

---

[3] IA 1986, Sch B1, para 5.
[4] IA 1986, Sch B1, para 3(1).

(c) realising property in order to make a distribution to one or more secured or preferential creditors.'

18.6 Another substantial change introduced by the Enterprise Act 2002 was the abolition of the right of the Crown to rank ahead of unsecured creditors by reason of it being a preferential creditor. As well as the abolition of the Crown's preferential status, a new s 176A has been introduced into IA 1986 so that administrators and liquidators have to make a prescribed part of the debtor company's net property available for the satisfaction of unsecured debts in certain circumstances. An administrator will have to include in the proposals such information he has in respect of the prescribed part of the debtor company's net property.

CREDITORS' MEETINGS

18.7 No other insolvency process was intended to give the creditors so many rights and powers as administration, although these have been lessened by the frequent use of pre-packs. Nonetheless it remains the case that used intelligently, the creditors' meeting can be a powerful mechanism for ensuring the accountability of the administrator. The meeting of creditors under this insolvency process takes place after the administrator has been appointed and is concerned with the approval of the proposals which should be directed at rescuing the debtor company in the interests of all creditors. If the meeting accepts the proposals, these then become the purposes which the administrator must seek to achieve and he may not subsequently change them without any revisions being accepted by a further creditors' meeting. If, however, the meeting rejects the proposals, then the outcome is placed in the hands of the court, which may terminate the administration or make such order as it thinks appropriate.

18.8 There are various types of creditors' meetings that may be held. There is the initial meeting,[5] a meeting to consider a revision of the proposals put by the administrator to the creditors at the initial meeting,[6] a further creditors' meeting initiated by the creditors or the court[7] and a further meeting of creditors initiated by the administrator.[8] The provisions cater for the changes in legislation and new rules were introduced. In essence, unless there is nothing in the proposals for the unsecured creditors, the administrator must summon an initial meeting of creditors in order that he may present a statement setting out proposals for the creditors to reject, approve or modify.

---

[5] Pursuant to IA 1986, Sch B1, para 51.
[6] Pursuant to IA 1986, Sch B1, para 54(2).
[7] IA 1986, Sch B1, para 53(2).
[8] IA 1986, Sch B1, para 62.

18.9 This requires some elaboration. The legislative framework is at once subtle and complex. Pursuant to para 52(1) of Sch B1 to IA 1986, the obligation to put the proposals to the creditors' meeting does not apply if the administrator thinks either:

- that the company has sufficient property to enable each creditor of the company to be paid in full;

- that the company has insufficient property to enable a distribution to be made to unsecured creditors other than by virtue of s 176A(2)(a); or

- that neither of the objectives in para 3(1)(a) and (b) can be achieved, so the purpose of the administration is for the benefit of secured creditors.

RELATIONSHIP BETWEEN CREDITORS' VOTING RIGHTS AND THE ADMINISTRATOR'S DUTIES

18.10 As often as not, administrators are required to act quickly to prevent the destruction of a company's goodwill and to preserve value. Many important decisions have to be made prior to any creditors' meeting. Hence the development of the pre-pack. At first blush, this would appear to run counter to the very essence of the administration process – to place proposals before a creditors' meeting and then, if they are approved, to implement those proposals. What rights do the creditors have at their meeting to ensure accountability when, as is not uncommon,[9] an administrator sells some or all of the company's business or assets prior to obtaining the approval of the creditors? To answer this question, it is necessary to understand the duties which are imposed on administrators.

18.11 The Enterprise Act 2002 has imposed on administrators new duties, including a duty to:

- perform his functions as quickly and efficiently as is reasonably practicable;[10]

- exercise his powers in the interests of the creditors as a whole;[11]

- perform his functions in accordance with the series of interwoven duties created by para 3(3) and (4) of Sch B1; and

---

[9] See *Re Transbus International Ltd* [2004] 2 All ER 911.
[10] See IA 1986, Sch B1, para 4 – it would appear that this duty is owed to the company such that creditors' and members' individual rights to enforce this duty are granted only in a representative capacity.
[11] IA 1986, Sch B1, para 3(2).

- where applicable, explain why he thinks that the objective mentioned in para 3(1)(a) or (b) cannot be achieved.[12]

18.12 Further, under para 74(1), a creditor may apply to court claiming that the administrator has acted, is acting or proposes to act in a way that has caused or would cause 'unfair harm' to his interests.[13] Paragraph 74(2) empowers a creditor to apply to court claiming that the administrator is not performing his functions as quickly or efficiently as is reasonably practicable. Finally, under para 75, the court has power at the instance of a creditor or others to make an administrator personally liable for breach of duty.

18.13 Creditors need access to information to properly assess whether the administrator has acted in accordance with his duties. In the case of pre-packaged sales, SIP 16 requires administrators to provide creditors with a detailed explanation and justification of why the sale was undertaken.[14] SIP 16 lists the information to be disclosed, which includes:

- the source of the administrator's initial introduction;

- the extent of the administrator's involvement prior to appointment;

- any marketing activities conducted by the company and/or the administrator;

- any valuations obtained of the business or the underlying assets;

- the alternative courses of action that were considered by the administrator, with an explanation of possible financial outcomes;

- why it was not appropriate to trade the business, and offer it for sale as a going concern, during the administration;

- details of requests made to potential funders to fund the working capital requirements, and whether efforts were made to consult with major creditors;

- the date of the transaction, details of the assets involved and the nature of the transaction, and if the sale is part of a wider transaction, a description of the other aspects of the transaction;

- the consideration for the transaction, terms of payment and any condition of the contract that could materially affect the consideration;

- the identity of the purchaser;

---

[12] IA 1986, Sch B1, para 49(2)(b).
[13] For a case discussing para 74(1), see *Re Lehman Brothers International (Europe) (in administration)* [2008] EWHC 2869 (Ch).
[14] SIP 16, para 8. SIP 16 applies with effect from 1 January 2009.

- any connection between the purchaser and the directors, shareholders or secured creditors of the company;

- the names of any directors, or former directors, of the company who are involved in management or ownership of the purchaser, or of any other entity into which any of the assets are transferred;

- whether any directors had given guarantees for amounts due from the company to a prior financier, and whether that financier is financing the new business; and

- any options, buy-back arrangements or similar conditions attached to the contract of sale.[15]

18.14 It is only in exceptional circumstances that the above information may be withheld and, in such circumstances, the reason why the information is not provided should be stated. SIP 16 warns practitioners that in cases where the sale is to a connected party, it is unlikely that considerations of commercial confidentiality would outweigh the need for creditors to be provided with this information.

18.15 Creditors should receive this information with the first notification to creditors, and the administrator is to hold the initial creditors' meeting as soon as possible after his appointment.[16] Where no initial creditors' meeting is to be held and it is impracticable to provide the information in the first notification to creditors, it should be contained in the statement of proposals, which is required to be sent out as soon as practicable after the administrator's appointment.[17]

18.16 It follows that an administrator will dispose of assets or take other substantive steps prior to the initial creditors' meeting at his risk. Whilst it is highly unlikely that the creditors will be able to undo any pre-meeting transaction entered into by the administrator with a third party, the administrator can be personally accountable in respect of his various duties.[18] All in all, these duties provide considerable power to the creditors at their initial meeting. As a last resort, where the administrator was appointed by the company or its directors under Sch B1, para 22, a majority of creditors may simply replace him at the initial or any subsequent creditors' meeting.[19]

---

[15] SIP 16, para 9.
[16] SIP 16, para 11.
[17] SIP 16, para 11. Cf Sch B1, para 49(5), where the obligation is qualified by the word 'reasonably'.
[18] *Clydesdale Financial Services Ltd v Smailes (No 1)* [2009] EWHC 1745 (Ch), [2010] BPIR 62.
[19] IA 1986, Sch B1, para 97(2).

THE PROPOSALS

18.17 The statement containing the proposals must deal with such matters as may be prescribed and, as already mentioned, it must, where applicable, explain why the administrator thinks the objective[20] cannot be achieved.[21] The matters prescribed are contained in r 2.33 and include:

- details of the court where the proceedings are pending and the relevant court reference number;

- the full name, registered address, registered number and any other trading names of the debtor company;

- details relating to the appointment of the administrator, including the date of appointment and the person making the application or appointment and, where there are joint administrators, details of the matters set out in para 100(2);

- the names of the directors and secretary of the debtor company and details of their shareholdings in the debtor company (if any);

- an account of the circumstances giving rise to the appointment of the administrator;

- if a statement of the debtor company's affairs has been submitted, a copy or summary of the statement of affairs with the administrator's comments, if any;

- where no statement of affairs has been provided, the names and addresses of creditors, including details of debts owed and security held as well as up-to-date details of the debtor-company's financial position;

- the basis upon which the administrator is to be remunerated;

- a statement complying with r 2.33(2B) of any pre-administration costs charged or incurred by the administrator or, to the administrator's knowledge, by any other person qualified to act as an insolvency practitioner;

- an estimate of the value of the prescribed part and an estimate of the value of the debtor company's net value (not necessary where a CVA is proposed);

- how the administrator proposes to achieve the purpose of the administration and how it shall come to an end;

---

[20] See IA 1986, Sch B1, para 3(1).
[21] IA 1986, Sch B1, para 49(1) and (2).

- if the administrator decides not to call a meeting, the reason for not doing so;

- how the affairs of the debtor-company have been managed and financed (including details of any assets disposed of, where appropriate) since the administrator took office and how they will continue to be financed in the future; and

- whether the EC Regulation on insolvency proceedings[22] applies and, if so, whether the proceedings are main proceedings or territorial proceedings.

18.18 In addition, the statement should include full details of any connected party transactions undertaken or proposed in the 2 years prior to the making of the administration order and in the period since the making of that order.[23] The statement is sent to:

- the Registrar of Companies;

- every creditor of the debtor company of whose claim and address the administrator is aware of; and

- every member of the debtor company of whose address he is aware.[24]

Pre-administration costs

18.19 Prior to the introduction of r 2.33(2A) and 2.33(2B)[25] in 2010 the ability of an administrator to recover fees and expenses prior to his appointment was limited; thus if he had advised in relation to a pre-pack he could not recover the costs of doing so. The position is now that if an administrator wishes to recover pre-appointment costs he must include in the proposal the information set out in r 2.33(2B) including details of:

- any agreement under which the fees were charged and expenses incurred, including the parties to the agreement and the date on which the agreement was made;

- details of the work done for which the fees were charged and expenses incurred;

- an explanation of why the work was done before the company entered administration and how it would further the para 3 objectives;

- a statement of the amount of the pre-administration costs, setting out separately:

---

[22] Council Regulation 1346/2000/EC.
[23] SIP 13, para 6.5.
[24] IA 1986, Sch B1, para 49(4).
[25] Inserted by the Insolvency (Amendment) Rules 2010, SI 2010/686.

- the fees charged by the administrator;
- the expenses incurred by the administrator;
- the fees charged and expenses incurred by any other insolvency practitioner (to the administrator's knowledge);
- a statement of the amounts of pre-administration costs which have already been paid and the identity and amount of every paying party (if more than one set out separately);
- a statement of the amounts of unpaid pre-administration costs (set out separately as above).

18.20 The statement containing the proposals has to be sent out to the above as soon as reasonably practicable after the debtor company enters administration, and in any event before the expiry of 8 weeks beginning on the date the debtor company went into administration.[26] It is a serious matter if a statement of proposals is not sent within the statutory time frame set out in Sch B1 in that the administrator will have committed an offence unless he can show that there was a reasonable excuse not to comply.[27]

18.21 The current administration procedure is aimed at reducing unnecessary costs and increasing the speed and efficiency of administration, there are occasions when the initial meeting will not have to be called at all. As mentioned above, the initial meeting may be dispensed with if the administrator's statement of proposals states that the administrator thinks:[28]

- that the company has sufficient property to enable each creditor of the company to be paid in full;

- that the company has insufficient property to enable a distribution to be made to unsecured creditors other than by virtue of s 176A(2)(a); or

- that neither of the objectives specified in para 3(1)(a) and (b) can be achieved.

18.22 In other words, where the administrator thinks that there is nothing in it for the unsecured creditors or where it is not possible to achieve for them more than would be obtained in liquidation, then this body of creditors drop out of the picture. However, an administrator will have to summon an initial meeting if it is requested by creditors of the debtor company and those creditors represent at least 10% of the total debts.[29] Such notice must be in the prescribed form and be given within 8 business days from the date on which the administrators proposals are sent out.

---

[26] IA 1986, Sch B1, para 49(5). However, note the requirements of SIP 16 in the case of pre-packaged sales, see discussion at **18.13**.
[27] IA 1986, Sch B1, para 49(7).
[28] IA 1986, Sch B1, para 52(1).
[29] IA 1986, Sch B1, para 52(2).

18.23 An innovative measure introduced by the Enterprise Act 2002 (designed to save time and money) allows the administrator to obtain approval for his proposals by correspondence.[30] The term 'correspondence' is defined in para 111(1) of Sch B1 to include 'correspondence by telephonic or other electronic means'. This will include e-mail, fax and phone. If these methods of 'correspondence' are utilised by the administrator, it will be prudent to ensure that a full record is made in case the outcome or procedure is later challenged. Thus in larger cases (particularly retail administrations involving many thousands of creditors) the full documentation may be made available on a website to which creditors are referred; the courts have approved such an approach in the interests of saving resources, time and costs.

18.24 Where an initial meeting is to be held it must be conducted in accordance with the rules[31] and be held:

- as soon as reasonably practicable after the company enters administration; and

- in any event, within the period of 10 weeks beginning with the date on which the company enters administration.

18.25 It is possible for the administrator to delay the initial meeting of creditors[32] by making an application to the court pursuant to para 107 of Sch B1 to IA 1986 (a general provision allowing a prescribed period to be varied by the court on the application of an administrator) or to extend time on one occasion with the consent of the creditors.[33]

NOTICE

18.26 The notice provisions are divided into those dealing with the initial meeting and those concerning creditors' meetings generally.

18.27 The initial meeting of creditors must be summoned in the prescribed manner and the administrator has to give notice to every creditor of the company whose claim and address he is aware of.[34] The invitation to the creditors' meeting must accompany the proposals.[35] After notice of the meeting has been sent to the creditors an administrator must advertise the meeting in the *London Gazette* including details of the meeting and where and when it is to take place, the purpose of the meeting and a statement setting out a creditor's entitlement to vote.[36] If the administrator thinks it appropriate, he may

---

[30] IA 1986, Sch B1, para 58(3).
[31] IA 1986, Sch B1, para 50(3).
[32] IA 1986, Sch B1, para 51(4).
[33] IA 1986, Sch B1, para 108.
[34] IA 1986, Sch B1, para 50(1).
[35] IA 1986, Sch B1, para 49(4)(c).
[36] Rule 2.34(1) and 2.35(4A) (inserted by the Insolvency (Amendment) Rules 2010, SI 2010/686).

advertise in other newspapers to ensure that notice comes to the attention of all the creditors of the debtor company.[37] The court may order that notice of any meeting is given by advertisement alone and in making such an order will have regard to the assets available and the interests of creditors.[38]

18.28 The administrator must also give notice to the directors or officers of the debtor company whose presence at the meeting is, in the administrator's opinion, required. The notice must be in the prescribed form (Form 2.19B) and has to be sent to them at the same time as the advertisement is placed.[39]

18.29 A copy of any notice or other document required to be sent to a creditor of the debtor company must also be sent to the Financial Services Authority where the company is or has been an authorised person or carried out regulated activities within the meaning of the Financial Services and Markets Act 2000.[40] This can be checked on the FSA Register available on its website.[41]

18.30 The Insolvency Rules 1986[42] ('the Rules') provide that notice of all creditors' meetings shall be in Form 2.20B[43] (all creditors' meetings include the initial meeting, where the creditors request a meeting, revision of proposals meeting, further creditors' meetings and whenever the administrator needs to summon a meeting).

18.31 Unless the court otherwise directs, the meeting of creditors has to be held between 10 am and 4 pm on a business day.[44] The administrator has to give at least 14 days' notice to the creditors that are known to the administrator and who had claims against the debtor company at the date the debtor company entered administration (unless that creditor has subsequently been paid in full).[45] As well as giving the requisite notice, the administrator has to have regard to the convenience of the creditors when deciding when to hold the meeting.[46] The notice sent to creditors has to contain the following details and items:

- the reason for the meeting;

- a statement of the effect of r 2.38 (entitlement to vote); and

- forms of proxy.

---

[37] Rule 2.34(1A).
[38] Rule 2.37A.
[39] Rule 2.34(2).
[40] Section 362(3).
[41] www.fsa.gov.uk/fsaregister.
[42] SI 1986/1925.
[43] Rule 2.35(2).
[44] Rule 2.35(3).
[45] Rule 2.35(4).
[46] Rule 2.35(3).

18.32 If the administrator thinks it appropriate to conduct the meeting by correspondence, he must send a notice in Form 2.25B to every creditor who is entitled to be notified of a creditors' meeting under r 2.35(4) (that is those known to the administrator who had claims against the debtor company at the date the debtor company entered administration).[47]

CHAIRMAN[48]

18.33 The chairman at a creditors' meeting summoned by the administrator has to be either the administrator or a person nominated in writing by the administrator.[49] A nominated person can only be either:

- a person who is qualified to act as an insolvency practitioner in relation to the debtor company; or

- an employee of the administrator or his firm, who is someone who has experience in insolvency matters.[50]

18.34 The chairman has considerable power with respect to the proceedings. In particular, with respect to creditors' meetings in an administration, the chairman may admit or reject the whole or part of a creditor's claim to vote (r 2.39(1)). If, however, the chairman is in any doubt about whether a creditor has a right to vote or not, then the chairman ought to mark the claim as objected to but nevertheless allow the creditor in question to vote (r 2.39(3)). Any challenge in court to the chairman's exercise of these powers must be made within 14 days from the delivery by the administrator of the report on the outcome of the meeting to the court, which is required under para 53(2) of Sch B1 to IA 1986. The chairman may also allow[51] a creditor to vote even though he fails to comply with the Rules by failing to provide details of the debt claimed in advance of the meeting.[52] However, for the discretion to be exercised the creditor has to show that failure to comply with the Rules was beyond his control. Further, the chairman has a discretion to allow a creditor to vote even if the debt is for an unliquidated amount or is unascertained. The chairman in these circumstances puts an estimated minimum value on the debt for the purpose of the creditor's entitlement to vote.[53]

18.35 The Rules provide that the chairman of the meeting is under a duty to see that minutes of the meeting are kept (r 2.44A(1)) and retained by the chairman as passed to the records of the administration (r 2.44A(2)). The

---

[47] Rule 2.48.
[48] For a review of the case-law relating to the powers and duties of a chairman of a meeting, see *Link Agricultural Pty Ltd v Shanahan* (1988) 28 ACSR 498; and *Re Chevron Furnishers Pty Ltd* (1992) 8 ACSR 726.
[49] Rule 2.36(1).
[50] Rule 2.36(2)(a) and (b).
[51] The discretion is provided by r 2.38(2).
[52] Rule 2.38(1)(a).
[53] Rule 2.38(5).

minutes must include a list of the names and addresses of creditors who attended (either in person or by proxy), if a creditors' committee had been established the names and addresses of those elected to be members of the committee (r 2.44A(4)) and a record of every resolution passed.

ADJOURNMENT

18.36 The Rules lay down three circumstances in which the meeting may be adjourned.

- First, the chairman may, at the meeting convened to consider the administrator's proposals, exercise his discretion to, and if a resolution is passed to that effect shall, adjourn the meeting if there is not the requisite majority approving the administrator's proposals (the requisite majority is discussed at **18.41**). The meeting cannot be adjourned for more than 14 days on this ground (r 2.34(4)). The same applies to any other meeting of creditors (r.2.35(6C)–(6D)).

- Secondly, if within 30 minutes of the time fixed for the meeting there is no quorum the meeting may be adjourned to such a time and place as the chairman may fix.

- Thirdly, if there is no chairman within 30 minutes of the time set down for the commencement of the meeting, then the meeting is adjourned to the same time and place the following week. If the new time falls on a day which is not a business day (because, for example, it is a Bank Holiday), then the meeting is adjourned to the business day immediately following (r 2.35(5)).

VOTING

18.37 As has been noted above, the chairman has limited powers to allow a creditor to vote even if that creditor has failed to comply with the Rules, and wider powers to reject the whole or part of a creditor's claim to vote. Generally, however, those who are entitled to vote are:[54]

- those who have provided details in writing of the debt claimed;

- those whose claim has been admitted; and

- those who have lodged a proxy with the administrator.

18.38 Creditors have to give notice to the administrator no later than 12 noon on the business day before the day fixed for the meeting. The details that are required to be furnished include:

---

[54] Rule 2.38(1)(a)–(c).

- details of the claims due to him from the debtor company;

- details of sums claimed on behalf of creditors by a Member State of the EU liquidator in proceedings (in relation to the office he holds); or

- where the creditor is secured, holds a negotiable instrument or claims pursuant to a hire purchase agreement, conditional sale or chattel lease agreement details of the debt should be provided in accordance with rr 2.40–2.42.

18.39 As regards Member State liquidator claims,[55] the liquidator of a debtor company is authorised to prove in secondary proceedings in England and Wales where main and secondary proceedings have been opened in other member states if the liquidator has lodged claims in his own proceedings: see the EC Regulation, Art 32(2) and (3). The EC Regulation provides that the liquidator may represent his own creditors by attending creditors' meetings. The wording of Art 32(3) suggests that the power vested in the liquidator to attend a creditors' meeting only exists when he has lodged the creditors' claims, although this limitation is contrary to the central principle of co-operation and communication between Member States.

18.40 The votes are calculated according to the amount of the creditor's claim as at the date on which the debtor company entered administration (r 2.38(4)). Rules 2.40–2.42 deal with the entitlement to vote of secured creditors; holders of negotiable instruments; retention of title creditors; and hire purchase, conditional sale and chattel leasing agreements. In very general terms, they require creditors holding these types of interests to make an allowance in respect of the security which they hold. This allowance is deducted from the creditor's debt for the purpose of calculation of the creditor's vote.

18.41 The majority required is a simple one based on the value of those present and voting in person or by proxy (r 2.43(1)), but a resolution will not be valid where more than one-half in value of the creditors vote against it, provided that those creditors making up the half against the resolution are not, to the chairman's knowledge, persons connected with the company (r 2.43(2)). The application of these rules may require a relatively time-consuming calculation, especially since creditors might be entitled to split their vote on the basis of value.[56]

18.42 In addition, a person appointed by the Financial Services Authority shall be entitled to attend any meeting of creditors and to make representations as to any matter requiring a decision.[57]

18.43 Where the administrator chooses to use correspondence rather than summon a meeting, the Rules provide that the votes must be received before 12

---

[55] Introduced by SI 2002/1307.
[56] See, for example, *Re Polly Peck International Plc* [1991] BCC 503.
[57] Financial Services and Markets Act 2000, s 362(5).

noon on the business day before the closing date, which will be specified on Form 2.25B, but in any event shall not be less than 14 days from the date the Form 2.25B was issued.[58] The vote must be accompanied by a statement in writing of the entitlement to vote as required by r 2.38 (setting out details of the debt claimed). Failure to provide such a statement will result in the vote being disallowed.[59]

18.44 To have a valid meeting the administrator must have received at least one valid Form 2.25B by the specified closing date. In the absence of one valid return the administrator must summon a meeting of creditors in accordance with r 2.35.[60] On receipt of the Form 2.25B the creditors may decide that they would rather a meeting be summoned. They can require the administrator to summon a meeting if any single creditor or number of creditors can demonstrate that they hold at least 10% of the total debts owed by the debtor company and respond to the administrator within 5 business days from the date the resolution or proposals were sent out.[61] If the creditors reject the proposals by voting through the correspondence method, the administrator may call a meeting.[62]

ADMINISTRATOR'S REPORT

18.45 After the conclusion of the initial creditors' meeting to which the administrator's proposals are presented, the administrator must, as soon as reasonably practicable, produce a report.[63] The report is in the form of a prescribed notice (Form 2.23B) and should include the result of the meeting and details of any modifications that were approved. The administrator must send the report to:[64]

- the court;

- the Registrar of Companies;

- every creditor who received notice of the meeting and any other person who received a copy of the original proposals; and

- any creditor who did not receive notice of the meeting, but of whose claim the administrator became aware after the closing date.

Paragraph 53(2) of Sch B1 to IA 1986 and rule 2.46 list the persons to whom the administrator must send a report. The list includes 'such other persons as

---

[58] Rule 2.48(2)–(4).
[59] Rule 2.48(3).
[60] Rule 2.48(6).
[61] Rule 2.48(7).
[62] Rule 2.48(8).
[63] IA 1986, Sch B1, para 53(2).
[64] IA 1986, Sch B1, and rule 2.46.

may be prescribed'. It will be important for an administrator to ensure that those persons prescribed are sent the report as para 53(3) of the Schedule makes it an offence not to do so without reasonable excuse. The Rules do not specify that an administrator should report to the Financial Services Authority after the initial meeting, but a broader obligation rests with the administrator to send a report to the Financial Services Authority 'without delay' if it appears that the debtor company or partnership has carried on a regulated activity in contravention of the general prohibition.[65]

POST-MEETING REVISION OF PROPOSALS

18.46 It is possible that the administrator may wish to revise the proposals that have been approved by the creditors at the initial meeting (or by correspondence). Insubstantial revisions may be made without reference to the same creditors that approved the proposals. There is an ability to revise the terms of the proposal where the changes are substantial; however, the administrator has to call a creditors' meeting in order to approve the revision.[66] The administrator will have to send to the creditors and to all those to whom he is required a statement setting out the proposed revisions to the proposals and attach a prescribed form (Form 2.22B). The statement of revised proposals has to include the matters contained in r 2.45(2). In addition, the statement of revised proposals should be sent to the members of the debtor company within 5 days of sending the same to the creditors.[67] The administrator should also publish a notice of the meeting in a newspaper[68] as soon as reasonably practical. Like the initial meeting, the meeting to deal with the revised proposals may be held through correspondence.[69]

CREDITORS' COMMITTEE

18.47 IA 1986, Sch B1, para 57 provides that the creditors' meeting may establish a creditors' committee in order that it may carry out the functions conferred on it by or under IA 1986 and assist the administrator in carrying out his functions. Once established, the administrator must call a creditors' committee meeting within 6 weeks.[70]

---

[65] Financial Services and Markets Act 2000, s 261.
[66] Jurisdiction for this is provided by IA 1986, Sch B1, para 54.
[67] Rule 2.45(3).
[68] Rule 2.45(4).
[69] Rule 2.48(8).
[70] Rule 2.52(3).

Chapter 19

ADMINISTRATIVE RECEIVERSHIP

19.1 For the most part, administrative receivership has been abolished by the Enterprise Act 2002 in respect of debentures created on or after 15 September 2003. This procedure was widely regarded as giving too much power to secured creditors, who lacked sufficient incentive to rescue companies. Nevertheless, for many years there will remain in circulation pre-Act debentures entitling their holders to appoint an administrative receiver. Further, by the Insolvency Act 1986 (IA 1986), ss 72B–72H there is a comprehensive list of specific exceptions to the general prohibition – making the appointment of an administrative receiver permissible even in respect of post-Enterprise Act 2002 debentures. The abolition has meant that there has been little jurisprudential development in respect of meetings since the last edition.

19.2 The meeting of creditors in an administrative receivership is more concerned with the communication of information to unsecured creditors than anything else. In particular, unsecured creditors are not in the driving seat as their approval is not required by the administrative receiver.

CREDITORS' MEETING

19.3 The administrative receiver has to submit a detailed report to certain parties and call a meeting, the details of which are set out below. However IA 1986, s 48(7) makes clear that those requirements do not apply in relation to the appointment of an administrative receiver to act with an existing administrative receiver, or in place of an administrative receiver who dies or ceases to act.

19.4 The substantive requirements are governed by s 48 of IA 1986. This provides that within 3 months of his appointment, an administrative receiver must send a report to the Registrar of Companies, and to any trustees for secured creditors and (so far as he is aware of their addresses) to all the secured creditors. The court may allow an extended period. If the debtor company is or has been an authorised person, is or has been an appointed representative or is carrying on, or has carried on, a regulated activity within the meaning of the Financial Services and Markets Act 2000, the administrative receiver must send a report to the Financial Services Authority[1] in addition to the secured creditors. Copy reports should be sent to unsecured creditors if their addresses are known within the 3-month period. If addresses are not known, IA 1986,

---

[1] Financial Services and Markets Act 2000, s 363(4).

s 48(2) provides for a practical alternative: publishing a notice stating an address which unsecured creditors may contact to obtain a copy of the report. If the debtor company has gone into liquidation or subsequently goes into liquidation the administrative receiver must send a copy of the report to the liquidator.[2]

19.5 Having sent (or published notice of) a report, the administrative receiver is then required, unless the court directs otherwise, to lay a copy of the report before a meeting of the unsecured creditors of the debtor company.[3] The court cannot give a direction to dispense with the meeting unless the administrative receiver's report expressly states that he intends to apply for such a direction and a copy of the report is sent to all the unsecured creditors (whose addresses are known) or a notice is published not less than 14 days prior to the hearing[4] for directions. The meeting of unsecured creditors may also be dispensed with, without the need for a direction from the court, if the debtor company has gone into liquidation and the administrative receiver has complied with the requirements of IA 1986, s 48(4).

19.6 As stated above, the report itself is detailed. It must include the following matters:[5]

- the events leading up to the appointment of the administrative receiver (so far as he is aware of them);

- the disposal or proposed disposal by him of any property of the company and the carrying on or proposed carrying on by him of any business of the company;

- the amounts of principal and interest payable to the debenture holders by whom or on whose behalf he was appointed and the amounts payable to preferential creditors;

- the amount (if any) likely to be available for the payment of other creditors;

- a summary statement of affairs; and

- full details regarding any connected party transactions made prior to the meeting.[6]

---

[2] IA 1986, s 48(4).
[3] IA 1986, s 48(2).
[4] IA 1986, s 48(3).
[5] This list is compiled from the requirements set out in s 48(1), (5) and SIP 13, para 6.5.
[6] IA 1986, s 48(2).

NOTICE

19.7 Notice of the meeting to consider the report is regulated by r 3.9 of the Insolvency Rules 1986[7] ('the Rules'). This rule sets out the following matters in respect of notice:

- when fixing the date of the meeting, the administrative receiver shall have regard to the convenience of the persons who are invited to attend;

- for added convenience the meeting shall be summoned to start between 10 am and 4 pm on a business day, unless the court directs otherwise;

- the administrative receiver must give at least 14 days' notice of the meeting giving the time, date and venue to all the creditors identified in the statement of affairs or who are otherwise known to the administrative receiver and had claims against the debtor company at the date he took the appointment; and

- every notice sent summoning the meeting must contain a form of proxy.

19.8 The notice, which must state the venue of the meeting, must be gazetted and may also be advertised in such manner as the administrative receiver sees fit.[8] The newspaper advertisement and the notice itself must include a statement to the effect that the creditors whose claims are wholly secured are not entitled to attend or be represented at the meeting[9] (reflecting the intention that the meeting is for unsecured creditors) and a statement of the effect of the voting rights as contained in r 3.11(1).[10]

THE RIGHT TO PARTICIPATE IN THE VOTING AT A CREDITORS' MEETING

19.9 The right to vote at a creditors' meeting where the debtor company is in administrative receivership is regulated by r 3.11 and r 3.11A. As already noted, the meeting is a meeting of unsecured creditors. This means that secured creditors may only vote in respect of the balance of the debt due after deducting the value of the security held.[11] So far as creditors whose debt is secured by a bill of exchange or a promissory note are concerned, they may only vote if they are willing to treat the liability of every person liable antecedently to the company as security, or if they are prepared to estimate the value of the security and deduct it from their claim against the company for the purpose of calculating voting rights.[12] There are special rules relating to those

---

[7] SI 1986/1925.
[8] Rule 3.9(6).
[9] Rule 3.9(5) and (6A).
[10] Rule 3.9(7).
[11] Rule 3.11(6).
[12] Rule 3.11(7).

creditors who have unliquidated claims. Such a creditor may not vote in respect of a debt for an unliquidated amount or any debt whose value is not ascertained, except where the chairman agrees to put upon the debt an estimated minimum value for the purpose of entitlement to vote and admits the claim for that purpose.[13]

19.10 No creditor qualified to vote may vote at the meeting unless they have given the administrative receiver details of the debt claimed to be due by 12 noon on the business day before the meeting and the claim has been admitted under r 3.11 (r 3.11(1)(a)). The following matters must be stated in a creditor's claim (r 3.11A):

(a) the creditor's name and address, and, if a company, its company registration number;

(b) the total amount of the claim (including any value added tax) as at the date of the appointment of the receiver, less all trade and other discounts available to the company, or which would have been available to the company but for the appointment, except for any discount for immediate, early or cash settlement;

(c) whether or not that amount includes outstanding uncapitalised interest;

(d) particulars of how and when the debt was incurred by the company;

(e) particulars of any security held, the date when it was given and the value which the creditor puts upon it;

(f) details of any reservation of title in respect of goods to which the debt refers;

(g) the name, address and authority of the person making out the claim (if other than the creditor himself); and

(h) any documents by reference to which the debt can be substantiated, but it is not essential that such documents be attached to the claim or submitted with it.

Where a creditor wishes to vote by proxy, the proxy must be lodged with the administrative receiver.[14]

---

[13] Rule 3.11(5).
[14] Rule 3.11(1)(b).

THE CHAIRMAN

19.11 The chairman at the meeting is the administrative receiver or a person nominated by the administrative receiver.[15] The administrative receiver may only nominate another person to be the chairman if that person is a qualified insolvency practitioner in relation to the company, or an employee of the receiver or the receiver's firm who is experienced in insolvency matters.[16]

19.12 As with the other insolvency procedures, the Rules confer on the chairman a number of specific powers in addition to the chairman's usual powers to regulate the meeting. Most of the additional powers relate to qualification for voting. The chairman has, for instance, discretion to allow a creditor who has failed to submit details in writing of the debt due from the company before 12 noon on the business day preceding the meeting to vote notwithstanding this omission if satisfied that the failure was due to 'circumstances beyond his control'.[17] The chairman may also call for the production of documents or evidence to support a creditor's claim.[18] The chairman may, whether he has called for the production of documents or other evidence or not, reject the whole or part of a creditor's entitlement to vote;[19] or, if unsure about the admissibility of a claim to be entitled to vote, mark it as objected to but allow it to proceed in the first instance.[20] The chairman's decision on entitlement to vote is subject to an appeal by any creditor to the court,[21] and if the chairman's decision is varied on appeal the court may summon another meeting or make any such order as it considers just[22] (see also r 3.12(5) which provides a general rule that the chairman shall not be liable for the costs of the appeal but the court may direct otherwise). Finally, the chairman is charged with the duty of ensuring that a record of the proceedings is made.[23] The record must show the names of the creditors attending in person or by proxy and, if a committee of creditors is appointed, the names and addresses of its members.[24]

ADJOURNMENT

19.13 Generally the creditors' meeting cannot be adjourned. This is the case even if the meeting is not quorate. The Rules provide that if there is no quorum and the meeting goes ahead it will be deemed to be duly summoned and held. If, however, the chairman thinks it desirable to adjourn the meeting, he may do

---

[15] Rule 3.10(1).
[16] Rule 3.10(2).
[17] Rule 3.11(2).
[18] Rule 3.11(3).
[19] Rule 3.12(1).
[20] Rule 3.12(3).
[21] Rule 3.12(2).
[22] Rule 3.12(4).
[23] Rule 3.15(2).
[24] Rule 3.15(3).

so to such date, time and place as he thinks fit.[25] As regards what constitutes a quorum, r 12.4A(2) provides that in the case of creditors' meetings at least one creditor entitled to vote is required to form a quorum.

VOTING

19.14 Resolutions at a creditors' meeting will be carried if a simple majority (of either those present or those who have voted by way of proxy) vote in favour.[26] As with other types of insolvency procedures, voting at the creditors' meeting is by reference to the value of the unsecured amount owing to the creditor after deducting any amounts paid in respect of that debt after the date the administrative receiver was appointed.[27] Since the size of the debt is relevant to making the calculation on voting power, a vote may not be cast in respect of an unliquidated or unascertained debt, unless the chairman agrees to an estimated minimum value for the purpose of calculating the voting power of a creditor holding such a debt.[28] The power to estimate a minimum value is also subject to appeal to the court under r 3.12(2).

CREDITORS' COMMITTEE

19.15 The creditors' meeting in an administrative receivership may establish a creditors' committee to assist the administrative receiver in the discharge of his functions.[29] The proceedings at the meetings of such a committee are governed by rr 3.18–3.30A.

---

[25] Rule 3.14(1).
[26] Rule 3.15(1).
[27] Rule 3.11(4).
[28] Rule 3.11(5).
[29] IA 1986, s 49 and r 3.18(1).

Chapter 20

CREDITORS' VOLUNTARY WINDING UP

MEETINGS TO BE HELD

20.1 A voluntary winding up is a creditors' voluntary winding up[1] where the company is insolvent in that the directors have not made a declaration of solvency in accordance with the Insolvency Act 1986 (IA 1986), s 89 (IA 1986, s 90). There is also provision for a members' voluntary winding up to be converted to a creditors' voluntary winding up (IA 1986, s 96). It is also a collective insolvency proceeding within the scope of the EC Regulation. The general idea of a creditors' voluntary winding up is to give as much control of the process as possible to the creditors. For example, they choose the liquidator and if there is a conflict between the insolvency practitioner nominated by the company and the person nominated by the creditors it is the creditors' choice of liquidator which takes precedence (IA 1986, s 100).

20.2 The first meeting to be held in a creditors' voluntary winding up is the meeting of the members at which a resolution is passed to voluntarily wind up the company. In a creditors' voluntary winding up, once the initial resolution has been passed by the company, the next meeting required is of the creditors (IA 1986, s 98), at which the directors must lay a statement of affairs before the creditors in accordance with IA 1986, s 99. This first meeting of creditors may also appoint a liquidator (IA 1986, s 100; see s 100(3) with respect to the situation where the creditors' and the members' meetings nominate different liquidators) and a liquidation committee (IA 1986, s 101). The business of the first meeting of creditors is restricted to the matters set out in the Insolvency Rules 1986[2] (the Rules): see r 4.53. IA 1986 provides for the position where a vacancy in the post of liquidator arises due to death, resignation or otherwise by permitting (unless the liquidator was appointed by the court or at the direction of the court) a creditors' meeting to be called to fill the vacancy (IA 1986, s 104). If the winding up has been converted from a members' voluntary winding up to a creditors' voluntary winding up, then the first creditors' meeting does not need to be held as its function will already have been satisfied by the creditors' meeting held in accordance with IA 1986, s 95, which is necessary for the conversion to a creditors' voluntary winding up (IA 1986, s 96). The other meetings which must be held in a creditors' voluntary winding up are the final creditors' and members' meetings prior to dissolution. The

---

[1] Specific guidance to insolvency practitioners on summoning and holding meetings of creditors convened pursuant to s 98 of IA 1986 can be found in SIP 8, which provides a thorough overview of the conduct of such meetings.
[2] SI 1986/1925.

requirement to hold annual meetings was replaced by imposing a duty on a liquidator to report annually to the creditors on the progress of the liquidation (IA 1986, s 104A).[3]

20.3 The liquidator may also, at any time, summon a meeting of creditors and contributories in order to ascertain their wishes (see r 4.54). Similarly, creditors may requisition meetings (see r 4.57). The procedure for the holding of all the members' meetings in a creditors' voluntary winding up is the same as that discussed at **22.2ff** in relation to a members' voluntary winding up. The creditors' meetings are, however, subject to special provisions in both IA 1986 and the Rules. SIP 12 provides guidance and recommends that the responsible insolvency practitioner should always create a record of the meeting and that the record should be prepared in accordance with the provisions set out in SIP 12.

THE SECTION 98 MEETING

20.4 The first meeting of creditors under IA 1986, s 98 must be summoned by the company within 14 days from the day upon which the resolution for winding up is to be proposed (IA 1986, s 98(1A)(a)). Unless the court makes an order under r 4.59 that the notice of the meeting is to be given by public advertisement rather than individually, the notice must be sent to the creditors at least 7 days before the day on which the meeting is to be held (IA 1986, s 98(1A)(b)) and the notice must be advertised in the *Gazette* (IA 1986, s 98(1A)(c)) and notice of the meeting may be advertised in such other manner as the directors think fit (IA 1986, s 98(1A)(d)) (and IA 1986, s 98(3) and (4) which apply where the company has more than one principal place of business or the principal place of business is not in the UK). It is incumbent upon the management of the debtor company to appoint one of the directors to attend the meeting and preside over it: IA 1986, s 99(1). Where the Financial Services Authority has an interest, an appointed person is entitled to attend any creditors' meeting.[4]

20.5 The notice to creditors must specify the time and place of the meeting and the place where proxies are to be lodged (r 4.51(2)). The first meeting of creditors must be held between 10 am and 4 pm on a business day (r 4.60(2)). The venue must be fixed with regard to the convenience of the creditors (r 4.60(1)). The notice must specify the name and address of a person qualified to act as an insolvency practitioner in relation to the company who, during the period before the day on which that meeting is to be held, will furnish creditors free of charge with such information concerning the company's affairs as they may reasonably require (IA 1986, s 98(2)(a))[5] or an address at which, during the 2 business days preceding the date of the meeting, a list of the names and

---

[3] Inserted by the Legislative Reform (Insolvency) (Miscellaneous) Order, SI 2010/18.
[4] Financial Services and Markets Act 2000, s 371(4)(a) and r 4.72.
[5] This will normally include information included in the statement of affairs and the list of creditors, when available.

addresses of the company creditors will be available free of charge (IA 1986, s 98(2)(b)). The notice must be accompanied by a proxy form (r 4.60(3)).

20.6 A summary or a copy of the directors' sworn statement of affairs should be handed to all those attending the meeting, including a list of the names of the major creditors and the amounts owing to them. Guidance as to the information to be given to the meeting is set out in SIP 8 (para 35) which should include:

- details of any prior involvement of the insolvency practitioner with the company or its directors;

- a detailed report of the previously held shareholders' meeting;

- details of the costs paid or payable by the company for the statement of affairs and the convening of the meeting and any insolvency advice received;

- a detailed account of the company's relevant trading history;

- an explanation as to the contents of the statement of affairs; and

- details of transactions with connected persons during the period of one year prior to the resolution of the directors that the company should be wound up.[6]

SUBSEQUENT MEETINGS: NOTICE

20.7 The Official Receiver or the liquidator may at any time summon and conduct meetings of creditors for the purpose of ascertaining their wishes (r 4.54(1)). They must give at least 14 days' notice specifying the purpose of the meeting (r 4.54(3)) to all creditors known to the liquidator (r 4.54(2)(a)) although the court may order the notice of meetings to be by public advertisement only (r 4.59). The place of the meeting must be fixed having regard to the convenience of the creditors (r 4.60(1)) and it must be held between 10 am and 4 pm on a business day (r 4.60(2)). In addition to stating these matters, the notice must state that proofs and (if applicable) proxies must be lodged at a specified place not later than midday on the business day before the date fixed for the meeting in order for creditors to be entitled to vote at the meeting (r 4.54(5)). A proxy form must accompany the notice (r 4.60(3)). No proxy form shall be pre-completed by the insertion in it of the name or description of any person (ie for appointment as an insolvency office holder or

---

[6] This is recognised as such an important area of potential concern to creditors attending the meeting that it is subject to separate practice guidance (SIP 13) entitled 'Acquisition of assets of insolvent companies by directors' (see in particular paras 4.2 and 5, which deal with recommended advice and disclosure which the insolvency practitioner should give to the directors and creditors respectively).

for appointment as a member of a committee or as proxy holder) (r 8.2). Rules 8.1–8.7 deal generally with representation of a creditor by proxy. There is a requirement for proxies to be signed by the principal or by a person authorised by him, in which case the nature of the authority must be stated. Proxies which are unsigned, or which do not explain the authority under which they are signed, will be invalid.

20.8 At least 28 days' notice of the final meeting before dissolution must be given to all creditors who have proved their debts (r 4.126(1)). An advertisement stating the time, place and object of the meeting must also be published in the *Gazette* at least one month before the meeting (IA 1986, s 106(2)) (see below). .

CREDITORS' MEETINGS: CHAIRMAN

20.9 Except at the first meetings of creditors, at which the director will preside, where IA 1986, s 99(1) applies as set out above, the chairman at meetings of creditors in a creditors' voluntary winding up should be the liquidator or a person nominated by the liquidator (r 4.56). A person nominated by the liquidator must be a qualified insolvency practitioner in relation to the company, or an employee of the liquidator or the liquidator's firm with experience in insolvency matters (r 4.56(2)).

20.10 If the directors (or one of them where one has been nominated) of the debtor company fail to attend and preside at the first creditors' meeting they will be guilty of an offence and liable to a fine (IA 1986, s 99(3)).[7] In those circumstances the meeting may still progress by those attending appointing their own nominee as chairman.[8]

20.11 The Rules confer specific powers and duties on the chairman of a creditors' meeting. The chairman has a discretion in relation to adjourning the meeting, which is discussed below; a discretion in relation to admitting the votes of creditors who have failed to satisfy the rules on lodging proofs where the chairman believes that the failure was beyond the creditor's control (r 4.68); and a discretion to admit or reject any creditors' proof with respect to entitlement to vote (r 4.70(1)) or to mark a proof as objected to (when he is in doubt) in the usual way (r 4.70(3)). The chairman's decisions on entitlement to vote may be appealed to the court by any creditor or contributory (r 4.70(2)). On such an appeal, the court is not limited to consideration of the evidence which was before the chairman, but may come to a conclusion on all the evidence subsequently filed at court whether on balance a creditor's proof should be admitted in whole or in part for voting purposes.[9]

---

[7] For a review of the case-law relating to the powers and duties of a chairman of a meeting, see *Link Agricultural Pty Ltd v Shanahan* (1998) 28 ACSR 498. See also *Re Chevron Furnishers Pty Ltd* (1992) 8 ACSR 726.
[8] *Re Salcombe Hotel Development Corporation Ltd* [1991] BCLC 44.
[9] *Re A Company (No 004539 of 1993)* [1995] BCC 116, at 120F–120G.

20.12 Where the chairman holds a proxy instructing the chairman to vote for a particular resolution and that resolution is not proposed by anyone else, then the chairman is required to propose it, unless there is a good reason, in the chairman's view, for not doing so (r 4.64(a)). If the chairman does not propose a resolution in these circumstances, he must notify the appointor of the proxy of the reason for this immediately after the meeting (r 4.64(b)).

20.13 The other specific duties imposed on the chairman are keeping minutes as part of the record of the liquidation (r 4.71(1)) and keeping a list of all creditors attending the meeting (r 4.71(2)). This list should be made available for inspection to anyone attending the meeting.

20.14 Nominations for the appointment of a liquidator should be requested before any vote is taken. The holder of a proxy requiring him to vote for a particular liquidator is required to nominate that person, and it is therefore possible that the chairman or any other holder of such proxies may need to make more than one nomination.[10] It is acceptable in the first instance for a vote to be taken on an informal show of hands and, if the result is accepted by all interested parties, the chairman may conclude that a resolution has been passed. If a formal vote becomes necessary, it should be conducted by stating the names of all those nominated and by the issue of voting papers on which those wishing to vote will be required to show their name, the name of the creditor they are representing, the amount of the creditor's claim and the name of the nominated person for whom they wish to vote. When all votes have been counted, the chairman should announce the result to the meeting, giving details of the total value of votes cast in favour of each nomination. He should also give details of votes which have been rejected, either in whole or in part, and should also state which nomination those creditors supported and the reasons for the rejection. An absolute majority is required and if the first poll is not conclusive, the nominee receiving the least votes will be excluded from the next (and each successive) poll where no other nominee has withdrawn. The meeting should be told of its right to appoint a liquidation committee and of the nature of the committee's functions, including its rights in relation to the liquidator's remuneration.[11]

CREDITORS' MEETING: ADJOURNMENT AND SUSPENSION

20.15 The chairman of a creditors' meeting has power, not only to adjourn the meeting at his discretion (r 4.65(3) and (4)), but also, during the course of the meeting, to suspend it once for up to one hour (r 4.65(2)). The chairman must adjourn the meeting if the meeting so resolves (r 4.65(3)). The adjourned meeting will be held at such time or place as the chairman determines (r 4.65(3) and (4)). However, this discretion is qualified to the extent that the

---

[10] SIP 8, para 42.
[11] SIP 8, paras 44–48. As to the appointment of a creditors' committee, see ibid, para 48.

adjournment may not be for more than 14 days and the usual rules (r 4.60(1) and (2)) as to fixing the time and place of meetings apply (r 4.65(5)). The meeting stands adjourned where there is no person present to act as chairman present (r 4.65(6A)). In this case, the adjournment will be to the same time and place in the following week, unless that falls on a day which is not a business day, in which case the meeting will be adjourned to the next business day following that day (r 4.65(6A)). Where the meeting has been adjourned, proofs and proxies may be lodged any time before midday on the business day before the adjourned meeting (r 4.65(7)).

20.16 Finally, it should be noted that a special provision is made with respect to the circumstances where the meeting of the company at which the resolution to wind up is to be proposed under IA 1986, s 84 is adjourned and the first meeting of creditors takes place before it. Where this happens, any resolution passed at the first meeting of creditors will not take effect until the company passes a resolution to wind up (r 4.53A).

CREDITORS' MEETING: VOTING

20.17 A person is only entitled to vote at a creditors' meeting in a creditors' voluntary winding up if he has lodged a proof of debt and the claim to vote has been admitted by the chairman under r 4.70(1) (r 4.67(1)(a)). If a creditor wishes to vote by proxy he must also lodge the proxy as required in the notice for the meeting (r 4.67(1)(b)). The chairman's power to allow a creditor to vote without proving their debt (r 4.68) has been noted above. The court also has the power in exceptional circumstances to allow creditors, or a class of creditors, to vote without proving their debts (r 4.67(2)).

20.18 As in other types of creditors' meetings considered in this Part, voting power is calculated by reference to the value of the debt owed (r 4.63(1)). Similarly, for the purpose of calculating voting rights, deductions must be made in respect of any type of security (r 4.67(4) and (5)(b)) or the holders of bills of exchange and promissory notes must treat the liability of those antecedent to the company as security (r 4.67(5)(a)), and an estimated minimum amount must be placed upon unliquidated or unascertained debts (r 4.67(3)).

20.19 The required majority is a simple majority in value of those voting (r 4.63(1)), although on any resolution affecting the office of liquidator the vote of the liquidator or any partner or employee of the liquidator cannot be counted as part of the majority (r 4.63(4)).

RESOLUTIONS BY CORRESPONDENCE

20.20 The rules were changed with effect from 6 April 2010 to enable a liquidator to seek the passing of creditors and contributories resolutions by correspondence(r 4.63A).[12] The Rules now provide that a liquidator may seek to obtain the passing of such a resolution without holding a meeting by giving notice of the resolution to every creditor or contributory who is entitled to be notified of a meeting at which the resolution could be passed.

20.21 In order to be counted, votes must be received by the liquidator in writing by midday on the closing date specified in the notice, and in the case of votes cast by creditors must be accompanied by a proof of debt as required by r 4.67(1)(a) unless it has already been lodged under that rule.

20.22 If any vote cast by a creditor is received without a proof of debt, or the liquidator decides that the creditor or contributory is not entitled to vote according to rr 4.67 to 4.70, then that creditor's or contributory's vote must be disregarded.

20.23 The closing date is set at the discretion of the liquidator; but in any event it must not be less than 14 days from the giving of notice.

20.24 For the resolution to be passed, the liquidator must receive at least one valid vote by the closing date specified in the notice. If no valid vote is received by the closing date specified, the liquidator must call a meeting of creditors or contributories at which the resolution could be passed.

20.25 Creditors whose debts amount to at least 10% of the total debts of the company may, within 5 business days from the giving of notice, require the liquidator to summon a meeting of creditors to consider the resolution. Similarly, contributories representing at least 10% of the total voting rights of all contributories having the right to vote at a meeting of contributories may, within 5 business days from the giving of notice, require the liquidator to summon a meeting of contributories to consider the resolution.

FINAL MEETING

20.26 The rules in relation to final meetings have been substantially changed by the Insolvency (Amendment) Rules 2010, SI 2010/686 with effect from 6 April 2010, largely to ensure that creditors are provided with sufficient information in respect of a liquidator's fees and remuneration.

20.27 At least 8 weeks before the holding of the final meeting of creditors the liquidator must send to each creditor known to him a draft of the report which the liquidator intends to place before the final meeting of creditors (r 4.49D(1)), except where the liquidator is the Official Receiver (r 4.49D(5)). Any secured creditor, 5% in value of creditors or 5% of the total voting members may request, within 21 business days of receipt of the draft report, further information about the liquidator's remuneration and expenses

---

[12] Inserted by the Insolvency (Amendment) Rules 2010, SI 2010/686 with effect from 6 April 2010.

(r 4.49E(1) and 4.49E(2)).[13] A liquidator complies with this requirement if, within 14 days, he provides the information or, if he considers that the costs of preparing the information would be excessive or would be prejudicial to the liquidation or lead to violence against any person or he is subject to an obligation of confidentiality in respect of the information, he states his reasons for not doing so (r 4.49E(3)). Any creditor or member, within 21 days of receipt of the reasons for not providing all of the information requested or the 14-day initial period, may apply to the court which may make such order as it thinks just (r 4.49E(4)).

20.28 A final meeting cannot take place in the absence of compliance with r 4.49D (r 4.126(1D)). The liquidator shall give at least 28 days' notice of the final meeting of creditors to be held under IA 1986 s 106 to all creditors who are known to the liquidator.

20.29 In addition the liquidator must place an advertisement in the Gazette at least one month before the meeting giving the time, place and objects of the meeting (IA 1986, s 106(2)). The advertisement must also include the time and date by which, and place at which, creditors must lodge proxies and hitherto unlodged proofs in order to be entitled to vote at the meeting (r 4.126(1A)[14]). In addition the liquidator may advertise notice of the meeting in such other manner as he thinks fit. The advertisement must state the purpose of the meeting, the venue fixed for the meeting; and the time and date by which, and place at which, creditors must lodge proxies and hitherto unlodged proofs in order to be entitled to vote at the meeting.

20.30 The liquidator's report laid before the meeting of creditors under s 106 must contain (r 4.126(1E)) an account of the liquidator's administration of the winding up, in particular his financial dealings with the company and the remuneration charged including:[15]

- a summary of the liquidator's receipts and payments, including details of all receipts from trading, expenses incurred (including the cost of employing a solicitor);

- a breakdown of the liquidator's remuneration and details of the basis fixed for the liquidator's remuneration and by whom it was fixed.

If the liquidator has sent out an annual report the information provided above need only relate to the period from the last annual report (r 4.126(5)).

20.31 At the final meeting, the creditors may question the liquidator with respect to any matter contained in the account (r 4.126(2)) and may resolve

---

[13] Any unsecured creditor or member who do not cross the 5% threshold may also seek such further information with the permission of the court (r 4.49E(1)(b).
[14] Rule 126 was substantially amended by the Insolvency (Amendment) Rules 2010, SI 2010/1986 with effect from 6 April 2010.
[15] For full details see r 4.126(1E).

against the liquidator having his release (4.126(3)). Where the creditors have so resolved, he must obtain his release from the Secretary of State and rule 4.122 – CVL applies accordingly.

RETURN TO REGISTRAR ON FINAL MEETINGS PRIOR TO DISSOLUTION

20.32 The liquidator must send a copy of the account of the liquidation which has been laid before the final members' meeting and the final creditors' meeting and a return concerning both meetings to the Registrar in the same way as required in respect of the final members' meeting in a members' voluntary winding up (IA 1986, s 106).

20.32 As in a members' voluntary winding up, this triggers the dissolution of the company which will occur within 3 months of the filing (IA 1986, s 201(2)), subject to the court's power to defer the date of dissolution (s 201(3) and (4)).

Chapter 21

WINDING UP BY THE COURT

MEETINGS TO BE HELD

21.1 The circumstances in which a company may be wound up by the court are contained in the Insolvency Act 1986 (IA 1986), s 122. One of those circumstances is that the company has resolved by special resolution to that effect (s 122(1)(a)). Where this is relevant, the special resolution should be passed in the same manner as any other special resolution of the company. A special resolution under the Companies Act 2006, s 283 is a resolution passed by a majority of not less than 75% (it is no longer a requirement for a special resolution that 21 days' notice of the meeting is given). There are six other possible circumstances within IA 1986, s 122(1) that could lead to a winding up by the court; thus, in many cases it is not unlikely that there will be no initial meeting of the company to pass a special resolution for winding up by the court.

21.2 Once winding up by the court has commenced, the official receiver must, as soon as is practicable in the period of 12 weeks beginning on the day the winding-up order was made, decide whether or not to exercise the power under IA 1986, s 136(4) to summon separate meetings of creditors and contributories, for the purpose of choosing someone other than the official receiver to be the liquidator (s 136(5)(a)). The official receiver is required to exercise the power to call such meetings when requested to by one-quarter in value of the company's creditors. The choice of the liquidator at such meetings of creditors and contributories is governed by IA 1986, s 139. At the meeting the creditors may also establish a liquidation committee (IA 1986, s 141; see, further, r 4.52 of the Insolvency Rules 1986[1] (the Rules) as to the business of such meetings). Meetings summoned by the official receiver under the power in IA 1986, s 136(4) are referred to in the Rules (and in this chapter), respectively, as 'the first meeting of creditors' and 'the first meeting of contributories' and together as 'the first meetings in liquidation' (r 4.50(7)).

21.3 Where the liquidator is not the official receiver, a final meeting of creditors must be summoned by the liquidator, at which the liquidator's report on the winding up should be presented and the meeting should determine whether to release the liquidator (IA 1986, s 146(1)). As in a creditors' voluntary winding up, the official receiver or the liquidator also has the power to call meetings of creditors or of contributories in order to ascertain their wishes (r 4.54); and the creditors or contributories may also requisition a

---

[1] SI 1986/1925.

meeting (r 4.57). There are a number of similarities in the rules on meetings of creditors in a creditors' voluntary winding up and meetings of creditors or contributories in a winding up by the court. The discussion below seeks to highlight the differences rather than repeating provisions in the Rules common to both types of winding up.

CONTRIBUTORIES

21.4 A contributory is any person liable to contribute to the company in the event of its winding up (IA 1986, s 79).

NOTICE

21.5 Where the official receiver decides to exercise the power to call first meetings of creditors and contributories, he must fix venues for each meeting within 4 months of the winding-up order (r 4.50(1)). Where the official receiver is required by the creditors to call first meetings under IA 1986, s 136(5)(c), he must fix a venue within 3 months of the receipt of the request (r 4.50(6)(b)). At least 14 days' notice of each meeting must be given to the court and, respectively, to every creditor known to the official receiver or identified in the statement of affairs, and to every person appearing in the company's books or otherwise as a contributory (r 4.50(2)). The notices must specify the usual matters regarding time and place which must be convenient for attendees and take place between 10 am and 4 pm on a business day (r 4.60(1) and (2)) and must be accompanied by a proxy form (r 4.60(3)). Additionally, the notice must state that proofs and (if applicable) proxies must be lodged at a specified place not later than 12.00 hours on the business day before the date fixed for the meeting in order for creditors to be entitled to vote at the meeting; and the same applies in respect of contributories and their proxies. (r 4.50(4)). Notice of the meetings must also be publicly advertised (r 4.50(5) and (5A)).

FINAL MEETING

21.6 At least 8 weeks before the holding of the final meeting of creditors the liquidator must send to each creditor known to him a draft of the report which the liquidator intends to place before the final meeting of creditors (r 4.49D(1)), except where the liquidator is the Official Receiver (r 4.49D(5)). Any secured creditor, 5% in value of creditors or 5% of the total voting members may request, within 21 business days of receipt of the draft report, further information about the liquidator's remuneration and expenses (r 4.49E(1) and 4.49E(2)).[2] A liquidator complies with this requirement if, within 14 days, he provides the information or, if he considers that the costs of preparing the information would be excessive or would be prejudicial to the

---

[2] Any unsecured creditor or member who do not cross the 5% threshold may also seek such further information with the permission of the court (r 4.49E(1)(b)).

liquidation or lead to violence against any person or he is subject to an obligation of confidentiality in respect of the information, he states his reasons for not doing so (r 4.49E(3)). Any creditor or member, within 21 days of receipt of the reasons for not providing all of the information requested or the 14-day initial period, may apply to the court which may make such order as it thinks just (r 4.49E(4)).

21.7 A final meeting cannot be convened in the absence of compliance with r 4.49D (r 4.125A). For the final meeting of creditors, at least 28 days' notice must be given to all creditors who have proved their debts and the notice should also appear in the *Gazette* at least one month before the meeting (r 4.125(1)).

21.8 The liquidator's report laid before the final meeting shall contain an account of the liquidator's administration of the winding up, including (r 4.125(2)):

- a summary of his receipts and payments, including details of remuneration charged and expenses incurred by the liquidator;

- details of the basis fixed for the liquidator's remuneration;

- a statement by him that he has reconciled his account with that which is held by the Secretary of State in respect of the winding up; and

- a statement as to the amount paid to unsecured creditors by virtue of the application of s 176A (prescribed part) (r 4.125A).

CHAIRMAN

21.9 Where a meeting in a winding up by the court is convened by the official receiver, as will be the case for the first meetings in liquidation, then the official receiver or a person nominated in writing by the official receiver is the chairman (r 4.55(2)).[3] A written nomination is not necessary where the person nominated is another official receiver or a deputy official receiver. Where the convenor is not the official receiver, as will be the case for the final meeting summoned by the liquidator under IA 1986, s 146, then the convenor or a person nominated in writing by the convenor is the chairman (r 4.55(3)). However, where the convenor is not the official receiver, the convenor may only nominate another person as chairman if that person is a qualified insolvency practitioner in relation to the company or an employee of the liquidator or the liquidator's firm experienced in insolvency matters (r 4.55(3)).

21.10 The powers and duties of the chairman in creditors' and contributories' meetings in a winding up by the court are the same as those in a creditors'

---

[3] For a review of the case-law relating to the powers and duties of a chairman of a meeting, see *Link Agricultural Pty Ltd v Shanahan* (1998) 28 ACSR 498. See also *Re Chevron Furnishers Pty Ltd* (1992) 8 ACSR 726.

voluntary winding up, except for the following two matters. First, in a winding up by the court the chairman does not have a discretion to allow a creditor to vote if the creditor has failed to comply with the rules on lodging proofs of debt by a certain time, although the chairman still has the same power to admit or reject a proof for the purpose of entitlement to vote (r 4.70(1)). A creditor who fails to comply with the requirements of r 4.67(1)(a) will have to make an application to the court if he wishes to vote, but exceptional circumstances will have to be shown: r 4.67(2).[4] Secondly, in a winding up by the court the chairman must not only make a record of resolutions passed (r 4.71(3)), he must also file certified particulars of such resolutions in court within 21 days of the meeting (r 4.71(4)).

ADJOURNMENT

21.11 The rules on adjournment are the same for creditors' and contributories' meetings in a winding up by the court as they are for creditors' meetings in a creditors' voluntary winding up.

VOTING

21.12 Subject to the absence of the chairman's discretion to allow a creditor to vote where the creditor has failed to lodge a proof by the due date (as discussed above), the rules on voting are the same for creditors' and contributories' meetings in a winding up by the court as they are for creditors' meetings in a creditors' voluntary winding up.

RESOLUTIONS BY CORRESPONDENCE

The rules in relation to the passing of resolutions by correspondence are the same as in the case of a creditors' voluntary winding up.

REPORT TO THE COURT

21.13 After the final meeting of creditors required under IA 1986, s 146 has been held, the liquidator must give notice to the court of the holding of the meeting and a copy of the report must be sent to the official receiver. The notice must state whether or not the meeting has resolved to release the liquidator and must be accompanied by a copy of the report laid before the final meeting by the liquidator (r 4.125(4)). This report must give an account of the winding up including, in particular, a summary of receipts and payments and a statement by the liquidator that the account given has been reconciled

---

[4] If the chairman accepts a creditor's proof for voting purposes, that does not mean that the proof is conclusive for purposes other than voting: *Assico Engineering Ltd* [2002] BCC 481, following *Company No 004539 of 1993* [1995] BCC 116.

with that held by the Secretary of State with respect to the winding up (r 4.125(2)). If the final meeting is inquorate, the liquidator must report this fact to the court, in which case the meeting is deemed to have been held and the liquidator is deemed released (r 4.125(5)).

Chapter 22

MEMBERS' VOLUNTARY LIQUIDATION

THE REQUIREMENTS TO BE SATISFIED FOR A MEMBERS' VOLUNTARY LIQUIDATION

22.1 If a company is solvent, the company may pass a resolution at a duly convened meeting of its members to place it into what is known as 'members' voluntary liquidation'. This may be done for a variety of reasons, such as reconstruction of a group, or it may be simply that the directors no longer wish to trade. Often, the process is entirely tax-driven. In order to effect a members' voluntary winding up a declaration has to be made by a majority of directors at a meeting to the effect that they have formed the opinion that the company will be able to pay its debts in full together with interest at the official rate within a 12-month period from the commencement of the winding up. The declaration can only be made if the directors are able to state that the opinion of solvency is based on information gained after a full inquiry into the company's affairs has taken place.[1] The declaration will have no effect unless it is made within 5 weeks before the resolution is passed to wind up the company or on that date, but before the passing of the resolution, and it embodies a statement of the company's assets and liabilities[2] as at the latest practical date before the making of the declaration.[3] The declaration of solvency has to be filed with the Registrar of Companies within 15 days from the date on which the resolution to wind up was made.[4] If the declaration is not lodged within the specified period, the company and every officer will have committed an offence as a result of the default and will be liable to a fine.[5] Similarly, if a director making the declaration of solvency does so without having reasonable grounds for his opinion, he may be liable to imprisonment, a fine or both.[6] Minor inaccuracies in the statement of assets and liabilities relied upon by the directors in making the declaration of solvency do not invalidate it.[7]

MEETINGS AND RESOLUTIONS

22.2 A number of company meetings are required in order to effect a members' voluntary winding up. First, there must be a meeting in which it is

---

[1] Insolvency Act 1986 (IA 1986), s 89.
[2] The statement should be as accurate as possible to reduce the risk of a later challenge.
[3] IA 1986, s 89(2).
[4] IA 1986, s 89(3). The declaration should be made using Form 4.70.
[5] IA 1986, s 89(6).
[6] IA 1986, s 89(4).
[7] *Re New Millennium Experience Co Ltd* [2004] 1 All ER 687.

resolved to wind the company up. This meeting must pass an ordinary resolution that the company be wound up either where the life of the company as fixed by the articles has expired or an event occurs which, under the articles, triggers a dissolution of the company;[8] or a special resolution that the company be wound up voluntarily.[9] Secondly, the company must hold a meeting to appoint a liquidator (joint liquidators may be appointed).[10] As with CVL's the requirement to hold annual meetings was replaced by imposing a duty on a liquidator to report annually to the creditors on the progress of the liquidation.[11] Finally, once the company's affairs are fully wound up the liquidator must call a final meeting and lay before it an account of the winding up of the company's affairs.[12] In the course of the final meeting the liquidator may give a full explanation of his dealings during the liquidation and may wish to fix his remuneration if this has not already been done.

NOTICE

22.3 A resolution of the members of a company is validly passed at a general meeting if (a) notice of the meeting and of the resolution is given and (b) the meeting is held and conducted in accordance with the provisions of the Companies Act 2006 (CA 2006), Part 13, Chapter 3 (and, where relevant, Chapter 4) and the company's articles.[13] Notice of the members' meeting should be given in accordance with the rules discussed in chapter 6, save as highlighted below. It is likely that any appointment on made following an invalidly convened meeting, or one which is flawed for another reason, will be void.[14]

22.4 In addition, written notice has to be given to any qualifying floating charge holder to which s 72A of the Insolvency Act 1986 (IA 1986) applies, before the company passes a resolution for voluntary winding up.[15] If notice is served on a qualifying floating charge holder, then a resolution to wind up the company cannot be passed until the end of the period of 5 business days beginning with the day on which the notice was given, unless the holder of the qualifying floating charge has consented in writing to the passing of the resolution.[16]

---

[8] IA 1986, s 84(1)(a).
[9] IA 1986, s 84(1)(b).
[10] IA 1986, s 91(1).
[11] IA 1986, s 104A, inserted by the Legislative Reform (Insolvency) (Miscellaneous) Order, SI 2010/18.
[12] IA 1986, s 94(1).
[13] CA 2006, s 301.
[14] *Re Minmar (929) Ltd* [2012] 1 BCLC 798 which although relating to the appointment of administrators, there is no reason to suppose that the same reasoning would not apply to liquidations.
[15] IA 1986, s 84(2A), as inserted by SI 2003/2096 with effect from 15 September 2003.
[16] IA 1986, s 84(2B).

22.5 A time and venue have to be selected for the members' meeting, and, under the Insolvency Rules 1986, the person calling the meeting has to have regard to the convenience of the members when fixing the time, date and venue.[17] Unless the court otherwise directs, the meeting has to start between 10 am and 4 pm on a business day.[18]

22.6 Once an insolvency practitioner has been appointed as liquidator, the chairman of the members' meeting must certify the appointment,[19] but should not do so until the insolvency practitioner has provided the chairman with a written statement to the effect that he is an insolvency practitioner, duly qualified under IA 1986 to be a liquidator and that he consents so to act. The certificate is to be sent to the liquidator who is under an obligation to keep the certificate as part of the liquidation records.[20] Any meetings held subsequent to the appointment of the insolvency practitioner as liquidator shall be chaired by the liquidator as the powers of the directors will have ceased upon his appointment.

VOTING

22.7 A company may be wound up voluntarily by ordinary or special resolution.[21]

PROCEDURE AND MEETINGS SUBSEQUENT TO THE PASSING OF THE RESOLUTION TO WIND UP

22.8 As the meeting is of members, it is the members who select and appoint the liquidator by (ordinary) resolution.[22] Section 85 of IA 1986 provides that when a company has passed a resolution voluntarily to wind up, it shall within 14 days after the passing of the resolution give notice of the resolution by advertisement in the *Gazette*. Failure to do so makes the company and every officer of it who is in default liable to a fine and, for continued contravention, a daily default fine.[23] The appointed liquidator is also under an obligation to publish notice (in the prescribed form) of his appointment and may advertise it in such manner as the liquidator thinks fit.[24] This also applies to any liquidator appointed to fill a casual vacancy. Where a meeting has to be held to fill such a casual vacancy, this must be convened by a contributory or by any continuing liquidator.[25] The reason for this is that at the time of the initial appointment of

---

[17] See r 4.60(1) of the Insolvency Rules 1986, SI 1986/1925 ('the Rules').
[18] Rule 4.60(2).
[19] Rule 4.139(2).
[20] Rule 4.139(3).
[21] IA 1986, s 84.
[22] IA 1986, s 91(1).
[23] IA 1986, s 85(2).
[24] IA 1986, s109 and r 4.106 of the Rules.
[25] IA 1986, s 92(2).

a liquidator the directors' powers generally cease.[26] Aside from the special arrangements for convening a meeting to fill a casual vacancy in the office of liquidator, such a meeting is held in the usual manner unless otherwise determined by the court.[27]

22.9 Any general meetings of the company called, and also the final meeting prior to dissolution, must be convened by the liquidator. This is a consequence of the cessation of the directors' powers. Certain other deviations from the normal procedure are also prescribed in respect of the final meeting of the company prior to dissolution. No meeting of creditors is required. First, the meeting is to be called by an advertisement in the *Gazette,* published at least one month before the meeting, specifying its time, place and object.[28] Secondly, within one week of holding the meeting, the liquidator must make a return to the Registrar specifying that the meeting took place on a certain date and must send the Registrar a copy of the account laid before the final meeting.[29] If the final meeting is inquorate, then the liquidator's return should note that the meeting was duly summoned but was inquorate.[30] The filing of the final account and return with the Registrar starts the process of dissolution of the company which, in the ordinary case, is deemed to have occurred within 3 months of the filing,[31] although the 3-month period is not absolute as the court has a power to defer the date of dissolution.[32]

---

[26] IA 1986, s 91(2).
[27] IA 1986, s 92(3).
[28] IA 1986, s 94(2).
[29] IA 1986, s 94(3) and see Form 4.71 of the Rules as to the form of the return.
[30] IA 1986, s 94(5).
[31] IA 1986, s 201(2).
[32] IA 1986, s 201(2).

Chapter 23

CREDITORS' SCHEMES UNDER PART 26 (SS 895–901) OF THE COMPANIES ACT 2006

INTRODUCTION

23.1 A company may seek to make a compromise or arrangement with (1) its member and/or (2) its creditors (or any class of them) by way of a scheme of arrangement. A scheme may take any form acceptable to the parties.[1] It is not a condition of a scheme that the company is or is likely to become insolvent. A scheme can only be entered through a statutory procedure gateway as described below.

23.2 The relevant statutory procedure has been incorporated into the Companies Act 2006. On 6 April 2008, the relevant provisions of the Companies Act 1985 (CA 1985) relating to schemes and reconstructions (ss 425–427) were repealed and replaced by the provisions contained in Part 26 of the Companies Act 2006 (CA 2006) (ss 895–899). The Companies Act 2006 is not a consolidation measure: 'It is evident that the current provisions have remained essentially unchanged since they first appeared in the 1870 Act and there is nothing to suggest that Parliament has recently intended to give them any different or wider meaning.'[2] Accordingly the jurisprudence and case-law which has grown up around s 425 (and, for that matter, its predecessors going back to the 1870 Act) remain relevant and applicable to Part 26 of CA 2006.

23.3 Schemes under Part 26 can be and are used for a variety of purposes, including the restructuring of a company's debt.

23.4 Where a compromise or arrangement[3] is proposed between a company and its creditors, or any class of them, or between the company and its members, or any class of them, the court may on the application[4] of the

---

[1] *IRC v Adam & Partners Ltd* [2001] 1 BCLC 222, [2000] BPIR 986, CA; and *IRC v Bland and Sargant* [2003] EWHC 1068 (Ch), [2003] BPIR 1274.
[2] *Re Lehman Brothers International (Europe) (In Administration)* [2010] Bus LR 489, [2010] BCC 272, [2010] 1 BCLC 496.
[3] Especially in insurance and other similar companies where there are many contingent claims (see *Re Equitable Life Assurance Society* [2002] 2 BCLC 510; *Re Marconi Corporation plc* [2003] EWHC 663 (Ch); and *Re MyTravel Group plc* [2004] EWCA Civ 1734).
[4] By a claim form issued in accordance with the Civil Procedure Rules, SI 1998/3132, Part 8: see CPR, r 49.1 as amended by the Civil Procedure (Amendment) Rules 2009, SI 2009/2092 and CPR Practice Direction 49B, para 7.

company or any creditor or member of it or, in the case of a company being wound up, an administration order being in force in relation to a company, of the liquidator or administrator, order a meeting of the creditors or class of creditors, or of the members of the company or class of members (as the case may be), to be summoned in such manner as the court directs.

23.5 The meeting works on the principle of a three-fourths majority having a binding effect such that if a majority in number representing three-fourths in value[5] of the creditors or class of creditors or members or class of members (as the case may be), present and voting either in person or by proxy at the meeting, agree to any compromise or arrangement, the compromise or arrangement, if sanctioned by the court, is binding on all the creditors or the class of creditors, or on the members or class of members (as the case may be), and also on the company or, in the case of a company in the course of being wound up, on the liquidator and contributories of the company.

23.6 The sanctioning of a scheme of arrangement was one of the statutory purposes for which a petition could be presented for an administration order under Part II of the Insolvency Act 1986 (IA 1986). After the coming into force of the corporate provisions of the Enterprise Act 2002, the old statutory purposes (set out in the former s 8(3)(c) of IA 1986) have been abolished in respect of administrations commenced after 15 September 2003. However, the new single purpose or primary objective of administrations set out in para 3(1) of Sch B1 to IA 1986 can still be achieved by the creditors of the company meeting to agree that the company should enter into a company voluntary arrangement (CVA) or a scheme of arrangement under Part 26.

23.7 For a host of reasons, many of which are particularly relevant in the larger insolvency cases,[6] the most appropriate method of achieving a solution for creditors of an insolvent company might be to bypass the insolvency

---

[5] These have been considered by numerous courts in a number of different common law jurisdictions over more than a century. In England, see *Re Alabama, New Orleans, Texas and Pacific Junction Railway Co* [1891] 1 Ch 213, CA; *Sovereign Life Assurance Co v Dodd* [1892] 2 QB 573, CA, at 579–580, per Lord Esher MR, and 582–583, per Bowen LJ; *Re United Provident Assurance Co Ltd* [1910] 2 Ch 477; *Re Hellenic & General Trust Ltd* [1976] 1 WLR 123; *Re BTR plc* [2000] 1 BCLC 740, CA, at 745–748, per Chadwick LJ; *Re Hawk Insurance Co Ltd* [2001] EWCA Civ 241, at [13]–[33], per Chadwick LJ; *Re MyTravel Group plc* [2004] EWCA Civ 1734. In Hong Kong, see *Re Industrial Equity (Pacific) Ltd* [1991] 2 HKLR 614, at 620–625, per Nazareth J. In Australia, see *Re Chevron (Sydney) Ltd* [1963] VR 249; *Re Jax Marine Pty Ltd* [1967] 1 NSWR 145, at 148–149; *Re Landmark Corporation Ltd* [1968] 1 NSWR 759, at 766; *Nordic Bank plc v International Harvester Australia Ltd* [1983] 2 VR 298, at 303; *Re Linter Textiles Corporation Ltd* [1991] 2 VR 561, at 565; *Re Bond Corporation Holdings Ltd* (1991) 5 ACSR 304, at 313–317; *Re NRMA Ltd* (1999–2000) 33 ACSR 595, at 616–617. In South Africa, see *Rosen v Bruyns, NO* [1973] 1 SALR 815, at 820–821; and *Borgelt v Millman NO* [1983] 1 SALR 757, at 769.

[6] In *Re MyTravel Group plc* [2004] EWHC 2741 (Ch), Mann J was of the view that bondholders whose debts were subordinated in the event of liquidation of the company did not have an economic interest in the company sufficient to require them to be a party to the scheme or a member of a relevant class, because the only alternative to the scheme was a liquidation and, in a liquidation, their subordinated status and the deficiency of assets meant that they had no prospect at all of recovering any of the sums due under the bonds (the Court of Appeal

procedures and effect a creditors' scheme under Part 26. Indeed, these provisions have been increasingly regarded as a flexible tool in the restructuring world, particularly for large rescues involving a need to compromise with various different creditors and shareholders. This is a specialised area and what follows is no more than a thumbnail sketch. At the heart of this jurisdiction are the principles upon which the creditors or members should be grouped into classes for the purpose of a scheme of arrangement.[7] The fact that a three-quarters majority of creditors having an interest in the outcome may 'cram down' dissenting creditors means that dissenting creditors cannot hold the ailing corporation to ransom. This, in turn, places considerable importance at the outset on a correct ascertainment of the relevant class or classes and identifying those with an economic interest in the outcome of the scheme.[8] That said, a scheme can only bind existing (including contingent) creditors of the company and not future creditors, who might have a claim in the future but had no existing rights.[9] The court has a wide jurisdiction to sanction a proposed scheme of arrangement in respect of a company whose principal place of business is not in England and Wales.[10]

THREE STAGES

Overview

23.8 The application for an order to convene meetings of members or creditors pursuant to CA 2006, s 896 will usually be heard by a Registrar in the Companies Court, unless it is thought that issues of difficulty may arise, in which case it can be heard by a judge. The application to sanction the scheme has to follow a meeting of members and or creditors where approval has been provided. This application is made by the original claim form and will be heard by a judge. On occasions the applicant will seek confirmation as to a reduction of capital. In these situations the first hearing will be heard by a Registrar. Otherwise the application will be heard by a judge.

23.9 The overview accords with what Chadwick LJ observed in *Re Hawk Insurance Co Ltd*,[11] where he explained that there are three stages in the process

---

considered that it was premature and unnecessary to decide whether the judge was correct, see *Re MyTravel Group plc* [2004] EWCA Civ 1734).

[7] [2001] EWCA Civ 241, [2001] 2 BCLC 480 (and see his earlier judgment in *Re BTR plc* [2000] 1 BCLC 740, at 742).

[8] Although recent litigation involving bondholders has given rise to early intervention in the process in which the court has had to decide a variety of issues at this first stage (see, for example, *Re Telewest Communications plc* [2004] EWHC 924 (Ch), [2004] BCC 342; *Re MyTravel Group plc* [2004] EWHC 2741 (Ch), [2004] EWCA Civ 1734).

[9] *Re T&N Ltd* [2005] EWHC 2870 (Ch), [2006] 1 WLR 1728.

[10] *Re La Mutuelle Du Mans Assurance Iard* [2005] EWHC 1599, [2006] BCC 11; *Re Drax Holdings Limited* [2003] EWHC 2743 (Ch), [2004] 1 All ER 903, [2004] 1 BCLC 10.

[11] Compare the questions addressed by and the approach of David Richards J at the first stage in *Re Telewest Communications plc* [2004] EWHC 924 (Ch) and at the third stage [2004] EWHC 1466 (Ch) of the same scheme.

by which a Part 26 scheme between a company and its creditors or a class of its creditors may become binding on dissentients:

- First, there must be an application to the court for an order that one or more meetings of the creditors be summoned. The application is generally made by the company without notice to any other party or to any creditors.

- Secondly, the proposals must be put to the meeting or meetings, considered and approved by a majority in number representing 75% in value of the claims of those present and voting in person or by proxy.

- Thirdly, if (but only if) they are approved by the requisite majority, then the court may sanction them, though it is not bound to do so.

23.10 At the first stage the court does not generally address the question whether it is necessary to order more than one meeting.[12] The only alternative would be to require the initial application to be made on notice to creditors and others and for notice of the application together with a copy of the scheme to be given to everyone potentially affected by it, with the risk of incurring the costs of a contested hearing and possible appeals before it could be known whether the scheme was likely to attract sufficient support in any event. The present practice ensures that those advising the company take their responsibility seriously, since an error on their part will be fatal to the scheme. At the same time it leaves the question, which goes to the jurisdiction of the court to sanction the scheme, to be decided at the appropriate time, that is to say, when the court is asked to sanction it. By then the outcome of the meeting or meetings will be known and the question, which will no longer be hypothetical, can be argued between the appropriate parties, that is to say, the company, on the one hand, and those who object to the scheme, on the other.[13] The formal position is as follows.

SUMMONING OF MEETING(S)

23.11 When giving directions as to the summoning of such a meeting or meetings, the court is primarily to decide whether there should be one meeting or more than one and to ensure that reasonable steps have been taken to notify the creditors or other interested parties of the meeting. Diverting for a moment to notification of creditors, there can be occasions when one or more persons have not received notice. The question will then arise as to whether the meeting

---

[12] 'Arrangement' includes a reorganisation of the company's share capital by the consolidation of shares of different classes or by the division of shares into shares of different classes, or by both of those methods.

[13] In June 2001, after a detailed review and consultation process, the Department for Trade and Industry published its final report *Modern Company Law for a Competitive Economy: Final Report (2001)*, recommending that this requirement be dispensed with, so that a threshold of three-fourths in value alone would apply.

has been properly convened. Vos J[14] was recently prepared to apply CA 2006, s 313 where the scheme documents had not been sent to 306 shareholders. The section provides that an accidental failure to give notice to one or more persons of a meeting is to be disregarded for the purpose of determining whether notice of the meeting has been duly given (and s 313 is applied to a class meeting by s 334). Accordingly, the court was willing to sanction the scheme. On the facts of that case the omission was rectified in time for those shareholders to vote for or against the scheme.

23.12 Returning to summoning a meeting, when determining whether to summon a meeting the court is not concerned with the merits of the scheme.[15] However, complex issues as to jurisdiction or other legal difficulties relating to the convening or conduct of the meetings should be addressed as early as possible with a view to minimising later unnecessary cost and delay.[16]

INFORMATION FOR THE MEETING

23.13 This is strictly a court process such that any order will have no effect until an office copy of it has been delivered to the Registrar of Companies for registration; and a copy of every such order shall be annexed to every copy of the company's memorandum issued after the order has been made or, in the case of a company not having a memorandum, of every copy so issued of the instrument constituting the company or defining its constitution.

23.14 Where a meeting of creditors or any class of creditors, or of members or any class of members, is summoned under Part 26, certain information must be circulated. With every notice summoning the meeting which is sent to a creditor or member there shall be sent also a statement explaining the effect of the compromise or arrangement and, in particular, stating any material interests of the directors[17] of the company (whether as directors or as members or as creditors of the company or otherwise) and the effect on those interests of the compromise or arrangement, insofar as it is different from the effect on the like interests of other persons.

23.15 If the compromise affects debenture holders' rights, the statement shall give the like explanation as regards the trustees of any deed for securing the issue of the debentures as it is required to give in respect of the company's directors.

---

[14] *Re Halcrow Holdings Ltd* [2011] EWHC 3662 (Ch).
[15] *Re British Aviation Insurance Co* Ltd [2006] 1 BCLC 665.
[16] *Re T&N Ltd (No 4)* [2007] Bus LR 1411 – this case also demonstrates the type of practical considerations which the court might need to address when giving directions as to meetings (see at [127]–[130} of the judgment of David Richards J).
[17] *Rankin & Blackmore* [1950] SC 218; *City Property Investment Trust Corporation Ltd* [1951] SLT 371.

23.16 Where a notice given by advertisement includes a notification that copies of a statement explaining the effect of the compromise or arrangement proposed can be obtained by creditors or members entitled to attend the meeting, every such creditor or member shall, on making an application in the manner indicated by the notice, be furnished by the company free of charge with a copy of the statement.

23.17 If a company makes default in complying with any of these requirements of Part 26, the company and every officer of it who is in default is liable to a fine; and for this purpose a liquidator or administrator of the company and a trustee of a deed for securing the issue of debentures of the company is deemed an officer of it.[18]

SINGLE MEETING OR SEPARATE CLASS MEETINGS?

23.18 The object of the class meeting is to enable creditors or members as the case may be to consult together with a view to their common interest.[19] Chadwick LJ observed in *Re Hawk Insurance Co Ltd*,[20] the question whether a single meeting is sufficient or separate class meetings must be held depends on whether it can be said that the company is entering into a single composite arrangement with all the creditors or members affected by the scheme or whether it is in reality entering into separate but interdependent arrangements with different classes of its creditors or members. While this provides the rationale for the summoning of one or more meetings, it does not provide a test by which the question can be determined.

23.19 The principle upon which the classes of creditors or members are to be constituted is that they should depend upon the similarity or dissimilarity of their rights against the company and the way in which those rights are affected by the scheme, and not upon the similarity or dissimilarity of their private interests arising from matters extraneous to such rights.

23.20 Lord Millett has summarised the following principles derived from the authorities:[21]

'(1) It is the responsibility of the company putting forward the Scheme to decide whether to summon a single meeting or more than one meeting. If the meeting or meetings are improperly constituted, objection should be taken on the application for sanction and the company bears the risk that the application will be dismissed.

(2) Persons whose rights are so dissimilar that they cannot sensibly consult together with a view to their common interest must be given separate meetings.

---

[18] However, a person is not liable for breach of these provisions if he shows that the default was due to the refusal of another person, being a director or trustee for debenture holders, to supply the necessary particulars of his interests.
[19] *Re Cortefiel SA* [2012] EWHC 2998 (Ch).
[20] [2001] EWCA Civ 241, [2001] 2 BCLC 480.
[21] In *UDL Argos Engineering v Li Lo Lin* [2001] HKCFA 53.

Persons whose rights are sufficiently similar that they can consult together with a view to their common interest should be summoned to a single meeting.

(3) The test is based on similarity or dissimilarity of legal rights against the company, not on similarity or dissimilarity of interests not derived from such legal rights. The fact that individuals may hold divergent views based on their private interests not derived from their legal rights against the company is not a ground for calling separate meetings.

(4) The question is whether the rights which are to be released or varied under the Scheme or the new rights which the Scheme gives in their place are so different that the Scheme must be treated as a compromise or arrangement with more than one class.

(5) The Court has no jurisdiction to sanction a Scheme which does not have the approval of the requisite majority of creditors voting at meetings properly constituted in accordance with these principles. Even if it has jurisdiction to sanction a Scheme, however, the Court is not bound to do so.

(6) The Court will decline to sanction a Scheme unless it is satisfied, not only that the meetings were properly constituted and that the proposals were approved by the requisite majorities, but that the result of each meeting fairly reflected the views of the creditors concerned. To this end it may discount or disregard altogether the votes of those who, though entitled to vote at a meeting as a member of the class concerned, have such personal or special interests in supporting the proposals that their views cannot be regarded as fairly representative of the class in question.'

23.21 There has now been a change in practice to avoid, if possible, the waste of costs and court time illustrated in *Re Hawk Insurance Co Ltd*.[22] A new Practice Statement was issued in 2002.[23]

IDENTIFICATION AND RESOLUTION OF CREDITOR ISSUES

23.22 The purpose of the Practice Statement was to enable issues concerning the composition of classes of creditor and the summoning of meetings to be identified and, if appropriate, resolved early in the proceedings. It is the responsibility of the applicant to determine whether more than one meeting of creditors is required by a scheme and if so to ensure that those meetings are properly constituted by a class of creditor so that each meeting consists of creditors whose rights against the company are not so dissimilar as to make it impossible for them to consult together with a view to their common interest. The present practice whereby the applicant may bring an application before either the judge or the registrar will continue, but applications in respect of substantial schemes will be listed before a judge. In appropriate cases

---

[22] [2001] 2 BCLC 480.
[23] Practice Statement (Chancery Division): Schemes of Arrangement with Creditors [2002] 1 WLR 1358, replacing the *Practice Note* [1934] WN 142.

applications brought before the registrar should be adjourned to a judge. Where possible, the judge before whom the application is first brought on should retain carriage of the scheme throughout.

23.23 It is the responsibility of the applicant by evidence in support of the application or otherwise to draw to the attention of the court as soon as possible any issues which may arise as to the constitution of meetings of creditors or which otherwise affect the conduct of those meetings ('creditor issues'). For this purpose, unless there are good reasons for not doing so, the applicant should take all steps reasonably open to it to notify any person affected by the scheme that it is being promoted, the purpose which the scheme is designed to achieve, the meetings of creditors which the applicant considers will be required and their composition. In considering whether or not to order meetings of creditors ('a meetings order') the court will consider whether more than one meeting of creditors is required and, if so, what is the appropriate composition of those meetings. Where a creditor issue has been drawn to the attention of the court it will also consider whether to give directions for the resolution of that issue, including if necessary directions for the postponement of meetings of creditors until that resolution has been achieved. Directions for the resolution of creditor issues may include orders giving anyone affected by a meetings order a limited time in which to apply to vary or discharge that order with the creditors meetings to take place in default of any such application within the time prescribed. While creditors who consider that they have been unfairly treated will still be able to appear and raise objections on the hearing of the petition to sanction the scheme, the court will expect them to show good reason why they did not raise a creditor issue at an earlier stage. The court has inherent power to direct how the meeting should be held and also as to its conduct.

23.24 In the absence of evidence that there existed only one creditor in any particular class the attendance of one creditor would not constitute a meeting for the purposes of Part 26.[24]

PROXIES

23.25 The order directing the convening of meeting(s) will provide for proxy forms to be sent out in well-established form. There should be a deadline for the submission of proxies and provision for the discretionary admission of late proxies, although proxies arriving after a deadline approved by a court are likely to be rejected.[25] The proxy is usually the insolvency office-holder or, if different, the chairman of the meeting. There is no requirement that a proxy should be a member of the relevant class in respect of which the meeting where he will vote is to be held. Proxies settled by the court do not tend to allow the

---

[24] *Re Altitude Scaffolding Ltd (T&N Ltd)* [2006] EWHC 1401 (Ch), [2007] 1 BCLC 199.
[25] *Re Equitable Life Assurance Society* [2002] 2 BCLC 510.

holder any discretion but simply direct him which way to vote. It will, however, allow him to vote on ancillary matters, including as to whether there should be an adjournment.

Human rights

23.26 Creditors whose claims are affected by a scheme might well have rights under the European Convention on Human Rights (the Convention): see s 1 of and Sch 1 to the Human Rights Act 1998 (HRA 1998). Article 1, Protocol 1 (A1FP) provides:

> 'Every natural or legal person is entitled to the peaceful enjoyment of his possessions. No one shall be deprived of his possessions except in the public interest and subject to the conditions provided for by law and by the general principles of international law.
>
> The preceding provisions shall not, however, in any way impair the right of a State to enforce such laws as it deems necessary to control the use of property in accordance with the general interest or to secure the payment of taxes or other contributions or penalties.'

23.27 Article 6(1) provides:

> 'In the determination of his civil rights and obligations or of any criminal charge against him, everyone is entitled to a fair and public hearing within a reasonable time by an independent and impartial tribunal established by law. Judgment shall be pronounced publicly but the press and public may be excluded from all or part of the trial in the interest of morals, public order or national security in a democratic society, where the interests of juveniles or the protection of the private life of the parties so require, or to the extent strictly necessary in the opinion of the court in special circumstances where publicity would prejudice the interests of justice.'

23.28 Article 14 provides:

> 'The enjoyment of the rights and freedoms set forth in this Convention shall be secured without discrimination on any ground such as sex, race, colour, language, religion, political or other opinion, national or social origin, association with a national minority, property, birth or other status.'

23.29 Moreover, s 6 of HRA 1998 provides that '[i]t is unlawful for a public authority to act in a way which is incompatible with a Convention right'. Section 6(3)(a) provides that 'public authority' includes 'a court or tribunal' and, further, the TiB is also a 'public authority'.

23.30 A scheme or arrangement under Part 26 is a court-driven process.[26] Insolvency office-holders such as administrators are also officers of the court. A claim in a scheme might constitute a 'possession' within the meaning of

---

[26] Cp *GJ v Luxembourg* [2000] BPIR 1021.

A1FP, and, as such, decisions affecting such a claim might involve a substantial interference[27] with its enjoyment. There have been unsuccessful attempts to challenge a scheme under A1FP. In *Re Waste Recycling Group Plc*[28] a scheme was approved by shareholders, representing 99.7% of the value of the shares. The majority shareholder, however, objected to the scheme on the grounds that the company should not pass into private ownership. He claimed that if the scheme were to proceed it would amount to compulsory acquisition of his possessions and that would infringe his A1FP rights. The court found that it was not possible or necessary in proceedings under s 425 of the 1985 Act to draw a distinction between those who viewed their shareholding as a way to call the board of directors of a company to account on environmental issues and those who viewed them as a financial interest. It was established that A1FP did not affect the approval of decisions under s 425 of the 1985 Act in cases where the shareholders' interest in the shares was purely financial. Furthermore a challenge to a scheme based on A1P1 failed in *Re T & N Ltd*[29] on the grounds that the claims of the creditors in question were not existing but possible future claims.

23.31 This is a nascent area of the law and it is inappropriate to theorise here as to its potential impact on schemes or arrangements effected under Part 26. It is sufficient to voice that there is potential for a successful claim if the facts support a real infringement.

SCHEMES VERSUS CVAS

23.32 The combined effect of the recent development of the restructuring industry in the UK and the emergence of litigious bondholders in the process has been a greater involvement of the courts. By the end of 2004, restructuring specialists had started to look favourably at the CVA[30] as a tool for achieving a more effective cram-down of the rights and interests of dissenting creditors in the larger insolvencies.[31] Each process has its merits and demerits:

---

[27] A1FP is well recognised in the Strasbourg case-law to contain 'three parts', or rather three different classifications of interference with the right to property as protected by this Article. These classifications of interference are: (i) an interference in peaceful enjoyment (A1FP, para 1, first sentence); (ii) a deprivation (A1FP, para 1, second sentence); and (iii) a control of use (A1FP, para 2). See *Sporrong v Sweden* (1982) 5 EHRR 35, at para. 61: 'This Article comprises three distinct rules.' However, as the European Court of Human Rights said in *Jacobsson v Sweden* (1989) 12 EHRR 56: 'The three rules are not "distinct" in the sense of being unconnected ...'

[28] [2004] 1 BCLC 352.

[29] [2005] EWHC 2870 (Ch), [2006] 1 WLR 1728.

[30] Traditionally the process used in smaller, simple cases.

[31] For example, the issue as to the appropriate test to determine whether a creditor has an 'economic interest' in a scheme is moot and is likely to re-emerge in one of the future battles between bondholders and those proposing a scheme. It emerged in *Re Bluebrook Ltd* [2010] 1 BCLC 338 where it was held that there was no need to include creditors whose rights were not sheltered by a scheme. If there was a dispute about that, then the court was entitled to ascertain whether a purported class actually had an economic interest in a real, as opposed to a theoretical or merely fanciful, sense, and take action accordingly. The 'economic interest' test

- there are no immediate class issues in a CVA and there is more flexibility allowed when drafting proposals;

- once approved, a scheme achieves finality, whereas a CVA is not court-driven and creditors have statutory rights of challenge notwithstanding approval by the creditors; and

- due to the requirement that the court must itself approve a scheme as fair, schemes are said to be more readily recognised by foreign courts.

23.33 This is a dynamic and complex area of the law relating to insolvency meetings and it is easy to sympathise with the individual creditor who wishes to understand and protect his rights in such a process.

---

appears to be judged by reference to what that creditor would receive in a liquidation (as considered, obiter, by Mann J in *Re MyTravel Group plc* [2004] EWHC 2741 (Ch)). In *Re Tea Corp Ltd* the court had regard to those who had a present interest in the assets of the company opining that preference shareholders may have an interest whereas ordinary shareholders may not. If that was the situation it would be immaterial how the ordinary shareholders voted. There is a view that, given that the enterprise will survive as a going concern under the proposed scheme, it should be accorded an 'enterprise value' for the purpose of determining who has an economic interest in the outcome of the scheme (and therefore should be entitled to vote for or against it).

Chapter 24

BANKRUPTCY

INTRODUCTION

24.1 The continuing high level of consumer debt, and unemployment at high levels and the 'fresh start' principles underlying the bankruptcy reforms introduced by Part X of the Enterprise Act 2002, in particular the automatic discharge after one year, have led to bankruptcy becoming a quick and efficient procedure adopted by debtors to rid themselves of debt with little or no stigma. For the vast majority of bankrupts, they will meet once with a manager of their local official receiver and be discharged by the first anniversary of the bankruptcy order. It follows that, if they happen at all, the great majority of meetings concerning a bankrupt's affairs, once acrimonious and hotly contested battlegrounds, have become a formality. However, the sheer weight of numbers of individuals becoming bankrupt means that the incidence of such meetings taking place is not low. In this chapter, a broad outline is given of what a creditor might expect out of that process which, in turn, will depend largely on whether the official receiver should decide to call a first creditors' meeting.

WHETHER TO HOLD A FIRST CREDITORS' MEETING

24.2 Within a few weeks of the bankruptcy order, creditors should expect to receive a report giving estimates of the bankrupt's assets and liabilities and what the causes of the bankruptcy are considered to be. If they think that a bankrupt is withholding information about his assets, creditors are encouraged to write to the particular official receiver dealing with the case. The official receiver will notify all known creditors (within 12 weeks of the date of the bankruptcy order) whether a meeting of creditors will be held and any such meeting must be held within 4 months of the bankruptcy order.[1] No meeting needs to be held where a trustee in bankruptcy other than the official receiver has already been appointed by the court on the making of the bankruptcy order, for example, an order made on a criminal bankruptcy petition, or where the court appoints the former supervisor of a voluntary arrangement as trustee. Otherwise, the official receiver will decide to hold a meeting if there are significant assets or other issues which a private insolvency practitioner might be required to resolve. Indeed, the Insolvency Service has a policy of retaining and dealing with cases where the asset realisations are straightforward and, in the majority of cases, this will provide a greater return to creditors. Where the

---

[1] Insolvency Rules (IR 1986), SI 1986/1925, r 6.79(1).

assets to be taken into account are more complex including, for example, the prospect of civil actions (for the recovery of monies, eg for preferences or undervalue transactions), it will usually be an independent insolvency practitioner who will take over the appointment as trustee in bankruptcy from the official receiver at the first meeting of creditors (see below), provided funding is likely to be available to finance such actions, whether from creditors generally or from a particular creditor or creditors or by means of a conditional fee agreement with willing lawyers.

24.3 As appears below, to make a claim, a creditor should complete a proof of debt form and return it to the official receiver. The form is sent along with the notice to creditors. As in all formal insolvency procedures, the unsecured creditors will usually only be paid when the fees and charges of the insolvency procedures and the claims of secured and preferential creditors have been paid.

24.4 The official receiver shall, at least once after the making of a bankruptcy order, report to creditors dealing with the bankruptcy proceedings and the affairs of the bankrupt.[2] If a statement of affairs has been submitted by or on behalf of the bankrupt the official receiver's report must contain a summary of that statement of affairs and such observations as he thinks fit.[3]

NOTICE OF FIRST MEETING OF CREDITORS[4]

24.5 If the official receiver decides to convene the 'first meeting of creditors'[5] pursuant to IA 1986, s 239 the primary purpose in the official receiver summoning first meetings is to secure the appointment of an insolvency practitioner as trustee. From 6 April 2010 the official receiver is no longer required to send a copy of the notice for first meeting to the court. Notices must be sent to the following:

- in the case of a creditors' meeting, to every creditor who is known to the official receiver;

- the bankrupt.[6]

In all cases the notice of first meetings must be published in the *Gazette*, and may be advertised in such other manner as the official receiver thinks fit. The Insolvency Rules specify standard contents for all *Gazette* notices and other advertisements.

24.6 Notices should be sent at least 14 days before the date fixed for the meeting. As soon as reasonably practicable the official receiver should also aim

---

[2] IR 1986, r 6.73.
[3] IR 1986, r 6.75.
[4] IR 1986, r 6.79(2).
[5] This is the official term for the meeting: IR 1986, r 6.79(7).
[6] IR 1986, r 6.84(1).

for the advertisement of first meetings to appear no less than 14 days before the meeting. In calculating the 14-day notice period, official receivers should additionally take in to account any service period applicable to the postage method used. Notices including proofs and proxies for use by foreign creditors should be dispatched as early as possible to allow extra time for their return prior to the meeting. The official receiver is permitted to send notice of meetings to creditors and contributories by electronic means,[7] provided that the intended recipient has consented to electronic delivery and has provided an electronic address for delivery. Where the official receiver issues a notice by electronic means, the document must contain or be accompanied by a statement informing the recipient that they may request a hard copy and providing a telephone number, e-mail address and postal address for making such a request. Where a hard copy of the notice is requested, it must be sent within 5 business days of receipt of the request.

24.7 The official receiver may also satisfy the requirement to give notice of a meeting to creditors by the notice being available for viewing or downloading on a website. The official receiver is required to notify creditors and contributories of the address of the website together with any password required to access or download the document. The notice given to creditors and contributories must also contain a statement informing the recipient of their entitlement to request a hard copy of the report and specifying a telephone number, e-mail address and postal address to make such a request. Where a hard copy is requested this must be issued within 5 business days of the receipt of the request.

24.8 Where a notice to creditors and/or contributories is issued informing them of a website address where they can view a meeting notice, the meeting notice must be available on the website for a period of not less than 3 months after the date on which the notice was sent.

24.9 The notice must state that proofs and, where applicable, proxies must be lodged at a specified place not later than midday on the business day before the date fixed for the meeting, in order for creditors to be entitled to vote at the meeting.[8] The official receiver can, should he wish, require a bankrupt's presence at the meeting or to be in attendance (ie at the venue).[9]

24.10 Where it is necessary to use a place other than the official receiver's office for the holding of meetings, consideration is given to where the majority of the creditors are situated.[10] It should, however, only be necessary in exceptional cases to hold meetings away from the official receiver's office.

---

[7] The Legislative Reform (Insolvency) (Miscellaneous Provisions) Order 2010, SI 2010/18 and Insolvency (Amendment) Rules 2010, SI 2010/686.
[8] IR 1986, r 6.79(4).
[9] IR 1986, r 6.84(3).
[10] IR 1986, r 6.86.

24.11 If the notices of meetings are served in accordance with the required time-limits detailed above, any meeting held is presumed to have been duly summoned and held. This is not altered in the event that certain creditors have not received the notices.

24.12 If the official receiver does not believe the assets available are enough to attract an insolvency practitioner, he will usually send notice to all creditors that no first meeting is to be held and as a result the official receiver will remain trustee. Thereafter, there is not likely to be a meeting before the final meeting is called.

CREDITORS' REQUISITION OF A MEETING[11]

24.13 In addition, the official receiver must hold a first meeting if it is requested by one-quarter in value of the creditors.[12] A creditors' requisition should be on Form 6.34. The requisition need not be accepted if not in the style laid down in the relevant form.[13] However, if a requisition by ordinary letter contains all of the information which would normally be found in the prescribed form, the official receiver may accept this as a valid requisition. The appropriate requisition form should be accompanied by:

(1) where the requisitioning creditor's debt alone is insufficient, a list of the creditors concurring with the request, and the amount of their respective claims in the proceedings;

(2) written confirmation of concurrence from each creditor concurring with the request, where more than one creditor requisitions the meeting; and

(3) a statement of the purpose of the requisitioned meeting. A creditor may only request a first meeting for the purpose of appointing a trustee other than the official receiver.

24.14 If the creditors request a meeting, they will have to lodge a deposit for the costs of the meeting with the official receiver.[14] If the creditors do not choose an insolvency practitioner at the meeting, the official receiver can apply to the Secretary of State to make an appointment or to remain as trustee.[15] The official receiver can also apply to the Secretary of State when an appointment of an insolvency practitioner is needed in an emergency, for example, to deal with urgent transactions involving assets or to continue to trade a business operated by the bankrupt. When this happens, the insolvency practitioner must notify the creditors. This may be done by advertisement in a newspaper if the court allows, for example, where there is a large number of creditors.

---

[11] IR 1986, r 6.83.
[12] IA 1986, s 294.
[13] IR 1986, r 6.83(2).
[14] IR 1986, r 6.87(1).
[15] IA 1986, s 295.

PROXIES

24.15 A creditor may normally only vote at a meeting if he has returned his proof of debt to the official receiver within the time stated in the notice. He can vote at the meeting without attending personally, but he must also have submitted a proxy form. The creditor (as principal) can only give one proxy for a person over 18 to be present at any one meeting at which he wishes to be represented, although he may specify on the proxy one or more alternative individuals to be proxy-holder at that meeting.[16] A proxy for a particular meeting may be given to the official receiver or, if different, the chairman of the meeting. A proxy may be either specific or general.[17] A general proxy entitles the proxy-holder to vote in favour of or against any resolution proposed and entitles the proxy-holder to propose resolutions, including one for the appointment of an insolvency practitioner as trustee. A specific proxy gives directions how the proxy-holder must vote, although this does not, unless the proxy states otherwise, preclude the proxy-holder from voting at his discretion on resolutions put to the meeting which are not dealt with in the proxy.

24.16 The form is supplied by the official receiver at the same time as the notice calling the creditors' meeting[18] and it must be returned by the time specified. The proof of debt and proxy form must be signed by the same person. A proof sent by fax or e-mail can be accepted for the purposes of a meeting, provided the fax is received within the time-limits set for the acceptance of proofs of debt. The official receiver should still, where possible, obtain the original proof of debt from the creditor, which should be retained on file together with the faxed copy. Where it has not been possible to obtain the original proof from the creditor, this should not prevent administration of the case.

24.17 A proxy sent by fax can be accepted for the purposes of a meeting provided the fax is received within the time limits set for the acceptance of proxies. The proxy will still be considered valid if it is faxed via an intermediary such as an insolvency practitioner who does not hold an original proxy having been instructed by fax, as long as that intermediary is duly authorised by the creditor.

24.18 A faxed proxy form will be validly signed because when a creditor faxes a proxy to the chairman of a meeting he transmits both the contents of the proxy and his signature applied to it.[19]

24.19 The Insolvency (Amendment) Rules 2010[20] introduced provisions enabling the submission of information to the official receiver, amongst others,

---

[16] IR 1986, r 8.1(3).
[17] IR 1986, r 8.1(4).
[18] IR 1986, r 6.86(3).
[19] *IRC v Conbeer* [1996] BCC 189.
[20] SI 2010/686.

by electronic means from 6 April 2010. These provisions[21] enable proxies to be submitted electronically provided that the following criteria are met:

- the convener of the meeting must have agreed to receipt of the proxy electronically;

- further they must be satisfied with the format by which the proxy is being sent;

- the electronic submission must contain all of the information that would have been required in the prescribed form; and

- the recipient must be able to provide the information submitted in a legible form.

To satisfy the requirements for authentication of documents submitted by electronic means, the identity of the sender must be confirmed in a way specified by the recipient. If the recipient has not specified how the sender's identity should be confirmed, the proxy or information is sufficiently authenticated if it is accompanied by a statement of the identity of the sender and the recipient has no reason to doubt the truth of that statement.

24.20 In practice, a scanned proxy containing an original signature and submitted to the official receiver by e-mail can be accepted for the purposes of a meeting provided that the official receiver has no reason to doubt its authenticity. Similarly, a proof received electronically from the creditor or their intermediary, and containing an electronic signature (authentication), may be accepted if the named individual can be traced to the originating organisation and is a known party within that organisation.

24.21 Where there have been amendments made to the proxy form by the intermediary prior to it being forwarded to the chairman and these amendments are made with the authority of the principal, they should be accepted by the chairman as binding the creditor. Where the chairman has concerns regarding the existence of such authority he should contact the creditor in order to clarify the position.

24.22 A proxy given for a particular meeting may be used at an adjournment of that meeting.

24.23 It has been held[22] that a creditor who is entitled to appoint a proxy, is also entitled to revoke that proxy and resubmit it with amended instructions, or appoint a different proxy, during an adjournment of a creditors' meeting. The court stated that appointing a proxy was no more than the giving of authority to act on a party's behalf at a particular meeting, which authority could be

---

[21] IR 1986, r 12A.31.
[22] *Re Cardona* [1997] BCC 697.

varied or revoked at any time prior to the meeting or relevant decision provided that any relevant requirements were complied with. The principal may therefore withdraw his authority for a proxy-holder to act at a particular meeting or withdraw authority for a proxy-holder to vote in a particular way, at any time and may, subject to the time-limits stated in the notice of the meeting, submit a new proxy form.

24.24 Any creditor who has submitted a proof of debt (which has not been wholly rejected) may inspect the proxies submitted for the meeting of creditors. An insolvency practitioner holding an appropriate authority may inspect the proxies. The bankrupt may also inspect the proxies regarding inspection of proofs of debt.

24.25 Creditors may inspect proxies relevant to their meeting. Such inspection may be carried out at the meeting itself. Any person with a right of inspection may take copies of the documents concerned. The official receiver is entitled (but tends not) to charge 15p per A4 or A5 page and 30p per A3 page where he supplies such copies.

ADMISSION OR REJECTION OF PROOFS FOR VOTING PURPOSES[23]

24.26 The chairman of the meeting needs to decide, for each proof of debt submitted, whether to admit it or reject it for voting purposes, either in full or in part. A decision to accept a creditor's proof for voting purposes is not binding for other purposes, such as payment of a dividend and further evidence may subsequently be requested in this regard. It has been held[24] with regard to meetings in relation to an individual voluntary arrangement that the chairman should reject claims that were clearly bad, admit claims that were clearly good and admit claims that were doubtful subject to being marked as objected to. A similar standard of judgment is expected of the chairman in relation to creditors' meetings in bankruptcy. A proof for a disputed debt should not be admitted for voting purposes if the evidence in support of it is clearly insufficient. If the chairman has any doubt as to whether a proof should be admitted or rejected, he should mark it as objected to and allow the creditor to vote, subject to the vote being subsequently declared invalid if the objection to the proof is sustained.

24.27 Debts for an unliquidated amount[25] or those whose value is not ascertained should not be rejected or objected to solely by their nature, in being of an unknown value. The chairman may reject or mark as objected to (either wholly or in part) claims of creditors with such debts for other reasons, such as being statute barred or in as far as they relate to costs after the insolvency order date.

---

[23] IR 1986, r 6.94.
[24] *Re a Debtor (No 222 of 1990) ex parte Bank of Ireland* [1992] BCLC 137, Harman J.
[25] IR 1986, r 6.93(3).

24.28 A decision of the chairman in relation to admission or rejection of a proof of debt (either wholly or in part) may be subject to an appeal to the court by any creditor or the bankrupt.[26] Such an appeal should be made within 28 days of being notified of the decision by the chairman. The chairman (where the official receiver or a person nominated to act on his behalf) is not personally liable for costs in respect of such an application unless the court otherwise orders. The court is not restricted, in considering whether the chairman was right to admit or reject a proof for voting purposes, by the evidence available to the chairman at the meeting and may consider any subsequent evidence that comes to light.

24.29 Where on appeal the chairman's decision is reversed or varied, or a creditor's vote is declared invalid, the court may order that a further meeting be summoned, or make any such other order as it thinks just. The court is likely to have regard to whether the outcome of the meeting would be changed; if not it is unlikely to order that a further meeting be convened.

24.30 Objections to a proof by the chairman, a creditor or any other interested person (including a bankrupt) should, where possible, be dealt with before the business of the meeting is started. The chairman should make a record of all objections so that if need be he can report fully and accurately to the court. If the chairman decides to reject, or mark as objected to, the whole or any part of a creditor's proof, he should detail this within his report to the court of the result of the meeting.

VOTING

24.31 When dealing with smaller meetings and/or the proofs and proxies submitted indicate there is unlikely to be any dispute over the matter being resolved upon, the chairman may take a vote via an informal show of hands indicating each creditor's intention should a formal vote subsequently be taken. Where the show of hands indicates that a certain result will be carried by a majority of creditors and there is no objection otherwise, the outcome may be taken as conclusive. Otherwise, a resolution is normally passed when a majority (in value) of those present and voting, in person or by proxy, vote in favour of the resolution, regardless of the extent of the majority.

24.32 Nominations for the appointment of a trustee in bankruptcy should be requested before any vote is taken. A proxy-holder with a special proxy requiring him to vote for the appointment of a particular insolvency practitioner is required to nominate that person. It is also possible that the chairman of the meeting may need to make more than one nomination where he holds such proxies.

---

[26] IR 1986, r 6.94.

24.33 Unless the chairman has good reason for suspecting that a person nominated to act as trustee is not qualified to act as an insolvency practitioner, he must accept all nominations and put them to the meeting. There should be no nomination at either meeting for the appointment of the official receiver as trustee as no such resolution may be passed.

24.34 Where on any vote there are two nominees for appointment, the person who obtains the most support is appointed.[27] Where there are three or more nominees, those entitled to vote are invited to support their favoured candidate, rather than voting for or against each one.[28] If one nominee has a clear majority in value, over both or all of the others together, that nominee will be appointed as trustee. Where there are three or more nominees for trustee, but after the first round of voting no one nominee has more support in value than all the others put together, the candidate with the least support is eliminated from the next round of voting (unless one of the other candidates withdraws, in which case the nominee with least support has another chance). Depending on the number of original candidates, further rounds of voting on the same basis take place, with one candidate being eliminated each time, until either one nominee has more support than all the others remaining put together, or there are only two candidates left and one has more support than the other.[29]

24.35 If a proxy-holder is entitled by the proxy he holds to vote for only one particular insolvency practitioner and the terms of the proxy preclude him from voting in any other way, if that insolvency practitioner is eliminated in a round of voting, the proxy-holder will not be entitled to vote in the next round. The value of the proxy-holder's principal's claim need not be counted as being entitled to vote for the purposes of the next round of voting.

24.36 The trustee nominated should be impartial, and if the chairman knows that some objection might be taken to a nominee, he should inform the meeting(s) of this, so that those present may take it into account when making their nominations. This may arise where a nominee has had previous dealings with the bankrupt or is thought to be an accounting party (for example, a creditor or debtor in the proceedings).

24.37 There is provision for the passing of resolutions by correspondence alone, without the requirement of holding a meeting. The exception to this rule is where the Insolvency Act requires that a particular resolution be passed at a meeting, therefore, this provision could not be used to effect the appointment of a trustee.

---

[27] IR 1986, r 6.88(2)(a).
[28] IR 1986, r 6.88(2)(b).
[29] IR 1986, r 6.88(2)(c).

CHAIRMAN

24.38 Where the convenor of a meeting is the official receiver, he, or a person nominated by him, shall be chairman.[30] The chairman has various responsibilities associated with the conduct of meetings, including decisions as to who will be in attendance at the meeting; which proofs of debt will be admitted for voting purposes; which proxies are valid;[31] which resolutions will be put to the meeting; and which questions if any may be asked of the bankrupt. Where the official receiver nominates someone other than another official receiver or a deputy official receiver to be chairman of a meeting (ie a senior examiner or an examiner), that nomination must be evidenced in writing.

24.39 Together with the bankrupt, creditors and their respective proxy-holders are the only persons entitled to be present and take part in meetings. A creditor who has not been notified of a meeting but discovers the existence of the meeting by some other means is not excluded from attending. Any creditors who have not proved, or whose proof has been wholly rejected, may be admitted to the meeting, but will not be allowed to take part in the proceedings. The chairman may wish to obtain the views of such creditors where relevant either before or after the meeting. A list of all those attending the meetings must be recorded whether or not they are entitled to vote.

24.40 If within 30 minutes from the time appointed for the meeting to commence, there is no suitable person present to act as chairman of the meeting, the meeting is automatically adjourned to the same time and place in the following week, or if that is not a business day, to the business day immediately following.[32]

CHAIRMAN AND PROXIES[33]

24.41 When the chairman (or official receiver) is given a proxy to speak and vote on behalf of a creditor at meetings, he cannot decline to be the proxy-holder and must act in accordance with the terms of the proxy. Where a creditor has given the chairman a proxy requiring that he vote for a particular resolution and no other person proposes the resolution, the chairman must do so, unless there is good reason for not doing so. If the chairman does not propose the required resolution he is required, immediately after the meeting, to inform the principal of the reason why. Where the chairman holds general proxies he may support nominations from others, or vote for or against any

---

[30] IR 1986, r 6.82(1).
[31] The chairman of the meeting needs to consider the wording of the proxy to ensure that the proxy-holder is acting in accordance with his principal's wishes, particularly if the proxy-holder is proposing the nomination of an insolvency practitioner under a general proxy. If two or more proxies are received on behalf of the same creditor, the chairman of the meeting will have to consider which proxy is the valid one.
[32] IR 1986, r 6.91(4A). This only applies to cases after 6 April 2010.
[33] IR 1986, r 6.89.

resolution, when he believes that in so doing he is securing the best interests of the majority of the creditors. The chairman should avoid using his general proxies to nominate a trustee, unless there is no other nomination leading to an appointment, when he may use the general proxies held to nominate an insolvency practitioner by reference to his rota.

24.42 The chairman should not normally use proxies with a general voting discretion to support resolutions which would not otherwise be passed. The chairman must always have some independent basis for supporting a resolution and should make a file note to record clearly the basis and authority on which he acts.

QUORUM

24.43 A quorum is established at a meeting of creditors where at least one creditor is entitled to vote. Where the creditors' meeting consists of only one creditor entitled to vote, either present or represented by proxy (including by the chairman), the chairman should review the list of creditors to establish the comparative value of the creditor's claim and the total number and value of creditors. Where there are other creditors with significant claims, who would be entitled to prove, but these creditors have not complied with all the necessary formalities, the meeting may be adjourned at the chairman's discretion to allow such creditors to prove should they wish to do so.

24.44 Where a quorum either is not expected, or cannot be achieved at the adjourned meeting of creditors, the meeting should not be further adjourned. Instead, an application to the Secretary of State should, if appropriate, be made for the appointment of the next insolvency practitioner on the official receiver's rota. If a quorum is not present at the meeting within 30 minutes of the time it was due to commence, the chairman may, at his discretion, adjourn the meeting.[34] Where there is a quorum at the meeting consisting of the chairman alone or with one other, and the chairman is aware of others (from the proofs and proxies submitted) being entitled to vote were they in attendance, he should delay the start of the meeting for at least 15 minutes.

OPENING THE MEETING

24.45 After satisfying himself that the persons present at a meeting are entitled to be there, or that there are no objections to other persons present, the chairman will usually start the proceedings by stating the purpose of the meeting and providing those present with a brief summary of the information in the report to creditors, if this has been sent out. It is not unusual for persons attending meetings to ask questions and, although the chairman has a discretion as to which questions he allows, this should be exercised with caution. If he decides to allow questions to be asked, he should only do so on

---

[34] IR 1986, r 6.91(2).

the clear understanding that such questions are to be put to him and that, if he does not already have answers to them, he will decide whether to seek information from the bankrupt.

24.46 In the event that the bankrupt is not in attendance, it is possible for the chairman, at his discretion or upon a resolution validly passed by the meeting, to adjourn the meeting in order to require the bankrupt to attend.[35] Questions permitted should be limited so far as possible to matters material to the purposes of the meeting, and the chairman should make a note of the questions and answers for future reference. Where any matter is raised which cannot be dealt with at the meeting, the chairman should seek to clear the point up by subsequent correspondence. It is usually preferable for persons seeking or offering information, which relates to confidential or contentious matters to be invited to a private interview with the office holder.

24.47 The resolutions, which may be taken at a first meeting of creditors, are limited by statute[36] to: (i) a resolution to appoint an insolvency practitioner as trustee, or two or more as joint trustees; (ii) a resolution to establish a creditors' committee; (iii) where there is no resolution to establish a creditors' committee, a resolution specifying the terms on which the trustee is to be remunerated, or to defer consideration of this matter; (iv) where a joint appointment of two or more insolvency practitioners has been resolved, a resolution specifying whether acts are to be done by both/all of them or only one; (v) where the meeting was requisitioned, a resolution authorising payment out of the assets, as an expense in the bankruptcy, of the cost of summoning and holding the meeting; (vi) a resolution to adjourn the meeting for not more than 14 days;[37] and (vii) any other resolution that the chairman thinks it right to allow for special reasons.

24.48 The chairman has discretion to suspend the meeting,[38] once, for any period up to one hour. This may prove useful where, for example, a proxy-holder needs to obtain further directions from his principal, or where, with a contentious meeting, a 'cooling-off' period is desirable.

24.49 A proof or proxy given for a meeting may be used at any adjournment of that meeting.[39] Any proofs and proxies for use at the adjourned meeting must be received by midday on the business day immediately before the adjourned meeting. Notice of the adjourned meeting should, if the chairman sees fit, be sent to the bankrupt, where they were not at the meeting. If at an

---

[35] IR 1986, r 6.91(1)
[36] IR 1986, r 6.80.
[37] In cases where the petition was presented before 6 April 2010 an adjournment must not be for more than 21 days.
[38] IR 1986, r 6.90.
[39] IR 1986, r 6.91(5).

adjourned meeting there is no quorum of creditors, the meeting should not normally be further adjourned. An adjournment should not be for a period of more than 14 days.[40]

24.50 All meetings have to be concluded not later than 14 days from the date the meeting was fixed to commence (subject, in first meetings, to any direction of the court). First meetings may be adjourned several times provided that they are completed before the 14-day limit. For general meetings, if there is to be a further adjournment it must be to the same time and place in the following week. However, if that day is not a business day or if it is more than 14 days after the date on which the meeting was originally to be held, the meeting must be adjourned to the same time and place on the business day immediately preceding the 14th day.[41]

24.51 Regard should always be had to the overall wishes of the creditors when considering an adjournment. Where there is a quorum and those present or represented wish to nominate a practitioner to act, the meeting should not be adjourned only because it is known that creditors not present or represented wish to make a different nomination. The exception to this general rule is where the chairman is aware of a creditor whose vote could be decisive, who wishes to nominate a practitioner to act as trustee, but the creditor has not complied with all of the necessary formalities.

24.52 There is no statutory duty to give notice of or advertise an adjourned meeting. If it is considered that lack of notice would tend to defeat the purpose of the adjourned meeting, such as where there was no quorum at the first meeting, notice should be given when the length of the adjournment permits.

NO RESOLUTION FOR THE APPOINTMENT OF A TRUSTEE

24.53 Where the creditors have not resolved on the appointment of an insolvency practitioner as trustee, but the first meeting has been closed or abandoned, the chairman will decide whether or not to apply to the Secretary of State for the appointment of an insolvency practitioner. In cases where an insolvency practitioner has been appointed following a resolution passed at a meeting, the bankrupt must be informed of the appointment of the trustee. The court must be notified of the outcome of the meeting.

24.54 Where an insolvency practitioner has been appointed trustee as a result of a meeting, the effective date of his appointment will be when the chairman certifies the appointment, following receipt of a written statement to the effect that the person nominated is an insolvency practitioner, is duly qualified, and

---

[40] IR 1986, r 6.91(3).
[41] IR 1986, r 6.91(4C). In respect of petitions presented before 6 April 2010 if there are repeated adjournments of the first meeting an application should be made to the court for directions for an order that there should be no further adjournment.

consents to act. The date of appointment is endorsed on the certificate of appointment when signed by the chairman.

24.55 A copy of the certificate of appointment is sent to the trustee by the chairman. This certificate of appointment may be produced in any proceedings as proof that the trustee is duly authorised to exercise the powers and perform the duties of his office.

24.56 Where the chairman is aware that the insolvency practitioner is authorised to act as such and is known to the official receiver, it may be possible to arrange for the handover to take place on the day of the meeting. From the date of appointment, not handover, the insolvency practitioner has a personal responsibility for the assets. If it appears likely in advance of a meeting that an insolvency practitioner will be appointed, which it should be in the majority of cases, there is no reason why all the papers cannot be prepared for handing over to the insolvency practitioner or his representative immediately after the conclusion of the meeting. If the official receiver is unaware whether the appointed insolvency practitioner is authorised to act, no documents should be handed over until that confirmation has been received.

CREDITORS' COMMITTEE

24.57 A creditors' committee can also be appointed at a meeting of creditors unless the official receiver remains as trustee. The committee supervises and assists the trustee on behalf of the creditors. In bankruptcies it is called a creditors' committee. The committee consists of at least three and not more than five elected creditors. An individual creditor who has been elected can act personally or appoint a representative. A creditor has a right to nominate himself or any other creditor as a member of a committee. He may also vote for himself.

24.58 If certain actions are proposed by the trustee, a creditors' committee must first give approval for them. Each committee has different powers, but they include agreeing to carry on the bankrupt's business and bringing or defending legal actions.

FURTHER (GENERAL) MEETINGS[42]

24.59 Where the official receiver decides not to summon a first meeting of the bankrupt's creditors, the official receiver becomes trustee from the date on which notice to that effect is given to the court. The official receiver may summon further (general) meetings at any time, in order to ascertain the wishes of creditors in any matter regarding the bankruptcy. The circumstances where such a meeting is likely to be warranted will be rare, especially where the official receiver is not the trustee. Nevertheless, general meetings of creditors are

---

[42] IR 1986, r 6.81.

sometimes held if the official receiver wants to find out the creditors' wishes in any matter relating to the insolvency proceedings, or if requested by 10% in value of the creditors. Where an insolvency practitioner is trustee, a final meeting of creditors will be called.

RELEASE[43]

24.60 If an official receiver is dealing with the case and a creditor has sent in a proof of debt, the official receiver will inform the creditor when he intends to apply to the Secretary of State for release. This means that the official receiver's role as trustee comes to an end. The creditors have a right to object to the official receiver's release. The release of the official receiver as trustee is not relevant to and does not affect a bankrupt's discharge. Generally, the official receiver's release can only be withheld if the official receiver has failed to realise assets that were available to be realised or has misapplied the proceeds of any assets realised. If an insolvency practitioner is dealing with the case and creditors have sent in a proof of debt, they will be sent a notice of the final meeting of creditors. At this meeting the insolvency practitioner will report on his conduct of the case and will give a summary of the receipts and payments. The creditors have a right to object to the insolvency practitioner's release.

KEEPING ADMINISTRATIVE RECORDS

24.61 Regulation 8 of IR 1986 (which had direct application to bankruptcies) has no counterpart in the 1994 Regulations which replaced them. Regulation 8 required the trustee to prepare and keep minutes of the proceedings at any meetings of creditors and of the creditors' committee (including a record of every resolution passed at such meetings), a copy of every resolution passed under r 6.162 (resolution by post), together with a note that the concurrence of the committee was obtained, and any other matters necessary to give an accurate record of his administration.

24.62 It remains a requirement[44] that:

(1) at a meeting of creditors 'minutes' or a 'record' of its proceedings are taken, or a 'report' is made;

(2) a list of all creditors attending the meeting is drawn up;

(3) at a meeting of a creditors' committee, every resolution passed is recorded in writing; and

---

[43] Insolvency Act 1986, s 299(2); IR 1986, r 6.136.
[44] By IR 1986, r 6.95.

(4) a copy of every resolution of a creditors' committee obtained by post, together with a note that the committee's concurrence was obtained, forms part of the record of the insolvency.

24.63 The chairman of the meeting is responsible for ensuring that the requirements at (1)–(3) above are met. It is also made necessary[45] that 'proxies used for voting at any meeting shall be retained by the chairman of the meeting', unless the chairman is not the responsible practitioner, in which case he shall deliver the proxies forthwith to the practitioner. Rule 12.5 of IR 1986 provides that a minute of proceedings at a meeting signed by 'a person describing himself as, or appearing to be, chairman of that meeting is admissible in insolvency proceedings without further proof'. The minute is prima facie evidence that the meeting was duly convened and held, that any resolutions were duly passed, and that all proceedings at the meeting duly took place.

24.64 There is, in any event, a practical *necessity*, regardless of any legislative requirements, to ensure that all stages in any insolvency process are fully documented and recorded, so that actions taken can be explained and justified, and that queries from a party interested in the proceedings, the court, or arising during a monitoring inspection, can be readily answered.

---

[45] By IR 1986, r 8.4.

Chapter 25

INDIVIDUAL VOLUNTARY ARRANGEMENTS

INTRODUCTION

25.1 For the large part, the law and practice of individual voluntary arrangements (IVAs) is the same as that pertaining to company voluntary arrangements (CVAs). The recommendations of the Cork Committee[1] which led to the introduction of IVAs were based on the need to provide an alternative to bankruptcy proceedings; a need not then met in practice by consensual deeds of arrangement – see, in particular, at para 359:

> '... a satisfactory form of proceedings for dealing with the insolvent debtor otherwise than directly through the machinery of the Bankruptcy Court ... would fulfil an important social need.'

In the case of debts less than £15,000 of unsecured debt, it is possible for a debtor to apply for a debt relief order, but this does not involve any meeting of creditors.

25.2 In common with CVAs, minority creditors can be forced down by the majority by s 260(2) of the Insolvency Act 1986 (IA 1986), which stipulates that those creditors who had notice of and were entitled to vote at the statutory meeting (or would have been so entitled if they had had notice of it) are bound by the arrangement 'as if they were parties', resulting in what has become known as a 'statutory binding'. Given that the effect of the approval of the proposal will be to bind the dissentient minority of creditors, the determination of the entitlement to vote at the meeting and the manner in which the meeting is conducted are of crucial importance.

THE PROPOSAL

25.3 A proposal for a voluntary arrangement must be made either by a debtor able to petition for his own bankruptcy or an undischarged bankrupt. An undischarged bankrupt may use the usual IVA scheme or may propose a fast track IVA with the Official Receiver as nominee. A discharged bankrupt may not propose an IVA that is effective against the creditors in his bankruptcy.[2]

---

[1] *Report of the Review Committee on Insolvency Law and Practice*, Cmnd 8558 (1982).
[2] See *Wright v Official Receiver* [2001] BPIR 196; *Re Ravichandran* [2004] BPIR 814; and *Demarco v Perkins* [2006] BPIR 645.

25.4 A proposal may be put to creditors either with the benefit of an interim order from the court or without an interim order.[3] The interim order imposes a moratorium which prevents a bankruptcy petition being presented against the debtor (or proceeded with) and the commencement or continuation of any other proceedings, execution or legal process, without the permission of the court.[4] It therefore provides a breathing space during which the creditors can consider the proposal at a duly convened creditors' meeting.

25.5 The proposal must provide a short explanation as to why, in the debtor's opinion, an IVA is desirable, and give reasons why the creditors may be expected to concur with such an arrangement.[5] It must state or deal with a further 17 specified matters.[6] The vast majority of proposals are in a standard form published by the Association of Business Recovery Professionals (R3) in 2002 and revised in 2004, amended as appropriate for the individual circumstances of the debtor.[7] Straightforward consumer-based IVAs are usually proposed pursuant to the IVA protocol which is a voluntary framework for dealing with IVAs and is in addition to the standard terms and conditions.

25.6 The common scheme is for the debtor to consult an insolvency practitioner, who becomes the nominee for the purposes of the IVA, and a proposal is prepared. The debtor then applies for an interim order, supported by the nominee's report stating whether in his opinion the proposal has a reasonable prospect of being approved and whether it has reasonable prospects of being implemented.[8] At the interim order hearing, the court must be satisfied that (a) the debtor intends to make a proposal for an IVA, (b) on the day of the application the debtor was an undischarged bankrupt or was able to present his own petition for his bankruptcy, (c) no application has been made by the debtor for a interim order in the preceding 12 months before the date of the application and (d) the nominee is authorised and willing to act.[9] The court may make an interim order if it thinks it would be appropriate to do so for the purposes of facilitating the consideration and implementation of the debtor's proposal.[10] Generally, the court must be satisfied that the proposal is serious and viable.[11] The interim order's duration will be specified and it will direct the date, time and place for the creditors' meeting.

---

[3] Section 256A(1) of IA 1986, inserted by the Insolvency Act 2000.
[4] Section 252(2) of IA 1986.
[5] Rule 5.3(1) of the Insolvency Rules 1986, SI 1986/1925 (IR 1986).
[6] Rule 5.3(2) of IR 1986.
[7] The R3 Standard Conditions for Individual Voluntary Arrangements are set out in *Individual Voluntary Arrangements* (Jordans), at Appendix 5A
[8] Section 256 of IA 1986 and rr 5.11–5.13 of IR 1986. The nominee must bring a considered opinion of the sort which one would expect of a professional accountant and a licensed insolvency practitioner to bear upon the nature of the proposals: see *Re a Debtor (No 222 of 1990)* [1992] BCLC 137, per Harman J.
[9] Section 255(1) of IA 1986.
[10] Section 255(2) of IA 1986.
[11] See *Hook v Jewson* [1997] BPIR 100; *Re a Debtor (No 103 of 1994)*, *Cooper v Fearnley* [1997] BPIR 20; *Knowles v Coutts & Co* [1998] BPIR 96; *Davidson v Stanley* [2005] BPIR 279 and *Tradition (UK) Limited v Ahmed* [2009] BPIR 626.

GIVING AND RECEIVING NOTICE OF THE MEETING

25.7 If in his report the nominee states that in his opinion a meeting of creditors should be summoned to consider the debtor's proposal, the date on which the meeting is to be held shall be:

(1) in a case where an interim order has not been obtained, not less than 14 days and not more than 28 days from that on which the nominee's report is filed in court under r 5.14 of IR 1986; and

(2) in a case where an interim order is in force, not less than 14 days from the date on which the nominee's report is filed in court nor more than 28 days from that on which the report is considered by the court.

25.8 Notices calling the meeting must be sent by the nominee, giving at least 14 days' clear notice before the date fixed for it to be held,[12] to all the creditors specified in the debtor's statement of affairs and any other creditors of whom the nominee is otherwise aware. It is clear that there is an obligation on the nominee to give notice to every creditor, whether entitled to vote or not and of whatever category. There can be no justification or excuse for failing to give notice to any creditor of whose existence the nominee or the debtor is aware. It follows, therefore, that the nominee, whether on his own initiative or at the request of the debtor, cannot pick or choose which creditors are to be given notice and should not, in any circumstance, make a deliberate decision not to give a particular creditor notice.[13] The nominee should not delegate the task of giving notice to the debtor. It is the nominee's responsibility to carry out this task.

25.9 There is no prescribed form but the notice must state the purpose of the meeting and the effect of the rule relating to requisite majorities.[14] Each creditor notified must be supplied with a copy of the proposal, a copy of the statement of affairs or, if the nominee thinks fit, a summary of it (the summary to include a list of the creditors and the amounts of their debts) and a copy of the nominee's comments on the proposal.[15] Where the proposal incorporates standard conditions, copies of those conditions should be sent. The strict requirements of IR 1986 are not exhaustive as to the advance documentation to be sent to creditors, and proof of debt forms and proxy forms should be supplied. If the circumstances so dictate, it may be appropriate to send the

---

[12] See r 5.17(2) of IR 1986; *Mytre Investments Ltd v Reynolds and Others (No 2)* [1996] BPIR 464, per Blackburne J. Fourteen days means '14 clear days'. If less notice is given, the creditor will not be bound. This means that, in effect, *at least* 17 days must elapse between the date of posting and the date of the meeting, ie if the notices are dispatched on the first of the month the meeting should not be held until the 18th of the month at the earliest. Note, however, s 260(2), as it now is, which can mitigate the effect of not giving notice, but this provision must not be used as an excuse for deliberately not giving notice.
[13] See *Re Debtors (Nos 400 IO and 401 IO of 1996)* [1997] BPIR 431.
[14] Rule 5.17(3) of IR 1986.
[15] Rule 5.17(3A) of IR 1986.

creditors copies of valuations, reports on ongoing litigation and such other material as may assist the creditors in making a proper decision.

25.10 The meeting must be summoned to start between 10 am and 4 pm on a business day, and the nominee must have regard to the convenience of creditors.[16] Normally, the nominee will summon the creditors' meeting to be held at his office or some other appropriate venue. The question of convenience will depend on the circumstances of each individual case. If the majority of creditors reside in the same area as the debtor and the place of the nominee's office, the nominee's office would normally be regarded as being convenient, but this would clearly be inconvenient if, for example, the nominee practised in London and the debtor and most of the creditors were located in Cornwall or Northumberland.

THE MEETING GENERALLY

25.11 Whilst neither IA 1986 nor IR 1986 require the debtor to attend the creditors' meeting, it will always be essential for him to do so. Creditors are likely to be unimpressed if the debtor fails to attend. It is more than a matter of courtesy. The debtor owes it to his creditors to attend, so that he can offer an explanation of his predicament and answer questions that may properly be put to him. Furthermore, the creditors' meeting may be asked to consider modifications to the proposal, which cannot be approved without the consent of the debtor.[17] Where a creditors' meeting is convened to consider two or more linked proposals, each debtor should attend. A creditor may vote against a proposal as a matter of principle if the debtor fails to attend without good reason.

25.12 Even if the nominee thinks that no creditors will attend in person, it is still, it is suggested, essential for the debtor to attend the meeting as, first, a creditor may well attend unexpectedly and, secondly, there is always the possibility of a late communication being received which puts forward a modification upon which the debtor's instructions will have to be taken.

25.13 Any modification may be proposed, and each one that is adopted must be specifically consented to by the debtor.[18] It is arguable that if the debtor does not give an actual and informed consent to each modification, then no valid arrangement has come into existence. Particular considerations arise if modifications are proposed at an adjourned meeting. It is normally just as important for a debtor to be present at an adjourned meeting as at the original meeting. Problems have arisen in practice where debtors have not been present at adjourned meetings. If modifications are proposed at a meeting which the debtor does not attend, which the nominee takes upon himself to agree, then,

---

[16] Rule 5.18 of IR 1986.
[17] See *Reid v Hamblin* [2001] BPIR 929.
[18] Section 258(2) of IA 1986 and any changes which affect the position of a secured creditor must be approved by that creditor.

prima facie, the creditors are entitled to assume that the nominee has the relevant authority from the debtor. In no circumstance should the nominee ever agree to a modification without first putting it fully to the debtor and explaining its consequences. If, in fact, the debtor does not give his consent to proposed modifications, then the purported IVA will be a nullity.[19]

25.14 The nominee should be the chairman of the meeting but, if for any reason he is unable to attend personally, he may nominate another person to act as chairman in his place. Any person so nominated must be either a duly qualified insolvency practitioner, an authorised person or an employee of the nominee or his firm who is experienced in insolvency matters. It is normally desirable for the nominee to be present personally, although this will often be impossible in the case of large insolvency practices which are at any given time involved on a large number of cases. Nevertheless, many creditors like to see the nominee himself and to be assured that he is taking a personal interest and concern in the case. If the nominee himself cannot be present, he must ensure that his replacement has sufficient knowledge of the particular case and general experience of handling creditors' meetings to ensure that the meeting is conducted properly. He should give his authority in writing. The nominee must, however, satisfy himself that the person chairing the meeting falls within the qualifications set out in the rules, namely such a person must be:[20]

(a) a person qualified to act as an insolvency practitioner in relation to the debtor;

(b) an authorised person in relation to the debtor; or

(c) an employee of the nominee or his firm who is experienced in insolvency matters.

25.15 The Rules provide for voting by proxy, which may be in favour of the chairman of the meeting or any other person. Under r 5.20 of IR 1986 the chairman is not by virtue of any proxy held by him able to vote to increase or reduce the amount of the remuneration or expenses of the nominee or the supervisor of the arrangement, unless the proxy specifically directs him to vote in that way. If the chairman uses a proxy contrary to such provision, his vote with that proxy does not count towards any required majority. Where the chairman is the nominated supervisor or someone authorised to act in his place, he is unable to vote on an open proxy, ie a proxy where there is no instruction to vote for or against the proposal. This is because r 8.6 of IR 1986 specifically forbids a proxy-holder with a financial interest in the result of a vote from voting in favour of a proposal unless he is specifically instructed to do so. The Statement of Insolvency Practice 3, at para 7, sets out important guidelines as to the conduct of creditors' meetings and, in particular, the use of proxies. Such guidelines must be followed.

---

[19] See *Reid v Hamblin* [2001] BPIR 929.
[20] Rule 5.19 of IR 1986.

25.16 For the purposes of voluntary arrangements, faxed proxies or those submitted by electronic means (where the nominee has consented to electronic delivery and provided an electronic address for delivery) are valid.[21]

25.17 The creditors' meeting may from time to time be adjourned. It may also be suspended only once and for up to 1 hour without the need for an adjournment.[22] If, at the first creditors' meeting, the requisite majority for approval of the arrangement with or without modifications has not been obtained, the chairman may or, if it is so resolved, must adjourn the meeting for not more than 14 days. If there are further adjournments, the final adjournment must not be to a day later than 14 days after the date on which the meeting was originally held.[23] If the meeting is adjourned, the chairman must give notice of that fact to the court, and it may be necessary to apply to the court for an extension of the interim order. If, after any final adjournment of the meeting, the proposal with or without modifications is not agreed to, it is deemed to be rejected. In certain circumstances, an adjournment may be necessary so as to afford the chairman and the debtor a proper opportunity either to consider proposed modifications and their effect on the arrangement generally or to deal with unforeseen matters arising at the creditors' meeting. It is prudent for all creditors to whom notice is given to be sent a written notice of the adjourned meeting.

The meeting: voting rights

25.18 The issue which has given rise to one of the greatest difficulties and controversy since the concept of the voluntary arrangement was born under IA 1986 has been that relating to voting rights. It is important to remember that one of the principal features of a voluntary arrangement is that when it takes effect it will bind every person who, in accordance with IR 1986, was entitled to vote at the meeting (whether or not he was present or represented at the meeting) and whether or not he had notice. The following principles apply:

(1) Subject to the limitations set out below, every creditor who was given notice of the creditors' meeting is entitled to vote at the meeting or any adjournment of it.[24] It is therefore important that notice is given to all known creditors. If a person purporting to be a creditor attends the meeting but has not been given notice, the nominee should make due inquiry as to that person's status and, if satisfied that he is a creditor, should permit him to attend and vote. If satisfied that the person is not a creditor, the nominee should not permit him to attend the meeting.

(2) A creditor's entitlement to vote is calculated as follows:[25]

---

[21] See *Commissioners of Inland Revenue v Conbeer and White* [1996] BPIR 398 and r 21.10A of IR 1986.
[22] Rule 5.24(4A) of IR 1986.
[23] Rule 5.24(3) of IR 1986.
[24] Rule 5.21(1) of IR 1986.
[25] Rule 5.21(2) of IR 1986.

(a) where the debtor is not an undischarged bankrupt and an interim order is in force, by reference to the amount of the debt owed to him as at the date of the interim order;
(b) where the debtor is not an undischarged bankrupt and an interim order is not in force, by reference to the amount of the debt owed to him at the date of the meeting; and
(c) where the debtor is an undischarged bankrupt, by reference to the amount of the debt owed to him as at the date of the bankruptcy order.

It follows that in all three situations care must be taken to ensure that, so far as is possible, the quantification of creditors' claims has been agreed at the commencement of the meeting, for the purposes of determining the entitlement to vote.[26]

(3) A creditor may vote in respect of a debt for an unliquidated amount or any debt whose value is not ascertained, and for the purposes of voting (but not otherwise) his debt should be valued at £1 unless the chairman agrees to put a higher value on it.[27] This provision in the rules should not be abused. If, when dealing with such a claim, the chairman is, properly, able to put a higher value on the claim then he should allow the creditors to vote for that higher value and not insist on the creditor voting for just £1.[28]

(4) The chairman has power to admit or reject a creditor's claim for the purpose of his entitlement to vote, and this power is exercisable in respect of the whole or any part of the claim.[29] However, the power to reject should only be exercised after the fullest possible inquiry and after permitting the creditor the opportunity to submit all relevant documentation and other evidence to substantiate his claim and to make the fullest possible representation.

(5) The chairman's decision on entitlement to vote is subject to appeal to the court by any creditor or by the debtor.[30] It follows that, if a creditor is aggrieved by the chairman's decision, the matter may be appealed to the court by either creditor or debtor. If on appeal the chairman's decision is reversed or varied, or a vote declared invalid, the court may order another meeting to be summoned, or make such order as it thinks just.[31]

---

[26] Which is not necessarily the same as the creditors' entitlement when it comes to the payment of a dividend or distribution.
[27] Rule 5.21(3) and see especially *Re Newlands (Seaford) Education Trust* [2006] EWHC 1511 (Ch), [2006] BPIR 1230, where the Chancellor had to consider whether the chairman of the meeting had properly valued at £1 a landlord's claim for future rent and historic dilapidations
[28] The Chairman is not obliged to value a claim at £1 if the evidence available suggests that it should be given a higher value: *Sofaer v Anglo Irish Asset Finance Plc* [2011] BPIR 1736 and *NatWest Bank plc v Yadgaroff* [2012] BPIR 371.
[29] Rule 5.22(4) of IR 1986.
[30] Rule 5.22(3) of IR 1986.
[31] Rule 5.22(4) of IR 1986.

(6) If the chairman is in doubt as to whether a claim should be admitted or rejected, he must mark it as objected to and allow the creditor to vote, subject to the creditor's vote being subsequently declared invalid if the objection to the claim is sustained.[32]

(7) The chairman is not personally liable for any costs incurred by any person in respect of an appeal under r 5.22 of IR 1986.[33]

The meeting: majorities

25.19 For a proposal to be approved, with or without modifications, there must be a majority in excess of three-quarters in value of creditors present in person or by proxy and voting.[34] By contrast, any other resolution requires only a majority in excess of one-half in value.[35] The proposal must also be approved by more than one-half in value of those who are associates of the debtor.[36]

After the meeting

25.20 The chairman of the meeting, who may or may not be the nominee, must prepare a report. No form is specified, although the report must contain certain information, namely:[37]

(a) whether the proposal for the arrangement was approved or rejected and, if approved, with what (if any) modifications;

(b) the resolutions which were taken at the meeting and the decision on each one;

(c) a list of the creditors, with their respective values, who were present or represented at the meeting and an indication of how they voted on each resolution;

(d) whether, in the opinion of the supervisor: (i) the EC Regulation[38] applies; and (ii) if so, whether the proceedings are main proceedings, secondary proceedings or territorial proceedings; and

(e) such further information, if any, as the chairman thinks appropriate to make known to the court.

---

[32] Rule 5.22(4) of IR 1986.
[33] Rule 5.22(7) of IR 1986.
[34] Rule 5.23(1) of IR 1986.
[35] Rule 5.23(2) of IR 1986.
[36] Rule 5.23(4) of IR 1986.
[37] Rule 5.27(2) of IR 1986.
[38] EC Regulation on Insolvency Proceedings (1346/2000).

25.21 A copy of the report must be filed with the court within 4 business days of the meeting and the court must cause that copy to be endorsed with the date of filing.[39] Where there has been an interim order then the order of the court directing the creditors' meeting to be held will specify the date, place and time for the court to give consideration to the chairman's report. If there has been no interim order then the court does not consider the report unless an application is made to the court.

25.22 If the arrangement is approved, the hearing will normally be a formality, and most courts will permit the matter to be dealt with without attendance. If the report states that the meeting has rejected the proposal, the court has a discretionary power to discharge any interim order which is in force in relation to the debtor, and it will always do so unless there is a challenge.

25.23 Notice of the result is to be given to all those who were sent notice of the meeting and any other creditor of whom the chairman is aware.[40] Where the debtor is an undischarged bankrupt notice must be given to the Official Receiver and (if any) the trustee. Immediately after a copy of the report has been filed in court, the chairman must report to the Secretary of State details of the arrangement, and the supervisor must give notice of his appointment to the Secretary of State.[41] In the event of the arrangement being rejected, the chairman may, but is not required to, include brief reasons why, in his opinion, the creditors declined to accept the proposal.

Effect of approval

25.24 The approved arrangement takes effect as if made by the debtor at the meeting.[42] It is binding on every person who in accordance with IR 1986 (i) was entitled to vote at the meeting (whether or not he was present or represented at it) or (ii) would have been so entitled if he had had notice of it, as if he were a party to the arrangement.[43] It follows that failure to give notice to a creditor or, indeed, a number of creditors, is no longer as potentially fatal as was previously the case.

25.25 In the vast majority of cases, the effect of the approval of the proposal will mean that unsecured creditors will see their claim against the debtor replaced with a right to receive a dividend or distribution of the assets the

---

[39] Rule 5.27(3) of IR 1986.
[40] In a case where there is an interim order the notice must be sent as soon as reasonably practicable after filing of the chairman's report with the court (r 5.27(4A)(a) of IR 1986); or in the case where no interim order was obtained notice must be sent to creditors within 4 business days of the meeting being held.
[41] Rule 5.29 of IR 1986.
[42] Section 260(2)(a) of IA 1986.
[43] Section 260(2)(b) of IA 1986, as amended by the Insolvency Act 2000.

subject of the IVA. The effect on existing litigation between a creditor and the debtor will depend upon the express terms of the IVA, although usually further conduct of the claim will be stayed.[44]

Challenging the decision of the meeting

25.26 There are three methods of challenging the outcome of the meeting. As indicated at **25.18**(5), any creditor may appeal to the court against the chairman's decision on a creditor's entitlement to vote or on any value he puts on an unliquidated or unascertained debt or on any decision made on whether to leave a vote out of account.[45] Additionally, under IA 1986:

(1) an application may be made to the court on the ground that the IVA approved by the creditors' meeting unfairly prejudices the interests of a creditor of a debtor;[46] or

(2) an application may be made to the court on the ground that there was some material irregularity at or in relation to the creditors' meeting.[47]

25.27 Such applications under s 262(1) of IA 1986 may only be made by:[48]

(a) the debtor;

(b) a person who:

　(i) was entitled, in accordance with the rules, to vote at the creditors' meeting; or
　(ii) would have been so entitled if he had had notice of it;

(c) the nominee (or his replacement under s 256(3), 256A(4) or 258(3)); and

(d) if the debtor is an undischarged bankrupt, the trustee of his estate or the official receiver.

---

[44] But not necessarily. Continuation of a claim may be permitted, albeit that enforcement against the debtor's assets prevented: see *Alman v Approach Housing Ltd* [2001] BPIR 203.

[45] Rule 5.22 of IR 1986. Such an appeal shall not be made after the expiry of 28 days after the submission of the chairman's report to the court or notice of the outcome of the meeting was given to creditors. In relation to IVAs, the period may be extended under the court's discretion to extend time-limits, when it will consider the length of the delay, the reasons for the delay, the apparent merit of the application and the prejudice that might be caused to each side were time to be extended: see *Tager v Westpac Banking Corp* [1997] BPIR 543.

[46] Section 262(1)(a) of IA 1986.

[47] Section 262(1)(b) of IA 1986.

[48] Section 262(2) of IA 1986.

25.28 An application under s 262(1) of IA 1986 shall not be made:[49]

(a) after the end of the period of 28 days beginning with the day on which the report of the creditors' meeting was made to the court under s 259 of IA 1986; or

(b) in the case of a person who was not given notice of the creditors' meeting, after the end of the period of 28 days beginning with the day on which he became aware that the meeting had taken place,

but (subject to that) an application made by a person within s 262(2)(b)(ii) on the ground that the arrangement prejudices his interests may be made after the arrangement has ceased to have effect, unless it has come to an end prematurely.

25.29 Where on an application under s 262(1) of IA 1986 the court is satisfied that there has been such unfair prejudice and/or material irregularity, it may do one or both of the following, namely:[50]

(a) revoke or suspend any approval given by the meeting; and/or

(b) give a direction to any person for the summoning of a further meeting of the debtor's creditors to consider any revised proposal he may make or, in a case falling within s 262(1)(b) of IA 1986, to reconsider his original proposal.[51]

25.30 Where at any time after giving a direction under s 262(4)(b) of IA 1986 for the summoning of a meeting to consider a revised proposal the court is satisfied that the debtor does not intend to submit such a proposal, the court shall revoke the direction and revoke or suspend any approval given at the previous meeting.[52] Where the court gives a direction under s 262(4)(b), it may also give a direction continuing or, as the case may require, renewing, for such period as may be specified in the direction, the effect in relation to the debtor of any interim order.[53] In any case where the court, on an application made under s 262 with respect to a creditors' meeting, gives a direction under s 262(4)(b) or revokes or suspends an approval under s 262(4)(a) or (5), the court may give such supplemental directions as it thinks fit, and, in particular, directions with respect to:[54]

---

[49] Section 262(3) of IA 1986.
[50] Section 262(4) of IA 1986.
[51] The court is not bound simply to apply the appropriate sums mathematically that ought to have been voted in considering if a further meeting should or should not be ordered, especially if there is a suggestion that, had there been no unfair prejudice of material irregularity, creditors might have applied their votes differently: see *Monecor (London) Ltd v Ahmed* [2008] BPIR 458. See also *Tradition (UK) Limited v Ahmed* [2009] BPIR 626.
[52] Section 262(5) of IA 1986.
[53] Section 262(6) of IA 1986.
[54] Section 262(7) of IA 1986.

(a) things done since the meeting under any voluntary arrangement approved by the meeting; and

(b) such things done since the meeting as could not have been done if an interim order had been in force in relation to the debtor when they were done.

25.31 Except in pursuance of the provisions of s 262 of IA 1986, an approval given at a creditors' meeting is not invalidated by any irregularity at or in relation to the meeting.

25.32 As regards the unfair prejudice ground, it must be established that the unfairness relates only to the terms of the IVA itself.[55] Thus a claimant who wished to pursue the debtor to judgment in order to obtain the benefit of the Third Party (Rights Against Insurers) Act 1930 as against the debtor's insurer, but was prevented from doing so by the moratorium on further proceedings imposed by the terms of the IVA, might be unfairly prejudiced.[56] An attempt to fetter a landlord's right to proceed against third parties (such as previous tenants or guarantors) would constitute unfair prejudice unless the landlord agreed.[57] In normal situations, if a tenant debtor were to continue occupying the creditor landlord's property for the purposes of trading under the voluntary arrangement, it should normally expect to pay the full rent to which the landlord was contractually entitled. A voluntary arrangement should so provide and, if it does not, in the absence of special circumstances, the landlord might well be entitled to object to the proposal on the grounds of unfair prejudice.[58]

25.33 A material irregularity would seem to include any failure to comply with the requirement of IA 1986 or IR 1986. If there has been a defect in procedure which, if followed correctly, would have made no difference to the outcome, such an irregularity is not material.[59] Obvious instances of material irregularity would be:

(1) changing the venue of the creditors' meeting without proper notice to all creditors or a failure to carry out the strict terms of any order made by the court as to the date, time and venue of the creditors' meeting;[60]

(2) failure to supply the required information;[61]

---

[55] See *Re a Debtor (No 259 of 1990)* [1992] 1 WLR 226; *IRC v Wimbledon Football Club Ltd* [2004] EWCA Civ 655, [2004] BCC 638; and *SISU Capital Fund Ltd v Tucker* [2005] EWHC 2170 (Ch), [2006] BPIR 154.
[56] See *Sea Voyager Maritime Inc v Bielecki* [1999] 1 All ER 628, [1998] BPIR 655; and *Jackson v Greenfield* [1998] BPIR 699.
[57] See *Prudential Assurance Company Ltd v PRG Powerhouse Ltd* [2007] EWHC 1002 (Ch), [2007] BCC 500, [2007] BPIR 839.
[58] See *Thomas v Ken Thomas Ltd* [2006] EWCA Civ 1504, [2007] Bus LR 429, [2007] BPIR 959.
[59] See *Re Trident Fashions Plc (in administration) (No 2)* [2004] EWHC 293, [2004] 2 BCLC 35.
[60] See *Re N* [2002] BPIR 1024.
[61] See *Fender v Commissioners of Inland Revenue* [2003] BPIR 1304, considered in detail below.

(3) breaches of IR 1986 relating to the admissibility of claims[62] or to voting rights[63] and majorities;

(4) failure of the chairman to adjourn if bound to do so;

(5) failure to deal correctly with modifications put forward by creditors;

(6) failure to disclose full extent of debts;[64]

(7) fabrication of claims in order to ensure that the requisite majority in favour of the proposal was achieved;[65] and

(8) failure to disclose private deals between creditors reached in order to achieve approval of the proposal.[66]

25.34 It is common for an allegation of material irregularity to be made tighter with an appeal under r 5.22 of IR 1986, especially where the complaint relates to the ascribing of values to the creditor's right or entitlement to vote.

CREDITOR RIGHTS IN PRACTICE: AN EXAMPLE

25.35 The facts of *Fender v Commissioners of Inland Revenue*[67] demonstrate the similarities with CVAs and the nature and extent of creditors' rights arising out of the meeting convened to approve proposals. The debtor proposed an IVA with an insolvency practitioner as his nominee. The nominee chaired the meeting at which the creditors approved the proposal. The proposal was approved by three creditors: Barclaycard (£160,000); Greville (£141,000); and ALP (just under £150,000), who made up 84.4% of the creditors by value. The debtor owned 99% of the shares in ALP and was associated with Greville, but it was not a connected party for voting purposes. The creditors who rejected the proposal, including the Inland Revenue, totalled £56,500. The Inland Revenue applied (i) under s 262(1)(a) of IA 1986 on the ground that the IVA unfairly prejudiced its interests; (ii) under s 262(1)(b) on the ground that there had been some material irregularity at or in relation to the creditors' meeting; and (iii) under r 5.17(7) of IR 1986 on the ground that the nominee had wrongly admitted Greville to vote. It argued that there had been a material irregularity in that (i) the nominee had concluded that there had been no transactions liable to be set aside as a transaction at an undervalue under s 339 of IA 1986 despite the fact that the IVA proposal disclosed that in a transaction with his wife, the debtor had exchanged his 50% interest in a property valued at £775,000 for a 50% interest in a property owned by his wife, valued at £175,000; (ii) the debtor

---

[62] See *Robert v Pinnacle Entertainment Ltd* [2003] EWHC 2394, [2004] BPIR 208.
[63] See, for example, *Re A Debtor (No 222 of 1990)* [1992] BCLC 137, [1993] BCLC 233.
[64] See *Bradburn v Kaye* [2006] BPIR 605.
[65] See *Tradition (UK) Ltd v Ahmed* [2008] EWHC 2946 (Ch).
[66] See *Somji v Cadbury Schweppes plc* [2001] BPIR 172.
[67] [2003] BPIR 1304.

had failed to disclose his 99% shareholding in ALP and the nominee had failed to place a value on it; and (iii) the nominee had failed to place a value on some excluded assets that were disclosed.

25.36 The court held that a debtor who put forward an IVA had to be honest and should take care to put all the relevant facts before the creditors. In performing his role as nominee, the nominee had a duty to exercise a professional independent judgment, informed by his qualifications and skills. Whilst a nominee was heavily reliant upon a debtor, if doubts reasonably arose as to the reliability or sufficiency of information provided, the nominee must satisfy himself that he has enough information of adequate quality to arrive at a fair provisional view as to whether a claim should be admitted. However, personal verification of every figure was not required, and the nominee would only be required to take reasonable steps. A material irregularity might occur in the proposal, the statement of affairs, the nominee's report or in the nominee's chairmanship of the creditors' meeting. An irregularity is material if it is one that would be likely to have made a material difference to the way in which the creditors would have considered and assessed the terms of the IVA.

25.37 The court further held that if the chairman's decision is challenged under s 262(1)(b) of IA 1986, or under r 5.17(5) of IR 1986, the court must at the hearing assess the merits of the dispute on the evidence adduced. On the evidence, the Greville debt was a contingent liability in respect of an unascertained sum. The judge found that the nominee had misunderstood his role under r 5.17(3) in assessing the debt, having concluded that he had a total discretion over the admission of votes. He had wrongfully included it and there was no evidence upon which he could even put a minimum value on it. Therefore, the approval of the IVA had been obtained by the wrongful admission of the Greville debt. Further, the judge found that the nominee had not considered the potential transaction at an undervalue and had told the creditors that there were no such issues by a clerical error. That was a material irregularity, as the creditors would have wanted to consider the potential claims. Pragmatically, the judge found that the non-disclosure of the shares in ALP was not an irregularity and was not material as they had no value. The approval of the IVA was revoked and no further meeting was directed.[68]

THE IVA PROTOCOL

25.38 The explosion in the nature and extent of consumer debt in the twenty-first century led to an increase in the numbers of IVAs and the development of a perceived tension between insolvency practitioners, debtors and creditors in the use of what have become known as 'consumer IVAs'. After discussions between the Insolvency Service, the British Bankers' Association and creditor and debtor organisations, a Protocol was agreed with the stated

---

[68] For further comment on the fact that the nominee's objectivity and independence must not be compromised, see in particular, the comments of Jacob LJ in *Smurthwaite v (1) Simpson-Smith (2) Mond (No 1) and (No 2)* [2006] EWCA Civ 1183, [2006] BPIR 1504.

purpose of facilitating the efficient handling of 'straightforward consumer individual voluntary arrangements'. The Protocol is a voluntary code aimed at assisting people to manage their debts effectively by paying off an agreed sum to creditors over a period which generally will be 5 years. This voluntary code is designed to ensure that the process that leads to the approval of the debtor's proposal will be transparent. It includes a form of standard terms and conditions[69] that are to be utilised with Protocol-compliant IVAs. It is also designed to provide greater certainty as regards dealing with the debtor's home and greater reassurance for creditors and debtors that the best option has been presented. Where the Protocol applies, the nominee must utilise the standard terms and conditions and summary sheet. There is no standard format for the IVA proposal itself other than regards these two documents. The documentation must state that the Protocol is being invoked and must state that the agreed documentation has been used. Since one of the purposes of the Protocol is to improve efficiency in the IVA process and reduce modifications, creditor-suggested modifications are to be expected to be kept to a minimum, especially as the intention is that creditors supporting the initiative are expected to abide by the nominee's assertion that the proposed IVA is Protocol-compliant. The protocol is a statement of best practice. It does not seek to set out the terms of any contract by which the IVA provider and the creditors, electing to operate the protocol, are to be bound in law.[70]

FAST-TRACK IVAS

25.39 The Enterprise Act 2002 introduced the concept of a fast-track IVA (FTVA). This is still a binding agreement with a debtor's creditors to pay all or part of the money he owes them. A debtor can only enter into it after he has been made bankrupt. In a FTVA the Official Receiver acts as nominee; that is, he helps the bankrupt prepare a proposal to put to his creditors and, if they accept the proposal, acts as supervisor, looking after the arrangement and making payments to creditors in accordance with the proposal.

25.40 The Official Receiver's fee to act as nominee is £300, and as supervisor he also charges 15% of all sums realised. In addition, the bankrupt will have to pay a registration fee of £35 for his FTVA to be recorded on the public register of all IVAs.

25.41 Once the creditors have approved the FTVA, the Official Receiver will apply to court for the bankruptcy order to be annulled (ie treated as if it had never existed). This will usually happen about 5 to 7 weeks after the FTVA has started. Once the bankruptcy order has been annulled, the bankrupt will no longer be subject to any of the bankruptcy restrictions, and if any assets (such as his home) were not included in his FTVA for distribution to the creditors, these will be returned to the bankrupt. The Official Receiver will tell anyone he notified of the bankruptcy order that the bankrupt is no longer bankrupt.

---

[69] See *Individual Voluntary Arrangements* (Jordans), at Appendix E6.
[70] *Mond v MBNA Europe Bank Ltd* [2011] Bus LR 513.

Details of the bankruptcy will be removed from the individual insolvency register, but the register does contain details of those in an IVA.

25.42 It is for the bankrupt to draw up a proposal to his creditors to pay part or all of his debts. The proposal must contain:

- details of the debts;
- the assets available to be sold;
- payments he is willing to make to his creditors;
- how long he will take to make these payments; and
- details of the fees and costs of administering the FTVA.

25.43 The Official Receiver, as nominee, will put the proposal to the creditors so that they can vote on whether or not to accept it. If they accept it, the agreement is binding and prevents them taking legal action to enforce their debts. The bankrupt, in turn, must deliver up the assets and make the payments offered in the proposal.

25.44 The bankrupt commits a criminal offence if he makes any false statement or fraudulently does or omits to do anything to get his creditors' approval of a FTVA.

25.45 The Official Receiver will send a copy of the proposal to each of the creditors so that they may vote on whether to accept it. Creditors who receive notice of the proposal will be bound by the FTVA. If the bankrupt does not name a particular creditor, that creditor would be able to apply for the FTVA to be revoked once they became aware of it. For the FTVA to be accepted, 75% or more of the creditors who vote must agree to the proposal. After that, the Official Receiver becomes supervisor of the FTVA and is responsible for realising the assets, collecting payments due under the arrangement and then paying that money to creditors. The bankrupt/debtor must co-operate in helping the supervisor to realise his assets and by making the agreed payments.

Part 3
LOCAL AUTHORITIES

Chapter 26

LOCAL AUTHORITY MEETINGS

INTRODUCTION

26.1 This chapter mainly deals with councils. There have always been close links between local authorities and the health sector, and the provisions of the Health and Social Care Act 2012 have increased the need for joint working. An understanding of the rules relating to meetings of health bodies may therefore be highly relevant, and whilst most of this Chapter deals with local authorities, it also briefly covers the provisions relating to meeting of health bodies.

Local authorities are democratically elected statutory corporations, exercising specific functions and powers in specific geographical areas. They cover everything from large county councils and city councils – Birmingham City Council is reputedly the largest local authority in Europe; to small district councils. County councils, borough and district councils (this includes all unitary councils such as Metropolitan District Councils), and London Boroughs are called principal councils in the legislation.

26.2 Different types of local authorities exercise different functions (for example, county councils deal with education and social services, but do not exercise housing functions). However, the law relating to how local authorities undertake their business at meetings generally applies to all types of authority and all different functions.

26.3 There are detailed legislative requirements as to how meetings are conducted in the local government context. Also, general statutory provisions impact on local government meetings in the same way as many other meetings, for example, human rights issues, equalities, defamation etc.

26.4 The Local Government Act 1972 (LGA 1972) is the starting point for understanding both the structure of local government in England and Wales and the fundamental rules about how much of local authority business is transacted at meetings. Schedule 12 to the LGA 1972 is particularly important. It deals with 'Meetings and Proceedings of Local Authorities'.

26.5 Since 1972, there have been many changes to the structure of local government. In 2000, the Local Government Act 2000 was passed, which fundamentally changed the internal decision-making arrangements for local authorities in England and Wales and had an impact on the running of their meetings. The Localism Act 2011 made several more changes to the legislation affecting local government and significantly changed some of the matters which had been brought in by the 2000 Act, particularly in relation to the Code of Conduct and the Standards regime. This introduction looks briefly at this overall picture, before going on to explore the detail of the law relating to local authority meetings.

Local government structure

26.6 LGA 1972 established the overall structure of local government in England and Wales. Councils were constituted as 'county councils' or 'district councils' (which legal definition also covered city councils and borough councils). The London Government Act 1963 established London boroughs.

26.7 There was further reform in the 1980s and 1990s to abolish metropolitan county councils and the Greater London Council, establish unitary authorities in England for the first time outside metropolitan areas and change the local government structure of Wales into 22 unitary authorities. The last round of changes in England took place with effect from 2009.

26.8 All of these local authorities (whether a county council, district council, city council, borough council, London borough, metropolitan council or unitary council) are known as 'principal councils'. This definition is important for understanding the law of meetings, as different rules apply to local authorities which are principal councils than to those which are not.

26.9 In most parts of England and Wales there is another tier of local government below principal councils. These are parish councils (in England) and community councils (in Wales).

26.10 Every parish or community has a parish/community meeting and some have a council. The rules relating to the meetings of these councils will be referred to within this chapter, but the main concentration will be on the law relating to the meetings of principal councils.

Local government equals meetings!

26.11 Local government is famous for its meetings. There is still a stereotypical image of local government holding meetings in a dusty council chamber, with arcane points of order and a sparsely populated public gallery attending the meeting with a vain hope of influencing decisions.

26.12 This is far from the position today. There have been huge changes in the way that local authorities organise their business and recent legislative changes have accelerated this.

26.13 Meetings have always been of fundamental importance to local government, primarily because, until LGA 2000, decisions could not be taken by elected councillors on their own. Decisions could only be taken by the full council (ie all the elected councillors meeting together), committees or subcommittees, or individual members of staff of the council to whom a decision had lawfully been delegated.

26.14 Elected councillors are also known as elected members: councillors hold office but are not employed by the council; staff employed by the council are nowadays all known as officers. The terms 'members' and 'officers' are used here.

26.15 The procedure for holding meetings and transacting business therefore became extremely important. As public authorities are capable of being taken to judicial review, it was also essential that local authorities adhered to their own procedures, as failure to do so could give rise to judicial challenge.

Types of meeting

26.16 Not all local authority meetings are the same. It is important to distinguish between different types as different rules apply to their conduct. Local authorities are involved in dozens of meetings every week in their area. These can range from a meeting of the full council (which could be 60 or 70 elected members meeting together) to a consultative meeting arranged with a small group of local residents on a particular proposal for their area.

26.17 Although not legally defined in this way, it may be helpful to think of local authority meetings in the following terms:

(1) meetings of elected councillors where decisions are taken and functions of the local authority are exercised;

(2) formal meetings arranged by the council for consultation, discussion, engagement with the public, members of the community, other public bodies, for example, local area meetings, tenants' forums; site visits; and

(3) meetings arranged by the local authority for a one-off/particular purpose, for example, a consultation meeting in a particular area to discuss a proposal for changes in services, a public meeting arranged by the council to facilitate debate about a contentious issue.

26.18 It will only be the first type of meeting described here (ie formal decision-making meetings) which is covered by the detailed legal framework outlined in this chapter. It will usually be the local authority's own internal rules (standing orders) which will govern the running of other types of meeting and a section on these is included at **26.32ff**.

26.19 With certain very limited exceptions laid down in statute, all voting members of a local authority committee must be elected members of the authority. An authority may co-opt members onto a committee who may participate but cannot vote. One of the exceptions to this is Health and Well

Being Boards, established by the Health and Social Care Act 2012. These are, by statute, committees of the Council yet the membership includes officers of the council, members of the relevant Clinical Commissioning Groups, and a member from local Healthwatch. At the time of writing the regulations concerning Health and Wellbeing Boards had not been produced, but the government had indicated that its intention was that all members would exercise voting rights.

26.20 It should be mentioned at this point that there can be debate over whether a gathering of a particular nature or the consideration of an issue in a particular way constitutes a meeting or not. In the case of *R v Secretary of State ex parte London Borough of Hillingdon*,[1] this issue was considered. It was held that delegation to a committee of one under s 101 of LGA 1972 was ultra vires. The word 'committee' could not be construed to permit a committee of one. It can also be important to know whether the meeting is a meeting of councillors, in which case the rules in this chapter will usually apply; or if it is a joint meeting with officers, in which case the rules are different. Generally, meetings held jointly with officers do not attract the same rules in relation to notice and access to the public as do member meetings.

26.21 The 1972 Act, (Sch 12, para 39(1)) requires that all questions coming before a local authority shall be decided by a majority of the members present and voting. To date this means physically present and so rules out the possibility of members being involved in meetings 'virtually', via a video link, for example. The government consulted about the possibility of changing this in the past, but nothing to change the legislation has appeared, and to the contrary, recent changes to the legislation appear to have made such innovations less likely.

Impact of the Local Government Act 2000

26.22 The Local Government Act 2000 (LGA 2000) was the most wide-ranging and fundamental change to the internal running of local government for decades. The Local Government and Public Involvement in Health Act 2007 (LGPIHA 2007) made changes to local government structure and operation. The Localism Act 2011 has made further changes. There are also some sets of regulations which are very important. It is worth looking briefly at the changes which these two key Acts introduced to the whole decision-making structure of local government before going on to look at the law relating specifically to meetings.

26.23 Prior to LGA 2000, the traditional approach of local authorities was to have a set of committees dealing with particular services, for example, a social services committee, a housing committee etc. Virtually all decision-making was delegated from the full council to these committees, which followed clear rules about how they ran.

---

[1] [1986] 1 All ER 273.

26.24 The full council got together periodically to make major decisions (usually every 6 or 8 weeks) and *had* to meet every year at the annual meeting.

26.25 LGA 2000 changed the committee structure for most authorities. All authorities except those district councils with a population of under 85,000 had to adopt one of three models of executive decision making, and so only some smaller district councils continue a modified version of the committee approach. The Localism Act 2011 changed this so that all councils could choose to change their governance structure back to a committee structure if they wished, in a straightforward way, although they have to observe the provisions of Sch 2 of the Localism Act. A petition of residents can also cause a referendum to be held about the issue.

26.26 In most authorities 'executive decision-making' was adopted and remains the case. This moved the control and power into the hands of a small group of elected members (the executive or cabinet) with a leader of the council. Some councils decided to have an elected mayor. At the time there was also a third option, of a mayor and council manager model. This was adopted by the City of Stoke-on-Trent but was not considered to be a successful model and so was abolished in LGPIHA 2007. Even the new model of elected mayor is only in place in a handful of councils across the country, although the Coalition Government required referendums to be held in 11 cities in May 2012. In 10 of the cities, the voters voted against an elected mayor. The exception was Bristol, which voted yes and held elections for an elected mayor in November 2012. (The law relating to the meetings of council with an elected mayor is not fundamentally different and so is not dealt with specifically in this chapter.)

26.27 The vast majority of authorities opted (after public consultation) for an executive and leader model. This involves an executive (also called a cabinet, which term will be used here) of up to ten elected members with the leader heading the cabinet.

26.28 The two most profound changes introduced by LGA 2000 which impact on meetings of local authorities are:

(1) It is possible for a local authority to have a cabinet comprised solely of one political party (if they have the majority of votes at council or this is agreed). Prior to this, all committees had to be politically balanced according to the overall political balance of the authority. In order to provide a check and balance to this potentially powerful cabinet, new committees called 'overview and scrutiny committees' have to be established. These can call in and review cabinet decisions.

(2) It is possible to delegate the power to make decisions to individual cabinet members, ie some core operational decisions of the local authority can be made without a meeting being held at all.

26.29 Alongside the executive/scrutiny approach, local authorities have still had to retain both the council as a whole, and provide for it to meet to be able to exercise the functions which it cannot delegate. There are some matters which can only be decided by full council. This includes the appointment or dismissal of the Head of Paid Service; the setting of the council tax and the council's budget, and the approval of matters such as a change in governance arrangements.

26.30 Councils will also tend to have a more traditional committee structure for dealing with certain functions, particularly those of a quasi-judicial nature or where individual applications are considered. These include dealing with planning applications and licensing applications. The LGA 1972, s 101 permits the council to delegate the discharge of their functions to a committee or sub committee or to an officer, provided that the delegation is not forbidden by any other legislation. For these committees the rules in relation to political balance set out in s 15 of the 1989 Act continue to apply.

26.31 The 2000 Act meant that it was important to know which functions were 'executive' functions and which functions belonged to the cabinet. The general rule is that any function of an authority which is not specified in regulations is to be the responsibility of the executive (LGA 2000, s 9D(2)). The relevant Regulations are the Local Authorities (Functions and Responsibilities) (England) Regulations 2000[2] which should be consulted whenever the question of responsibility for functions is in issue.

Internal rules – constitution and standing orders

26.32 External statutory provisions which apply to the way in which local authorities hold their meetings are supplemented by the authority's own internal rules on the conduct of business.

26.33 Section 37 of LGA 2000 requires local authorities to prepare and keep up to date a 'Constitution', which must contain information that the Secretary of State may direct, together with a copy of the local authority's standing orders. Local authorities must ensure that copies of the constitution are available free of charge for inspection by members of the public at their principal office, and copies of the constitution can be supplied on payment of a reasonable fee. These days all councils have their constitution available on their website for the public to see.

26.34 Paragraph 42 of Sch 12 to LGA 1972 allows local authorities to make standing orders 'for the regulation of their proceedings and business' and also allows them to vary or revoke any such standing orders. There are also more specific powers in LGA 1972 relating to standing orders, for example, the power in s 106 to make standing orders for committees and joint committees.

---

[2] SI 2000/2853.

26.35 For many years it was a matter of complete discretion for local authorities as to what internal rules they put in their standing orders. However, s 20 of the Local Government and Housing Act 1989 gave the Secretary of State power to make regulations which could require local authorities to incorporate into their standing orders certain prescribed matters for regulating proceedings and business. Section 20(2) gives examples of the sort of matters that any regulations could cover, including the ability of individual members to requisition meetings of the authority, to require a vote etc.

26.36 The Local Authorities (Standing Orders) (England) Regulations 2001[3] (and equivalent 2006 Regulations in Wales[4]) have been made under this section and prescribe the contents of standing orders of local authorities operating executive arrangements. The standing orders that *have* to be incorporated relate to staffing matters and conduct of certain business; they do not directly affect the conduct of meetings, but in some circumstances control the membership of committees.

26.37 Standing orders cannot depart from any statutory requirements for the holding or running of meetings, but otherwise it is up to individual authorities to decide what detail goes in their standing orders relating to meetings.

26.38 Provisions included within standing orders can be challenged – see *R v Flintshire County Council ex parte Armstrong-Braun*.[5] Here, the Court of Appeal upheld an appeal by a councillor representing the Green Party on Flintshire County Council who challenged the proposed inclusion of a new standing order requiring that notice of every motion to the full council should be seconded. As the only representative of his political party on the county council, he argued that this was inconsistent with the principles of openness, accountability and representation, as he was unlikely ever to find another member to second his motions. The Court of Appeal held that, in principle, a standing order could be quashed as falling outside the policy and objectives of LGA 1972 and being 'otherwise legally objectionable'. It did not determine whether the particular standing order was ultra vires, but remitted the matter back to the council to give full consideration to the implications of including it in their standing orders.

26.39 If a local authority departs from its own standing orders, this is capable of judicial review (see **26.198**).

26.40 The next sections of this chapter look at the detailed statutory provisions which apply to local authority decision-making and formal meetings.

---

[3] SI 2001/3384.
[4] Local Authorities (Standing Orders) (Wales) Regulations 2006, SI 2006/1275.
[5] [2001] EWCA Civ 345.

CONVENING MEETINGS

26.41 In this section we will look at the meetings local authorities have to convene, where meetings can be held and the rules relating to the notice and agenda for meetings.

What meetings must local authorities hold?

26.42 Although the manner in which local authorities conduct their business using meetings (for example, the frequency, venue and arrangements for them) is largely a matter for each authority, there are some meetings that they *must* hold.

26.43 Principal councils must hold an annual meeting in March, April or May of every year, at 12 noon if no time is specifically fixed. This is required by para 1 of Sch 12 to LGA 1972. If the year in question is one when an election is taking place, the annual meeting must be held on the eighth day after the day of retirement of councillors or such other day within 21 days following the day of retirement as the council fixes.

26.44 In addition to this statutory requirement to hold an annual full council meeting, an authority can hold such others during the year as it thinks fit. Now that so many functions are dealt with by the executive many councils arrange to hold meetings as infrequently as every other month, although they are able to hold extraordinary meetings if necessary.

26.45 Schedule 12 to LGA 1972 also sets out circumstances where a meeting *must* be held if a requisition requiring a meeting signed by five members of the council has been presented to the chairman and he fails to call an extraordinary meeting within 7 days after this request (Sch 12, para 3).

26.46 There are slightly different rules for parishes and communities.

26.47 Parish and community councils must hold one annual meeting every year, which must be in May and, if no time is fixed, it must be at 6 pm. If it is an election year, the annual meeting must be held on or within 14 days after the day on which councillors elected at the election take office.

26.48 Parish councils must, in addition to the annual meeting, hold at least three meetings. These can be at such hour and on such days as the councils themselves decide.

26.49 Community councils have more flexibility and can hold additional meetings during the year at such times and dates as they think fit.

26.50 These requirements are set out for parish councils in Part II of Sch 12 to LGA 1972 and for community councils in Part IV of Sch 12.

26.51 Both parish council and community council meetings can be requisitioned by two members of the council presenting a request to the chairman of the council and him refusing to call a meeting within 7 days.

26.52 Parish meetings (ie small parishes which do not have a parish council) are covered by Part III of Sch 12 to LGA 1972. This requires that the parish meeting of a parish must assemble annually on some day between 1 March and 1 June (inclusive) every year. The meetings can be held on such days and at such times as are fixed by the parish council or, if there is no council in the parish, by the chairman of the parish meeting. The meeting must not commence earlier than 6 pm.

26.53 For community meetings, Part V of Sch 12 to LGA 1972 details the requirements. There is no requirement on a community meeting to be held at any time. A meeting can be convened in particular circumstances and by particular people (see below).

Where should meetings be held?

26.54 Principal councils can hold meetings wherever they determine. Paragraph 4 of Sch 12 to LGA 1972 allows meetings to be held either within or outside the local authority area. Section 132 of LGA 1972 gives principal councils the power to acquire premises for the purposes of holding meetings and s 134 allows parish and community councils to use rooms in schools maintained by the LEA for specific meetings.

26.55 Meetings of parish or community councils, or parish or community meetings, can be held anywhere the council determines, but should not be held in licensed premises unless no other suitable room is available either free of charge or at a reasonable cost.

26.56 Clearly, the drafters of the 1972 legislation did not think it was feasible to restrict a meeting of a principal council in the same way!

Notice of meetings

26.57 The general presumption that the conduct of local government should be open and transparent demands that the public have access to meetings. This is dealt with in detail at **26.114ff**. This right would be substantially prejudiced if councils were not required to give clear advance notice of when, where and for what purposes meetings were to be convened. Therefore, there are very strict requirements about the convening of meetings and notice which must be given. These were varied for meetings of the executive with effect from September 2012 through the Local Authorities (Executive Arrangements) (Meetings and Access to Information) (England) Regulations 2012[6] (see **26.63**). These must be observed in relation to meetings of executive bodies; which are defined as

---

[6] SI 2012/2089.

meetings of the executive; a committee of the executive; a joint committee composed of meetings of a local authority executive; a sub committee of such and an area committee of a local authority executive.

26.58 Section 100A(6)(a) of LGA 1972 requires that principal councils must give public notice of the time and place of the council meeting by posting it at the offices of the council at least 5 clear days before the meeting. The requirement to give 5 days' advance notice was brought in in 2002 in England in place of the previously required 3 days' notice. This seems to have created an inconsistency in the legislation in that para 4(2) of Sch 12 to LGA 1972 requires that a principal council must give 3 clear days' notice by publishing notice of this at the council's offices and by sending a summons to attend the meeting specifying the business to be transacted to the usual place of residence of every member of the council. In Wales, the requirement in both pieces of the legislation is for 3 clear days' notice.

26.59 The calculation of the days has been the subject of dispute. In *R v Swansea City Council ex parte Elitestone Ltd*,[7] the Court of Appeal decided that the period was exclusive of the day of notice and the meeting itself and also excluded Saturdays and Sundays. The notice requirements under s 100A (5 clear days' public notice for England and 3 clear days' public notice for Wales) apply not only to meetings of the full council of principal councils, but also to meetings of committees and subcommittees which are open to the public in the same way and require the same notification (s 100E(1)).

26.60 Requirements for convening parish and community council meetings are set out in Parts II–IV of Sch 12 to LGA 1972 and broadly require 3 clear days' notice of the time and place of the meeting to be fixed in some conspicuous place in the area and a summons to attend the meeting to be sent to all members giving the same notice.

26.61 For parish meetings and community meetings, not less than 7 clear days' notice has to be given of a meeting by posting a notice in a conspicuous place in the area and by giving any other publicity to the holding of the meeting that appears reasonable. If there is particular business to be transacted at a parish or community meeting involving changes to the grouping of the parish or the establishment or dissolution of a parish/community meeting, additional notice of the meeting has to be given. For parish meetings this is 14 clear days and for community meetings, 30 clear days.

26.62 The introduction of executive decision-making to local government in England and Wales under LGA 2000 required specific consideration of the arrangements for convening and accessing the new type of meetings brought in by this form of decision-making.

---

[7] [1993] 66 P&CR 422.

26.63 The Local Authorities (Executive Arrangements) (Access to Information) (England) Regulations 2000[8] introduced provisions relating to executive decision-making. This included the concept of 'key decisions' in England, ie a decision of some significance in financial or service delivery implications. In September 2012 these regulations were revoked and replaced by the Local Authorities (Executive Arrangements) (Meetings and Access to Information) (England) Regulations 2012.[9] These made some significant changes to the 2000 Regulations and set out the process that local authorities in England must complete before they can take an executive decision, and the rights of councillors and members of the public to attend meetings and to inspect the agenda, reports and background papers relating to executive decisions. Failure to comply with the detail of these regulations can prevent an authority from taking a decision, or render that decision open to being held to be void on judicial review.

26.64 The new regulations only apply to executive decisions and not to decisions to be taken by the council, or a committee or an officer on behalf of the council. Similar, but significantly different processes apply to decision-making by or on behalf of the council, and these processes are set out in ss 100A to 100K of the LGA 1972.

26.65 The agenda setting out the items of business to be transacted at the meeting, together with any written reports, must be sent to the cabinet members at least 5 clear days in advance of the meeting, and must be made available for public inspection at the same time.

26.66 The sections below look at the impact of key decisions on whether members of the public are able to attend meetings, but where such a meeting is to be held, an item of business can only be considered at it where a copy of the agenda or part of the agenda including the item has been available for inspection by the public for at least 5 clear days before the meeting or, if the meeting is convened at shorter notice (which is allowed where there are exceptional circumstances and special urgency), the item must have been available for inspection by the public from the time the meeting was convened.

26.67 A copy of the agenda and report for a public meeting has to be available for inspection by the public at the offices of the local authority at the same time as they are made available to members of the executive or decision-making body responsible for making the decisions to which the papers relate. Previously, there was a requirement to publish a Forward Plan once a month, at least 14 days before the start of the month, and setting out prescribed details of all the key decisions which the authority anticipated making in the next 4 months and who will be taking each decision. This has been replaced by a requirement to publish 28 days' notice of any intended key decision, and the requirement to publish a formal Forward Plan has gone. The authority then

---

[8] SI 2000/3272.
[9] SI 2012/2089.

has discretion whether it wishes to give notice separately for each intended key decision or to publish regular 'bulletins'. The notice must now not just be available for inspection, but must be available on the Council's website.

26.68 The authority cannot take a key decision unless it has given the required 28-day notice. If a matter is urgent, reg 10 allows the authority to take an urgent key decision without giving 28 days' notice where it is impracticable to give the full notice, provided that the authority give at least 5 clear days' notice to all members of the relevant Overview and Scrutiny Committee of the authority, which can then call in the decision to check that it was genuinely urgent.

26.69 Where the key decision is so urgent that there is not even time to give 5 clear days' notice, reg 11 allows the authority to take the decision without that notice if the Chairman of the relevant Overview and Scrutiny Committee has agreed that the key decision is urgent and cannot reasonably be deferred.

26.70 This notice requirement applies whether the key decision is to be taken by the cabinet at a meeting, or by the executive leader or the executive mayor or by another cabinet member, or by an officer without a meeting taking place.

26.71 The replacement of the requirement for a key decision to be in a Forward Plan published at least 14 days before the month in which the key decision is to be taken by a requirement for 28 clear days' notice of each key decision.

26.72 The position in Wales is slightly different and is governed by the Local Authorities (Executive Arrangements) (Decisions, Documents and Meetings) (Wales) Regulations 2001,[10] which do not incorporate the concept of 'key decisions' but deal with meeting arrangements for executives and committees in Wales.

Agenda for meetings

26.73 In relation to principal councils, the notice of the meeting and the summons to attend the meeting must specify the business which is proposed to be transacted at that meeting (para 4(2) of Sch 12 to LGA 1972).

26.74 Paragraph 4(5) states that, with two exceptions, only the business which is specified in the summons can actually be transacted at the meeting. The two exceptions are:

(1) business which is required by statutory provision to be transacted at the annual meeting of the council; and

---

[10] SI 2001/2290.

(2) any other business brought before the meeting as a matter of urgency in accordance with the council's standing orders.

26.75 Section 100B of LGA 1972 states that copies of the agenda for a meeting of a principal council and (unless the matter is of a confidential nature – see **26.126**) any reports to be considered at the meeting must be open for inspection by members of the public for at least 5 clear days before the meeting (unless the meeting has been convened at shorter notice).

26.76 Section 100B(4) expands on the provisions of Sch 12 to LGA 1972 in dealing with access to the agenda and urgent items. It reinforces that an item of business cannot be considered at a meeting unless a copy of the agenda which includes that item has been open to the public for inspection for at least 5 clear days before the meeting (or for a shorter time if the meeting is convened more urgently). This does not apply where an item has been added to the agenda as a matter of urgency. Section 100B(4)(b) states that urgent items can be added to the agenda of a meeting of a principal council only if the chairman of the meeting is of the opinion that the item should be considered as a matter of urgency by reason of special circumstances and that these reasons must be included in the minutes of the meeting. This is one of the very rare examples of a statutory power being held by the chairman of a local authority meeting, who has absolute discretion to determine what constitutes special circumstances and to agree or refuse to accept an urgent item on the agenda of a meeting. A decision which was potentially unreasonable would be judicially reviewable.

26.77 It is difficult to challenge a situation where a local authority proceeds to consider an item of business which is not on the agenda but is not added as an urgent item.

26.78 In the case of *Ayles v Romsey and Stockbridge Rural District Council*,[11] a builder challenged the decision of a local authority to refuse him planning permission on the basis that the summons to the council meeting had not mentioned his particular application. The court decided that he had no locus on which to challenge the decision and, in any event, the notice convening the meeting referred to various building plans having been passed and this was sufficient. The court took a hard line that it should not be open to anybody to challenge the lack of specific reference to a matter on an agenda as it would 'expose public bodies of this kind to the greatest risk, and it would expose to the greatest of risk persons who deal with such bodies'. The court did agree that elected councillors may have the right to complain in these circumstances.

26.79 This case is old authority now and it is likely that the courts would take a more robust approach to a council which sought to rely on a vague or blanket agenda item if the consequence of this was the lack of awareness by persons affected of the nature of the business to be transacted.

---

[11] (1944) 42 LGR 210.

26.80 In relation to meetings of parish and community councils, Part II of Sch 12 to LGA 1972 is silent in relation to the limitation on considering at a properly convened meeting only those items of business that have been included in the agenda sent out with the summons for the meeting.

RUNNING MEETINGS

26.81 In this section, we will look at chairing of meetings, rules relating to voting and quorum provisions.

Chairing meetings

26.82 At a meeting of a principal council, if the chairman of the meeting is present, he must preside (Sch 12, Part I, para 5 to LGA 1972). If the chairman is absent from a meeting of the full council, the vice-chairman shall preside if present or, if not, another member of the council chosen by the members present shall preside. LGA 2000 added a rider to this which prevents a member of the cabinet of a principal council being chosen to preside at the meeting of the principal council in these circumstances. There are specific provisions relating to the chairing of the council meeting of a London borough which allow the mayor or, in his absence, the deputy mayor, to preside.

26.83 In parish and community councils, the chairman or vice-chairman must preside at a meeting of the council and, in both their absences, any councillor as the members present choose.

26.84 In relation to parish meetings, where the parish has a separate council, the chairman of that council, if he is present, must preside at a parish meeting and, in his absence, the vice-chairman of that council if he is present must preside. If there is no separate parish council for the parish, the chairman of the parish meeting chosen for the year, if present, must preside. If all of these people are not present at a parish meeting, then the meeting can appoint any person present to take the chair.

26.85 In relation to community meetings, where there is a community council, the chairman of that council if present must preside. In any other case, a person present at the meeting can be appointed to chair that meeting.

26.86 There is little statutory regulation of the roles and responsibilities of the chair of local authority meetings. We have already seen that the chairman has power to decide on adding urgent business to the agenda. There are also powers relating to voting (see below).

Voting at meetings

26.87 Schedule 12 to LGA 1972 deals with the rules relating to voting at local authority meetings. The same basic rules apply to meetings of all local authorities.

26.88 Schedule 12, Part VI, para 39 states that, subject to the provisions of any enactment, all matters to be considered by a local authority shall be decided by a majority of the members of the authority present and voting at the meeting. This applies to meetings of council, committees and of the executive. Because of this provision, councillors who do not attend in person any particular meeting cannot vote by proxy, postal or other means of voting. If there is an equality of votes, then the general rule is that the Chairman, or other person presiding at the meeting is to have a second or casting vote. These rules mean that councils are not able to provide that, for example, decisions must be made unanimously or by a certain majority if this differs from the provisions in the Act.

26.89 The effect of these provisions was considered by the Court of Appeal in *R (Friends of Hethel) v South Norfolk District Council*.[12] In this case, the terms of reference of an area planning committee ('APC') provided that if officers recommended a grant of planning permission, the APC could only refuse permission if a two-thirds majority voted for refusal. In respect of one application, officers had recommended that planning permission be granted. A simple majority voted to refuse permission. The council's planning committee then voted to grant permission (by a simple majority) on the basis that the two-thirds majority had not been achieved. The Court of Appeal quashed the planning permission, on the basis that permission had been validly refused by the APC. The requirement in the APCC's terms of reference for a two-thirds majority was unlawful, because it contravened the statutory rules set out in Sch 12 to the 1972 Act. The Court of Appeal went on to consider an argument that the effect of that unlawful requirement in the APC's terms of reference was that any decision it reached under those terms of reference was unlawful, and so would mean that its decision to refuse planning permission was unlawful. That argument was rejected. The court held that the arrangements by which the decision had been delegated to the APC were in principle lawful, and the only aspect of those arrangements which was unlawful was the requirement for a two-thirds majority in favour of refusal, if officers recommended in favour of the application. Accordingly the decision of the APC to grant the planning permission by a simple majority was valid.

26.90 There are circumstances where statute requires other than a simple majority vote, for example, s 239 of LGA 1972, which requires a special majority for a resolution to promote or oppose a Local Act of Parliament.

---

[12] [2010] EWCA Civ 894, [2011] 1 WLR 1216.

26.91 If the vote is equal, para 39(2) states that the person presiding at the meeting will have a second or casting vote. A second vote would apply where he had already voted. A casting vote would be where he had not voted initially and the vote remained equal.

26.92 The circumstances in which it is or is not appropriate for the chairman of a meeting to exercise the second or casting votes was considered in *R v Bradford Metropolitan City Council ex parte Wilson*.[13]

26.93 Here, a decision by the council was challenged on the basis that the Lord Mayor (who was presiding over the full council meeting) had exercised his casting vote along party political lines and was therefore in breach of the council's standing orders and contrary to the legitimate expectation of the applicant. An argument was made that the second or casting vote in these circumstances should be exercised without regard to party political considerations and that the chairman in these circumstances was in an analogous position to the position as the Speaker of the House of Commons and should operate apolitically.

26.94 The Divisional Court rejected this argument and decided that the purpose of the casting vote was simply to avoid the deadlock which would otherwise ensue. It was expected that the chairman in these circumstances should properly exercise the casting vote and should make his decision honestly and in the light of his conscience as to what was the best resolution for the citizens of the area. If his motivation had solely been to enable the leader of the Conservative group to run the council, this may have affected the decision.

26.95 Lord Justice Bingham stated as follows:[14]

> 'I would not, however, wish to encourage the view that a casting vote should be exercised unadvisedly, lightly or wantonly. It should be exercised with great circumspection, taking the broadest view of what the public interest requires and bearing in mind that what is sauce for today's goose may be sauce for tomorrow's gander, but cases in which the law will intervene will be rare. In any ordinary case the guarantee of propriety must be found not in legal sanctions but in the wisdom, judgement and sense of civic responsibility of the individual office-holder.'

26.96 The court also decided that it would have been unlawful for the council to agree to include in their standing orders a proposal that the use of the casting vote should only be used in exceptional circumstances and in any case could not be used to change the status quo. This would put an unlawful fetter on the discretion given by Parliament to the chairman as to how to exercise his vote in these circumstances.

26.97 In relation to the *method* of voting, standing orders of the relevant local authority will usually provide for this. In the case of parish and community

---

[13] [1990] 2 QB 375.
[14] [1990] 2 QB 375, at 383.

councils, Sch 12, paras 13 and 29 state that the manner of voting should be by a show of hands unless the council's standing orders say otherwise.

26.98 In many meetings, non-controversial issues are dealt with very quickly and without necessarily a formal showing of hands leading to an announced result. The courts have considered these rather casual approaches to voting and have decided that a resolution may be validly passed even without a show of hands or ballot: see, for example, *R v Highbury Corner Magistrates' Court ex parte Ewing*,[15] where a non-controversial resolution was passed without dissent 'on the nod'.

26.99 The 2004 case of *R (Tromans) v Cannock Chase District Council*[16] saw the Court of Appeal intervening in an unprecedented way in the internal procedures and voting arrangements of a council.

26.100 Cannock Chase's Planning Committee voted on a contentious planning application. The Committee chairman declared the vote as seven to six in favour of granting planning permission. The Council's solicitor and the Committee clerk similarly recorded the vote as seven to six in favour of granting planning permission. Mrs Tromans, a local resident who was opposed to the development and attended the Committee meeting, and two parish councillors present recorded the vote as seven to six against granting planning permission. Some time later, the Committee took a short recess and Mrs Tromans approached the district planning officer and said that she thought that the chairman had counted the vote incorrectly. The district planning officer said that he thought that the chairman had counted the vote correctly. He did not raise the issue with the Committee chairman and the Committee re-convened after the recess and completed its other business.

26.101 There was a side issue in that one member of the Committee had left the room during the course of the consideration of this planning application and had returned just in time for the vote. Members had previously been advised by the Council's solicitor that they must not vote on a planning matter unless they had been present for the whole of the discussion of that matter. The chairman and the officers were clear, and recorded, that this member had not participated in the vote, but Mrs Tromans was under the impression that she had voted against the application.

26.102 It would have been open to any member of the Committee who had concerns about the accuracy of the vote to request the chairman to confirm the result, but no member of the Committee made such a request. It would also have been open to any member of the Committee, under the council's standing orders, to ask that his vote for or against the application be recorded and to urge other members of the Committee to record their votes, thus demonstrating the accuracy or inaccuracy of the declared result. Further, the

---

[15] [1991] 1 WLR 388.
[16] [2004] EWCA Civ 1036; [2004] All ER (D) 504 (Jul), CA.

Committee is required to vote at its next meeting to confirm the accuracy of the minutes of its last meeting. So there was an existing mechanism whereby Mrs Tromans could have expressed her concerns to a member of the Committee, who could then have asked individual members how they had voted, and could then have moved a correction to the minute if he were still persuaded that the chairman had declared the vote incorrectly.

26.103 Despite this, the Court of Appeal felt that there were no statutory or other provisions in relation to the voting of a committee which would assist. The fact that such mechanisms existed for ensuring the accuracy of the decision of the Committee, and that no member of the Committee had felt it necessary to question the accuracy of the decision, did not deter the Court of Appeal from concluding that, where a member of the public raised with an officer an issue as to the accuracy of the vote, there was a duty upon the officer to relay the concerns of a member of the public to the chairman, and then a duty upon the chairman to consider whether there was any doubt about the accuracy of the vote. Accordingly, the Court of Appeal quashed the decision of the Committee.

26.104 This raises difficult practical issues for the administration of committee meetings.

26.105 Taken at face value, it now appears to be necessary for the chairman, at the end of each meeting, to ask the officers and members present, and perhaps any members of the public, whether they have any concerns about the accuracy of any of the votes taken at that meeting. The Court of Appeal did not provide any assistance to chairmen as to how they might confirm such accuracy later in the meeting, when some of those members of the Committee who took part in the vote may already have left the council chamber or committee room.

26.106 The Court of Appeal's judgment in this case flies in the face of the Local Government Acts, which are very clear in limiting participation in decision-making in local authorities to the duly elected or co-opted members of the relevant authority. In effect, it extends to members of the public a right of challenge at the meeting.

26.107 The House of Lords refused to allow an appeal on the basis that this case raised no matter of public interest, which is a surprising conclusion.

26.108 The council's Constitution will provide for the circumstances in which a named or recorded vote can be called for. It is usual for a number of members to have to request this before it is done, as it is a rather lengthy and cumbersome process. When a named vote is called for, the clerk to the meeting will read out the names of individual members and they will declare if they are for or against the matter.

26.109 In local authorities voting almost never takes place secretly. The exception to this, which is by custom and practice rather than through legislation, is when there is a contest for the chairmanship of the Council or a committee of the council, when it is usual for members to vote secretly in order for future business not to be affected.

2.110 In parish and community councils, members also have the statutory right to have the voting recorded on any particular question so as to record what each councillor voted in respect of a particular resolution. In principal councils, this provision is usually incorporated through their standing orders.

Quorum at meetings

26.111 For principal councils, Sch 12, para 6 states that one-quarter of the whole number of members of the council must be present. The only circumstance in which this does not apply is where more than one-third of members of the authority become disqualified from voting at the same time. In these circumstances, the quorum of the authority is determined by reference to the number of members of the authority remaining qualified rather than by reference to the whole authority (Sch 12, para 45).

26.112 When calculating the whole number of members, this includes vacant seats.[17]

26.113 In relation to parish and community councils, the quorum is at least one-third of the whole number of members of the council. The provision relating to disqualification levels also applies, but the quorum in any circumstances can never be less than three.

PUBLIC INVOLVEMENT

26.114 The provisions relating to the public's right to attend and participate at meetings have developed over the years both through statutory provision (for example, the Local Government (Access to Information) Act 1985, which amended LGA 1972) and also by local authorities themselves actively encouraging greater public involvement in their meetings. This section of the chapter looks at public participation under three headings – the Right to attend meetings, the Right to participate at meetings and Rights of the press.

Right to attend

26.115 In 1908, in *Tenby Corporation v Mason*, the courts decided that neither the press nor the public had a statutory right to attend local authority meetings.[18] This limited approach was partly remedied by the Local Authorities (Admission of the Press to Meetings) Act 1908 (the 1908 Act), which was

---

[17] *Newhaven Local Board v Newhaven School Board* (1885) 30 ChD 350.
[18] [1908] 1 Ch 457.

passed in direct and rapid response to the *Tenby* case and which granted press rights to attend local authority meetings.

26.116 However, these access rights were often thwarted by local authorities resolving to exclude them or by holding committee meetings rather than full council meetings to which the statutory right of access did not apply.

26.117 In addition, the 1908 Act only applied to the press, and the general public had no statutory right to attend.

26.118 In 1960, the Public Bodies (Admission to Meetings) Act 1960 (the 1960 Act) was passed, which gave rights to the press and public to attend meetings of local authorities (and other public bodies).

26.119 Section 100 of LGA 1972 applies the provisions of the 1960 Act to all meetings of committees of local authorities as well as meetings of the local authorities themselves, and to joint committees.

26.120 The 1960 Act still applies to parish and community councils (and to all other public bodies listed in the Act or subsequently added by statutory instrument). However, in 1985, the Local Government (Access to Information) Act 1985 introduced substantial new provisions into LGA 1972 dealing with principal councils. This now provides a comprehensive code to access by the public to meetings of local authorities. The 1985 Act inserted a new Part VA 'Access to Meetings and Documents of Certain Authorities, Committees and Sub Committees' (ss 100A–100K of LGA 1972). Section 237 of LGPIHA 2007 also added a new s 100EA to deal with issues relating to decision-making by individual members.

26.121 Section 100A requires that a meeting of a principal council must be open to the public except to the extent that they can be excluded in specified circumstances. The Local Authorities (Executive Arrangements) (Meetings and Access to Information) (England) Regulations 2012[19] have introduced an entirely new requirement for the authority to publish 28 clear days' notice of the intention to hold a private meeting (or part of a meeting) of Cabinet. There is no need to hold a meeting in order to resolve that the main meeting will be in private as, in practice, the Proper Officer will maintain a list of anticipated Cabinet reports and will give the required 28 days' notice where he is aware of a pending decision which is likely to be taken in private session.

26.122 The 28-day notice must then be reinforced by a 5-day notice which sets out the reasons for the meeting to be held in private and details of any representations received as to why the meeting should be in open court and the authority's response to those representations.

---

[19] SI 2012/2089.

26.123 Again, inevitably some issues meriting consideration at a private meeting arise at less than 28 days' notice, so there is an urgency procedure, under which the authority can decide the matter at less than 28 or 5 days' notice, provided that it has first obtained the consent of the chair of the relevant Overview and Scrutiny Committee that the date by which the meeting must be held makes it impracticable to give the 28 and 5 clear day notices and that the meeting cannot reasonably be deferred.

26.124 This is slightly different from the urgency provisions on the advance notice of key decisions, as the 'moderately urgent' reg 10 option of giving 5 clear days' notice to all members of the Scrutiny Committee is omitted, and the urgency must be justified in terms of the inability to defer the meeting. This would clearly cover a case where there is a statutory deadline by which a decision must be taken, such as the requirement to set council tax by 11 March, but might reasonably extend to the position where, for example, a tender must be accepted while the tenders are still valid.

26.125 Where a public meeting is to be held notice must be given at least 5 clear days before the meeting and an item of business can only be considered if a copy of the agenda has been made available.

26.126 There are two broad areas where the public can be excluded:

(1) where confidential information is to be discussed – defined in s 100A(3) very narrowly as information from the government supplied on terms which forbids disclosure or information which the authority is prohibited from disclosing; and

(2) where exempt information is to be discussed.

26.127 Exempt information is defined in s 100I and Sch 12A to LGA 1972 and was amended by the Local Authorities (Access to Information) (Variation) Order 2006.[20] The descriptions of exempt information now vary for England and Wales.

26.128 The description of exempt information in England is now as follows:

(1) information relating to any individual;

(2) information which is likely to reveal the identity of an individual;

(3) information relating to the financial or business affairs of any particular person (including the authority holding that information) (unless such information is required to be publically registered under the Companies Acts or Charities Acts etc);

---

[20] SI 2006/88.

(4) information relating to any consultations or negotiations, or contemplated consultations or negotiations, in connection with any labour relations matter arising between the authority or a Minister of the Crown and employees of, or office-holders under, the authority;

(5) information in respect of which a claim to legal professional privilege could be maintained in legal proceedings;

(6) Information which reveals that the authority proposes:

   (a) to give under any enactment a notice under or by virtue of which requirements are imposed on a person; or
   (b) to make an order or direction under any enactment; and

(7) information relating to any action taken or to be taken in connection with the prevention, investigation or prosecution of crime.

26.129 An important new test which was introduced in 2006[21] is that information which falls within any of the seven paragraphs above is only exempt if, and so long as, in all the circumstances of the case, the public interest in maintaining the exemption outweighs the public interest in disclosing the information. This is to bring the access to information provisions in England more in line with the provisions of the freedom of information and human rights legislation which apply to public bodies, including local authorities. Accordingly, the members must consider this issue and agree that the fact that the information contained within a matter, is not only within one of the categories listed as exempt, but also that the public interest in not disclosing outweighs the public interest in disclosing. It is good practice for this to be made explicit when the agenda item is being considered to show that the minds of members have addressed this issue.

26.130 In so far as executive meetings are concerned, reg 4 of the 2012 Regulations provides that the public *must* be excluded whenever the cabinet resolves to exclude the public during the item where it is likely that, if they remained present, exempt information would be disclosed.

26.131 The description of exempt information in Wales is as follows:

(1) information relating to a particular employee, former employee or applicant to become an employee of, or a particular office-holder, former office-holder or applicant to become an office-holder under the authority;

(2) information relating to a particular employee, former employee or applicant to become an employee of, or a particular officer, former officer or applicant to become an officer appointed by:

---

[21] LGA 1972, Sch 12A, para 10.

(a) a magistrates' court committee;
(b) a probation committee within the meaning of the Probation Service Act 1993; or
(c) a local probation board within the meaning of the Criminal Justice and Court Services Act 2000;

(3) information relating to a particular chief officer, former chief officer or applicant to become a chief officer of a local probation board within the meaning of the Criminal Justice and Court Services Act 2000;

(4) information relating to any particular occupier or former occupier of, or applicant for, accommodation provided by or at the expense of the authority;

(5) information relating to any particular applicant for, or recipient or former recipient of, any service provided by the authority;

(6) information relating to any particular applicant for, or recipient or former recipient of, any financial assistance provided by the authority;

(7) information relating to the adoption, care, fostering or education of any particular child;

(8) information relating to the financial or business affairs of any particular person (other than the authority) (unless such information is publically registered, for example, under the Companies Acts, Charities Acts etc);

(9) the amount of any expenditure proposed to be incurred by the authority under any particular contract for the acquisition of property or the supply of goods or services;

(10) any terms proposed or to be proposed by or to the authority in the course of negotiations for a contract for the acquisition or disposal of property or the supply of goods or services (provided the disclosure of such terms would prejudice the authority in those or any other negotiations concerning the property or goods or services);

(11) the identity of the authority (as well as of any other person, by virtue of (7) above) as the person offering any particular tender for a contract for the supply of goods or services;

(12) information relating to any consultations or negotiations, or contemplated consultations or negotiations, in connection with any labour relations matter arising between the authority or a Minister of the Crown and employee of, or office-holders under, the authority (provided the disclosure to the public of such information would prejudice the authority in those or other consultations or negotiations);

(13) any instructions to counsel and any opinion of counsel (whether or not in connection with any proceedings) and any advice received information obtained or action to be taken in connection with:

(a) any legal proceedings by or against the authority; or
(b) the determination of any matter, affecting the authority
(whether in either case, proceedings have been commenced or are in contemplation);

(14) information which, if disclosed to the public, would reveal that the authority proposes:

(a) to give under any enactment a notice under or by virtue of which requirements are imposed on a person; or
(b) to make an order or direction under any enactment
(provided that disclosure to the public might afford an opportunity to a person affected by the notice, order or direction to defeat the purpose or one of the purposes for which the notice, order or direction is to be given or made);

(15) any action taken or to be taken in connection with the prevention, investigation or prosecution of crime; and

(16) the identity of a protected informant.

26.132 In every situation where a local authority decides to exclude the public from the meeting because it is discussing exempt information, the authority must explicitly pass a resolution specifying which part of its business is covered by this exclusion and the paragraph which relates to it. The Local Authorities (Executive Arrangements) (Meetings and Access to Information) (England) Regulations 2012 apply different rules in relation to what the regulations call 'Private' meetings which are those where 'exempt' information is being considered. From September 2012 where a meeting or part of a meeting is to be held in private, the authority must publish – by making available at its offices at least 28 days beforehand – a notice of its intention to hold the meeting in private. The notice must include a statement of the reasons for the meeting to be held in private. Furthermore, at least 5 clear days before the private meeting the decision-making body must make available at the offices of the decision-making body a further notice of its intention to hold the meeting in private and publish the notice. This notice must include a statement of the reasons for the meeting to be held in private as well as details of any representations received about why the meeting should be open to the public and its response to any such representations.

26.133 When matters make compliance with these rules impracticable, the meeting may only be held in private when agreement has been obtained from the chairman of the relevant Overview and Scrutiny Committee or, if there is no such person from the chairman of the authority; or the vice chairman if neither is in place; that the meeting is urgent and cannot reasonably be deferred.

26.134 In these instances, as soon as the council has obtained agreement to hold the meeting in private it must publish a notice setting out why the meeting is urgent and cannot reasonably be deferred.

26.135 There have been a number of cases looking at the legitimacy of authorities seeking to exclude the public, and although most of these related to an earlier set of definitions of exempt information, many continue to be relevant under the current regulations.

26.136 In *R v Wandsworth London Borough Council ex parte Darker Enterprises Ltd*,[22] the court decided that it was legitimate for Wandsworth Council's licensing subcommittee to consider an application to renew a sex establishment licence in private, although it was difficult to stretch one of the descriptions of exempt information easily to cover the case. Also, the council had given reasons for its decision so the applicants were unable to point to any detriment that they had suffered as a consequence of the council's determination.

26.137 There can be circumstances where a council is dealing with an application or a particular case by an individual and wishes to consider the matter in private session by using one of the classifications of exempt information. In these circumstances, the council does have a discretion as to whether to allow the particular individual affected by the consideration to remain in the meeting. In *R v Kensington and Chelsea Royal London Borough Council ex parte Stoop*,[23] it was held that a planning committee meeting was entitled to go into private session to hear the legal advice even where both the developer and objectors were present at the meeting.

26.138 The requirement that meetings should be open to the public save in specified circumstances can raise practical difficulties for councils where a particularly contentious issue is being discussed or many members of the public wish to attend a meeting. In the case of *R v Liverpool City Council ex parte Liverpool Taxi Fleet Operators Association*,[24] the court decided that there could be circumstances where unexpected demand for public attendance meant that the public could not be admitted. If this was done deliberately to ensure a situation where the public could not get to the meeting, this would be in bad faith and be challengeable.

26.139 The public's right to attend meetings is without prejudice to any power of exclusion in the event of disorderly conduct (see below).

---

[22] (1999) 1 LGLR 601.
[23] [1992] 1 PLR 58.
[24] [1975] 1 All ER 379.

26.140 At a meeting of a principal council, there must be a reasonable number of copies of the agenda and the reports to be considered at the meeting available (s 100B(6) of LGA 1972).

26.141 Section 100A(7) of LGA 1972 deals with a matter which had been controversial prior to this clarification. It states that nothing in the section requiring access by the public to meetings requires a principal council to permit the taking of photographs or recordings at the meeting itself. Many local authorities have a provision within their standing orders which deals with this. Some councils allow filming and recording in certain circumstances or with particular clearance in advance, and many council meetings are now streamed via the internet. However, this is the choice of the council, and the Local Authorities (Executive Arrangements) (Meetings and Access to Information) (England) Regulations 2012 repeated that councils were not required to permit the taking of photographs or recording of proceedings.

26.142 In relation to the right to attend parish and community councils, the Public Bodies (Admission to Meetings) Act 1960 continues to apply. It requires meetings to be open to the public, but the council can pass a resolution excluding the public where publicity would be prejudicial to the public interest because of the confidential nature of the business or further stated special reasons that arise from the nature of the business.

Right to participate

26.143 There is no statutory right for the public to participate in (as opposed to attend) local authority meetings. However, many local authorities actively encourage both attendance and contributions by the public. This can be structured into meetings in different ways, for example, by giving a specified part of the agenda over to members of the public who have indicated in advance that they wish to make a presentation, by allowing questions from the public gallery or by the submission of petitions. Local authority standing orders will deal with this in some detail. However, there are some legal constraints and issues which affect the right to participate.

26.144 Once councils create circumstances in which members of the public have an advertised right to attend and make representations, care must be exercised in how these rights are operated. In *R v Alnwick District Council ex parte Robson*,[25] Mr Justice Sedley overturned the grant of a planning permission where a potential objector had missed his opportunity to voice his objections at the planning committee because of the confusing wording in the leaflet telling the public of their right to attend and speak at planning committees.

---

[25] [1997] EGCS 144.

26.145 In the case of *R (On the Application of WB) v Leeds School Organisation Committee*,[26] the court considered whether the principles of natural justice imposed a duty on a school organisation committee to give consideration to whether it should exercise its power to hear objectors even if it had no obligation to do so. In this case, inadequate notice had been given of a meeting and a parents' action group had not been informed of it. The court decided that failure to invite or accept particular oral submissions could amount to an error of law depending on the circumstances of the case.

26.146 The European Convention on Human Rights is now largely incorporated into English law by virtue of the Human Rights Act 1998. This has an impact on the way in which public authorities conduct themselves and could have a bearing on the procedures for local authority meetings. In particular, the right to a fair hearing under Art 6 has raised the prospect of further procedural standards being applied to local authority meetings which fall within the remit of this Article. The right to a fair hearing applies in the determination of civil rights and obligations and provides for the right to a fair and public hearing within a reasonable time by an independent and impartial tribunal established by law.

26.147 In assessing whether this right is of direct relevance to any local authority meeting, there needs to be consideration of whether the matter in question is dealing with a civil right or obligation. European case-law has concluded that a number of aspects of local authority decision-making could fall within the remit of this Article, including a licensing decision and a decision relating to parental choices on education.

Press rights

26.148 The press were first given rights of access to council meetings by the Local Authorities (Admission of the Press to Meetings) Act 1908, which is referred to at **26.115**.

26.149 The Public Bodies (Admission to Meetings) Act 1960, as well as extending the ability of the public to attend local authority meetings (see above), also brought in specific provisions in relation to attendance of the press.

26.150 Section 1(4)(c) states that while a meeting is open to the public under the provisions of the Public Bodies (Admission to Meetings) Act 1960:

> '... duly accredited representatives of newspapers attending for the purpose of reporting the proceedings for those newspapers shall, so far as practicable, be afforded reasonable facilities for taking their report and, unless the meeting is held in premises not belonging to the body or not on the telephone, the telephoning of the report at their own expense.'

The reference to newspapers covers news agencies or other news organisations.

---

[26] [2002] EWHC 1927.

26.151 The 1960 Act specifically stated that the extension of access to the press did not require the public body to allow the taking of photographs of any proceedings or the simultaneous transmission of any proceedings.

26.152 Although the language of the 1960 Act now seems quaint in relation to the modern arrangements for telecommunications, its provisions still apply to meetings of parish and community councils.

26.153 In relation to principal councils, LGA 1972, as amended by the Local Government (Access to Information Act) 1985, now deals with press access to meetings open to the public.

26.154 Section 100A(6)(c) makes provision for accredited members of the press to be given reasonable facilities for reporting the proceedings and has the same restrictions as the 1960 Act relating to the use of photographs. The same provisions apply to committees and subcommittees open to the public.

26.155 Section 100B(7) enables newspapers/news agencies to be provided with copies on request of:

(1) the agenda for a meeting;

(2) any further statements or particulars as are necessary to indicate the nature of the items included in the agenda; and

(3) if the proper officer thinks fit, copies of any other documents supplied to members of the council in connection with the items.

These documents are to be provided on request and on payment of any necessary postage or other charge.

ISSUES ARISING DURING THE MEETING

Conflicts/declarations of interest

26.156 A formally constituted local authority meeting should follow the order of business set out on its agenda.

26.157 One of the features of local authority meetings is the need for councillors to consider whether or not they have an interest which needs to be declared at the meeting and, if so, whether this is of such a nature that it requires them to withdraw from participation in the meeting and leave the meeting room.

26.158 Until 2012 there was a detailed Code of Conduct with which members had to comply, but this was abolished by the Localism Act 2011. Details of the new regime appear below. It should be noted, however, that these rules do not affect the need for decisions to be made properly and without bias of any kind, including predetermination. If a decision is made where the decision maker is perceived to be biased it is possible that it could be successfully challenged via judicial review.

26.159 LGA 2000 introduced a new code of conduct and framework for the regulation of local authority member interests which was abolished by the Localism Act 2011 which introduced the concept of 'disclosable pecuniary interests' and required all authorities to have a Code of Conduct even though the Act did not cover the sanctions that could be imposed upon members for breaches of this. This is not within the subject area of this book, but the following paragraphs set out very briefly the implications for elected members.

26.160 If a member has a disclosable pecuniary interest (see **26.161**) in a matter, he is not entitled to participate and vote in the matter unless he had been granted a dispensation. Unless he has registered the interest he must declare it at the meeting. The Localism Act allows local authorities to make standing orders requiring that members must leave the council chamber or committee room whilst the matter is being discussed.

26.161 In so far as meetings are concerned, the main provisions concern members who have a Disclosable Pecuniary Interest, introduced via Chapter 7 of the Localism Act 2011. This provides that members have duties to register, disclose and not to participate in respect of any matter in which they have a disclosable pecuniary interest. These are defined in the Relevant Authorities (Disclosable Pecuniary Interests) Regulations 2012, Sch 1[27] as follows:

Subject	Prescribed description
Employment, office, trade, profession or vocation	Any employment, office, trade, profession or vocation carried on for profit or gain.
Sponsorship	Any payment or provision of any other financial benefit (other than from the relevant authority) made or provided within the relevant period in respect of any expenses incurred by M in carrying out duties as a member, or towards the election expenses of M.
	This includes any payment or financial benefit from a trade union within the meaning of the Trade Union and Labour Relations (Consolidation) Act 1992.

---

[27] SI 2012/1464.

Contracts	Any contract which is made between the relevant person (or a body in which the relevant person has a beneficial interest) and the relevant authority –

(a) under which goods or services are to be provided or works are to be executed; and

(b) which has not been fully discharged. |
| Land | Any beneficial interest in land which is within the area of the relevant authority. |
| Licences | Any licence (alone or jointly with others) to occupy land in the area of the relevant authority for a month or longer. |
| Corporate tenancies | Any tenancy where (to M's knowledge) –

(a) the landlord is the relevant authority; and

(b) the tenant is a body in which the relevant person has a beneficial interest. |
| Securities | Any beneficial interest in securities of a body where –

(a) that body (to M's knowledge) has a place of business or land in the area of the relevant authority; and

(b) Either –

  (i) the total nominal value of the securities exceeds £25,000 or one hundredth of the total issued share capital of that body; or |

(ii) if the share capital of that body is of more than one class, the total nominal value of the shares of any one class in which the relevant person has a beneficial interest exceeds one hundredth of the total issued share capital of that class.

The terms are defined in reg 1. For this purpose:

'"body in which the relevant person has a beneficial interest" means a firm in which the relevant person is a partner or a body corporate of which the relevant person is a director, or in the securities of which the relevant person has a beneficial interest;

"director" includes a member of the committee of management of an industrial and provident society;

"land" includes an easement, servitude, interest or right in or over land which does not carry with it a right for the relevant person (alone or jointly with another) to occupy the land or to receive income;

"M" means the person M referred to in section 30 of the Act;

"member" includes a co-opted member;

"relevant authority" means the authority of which M is a member;

"relevant period" means the period of 12 months ending with the day on which M gives a notification for the purposes of section 30(1) of the Act;

"relevant person" means M or any other person referred to in section 30(3)(b) of the Act;

"securities" means shares, debentures, debenture stock, loan stock, bonds, units of a collective investment scheme within the meaning of the Financial Services and Markets Act 2000 and other securities of any description, other than money deposited with a building society.'

Failure by a member to declare a disclosable pecuniary interest does not mean that the decision is invalid. However, if by failing to observe the requirements of the regulations a member invalidated the decision in some other way, eg by bias, the decision could be challenged.

The position in Wales

26.162 The Welsh Code of Conduct has not been changed by the Localism Act. The Local Authorities (Model Code of Conduct) (Wales) Order 2008[28] repealed the earlier codes and now sets out the Model Code for local authorities and community councils in Wales. The provisions relating to the general rules of conduct in the Welsh Code are very similar but not exactly the same as the previous English Code. In relation to the declaration of interests and the consequences for attendance at meetings and withdrawal etc, the Welsh Code now follows the former English approach of personal and prejudicial interests. Members are bound by the Code when they are acting, claiming to act or giving the impression that they are acting as a member or a representative of their authority.

Disorder at the meeting

26.163 Occasionally at a local authority meeting, a matter is discussed which provokes intense views and heated debate. There have been situations (for example, the setting of poll tax levels) where there have been outbreaks of extreme public disorder requiring the involvement of the police.

26.164 The general provisions relating to the ability of members of the public and press to attend meetings (outlined above) are without prejudice to the general common law power of exclusion of members of the public in extreme circumstances. Section 100A(8) of LGA 1972 states that the admission to meetings of principal councils is without prejudice to 'any power of exclusion to suppress or prevent disorderly conduct or other misbehaviour at a meeting'.

26.165 Virtually identical provisions are contained within s 1(8) of the Public Bodies (Admission to Meetings) Act 1960, which still apply to parish and community councils.

26.166 Two cases involving public authorities in Brent have considered these provisions.

26.167 In *R v Brent Health Authority ex parte Francis*,[29] the court considered the application of the 1960 Act and decided that although there was no express power in the statute, at common law there was power to exclude the public in the extreme circumstances such as applied in this case. It involved the consideration of government spending cuts by a health authority where three meetings had been disrupted by unruly behaviour by members of the public. The health authority decided, as a last resort, to exclude the public, other than inviting members of the press and one member of the Community Health Council into the debate.

---

[28] SI 2008/788.
[29] [1985] 1 All ER 74.

26.168 In *R v Brent London Borough Council ex parte Assegai*,[30] the local authority banned the applicant from the council premises as a result of a scene at a council meeting. The decision was set aside by the court on the basis that the applicant had not been given an opportunity to make representations before this ban was made and also it was out of proportion to anything done by the individual. This reinforces that any decision to exclude either individuals or the public en masse must be taken with due regard to the rules of natural justice.

26.169 At a meeting the chairman has an inherent power and duty to keep order. This can involve calling for order, seeking assistance from officers, utilising the provisions of standing orders to adjourn/suspend the meeting and, if necessary, calling the police to intervene to end or prevent a breach of the peace. The police can enter council premises if they believe a breach of the peace is being committed.

26.170 If members are responsible for the disorderly conduct, standing orders will usually provide for individual members to be asked to desist, then to leave and if necessary to suspend the meeting while order is restored.

26.171 If the members' conduct is aggressive, extreme or persistent they could be reported to the Standards Board for England or the Ombudsman in Wales, on the basis that they are in breach of the Code of Conduct.

Defamation

26.172 There can be occasions where verbal statements made at local authority meetings, or written statements circulated in the agenda or papers or minutes of the meeting, are considered defamatory.

26.173 A defamatory statement (defined by *Halsbury's Laws of England*) is:

> 'A statement which tends to lower a person in the estimation of right thinking members of society generally, or to cause him to be shunned or avoided or to expose him to hatred, contempt or ridicule, or to convey an imputation on him disparaging or injurious to him in his office, profession, calling, trade or business.'

26.174 In most cases, it is not necessary to prove a malicious intention in making what could amount to a defamatory statement. However, the concept of absolute or qualified privilege against defamation actions has been established to recognise that there are circumstances where open and robust discussion is needed.

26.175 Certain circumstances give rise to absolute privilege, ie there can be no liability for defamation; these include statements made in Parliament or in courts of law.

---

[30] (1987) *The Times*, June 18.

26.176 Qualified privilege applies in certain other circumstances and would cover statements made in council or committee meetings. It broadly covers situations where the person making the statement has an interest or a duty (legal, social or moral) to make it, and the person to whom it is made has the corresponding interest or duty to receive it.

26.177 If a situation is covered by qualified privilege, malice in the person making the statement has to be proved in order for an action of defamation to succeed.

26.178 The Public Bodies (Admissions to Meetings) Act 1960 and LGA 1972 explicitly provide for any defamatory matter in the agenda for meetings or further statements or particulars provided, and for documents supplied to a member of the public or for the benefit of the press, to be covered by privilege (unless the publication is proved to be made with malice).

26.179 In the case of *Horrocks v Lowe*,[31] the House of Lords considered the circumstances of a defamation action brought by one councillor against another. In the course of a lengthy speech of criticism, offensive personal observations were made about a councillor who (having declared an interest in the matter) was not present to hear them. These included 'I don't know how to describe his attitude, whether it was brinkmanship, megalomania or childish petulance'.

26.180 The House of Lords decided that the defendant had not misused the privileged occasion by using it for some purpose other than that for which the privilege was accorded to him in the public interest. He had a positive belief in the truth of what he said and he was therefore entitled to succeed in his defence of qualified privilege. There could be circumstances whereby the qualified privileged occasion was used for improper purposes, for example, expressions of 'personal spite or ill-will or private advantage unconnected with the duty or interest which constitutes the reason for the privilege'.

26.181 There are other defences which apply to defamation actions including that the comments were justified or were fair comment on the matter.

AFTER THE MEETING

Minutes

26.182 Schedule 12, Part VI, para 40 to LGA 1972 requires that the names of members present at a meeting of any local authority shall be recorded.

---

[31] [1975] AC 135.

26.183 Paragraph 41 requires that minutes of the proceedings of any local authority meetings should be drawn up and kept in a minute book. The minutes should be signed at that meeting (or the next suitable meeting) by the 'person presiding'.

26.184 The minutes of any local authority meeting may be recorded on consecutively numbered loose leaves, each initialled.

26.185 Any minutes signed by the person presiding shall be considered acceptable in evidence.

26.186 The same provisions apply to committees and subcommittees as to full council meetings.

26.187 Where a minute of a committee or subcommittee has been signed in accordance with Part VI, the meeting is deemed to have been duly constituted, duly convened, to have had power to deal with the matters in the minutes and the members present to be duly qualified.

26.188 Section 100C(1) of LGA 1972 gives local government electors the right to inspect and make copies of or extracts from minutes of principal councils and s 228(1) of the Act gives equivalent rights in respect of parish and community councils.

26.189 Section 41 of the Local Government (Miscellaneous Provisions) Act 1976 provides that a copy of the minutes of the proceedings at a meeting of a local authority certified by the proper officer stating that the minutes were signed in accordance with para 41 of Sch 12 to LGA 1972 (see **26.183**) shall be evidence of the matters stated in the certificate and the minutes in question.

Access to papers

26.190 Section 100C of LGA 1972 requires that certain documents of a principal council be kept available for inspection by members of the public for 6 years from the date of the meeting.

26.191 The documents are:

- the minutes of the meeting;

- a summary of any matters considered in exempt session;

- the agenda for the meeting; and

- any open reports considered at the meeting.

26.192 In the case of principal councils, s 100D of LGA 1972 requires that each report for a meeting which is required to be open to members of the public shall include a list of 'background papers'. These are papers which disclose any facts or matters on which the report (or an important part of it) was based and have been relied on to a material extent in preparing the report.

26.193 These background papers must be available for 4 years from the date of the meeting which considers the report.

CHALLENGING DECISIONS

26.194 There are a number of different ways in which decisions made at local authority meetings can be challenged, appealed or reviewed. Some of these routes involve internal reviews by another part of the local authority (for example, by a scrutiny committee), some involve a statutory right of appeal (for example, against the refusal of licensing panels), some are external administrative considerations of decisions (for example, by an ombudsman) and some involve the judicial review by the High Court of the way in which a decision has been reached (not the merits of it).

26.195 The main routes of challenge are now considered.

Overview and scrutiny

26.196 LGA 2000 introduced requirements for overview and scrutiny committees to be established by principal councils. These provisions were changed by the Localism Act 2011, but every principal authority is required to have one or more Overview and Scrutiny committees. Each authority's standing orders and constitution will provide for circumstances in which an overview and scrutiny committee can review (or sometimes call in) decisions or proposals of the executive of the council. Each authority will have different provisions specifying when decisions can be reviewed. However, the overview and scrutiny committee has no decision-making powers so can only recommend a reconsideration of the decision by the executive, or can make a referral to the full council meeting so that the council makes the decision.

Referral within the council

26.197 Some principal authorities' standing orders or constitutions allow for decisions of certain meetings to be 'referred up' to other bodies. This means that a committee meeting may appear to make a final decision, only for the matter to be referred on to another meeting (usually the full council meeting). Implementation of the decision is put on hold until final determination. An authority's standing orders will set out the details of how a matter can be 'referred up'. This will usually require that an individual member (or a minimum number of members) indicates their wish for the matter to be referred before the next item of business is started. This must all be recorded in the minutes of the meeting.

Statutory routes of appeal/review

26.198 There are a number of areas of local government function where there are specific statutory routes of appeal/review following decisions. The main ones of these are as follows

(1) *Right of appeal against planning decision*: Town and Country Planning Act 1990, s 78.
    Appeal against refusal of planning permission, or refusal of any consent, agreement or approval required by a planning condition, or refusal of approval required under a development order, is by notice to the Secretary of State.

(2) *Right of appeal against decision of licensing authorities under the new licensing procedures*: Licensing Act 2003, s 181 and Sch 5.
    Appeal is to the magistrates' court.

(3) *Appeal against decision regarding the authority's duty to secure accommodation for homeless persons*: Housing Act 1996, ss 202 and 204.
    Right to request review of decision (s 202). A person who is dissatisfied with the decision on review may appeal to the county court on a point of law (s 204).

(4) *Appeal against decision not to make a statement of special educational needs*: Education Act 1996, s 325.
    Appeal to the Special Educational Needs and Disability Tribunal.

Judicial review

26.199 Local authorities are public bodies carrying out public acts and duties and quasi-judicial functions. Their decisions are therefore capable of being challenged in the High Court through proceedings for judicial review.

26.200 This means that the court will review the decision-making process (not the merits of the decision itself), ie the court looks at *how* the decision was made, not *what* decision was made. A decision can be challenged on the basis that it was not made lawfully. There are a number of aspects to this.

(1) that it is illegal, ie the decision-maker had not correctly applied the law in reaching the decision;

(2) that it is irrational, ie no reasonable local authority could have come to that decision; or

(3) that the procedure applied in making the decision was incorrect (this is obviously particularly relevant in relation to the importance of local authorities following correct procedures in the conduct of their meetings).

26.201 Judicial review proceedings may only be brought by a person with a sufficient interest in the decision to have standing to challenge it. It is often used by third parties aggrieved by the grant of planning permission. The courts have taken an increasingly generous view of standing in recent years and have permitted pressure groups, neighbours and even commercial rivals to contest decisions. It is unlikely that a court will refuse to hear an applicant unless the person proposing to bring the challenge really has no connection with the matter at all.

26.202 Judicial review proceedings must be brought very promptly and in any event within 3 months of the claim arising (usually this will be the date of the meeting making the decision).

26.203 Before a judicial review action is commenced the pre-action protocol must be complied with. The protocol's objective is to avoid unnecessary litigation. A potential claimant must therefore send a letter to the defendant (in this case the local authority). The letter must identify the issues in dispute and establish whether litigation can be avoided. The defendant should reply within 14 days.

26.204 Permission to proceed judicial review is a two-stage process: it involves a permission stage and then, if granted, a full hearing. The purpose of the permission stage is to weed out claims without any merit.

26.205 If a person proposes to bring judicial review proceedings, they must do so within the time-limits set out above and then serve notice upon the local authority and other interested parties. Such interested parties are required to serve an acknowledgement of service within 21 days of receipt of the papers if they wish to play any further part in the permission stage. The acknowledgement must state whether they challenge the application and, if they do, their grounds for doing so.

26.206 The application for judicial review and the acknowledgements of service will be considered by a single judge – initially just on paper – for him to decide whether to grant permission to bring the proceedings. The judge has three choices:

- to grant permission;
- to refuse permission; or
- to defer the matter to an oral hearing before a judge.

26.207 If permission is refused on a paper consideration the applicant also has the right to request an oral hearing. At such a hearing the applicant and any interested parties who have returned an acknowledgement of service form have a right to appear and make representations as to whether permission should be granted. It is usual for an application for permission to be decided within 3 months of the application – unless the matter is either urgent or an oral hearing is required.

26.208 Assuming that permission is granted to bring a judicial review, the defendant council and other interested parties are all entitled to submit evidence as to why the application should be refused. All evidence is usually in paper form, rather than witnesses. The full hearing therefore consists of legal submissions from counsel on each side, drawing upon the evidence that has been submitted by all the parties. The decision upon the application is made by a single judge.

26.209 Judicial review can be a very powerful tactical tool for aggrieved parties as it results in a great deal of uncertainty for the affected local authorities and applicants. Normally, if the proceedings succeed, the court will quash the authority's decision and direct it to re-determine (if it is still capable of legally doing so) the matter, this time ensuring that it complies with all relevant matters.

26.210 This could result in the same decision being made. In such cases the proceedings could be seen as being a pyrrhic victory, but the original applicant for judicial review proceedings may have had other good reasons which in their view justified bringing the proceedings even if this resulted in the same conclusion.

26.211 Conduct of elected members at meetings can be the basis of judicial review proceedings in the High Court (for example, where there are allegations of predetermination of an issue), as well as potentially leading to a complaint about a breach of the Code of Conduct for councillors.

26.212 There have been a number of cases in recent years exploring how members' conduct at (or in connection with) meetings can lead to allegations of bias, predetermination or predisposition and what this means for the legality of the decision taken.

26.213 In *National Assembly for Wales v (1) Elizabeth Condron (2) Miller Argent (South Wales) Ltd*,[32] the Court of Appeal considered the implications of a comment made by an Assembly member on his way into a meeting of the National Assembly's Planning Decision Committee.

26.214 As he was going in to a meeting at which the Committee was to consider whether to agree or not with the report of a planning inspector into a controversial planning application, the Assembly member was alleged to have said to a demonstrator, 'I am going to go with the report of the inspector'. The Court of Appeal decided that this comment went no further than indicating a predisposition to follow the inspector's report and did not indicate a 'closed

---

[32] [2006] EWCA Civ 1573.

mind', which would have shown predetermination and make the decision open to challenge. The court also commented that the members of the committee had had training in their role and that the nature of their discussions was unusually prolonged; all circumstances lead to the view that the Assembly member in question was not biased.

26.215 In the case of *R (on the application of Island Farm Development Ltd) v Bridgend County Borough Council*,[33] also decided in 2006, Mr Justice Collins decided that there was no apparent bias or predetermination by a newly elected local authority when it reached a decision to discontinue negotiations for a sale of land which the previous political administration had agreed would proceed. In reaching this view, the court looked carefully at the way in which the meeting was conducted, including the way in which the members had prepared for the meeting and the way they voted. The conclusion was that members were entitled to have regard to and apply policies they believed in, particularly where these policies were clearly part of a political manifesto on which they had been elected. There was no positive evidence of a closed mind and the meeting looked at the report fairly and openly. The test is that members must:

> 'approach their decision-making with an open mind in the sense that they must have regard to all material considerations and must be prepared to change their views if persuaded that they should.'

26.216 A third case from Wales, decided in 2007, explored events at a meeting of a committee at Neath Port Talbot County Borough Council.[34] A challenge was made to the decision of a planning committee on the basis (inter alia) that elected members had been wrongly advised and had abstained from voting under a misapprehension of law. This had related to advice given to them by the legal officer of the authority, and the court in the first instance found that this had been wrong advice and also that the members had felt under pressure not to participate in the voting.

26.217 The Court of Appeal overturned this decision and held that there was no procedural irregularity. The elected members had been left to make their own decision and not been pressurised to abstain. Also, the legal advice they had received was correct.

26.218 A case decided in 2008 unusually considered whether the timing of a meeting of a local authority could give rise to a judicial review challenge. In *Persimmon Homes Teesside Limited v R (on the application of Kevin Paul Lewis)*,[35] the Court of Appeal allowed an appeal and reinstated a decision of the Planning Committee of Redcar and Cleveland Borough Council. The case involved the granting of planning permission and was challenged on a number of grounds by opponents of the development. The leading ground was that the meeting at which the decision had been taken had been held very close to the

---

[33] [2006] EWCA 2189 (Admin).
[34] *Neath Port Talbot CBC v Ware* [2007] EWCA Civ 1359.
[35] [2008] EWCA Civ 746.

local council elections. The judge at first instance found that, for a number of reasons, including this, there had been a real possibility of bias or predetermination on the part of the Committee and quashed the decisions as unlawful.

26.219 The Court of Appeal disagreed and held that the authority's decision should stand as the members had considered it properly and openly. Central to the conclusion was a recognition that: 'Councillors are not in a judicial or quasi judicial position but are entitled to provide and pursue policies.' Members of planning committees would be entitled, and indeed expected, to have expressed views on planning issues. The timing of the election was not a factor to warrant the conclusion that members had closed minds to the issue. Nor was the fact that there was unanimity of seven coalition members on the authority when voting on the decision at the meeting.

26.220 The issue of the party whip was considered further in *R v Local Commissioner for Local Government for North and North East England, ex parte Liverpool City Council*.[36] This was a case concerning an application by Liverpool Football Club to build a stand. It was alleged that the Labour party had agreed their view on the applications before the meeting, and in an investigation by the Ombudsman members agreed that this had happened and that the party had caused them to vote differently from how they would have done if given a choice. It was held that 'The line is clear – a local authority councillor is entitled to give weight to the views of party colleagues but should not abdicate responsibility by voting blindly in support of party policy or party whip' (Henry LJ).

26.221 The Localism Act 2011 attempted to put some statutory protection around the ability of members to form a view before the decision was taken without the risk of successful challenge. Section 25(2) provides that:

> 'An elected or co-opted member is not to be taken to have had, or to have appeared to have had, a closed mind when making a decision just because –
>
> (a) The decision-maker had previously done anything that directly or indirectly indicated what view the decision-maker took or would or might take, in relation to a matter, and
> (b) The matter was relevant to the decision.'

This has yet to be tested in the courts.

Local Government Ombudsman

26.222 The role of the Local Government Ombudsman (LGO) (or, more correctly, the Commissioner for Local Administration) was established by the Local Government Act 1974. There are three LGOs for England, divided by

---

[36] [2000] LGR 571.

geographic area, and one for Wales (which hasa remit to cover issues across the whole public sector in Wales as the Public Services Ombudsman).

26.223 LGPIHA 2007, Part 9 introduced a number of changes to the Ombudsman's jurisdiction and operation in England. The LGO's jurisdiction covers all local authorities (excluding town and parish councils) and police authorities. They may investigate complaints by members of the public who consider that they have been caused injustice by maladministration or by service failure in connection with action taken by, or on behalf of, authorities within the LGO's jurisdiction in the exercise of their administrative functions. Members of the public are able to complain on their own behalf, and there is no need for them to be referred by a councillor.

26.224 There is no statutory definition of maladministration and little judicial authority on the subject. In piloting the Parliamentary Commissioner Act 1967 through Parliament, Richard Crosman referred to 'bias, neglect, inattention, delay, incompetence, ineptitude, perversity, turpitude, arbitrariness and so on'.[37] The main test of whether there has been maladministration is whether an authority has acted reasonably in accordance with the law, its own policies and generally accepted standards of local administration. The LGO is concerned with the way a decision is reached, not with the *merits* of decisions.

26.225 The Local Government Act 1974, ss 26 and 27 impose limitations on the LGO's jurisdiction:

- the complaint should be made 'in time'; and

- the complaint must first be brought to the notice of the authority to which the complaint relates and the authority must have been given a reasonable opportunity to investigate and reply to the complaint.

In addition, the LGO may not investigate a complaint in certain circumstances, including:

- where there is an alternative remedy, ie a right of appeal or by way of proceedings in a court of law;

- a complaint about action which affects all or most of the inhabitants of the authority's area:
    - concerning matters listed in Sch 5 to the 1974 Act (as amended by LGPIHA 2007) including the commencement of conduct of court proceedings; action in respect of personnel matters; action conduct, curriculum, internal organisation, management or discipline in any school;
    - relating to anything done before 1 April 1974; or

---

[37] HC Deb, vol 734, col 51 (18 October 1966).

– made by a body constituted for the purpose of the public service or by any other body whose members are appointed by the Queen or a minister or whose revenues consist wholly or mainly of money provided by Parliament.

One of the potential areas of maladministration which the Ombudsman can investigate concerns allegations of bias by local authority members in making decisions at meetings.

It was anticipated that the changes to the Code of Conduct rules brought in by the Localism Act 2011 may increase referrals to the Ombudsman, but at the time of writing it is too soon to tell.

26.226 In Wales the Ombudsman investigates complaints that members of local government bodies have behaved wrongly and breached the Code of Conduct. Following his investigation he will send a formal report either to the authority's standards committee or to the Adjudication Panel for Wales, who will decide upon the complaint. The maximum penalty for breach of the Code of Conduct is 5 years' disqualification from office.

HEALTH BODIES

26.227 There are a number of different statutory provisions which apply to the meetings of different types of statutory health body, and care must be taken to ensure that the correct set of rules are applied to the body concerned.

26.228 From 1 April 2013 there are five main types of body which practitioners will be likely to encounter:

- non departmental public bodies, including the NHS Commissioning Board, and the Care Quality Commission;

- special health authorities such as the NHS Trust Development Authority;

- NHS Trusts formed under s 25 of the NHS Act 2006;

- NHS Foundation Trusts formed under s 33 of the NHS Act 2006;

- NHS Clinical Commissioning Groups (CCGs) formed under s 14Aff of the 2006 Act as amended by the Health and Social Care Act 2012.

Primary Care Trusts and Strategic Health Authorities have now been abolished, and the intention is that all NHS trusts will either become NHS Foundation Trusts or otherwise cease to exist although the original timetable for this of April 2014 is already slipping.

Bodies subject to the Public Bodies (Admission to Meetings) Act 1960

26.229 Special health authorities, NHS trusts and the NHS Commissioning Board are subject to the provisions of the Public Bodies (Admission to Meetings) Act 1960, and the same rules apply to them as apply to other bodies as described above. In practice most such bodies go further than the requirements of the Act in publishing information and board papers on their websites and indeed the Commissioning Board goes so far as to live-stream its board meetings to enable the public to observe via the internet.

26.230 The Care Quality Commission and Monitor are also subject to the 1960 Act.

26.231 Areas where the application of the Act can be more troublesome are around the legitimacy of decisions to exclude the public and press, and the extent to which matters are dealt with outside the formal board meeting. As regards the former, there are clearly some issues or topics where duties of confidentiality to third parties, whether employees or patients, may come into play. For employees this is a relatively rare issue where a dismissal or grievance appeal is being reported to the Board, and in most cases there is no controversy about that being dealt with in private session, although where the employee concerned is very senior for the circumstances are a matter of public concern it may be necessary to take a more limited item in the public session of the Board as a matter of report. More problems arise in connection with individual complaints or service failures. However, there is a need for the Board to be seen to be taking quality of service seriously, and accordingly should either use anonymised information, or where appropriate, seek consent of the parties to disclose names; the former may well be the best way of dealing with, for example, receiving reports from the Health Service Ombudsman into a complaint against the Trust.

26.232 Commercial confidentiality is often used as a ground for the exclusion of the press and public, and can be perfectly legitimate; but bodies need to be careful not to overuse the 'commercial' interests of the organisation.

26.233 A further problem has arisen from time to time with NHS bodies as to what constitutes a meeting of the Board, particularly in the context of meetings of the board members where, although no decisions are taken, the Board is discussing issues in private. This is clearly open to abuse where in effect the debate and decisions are taken in private session but the formalities then take place in public. Similar effects can be created by the overuse of delegation to powerful committees, which may call into question whether the board is functioning effectively. It may be of relevance here to note the criticism of the Board of the Mid-Staffordshire NHS Foundation Trust for conducting too much of its business in private session, and thus undermining accountability even though at the time there was no obligation to hold meetings in public at all.

NHS Foundation Trusts

26.234 The statutory framework of NHS Foundation Trusts requires them to have a relatively complex governance structure. They must have a constitution compliant with Sch 7 of the NHS Act 2006, with members, and both a board of directors, and a council of governors. The powers of the Foundation Trust are substantially vested in the board of directors who are accountable to the council of governors. The members are members of the public or patients, and employees who have either applied, or in the case of employees in some trusts, have not opted out of membership. The members elect a majority of the governors.

26.235 Historically, some Foundation Trusts included provision for members meetings, but unless the constitution provided them with any rights (such as the right to approve amendments to the constitution) they were primarily information and engagement meetings rather than decision-making meetings. Now an annual meeting of the members is required; it must be open to the public, with no provision for exclusion. At least one director of the Trust must attend and present the annual accounts, the auditors' report and the Trust's own annual report. The meeting also has the specific function of endorsing (or otherwise) changes to the constitution which have an impact on the powers and duties of the council of governors, or the role of the council in the Trust. Such amendments may be validly made, but if they are, a governor must attend the meeting and present it to the members who vote on whether or not to approve it. If they do, by a simple majority it remains in force; otherwise it falls and the constitution has to be re-amended.[38]

26.236 Meetings of the council of governors must be held in accordance with the constitution, and are normally at least three times a year, and meetings must be open to the public, although the public may be excluded for 'special reasons'. It is unclear what the significance of using this formulation rather than the 1960 Act version is intended to carry, but the form of words reappears in more recent health legislation. The requirements of notice of the meeting or the agenda are not carried across.

26.237 From establishment in 2004 until 2013, meetings of boards of directors of Foundation Trusts were not required to be open to the public. The belief appears to have been that as semi-independent bodies, they should be treated more like private institutions. As a result there was quite a wide variation of the approaches taken, both in terms of constitutional provisions and practice, as to whether Foundation Trusts took advantage of this. However the 2012 Act reversed this and inserted a requirement for the constitution to provide for meetings in public, subject again to the power to include a right to exclude the public 'for special reasons'.[39]

---

[38] National Health Service Act 2006, Sch 7, para 27A.
[39] National Health Service Act 2006, Sch 7, para 18E.

26.238 There is no explicit guidance on the meaning of special reasons, although in the context of 'other special reasons justifying the exclusion of the public, in *R v Liverpool City Council ex parte Liverpool Taxi Fleet Operators Association*,[40] potential overcrowding was held to be a sufficient justification.

26.239 When there is a meeting of the directors, although there is no formal requirement to publish notice of the meeting, there is a requirement to send a copy of the agenda to the council governors in advance of the meeting, and as soon as practicable after the meeting a copy of the minutes. The Act does not address the question of the items on the agenda where the public have been excluded either in the context of the agenda or the minutes, and this may create tension between any duties of confidence owed to the Trust and the need for the governors to feel that they are acting as a necessary channel of information to the members and the wider public.

Clinical Commissioning Groups

26.240 These bodies are created by the amendments to the NHS Act 2006 introduced by the Health and Social Care Act 2012. They are also complex structures, with membership comprised of the holders of primary medical care contracts in their area. They must have a governing body which has statutory functions in relation to the group, and may or may not have a range of other responsibilities vested in it. Currently the model appears to be for the powers and functions of the CCG to largely devolve on the governing body, but in some cases significant powers are retained by the members or sub-groups of the members.

26.241 The Act requires the group to specify in its constitution the procedures to be followed in making decision, and for ensuring transparency about decisions of the group and the manner in which they are made. There is no formal requirement in the Act for meetings of the group – ie the members to be in public as such.

26.242 Similar provisions apply to the decision making and meetings of the governing body, although these are subject to the express provision that this must include provision for the meetings of the governing body to be held in public, except where the Group considers that it would not be in the public interest to permit members of the public to attend a meeting or part of a meeting. In practice the decision about whether to exclude the public is delegated to the governing body itself, but the provision introduces a third slightly separate test for exclusion of the public.

26.243 Both Foundation Trusts and CCGs also have explicit statutory provision dealing with the need to have provisions in place concerning conflict of interest. The Foundation Trust model is derived from the Companies

---

[40] [1975] 1 WLR 701.

Act 2006, and is more explicit, but there is a clear area of concern over the declaration of interests and the need to take appropriate steps.

Part 4

MEETINGS OF PRIVATE ORGANISATIONS

Chapter 27

MEETINGS OF PRIVATE ORGANISATIONS

BACKGROUND

27.1 In this chapter the words 'private organisation' refer to an unincorporated association of people, pursuing a common, non-commercial objective together. Examples include associations and clubs formed for sporting, voluntary or social reasons, or to pursue a hobby or an area of learning.

27.2 It does not include associations regulated by specific legislation or rules, such as trade unions, Friendly Societies, charitable associations or investment clubs; or groups of customers benefiting as the result of actions of a supplier, such as 'clubs' of large or loyal customers to whom special deals are offered, or Christmas clubs. It does not include what are often called 'proprietary clubs' – set up by an owner to make a profit.

27.3 This chapter assumes that the activities of the organisation's members (acting in that capacity) create legal relations between them, and/or between the members and third parties, that would not exist otherwise. For example, each member may contribute to some common fund (for example, by paying membership subscriptions) so that a court will intervene to protect his right or interest in that fund against other members. The organisation's members may need to buy, rent or hire premises, goods or services to enable them to pursue the organisation's objectives, and borrow money to do so, so that there are contractual relations with third parties. Activities may create a liability to third parties, such as a liability for injury to spectators if a sporting event is held. There may be a liability to pay tax, such as VAT.

27.4 Where such legal relations exist, the members of such an organisation may have established a written contract, setting out their respective rights and obligations as members, and how the organisation will deal with third parties.

27.5 If they have not, the law will probably imply the terms of such a contract, inferring its terms from, for example, correspondence, minutes and other records and the acts and omissions of the members. This is deeply unsatisfactory in the event of a dispute, so a written contract is usually drawn up. This contract is often called a constitution. (It may also be known by other names, such as 'rules', 'statutes', 'governing document' or 'standing orders' – these all mean the same.)

27.6 Since the constitution of a private organisation constitutes a contract between all the members of an unincorporated association, each member is bound by and entitled to the benefits conferred by the constitution as amended from time to time. The constitution can only ever be amended by the members and, in default of a contrary provision in the document itself which allows amendments to the constitution by a lesser majority, the consent of all members will be required for it to be amended.

27.7 The constitution will usually say what the name and objects of the private organisation are to be, specify the members' liability to contribute to the organisation's funds and regulate how contracts are to be concluded and property held on its behalf. More to the point, it will often set out how decisions are to be made, and the part that meetings play in that process.

27.8 Theoretically, the constitution could provide that all decisions must be made by unanimous agreement of all the members. This is not usually practical, even in the smallest organisations. Instead, the constitution of a small private organisation will often permit the members to appoint officers, such as a secretary and treasurer, and delegate authority to them to deal with certain acts or decisions. For example, a treasurer may be authorised to deal with suppliers and operate the organisation's bank account. Anything not delegated to officers must, however, still be decided by all the members (or those members entitled to vote – dividing members up into classes, with different voting and other rights is common in, for example, full, honorary, junior, associate etc members).

27.9 A private organisation does not have to be very large before the members (and often the officers themselves) decide that delegating to individual officers is not ideal. It places too much responsibility on the officers and makes it hard for members to supervise their activities. The constitution may therefore provide for a body, akin to the board of directors in a limited company, to whom the members delegate the majority of day-to-day decisions.[1] This body is often called the executive committee (but other terms, such as 'management committee' or 'governing body', may be used). The constitution will define how the executive committee is elected, its powers and how it may exercise them. It will give the executive committee general powers to run the organisation, requiring the committee to refer a decision back to the members in specified circumstances.

27.10 This does not mean that a private organisation with an executive committee will have no officers. The executive committee's powers may include the power to delegate further – to officers such as a secretary, treasurer and/or steward. These may be executive committee members or third parties. The

---

[1] The constitution may also provide for the appointment of trustees from among the executive committee, for example, to hold title to assets, such as premises or investments, on behalf of the organisation's members. Meetings of such trustees are not covered in this book.

officers are now, however, working to the executive committee rather than to the members as a whole. This is much more satisfactory. Officers are more accountable, but less exposed.

27.11 The balance struck between matters the members choose to reserve to themselves in the constitution and those they delegate to the executive committee will depend on the size and nature of the organisation, and the relationship between the members and executive committee. Some constitutions delegate power to make virtually all day-to-day decisions to the executive committee. Only decisions relating to changes to the constitution itself, the decision to dissolve the organisation and the election and removal of members of the executive committee are reserved to the members. Others reserve a far broader range of decisions to the members.

27.12 It is common for the constitutions of private organisations to authorise the executive committee to make rules, supplemental or ancillary, to the main constitution, setting out how it will exercise the powers delegated to it. These are often called 'by-laws'. The by-laws regulate detailed day-to-day matters concerning the internal affairs of the organisation – matters such as charges for use of the organisation's facilities and rules regarding admission of guests to its events and premises. They often also regulate matters pertaining to convening and conduct of executive committee meetings. If by-laws are inconsistent with the constitution, the constitution prevails.

27.13 It would be possible, but unusual, for the by-laws to regulate the convening and conduct of members' meetings. But the rules regarding, for example, the manner in which notice of members' meetings are to be given, notice, quorum, chairing and recording of events at members' meetings are more likely to be set out in the constitution, alterable only with the approval of a members' resolution, than the by-laws, alterable at the whim of the executive committee.

27.14 If neither the constitution nor the by-laws make provision for meetings, or their provisions are unclear, there is no underlying statute law for the members or executive committee to fall back on. (This differs from limited companies where much of the procedure relating to members' meetings, and some relating to directors' meetings, is set out in the Companies Act 2006 or the Insolvency Act 1986 and regulations made under them, so no specific provision need be made in a company's memorandum and articles in respect of matters covered by the Acts.)

27.15 In those circumstances, the members and executive committee will need to consider case-law relating to meetings of unincorporated associations. For example, even if there is no provision in the constitution or by-laws, case-law means there is probably an inherent right for members of a private organisation to meet together, so the ability to call a special meeting would be implied into the constitution. But case-law only provides a certain, complete answer if the circumstances that have arisen exactly match those that arose in the relevant case-law. This is rare, so cases can usually provide only principles and guidance that the organisation can try to apply.

27.16 To avoid this uncertainty, a private organisation should make full provision for calling and holding of members' meetings and executive committee meetings in its constitution and/or by-laws, and rely on case-law as little as possible.

MEMBERS' MEETINGS

The annual general meeting

27.17 At the very least, a private organisation will want to provide for an annual general meeting of the members every calendar year in its constitution, at which members can question the executive committee about its management of the organisation.

Special meetings

27.18 If the constitution says that a matter must be dealt with at a members' meeting 'called for the purpose', it cannot be put to the annual general meeting, as that is not called for that purpose.[2] A 'special' or 'extraordinary' members' meeting would be needed.

27.19 The constitution should provide for special members' meetings to be convened and held in any event, to deal with issues requiring a decision of the members that arise between annual general meetings. If the constitution requires a special meeting to make a particular decision, it is not sufficient if that decision is made at an ordinary or annual general meeting.[3]

Who can call members' meetings?

27.20 For the annual general meeting, the constitution may specify the day in each year upon which the annual general meeting is to be held, at the same time and venue. The executive committee is therefore obliged to convene the annual general meeting for that date in accordance with the rules. Giving of further notice may not be required, but this is unusual. Notice of the meeting, and financial and other information about the organisation's affairs, must usually be sent to, circulated or otherwise made available to members for a certain period before the meeting.

27.21 The constitution will usually provide that special members' meetings can be called by the executive committee, or upon the requisition of a specific number or proportion of the members. If it does not, there is case-law that says

---

[2] *Harington v Sendall* [1903] 1 Ch 921.
[3] *Fisher v Keane* (1878) 11 ChD 353.

there is no residual power to require the calling of a members' meeting.[4] However, it is hard to see how a requisition submitted by or on behalf of every member could be ignored by the executive committee. If it was, it is hard to conceive how a meeting convened by all the members acting in unison could be challenged.

27.22 Company law provides that a general meeting of members of a limited company can be requisitioned by members holding not less than 5% of the voting rights in the company.[5] Subject to an organisation's particular circumstances, something between 5% and 10% of the voting membership seems a reasonable proportion for the purposes of requisitioning a special meeting of members of a private organisation. Company law requires that the requisition (or 'request', as it is referred to in CA 2006, even though it is mandatory to comply with it) be in writing, signed by or on behalf of the requisitioning members. Many organisations' constitutions have borrowed from company law in this respect too.

Notice period

27.23 The notice period is the period before the proposed date of the meeting during which notice must be given. If the rules do not specify the notice period for the annual and special meetings, then 'reasonable' notice is required. There have been cases specifying 7 days as reasonable in the particular circumstances. But private organisations are better advised to specify a particular notice period rather than rely on the 'reasonableness' test. Fourteen or 21 days' notice is common. The constitution should specify whether the day of service is to be counted and/or the day of receipt (or deemed receipt – see below). If neither is to be counted (as would be usual) the rules should specify that 'clear days' notice' is required.[6]

How notice is to be given

27.24 If the constitution makes no provision regarding notice, the executive committee can probably determine how it shall be given[7] but, to avoid uncertainty, the rules should also set out the manner in which notice is to be given. For example, the rules may provide that notice is to be given by advertisement in a newspaper circulating in the area local to the organisation's premises or where the members live, or by placing it in a specified or prominent place to which members have access and where they are likely to see it, such as a notice-board in a communal area. More likely, the rules will specify that notice is to be given personally or by post.

---

[4] *Pedley v Inland Waterways Association Ltd* [1977] 1 All ER 209.
[5] Companies Act 2006, s 303 as amended by reg 3 of the Companies (Shareholders' Rights) Regulations 2009, SI 2009/1632.
[6] *R v Turner* [1910] 1 KB 346, CA.
[7] *Labouchere v Earl of Wharncliffe* (1879) 13 ChD 346.

27.25 In *Labouchere v Earl of Wharncliffe*,[8] a case in which a special meeting was called to consider the expulsion of a member, the rules required a fortnight's notice of the meeting. The executive committee gave notice by posting a hard copy in the coffee-room of the organisation and sending a circular to each of the members.

27.26 Sir George Jessel MR said that he was not aware of any common law rule saying how private organisations (in this case, a club) should give notice. If there was nothing in the organisation's rules 'it is within the general functions of a committee of a club to say how notices should be given on each particular occasion'.

27.27 In exercising their discretion, the judge said that committees should distinguish between matters concerning only those who habitually use the organisation's premises, in which case posting the notice in a public part of the premises (in this case, the coffee-room or the library) was sensible, and more important matters. These might include:

> '... matters relating, perhaps, to some organic change – matters connected with the general mode of conducting the club – matters connected with the conduct of a particular member; and in such cases it is only right to give notice by circular to those who do not habitually or daily use the club that these matters are coming on for consideration, in order that they may attend and take part in the discussion.'

The court held the expulsion was an important matter and notice had not therefore been properly given. (The full fortnight's notice had not been given either.) The meeting was therefore not valid.

27.28 To avoid committees having to exercise this sort of judgment, the constitution will usually make clear, unambiguous provision for the manner in which notice is to be given. Common provisions are for notice to be given personally, or by post to the member's address as stated in the organisation's register of members. It is now possible to give notice electronically, and it is suggested that the rules discussed in Chapter 11 in relation to limited companies can be adapted for this purpose.

The form of the notice

27.29 A notice of a special, or the annual general, members' meeting should specify the time, date and place of the meeting. If a meeting is called for a place, date and time with the intention of excluding a member, or is generally unreasonable, a member may challenge the validity of the meeting.[9]

---

[8] (1879) 13 ChD 346.
[9] *Cannon v Trask* (1875) LR 20 Eq 669.

27.30 The notice should contain sufficient detail, and be sufficiently clear, for a member to be able to decide whether he should attend the meeting, and, if necessary, ask questions; or whether he may allow the meeting to pass the resolution without his attendance.

27.31 Best practice for special meetings is for each item of business to be put to a members' meeting to be stated on the notice exactly as it is to be put to the members.[10] Certainly, express mention is required of any unusual items on the agenda.[11]

27.32 The business for members at the annual general meeting will usually be:

- to consider reports from the executive committee (including, in particular, reports from the secretary and treasurer);

- to receive the organisation's accounts and to agree financial contributions to be made by the members (such as subscription fees); and

- to deal with the election, re-election and resignation of members of the executive committee in accordance with the rules in the constitution (if any).

27.33 The annual general meeting of the organisation may also want to consider plans for the year to come. The meeting will usually end with the chairman asking members if they wish to raise 'any other business'. Unless the constitution says otherwise, members cannot use this as an opportunity to raise an issue that is not directly connected with the business of the meeting.

27.34 Some constitutions draw a distinction between ordinary and special business at the annual general meeting. The items listed above are usually specified as ordinary business. Everything else is, by default, special business. The significance of this is that the constitution will usually go on to say that notice need only be given of special business to be conducted at the annual general meeting. The fact that the ordinary business will be conducted can be taken as read. This practice originally mirrored company law, but has now fallen into disuse in company law.

Service of the notice

27.35 If no provision is made in the rules, case-law suggests that a notice is only given once it is actually received.[12] The organisation can be sure notices personally handed to members have been received, but what if the rules permit the sending of notices by post or electronically? There is no guarantee the notice has actually been received. Indeed, cases in which notices sent by post

---

[10] *Young v Ladies Imperial Club* [1920] 2 KB 523.
[11] *Harington v Sendall* [1903] 1 Ch 921.
[12] *Beanby Estates Ltd v Egg Stores (Stamford Hill) Ltd* [2003] 1 WLR 2064; *Blunden v Frogmore Investments Ltd* [2002] 2 EGLR 29.

have been returned undelivered,[13] or in which notice was held likely, on a balance of probabilities, not to have been received,[14] have decided that notice was never validly given. The rules should therefore make clear the circumstances in which a notice is deemed received – for example, within 48 hours after it is posted – even if never actually received. In a case in which a member of a limited company with corresponding provisions in its articles of association did not receive a notice in good time due to a postal strike, however, the court granted him an injunction to restrain the holding of the meeting.[15]

Who is entitled to notice?

27.36 Case-law requires that notice be given to all members. Omission to give notice to a member makes the meeting invalid[16] unless all members ratify decisions made at it,[17] or acquiesce in them.[18]

The chairman

27.37 The rules should provide for a chairman to preside over members' meetings. This may be the chairman of the executive committee who, being appointed or elected for a term, is entitled to preside at both executive committee and members' meetings during that term. Alternatively, it may be a person appointed from among the executive committee members present to preside just at that meeting.

27.38 If a person is entitled to chair a meeting but is not present within, say, 5 minutes of the starting time for the meeting, the rules often provide for those present to appoint a chairman from among their number, choosing from executive committee members first. Only if no committee members are present, or those present are unwilling to preside, should appointment of a member be considered.

27.39 If the rules make no provision for appointment of a chairman, the members present should choose the chair from among their number.[19]

27.40 See Chapter 7 for case-law on the chairman's powers and authority.

---

[13] *R v County of London Quarter Sessions Appeals Committee ex parte Rossi* [1956] 1 QB 682.
[14] *R v Tavistock Commissioners ex parte Adams* (1969) 46 TC 154.
[15] *Bradman v Trinity Estates plc* [1989] BCLC 757.
[16] *Smyth v Darley* (1849) 2 HLC 789; *Young v Imperial Ladies Club Limited* [1920] 2 KB 523 CA; *John v Rees* [1970] Ch 345.
[17] *Re Sick and Funeral Society of St John's Sunday School, Golcar* [1973] 1 Ch 51.
[18] *Abbatt v Treasury Solicitor* [1969] 1 WLR 1575, CA.
[19] This would also apply to subcommittees where, more often than not, the chairman of the organisation would not be part of its composition.

Quorum

27.41 The first job of the chairman is to ensure that a quorum is present. The quorum is the number of members needed before the meeting can validly transact business that binds all members, even if not present. If the rules make no provision, a majority of the members must attend for there to be a quorum.[20] In many private organisations, attendance of more than half the members at a members' meeting would be quite an achievement, so the quorum is often lower. Yet it should not be too low, as that could allow a small group of activists to take over. The rules often set a less ambitious quorum such as one-fifth or one-tenth of the members.

27.42 If a quorum is not present at the official time for starting the meeting, rules often provide that the chairman may wait 5 minutes. Even if the rules are silent, it is likely that the chairman has implied power to delay the start of the meeting for a few minutes in the interests of those who have turned up – who may have travelled or otherwise inconvenienced themselves to attend.[21]

Voting

27.43 It is crucial to provide a mechanism to allow the members to change the constitution itself. In the absence of an express provision in the rules, unanimity is required for any change, under the usual rules governing variation of a contract.

27.44 To avoid the practical difficulties that this can cause, the rules should specify the proportion of votes required to pass different resolutions of the members. They will usually provide for a simple majority, or a majority of 75% or more, of the votes cast if a resolution is to be treated as passed.[22] (It is permissible for the rules to provide for different majorities for different types of resolution.) The majority is therefore calculated by reference to those who attend and vote. Absentees and abstainees are not counted. (Even if the rules do not specify that only those who attend and vote are counted, this is probably implied.[23])

27.45 A chairman may vote unless the rules prohibit this.[24] In many organisations, the rules confer a casting or second vote on the chairman in the event of a tie.[25] The fact that the chairman has an interest in the outcome of a decision does not, in itself, impugn the integrity of the process at a meeting. It

---

[20] *Ellis v Hooper* (1859) 28 LJ Ex 1 [C].
[21] See *John v Rees* [1970] Ch 345, at 383A.
[22] The case of *Morgan v Driscoll* (1922) 38 TLR 251 provides that an amendment must not be incompatible with the fundamental objects of the organisation. It is hard to see why not, if the members unanimously agree it.
[23] *Knowles v Zoological Society* [1959] 1 WLR 823.
[24] *Nell v Longbottom* [1894] 1 QB 767, at 771C.
[25] There is no common law right to a casting vote: *Nell v Longbottom* [1894] 1 QB 767.

would be impractical to require the chairman to be totally disinterested in every matter, and he is presumed to act in good faith unless it is proven otherwise.[26]

27.46 The rules will usually provide for voting on a show of hands – it would be unusual for any member of a private organisation to have more than one vote. Some constitutions provide that a member may not vote if his subscriptions are in arrears.

27.47 Other means of voting that may appear in an organisation's rules are by acclamation, poll or ballot. A decision by acclamation occurs when the chairman honestly and reasonably believes that the sense of the meeting is for or against a particular decision, so that a formal vote is not necessary.[27]

27.48 In some organisations, the rules provide for a vote by poll.[28] A poll records the number of votes, either by an individual voting slip or by signing a voting list, and is a more accurate way of establishing the true vote than a show of hands. In the event that a member considers that the results of a vote taken by a show of hands is incorrectly declared, he can probably demand a poll in any event.[29] A valid request for a poll invalidates the results of any show of hands.[30] Unless the rules say otherwise, a poll has to be taken of all the members entitled to vote[31] so that this will usually require the adjournment of the meeting.

27.49 In company law, members of a company limited by shares have the right to appoint a proxy to attend members' meetings on their behalf. In the absence of a specific power in the constitution, members of a private organisation may not appoint a proxy.[32]

27.50 Some private organisations' rules provide for officers to be elected by secret ballot.

27.51 In the absence of a power to do so in the constitution, a member has no right to appoint a proxy to attend and vote at members' meetings on his behalf.

27.52 A member's vote at a special meeting must be given on proper information, as it binds both dissentient and absent members. This rule is

---

[26] *Blair v Consolidated Enfield Corporation* [1995] 4 SCR, on appeal from the Court of Appeal for Toronto.
[27] *Re Citizens Theatre* [1946] SC 14 at 17C. This voting is sometimes recorded in the minutes as 'Nem Con'. This is shorthand for *'Nemine contradicente'*, ie with no one dissenting. This is not the same thing as a unanimous decision in favour.
[28] *R v Rector of Birmingham* (1837) 7 A & E 254C.
[29] *Re Wimbledon Local Board* (1882) 8 QBD 459C.
[30] *R v Cooper* (1870) LR 5 QB 457.
[31] *R v Rector of St Mary, Lambeth* (1838) 8 A & E 356.
[32] *Harben v Phillips* (1883) 23 ChD 14; *Woodford v Smith* (1970) 120 LJ News 333.

consistent with the general principle that matters must be fairly put before the meeting and the meeting itself must be conducted in the fairest possible manner.[33]

Amendments

27.53 In *Betts & Co v MacNaghten*, a company law case,[34] the court considered a notice stating that the meeting was for the purpose of considering the resolution 'That A, B, and C be appointed directors'. The resolution allowed for such amendments and alterations as should be determined upon at the meeting. At the meeting, two further directors were appointed in addition to A, B and C. It was held that the notice sufficiently indicated the business to be transacted, and that the particularity of the names did not put greater restriction upon the meeting than there would have been had the notice been in general terms. Accordingly, all five were properly appointed.

27.54 It is hard to see why that case would not also have been followed in the case of a private organisation. In that case, however, notice was given of the resolution with the addition of the words 'with such amendments as shall be determined on at the meeting', so the court may have been more than usually ready to find that an amendment to the ordinary resolution which had been set out in the notice would not invalidate the resolution.

27.55 Also, the power to amend resolutions at a members' meeting will usually only apply if the amendment at the meeting renders the resolution less, and not more, onerous to the company or its members; for example, where the subscription proposed in the amendment is lower than that proposed in the notice.[35] The reason for this is that a member may have decided not to attend because they were content with the stated proposal, but might have wanted to attend had the amendment increased subscriptions in their absence.

27.56 A proposed amendment should be sufficiently definite.[36] It need not be seconded unless the articles specifically require this. 'If the chairman put the question without its being proposed or seconded by anybody, that would be perfectly good.'[37] A chairman is, therefore, not justified in refusing a motion or amendment because there is no seconder unless the rules expressly provide that all motions and amendments shall be seconded.

27.57 Where there is more than one amendment, these should be put to the meeting in the order in which they affect the main resolution. The main resolution, as finally amended, should then be put to the meeting. Strict

---

[33] *Tiessen v Henderson* [1899] 1 Ch 861.
[34] [1910] 1 Ch 430.
[35] *Torbuck v Westbury (Lord)* [1902] 2 Ch 871. The resolution in this case was a special resolution, and the section of the Companies Act 1862 relating to special resolutions differed from s 283 of the Companies Act 2006.
[36] *Henderson v Bank of Australasia* (1890) 45 ChD 330.
[37] *Horbury Bridge Coal Co* (1879) 11 ChD 109, at 118.

adherence to the formality of putting motions and amendments is not essential, provided they are put to the meeting in such a way that those present understand what they are called upon to decide.[38]

27.58 If there is the slightest doubt as to whether an amendment is in order or not, it should be allowed to be put. The chairman is bound to allow the proposal of all legitimate and germane resolutions and amendments, and a refusal to do so will invalidate that part of the proceedings, because such refusal may amount to the withdrawal of a material and relevant question from the meeting. In *Henderson v Bank of Australasia*, a company law case, Cotton LJ observed:[39]

> '... the chairman was entirely wrong in refusing to put the amendment, and ... the resolutions which were passed cannot be allowed to stand, because the chairman, under a mistaken idea as to what the law was which ought to have regulated his conduct, prevented a material question from being brought before the meeting.'

27.59 Where the chairman does rule an amendment out of order, there is no obligation on the part of the mover of the amendment to contest that ruling or to leave the meeting. It is not necessary for the mover to keep up an altercation with the chairman, nor does the mover lose any right to later object by acting under the ruling of the chairman.[40]

Adjournments

27.60 Where the rules make no provision for adjournment, the power of adjournment is vested in the meeting.[41] The chairman cannot adjourn the meeting without its authority. If he purports to do so, the meeting may proceed in any event. Motions for adjournment can generally be brought forward at any period of the meeting, and take precedence over any matter then under consideration.

27.61 Usually, the constitution will provide for meetings to be adjourned in certain circumstances, such as if a certain number or proportion of the members at the meeting demand it. But the chairman must always adjourn the meeting if he believes that to be the will of a majority of the members present at a meeting, even in the absence of an express power in the constitution.[42]

27.62 In the unusual situation where the meeting is in total disorder, so the views of the members cannot be ascertained (even after 'earnest and sustained efforts'[43]), the chairman has an inherent power (whatever the provisions of the rules) to adjourn the meeting. This should be for as short a time as possible,

---

[38] *Stevens ex parte* (1852) 16 JP 632.
[39] (1890) 45 ChD 330, at 346.
[40] *Henderson v Bank of Australasia* (1890) 45 ChD 330.
[41] Cf *R v Grimshaw* (1847) 11 Jur 965; *Stoughton v Reynolds* (1736) 2 Strange 1044; *National Dwellings Society v Sykes* [1894] 3 Ch 159.
[42] *John v Rees* [1970] Ch 345.
[43] Ibid.

and he should take steps, so far as possible, to ensure that all present know of the adjournment.[44] In some circumstances he will have a duty to adjourn – where, for example, the safety of members is at risk.

27.63 The date and time of the adjourned meeting is usually fixed at the time of the original adjournment. If the constitution is silent, there is no need to give notice of the adjourned meeting.[45] This is because the adjourned meeting is treated as merely a continuation of the original meeting[46] (although resolutions passed at the adjourned meeting are treated as passed on the date the adjourned meeting is held). Business is therefore confined to that specified in the original notice.[47] This means that members who did not attend the meeting will not know of the adjourned meeting. It is therefore good practice to include a provision in the organisation's constitution (mirroring the company law provision[48]) saying that, if the adjournment is for 14 days or more, notice of the adjourned meeting will be sent to all members.

EXECUTIVE COMMITTEE MEETINGS
When held, and notice period

27.64 The rules will often provide that regular meetings of the executive committee must be held – for example, on the second Tuesday of every month at a specified time and place. If so, that is sufficient notice – no notice need be given before each individual meeting.

27.65 Alternatively, and more commonly, the executive committee of a private organisation will decide when the next meeting is to be held at the end of each preceding meeting. Notice of the new date is given to those committee members who did not attend the original meeting by including it in the minutes of that meeting, containing the new date.

27.66 Unusually, the rules may require that a member of the executive committee must request a meeting – perhaps of the secretary – before one is convened, and that notice of the meeting must be drawn up and sent out. In that case, in the absence of an express rule, reasonable notice must be given of the meeting. This will depend on the facts in any particular case, but the members of the executive committee must have sufficient time before the meeting to consider any information sent to them. If, however, a practice develops of giving a particular period of notice, this will be held to be reasonable in the absence of any particular circumstances which would make that period inappropriate. But in *Re Homer Gold Mines*,[49] a company law case,

---

[44] Ibid; *Byng v London Life Association Ltd* [1989] BCLC 400.
[45] *Wills v Murray* [1850] 4 Ex 843; *Scadding v Lorant* [1851] 3 HLC 418.
[46] *Scadding v Lorant* (1851) 3 HLC 418.
[47] *Kerr v Wilkie* (1860) 1 LT 501.
[48] See the model form articles under CA 2006 and, for companies with older articles, Table A to the Companies Act 1985.
[49] (1888) 39 ChD 546.

shorter notice than any previously given was held invalid because the court decided that shorter notice had been given with a view to excluding certain directors. A notice period may, however, be extremely short if all the executive committee members are able to attend, and if any member wishes to object to the shortness of the notice, that member should make such an objection at once.[50]

27.67 Sending out an agenda and papers in advance of each meeting is desirable, but committees tend to develop their own procedures for achieving this. The key requirements are that members of the executive committee receive enough information to decide whether to attend or not, and that all members receive the same information – there is equality.

To whom should notice be given?

27.68 If notice is required, it is highly desirable that it be given to all members of the executive committee, whether the rules require this or not.

The form of the notice

27.69 The notice need not be in writing unless the rules so provide.[51] It can be oral if, for example, given by telephone.

27.70 Executive committee members can deal with all the affairs of the organisation that require attention or arise at any of their meetings, irrespective of whether they have been specified in the notice or not, provided:

- they do not exceed their powers; and

- by doing so, they are not acting unfairly towards a committee member who has decided, on the strength of the notice (if any) not to attend.[52]

27.71 In some private organisations, therefore, the practice is not to give any indication of the nature of the business, unless there is something unusual to be considered, and no agenda are included in or attached to notices of meetings.

27.72 However, certain cases, inconsistent with this practice, have been decided on the basis that the object of requiring proper notice of the purposes for which the meeting is to be held is to enable a person entitled to attend to exercise his own judgment as to whether to attend. For example, in company law it has been held that the heading 'Any other business' in a notice will generally authorise the transaction of business of a purely formal nature but not business of any substantial importance. In *Young v Ladies' Imperial Club*,[53] it was held that, as the notice of a meeting did not state the object of the

---

[50] *Browne v La Trinidad* (1887) 37 ChD 1.
[51] *Browne v La Trinidad* (1887) 37 ChD 1.
[52] *La Compagnie de Mayville v Whitley* [1896] 1 Ch 788.
[53] [1920] 2 KB 523.

meeting with sufficient particularity, it was invalid and consequently the proceedings of that meeting were invalidated. It has also been held that a notice may be good in part and bad in part, and it is not wholly invalid because it extends to something which cannot be done at the meeting.[54]

27.73 A better view, therefore, is that the notice must provide, or be accompanied by, a description of the nature of (all) the proposed business of the meeting, in sufficient detail for the executive committee member to decide whether or not to attend, and that the meeting cannot, in ordinary cases, go outside the business described in that notice.[55] Such a notice or agenda gives members an opportunity to consider issues in advance and can shorten meetings by reducing ill-informed discussion or misapprehensions based on insufficient information.

Service of the notice

27.74 This is not usually dealt with in the rules – the executive committee may establish its own rules regarding service.

Conduct of the meeting

27.75 If there is no provision in the rules, the executive committee has, subject to its having express or implied authority to decide a matter (and unless the conduct of a member is under consideration so the rules of natural justice apply), an absolute discretion as to the procedure it adopts when making its decisions.[56] However, the rules will often specify how the committee is to operate in certain respects.

The chairman

27.76 The rules generally provide that the committee may elect a chairman of its meetings and determine the period for which the chairman is to hold office. If no chairman is elected, if the chairman is unwilling to preside or if at any meeting the chairman is not present within 5 minutes after the time appointed for holding the meeting, the members of the committee present may choose one of their number to be chairman of the meeting.

27.77 The election of a chairman may be a general one or merely for a particular meeting. It is important that a clear record of this is kept in the minutes, since confusion and dispute will often result if it is not clear who the chairman is – especially if the articles give the chairman a casting vote, as they sometimes do.[57]

---

[54] *Cleve v Financial Corporation* (1873) LR 16 Eq 363.
[55] *Longfield Parish Council v Wright* (1919) 88 LJ (Ch) 119.
[56] *Cassel v Inglis* [1916] 2 Ch 211.
[57] For example, reg 13 in the model form articles for a private company limited by shares prescribed under CA 2006.

Quorum

27.78 The rules usually prescribe a quorum for executive committee meetings, without which the meeting is invalid. If they do not, it is likely that a majority of the members must attend for there to be a quorum (or any other number that has become legitimised by normal practice of the committee).[58]

Voting

27.79 Unless the rules provide otherwise, each committee member has only one vote at a meeting. In the event of a disagreement the majority view will prevail, though the chairman may have a casting vote.

27.80 The members of the organisation may wish to include a provision in the rules requiring executive committee members who have a personal interest in a matter under discussion to declare their interest to the committee. By analogy with company law, it is open to require that executive committee members may not vote on matters in which they have such an interest.

27.81 The rules may, however, provide that a member of the executive committee may act, or his firm may act, in a professional capacity for the organisation, and that the member of the committee or his firm shall be entitled to remuneration for professional services as if that person were not a member of the executive committee.

Delegation to subcommittees

27.82 The rules may allow the executive committee to establish subcommittees to which they delegate specific tasks, such as dealing with membership issues – admission, expulsion etc. 'A (sub)committee means a person or persons to whom powers are committed which would otherwise be exercised by another body.'[59] It exercises limited powers, which may be modified or withdrawn by its appointing authority. The powers of subcommittees should be clearly set out in their appointment.

27.83 Ordinarily, the executive committee will specify the way the subcommittee is to operate – usually by saying that it will operate like the executive committee save that it will have, perhaps, a smaller quorum. If no quorum is specified, the quorum for subcommittee meetings will be the entire committee because powers are delegated to the subcommittee itself, not to its individual members.[60] Rules setting a more achievable quorum are strongly recommended.

---

[58] *Regent's Canal Ironworks* [1867] WN 79.
[59] *Re Taurine Co* (1883) 25 ChD 132.
[60] *Brown v Andrew* (1849) 18 LJ QB 153 [C]; *R v Liverpool City Council ex p Professional Association of Teachers* (1984) *The Times*, March 22.

27.84 Where a subcommittee is exercising a power to discipline members, for example, by expulsion under the constitution, it is acting in a quasi-judicial capacity and must therefore act fairly in accordance with the rules of natural justice.[61] Strict legal procedures do not have to be followed,[62] but the rules of natural justice do require that the member be given precise grounds for the allegations being made against him and the opportunity to be heard on them. The committee should act in good faith on the evidence before it, assessing its weight (or lack of it).[63]

MINUTES AND RECORDS

27.85 The members should specify in the rules that minutes must be kept of both members' and executive committee meetings, to avoid disputes. The following applies to both types of meeting unless stated otherwise.

27.86 One purpose of minutes is to provide an accurate record of what was decided at the meeting. This does not mean that it is always necessary to record the speeches or arguments at the meeting. The minutes will often record only what was agreed upon. If the organisation wants a record of what was said, this record can be created as a separate report, outside the minutes.

27.87 There may, however, be occasions when recording reasons for a decision, or key points made during debate at the meeting, is appropriate. It is open to the meeting to decide the form and content of the record of the meeting they want, and they can require inclusion of such background information if they wish.[64] If they do so, the resulting minutes are usually called 'minutes of narration'. Minutes of narration may be indicated because a matter is important or contentious. If the organisation is in financial difficulties, the executive committee may be keen to demonstrate the reasoning behind their decisions.

27.88 Another function of the minutes of an executive committee meeting is to record any necessary declarations of their personal interests by members of the committee, if required by the rules.

27.89 A function of minutes of all meetings is to show that decisions have been taken properly and in accordance with the statutory rules, articles, operating procedures and customs of the organisation, and the common law. The minutes should be:

---

[61] *Annamunthodo v Oilfield Workers Trade Union* [1961] AC 945.
[62] For example, there is no right to legal representation: *Enderby Town Football Club v The Football Association* [1971] Ch 591.
[63] *Abbot v Sullivan* [1952] 1 KN 189; *Byrne v Kinematograph Renters Society Ltd* [1958] 2 All ER 579; *Ceylon University v Fernando* [1960] 1 WLR 223; *Mahon v Air New Zealand* (1983) *The Times*, October 21.
[64] *Re Land Credit Co* (1869) LR 4 Ch App 460, at 473.

(1) an exact account of what was actually agreed upon;

(2) sufficiently detailed and complete, so that a member who was absent can fully understand what was decided at that meeting; and

(3) concise.

27.90 The minutes should contain, among other things:

(1) the names of those present;

(2) identification of all papers presented to the meeting (these should be retained for reference);[65]

(3) full and exact details of all contracts and questions involving financial considerations;

(4) the wording of resolutions passed; and

(5) instructions to officers, and all transactions authorised at that meeting.

27.91 Ideally, minutes should be kept in a secure place, such as a fireproof safe or other like place, or as a computer record. The rules may specify who may inspect minutes.

27.92 It is good practice for minutes to be signed by the chairman of that meeting or by the chairman of the next succeeding meeting.

27.93 Rules sometimes provide that the minutes of a meeting if purporting to be signed by the chairman shall be 'conclusive evidence without any further proof of the facts therein stated'. According to the only reported decision on such an article, evidence cannot be given in such a case to contradict minutes so signed unless it can first be shown that the minutes have been written up fraudulently.[66] There is much doubt whether this decision is correct, and a rule framed in this way is inadvisable.

27.94 Best practice is also to circulate their respective minutes to members and executive committee members. Common practice is for minutes to be read or, if previously circulated to the members of the meeting (which is more likely), taken as read, at the next following meeting. They are then submitted to the meeting for approval. If regarded as a correct report of the proceedings by those present at that meeting, they are signed by the chairman. If considered

---

[65] For limited company board meetings, this is a recommendation of the Institute of Chartered Secretaries and Administrators 'Good Boardroom Practice. A Code for Directors and Company Secretaries' guidelines, available from the Information Centre, ICSA, 16 Park Crescent, London W1B 1AH or e-mail informationcentre@icsa.org.uk. See also www.icsa.org.uk.

[66] *Kerr v John Mottram Ltd* [1940] Ch 657.

incorrect, they may be modified and then signed. Any discussion on the minutes, except as to their accuracy, is out of order, and the chairman should rule accordingly.

27.95 If there is a conflict of opinion about the accuracy of the minutes, an amendment to the motion that they are correct, setting out any suggested alteration, should be put to the meeting. Those who were not present at the preceding meeting should not take part in the discussion or vote.

27.96 The approval of the minutes by a meeting merely verifies their accuracy; it does not necessarily mean that such minutes are adopted or that the resolutions therein have been confirmed or ratified by the subsequent meeting.

27.97 There is no statutory requirement that the minutes be approved by the attendees at the meeting to which they relate, or at the next succeeding meeting, before they are signed by the chairman. They can be signed at any time. This means that minutes can still be signed in the event of an emergency. However, best practice is for the minutes to be put before the members or executive committee at the next succeeding meeting before they are signed, if possible.

27.98 The benefits of holding a set of minutes signed by the chairman mean it is undesirable to keep computerised records of minutes without also printing out a hard copy of those minutes and obtaining the signature of the chairman to them.

Appendix 1

SUMMARY OF MAIN MATTERS TO BE DEALT WITH BY MEMBERS UNDER THE COMPANIES ACT[1]

AMENDMENT OF ARTICLES TO ADD, REMOVE OR ALTER OBJECTS[2]

A1.1 A company may amend its articles of association to add, remove or alter any statement of the company's objects in those articles (or treated as being in those articles by virtue of saving provisions introduced under the Companies Act 2006) by passing a special resolution. Note that the alteration does not take effect until the company has given notice of the amendment to the Registrar of Companies and the Registrar has entered it on the register.

OTHER ALTERATIONS OF ARTICLES

A1.2 Subject to the provisions of the Companies Acts a company may alter any other provision of its articles by passing a special resolution.

CHANGE OF NAME

A1.3 A company may change its name by passing a special resolution. Note the change does not take effect until the Registrar of Companies issues a certificate of incorporation on change of name. Note that a company may also change its name by any other means provided for in its articles of association.

---

[1] Note: this is not an exhaustive list.
[2] Under CA 2006 companies have a single constitutional document – their articles of association. If the members of a company wish to restrict the activities it can carry on, they can include appropriate restrictions in the articles. Otherwise, the company's constitution will not contain any objects so it can carry on any lawful business activities. For companies incorporated under previous Companies Acts, which had to include their objects in their memorandum of association, those objects are deemed, from 1 October 2009, to be part of their articles of association unless altered or removed by the members.

ALTERATIONS TO CAPITAL

A1.4 A company may, by ordinary resolution passed in general meeting:

(1) re-denominate its share capital;[3]

(2) consolidate and divide all or any of its share capital into shares of larger amount than its existing shares;

(3) reconvert any of its paid-up shares converted into stock back into paid-up shares of any denomination;

(4) subdivide any of its shares into shares of a smaller amount;

A1.5 Shares are subdivided if, for example, one share of £1 is turned into ten shares of 10p. Shares are consolidated if, for example, five shares of £1 each are turned into one share of £5. When consolidating shares in this way, care must be taken to ensure that each shareholder will end up with a whole number of shares.

REDUCTION OF CAPITAL SUPPORTED BY SOLVENCY STATEMENT[4]

A1.6 A *private* company limited by shares may reduce its share capital by special resolution supported by a solvency statement made by the directors. This acts as an alternative to the possibility of reducing share capital by special resolution confirmed by the court (see below). In appropriate cases the reduction supported by solvency statement is likely to be substantially simpler than the alternative procedure requiring an application to the court.

REDUCTION OF CAPITAL – CONFIRMED BY COURT ORDER

A1.7 A company may pass a special resolution to reduce its capital – an application to the court for an order to confirm the reduction must then be made. There are various detailed and complex procedures laid down in CA 2006 in connection with a reduction of capital, especially concerning publicity for the proposal. Therefore the alternative administrative procedure for reduction supported by a solvency statement (see above) is usually a simpler option for a private share company wishing to reduce its capital.

---

[3] This means the conversion of shares from having a fixed nominal value in one currency to having a fixed nominal value in another currency. This is subject to the company satisfying a number of other, strict, procedural requirements, and to the company's articles, which may prohibit or restrict the power.

[4] This option was introduced under the Companies Act 2006 reforms, see ss 642–644 of the Companies Act 2006.

DISAPPLICATION OF PRE-EMPTION RIGHTS ON ALLOTMENT OF SHARES[5]

A1.8 In certain circumstances a company may be able to disapply the statutory pre-emption rights in favour of existing members that would otherwise apply by passing a special resolution to that effect.

APPROVAL OF AGREEMENT TO TRANSFER NON-CASH ASSET IN PAYMENT FOR ALLOTMENT OF SHARES IN A PUBLIC COMPANY

A1.9 In certain restricted circumstances the members of a public company must approve, by ordinary resolution, the terms of an agreement entered into with a subscriber to the company's memorandum under which they will pay for shares allotted to them by transferring non-cash assets to the company equal in value to one-tenth or more of the company's total issued share capital.

A1.10 Public companies must hold an AGM within 6 months of the financial year end.

DECLARATION OF DIVIDENDS

A1.11 Subject to the provisions of its own articles, a company usually declares dividends after the end of an accounting reference period by passing a resolution in general meeting to declare a full dividend. However, the articles often allow the directors of the company to pay an 'interim' dividend during the course of an accounting reference period without referring the matter to the shareholders.

GIVING AUTHORITY TO THE DIRECTORS TO ALLOT SHARES

A1.12 Under CA 2006, the directors of a public company, or a private company with more than one class of share capital, cannot allot any shares unless they have been given authority to do so either by the company's articles or by ordinary resolution passed in general meeting. If the directors of a private company with only one class of shares still have an authority to allot shares, given before the relevant provisions of CA 2006 came into force, the members can pass an ordinary resolution to the effect that the directors shall have the powers given by s 550 (and therefore that the authority, and the restrictions in it, no longer apply).

---

[5] This will only be relevant to a company incorporated before 1 October 2009, which has a memorandum of association.

REMOVAL OF A DIRECTOR

A1.13 A company may, by ordinary resolution of which special notice has been given, remove a director from the office of director at any time regardless of anything in its articles or in any agreement between it and the director. Note this removes the director from office, but does NOT end his or her employment, where the director in question is also an employee of the company.

A1.14 At least 28 days before the meeting at which such a resolution is to be proposed, special notice of the resolution must be given to the company by the shareholder(s) proposing it and the company must then give at least 21 days' notice of the meeting to all its shareholders.

A1.15 A director should not be removed unless professional advice has been taken.

AUTHORISING THE GIVING OF FINANCIAL ASSISTANCE

A1.16 The Companies Act 2006 has abolished the previous restrictions on the giving of financial assistance by a private company for the acquisition of shares in that company or its holding company. However, the legal restrictions continue to apply to public companies, so advance approval by special resolution of the members would be needed for such a transaction involving a public company.

AUTHORISING A PURCHASE BY THE COMPANY OF ITS OWN SHARES

A1.17 In certain circumstances, a company can purchase its own shares from a shareholder.

A1.18 If a private or public company is proposing to do so and the purchase money is to come from its distributable profits then the contract for the purchase must be approved by a special resolution of the company.

A1.19 If a private company is proposing to do so and the purchase money is to come from capital that payment out of capital must be approved by a special resolution of the company. (Note that if the proposed payment is to be made from capital the company's creditors or any dissenting shareholder can apply to the court for cancellation of the special resolution. Note also that there are complex procedural requirements in respect of a purchase of a company's own shares which must be observed – the requirements are particularly stringent in the case of a purchase from capital.)

APPOINTMENT OF AUDITORS (IF REQUIRED)

A1.20 An auditor of a private company must be appointed for each financial year, unless the directors reasonably resolve otherwise on the ground that audited accounts are unlikely to be required. The Companies Act 2006 contains detailed provisions about who should appoint the auditor, when the appointment should be made and in what circumstances the auditor is deemed re-appointed.

A1.21 In practice, unless the directors resolve that audited accounts are unlikely to be required, it is likely to be easiest if the members appoint the auditor by ordinary resolution. After that, the auditors will usually be deemed re-appointed. Some may prefer the auditors to be initially appointed by the directors and afterwards re-appointed (perhaps each year) by the members.

FIXING OF AUDITORS' REMUNERATION

A1.22 The remuneration of an auditor appointed by the directors must be fixed by the directors. The remuneration of an auditor appointed by the members must be fixed by the members by ordinary resolution or in such manner as the members may by ordinary resolution determine. In practice, the members may choose to delegate to the directors the power to fix the auditor's remuneration.

REMOVAL OF AUDITORS

A1.23 A company may remove its auditor before the expiration of the auditor's term of office, regardless of anything in any agreement between the auditor and the company, by passing an ordinary resolution of which special notice has been given.

DIRECTOR'S CONTRACT OF EMPLOYMENT FOR MORE THAN 2 YEARS

A1.24 Where it is proposed that a provision should be included in an agreement whereby a director's employment is to continue (or may continue) for a period of more than 2 years and during that time the employment:

(1) cannot be terminated by the company by notice; or

(2) can be terminated only in specified circumstances,

then that provision must have the prior approval of the company given by a resolution passed in general meeting.

SUBSTANTIAL PROPERTY TRANSACTIONS INVOLVING DIRECTORS

A1.25 The prior approval of the shareholders must be given by a resolution in general meeting before a company enters an agreement:

(1) whereby a director or a person connected with a director, acquires or is to acquire one or more non-cash assets of a specified value; or

(2) whereby the company acquires or is to acquire one or more non-cash assets of a specified value from a director or a person connected with a director.

A1.26 Professional advice will be required with regard to the 'specified value' and note that there are some exceptions to this rule.

SHAREHOLDERS' VOLUNTARY WINDING UP

A1.27 If a company is solvent, its shareholders can pass a special resolution that the company should be wound up. During the course of the winding up there will be periodic meetings of the company's shareholders and eventually there will be a final general meeting.

VOLUNTARY ARRANGEMENT UNDER THE INSOLVENCY LEGISLATION OF 1986

A1.28 A liquidator, administrator or the directors of a company may propose a composition in satisfaction of the company's debts or a scheme of arrangement of its affairs which is to be implemented under the supervision of a qualified insolvency practitioner. That qualified insolvency practitioner may summon meetings of the shareholders to consider the proposal and to approve or modify or reject it.

APPLICATION FOR RE-REGISTRATION OF A PRIVATE COMPANY AS A PUBLIC COMPANY

A1.29 A private company may apply to the Registrar of Companies for re-registration as a public company. Before making such an application the shareholders must pass a special resolution that the company should be so re-registered, and comply with other detailed procedural requirements.

APPLICATION FOR RE-REGISTRATION OF A LIMITED COMPANY AS AN UNLIMITED COMPANY

A1.30 A private company registered as a limited company can apply to the Registrar of Companies for re-registration as an unlimited company. Every shareholder must sign a statutory 'Form of Assent', agreeing to the company being so re-registered.

Appendix 2

BUSHELL V FAITH CLAUSE

EDITOR'S NOTE

A2.1 The wording below could be used if the company's articles apply the new model articles for a private company limited by shares (which take effect for new incorporations on or after 1 October 2009, see SI 2008/3229). The wording should be modified as appropriate if the articles use an older model, such as a previous version of Table A, in which case one or more specific provisions of Table A may need to be modified or disapplied.

ENHANCED VOTING RIGHTS FOR DIRECTORS

A. Every director for the time being of the Company who is a member of the Company shall have the following rights:

    A.1 if at any general meeting a poll is duly demanded on a resolution to remove him from office, to ten votes for each share of which he is the holder; and

    A.2 if at any general meeting a poll is duly demanded on a resolution to delete or amend the provisions of this article, to ten votes for each share of which he is the holder if voting against such resolution.

B. The voting provisions of these Articles with regard to voting at general meetings shall be modified accordingly.

Appendix 3

THE UK CORPORATE GOVERNANCE CODE

THE MAIN PRINCIPLES OF THE CODE

Section A: Leadership

A.1: The Role of the Board

Main Principle

Every company should be headed by an effective board which is collectively responsible for the long-term success of the company.

Supporting Principles

The board's role is to provide entrepreneurial leadership of the company within a framework of prudent and effective controls which enables risk to be assessed and managed. The board should set the company's strategic aims, ensure that the necessary financial and human resources are in place for the company to meet its objectives and review management performance. The board should set the company's values and standards and ensure that its obligations to its shareholders and others are understood and met.

All directors must act in what they consider to be the best interests of the company, consistent with their statutory duties.[1]

Code Provisions

A.1.1. The board should meet sufficiently regularly to discharge its duties effectively. There should be a formal schedule of matters specifically reserved for its decision. The annual report should include a statement of how the board operates, including a high level statement of which types of decisions are to be taken by the board and which are to be delegated to management.

A.1.2. The annual report should identify the chairman, the deputy chairman (where there is one), the chief executive, the senior independent director and

---

[1] For directors of UK incorporated companies, these duties are set out in the Sections 170 to 177 of the Companies Act 2006.

the chairmen and members of the board committees.[2] It should also set out the number of meetings of the board and those committees and individual attendance by directors.

A.1.3. The company should arrange appropriate insurance cover in respect of legal action against its directors.

A.2: Division of Responsibilities

Main Principle

There should be a clear division of responsibilities at the head of the company between the running of the board and the executive responsibility for the running of the company's business. No one individual should have unfettered powers of decision.

Code Provision

A.2.1 The roles of chairman and chief executive should not be exercised by the same individual. The division of responsibilities between the chairman and chief executive should be clearly established, set out in writing and agreed by the board.

A.3: The Chairman

Main Principle

The chairman is responsible for leadership of the board and ensuring its effectiveness on all aspects of its role.

Supporting Principle

The chairman is responsible for setting the board's agenda and ensuring that adequate time is available for discussion of all agenda items, in particular strategic issues. The chairman should also promote a culture of openness and debate by facilitating the effective contribution of non-executive directors in particular and ensuring constructive relations between executive and non-executive directors.

The chairman is responsible for ensuring that the directors receive accurate, timely and clear information. The chairman should ensure effective communication with shareholders.

---

[2] Provisions A.1.1 and A.1.2 overlap with FSA Rule DTR 7.2.7 R; Provision A.1.2 also overlaps with DTR 7.1.5 R (see Schedule B).

Code Provisions

A.3.1. The chairman should on appointment meet the independence criteria set out in B.1.1 below. A chief executive should not go on to be chairman of the same company. If exceptionally a board decides that a chief executive should become chairman, the board should consult major shareholders in advance and should set out its reasons to shareholders at the time of the appointment and in the next annual report.[3]

A.4: Non-executive Directors

Main Principle

As part of their role as members of a unitary board, non-executive directors should constructively challenge and help develop proposals on strategy.

Supporting Principles

Non-executive directors should scrutinise the performance of management in meeting agreed goals and objectives and monitor the reporting of performance. They should satisfy themselves on the integrity of financial information and that financial controls and systems of risk management are robust and defensible. They are responsible for determining appropriate levels of remuneration of executive directors and have a prime role in appointing and, where necessary, removing executive directors, and in succession planning.

Code Provisions

A.4.1. The board should appoint one of the independent non-executive directors to be the senior independent director to provide a sounding board for the chairman and to serve as an intermediary for the other directors when necessary. The senior independent director should be available to shareholders if they have concerns which contact through the normal channels of chairman, chief executive or other executive directors has failed to resolve or for which such contact is inappropriate.

A.4.2. The chairman should hold meetings with the non-executive directors without the executives present. Led by the senior independent director, the non-executive directors should meet without the chairman present at least annually to appraise the chairman's performance and on such other occasions as are deemed appropriate.

A.4.3. Where directors have concerns which cannot be resolved about the running of the company or a proposed action, they should ensure that their concerns are recorded in the board minutes. On resignation, a non-executive

---

[3] Compliance or otherwise with this provision need only be reported for the year in which the appointment is made.

director should provide a written statement to the chairman, for circulation to the board, if they have any such concerns.

Section B: Effectiveness

B.1: The Composition of the Board

Main Principle

The board and its committees should have the appropriate balance of skills, experience, independence and knowledge of the company to enable them to discharge their respective duties and responsibilities effectively.

Supporting Principles

The board should be of sufficient size that the requirements of the business can be met and that changes to the board's composition and that of its committees can be managed without undue disruption, and should not be so large as to be unwieldy.

The board should include an appropriate combination of executive and non-executive directors (and, in particular, independent non-executive directors) such that no individual or small group of individuals can dominate the board's decision taking.

The value of ensuring that committee membership is refreshed and that undue reliance is not placed on particular individuals should be taken into account in deciding chairmanship and membership of committees.

No one other than the committee chairman and members is entitled to be present at a meeting of the nomination, audit or remuneration committee, but others may attend at the invitation of the committee.

Code Provisions

B.1.1. The board should identify in the annual report each non-executive director it considers to be independent.[4] The board should determine whether the director is independent in character and judgement and whether there are relationships or circumstances which are likely to affect, or could appear to affect, the director's judgement. The board should state its reasons if it determines that a director is independent notwithstanding the existence of relationships or circumstances which may appear relevant to its determination, including if the director:

- has been an employee of the company or group within the last five years;

---

[4] .3.1 states that the chairman should, on appointment, meet the independence criteria set out in this provision, but thereafter the test of independence is not appropriate in relation to the chairman.

- has, or has had within the last three years, a material business relationship with the company either directly, or as a partner, shareholder, director or senior employee of a body that has such a relationship with the company;

- has received or receives additional remuneration from the company apart from a director's fee, participates in the company's share option or a performance-related pay scheme, or is a member of the company's pension scheme;

- has close family ties with any of the company's advisers, directors or senior employees;

- holds cross-directorships or has significant links with other directors through involvement in other companies or bodies;

- represents a significant shareholder; or

- has served on the board for more than nine years from the date of their first election.

B.1.2. Except for smaller companies,[5] at least half the board, excluding the chairman, should comprise nonexecutive directors determined by the board to be independent. A smaller company should have at least two independent non-executive directors.

B.2: Appointments to the Board

Main Principle

There should be a formal, rigorous and transparent procedure for the appointment of new directors to the board.

Supporting Principles

The search for board candidates should be conducted, and appointments made, on merit, against objective criteria and with due regard for the benefits of diversity on the board, including gender.

The board should satisfy itself that plans are in place for orderly succession for appointments to the board and to senior management, so as to maintain an appropriate balance of skills and experience within the company and on the board and to ensure progressive refreshing of the board.

---

[5] A smaller company is one that is below the FTSE 350 throughout the year immediately prior to the reporting year.

Code Provisions

B.2.1. There should be a nomination committee which should lead the process for board appointments and make recommendations to the board. A majority of members of the nomination committee should be independent non-executive directors. The chairman or an independent non-executive director should chair the committee, but the chairman should not chair the nomination committee when it is dealing with the appointment of a successor to the chairmanship. The nomination committee should make available its terms of reference, explaining its role and the authority delegated to it by the board.[6]

B.2.2. The nomination committee should evaluate the balance of skills, experience, independence and knowledge on the board and, in the light of this evaluation, prepare a description of the role and capabilities required for a particular appointment.

B.2.3. Non-executive directors should be appointed for specified terms subject to re-election and to statutory provisions relating to the removal of a director. Any term beyond six years for a nonexecutive director should be subject to particularly rigorous review, and should take into account the need for progressive refreshing of the board.

B.2.4. A separate section of the annual report should describe the work of the nomination committee,[7] including the process it has used in relation to board appointments. This section should include a description of the board's policy on diversity, including gender, any measurable objectives that it has set for implementing the policy, and progress on achieving the objectives. An explanation should be given if neither an external search consultancy nor open advertising has been used in the appointment of a chairman or a non-executive director. Where an external search consultancy has been used, it should be identified in the annual report and a statement made as to whether it has any other connection with the company.

B.3: Commitment

Main Principle

All directors should be able to allocate sufficient time to the company to discharge their responsibilities effectively.

Code Provisions

B.3.1. For the appointment of a chairman, the nomination committee should prepare a job specification, including an assessment of the time commitment

---

[6] The requirement to make the information available would be met by including the information on a website that is maintained by or on behalf of the company.
[7] This provision overlaps with FSA Rule DTR 7.2.7 R (see Schedule B).

expected, recognising the need for availability in the event of crises. A chairman's other significant commitments should be disclosed to the board before appointment and included in the annual report. Changes to such commitments should be reported to the board as they arise, and their impact explained in the next annual report.

B.3.2. The terms and conditions of appointment of non-executive directors should be made available for inspection.[8] The letter of appointment should set out the expected time commitment. Non-executive directors should undertake that they will have sufficient time to meet what is expected of them. Their other significant commitments should be disclosed to the board before appointment, with a broad indication of the time involved and the board should be informed of subsequent changes.

B.3.3. The board should not agree to a full time executive director taking on more than one non-executive directorship in a FTSE 100 company nor the chairmanship of such a company.

B.4: Development

Main Principle

All directors should receive induction on joining the board and should regularly update and refresh their skills and knowledge.

Supporting Principles

The chairman should ensure that the directors continually update their skills and the knowledge and familiarity with the company required to fulfil their role both on the board and on board committees. The company should provide the necessary resources for developing and updating its directors' knowledge and capabilities.

To function effectively all directors need appropriate knowledge of the company and access to its operations and staff.

Code Provisions

B.4.1. The chairman should ensure that new directors receive a full, formal and tailored induction on joining the board. As part of this, directors should avail themselves of opportunities to meet major shareholders.

B.4.2. The chairman should regularly review and agree with each director their training and development needs.

---

[8] The terms and conditions of appointment of non-executive directors should be made available for inspection by any person at the company's registered office during normal business hours and at the AGM (for 15 minutes prior to the meeting and during the meeting).

B.5: Information and Support

Main Principle

The board should be supplied in a timely manner with information in a form and of a quality appropriate to enable it to discharge its duties.

Supporting Principles

The chairman is responsible for ensuring that the directors receive accurate, timely and clear information. Management has an obligation to provide such information but directors should seek clarification or amplification where necessary.

Under the direction of the chairman, the company secretary's responsibilities include ensuring good information flows within the board and its committees and between senior management and non executive directors, as well as facilitating induction and assisting with professional development as required.

The company secretary should be responsible for advising the board through the chairman on all governance matters.

Code Provisions

B.5.1. The board should ensure that directors, especially non-executive directors, have access to independent professional advice at the company's expense where they judge it necessary to discharge their responsibilities as directors. Committees should be provided with sufficient resources to undertake their duties.

B.5.2. All directors should have access to the advice and services of the company secretary, who is responsible to the board for ensuring that board procedures are complied with. Both the appointment and removal of the company secretary should be a matter for the board as a whole.

B.6: Evaluation

Main Principle

The board should undertake a formal and rigorous annual evaluation of its own performance and that of its committees and individual directors.

Supporting Principles

Evaluation of the board should consider the balance of skills, experience, independence and knowledge of the company on the board, its diversity, including gender, how the board works together as a unit, and other factors relevant to its effectiveness.

The chairman should act on the results of the performance evaluation by recognising the strengths and addressing the weaknesses of the board and, where appropriate, proposing new members be appointed to the board or seeking the resignation of directors.

Individual evaluation should aim to show whether each director continues to contribute effectively and to demonstrate commitment to the role (including commitment of time for board and committee meetings and any other duties).

Code Provisions

B.6.1. The board should state in the annual report how performance evaluation of the board, its committees and its individual directors has been conducted.

B.6.2. Evaluation of the board of FTSE 350 companies should be externally facilitated at least every three years. The external facilitator should be identified in the annual report and a statement made as to whether they have any other connection with the company.

B.6.3. The non-executive directors, led by the senior independent director, should be responsible for performance evaluation of the chairman, taking into account the views of executive directors.

B.7: Re-election

Main Principle

All directors should be submitted for re-election at regular intervals, subject to continued satisfactory performance.

Code Provisions

B.7.1. All directors of FTSE 350 companies should be subject to annual election by shareholders. All other directors should be subject to election by shareholders at the first annual general meeting after their appointment, and to re-election thereafter at intervals of no more than three years. Non-executive directors who have served longer than nine years should be subject to annual re-election. The names of directors submitted for election or re-election should be accompanied by sufficient biographical details and any other relevant information to enable shareholders to take an informed decision on their election.

B.7.2. The board should set out to shareholders in the papers accompanying a resolution to elect a nonexecutive director why they believe an individual should be elected. The chairman should confirm to shareholders when proposing re-election that, following formal performance evaluation, the individual's performance continues to be effective and to demonstrate commitment to the role.

Section C: Accountability

C.1: *Financial and Business Reporting*

Main Principle

The board should present a fair, balanced and understandable assessment of the company's position and prospects.

Supporting Principle

The board's responsibility to present a fair, balanced and understandable assessment extends to interim and other price-sensitive public reports and reports to regulators as well as to information required to be presented by statutory requirements.

The board should establish arrangements that will enable it to ensure that the information presented is fair, balanced and understandable.

Code Provisions

C.1.1. The directors should explain in the annual report their responsibility for preparing the annual report and accounts, and state that they consider the annual report and accounts, taken as a whole, is fair, balanced and understandable and provides the information necessary for shareholders to assess the company's performance, business model and strategy. There should be a statement by the auditor about their reporting responsibilities.[9]

C.1.2. The directors should include in the annual report an explanation of the basis on which the company generates or preserves value over the longer term (the business model) and the strategy for delivering the objectives of the company.[10]

C.1.3. The directors should report in annual and half-yearly financial statements that the business is a going concern, with supporting assumptions or qualifications as necessary.[11]

---

[9] This requirement may be met by the disclosures about the audit scope and responsibilities of the auditor included, or referred to, in the auditor's report pursuant to the requirements of ISA (UK and Ireland) 700, "The Auditor's Report on Financial Statements". Copies are available from the FRC website.

[10] It would be desirable if the explanation were located in the same part of the annual report as the Business Review required by Section 417 of the Companies Act 2006. Guidance as to the matters that should be considered in an explanation of a business model is provided in "Reporting Statement: Operating And Financial Review". Copies are available from the FRC website.

[11] "Going Concern and Liquidity Risk: Guidance for Directors of UK Companies 2009" suggests means of applying this part of the Code. Copies are available from the FRC website.

C.2: Risk Management and Internal Control[12]

Main Principle

The board is responsible for determining the nature and extent of the significant risks it is willing to take in achieving its strategic objectives. The board should maintain sound risk management and internal control systems.

Code Provision

C.2.1. The board should, at least annually, conduct a review of the effectiveness of the company's risk management and internal control systems and should report to shareholders that they have done so.[13] The review should cover all material controls, including financial, operational and compliance controls.

C.3: Audit Committee and Auditors[14]

Main Principle

The board should establish formal and transparent arrangements for considering how they should apply the corporate reporting and risk management and internal control principles and for maintaining an appropriate relationship with the company's auditors.

Code Provisions

C.3.1. The board should establish an audit committee of at least three, or in the case of smaller companies[15] two, independent non-executive directors. In smaller companies the company chairman may be a member of, but not chair, the committee in addition to the independent non-executive directors, provided he or she was considered independent on appointment as chairman. The board should satisfy itself that at least one member of the audit committee has recent and relevant financial experience.[16]

C.3.2. The main role and responsibilities of the audit committee should be set out in written terms of reference[17] and should include:

---

[12] "Internal Control: Guidance to Directors" suggests means of applying this part of the Code. Copies are available from the FRC website.
[13] In addition FSA Rule DTR 7.2.5 R requires companies to describe the main features of the internal control and risk management systems in relation to the financial reporting process.
[14] "Guidance on Audit Committees" suggests means of applying this part of the Code. Copies are available from the FRC website.
[15] See footnote 6.
[16] This provision overlaps with FSA Rule DTR 7.1.1 R (see Schedule B).
[17] This provision overlaps with FSA Rules DTR 7.1.3 R (see Schedule B).

- to monitor the integrity of the financial statements of the company and any formal announcements relating to the company's financial performance, reviewing significant financial reporting judgements contained in them;

- to review the company's internal financial controls and, unless expressly addressed by a separate board risk committee composed of independent directors, or by the board itself, to review the company's internal control and risk management systems;

- to monitor and review the effectiveness of the company's internal audit function;

- to make recommendations to the board, for it to put to the shareholders for their approval in general meeting, in relation to the appointment, re-appointment and removal of the external auditor and to approve the remuneration and terms of engagement of the external auditor;

- to review and monitor the external auditor's independence and objectivity and the effectiveness of the audit process, taking into consideration relevant UK professional and regulatory requirements;

- to develop and implement policy on the engagement of the external auditor to supply non-audit services, taking into account relevant ethical guidance regarding the provision of non-audit services by the external audit firm; and to report to the board, identifying any matters in respect of which it considers that action or improvement is needed and making recommendations as to the steps to be taken; and

- to report to the board on how it has discharged its responsibilities.

C.3.3. The terms of reference of the audit committee, including its role and the authority delegated to it by the board, should be made available.[18]

C.3.4. Where requested by the board, the audit committee should provide advice on whether the annual report and accounts, taken as a whole, is fair, balanced and understandable and provides the information necessary for shareholders to assess the company's performance, business model and strategy.

C.3.5. The audit committee should review arrangements by which staff of the company may, in confidence, raise concerns about possible improprieties in matters of financial reporting or other matters. The audit committee's objective should be to ensure that arrangements are in place for the proportionate and independent investigation of such matters and for appropriate follow-up action.

---

[18] See footnote 7.

C.3.6. The audit committee should monitor and review the effectiveness of the internal audit activities. Where there is no internal audit function, the audit committee should consider annually whether there is a need for an internal audit function and make a recommendation to the board, and the reasons for the absence of such a function should be explained in the relevant section of the annual report.

C.3.7. The audit committee should have primary responsibility for making a recommendation on the appointment, reappointment and removal of the external auditors. FTSE 350 companies should put the external audit contract out to tender at least every ten years. If the board does not accept the audit committee's recommendation, it should include in the annual report, and in any papers recommending appointment or re-appointment, a statement from the audit committee explaining the recommendation and should set out reasons why the board has taken a different position.

C.3.8. A separate section of the annual report should describe the work of the committee in discharging its responsibilities.[19] The report should include:

- the significant issues that the committee considered in relation to the financial statements, and how these issues were addressed;

- an explanation of how it has assessed the effectiveness of the external audit process and the approach taken to the appointment or reappointment of the external auditor, and information on the length of tenure of the current audit firm and when a tender was last conducted; and

- if the external auditor provides non-audit services, an explanation of how auditor objectivity and independence is safeguarded.

Section D: Remuneration

D.1: *The Level and Components of Remuneration*

Main Principle

Levels of remuneration should be sufficient to attract, retain and motivate directors of the quality required to run the company successfully, but a company should avoid paying more than is necessary for this purpose. A significant proportion of executive directors' remuneration should be structured so as to link rewards to corporate and individual performance.

---

[19] This provision overlaps with FSA Rules DTR 7.1.5 R and 7.2.7 R (see Schedule B).

Supporting Principle

The performance-related elements of executive directors' remuneration should be stretching and designed to promote the long-term success of the company.

The remuneration committee should judge where to position their company relative to other companies. But they should use such comparisons with caution, in view of the risk of an upward ratchet of remuneration levels with no corresponding improvement in performance.

They should also be sensitive to pay and employment conditions elsewhere in the group, especially when determining annual salary increases.

Code Provisions

D.1.1. In designing schemes of performance-related remuneration for executive directors, the remuneration committee should follow the provisions in Schedule A to this Code.

D.1.2. Where a company releases an executive director to serve as a non-executive director elsewhere, the remuneration report[20] should include a statement as to whether or not the director will retain such earnings and, if so, what the remuneration is.

D.1.3. Levels of remuneration for non-executive directors should reflect the time commitment and responsibilities of the role. Remuneration for non-executive directors should not include share options or other performance-related elements. If, exceptionally, options are granted, shareholder approval should be sought in advance and any shares acquired by exercise of the options should be held until at least one year after the non-executive director leaves the board. Holding of share options could be relevant to the determination of a non-executive director's independence (as set out in provision B.1.1).

D.1.4. The remuneration committee should carefully consider what compensation commitments (including pension contributions and all other elements) their directors' terms of appointment would entail in the event of early termination. The aim should be to avoid rewarding poor performance. They should take a robust line on reducing compensation to reflect departing directors' obligations to mitigate loss.

D.1.5. Notice or contract periods should be set at one year or less. If it is necessary to offer longer notice or contract periods to new directors recruited from outside, such periods should reduce to one year or less after the initial period.

---

[20] As required for UK incorporated companies under the Large and Medium-Sized Companies and Groups (Accounts and Reports) Regulations 2008.

D.2: Procedure

Main Principle

There should be a formal and transparent procedure for developing policy on executive remuneration and for fixing the remuneration packages of individual directors. No director should be involved in deciding his or her own remuneration.

Supporting Principles

The remuneration committee should consult the chairman and/or chief executive about their proposals relating to the remuneration of other executive directors. The remuneration committee should also be responsible for appointing any consultants in respect of executive director remuneration. Where executive directors or senior management are involved in advising or supporting the remuneration committee, care should be taken to recognise and avoid conflicts of interest.

The chairman of the board should ensure that the company maintains contact as required with its principal shareholders about remuneration.

Code Provisions

D.2.1. The board should establish a remuneration committee of at least three, or in the case of smaller companies[21] two, independent non-executive directors. In addition the company chairman may also be a member of, but not chair, the committee if he or she was considered independent on appointment as chairman. The remuneration committee should make available its terms of reference, explaining its role and the authority delegated to it by the board.[22] Where remuneration consultants are appointed, they should be identified in the annual report and a statement made as to whether they have any other connection with the company.

D.2.2. The remuneration committee should have delegated responsibility for setting remuneration for all executive directors and the chairman, including pension rights and any compensation payments. The committee should also recommend and monitor the level and structure of remuneration for senior management. The definition of 'senior management' for this purpose should be determined by the board but should normally include the first layer of management below board level.

D.2.3. The board itself or, where required by the Articles of Association, the shareholders should determine the remuneration of the non-executive directors within the limits set in the Articles of Association. Where permitted by the Articles, the board may however delegate this responsibility to a committee, which might include the chief executive.

---

[21] See footnote 6.
[22] This provision overlaps with FSA Rule DTR 7.2.7 R (see Schedule B).

D.2.4. Shareholders should be invited specifically to approve all new long-term incentive schemes (as defined in the Listing Rules[23]) and significant changes to existing schemes, save in the circumstances permitted by the Listing Rules.

Section E: Relations with shareholders

E.1: Dialogue with Shareholders

Main Principle

There should be a dialogue with shareholders based on the mutual understanding of objectives. The board as a whole has responsibility for ensuring that a satisfactory dialogue with shareholders takes place.[24]

Supporting Principles

Whilst recognising that most shareholder contact is with the chief executive and finance director, the chairman should ensure that all directors are made aware of their major shareholders' issues and concerns.

The board should keep in touch with shareholder opinion in whatever ways are most practical and efficient.

Code Provisions

E.1.1. The chairman should ensure that the views of shareholders are communicated to the board as a whole. The chairman should discuss governance and strategy with major shareholders. Nonexecutive directors should be offered the opportunity to attend scheduled meetings with major shareholders and should expect to attend meetings if requested by major shareholders. The senior independent director should attend sufficient meetings with a range of major shareholders to listen to their views in order to help develop a balanced understanding of the issues and concerns of major shareholders.

E.1.2. The board should state in the annual report the steps they have taken to ensure that the members of the board, and in particular the non-executive directors, develop an understanding of the views of major shareholders about the company, for example through direct face-to-face contact, analysts' or brokers' briefings and surveys of shareholder opinion.

---

[23] Listing Rules LR 9.4. Copies are available from the FSA website.
[24] Nothing in these principles or provisions should be taken to override the general requirements of law to treat shareholders equally in access to information.

E.2: Constructive Use of the AGM

Main Principle

The board should use the AGM to communicate with investors and to encourage their participation.

Code Provisions

E.2.1. At any general meeting, the company should propose a separate resolution on each substantially separate issue, and should in particular propose a resolution at the AGM relating to the report and accounts. For each resolution, proxy appointment forms should provide shareholders with the option to direct their proxy to vote either for or against the resolution or to withhold their vote. The proxy form and any announcement of the results of a vote should make it clear that a 'vote withheld' is not a vote in law and will not be counted in the calculation of the proportion of the votes for and against the resolution.

E.2.2. The company should ensure that all valid proxy appointments received for general meetings are properly recorded and counted. For each resolution, where a vote has been taken on a show of hands, the company should ensure that the following information is given at the meeting and made available as soon as reasonably practicable on a website which is maintained by or on behalf of the company:

- the number of shares in respect of which proxy appointments have been validly made;
- the number of votes for the resolution;
- the number of votes against the resolution; and
- the number of shares in respect of which the vote was directed to be withheld.

E.2.3. The chairman should arrange for the chairmen of the audit, remuneration and nomination committees to be available to answer questions at the AGM and for all directors to attend.

E.2.4. The company should arrange for the Notice of the AGM and related papers to be sent to shareholders at least 20 working days before the meeting.

Schedule A: The design of performance-related remuneration for executive directors

The remuneration committee should consider whether the directors should be eligible for annual bonuses. If so, performance conditions should be relevant, stretching and designed to promote the long-term success of the company. Upper limits should be set and disclosed. There may be a case for part payment in shares to be held for a significant period.

The remuneration committee should consider whether the directors should be eligible for benefits under long-term incentive schemes. Traditional share option schemes should be weighed against other kinds of long-term incentive scheme. Executive share options should not be offered at a discount save as permitted by the relevant provisions of the Listing Rules.

In normal circumstances, shares granted or other forms of deferred remuneration should not vest, and options should not be exercisable, in less than three years. Directors should be encouraged to hold their shares for a further period after vesting or exercise, subject to the need to finance any costs of acquisition and associated tax liabilities.

Any new long-term incentive schemes which are proposed should be approved by shareholders and should preferably replace any existing schemes or, at least, form part of a well considered overall plan incorporating existing schemes. The total rewards potentially available should not be excessive.

Payouts or grants under all incentive schemes, including new grants under existing share option schemes, should be subject to challenging performance criteria reflecting the company's objectives, including nonfinancial performance metrics where appropriate. Remuneration incentives should be compatible with risk policies and systems.

Grants under executive share option and other long-term incentive schemes should normally be phased rather than awarded in one large block.

Consideration should be given to the use of provisions that permit the company to reclaim variable components in exceptional circumstances of misstatement or misconduct.

In general, only basic salary should be pensionable. The remuneration committee should consider the pension consequences and associated costs to the company of basic salary increases and any other changes in pensionable remuneration, especially for directors close to retirement.

Schedule B: Disclosure of corporate governance arrangements

Corporate governance disclosure requirements are set out in three places:

- FSA Disclosure and Transparency Rules sub-chapters 7.1 and 7.2 (which set out certain mandatory disclosures);

- FSA Listing Rules 9.8.6 R, 9.8.7 R, and 9.8.7A R (which includes the 'comply or explain' requirement); and

- The UK Corporate Governance Code (in addition to providing an explanation where they choose not to comply with a provision, companies must disclose specified information in order to comply with certain provisions).

These requirements are summarised below. The full text of Disclosure and Transparency Rules 7.1 and 7.2 and Listing Rules 9.8.6 R, 9.8.7 R, 9.8.7A R are contained in the relevant chapters of the FSA Handbook.

The Disclosure and Transparency Rules sub-chapters 7.1 and 7.2 apply to issuers whose securities are admitted to trading on a regulated market (this includes all issuers with a Premium or Standard listing). The Listing Rules 9.8.6 R, 9.8.7 R and 9.8.7A R and UK Corporate Governance Code apply to issuers of Premium listed equity shares only.

There is some overlap between the mandatory disclosures required under the Disclosure and Transparency Rules and those expected under the UK Corporate Governance Code. Areas of overlap are summarised in the Appendix to this Schedule. In respect of disclosures relating to the audit committee and the composition and operation of the board and its committees, compliance with the relevant provisions of the Code will result in compliance with the relevant Rules.

Disclosure and Transparency Rules

Sub-chapter 7.1 of the Disclosure and Transparency Rules concerns audit committees or bodies carrying out equivalent functions.

DTR 7.1.1 R and 7.1.3 R set out requirements relating to the composition and functions of the committee or equivalent body:

- DTR 7.1.1 R states than an issuer must have a body which is responsible for performing the functions set out in DTR 7.1.3 R, and that at least one member of that body must be independent and at least one member must have competence in accounting and/or auditing.

- DTR 7.1.2 G states that the requirements for independence and competence in accounting and/or auditing may be satisfied by the same member or by different members of the relevant body.

- DTR 7.1.3 R states that an issuer must ensure that, as a minimum, the relevant body must:

    1. monitor the financial reporting process;
    2. monitor the effectiveness of the issuer's internal control, internal audit where applicable, and risk management systems;
    3. monitor the statutory audit of the annual and consolidated accounts;

4. review and monitor the independence of the statutory auditor, and in particular the provision of additional services to the issuer.

DTR 7.1.5 R sets out what disclosure is required. Specifically:

- DTR 7.1.5 R states that the issuer must make a statement available to the public disclosing which body carries out the functions required by DTR 7.1.3 R and how it is composed.

- DTR 7.1.6 G states that this can be included in the corporate governance statement required under sub-chapter DTR 7.2 (see below).

- DTR 7.1.7 G states that compliance with the relevant provisions of the UK Corporate Governance Code (as set out in the Appendix to this Schedule) will result in compliance with DTR 7.1.1 R to 7.1.5 R.

Sub-chapter 7.2 concerns corporate governance statements. Issuers are required to produce a corporate governance statement that must be either included in the directors' report (DTR 7.2.1 R); or in a separate report published together with the annual report; or on the issuer's website, in which case there must be a cross-reference in the directors' report (DTR 7.2.9 R).

DTR 7.2.2 R requires that the corporate governance statements must contain a reference to the corporate governance code to which the company is subject (for companies with a Premium listing this is the UK Corporate Governance Code). DTR 7.2.3 R requires that, to the extent that it departs from that code, the company must explain which parts of the code it departs from and the reasons for doing so. DTR 7.2.4 G states that compliance with LR 9.8.6 R (6) (the "comply or explain" rule in relation to the UK Corporate Governance Code) will also satisfy these requirements.

DTR 7.2.5 R, DTR 7.2.7 R and DTR 7.2.10 R set out certain information that must be disclosed in the corporate governance statement:

- DTR 7.2.5 R states that the corporate governance statement must contain a description of the main features of the company's internal control and risk management systems in relation to the financial reporting process. DTR 7.2.10 R states that an issuer which is required to prepare a group directors' report within the meaning of Section 415(2) of the Companies Act 2006 must include in that report a description of the main features of the group's internal control and risk management systems in relation to the process for preparing consolidated accounts.

- DTR 7.2.6 R states that the corporate governance statement must contain the information required by paragraph 13(2)(c), (d), (f), (h) and (i) of Schedule 7 to the Large and Medium-sized Companies and Groups (Accounts and Reports) Regulations 2008 (SI 2008/410) where the issuer is subject to the requirements of that paragraph.

- DTR 7.2.7 R states that the corporate governance statement must contain a description of the composition and operation of the issuer's administrative, management and supervisory bodies and their committees. DTR 7.2.8 G states that compliance with the relevant provisions of the UK Corporate Governance Code (as set out in the Appendix to this Schedule) will satisfy these requirements.

Listing Rules

Listing Rules 9.8.6 R (for UK incorporated companies) and 9.8.7 R (for overseas incorporated companies) state that in the case of a company that has a Premium listing of equity shares, the following items must be included in its annual report and accounts:

- a statement of how the listed company has applied the Main Principles set out in the UK Corporate Governance Code, in a manner that would enable shareholders to evaluate how the principles have been applied;
- a statement as to whether the listed company has:
    - complied throughout the accounting period with all relevant provisions set out in the UK Corporate Governance Code; or
    - not complied throughout the accounting period with all relevant provisions set out in the UK Corporate Governance Code, and if so, setting out:
        i. those provisions, if any, it has not complied with;
        ii. in the case of provisions whose requirements are of a continuing nature, the period within which, if any, it did not comply with some or all of those provisions; and
        iii. the company's reasons for non-compliance.

The UK Corporate Governance Code

In addition to the "comply or explain" requirement in the Listing Rules, the Code includes specific requirements for disclosure which must be provided in order to comply. These are summarised below.

The annual report should include:

- a statement of how the board operates, including a high level statement of which types of decisions are to be taken by the board and which are to be delegated to management (A.1.1);
- the names of the chairman, the deputy chairman (where there is one), the chief executive, the senior independent director and the chairmen and members of the board committees (A.1.2);

- the number of meetings of the board and those committees and individual attendance by directors (A.1.2);

- where a chief executive is appointed chairman, the reasons for their appointment (this only needs to be done in the annual report following the appointment) (A.3.1);

- the names of the non-executive directors whom the board determines to be independent, with reasons where necessary (B.1.1);

- a separate section describing the work of the nomination committee, including the process it has used in relation to board appointments; a description of the board's policy on diversity, including gender; any measurable objectives that it has set for implementing the policy, and progress on achieving the objectives. An explanation should be given if neither external search consultancy nor open advertising has been used in the appointment of a chairman or a non-executive director. Where an external search consultancy has been used it should be identified and a statement made as to whether it has any other connection with the company (B.2.4);

- any changes to the other significant commitments of the chairman during the year (B.3.1);

- a statement of how performance evaluation of the board, its committees and its directors has been conducted (B.6.1). Where an external facilitator has been used, they should be identified and a statement made as to whether they have any other connection to the company (B.6.2);

- an explanation from the directors of their responsibility for preparing the accounts and a statement that they consider that the annual report and accounts, taken as a whole, is fair, balanced and understandable and provides the information necessary for shareholders to assess and provide the company's performance, business model and strategy. There should also be a statement by the auditor about their reporting responsibilities (C.1.1);

- an explanation from the directors of the basis on which the company generates or preserves value over the longer term (the business model) and the strategy for delivering the objectives of the company (C.1.2);

- a statement from the directors that the business is a going concern, with supporting assumptions or qualifications as necessary (C.1.3);

- a report that the board has conducted a review of the effectiveness of the company's risk management and internal controls systems (C.2.1);

- where there is no internal audit function, the reasons for the absence of such a function (C.3.6);

- where the board does not accept the audit committee's recommendation on the appointment, reappointment or removal of an external auditor, a statement from the audit committee explaining the recommendation and the reasons why the board has taken a different position (C.3.7);

- a separate section describing the work of the audit committee in discharging its responsibilities, including: the significant issues that it considered in relation to the financial statements, and how these issues were addressed; an explanation of how it has assessed the effectiveness of the external audit process and the approach taken to the appointment or reappointment of the external auditor, including the length of tenure of the current audit firm and when a tender was last conducted; and, if the external auditor provides non-audit services, an explanation of how auditor objectivity and independence is safeguarded (C.3.8);

- a description of the work of the remuneration committee as required under the Large and Medium-Sized Companies and Groups (Accounts and Reports) Regulations 2008, including, where an executive director serves as a non-executive director elsewhere, whether or not the director will retain such earnings and, if so, what the remuneration is (D.1.2);

- where remuneration consultants are appointed they should be identified and a statement made as to whether they have any other connection with the company (D.2.1); and

- the steps the board has taken to ensure that members of the board, and in particular the non-executive directors, develop an understanding of the views of major shareholders about their company (E.1.2).

The following information should be made available (which may be met by placing the information on a website that is maintained by or on behalf of the company):

- the terms of reference of the nomination, audit and remuneration committees, explaining their role and the authority delegated to them by the board (B.2.1, C.3.3 and D.2.1); and

- the terms and conditions of appointment of non-executive directors (B.3.2) (see footnote 9 on page 13).

The board should set out to shareholders in the papers accompanying a resolution to elect or re-elect directors:

- sufficient biographical details to enable shareholders to take an informed decision on their election or re-election (B.7.1);

- why they believe an individual should be elected to a non-executive role (B.7.2); and

- on re-election of a non-executive director, confirmation from the chairman that, following formal performance evaluation, the individual's performance continues to be effective and to demonstrate commitment to the role (B.7.2).

The board should set out to shareholders in the papers recommending appointment or reappointment of an external auditor:

- if the board does not accept the audit committee's recommendation, a statement from the audit committee explaining the recommendation and from the board setting out reasons why they have taken a different position (C.3.6).

Additional guidance

The FRC publishes guidance on going concern, risk management and internal control and audit committees, which contain further suggestions as to information that might usefully be disclosed in the statement that the business is a going concern (C.1.3), the statement on the board's review of the company's risk management and internal control systems (C.2.1) and the report of the audit committee (C.3.8) respectively. This guidance is available on the FRC website.

Appendix

Overlap between the Disclosure and Transparency Rules and the UK Corporate Governance Code

Disclosure and transparency rules	UK Corporate Governance Code
D.T.R 7.1.1 R Sets out minimum requirements on composition of the audit committee or equivalent body.	**Provision C.3.1** Sets out recommended composition of the audit committee.
D.T.R 7.1.3 R Sets out minimum functions of the audit committee or equivalent body.	**Provision C.3.2** Sets out the recommended minimum terms of reference for the audit committee.
D.T.R 7.1.5 R	**Provision A.1.2**

The composition and function of the audit committee or equivalent body must be disclosed in the annual report *DTR 7.1.7 R states that compliance with Code provisions A.1.2, C.3.1, C.3.2 and C.3.3 will result in compliance with DTR 7.1.1 R to DTR 7.1.5 R.*	The annual report should identify members of the board committees. **Provision C.3.8** The annual report should describe the work of the audit committee.
D.T.R 7.2.5 R The corporate governance statement must include a description of the main features of the company's internal control and risk management systems in relation to the financial reporting process. *While this requirement differs from the requirement in the UK Corporate Governance Code, it is envisaged that both could be met by a single internal control statement.*	**Provision C.2.1** The Board must report that a review of the effectiveness of the risk management and internal control systems has been carried out.
DTR 7.2.7 R The corporate governance statement must include a description of the composition and operation of the administrative, management and supervisory bodies and their committees. *DTR 7.2.8 R states that compliance with Code provisions A.1.1, A.1.2, A.4.6, B.2.1 and C.3.3 will result in compliance with DTR 7.2.7 R.*	This requirement overlaps with a number of different provisions of the Code: **A.1.1:** the annual report should include a statement of how the board operates. **A.1.2:** the annual report should identify members of the board and board committees. **B.2.4:** the annual report should describe the work of the nomination committee.

	C.3.8: the annual report should describe the work of the audit committee. **D.2.1:** a description of the work of the remuneration committee should be made available. *[Note: in order to comply with DTR 7.2.7 R this information will need to be included in the corporate governance statement].*

INDEX

References are to paragraph numbers.

Accounts
  annual general meeting, and   5.21–5.31
Adjournment of members' meetings   9.1
  articles, and   9.2, 9.3
  business at adjourned meetings   9.24–9.27
  chairman's power, exercise of   9.1
  continuation on later date   9.23
  court, powers of   9.12
  directors, and   9.21, 9.22
  fiduciary power   9.4, 9.5
  fresh notice   9.14–9.19
  meeting in total disorder   9.6–9.10
  procedure on   9.13
  proxy holders, and   9.20
  relevant matters   9.11
Administrative receivership   19.1
  creditors' committee   19.15
  creditors' meeting   19.3
    adjournment   19.13
    chairman   19.11, 19.12
    notice   19.7, 19.8
    report   19.5, 19.6
    right to participate in voting   19.9, 19.10
    substantive requirements   19.4
    voting   19.14
Annual general meetings   4.3–4.8
  accounts   5.21–5.31
  application for investigation   5.35–5.37
  appointing auditors   5.38–5.40
  auditors' reports   5.21–5.31
  authority to make market purchase of own shares   5.92
  balance sheets   5.21–5.31
  business of   5.10, 5.11
  circulation of members' resolutions   5.106
  circulation of members' statements   5.112
  committee of inspection   5.34
  CREST   5.136
  directors' authority to allot shares   5.56–5.72
  dividends   5.18–5.20
  election of directors in place of retiring   5.41–5.54
  explanatory circulars   5.137, 5.138
  fixing remuneration of auditors   5.38–5.40
  items that usually may be dealt with   5.18
  notice of   5.1, 5.2
    form   5.1, 5.2

Annual general meetings—*continued*
  notices   5.5–5.9
  ordinary business   5.12–5.17
  other business   5.55
  political contributions   5.102
  procedure at   5.32, 5.33
  special business   5.12–5.17
  statutory pre-emption rights, disapplying   5.73–5.86
  when held   5.3, 5.4
Articles of association   2.14
  Companies Act 2006   2.15–2.18
  differences in   2.35–2.37
  written resolutions, provision for   3.99
Auditors
  appointing   10.2
    annual general meeting, at   5.38–5.40
    private companies   10.3–10.11
    public companies   10.12–10.17
  audit concerns, rights to raise
    accounts meetings, at   10.47–10.52
  cessation of office
    requirements   10.37–10.44
  changing   10.20–10.22
    ordinary resolution   3.28–3.42
  meetings, rights in relation to   10.45, 10.46
  notice of general meeting to   6.64
  reappointing   10.2
  removal   10.19
    special notice   10.23–10.29
  remuneration   10.18
    annual general meeting, at   5.38–5.40
  resigning   10.30–10.36
    rights to require meeting   4.34
  resolutions, and   10.45, 10.46
  special written resolutions, and   3.91–3.95
Auditors' reports
  annual general meeting, and   5.21–5.31

Balance sheets
  annual general meeting, and   5.21–5.31
Bankruptcy
  administrative records   24.61–24.64
  admission of proofs for voting purposes   24.26–24.30
  chairman and proxies   24.41, 24.42
  chairman of meeting   24.38–24.40
  creditors' committee   24.57, 24.58

Bankruptcy—continued
creditors' requisition of meeting   24.13, 24.14
first creditors' meeting, whether to hold   24.2–24.4
further (general) meetings   24.59
nature of process   24.1
no resolution for appointment of trustee   24.53–24.56
notice of first meeting of creditors   24.5–24.12
opening meeting   24.45–24.52
proxies   24.15–24.25
quorum   24.43, 24.44
rejection of proofs for voting purposes   24.26–24.30
release   24.60
voting   24.31–24.37

Board meetings *see* Directors' meetings

Chairman
appointment   7.23–7.27

Chairman of general meeting   7.23
adjournment of meeting   7.51
appointment   7.23
authority   7.28–7.38
casting vote, exercising   7.53, 7.54
closing meeting with consent   7.50
disputing conduct   7.58
duties   7.28–7.38
poll, arrangements for taking   7.52
powers   7.28–7.38
proxies, receiving or rejecting   7.52
regulating course of proceedings   7.39, 7.40
     amendments to resolutions proposed   7.45, 7.46
     debate, relevance of   7.42
     keeping order   7.47
     order of speaking   7.43, 7.44
     points of order   7.48
     right to speak   7.39–7.41
     separate resolutions   7.49
result of voting, declaring   7.55–7.57

Class meetings   4.38–4.48, 4.50–4.52
company limited by guarantee   4.49
compensation to directors for loss of office   4.62
directions of court pursuant to s425   4.53–4.57
compromise or arrangement   4.53–4.57
separate class, and   4.58–4.61

Class shares
voting rights, and   8.5–8.13

Clinical Commissioning Groups   26.240–26.243

Commencement of litigation
company meetings, and   2.52

Committee of inspection   5.34

Company administrations   18.1
adjournment   18.36

Company administrations—continued
administrator's report   18.45
chairman   18.33–18.35
creditors' committee   18.47
creditors' meetings   18.7
     types   18.8, 18.9
Crown's preferential status   18.6
notice of meetings   18.26–18.32
origins   18.1
pre-administration costs   18.19, 18.20
proposals   18.18
     approval by correspondence   18.23
     dispensing with initial meeting   18.21, 18.22
     initial meeting   18.24
         delay   18.25
     post-meeting revision   18.46
purposes   18.2, 18.3
relationship between creditors' voting rights and administrator's duties   18.10, 18.15, 18.16
     Enterprise Act 2002   18.11
     goodwill, and   18.10
     SIP 16   18.13, 18.14
     'unfair harm'   18.12
rescue of debtor company   18.5
streamlined   18.4
voting   18.37, 18.38, 18.40–18.44

Company meetings   1.1
acts beyond directors' powers   2.47–2.51
commencement of litigation   2.52
Companies Act 2006   2.1–2.13
custom   2.39
debenture stockholders   4.63–4.67
decisions made without   3.62–3.64
directors, position of   2.44
elective resolutions *see* Elective resolutions
extraordinary resolutions *see* Extraordinary resolutions
general principles   2.40
how members make decisions   2.42
illegal act, agreement to   2.43
informal rules   2.38
limited companies   1.6
ordinary resolutions *see* Ordinary resolutions
rules or hierarchy   2.41
short notice   3.60, 3.61
special resolutions *see* Special resolutions
ultra vires acts   2.47–2.51

Company voluntary arrangements
calculation of creditor's voting rights   17.49–17.54
challenging decisions   17.64–17.69
Cork Committee, and   17.4–17.6
court-approved schemes   17.2, 17.3
creditors' meeting   17.8–17.10
meaning   17.1
meetings
     adjournments   17.39

Index

Company voluntary arrangements—*continued*
meetings—*continued*
  chairman 17.28–17.34
  meetings to be held prior to 17.7
  members' meetings 17.59–17.61, 17.63
    approval of arrangement 17.55
    outcome of 17.56–17.58
  moratorium procedure 17.8–17.10
  notice of meetings 17.13
  nominee administrator or
    liquidator, where 17.26, 17.27
  nominee not administrator or
    liquidator, where 17.13, 17.14, 17.16–17.25
  proxies 17.35–17.38
  purpose of meeting 17.15
  report to court 17.11
  voting at creditors' meeting 17.44, 17.48
  calculation of creditor's voting
    rights 17.43
    cause of action 17.47
    contingent creditor 17.45
    creditor 17.46
    creditor, meaning 17.40–17.42

Compromise or arrangement
  class meetings, and 4.53–4.57

Corporate representatives
  voting by 8.39–8.42

Creditors' schemes under Part 26 Companies Act 2006
  CVAs, and 23.32, 23.33
  flexible tool, as 23.7
  human rights 23.29, 23.31
  identification of creditor
    issues 23.22–23.24
  information for meeting 23.13–23.17
  proposed compromise or
    arrangement 23.1–23.6
  proxies 23.25
  resolution of creditor issues 23.22–23.24
  separate class meetings 23.18–23.21
  single meeting 23.18–23.21
  summoning of meetings 23.11, 23.12
  three stages 23.8–23.10

Creditors' voluntary winding up 20.1–20.3
  creditors' meeting
    adjournment 20.15, 20.16
    chairman 20.9–20.13
    nominations for liquidator 20.14
    suspension 20.15, 20.16
    voting 20.17–20.19
  final meeting 20.27–20.31
  meetings to be held 20.1–20.3
  resolutions by
    correspondence 20.20–20.25
  return to Registrar on final
    meetings prior to
    dissolution 20.32
  section 98 meeting 20.4–20.6
    directors' sworn statement of
      affairs 20.6
    notice 20.5

Creditors' voluntary winding up—*continued*
  subsequent meetings
    notice 20.7, 20.8

CREST
  annual general meeting, and 5.136

Debenture holders
  notice of general meeting 6.65, 6.66

Debenture stockholders
  meetings 4.63–4.67

Defamation
  local authority meetings 26.172–26.181

Directors
  authority to allot shares
    annual general meetings,
      and 5.56–5.72
  compensation for loss of office
    class meetings, and 4.62
    meetings, convened by 4.9
    notice of general meeting to
      proposal of compensation 6.63
      payments
    notice of 6.79–6.87
  removal of
    ordinary resolution, and 3.7–3.27
  retiring, election in place of
    annual general meeting, at 5.41–5.54

Directors' meetings
  alternate directors 12.111–12.115
  board, function of 12.1
  chairman 12.59
    appointment 12.61
    election 12.62, 12.63
    role 12.60
  UK Corporate Governance
    Code 12.64
  codified duties 12.8, 12.10, 12.11
  Combined Code 12.3–12.5
  committees 12.116–12.120
  conducting board meetings 12.33
  convening board meetings 12.33
  decisions reserved to board 12.12–12.16
  delegation of powers by
    board 12.12–12.16
  exercising power to delegate 12.24–12.28
  GBP Code 12.17–12.23, 12.34–12.36
  invalid appointments, effect 12.142, 12.143
  monitoring exercise of delegated
    powers 12.29–12.32
  nature of business to be
    conducted 12.52–12.58
  notice of 12.43–12.51
  obligation to meet 12.37–12.41
  quorum 12.65–12.77
    abuse of provisions 12.78
    failure to keep 12.79
    general rules 12.65–12.77
    minimum number of directors 12.80
  resolutions in lieu 12.121–12.127
  reviewing exercise of delegated
    powers 12.29–12.32

Directors' meetings—*continued*
  sole director, companies
    with   12.128–12.141
  statutory duties   12.6, 12.7
  UK Corporate Governance Code   12.2
  votes   12.81, 12.82
    personal interest, and   12.83–12.87
    articles, and   12.100–12.110
    declarations   12.88–12.90
    general notice   12.97, 12.98
    material interest   12.91–12.96
  who may summon   12.42
Directors' reports
  annual general meeting, and   5.21–5.31
Disability discrimination
  electronic communications, and   11.212
Dividends
  annual general meeting, and   5.18–5.20
Duomatic principle   3.65, 3.66, 3.100

Elective resolutions   3.55
  notice   3.56
  scope   3.55
  transitional provisions   3.57–3.59
Electronic board meetings   13.19
  authority   13.23, 13.24
  conditions for   13.25–13.27
  desirability   13.39
  key issues   13.20–13.22
  location   13.28–13.30
  participant number   12.34
  'problem' territory   13.31–13.36
  voting procedure   13.37, 13.38
Electronic communications   13.1–13.4
  ability to retain copy   11.21
  articles, and
    new rules, and   11.48–11.50
  authentication   11.188–11.191
  bankruptcy of member   11.69–11.71
  breakdowns in   11.223, 11.224
  'by electronic means'   11.16–11.20
  death of member   11.69–11.71
  deemed delivery   11.27
  deeming provision   11.42–11.44
  delivered, when   11.150–11.155
  documents   11.8–11.13
  general meetings involving   11.192
    entirely virtual general
    meetings   11.193–11.206
  hard copy version, right to
    require   11.163–11.165
  ICSA Guidance   11.40, 11.41, 11.45
  'in electronic form'   11.15, 11.17–11.20
  individual members, from   11.166–11.187
  information   11.8–11.13
  invitation and request, relationship
    between   11.111–11.113
  invitation to members to
    participate   11.72–11.75, 11.88–11.91
    contents   11.76
    finalising   11.86, 11.87
    ICSA Guidance   11.77–11.79

Electronic communications—*continued*
  invitation to members to
    participate—*continued*
    methods of
      communication   11.80–11.83
    size of documents   11.84, 11.85
  joint holders of shares or
    debentures   11.29–11.32
  methods   11.23
  methods of sending or supplying
    documents and information   11.14
  mutual, express agreement
    required   11.51–11.59
  new rules
    articles, and   11.24–11.26, 11.28, 11.33
  nominated persons   11.60–11.64
    indirect investor rights   11.65
    s145 CA 2006   11.66–11.68
  non-delivery   11.156–11.162
  non-statutory documents   11.47
  notices of general meetings   11.22
  practical issues   11.36–11.39
  previous rules   11.34, 11.35
  remote participation in physical
    meetings   11.207
    amendment of articles   11.213
    best interests of
      company   11.208–11.211
    conduct of meeting   11.220, 11.221
    Disability Discrimination Act
      1995   11.212
    entitlement to participate   11.215
    not mandatory   11.225–11.227
    notice of   11.214
    quorum   11.216, 11.217
    record keeping   11.222
    see, be seen, hear and be heard   11.218, 11.219
    voting   11.220, 11.221
    written resolutions in lieu of
      meeting   11.228–11.232
  review of articles   11.46
  sent, when   11.150–11.155
  statutory framework   11.4–11.7
  technological advances   11.1–11.3
  website
    deemed agreement to making
      documents available
      by   11.95–11.98
    ICSA guidance   11.104–11.110
    making documents and
      information
      available   11.92–11.94, 11.131–11.149
    notification that document is
      available on   11.114–11.130
      request   11.99–11.103
  written resolutions in lieu of
    meeting   13.40–13.43
Electronic notice   13.5, 13.6, 13.11
  agreement to   13.9, 13.10
  authorisation   13.8

Index

Electronic notice—*continued*
  e-mail attachment   13.18
  receipt, rules for   13.12–13.16
  Table A   13.7
  unauthorised access   13.17
Explanatory circular
  annual general meeting, and   5.137, 5.138
Expulsion from meetings   15.1, 15.2
  disorderly conduct   15.3–15.6
Extraordinary resolutions   3.48, 3.49
  notice of meeting   3.54
  passing   3.50, 3.51
  poll   3.52, 3.53
  transitional provisions   3.48

Fast-track IVA   25.39
  Official Receiver as nominee   25.39–25.41
  proposal   25.42

General meetings   4.1, 4.2
  chairman   7.1, 7.2, 7.23
  formal procedures   7.3–7.7
  notice of *see* Notice of general meetings
  quorum   7.1, 7.2, 7.8

Health bodies   26.227, 26.228
  bodies subject to 1960 Act   26.229–26.233

Individual voluntary arrangements
  approval, effect of   25.24, 25.25
  contents of notice   25.9
  Cork Committee, and   25.1
  creditor rights in practice   25.35–25.37
  creditors' meeting   25.11–25.13
    adjournment   25.17
    chairman   25.14
    challenging decision   25.26–25.30
    majorities   25.19
    proxies   25.14–25.16
    voting rights   25.18
  fast–track   25.39
  giving notice of meeting   25.7, 25.8
  material irregularity   25.33, 25.34
  minority creditors, and   25.2
  nominee, duty of   25.36, 25.37
  notice of result of meeting   25.23
  proposal   25.3
    common scheme   25.6
    explanation   25.5
    interim order, and   25.4
  Protocol   25.38
  receiving notice of meeting   25.7, 25.8
  report of meeting   25.20–25.22
  similarities with CVAs   25.35
  time and venue of meeting   25.10
  unfair prejudice   25.32
Informal corporate acts   3.65, 3.66, 3.100, 3.116
  absence of special notice, and   3.117, 3.118
  alteration of share capital, and   3.105

Informal corporate acts—*continued*
  consent   3.101–3.104
  declaration of dividends, and   3.114
  insolvent company, and   3.115
  limitation   3.106–3.112
  s143 CA 1985, and   3.113
Insolvency
  meetings in   1.8
Insolvency, meetings in
  chair   16.17
  delegation to creditors' committees   16.11, 16.12
  first meeting of creditors   16.13
  licensed insolvency practitioner   16.2, 16.3
  preferential creditors   16.19, 16.20
  'proof'   16.14, 16.15
  'prove'   16.14, 16.15
  range or procedures   16.1
  regulation of   16.10
  residuary supervisory role of court   16.16
  secured creditors   16.18
  SIPs   16.17
  will of creditor   16.4, 16.5, 16.9

Judicial review
  local authority meetings, and   26.199–26.203, 26.205–26.221

Limited companies   1.6
Listed companies
  notifications by   3.121–3.123
Local authorities
  meetings   1.9
Local authority meetings   26.1–26.5
  access to papers   26.190–26.193
  agenda   26.73–26.80
  appeal, statutory routes   26.198
  chairing   26.82–26.86
  challenging decisions   26.194, 26.195
  conflicts of interest   26.156–26.161
    Wales, position in   26.162
  constitution   26.32–26.40
  convening meetings   26.41
  declarations of interest   26.156–26.161
  defamation   26.172–26.181
  disorder at   26.163–26.170
  impact of Local Government Act 2000   26.22–26.31
  internal rules   26.32–26.40
  issues arising during   26.156–26.161
  judicial review   26.199–26.203, 26.205–26.221
  meetings which must be held   26.42–26.53
  minutes   26.182–26.189
  notice of   26.57–26.66, 26.68–26.72
    copy of agenda and report   26.67
  overview   26.196
  places where held   26.54–26.56
  press rights   26.148–26.155
  public involvement   26.114
  quorum   26.111–26.113
  referral within council   26.197
  review, statutory routes   26.198

Local authority meetings—*continued*	
right to attend	26.115–26.138, 26.140–26.142
disorderly conduct	26.139
right to participate	26.143–26.145, 26.147
running	26.81
scrutiny	26.196
standing orders	26.32–26.40
stereotypical image	26.11–26.15
types	26.16–26.21
voting at	2.110, 26.87–26.109
Local Government Ombudsman	26.222–26.226
Local government structure	26.6–26.10
Meetings	
collective communications	1.2, 1.3
electronic communications, and	1.4
insolvency, in	1.8
local authorities	1.9
origins	1.1
private members' organisations	1.10
regulation	1.5
Members' meetings	4.1, 4.2
adjournment *see* Adjournment of members' meetings	
court, ordered to be held by	4.25
application	4.26
class rights, and	4.28
powers of court	4.29
proxy voting	4.30–4.33
reasons for	4.27
directors, convened by	4.9
notice	4.10
Table A Reg 92	4.11
members, convened by	4.12
members, requested by	4.13
contents of request	4.16, 4.17
duties of directors	4.20–4.24
form of request	4.18
notice of resolution	4.19
required percentage	4.13–4.15
notice	4.10
proxies at *see* Proxies at members' meetings	
resigning auditors' rights to require	4.34
contents of statement	4.37
purpose	4.35, 4.36
types	4.1, 4.2
voting at *see* Voting at members' meetings	
Members' resolution	3.1
transitional provisions	3.2, 3.3
types	3.1
Members' voluntary liquidation	
chairman	22.6
meetings	22.2
meetings subsequent to passing of resolution to wind up	22.8, 22.9
notice	22.3
procedure subsequent to passing of resolution to wind up	22.8, 22.9
requirements to be satisfied	22.1

Members' voluntary liquidation—*continued*	
resolutions	22.2
time and venue of meeting	22.5
voting	22.7
Minutes of meetings	
background	14.1, 14.2
board meetings	14.5, 14.7, 14.9
contents	14.11
function of	14.10
listed companies	14.8
minute books	14.12–14.15
obligation to keep	14.1, 14.2
purpose	14.4
recording	14.3
resolutions agreed to by all members in lieu of meeting	14.32–14.34
rights to inspect	14.16–14.19
validating	14.20–14.31
NHS Foundation Trusts	26.234–26.239
Notice of general meetings	6.1–6.3
auditors	6.64
authentication	6.95, 6.96
circulation of statement given pursuant to s314	6.88–6.94
date	6.20–6.22
debenture holders	6.65, 6.66
form of	6.20–6.22
framing resolution	6.23, 6.24
hard copy	6.68
method of service	6.67, 6.69–6.72
notice of proposal to pay compensation to directors	6.79–6.87
ordinary resolutions	6.25–6.35
period of	6.4–6.19
place	6.20–6.22
proxies, statement regarding	6.44–6.54
signing	6.55
special resolutions	6.36–6.43
time	6.20–6.22
to whom sent	6.56–6.58
bankruptcy of member, persons entitled as result of	6.61, 6.62
death of member, persons entitled as result of	6.61, 6.62
directors	6.63
joint holders of shares	6.60
members	6.56–6.58
special classes of members	6.59
writing, in	6.73–6.78
Notifications	
listed companies, by	3.121–3.123
Official Receiver	
nominee, as	25.39–25.41, 25.43–25.45
Ordinary resolutions	3.4, 3.5
notice of	6.25–6.35
scope	3.6
special notice	3.7–3.27
changes in auditors	3.28–3.42

Index

Ordinary resolutions—*continued*
   special notice—*continued*
      removal of director   3.7–3.27

Political contributions
   annual general meetings, and   5.102
Poll
   voting at members' meetings   8.31–8.38
Private organisations
   annual general meeting   27.17
   business for   27.32–27.34
   by-laws   27.13, 27.14
   case-law   27.15, 27.16
   constitution   27.6–27.8
   delegation   27.9
   executive committee   27.9–27.12
   executive committee
      meetings   27.64–27.67
      chairman   27.76, 27.77
      conduct of   27.75
      delegation to
         subcommittees   27.82–27.84
      form of notice   27.69–27.73
      notice period   27.64–27.67
      quorum   27.78
      service of notice   27.74
      to whom notice should be given   27.68
      voting   27.79–27.81
      when held   27.64–27.67
   implied terms of contract   27.5
   legal relations between members   27.3, 27.4
   meaning   27.1, 27.2
   meetings   1.10
   members' meetings   27.17
      adjournments   27.60–27.63
      amendments   27.53–27.59
      chairman   27.37–27.39
      form of notice   27.29–27.31
      how notice to be given   27.24–27.28
      notice period   27.23
      quorum   27.41, 27.42
      service of notice   27.35
      voting   27.43–27.52
      who can call   27.20–27.22
      who is entitled to notice   27.36
   minutes   27.85
      approval   27.96–27.98
      circulation   27.94, 27.95
      contents   27.90–27.93
      purpose   27.86–27.89
      records   27.85
      special meetings   18.18, 27.18, 27.19
Proxies at general meetings
   general principles   8.1
Proxies at members' meetings   8.1
   adjournments, and   8.88
   amendments, and   8.89
   contents of notice   8.86
   contractual or fiduciary obligation
      to member   8.90
   expenses of sending out forms   8.84
   form for appointment   8.83

Proxies at members' meetings—*continued*
   form for specified meeting   8.112–8.115
   meaning   8.81, 8.82
   misdescription of meetings,
      and   8.112–8.114
   notice of invalidity   8.107
   prescribed formalities, effect   8.97–8.106
   proxy holder voting contrary to
      instructions   8.94
   proxy notice not complying with
      articles   8.95, 8.96
   revocation of proxy notice   8.108
   soliciting   8.91–8.93
   two or more forms, problems of
      validity   8.109–8.111
   two-way form   8.85, 8.87
   voting   8.20–8.30

Quorum at general meetings
   abuse of provisions   7.21, 7.22
   corporate member   7.15
   general rules   7.8
   one member   7.9
   one person meetings   7.16–7.19
   qualifying persons   7.8
   special class quorums   7.20
   throughout   7.10–7.13
   two joint holders   7.14

Registration of resolutions   3.119, 3.120
Resolutions
   circulation
      annual general meeting, and   5.106
   elective *see* Elective resolutions
   extraordinary *see* Extraordinary
      resolutions
   ordinary *see* Ordinary resolutions
   registration   3.119, 3.120
   Regulation 53 of 1985 Table A   3.96–3.98
   special *see* Special resolutions
   statutory written *see* Statutory
      written resolutions
   written
      provision in articles   3.99

Shareholders' meetings   4.38–4.52
   class meetings   4.38–4.52
Shares
   authority of company to purchase
      own
      annual general meeting, and   5.92
   authority of directors to allot
      annual general meeting,
      and   5.56–5.72
Sole director
   companies with
      directors' meetings   12.128–12.141
Special resolutions   3.43
   notice of   6.36–6.43
   passing   3.45–3.47

Statutory pre-emption rights
  disapplying
    annual general meeting,
      and   5.73–5.86
Statutory written resolutions   3.67
  accuracy of register of numbers,
    and   3.85, 3.86
  agreement to   3.82
  alternative procedures   3.72
  auditors, and   3.91–3.95
  authenticated document   3.82–3.84
  circulation date   3.80, 3.81
  procedure   3.68–3.71
  request for   3.87–3.90
  sending copies   3.73–3.75
  voting rights   3.76–3.79

Table A   2.19–2.21
  company limited by guarantee,
    and   2.26–2.30
  directors, powers of   2.45, 2.46
  Regulation 53   3.96–3.98
  variations   2.25
  versions   2.22–2.24
Table C   2.26–2.34
Third-party interests in shares
  voting rights, and   8.14–8.17

Voting at members' meetings
  announcing results of poll   8.76, 8.77
  class shares, and   8.5–8.13
  fraud on minority   8.2–8.4

Voting at members' meetings—*continued*
  objections to right to vote   8.18, 8.19
  poll   8.31–8.38
  poll, demanding   8.43–8.47, 8.49–8.52
    acceptance of   8.55–8.57
    challenge to   8.53, 8.54
    proxies   8.48
    withdrawing   8.58
  poll, taking   8.59–8.64, 8.72–8.75
    manner of   8.65, 8.66
    place of   8.59–8.64
    reasons for   8.67
    register of members, and   8.71
    scrutineers   8.69, 8.70
    time of   8.59–8.64
  report by independent assessor   8.78–8.80
  show of hands   8.20–8.30
  third-party interests in shares   8.14–8.17

Website *see* Electronic communications
Winding up by court   21.1
  adjournment of meetings   21.11
  chairman of meetings   21.9, 21.10
  contributions   21.4
  final meeting   21.6–21.8
  meetings to be held   21.1
  notice of meetings   21.5
  report to court   21.13
  summoning of meetings   21.2, 21.3
  voting at meetings   21.12
Written resolutions
  provision in articles   3.99